W0018297

ADVANCES IN INFORMATION PROCESSING AND PROTECTION

ADVANCES IN INFORMATION PROCESSING AND PROTECTION

Edited by

Jerzy Pejaś
Szczecin University of Technology
Szczecin, Poland

Khalid Saeed
Bialystock Technical University
Bialystock, Poland

 Springer

Jerzy Pejaś
Szczecin University of Technology
Faculty of Computer Science
Zolnierska 49
71 210 Szczecin
Poland
Email: jpejas@wi.ps.pl

Khalid Saeed
Bialystock Technical University
Faculty of Computer Science
Wiejska 45A
15-351 Bialystok
Poland
Email: aida@ii.pb.bialystock.pl

ISBN-13: 978-0-387-73136-0   e-ISBN-13: 978-0-387-73137-7

Library of Congress Control Number: 2007928497

© 2007 Springer Science+Business Media, LLC.
All rights reserved. This work may not be translated or copied in whole or in part without the written permission of the publisher (Springer Science+Business Media, LLC, 233 Spring Street, New York, NY 10013, USA), except for brief excerpts in connection with reviews or scholarly analysis. Use in connection with any form of information storage and retrieval, electronic adaptation, computer software, or by similar or dissimilar methodology now know or hereafter developed is forbidden.
The use in this publication of trade names, trademarks, service marks and similar terms, even if the are not identified as such, is not to be taken as an expression of opinion as to whether or not they are subject to proprietary rights.

Printed on acid-free paper.

9 8 7 6 5 4 3 2 1

springer.com

FOREWORD

The Computer Science is relatively new field which is developing very fast not only because due to the huge interest of scientists and the market request, but also because this science has created possibilities for people of investigation and solved many problems that some time ago seemed to be insolvable. Such problems had only been described in science fiction novels, like underwater journeys of captain Nemo described by Jules Verne in XIX century. At present, various human dreams are successively becoming reality exactly as the underwater journeys became possible in the XX century.

The proposed book gives you a view of the progress in such domains of Computer Science as Artificial Intelligence, Biometrics, Security of Information Technology, Computer Information Systems and Industrial Management. The works contained in the book describe the newest investigation results of devoted scientists from Europe and Asia.

The book is written in a hard scientific language. It is really valuable and I am sure it will deliver you many scientific benefits.

Professor Andrzej Piegat
Szczecin University of Technology
Faculty of Computer Science and Information Systems
and
University of Szczecin, Poland
Faculty of Economic Sciences and Management

ACKNOWLEDGMENTS

We would like to express our indebtedness to all professors and IPC Members who took upon themselves the task of reviewing the papers presented in this book.
  They are:

1) Bagiński Czesław
2) Bartkowiak Anna
3) Bielecki Włodzimierz
4) Dańko Wiktor
5) Dorogov Alexander
6) Choraś Ryszard S.
7) El Fray Imed
8) Facchinetti Gisella
9) French Roger Allan
10) Imada Akira
11) Kobayashi Shin-ya
12) Kompanets Leonid
13) Koszelew Jolanta
14) Kukharev Georgy
15) Kuriata Eugeniusz
16) Madani Kurosh
17) Mosdorf Romuald
18) Oniszczuk Walenty
19) Piegat Andrzej
20) Popov Orest
21) Rakowski Waldemar
22) Sosnowski Zenon
23) Stokłosa Janusz
24) Śmierzchalski Roman
25) Wierzchoń Sławomir T.
26) Yarmolik V. N.
27) Zieniuk Eugeniusz

We also acknowledge the authors' extensive efforts in preparing their works in the way that definitely will satisfy the readers. It is because of their valuable contributions, that this book has appeared in its really useful and precious form.
  Finally, our thanks go to the assistants and the publishers for their help in much of the editing work that led to what we have produced.

Editors
Jerzy Pejaś and Khalid Saeed

INTRODUCTION

This book presents selected papers given at an international conference on advanced computer systems. It brings a number of new concepts into the field, providing a very fundamental and formal approach to Artificial Intelligence, Computer Security, Safety, Image Analysis, Graphics, Biometrics, Computer Simulation, and Data Analysis. State-of-the-art theoretical and practical results in a large number of real problems are achieved with the techniques described.

All papers presented in this book are partitioning in the four topical groups
1. Artificial Intelligence,
2. Computer Security and Safety,
3. Image Analysis, Graphics, and Biometrics,
4. Computer Simulation and Data Analysis.

Section 1. Artificial Intelligence considers results of the science and engineering of making intelligent algorithms and computer programs and it includes papers concerned Humatronics, Fuzzy Logic, Robotics, Cell, Genetic, and Probabilistic Algorithms, Incomplete Data and Similarity Relations, Fast Neural Networks and others topics.

Section 2. Computer Security and Safety covers a wide range of issues: Error Detection in Block Ciphers, Parallelization of Encryption Algorithms, Visual Cryptography Methods, Neural Network for building Programmable Block Ciphers, Security and Safety in Distributed Computing Environments, Chaotic Product Cipher, and other questions.

Section 3. Image Analysis, Graphics, and Biometrics deals with difficult tasks of the study of the extraction of meaningful information from images as well as methods for uniquely recognizing humans based upon one or more intrinsic physical or behavioral traits. Papers presented in this section are concerned Word-Recognition, Signature Identification, Fingerprint Recognition, Biometric Images Pre-classification, and other issues.

Section 4. Computer Simulation and Data Analysis concerns computer programs that attempt to simulate an abstract model of a particular system and transforming data with the aim of extracting useful information and facilitating conclusions. It includes papers devoted to Processor Utilization on a Multi-Processor System, Computer-based training systems for operators of dynamic objects, Linked Computer Servers, Loops Parallelization in the .NET Environment to be used for simulation purposes, and other related topics.

I hope that the papers, presented in this book, will allow you to enlarge your knowledge in the field of advanced computer systems.

I wish you a satisfaction from reading the book.

Professor Włodzimierz Bielecki, Vice Dean
Faculty of Computer Science
Szczecin University of Technology

TABLE OF CONTENTS

PART I - ARTIFICIAL INTELLIGENCE

PART IV - COMPUTER SIMULATION AND DATA ANALYSIS

PART I

ARTIFICIAL INTELLIGENCE

Humatronics and RT-Middleware

Toru Yamaguchi and Eri Sato

Tokyo Metropolitan University, Dept. of System Design
6-6 Asahigaoka, Hino, Tokyo 191-0065 Japan
{yamachan, esato}@fml.ec.tmit.ac.jp

Abstract. This paper described Humatornics for symmetrical communication between a human and robots. Recently, we use various types of systems based on electronics. However, these systems are not useful and imposes burden. The electronics for solving these problems are called "Humatronics". Advanced humatronics are mostly needed for natural communication between human and system To realize humatronics, a system understands human using various sensor, architecture, and so on. Therefore we focused on Robot Technology Middleware (RTM). RT Middleware was developed by AIST (Agency of Industrial Science and Technology, Japan) for easily integrating robot systems by modularized software components. By constructing modules based on RT Middleware, we developed modules, which are functional elements to interact with human as components of easily system integration. Firstly this paper describes "Humatonics" and RT-Middleware. Secondly we show a system, which is based on humatronics concept using RT-Middleware.

1. Introduction

Nowadays various types of systems are used in daily life. We enjoy using the Internet at home, and helped by car navigation system when the driving. Users need to understand how to use most of these systems today. To obtain outputs, a user has to put correct inputs. However, information and systems are becoming increasingly complicated, we need more knowledge and skills to obtain outputs. Moreover, with the progress on computer technology various types of robots are developed and used. Frantic effort is needed to make full use of these systems. These systems are far from knowing intuitively. Then, 'humatronics' is spreading with a central focus on ITS [1]. Various sensor, tool or algorithm is needed for understanding a human. However, implementation of these sensor or algorithm for individual system is hard. Also, contractions of interaction robot or service robot which is constructed many parts is hard. Robot Technology Middleware (RT-Middleware) for easily integrating robot systems by modularized software components.

2. Humatronics

Various systems based on electronics, such as computers, cellular phones, cars and even robots, are used in our daily life. However, these systems are not useful, impose burdens, especially to elderly and handicapped people. We name the electronics for solving these problems "Humatronics". As shown in Fig 1, humatronics is divided into two stages. In this paper, we have researched on the first stage of the humatronics.

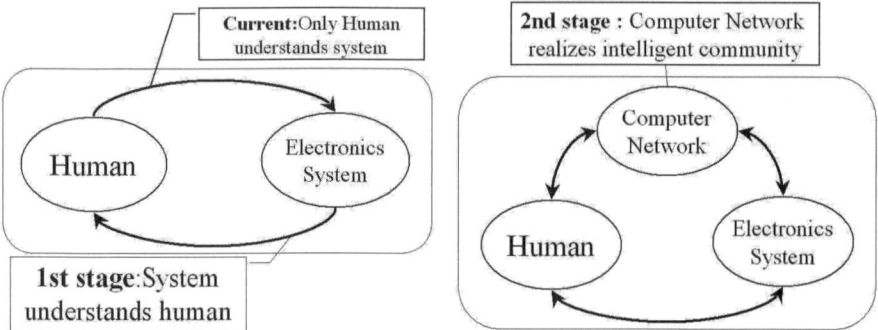

Fig. 1. Humatronics: Humatoronics is constructed two stages. The right figure showed 1st Stage. On the 1st stage, a system understands human and constructs a symmetrical interaction. On the other hand, the system forms an intelligent community on the 2nd stage. The intelligent community supports humans seamlessly.

To actualize the interaction between human and system, system must understand human intention first. Present interface, such as keyboard, mouse and so on, are unsuitable for intuitively operation or manipulation. Manipulation using natural motion based on human-to-human communication is needed. Therefore, system needs to understand human, and establish symmetrical interaction between human and system. Advance humatronics are mostly needed for natural communication between human and system. We think nonverbal communication is primitive and important for communication between human. So, we show step toward natural communication between human and robot based on interpersonal communication (Fig 2). We have researched human-robot interaction using hand motion considering situation [2], and natural interface using pointing movement [3][4].

Our laboratory has developed software, which track human motion using a camera. To recognize gesture, the system implement some cameras for calculate 3-dimensional coordinates. Additional the system include visible types robot that service to human physically. To develop a system such as collaborates tracking soft wares using camera and robots is hard. Thus, we used RT-Middleware to implement these sensor and robots in a system. In the next section, we describe RT-Middleware.

Fig. 2. Natural communication between humans and robots based on human communication.

3. RT-Middleware

NEDO (New Energy and Industrial Technology Development Organization) is leading with the standardization of robot elements as 21century robot challenging program. Recently, the committee has decided on groups to be commissioned. The group that headed by Prof. Tanie is going to develop a middle ware for modularity and an open architecture specification (RT-Middleware project). In our research, we focused on vision modules. We had studied about object tracking software using camera information. However, it is difficult to implement other systems. Firstly, we modularize this tracking software using OpenRTM-aist, which was developed by AIST (Agency of Industrial Science and Technology, Japan)[5][6][7]. Modularizing a sensor, controller, and so on as RT-component. Developers are able to connect these modules and build a system. Fig.4 showed the screenshot of Rtc-link. Rtc-link displayed each RT-component, which was connected naming server. The component (right side in Fig.4) calculates three-coordinates using the obtained coordinates from two modules (left side in Fig.4) by DTL method. In next section, we show the system that gesture recognition and obtaining object information, contacted based on RT-Middleware.

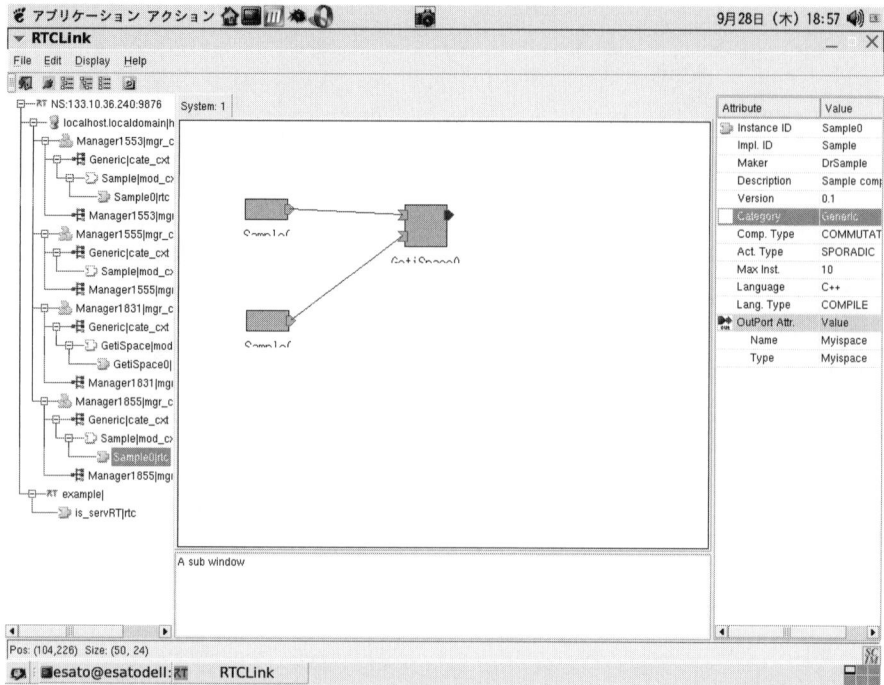

Fig. 4. Screenshot of RT-middleware: the right side modules calculate three coordinates using the coordinates, which was obtained by the left side modules.

4. Experiment of interaction system using gesture

We have researched human robot interaction using pointing movement. In the previous research, we constructed virtual room for interactive interface. Because, in actual object cannot react when a user attended it; the object in virtual room can be blink as a reaction when a user pointed out it. The user answered whether the object is what you want or not. Therefore, a user and the system can be attended same object interactively. To realize the interactive way in actual room, the system need to recognize feature of object, which a user attended. Thus, in this research, we focused on color information. If the system obtains color information of the object, for example, the system could ask whether the user pointed out something red as shown in Fig. 5. In this research, we constructed the system that obtains RGB information of pointed out object as the first step in this interaction.

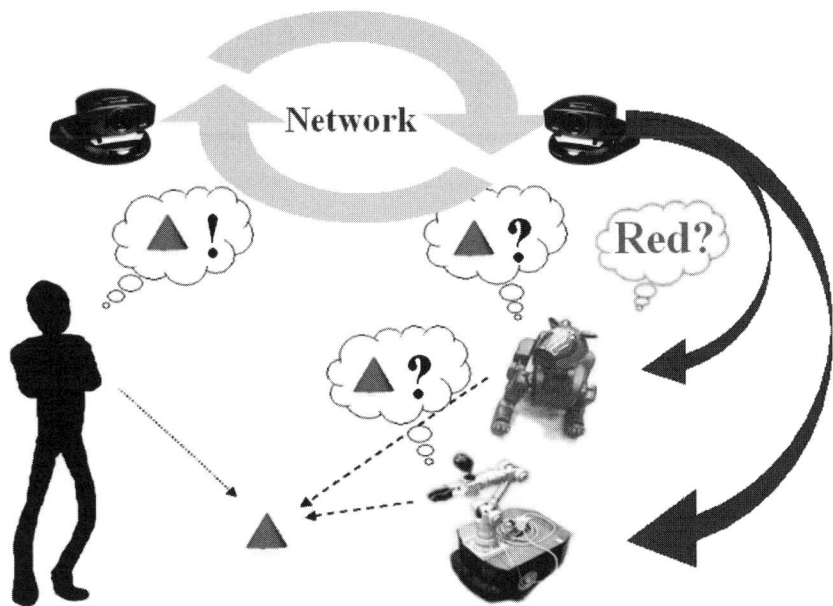

Fig. 5. Interaction using RGB information. In an actual room, robots show attended object using color information. The color information is obtained by tracking modules, which is composed a camera and PC and tracks human motions or observes the environment. Robots and tracking modules share the information by network

4.1 System outline and each components

In this system are constructed 4 steps. First step tracks a user's motion using camera. Second step calculate a 3 dimensional coordinates of user's head and hand by DLT method using 2-dimensional data, which was obtained at first part. Third step recognize indicating point using the 3-dimensional coordinates. Last step obtained RGB data on the picture, which was used at first step using 3 dimensional coordinates of indicating point. These steps related each other; it is difficult to improve each other under the previous construction method. For example, when some researcher proposes a new motion tracking we have to rewrite a program adapting our environment. Also, when we want to implement a new sensor in our system, we have to adapt the system. Therefore, we divided our system for four modules and constructed based on RT-Middleware.

We prepared two sets of equipment comprised of a camera and a PC that are a kind of unconscious robot in a room, as illustrated by Fig. 6. The users wore a cap and had a glove on their dominant hand. The unconscious robots track the cap, the glove, and the robot's markers. For tracking, we used iSpace, open source software that was developed in our laboratory for tracking objects with RGB information from cameras. 3-dimensional coordinates of the user's head and hand positions are calculated using

DLT method [8][9][10]. We describe DLT method late. The module obtained coordinates of indicated point and calculate the coordinates in picture. The system consists of 4 modules; these modules were developed using OpenRTM-aist-0.2.0. Each module in this system is connected as shown in Fig. 7.

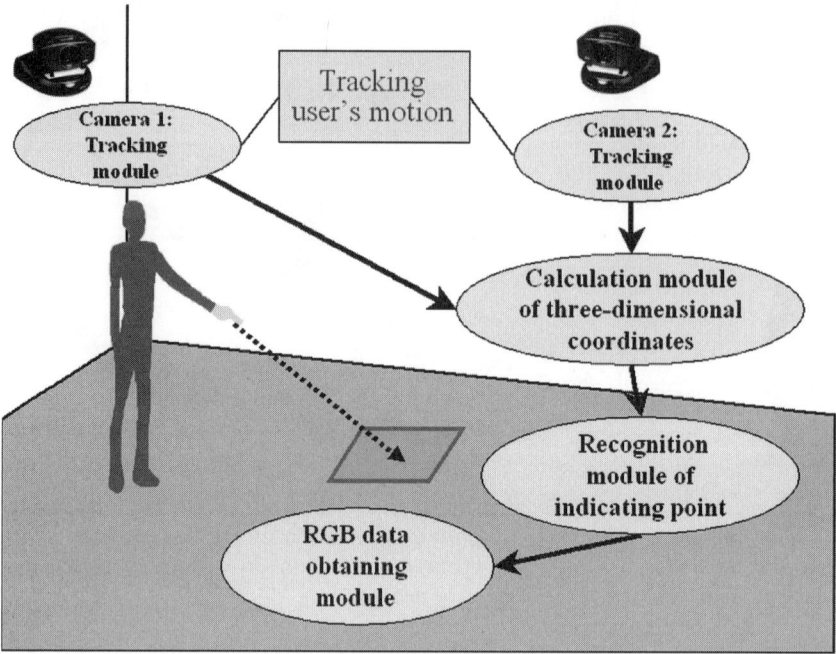

Fig. 6. Recognition of pointing movement and obtaining RGB information; Pointing movement was observed by two cameras. The cameras connected tracking module, which track user's head and hand motion. The tracking data was translated from 2 dimensional coordinates on image to 3 dimensional coordinates in real world. Indicated point on the floor was calculated by recognition module of indicating point.

Tracking module: Tracking module was used with iSpace, which can be track up to 8 objects. This module was interface to RT-modules of iSpace and has an OutPort. iSpace send tracking objects data, object no, 2-dimensional coordinates on image, and find flag as tracking status through this modules from OutPort. In this research, user's head and right hand was tracked.

3-dimensional coordinates calculation module: This module has two InPort and an OutPort. InPort received the 2-dimensional coordinates from tracking modules. DLT method was implemented this module. DLT method has few constraints that must be observed for calculating 3-dimensional coordinates. Generally, when we calculate 3-dimensional coordinates, we use two-dimensional coordinates by picture of two or more cameras. When we use to like this technique, we need to determine on many values called camera constants. Camera constants are, for example, distance between camera device and target object, established angle of cameras, binocular visions of camera lens, and so on. To exactly determine these values is difficult. DLT method has characteristic that not to determine them and to calculate camera constants using six points given 3-dimensional coordinates called control points.

Pointing movement recognition module: This module has an InPort and an OutPort. This module received 3-dimensional coordinates from the above module. In this research, indicated point the intersection point of floor with the line, which is connecting center of eyes with fingertip. The 3-dimensional coordinates of indicated point was output.

RGB data obtaining module: This module has an InPort as obtaining the 3 dimensional coordinates. This module translated the data from above module to 2 dimensional coordinates on image, and obtained RGB data of indicated point on the floor in image.

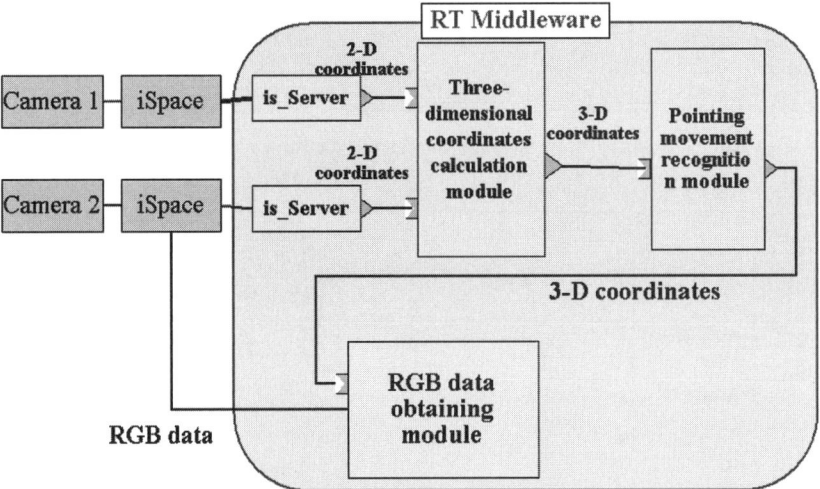

Fig. 7. Modules in this system; this system consists of 4 modules. These modules had InPort or OutPort to connect with other modules.

4.2 Result

We set on the three color papers, green, blue, and red, on the floor and participants pointed them as shown in Fig. 8. The participant pointed out, green, blue, and read continuously. Two cameras (Sony EVI-D30) are established 90 degrees each other in the room. A user wears a cap and has a glove on his right hand as markers for tracking. iSpace is booted on each Computer, and tracking modules and other modules run on Vine3.2. Fig. 9 shows experimental result. RGB data of the point, which was indicated by a user, is highest the color, green, blue, red. The color is intended point by a user every ten seconds.

Fig. 8. Experiment scenery; the participant pointed out the three color paper on the floor.

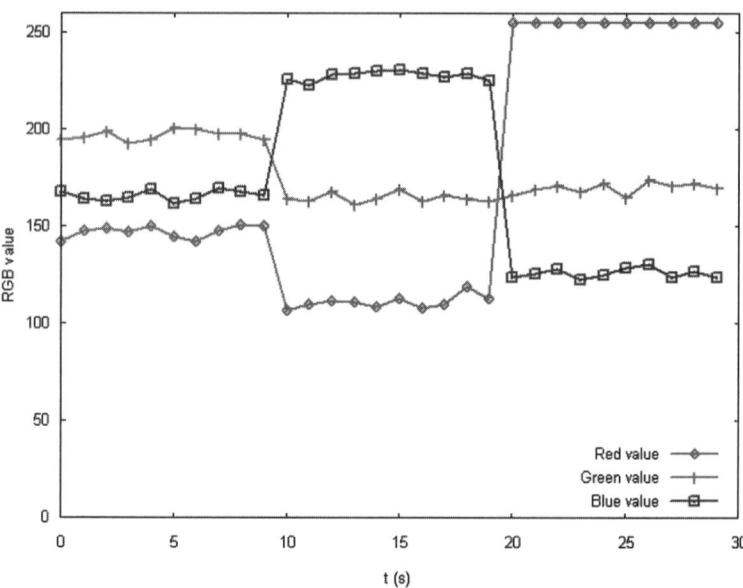

Fig. 9. Obtained RGB data. The graph shows RGB data of indicated point each sec. Each pointing movement is 10 sec approximately.

Conclusion

We describe "Humatronics" that a system understands a human and constructed symmetrical interaction. Additionally, the systems form an intelligent community for supporting human seamlessly. To realize humatronics, we showed RT-Middleware. RT-Middleware supports a robot integration using various sensors, tools and so on.

We focused on gesture interaction and developed a system, which recognize a user's pointing movement and obtained RGB information of an object using RT-Middleware. The system consisted of 4 components. Each component can be connect/disconnect on RTC-Link, which can be monitor components. Therefore, we improve the system on individual components easily. Each component will be reused when other system developed.

Step toward natural communication between human and robot, "Humatronics" is one of the important solutions. RT-Middleware supports not only an integration of robot but also construction a new system based on humatronics.

Acknowledgements

This research is being conducted as a part of the "Development Project for a Common Basis of Next-Generation Robots" consigned by New Energy and Industrial Technology Development Organization (NEDO).

Reference

[1] Special Sessions SS10. Humatronics -an automotive electronics which cooperate with human community. In 11th World Congress on ITS, page 32, 2004.

[2] T. Yamaguchi, E. Sato, and Y. Takama, "Intelligent space and human centered robotics," IEEE Transaction on Industrial Electronics, vol. 50, no. 5, pp. 881–889, 2003.

[3] E. Sato, A. Nakajima, T. Yamaguchi, and F. Harashima, "Humatronics(1) - natural ineraction between human and networked robot using human motion recognition," in 2004 IEEE/RSJ International Conference on Intelligent Robots and Systems, 8 2005, pp. 2794–2799.

[4] J. Nakazato, K. Kiyama, and T. Yamaguchi, "Intelligent networked mobility based on natural interaction for human support system," in 2006 RISP International Workshop on Nonlinear Circuits and Signal Processing, 3 2006, pp. 134–137.

[5] Noriaki Ando, et al, RT-Component Object Model in RT-Middleware – Distributed Component Middleware for RT (Robot Technology) –, CIRA2005 (CD-ROM)

[6] Noriaki Ando, et Al, RT-Middleware: Distributed Component Middleware for RT (Robot Technology), 2005 IEEE/RSJ International Conference on Intelligent Robots and Systems, pp.3555-3560

[7] RT Middleware Project (in Japanese), http://www.is.aist.go.jp/rt/.

[8] Y. I. Abdel-Aziz and H. M. Karara, "Direct linear transformation from comparator coordinates into object space coordinates in close-range photogrammetry," in Proceedings of the Symposium on Close-Range Photogrammetry, 1971, pp. 1–18.

[9] Y. Ikegami, S. Sakurai, and K. Yabe, "Dlt method," Japanese Journal of Sports Science, vol. 10, no. 3, pp. 191–195, 1991, (in Japanese).

[10] Y. Miyanokoshi, E. Sato, and T. Yamaguchi, "Suspicious behavior detection based on case-based reasoning using face direction," in SICEICASE International Joint Conference 2006, 2006, pp. 5429–5432.

A Fuzzy Way to Measure Quality of Work in a Multidimensional Perspective

Tindara Addabbo*, Gisella Facchinetti*,
Giovanni Mastroleo**, Giovanni Solinas*

*Università di Modena e Reggio Emilia; Dipartimento di Economia Politica
**Università della Calabria, Dipartimento di Scienze Aziendali
e-mail: addabbo.tindara@unimore.it, facchinetti.gisella@unimore.it,
mastroleo@unical.it; solinas.giovanni@unimore.it

Abstract: This paper focuses on the definition and measurement of quality of work (QL) by using a multidimensional approach, based on fuzzy logic. The multidimensional nature of quality of work has been widely acknowledged in economic and sociological literature and attempts at measuring its different dimensions can be found at European level in the work carried out by the European Foundation for the Improvement of living and working conditions. The European Commission and the International Labour Office have also identified different dimensions for quality of work and proposed new indicators to measure them. In this paper an attempt is made to maintain the complexity of the quality of work concept by using a technique that allows measurement without introducing too strong assumptions and makes the rules for judging the different dimensions of QL and their interactions explicit.

Introduction

The crucial role played by work in an individual's life has been widely stressed in the literature. In the words of Gallino (1993):

"Work produces an important share of material and immaterial culture, by greatly increasing the distance between human beings and all other species […]. By intervening in the natural environment and in the artificial environment, made of culture, work continuously changes human living conditions and therefore can be considered as one of the main agents of social evolution. [It can establish] social relations amongst people that materialize in the building of collectivity, groups, organizations characterized by different forms of cooperation, collaboration and integration. [In so doing] by requiring that everyone cooperates with others not by ideological persuasion but by an intrinsic need, work confers direction, aim, identity on individual life" (Gallino, 1993, p. 396, our trans.).

Hence work alters the environment, the characteristics of artefacts produced, and the very relations among persons. From this derives also the multidimensional character of the notion of quality of work.

More recently the multidimensional nature of quality of work has been widely acknowledged, as is visible in the research work carried out by the *European*

Foundation for the Improvement of living and working conditions (Merllié and Paoli 2001); the European Commission and the International Labour Office, too, have identified different dimensions for quality of work and proposed new indicators to measure them. (EC, 2001; ILO, 2003). Not only earnings but also other dimensions (like for instance safety at work, social protection, type of job contracts) appear relevant in an extended definition of quality of work. The literature has not only addressed the importance of extending the definition of quality of work to other than monetary dimensions, but has also dealt with questions regarding the existence of compensating differentials amongst the different elements that compose the quality (like for instance whether a lower paid job is characterized by better workplace relations or by safer work and if these elements compensate for the lower wage). If, conversely, the differentials are not such as to compensate — as occurs in the segmented labour markets — it becomes important to have available instruments that enable understanding (and measurement) as to which jobs (in terms of position, type of contract) and in which contexts (industry, type of enterprise, regional area) jobs characterized by different quality are concentrated, and whether there are individual and family characteristics more correlated to the risk of finding oneself in jobs or workplaces that can be defined as low quality.

In this paper we deal with the identification of the dimensions relevant to defining quality of work and the building of a system that accounts for different indicators of these dimensions.

The paper is the first result of an interdisciplinary partnership, between researchers in different disciplines (economists, sociologists, mathematicians) sharing a common view: since living and working conditions are intrinsically multidimensional and mediated by human interpretation and perceptions, their quantification is not well achieved by classical mathematics or statistics. Therefore the group used techniques able to tolerate vagueness and imprecision and capable of capturing the complex interrelated dimensions of quality of work according to individual perceptions.

2. Quality of work

In working on the scheme originally proposed by Gallino, we took into account six different dimensions that are defined by the combination of a relevant number of indicators and elementary variables. Each dimension allows one to analyse how, by starting from individual perception by the worker, work matches and sometimes comes into conflict with individuals' specific targets and needs. Work is of a high quality if according to Gallino every analytical dimension taken into account "shows properties aimed at significantly satisfying the corresponding needs" (Gallino, 1993, p. 393, our trans.). It is difficult to establish a ranking amongst the different dimensions and every dimension is involved in the determination of quality of work with the same weight.

The different dimensions that we will include in the definition of the quality of work are:

- Control dimension (Control): relation with colleagues, relation with management/entrepreneur, autonomy in managing working rhythms, possibility of direct agreement with colleagues.
- Economic dimension (EconomDim). In this dimension we consider earnings, seniority, job security, social insurance, profit sharing, wage, career perspectives and parental leaves and protection.
- Ergonomic dimension (ErgonDim): work environment (individual space, smokes and fumes, dust) pace and intensity, cognitive effort and stress.
- Complexity dimension (JobComplex): acknowledgment of one's capabilities, job variety and richness, effort required, training.
- Social dimension (SocialDim): In this dimension we include elements connected to others' esteem, acknowledgment of professional abilities, career perspectives, sharing firm's decision, work life satisfaction and job satisfaction.
- Work life balance (WorkLiBal): includes maternity protection, parental leaves, management and availability of paid holidays, participation of employees in management of working hours distribution and shifts, availability of family- friendly policies.

These different dimensions are the final inputs (built by means of intermediate systems that combine the elementary elements by giving different weights to each variable) of a fuzzy expert system and, for the reasons given above, every dimension in the model has the same weight.

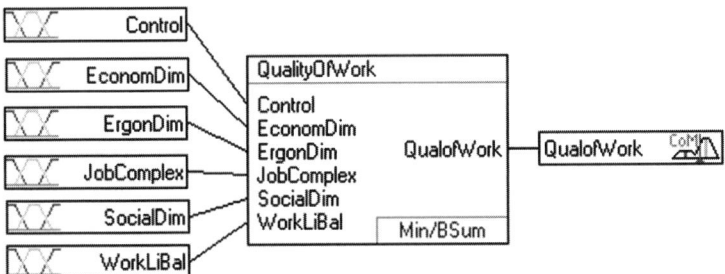

Fig. 1. Quality of work.

In turn, every dimension is the output of a fuzzy system. The sample of firms and the technique used to read the data enable one to understand how the quality of the workplace is constituted in the context of specific firms and how its elements, workplace relations and organizing structures can change with regard to the type of firm and the product market conditions.

3. Economic Dimension

In this paper we enter into details of the "Economic Dimension" system. The economic dimension is the output of these eleven inputs:

Table 1. Input variables

A01	Earnings
A02	Earnings related to seniority
A03	Job security
A04	Social insurance
A05	Profit sharing schemes
A06	Firm's pay differentials schemes
A07	Fringe benefits
A08	Learning and training
A09	Maternity protection
A10	Parental leaves
B07	Career perspectives

Each one of these elements refers to the worker's subjective perception of her job's characteristics with reference to the above elements. Fig. 2 shows the structure of the system.

In the structure of the fuzzy system some intermediate variables appear:

- 1st level of intermediate variables: career perspectives, earning level, earning variability, social protection and parental protection.
- 2nd level of intermediate variables: earnings and protections.

These are variables obtained by the partial aggregation of initial inputs, useful for better understanding of the evolution of the system. They may be defuzzified to obtain a partial output of the variables involved.

In relating input with intermediate variables and output, Fig. 2 shows the type of partition used. In building the economic dimension the elements that we have considered are: career, earnings and security.

- Career (1st level intermediate variable) synthesizes the opportunities and perspectives that are perceived by the individual together with training (input variables A08, B07).
- Earnings (2nd level intermediate variable) show workers' perception of gross income and wage differentials (1st level intermediate variables). Earnings include also fringe benefits (input variables A01, A07). Share of earning connected to seniority and to types of workers participation in firms' results as well as individual earnings differentials (input variables A02, A05, A06).
- 'Security' system (intermediate variable 2nd level) synthesizes both elements of stability and grant of job (input variable A03), and social security (input A04) and parental leaves (input variables A09, A10).

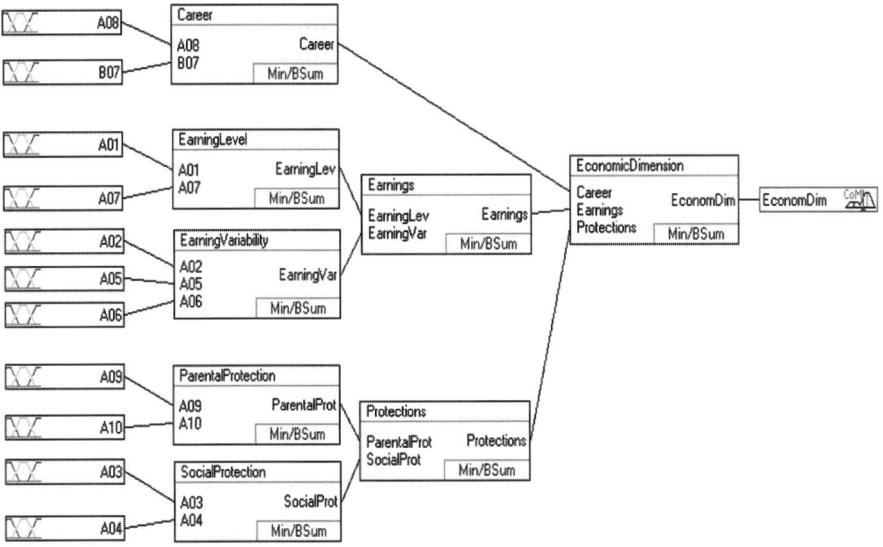

Fig. 2. System layout

In the analytical framework proposed the economic dimension will be considered of high quality if, according to the worker, it will be able to satisfy his needs, in terms of earnings, career and job stability. To close the system we had to specify weights. Weights range from 1 to 2. In creating intermediate variables of level 1 we have given more weight to the opportunities and perspectives felt by the employee than to the training content of the work. In defining earnings we have given more weight to the variable that refers to the level of gross earnings rather than to fringe benefits. We have given more weight to seniority in evaluating the dimension connected to wage variability. Variables on the job stability have a higher weight. Passing from 1st level variables to 2nd level variables we have given a greater weight to earnings level and social security than to earnings variation and parental protection.

All the inputs are described by three linguistic attributes low, medium, high:

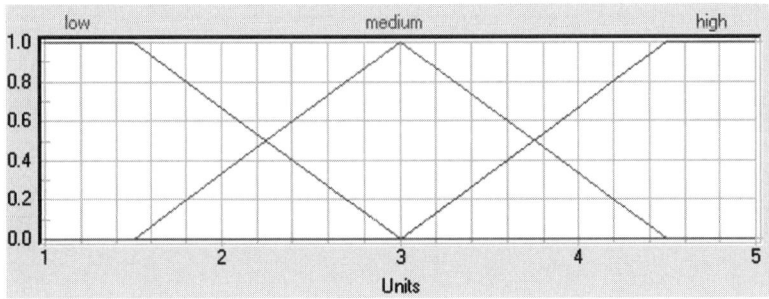

Fig. 3. Input variables layout

The first level of intermediate variables is described by five linguistic attributes like in the figure below that describes the Career variable.

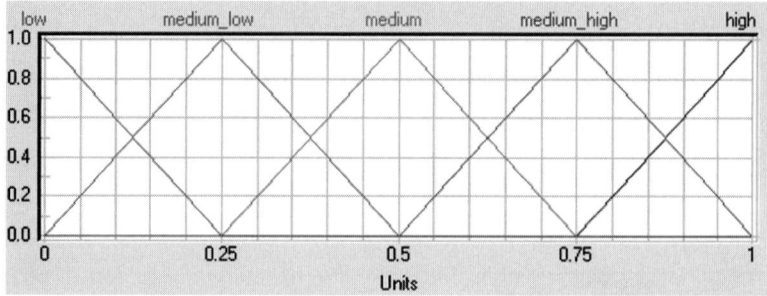

Fig. 4. First level of intermediate variables layout

The second level of intermediate variables are described by seven linguistic attributes like in the figure below that describes the variable earnings:

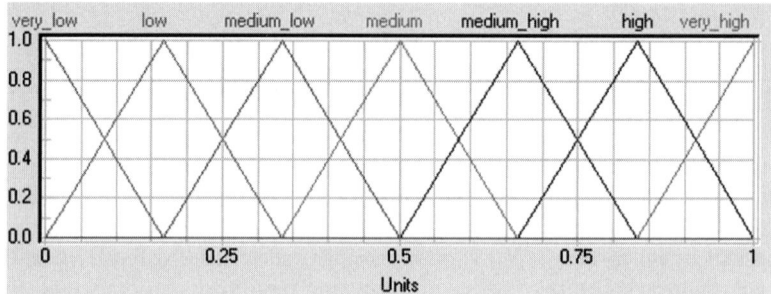

Fig. 5. Second level of intermediate variables layout

The "economic dimension" output is described by eleven linguistic attributes:

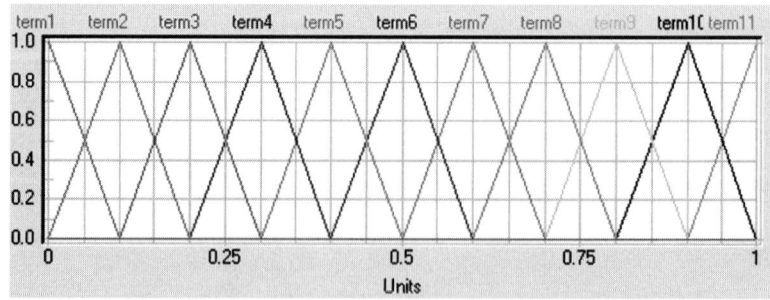

Fig. 6. Output layout

The system presents eight rule blocks for a total of 274 rules.

The rule blocks contain the control strategy of a fuzzy logic system. Each rule block confines all rules for the same context. A context is defined by the same input and output variables of the rules. The 'if' part of the rules describes the situation, for which the rules are designed. The 'then' part describes the response of the fuzzy system in this situation. The processing of the rules starts by calculating the 'if' part. The operator type of the rule block determines which method is used. We choose the MIN t-norm as AND operator.

Table 2. *Rules of the Rule Block "Career"*

IF		THEN
A08	B07	Career
low	low	low
low	medium	medium_low
low	high	medium
medium	low	medium_low
medium	medium	medium
medium	high	medium_high
high	low	medium
high	medium	medium_high
high	high	high

The fuzzy composition eventually combines different rules to one conclusion. We choose the Bounded Sum as fuzzy operator for the aggregation method of the result to enable all firing rules to be evaluated.

Different methods can be used for the defuzzification, resulting either in the 'most plausible result' or the 'best compromise'. We choose a 'best compromise' method like CoA (Center of Area).

Results

The sample that we used to test the model is made up of employees working in firms of different dimension and belonging to different industries (mechanical, building, services, food industry, information technology, textiles) in the same area (Modena) having a common economic and welfare system. We have tested our expert system with 719 records of employees of these firms. The statistics referred to in this Section must be considered as referring to the sample of firms not randomly selected from the population of firms in Modena. Each firm was analysed to reconstruct its structure and dimensions connected to quality of work, and it is possible to read the results of the output of the system both by firm and by the whole sample constructed. Deeper analyses of the results are currently in progress to match the richness of the fuzzy expert system outcome with the richness of case studies.

In Table 3 we report the value of the variables that compose the analysed dimension and some individual characteristics referring to the worst cases in terms of the economic dimension.[1] Amongst 10 employees at the bottom of the distribution of the economic dimension 9 are women, 5 were born in Southern Italy and 5 are in non-standard employment. They fare very badly in each component of the dimension, and a good degree of satisfaction shown by some of them in maternity protection is not sufficient to increase the value of the whole output of this dimension. By comparing the output of the fuzzy expert system with the mean of the different variables involved in the measurement of this dimension one may find that standard techniques tend to overestimate (with respect to the fuzzy expert output) the value of the economic dimension. By neglecting the connection existing with different dimensions and by simply summing up each indicator one tends to overestimate quality of work.

Table 3. Individual records ordered by the output of the economic dimension: last 10 according to output of economic dimension.

ID	Firm	1 Sex	2 Age	3 Class	4 Place of birth	5 Degree	6a Qualification	A01_Earnings	A02_Earnings related to seniority	A03_Job security	A04_Social insurance	A05_Profit sharing schemes	A06_Firm's pay differentials	A07_Fringe benefits	A08_Capabilities acknowledge	A09_Maternity protection	A10_Parental leaves	B07_Career perspectives	EconomDim	Average
175	2	0	29	1	6	5	3	1	1	1	1	1	1	1	1	2	1	1	0,000	0,023
10	3	0	31	2	2	6	7	1	1	1	1	1	1	1	1	1	1	1	0,000	0,000
18	3	0	30	1	1	6	7	1	1	1	1	1	1	1	1	1	1	1	0,000	0,000
259	2	0	25	1	6	4	1	1	2	2	1	1	1	1	1	1	3	1	0,033	0,091
17	3	0	.	4	1	2	3	1	1	1	1	2	1	2,72	1	3	2	1	0,033	0,130
19	3	0	28	1	3	5	7	1	1	1	1	1	1	1	2	1	1	1	0,033	0,023
258	2	0	44	3	6	3	1	1	1	1	1	1	1	1	1	4	2	1	0,060	0,091
14	6	1	36	2	1	4	3	2	2	3	1	1	1	2	1	2,22	3	1	0,060	0,187
232	2	0	29	1	6	5	3	1	1	1	1	2	1	1	1	4	1	1	0,075	0,091
90	2	0	42	3	6	2	7	2	2	3	2	1	1	3	1	3	3	1	0,083	0,250

In Table 4 we report the value of the variables connected to the best cases according to the ranking of the economic dimension. Women and men are equally present in this group. There is a prevalence of workers with more than 35, with high specialization and seniority; 4 of them are in apical positions. In this case the distance between the fuzzy output and the arithmetic mean of each indicator is lower than in the bottom end of the economic dimension distribution. [A deeper analysis on the distance of the two different measures along the distribution and for different groups of workers is required to test the implications of adopting different techniques for measuring the economic dimension.]

---

[1] Missing values have been replaced by average value for that variable computed for each firm and each job position.

Table 4. Individual records ordered by the output of the economic dimension: first 10 according to output of economic dimension

ID	Firm	1 Sex	2 Age	3 Class	4 Place of birth	5 Degree	6a Qualification	A01_Earnings	A02_Earnings related to seniority	A03_Job security	A04_Social insurance	A05_Profit sharing schemes	A06_Firm's pay differentials	A07_Fringe benefits	A08_Capabilities acknowledge	A09_Maternity protection	A10_Parental leaves	B07_Career perspectives	EconomDim	Average
110	2	0	40	2	1	3	7	5	5	5	5	5	5	5	5	5	5	5	1,000	1,000
51	5	1	50	3	6	2	5	5	5	5	5	5	5	5	5	5	5	5	1,000	1,000
23	5	1	57	4	6	4	5	5	5	5	5	5	5	5	5	5	5	5	1,000	1,000
24	1	1	0	2	1	4	3	5	4	5	5	5	4	5	5	5	5	5	0,940	0,955
152	5	1	54	4	6	4	5	5	5	5	4	4	5	5	5	2,56	4	5	0,917	0,876
32	12	0	39	2	1	2	1	5	5	5	5	1	1	5	5	5	5	5	0,900	0,818
96	2	0	35	2	1	5	3	5	4	5	5	5	4	4	5	5	5	4	0,900	0,909
67	1	0	45	3	1	4	6	4	3	4	5	4	2,67	5	5	5	5	5	0,875	0,833
145	5	1	65	4	7	1	2	5	5	5	5	5	5	5	4	4	4	4	0,875	0,909
99	23	0	21	.	3	2	1	5	5	5	5	5	5	2	4	5	5	5	0,867	0,909

Descriptive analyses on the distribution of quality of work and its dimensions across the sample of firms analysed show a high degree of variation.

Table 5. Correlation coefficients amongst the different dimensions of quality of work

Dimensions*	Complexity	Work-life balance.	Economic	Social	Ergonomic	Control	Quality of work
Complexity	1						
Work-life balance	0.4387	1					
Economic	0.6248	0.481	1				
Social	0.6402	0.6163	0.6662	1			
Ergonomic	0.3696	0.4609	0.2942	0.4117	1		
Control	0.6408	0.5271	0.4764	0.8389	0.4089	1	
Quality of work	0.7601	0.7146	0.7174	0.8524	0.6194	0.8027	1

* For dimensions' definitions see section 2

As Table 5 shows, the different dimensions (that have been measured by separate intermediate systems) are positively related and the final output of the system (variable quality of work) is positively related to all the dimensions, the correlation coefficients being high with respect to social and control dimensions. As far as the dimension that is central to this paper (the economic dimension) is concerned, the results of this correlation analysis show a higher correlation of the economic dimension with the complexity dimension and with the social dimension whereas the correlation with the ergonomic dimension is weaker.

This is not consistent with the literature on compensating differentials amongst the different elements that compose the quality of work and is more consistent with the existence of segmented labour markets.

Conclusions

In providing a synthesis of each dimension of quality of work, the fuzzy expert system that we have proposed here turns out to be a more flexible and powerful tool than traditional techniques used to define quality of work. The fuzzy expert system allows one to consider the relation amongst elementary variables/indicators and, therefore, amongst the analytical dimensions that we have defined, weighting and ranking them according to a system of rules that, step by step, can incorporate status of art, theoretical framework and researchers' views. The expert system can be used both to study individual cases, or particular types of work or to provide a comparative analysis of different labour markets.

The system allows one to investigate when a trade-off between the different dimensions arises. Traditional discussion on the compensating differentials between monetary and non-monetary characteristics and on segmented labour markets can therefore be tackled on completely different grounds. This technique proves to be superior to other techniques since it enables one to account for the interrelations amongst the different dimensions (it also allows the same variable to enter in different dimensions with different weight), to specify rules of judgement on the meaning of the values assumed by different variables and to relate the output of the system with individual characteristics (age, gender, education, work experience), job characteristics and characteristics of the firm (size, economic situation of the firm's good market, union presence). In other words, the system provides an output that captures labour market segmentation and could detect the dimensions, that endogenously contribute to determine segmentation.

References

Addabbo T. – Facchinetti G. - Mastroleo G. (2005). "A fuzzy expert system to measure functionings. An application to child wellbeing". In K. Saeed, R. Mosdorf, J. Pejas, P. Hilmola, Z. Sosnowsky (eds) *Proceeding of Image Analysis, Computer Graphics, Security Systems and Artificial Intelligence Applications*. Bialystok Vol. 1, 29-42.

European Commission (2001) "Employment and social policies: a framework for investing in quality" Communication from the Commission to the Council, the European Parliament, the Economic and Social Committee and the Committee of the Regions, COM (2001), Final, 20/06/2001.

Gallino L. (1993), *Dizionario di sociologia*, Torino, Utet (I ed. 1978)

International Labour Office (2003). *General Report, Seventeenth International Conference of Labour Statisticians*, Geneva, 24 November – 3 December 2003.

Merllié, D. - Paoli M. (2001) *Third European Survey on working conditions – 2000* European Foundation for the Improvement of Living and Working Conditions, Luxembourg: Office for Official Publications of the European Communities.

Piegat A. (2001), *Fuzzy modelling and control*. Springer-Verlag, Heidelberg-New York.

Application of the Peano Curve for the Robot Trajectory Generating

Marcin Pluciński and Marcin Korzeń

Faculty of Computer Science and Information Technology,
Szczecin University of Technology, Żołnierska 49, 71-210 Szczecin, Poland,
mplucinski@wi.ps.pl, mkorzen@wi.ps.pl

Abstract. One of many possible applications of mobile robots is using them to autonomous searching of the given area. There are two problems in such a task. The first one – how to generate a map of the searching area, the second – what shape should have a path of the robot which assures that the robot cover the whole area in the efficient way. The paper shows how this problem was solved for the miniature mobile Khepera^2 robot.

1. Introduction

One of many possible applications of mobile robots is using them to autonomous searching of the given environment. The main task of the robot is finding a polygon surrounding the area and running over all points inside it. Such a task must be solved, for example, by robots autonomously cleaning houses or mowing a grass.

There are two problems in the mentioned task. The first one – how to generate a map of the searching area, the second – what shape should have a path of the robot which assures that the robot cover the whole area in the efficient way. The paper shows how this problem was solved for the miniature mobile Khepera^2 robot.

2. Main parameters of the mobile Khepera^2 robot

Khepera^2 is the tiny two-wheeled mobile robot particularly useful in research and education. Its standard equipment and additional modules allows researching in trajectory planning, obstacle avoidance, processing of sensor information, group behaviour and cooperation of robots [6,7].

Below, there are listed the most important parameters of the Khepera^2 robot [4,7]:
- processor: Motorola 68331, 25 MHz,
- memory: RAM – 512 Kb, Flash – 512 Kb (programmable via serial port),
- motion: 2 DC motors,
- speed: min. ≈ 0.01 m/s, max. ≈ 1 m/s,
- sensors: 8 infra-red proximity and ambient light sensors,
- communication: standard serial port,

– size: diameter – 70 mm, height – 30 mm,
– weight: approx. 80 g,
– power: power adapter or rechargeable batteries.

The robot is equipped with 2 DC motors coupled with a wheel through a 25:1 reduction gearbox. An incremental encoder, placed on the motor axis, gives 24 pulses per revolution of the motor. Taking into account 25:1 reduction, the counter is increased by 600 pulses per revolution of the wheel. Next, taking into account the wheel size (radius 7.8 mm) it can be found that the counter is increased by 12 pulses per millimeter of a path of the robot (0.08 mm per 1 pulse) [4].

The main processor has the direct control on the motor power supply and can read the pulses of the incremental encoder. Both motors can be controlled by a PID controller used in one of two control modes. The position of wheels is controlled in the first mode. A given value of counters for each wheel is set (and in this way a given position of the robot). When given values are reached the robot stops. Such mode of a robot work isn't useful in a move control, so more often the second mode is used – the mode which a speed of the robot is controlled in.

In case of this controller, a given speed can be set for each wheel independently. The speed is given in pulses per 10 ms, so the minimal speed which can be set is equal 0.008 m/s (one pulse per 10 ms) and maximal – approx. 1 m/s (127 pulses per 10 ms). Robot wheels can move forward and backward and PID controller settings can be changed by user.

The Khepera[2] robot is equipped with 8 infra-red proximity sensors. Positions of sensors are shown in Fig. 1. They are placed in such a way to detect obstacles in all directions.

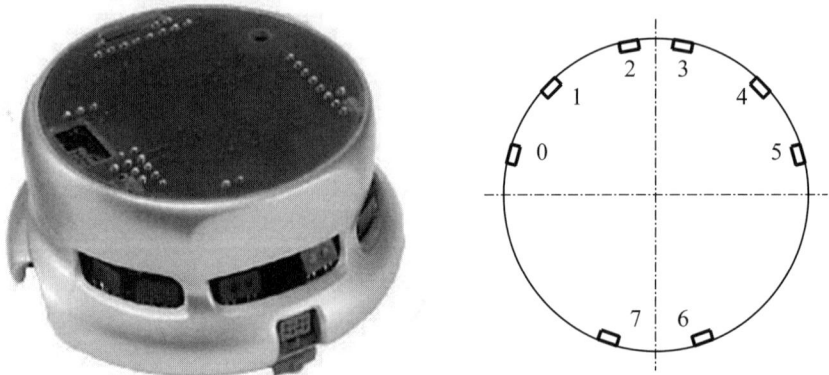

Fig. 1. The Khepera[2] robot and positions of the infra-red sensors

Each sensor has an infra-red light emitter and a receiver. Sensors allow two measures: the normal ambient light (made only by the receiver) and the light reflected by obstacles. Measurements are made every 20 μs and measured analogue values are converted into 10-bit digital values [1,4].

Sensors allows detecting obstacles from a distance approx. 6 cm. Results of a measurement of an infra-red light reflected by obstacles mostly depends on such factors like light conditions in an environment and a reflection degree of an obstacle (which depends on obstacle color, material and surface roughness). Exemplary characteristic of the sensor 2 (front-left) taken for white paper is presented in Fig. 2.

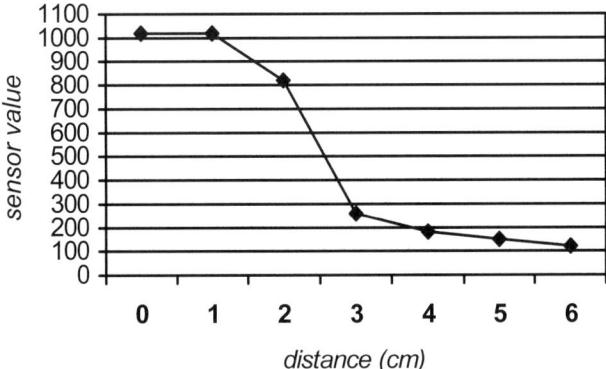

Fig. 2. Exemplary characteristic of the sensor 2

An appearance of the characteristic in Fig. 2 is demonstrative. Its shape will be different for other light conditions or obstacles made of other material. Moreover, sensor readings are disturbed by measurement noise what makes their interpretation more complicated. The standard deviation of this noise is approx. 10 (in sensor units) and that's why a precise localisation of obstacles around the robot is very difficult.

3. Navigation

A current robot position can be counted on the base of the way that left and right wheel traveled. After each sampling step, a state of both wheel counters is read. With the knowledge of a wheels diameter and a distance between them we can calculate the way traveled by the geometric center of the robot.

Let us introduce some notations:

R – radius of an arc covered by the robot center (line segments OA, OB),
b – distance between wheels (53 mm),
l_L – length of an arc covered by the left wheel,
l_P – length of an arc covered by the right wheel,
l – length of an arc covered by the robot center,
d – half of the line segment AB,
$\Delta\beta$ – change of the robot course,
β – robot course in the point A,
x_1, y_1 – local, moveable coordinate system connected with the robot.

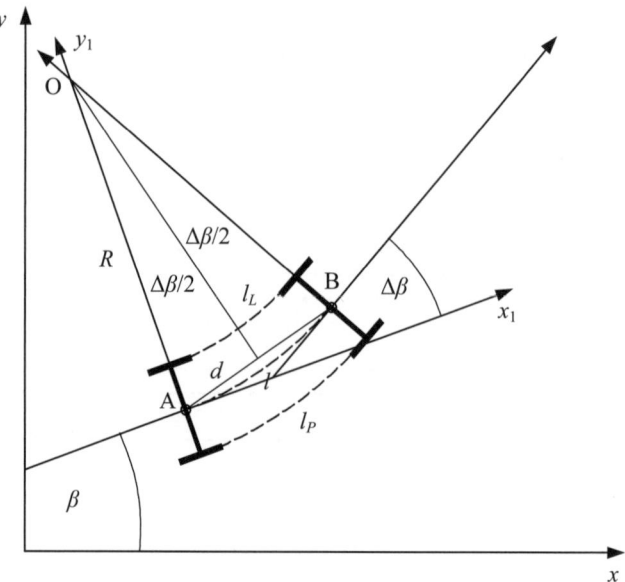

Fig. 3. Notations used for the robot position calculation

Now, we can count:

$$\Delta\beta = \frac{l_P - l_L}{b}, \quad l = \frac{l_P + l_L}{2}. \tag{1}$$

Equations (2) can be derived from formulas (1) and from geometric dependencies from Fig. 3.

$$x_B = l \cdot \frac{\sin(\Delta\beta/2)}{\Delta\beta/2} \cdot \cos(\beta - \Delta\beta/2) + x_A, \tag{2}$$

$$y_B = l \cdot \frac{\sin(\Delta\beta/2)}{\Delta\beta/2} \cdot \sin(\beta + \Delta\beta/2) + y_A.$$

With formulas (1) and (2) we can count a new robot position in each sampling step on the base of a previous position and a distance covered by wheels. Unfortunately, such position counting method cause that the position is known with an error increasing with time (but with available robot equipment there is no other method). Moreover, big errors may be caused by slide of wheels (for example, during collision with an obstacle).

4. Map of the environment

To generate a map, the robot must go round the given environment and register all met obstacles.

In the first phase of a movement, the robot moves forward until it finds an obstacle in a given distance (30 mm in experiments). An infra-red sensor which indicate the greatest value is closest to it. We know the bearings of sensors, so the robot can be turned in such a way to be positioned left side (sensor 0) near an obstacle.

The second phase of the movement consists in moving along the obstacle in the given distance. Speed of wheels is controlled here by special controller described below. Let us introduce some more notations:

p_0 – value of the sensor 0,

v_L, v_R – speed of the left and right wheel,

v_N – nominal speed,

W_{min}, W_{max} – range of sensor values, which represent an assumed distance from obstacles.

1. If $p_0 \in [W_{min}, W_{max}]$ then set the robot speed: $v_L = v_R = v_N$.

   The robot moves with the given distance from obstacles. To take into account measurement noise, the sensor value p_0 can belong to the specified range $[W_{min}, W_{max}]$ for the given distance from an obstacle. In such solution, the robot doesn't turn accidentally as a reaction on noise. In our experiments, we assumed $W_{min} = 180$ and $W_{max} = 220$. It assured that the robot moved approx. 30 mm from obstacles.

2. If $p_0 < W_{min}$ the robot drive away from an obstacle.

   Count an error: $e^- = W_{min} - p_0$ and set robot speeds:

   $v_L = v_N - K^- \cdot e^-$, $v_R = v_N + K^- \cdot e^-$.
   If $v_L \leq 0$ then set $v_L = 1$.

3. If $p_0 > W_{max}$ the robot approach an obstacle.

   Count an error: $e^+ = p_0 - W_{max}$ and set robot speeds:

   $v_L = v_N + K^+ \cdot e^+$, $v_R = v_N - K^+ \cdot e^+$.
   If $v_R \leq 0$ then set $v_R = 1$.

K^-, K^+ are gain coefficients of the control algorithm. They are taken experimentally and for the reason that sensor characteristics are nonlinear (Fig. 2) they have different values.

During a movement along an obstacle, a state of front sensors (2 and 3 in Fig. 1) must be checked. If an obstacle is detected in the given distance (30 mm in experiments) the robot stops and turns 90 degrees right.

Moving along obstacles, in each sampling step the robot saves a position of its center and a position of point located 75 mm left (35 mm for the robot radius + 30 mm for approx. distance to the obstacle). The robot moves until it came back near (with the given precision) the point where it started to go round the environment. A result of the movement is a recorded shape of boundaries of the searched area (a map) which consists with large amount of points.

In the end, the map must be simplified. We check all recorded points and if a next point is too close to a previous one (we assume a minimal distance) we remove it. Later, if the next point is placed in the beginning of a line segment which changes a direction in comparison with previous segment by a small angle (we assume a minimal angle) we remove it too. As the result, we get the map represented by small amount of points that really describe the boundaries shape of the searched area. In the same way we simplify the recorded path of the robot. A closed polygon obtained in this way will be used in generating of the future robot trajectory on which the robot will move during area searching.

5. Robot trajectory generating

The basic problem is to construct such a curve that will cover the surface of the polygon at a uniform rate. Historically, the first example of a curve that fills a surface, was a curve filling the surface of a square described in 1890 by G. Peano. It is known [5], that each compact and connected subset of n-dimensional space, is a continuous image of the unit interval.

The construction given by Peano is exact in a sense, that the image of that curve is a square. But from a practical point of view important is only the fact that the robot trajectory can pass sufficiently close to a given point of a considered area. In order to define, whether given curve fills the surface, let's define an ε-covering concept.

Assume that there is a given area X on the plane. We say that the set of points $\{x_1, x_2, \ldots, x_n\}$, are ε-covering of a given set X, if $X \subset \bigcup_{i=1}^{n} K(x_i, \varepsilon)$, where $K(x_i, \varepsilon)$ is the open ball of radius ε and centered at point x_i. Additionally, if the set of points $\{x_1, x_2, \ldots, x_n\}$ belongs to certain curve, we will say that curve ε-covers given polygon. In practice, the ε quantity depends on the radius of the robot. In the considered case this quantity is equal to 35 mm.

There are two ways of solving the problem: on-line (points of curve are computed currently while robot is moving) and off-line (whole trajectory is generated at the beginning, and after that robot moves). Both approaches have either advantages or disadvantages and difficulties with implementation.

In the paper we present off-line approach. In such case we must first find the vertices of an analysed area. It can be realised in the way presented in the first part of the paper. The next step is to generate trajectory on the basis of vertices. For that problem the algorithm in Fig. 4 is presented.

The illustration of the algorithm is presented in Fig. 5. In this case there is a given polygon with 6 vertices. First, we create the triangulation and set the beginning cycle – what mean the sequence of going through vertices in our case (1, 2, 3, 4, 5, 6).

In the next steps we add vertices in sequence. In the first step we include vertex no 7, which divides the current longest side connecting vertices 2 and 3. We update the tables describing graph, by removing edge connecting vertices 2 and 3 in table G, and adding in this place edges (2, 7), (3, 7) i (6, 7). In table V, we remove the edge 3 from the list of vertex 2 neighbours and add vertex 7, from the list of vertex 3 neighbours we remove vertex 2 and add vertex 7, there is also added a new vertex 7 with a list of neighbours (2, 3, 6). For the new created edges we count length.

Input:
        W – ordered set of vertices of a given area $W = \{w_i\}$
        r – radius of covering (radius of the robot)

Output:
        P – ordered set of vertices of a filling polygon curve

Initialisation:
      Find: T – triangulation of polygon
              G – set of edges of triangular partition
              V – list vertices of triangulation (each vertex is a structure:
                   (number of vertex, list of neighbours))
              Initiation of curve: $P_0 = W$

while (maxLengthOfEdge(P) > r)
        1. find (p,g) – the longest edge in graph G
        2. divide (p,g) in two, let c be middle point
        3. add new point c into graph and update arrays G, V
        4. add point c to curve P_{i+1}, insert it before or after one of its neighbours

end

return P

Fig. 4. Filling space curve construction algorithm

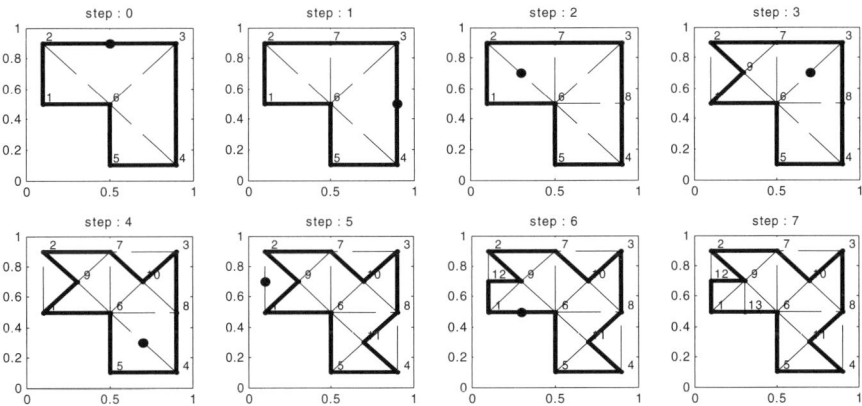

Fig. 5. Illustration of the algorithm from Fig. 4, the first eight steps of algorithm for a given area

The new added point no 7 is inserted to the cycle (point 4. of the algorithm) before or after one of the vertices 2, 3, 6 so that the created cycle was the shortest. In that case it is between vertices 2 and 3.

It is clear, that the vertices set of a curve generated in such way is ε-covering of a given polygon. More precisely, it means that a distance between any point of the polygon and the curve is less then r.

When the ε-covering of polygon is considered, the order of running vertices is not valid. It is important that robot visits each vertex at least once. But from practical point of view, such trajectory should have additional properties. First, it should be economical (i.e. short) and second, it should be easy to realise by a robot.

In the case of the Khepera robot we do not have possibility of precise measurement of its position. We can only measure positions of motor engines and determine a robot position by adequate summing. While robot moving, errors caused by large number of turnings are increasing. Therefore, it would be good to generate trajectory with possibly low number of turnings, which goes through the points generated by the algorithm.

Basing on the results obtained from the algorithm (Fig. 4), especially on discretisation given by points P and triangulation G, V, we can propose another trajectory generating algorithm. In each step it adds the next point, which is first on the left side in triangulation V. Added point is removed from triangulation. It means that vertex, for which the angle between current and following direction of move is the least, is chosen.

Comparison of these two approaches is presented in Fig. 6. We use spline Bezier curves in order to improve further properties of obtained trajectory. Both, either the original trajectory or the smoothed by Bezier splines trajectory are presented in Fig. 6.

6. Experiments

We realized a lot of experiments in which the robot searched environments with difficult complication degree. A robot movement trajectory was generated for each created map. Exemplary maps and trajectories are shown in Fig. 7. Real shapes of searched areas are shown on the top part of the figure.

Generated maps are turned by a small angle. It is a result of an assumption that in the beginning of an experiment geometrical center of the robot is placed in the origin of the global coordinate system and the course β of the robot equals 0. Imprecision start placement of the robot produces the effect of the map rotation.

Maps are not generated precisely. It results from small accuracy of infra-red sensors, differences of light conditions in different places of the environment, shadows and errors in counting of the global robot position.

7. Conclusions

Experiments proved an efficiency of all described algorithms in spite of small accuracy of sensors. Better results could be obtained for the robot equipped with better sensors (more exactly detecting obstacles from greater distance) and devices enabling exact navigation. Trajectory obtained in the second algorithm is not perfect and needs smoothing (line is broken due to triangulation).

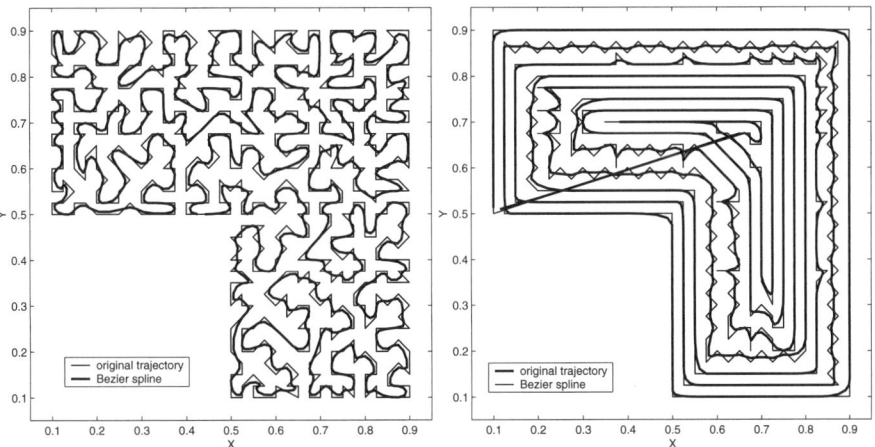

Fig. 6. Comparison of two described algorithms (after 642 steps) – both lines are smoothed by Bezier splines

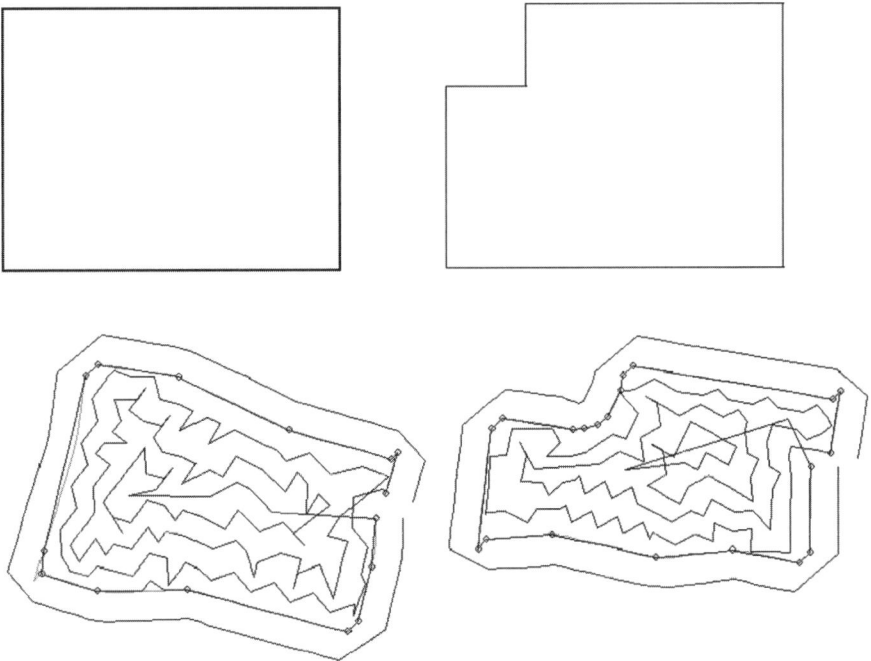

Fig. 7. Results of experiments – exemplary maps and generated trajectories

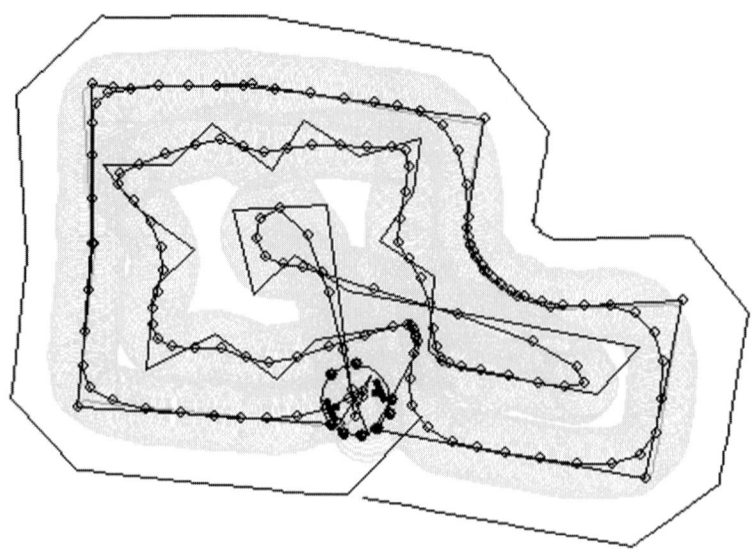

Fig. 8. Exemplary map, generated trajectory and covered area

Both trajectory generation algorithms are quite fast (computational complexity equals $O(n^2)$ – where n is the number of map points). Calculations for 2500 points of the map took approx. 1 s (on a computer with an Athlon 1.1 GHz processor). It should be enough to cover about 600 m^2 for a robot with a diameter equal to 0.5 m.

Future research will concern environments with not connected boundary. Next, we plan to improve the method of trajectory generating to enable an area searching by many robots.

References

[1] Bureau P.: Khepera[2] – IR sensors report, K-Team S.A., Switzerland (2000)
[2] Dulęba I.: Methods and algorithms of the mobile and manipulation robots movement (in polish), Akademicka Oficyna Wydawnicza EXIT, Warszawa (2001)
[3] Giergiel M., Hendzel Z., Żylski W.: Modeling and controlling of mobile wheel robots (in polish), Wydawnictwo Naukowe PWN, Warszawa (2002)
[4] Khepera[2] – user manual, K-Team S.A., Switzerland (2000)
[5] Kuratowski K.: Introduction to set theory and topology, Elsevier, 2 RevEd edition, (1972)
[6] Pluciński M.: Application of a probabilistic neural network to an identification of objects on the base of Khepera[2] robot infra-red sensor readings (in polish), Proceedings of the IX Informatics Symposium, Faculty of Computer Science and Information Technology, Szczecin University of Technology, Szczecin (2004)
[7] www.k-team.com – website of K-Team Corporation

On Some Properties of the B-Cell Algorithm in Non-Stationary Environments

Krzysztof Trojanowski, Sławomir T. Wierzchoń

Institute of Computer Sci., Polish Acad. of Sciences, Ordona 21, 01-237 Warsaw, Poland
{trojanow,stw}@ipipan.waw.pl

Abstract: Mammalian immune system and especially clonal selection principle, responsible for coping with external intruders, is an inspiration for a set of heuristic optimization algorithms. In this paper we focus our attention on an instance of a clonal selection algorithm called BCA. This algorithm admits very good exploratory abilities when solving stationary optimization problems. We try to explain this capability studying the behavior of the mutation operator being distinguishable feature of BCA. Later we apply it to solve non-stationary optimization problem.

1. Introduction

The task of non-stationary functions optimization is the identification of a series of optima that change their location (and possibly their value) in time. More formally we want to identify at least the global optimum of a function $f(x, t)$ where $x \in A \subset \mathbb{R}^n$, A is a given set of admissible solutions being a subset of the n-dimensional Euclidean space $\mathbb{R}^n$, and t represents time. Typically the domain A is the Cartesian product of the intervals $[x_i^{min}, x_i^{max}]$, $i = 1, .., n$, and sometimes it varies in time too. Evolutionary algorithms designed to cope with such stated task exploit one of the following strategies, [4, 7]: (a) the expansion of the memory in order to build up a repertoire of ready responses for environmental changes, or (b) the application of some mechanism for increasing population diversity in order to compensate for changes encountered in the environment. In this last case commonly used mechanisms are: random immigrants mechanism, triggered hypermutation or simply increasing the mutation rate within a standard genetic algorithm to a constant high level (for more details on the evolutionary techniques for optimization in dynamic environments see [2, 7, 9]). Recently, other swarm-based techniques – like ACO (Ant Colony Optimization, [8]) or PSO (Particle Swarm Optimization, [1]) – are proposed to deal with the problem.

In this paper we study the ability of an immune-based algorithm to trace varying positions of the global optimum of a multimodal function. The first immune algorithm, called Simple Artificial Immune System or Sais, to cope with pattern tracking in dynamic environment was proposed in [7]. These authors used very simple unimodal function whose maximum was changed cyclically. In our approach we study much more complicated environments described in Section 5. The general idea underlying immune algorithms is presented in Section 2 and a specific instance of such an algorithm – in Section 3.

2. Immune based algorithms for numerical optimization

The natural immune system (NIS for brevity) protects mammalian organisms against dangerous agents like fungi, viruses, bacteria, etc., called pathogens. Among many theories used to explain how the NIS copes with the antigens (i.e., a special group of pathogens) the most attractive and most simple is the clonal selection theory, [5, 6]. Namely, to destroy replicating antigens the immune cells, more precisely lymphocytes of type B (or B-cells in short), reproduce themselves asexually in a way proportional to their degree of recognition of the intruder. This degree is measured in terms of the affinity, i.e. the strength with which a B-cell binds the antigen. The offspring, or clones, of the B-cell are subjected mutation allowing them to become more adapted to the recognized antigen. In general the higher affinity of a given B-cell with the antigen, the more clones this cell produces, and the lower mutation rate is applied to its clones. This mechanism gave birth to the CLONALG algorithm which can be viewed as a basic clonal selection algorithm. As stated in [5] "this algorithm has all the steps involved in an evolutionary algorithm: reproduction and genetic variation, affinity (fitness) evaluation, and selection". The difference between immune and evolutionary algorithm is rather subtle: "clonal selection algorithms are primarily based upon affinity-proportionate reproduction, mutation and selection" (quotation from [5]). Review of different instances of the clonal selection algorithm can be found in [5] and [17].

The general idea of using an immune-based algorithm in an optimization problem is such that the problem is treated as an antigen and the aim of the algorithm is to produce B-cells coping with the antigen, i.e. solutions to this problem. Obviously when we are interested in finding the global optimum of a function $f(x)$ in the set of admissible solutions $A \subseteq R^n$, we are interested in obtaining a single B-cell $\mathbf{x}^*$ with the affinity as close as possible with the antigen $\mathbf{x}_{opt}$ i.e. $f(\mathbf{x}^*) \approx f(\mathbf{x}_{opt})$. When f is a multimodal function we are interested in finding as much as possible local optima; a successful representative of such an algorithm is `opt-aiNet` mentioned in [6]. In this case the size of the population of B-cells is not known in advance. Lastly, when the optimized (multimodal) function varies in time we are interested in tracing location of its global optimum. This last case is most complicated. We distinguish here two sub-cases: the function $f(x, t)$ is periodic or a-periodic. In both cases the algorithm should be able to explore constantly the search space A, and it should be possible to maintain a kind of memory allowing fast retrieval of already known positions. This last property is necessary for tracing optima in periodic functions. A first attempt to this problem is reported in [15]. In this paper we focus on another instance of the clonal selection algorithm called BCA (B-cell algorithm) proposed in [10]. We choose this algorithm because of its high efficacy in stationary optimization.

3. B-Cell Algorithm (BCA)

Our version of the BCA algorithm originates from [10]. It implements non-deterministic iterated process of exploring multidimensional search space and works with a population of tentative solutions called B-cells. Each B-cell is represented as n-dimensional vector of bit strings of length n_b.

The pseudo-code of the main loop of BCA is given in Figure 1. The symbol $x_i \in P$ represents i-th B-cell of the population P, $xc_{i,k}$ – k-th copy (clone) of the i-th B-cell subjected further mutation, $f(x_i)$ – B-cell affinity to the antigen, i.e. fitness of the B-cell x_i, and xc_i^* is the best mutated clone of the i-th B-cell, i.e. $f(xc_i^*) \geq f(xc_{i,k})$, $k \in \{1, .. c\}$ where c is the number of clones produced by the B-cell. Note that while in the CLONALG the number of clones produced by a given cell is proportional to its fitness, here each cell produces exactly the same number of clones.

The algorithm starts with a population of randomly generated solutions from the search space and performs the process of iterated improvement of the solutions by the execution of the main loop depicted in Figure 1. The loop obeys two main blocks: (i) affinity evaluation – step (a), and (ii) clonal selection and expansion – steps (b) - (f).

For each B-Cell $x_i \in P$
(a) compute its fitness i.e. the value of the objective function $f(x_i)$
(b) make c clones $xc_{i,k}$, $k \in \{1, .. c\}$ of x_i and place them in a clonal pool C_i
(c) randomize one clone $xc_{i,(j)}$ in the clonal pool C_i, where (j) stands for a number from $\{1, .. c\}$
(d) apply the contiguous mutation to all the remaining clones in $C_i \setminus \{ xc_{i,(j)}\}$
(e) for each clone in C_i compute its fitness
(f) the mutated clone xc_i^* with the highest fitness replaces the original B-Cell if $f(xc_i^*) > f(x_i)$.

Fig. 1. Pseudo-code of the main loop of BCA

The algorithm has three control parameters: $|P|$ – population size, c – number of clones in the clonal pool, and n_b – the length of binary string representing each of n components of a B-cell. Two interesting features of the BCA are [10]: (a) an efficient population size for many functions is low in contrast with other population-based algorithms (like e.g. genetic algorithm); typical size $|P| \in \{3, ..., 6\}$, and (b) the size of the clonal pool is typically the same as $|P|$. These features proved to be satisfactory when solving stationary optimization problems.

We also assume that the optimization system "knows" when its environment has changed. However the algorithm does not start from scratch then but reevaluates its population of solutions and continues the search process.

4. Contiguous mutation

The mutation operator works on solutions represented as binary strings. As showed in [13], BCA with a 64-bit double precision floating point coding (according to IEEE 754 standard) significantly outperformed BCA with 32-bit pure binary coding, therefore we decided to turn to the former approach.

In the first step the mutation operator randomly selects a bit in the string which will be a starting point hs_{cm} (called also *hot spot*) of the sequence of bits to be mutated. Then the length l_{cm} of the sequence is generated randomly too, i.e. $l_{cm} = U_i(0,63)$ where $U_i(0,63)$ is an integral random variable uniformly distributed over the interval $[0,63]$. Finally every bit of the sequence defined by hs_{cm} and l_{cm} is mutated individually: if $(U(0,1) > 0.5)$ then x[i]=1, else x[i]=0, where $i = hs_{cm}$, $hs_{cm} +1$, .., $hs_{cm} + l_{cm}$. If the mutation operator attempts to index outside the bound of the bit string, i.e., $i > 63$, the index i is reevaluated: $i = i \bmod 64$. Then the sequence continues from the beginning of the string.

To get an insight into the nature of the mutation operator, a number of simulations have been done. In Figure 2 four histograms are presented for mutations of four different values from the interval $[-10,10]$: -7.5, -0.7, 6.8 and 9.9. For each of these values we applied the contiguous mutation 10,000 times. Interestingly, some of the mutated values did not belong to the entire interval, and some of the offspring located near to zero (more precisely, in the interval $[-10^{-6},10^{-6}]$). These values are not presented in the histograms. Distribution of all the remaining values, i.e. those which belong to the interval $[-10,10] \setminus [-10^{-6},10^{-6}]$ is presented in Figure 2.

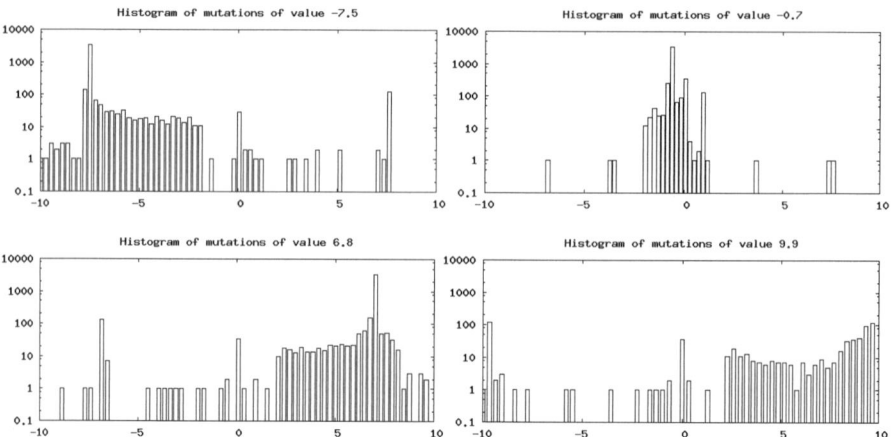

Fig. 2. Sample histograms for contiguous mutation of four different values

Numbers of mutated values presented and omitted in the histograms are shown in Table 1.

Table 1. Number of values presented and omitted in the histograms in Figure 2

Value	in the interval	out of the interval	too close to zero
-7.5	4118	3456	2426
-0.7	4500	2475	3025
6.8	3854	3748	2398
9.9	4260	3399	2341

The mutation operator must not generate values from out of the search domain, as well as the generated values should not converge to zero. Thus in our implementation the modification is repeated till the proper value is obtained.

5. Plan of experiments and applied measures

The algorithms are considered as comparable when the number of fitness function evaluations between subsequent changes in the environment is similar for each of the compared algorithms (see e.g. [3]). For comparison with results published by other authors, we assumed that the number of function evaluations equals approximately 5000. In our experiments we varied some of algorithm's parameters however for each of parameters' settings the constraint on maximum number of iterations was always satisfied. Particularly, we varied the population size, $|P|$ from 4 to 32 with step 2, and also for $|P| \in \{36, 42, 52, 64, 84, 126\}$ assigning the number of clones $c = \lfloor 248/|P| \rfloor$.

In case of the biggest size of the population, i.e. $|P| = 126$ the clonal pool is the smallest and consists of just one clone. Such a setting turns out the BCA algorithm into a local search algorithm where for each antibody only one successor is randomly generated. In opposite case there is a population of 4 B-Cells and each cell generates 62 clones. This time we have a strong selective pressure (61 mutated solutions plus one randomly generated) but a poor diversity.

The behavior of the algorithm was tested with six environments generated with two test-benchmarks. The first test-benchmark is a Test Case Generator[1] (or TCG) proposed in [14]. We created four testing environments with TCG; two of them with cyclic changes and two with non-cyclic ones. In case of cyclic changes a full run of a single experiment includes 5 cycles of changes in the environment. In case of non-cyclic environments the total number of changes for the full run was set to 25. The second test-benchmark is a Moving Peaks Benchmark (or MPB) generator [2,12]. Its description, sample parameters settings and a source code are available at the web page [2]. We created two testing environments with MPB called scenario 1 and 2, [2]. The total number of changes for the full run for each of the scenarios was 25 too.

Six groups of experiments were performed: two of them with cyclically changing environments and four others with non-cyclically changing environments. Table 2 shows the settings for each of the groups.

Table 2. Parameters of six groups of experiments. Here the symbol TCG_{10c} (resp. TCG_{20nc}) means the cyclic (resp. non-cyclic) environment with 10 (resp. 20) moving peaks generated by TCG; similarly MPB_5 stands for the environment with 5 moving peaks generated by the MPB

Environment	TCG_{10c}	TCG_{20c}	TCG_{12nc}	TCG_{20nc}	MPB_5	MPB_{50}
No. of dimensions	2	2	2	2	5	5
Environment type	10×10	10×10	6 × 6	10 × 10	1	2
No. of varying optima	10	20	12	20	5	50
No. of iterations	1000	2000	500	500	500	500

---

[1] Figures of sample environments generated with TCG are available at:
`http://www.ipipan.waw.pl/~stw/ais/environment/env.html`

The first row called *No. of dimensions* shows the number of dimensions of the search space where the optimization is performed. *Environment type* shows the identifier of the testing environment. In case of TCG the identifier describes the landscape for the 2-dimensional search space, e.g. 10×10 means that we have a "chessboard" with 100 fields (10 by 10) each with a single hill in the center. In case of MPB the identifier is a number of scenario. *No. of varying optima* shows the number of varying hills, peaks or cones in the optimization landscape. *No. of iterations* shows the number of iterations performed in one full run of a single experiment. In case of cyclic changes this number is equal to: number of cycles of changes multiplied by the number of changes in a cycle (i.e. no. of varying optima) and by the number of iterations between changes. For example, for environment TCG_{10c} it is: $5 \times 10 \times 20$.

To evaluate the results, we used three measures: average error, offline performance and offline error, [3]. Average error is the average deviation from the optimum of all evaluations performed in a single experiment. Offline performance is the average of all evaluations of the best evaluation since the last change of the environment and time. Simply every time the solution's fitness is evaluated, the value of an auxiliary variable is updated by the value of actually evaluated solution if it is better than any other since the last change or by the fitness of the best solution since the last change. When the experiment is finished the sum is divided by the total number of evaluation. The last measure, offline error, represents the average deviation of the best individual evaluated since the last change from the optimum. It is evaluated similarly to the offline performance, but instead of the fitness of the currently best solution its deviation from the optimum is computed. Every experiment was repeated 100 times and the mean values of these measures are presented in the Figures 3 – 5.

6. Results of experiments

There are three figures with the results. Each of them shows different quality index, i.e. offline error (Fig. 3), average error (Fig. 4) and offline performance (Fig. 5). Each of the figures includes three graphs for three types of environments: cyclic (top graph), non-cyclic (middle graph) and randomly changing environment (bottom graph).

The best values of the offline error (Fig. 3) were obtained for rather small size of clonal pool, i.e. for a population of 64 B-Cells where each of them generates just 3 clones and among them one was replaced by a random solution. This indicates that diversity in the population is more useful than the high selective pressure. This is in accordance with observations for other evolutionary approaches.

The average error (Fig. 4) shows the average distance from all the solutions created during the experiment and the optimum measured as a difference between fitness values of the individuals and the optimum. After every change in the fitness landscape all the B-Cells have to be reevaluated and it is obvious that at least some of them should be much worse than before the change. Therefore it is not expected that this measure will be close to zero. However if the number of the B-cells with low affinity to the antigen is small, we may say that the algorithm is sufficiently sensitive to detect different types of changes.

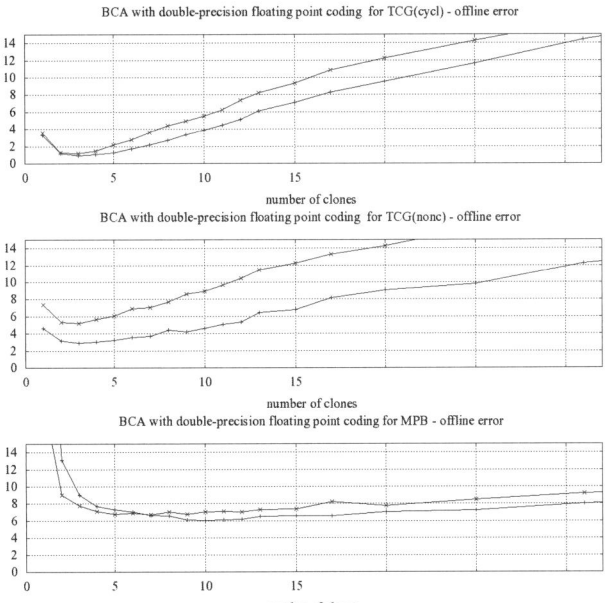

Fig. 3. Offline error obtained during experiments with BCA with double precision floating point coding. X axis represents number of clones.

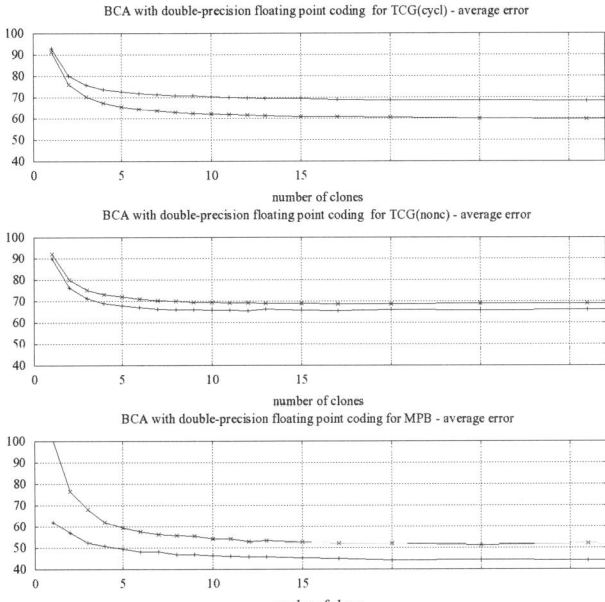

Fig. 4. Average error obtained during experiments with BCA with double precision floating point coding. X axis represents number of clones.

In Fig. 4 it can be seen that the value of the average error is high for small sizes of the clonal pool, and starts to stabilize for the clonal pool larger than 5. Comparing this with the best parameter settings for minimal value of the offline error, we can conclude that the lowest values of the average error do not really guarantee the best offline error value but rather average and stable albeit not very advantageous outcome. Thus it seems to be better to set the parameters to the values close before the stability area of average error (i.e. for the clonal pool it would be better to set the value close to 5 in case of Fig. 4). Simply it is better to have a higher value of the average error and a low value of the offline error than the opposite.

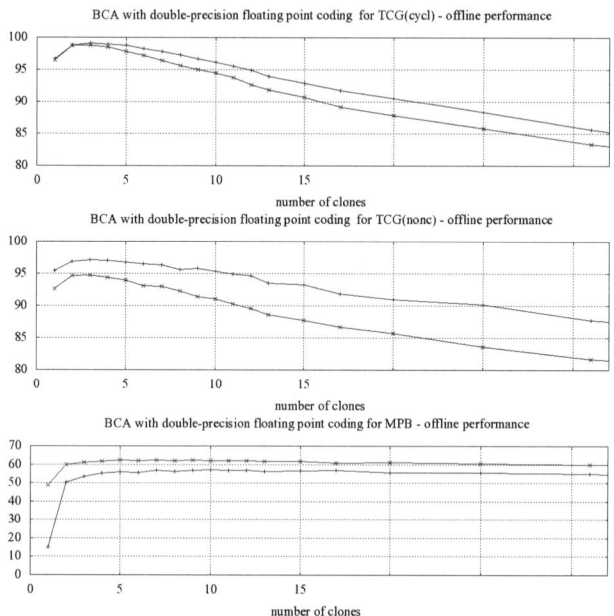

Fig. 5. Offline performance obtained during experiments with BCA with double precision floating point coding. X axis represents number of clones.

The last measure is the offline performance (Fig. 5) which helps to observe average value of the best fitness values obtained during the search process. This allows controlling the reaction of the algorithm to the environmental changes, and especially how fast it is able to return to the already attained quality, which was lost because of the change in the fitness landscape. Indications of the offline error almost completely agree with indications of the offline performance, however, the latter also gives us some more general information. Together with offline error it shows the proportion between the difference between the obtained best values and the absolute fitness value of the best solutions which could be useful for experts in case of a real-world problem. In our case the TCG tasks always have the optimum value set to 100 so the value of the offline performance is easy to evaluate since it is a difference between the optimum value and the offline error. In case of MPB the optimum value is defined as a value which is not constant but has just to fit into an interval which according to the specification of the two scenarios proposed by Branke [2] was in our case set to [30,70].

For those who always want a clear answer who is the best an additional ranking was prepared. In Table 3 the best mean values of evaluated measures obtained during experiments are presented. The results of offline error are comparable with the results obtained by other clonal selection based algorithms and presented in [13] and in case of cyclically changing environments are better than any of the tested algorithms.

Table 3. Best values obtained by BCA

Measure:	TCG_{10c}	TCG_{20c}	TCG_{12nc}	TCG_{20nc}	MPB_5	MPB_{50}
Offline error	0.91	1.19	2.87	5.23	6.07	6.74
Average error	67.78	59.08	65.42	68.40	43.17	50.77
Offline performance	99.09	98.81	97.13	94.77	57.11	62.26

7. Conclusions

In this paper we studied applicability of a version of clonal selection algorithm called BCA [10]. The algorithm is very simple and has a small number of parameters. However it converges very quickly when solving stationary optimization problems. According to its authors, this phenomenon may be caused by the contiguous hypermutation operator. Our considerations presented in Section 4 highlight slightly the nature of this operator, and explain, at least partially, its efficiency when solving static optimization problems.

Fast convergence of the algorithm can be treated as its perpetual readiness to explore "promising" regions of the search space. That is why we examined its behavior by solving a set of non-stationary optimization test-cases. It is important to stress that the strength of the algorithm and especially its mutation operator is closely connected with a way of coding of the binary strings where it is applied. Our earlier experiments with non-stationary optimization tasks [13, 16] showed that the results are not acceptable when the operator is applied to the strings with pure binary coding. However the results become much better and comparable with the results of other evolutionary algorithms when we turn to floating point coding. Particularly we were interested in the influence of the number of clones produced by each B-cell on the algorithm's ability to trace changing global maximum. Extensive tests of different configurations of the algorithm's parameters helped us to describe the optimal parameters setting and explain what makes them better than the others.

One more feature of the BCA algorithm needs further reflection. In our opinion BCA can be viewed as a family of parallel hill-climbers. Namely each B-cell x_i produces c offspring, and only these offspring compete with a given B-cell for surviving. This is just the hill-climbing strategy: only the best neighbor of the current best solution can replace it (if it is better than that current solution). Here we observe analogical behavior. Particularly, when each B-cell produces single copy and this copy is replaced by a randomly generated solution, we obtain the simplest stochastic search algorithm.

These properties will be examined in further our studies.

References

[1] T. Blackwell. Particle swarm optimization in dynamic environments. URL:
http://igor.gold.ac.uk/~mas01tb/papers/PSOdynenv.pdf

[2] J. Branke. The moving peaks benchmark. URL:
http://www.aifb.uni-karlsruhe.de/~jbr/MovPeaks/movpeaks/.

[3] J. Branke. *Evolutionary Optimization in Dynamic Environments*. Kluwer Academic Publishers, 2002.

[4] H.G. Cobb and J.J. Grefenstette. The immune learning mechanisms: Reinforcement and recruitment and their applications. In *Proceedings of the Fifth International Conference on Genetic Algorithms*. Morgan Kaufmann, 1993.

[5] L. N. de Castro. Immune, swarm, and evolutionary algorithms. part 1: Basic concepts, part 2: Philosophical comparisons. In: *Proc. of Internat. Conf. on Neural Info. Processing, ICONIP, Workshop on Artificial Immune Systems*, 2002, vol. 3, pp. 1464–1473.

[6] L. N. de Castro and J. Timmis. *Artificial Immune Systems: A New Computational Intelligence Approach*. Springer-Verlag, 2002.

[7] A. Gaspar and P. Collard. From GAs to artificial immune systems: Improving adaptation in time dependent optimization. In *Proc. of the Congress on Evolutionary Computation*, vol. 3, IEEE Press, Piscataway, NJ, 1999, pp 1859–1866.

[8] M. Guntsch, M. Middendorf, H.Schmeck. An ant colony optimization approach to dynamic TSP. In *Proc. Genetic Evol. Comput. Conf.* Morgan Kaufmann 2001, pp. 860-867

[9] Y. Jin, J. Branke. Evolutionary optimization in uncertain environments – A survey. IEEE Trans. on Evolutionary Computation, 4(2005)303-317

[10] J. Kelsey and J. Timmis. Immune inspired somatic contiguous hypermutation for function optimisation. In *Genetic Evol. Comput. Conf – GECCO 2003*, Springer, 2003, pp. 207–218.

[11] R.W. Morrison. *Designing Evolutionary Algorithms for Dynamics Environments*. Natural Computing Series. Springer, 2002.

[12] R. W. Morrison and K. A. De Jong. A test problem generator for non-stationary environments. In *Proc. of the Congress on Evolutionary Computation*, vol. 3, IEEE Press, Piscataway, NJ, 1999, pp. 1859–1866.

[13] K. Trojanowski. Clonal selection principle based approach to non-stationary optimization tasks. In *The 9th National Conference on Evolutionary Computation and Global Optimisation*. Oficyna Wydawnicza Politechniki Warszawskiej, Warszawa, 2006.

[14] K. Trojanowski and Z. Michalewicz. Searching for optima in non–stationary environments. In *Proc. of the Congress on Evolutionary Computation*, vol. 3, IEEE Press, Piscataway, NJ, 1999, pp. 1843–1850.

[15] K. Trojanowski and S. T. Wierzchoń. Studying properties of multipopulation heuristic approach to nonstationary optimisation tasks. In *IIS 2003: Intelligent Information Processing and Web Mining*, Springer, 2003, pp. 23–32.

[16] K. Trojanowski and S. T. Wierzchoń. A comparison of clonal selection based algorithms for non-stationary optimisation tasks. In *IIPWM 2006: Intelligent Information Processing and Web Mining*, Advances in Soft Computing 5, Springer, 2006, pp. 41–52.

[17] S.T. Wierzchoń. Function optimization by the immune metaphor. *Task Quarterly*, 6(2002)493–508.

The Grouping of Valuations in Probabilistic Algorithms

Anna Borowska

Bialystok Technical University, Wiejska 45A Street, 15-351 Bialystok, Poland
borowska.anna@interia.pl

Abstract. This paper is an extension of my previous publication [2]. The mainly aim of that paper was a comparison of two techniques of a reduction of valuations in probabilistic algorithms, namely the reduction by "identifying" and by "grouping". The first of these methods is exactly described in [8], [3]. The second one (cf. [7]) is known as a reduction of states in absorbing Markov chains. In [2] we justified that a grouping can be also applied to the certain class of probabilistic programs and we formulated conditions which if are fulfilled, we can use this method. Here we show, that this method is more universal than the first one. Also we add examples of statistics which we can move from Markov chains to probabilistic programs.

1. Introduction

The complexity of methods for verification probabilistic algorithms depends on a size of a transition matrix which corresponds to a given program. So, we are interested in manners of a reduction of these matrixes. In [8] there are presented two techniques. The first one (named "by identifying") consists in defining an interpretation of a program in a standard quotient structure, which is determined by congruence. The second technique defines conditions for a reduction of a number of looping valuations. We noticed, that both these methods are cases of the technique called the grouping for the sake of a partition, which is applied (in [7]) to absorbing Markov chains.

2. The Block Matrices

The method by grouping relies on properties of block matrixes. We are interested in block matrixes $A \in R^{n \times m}$ which additionally satisfy a following property. For each block, sums of elements in rows are equal. For more transparency, we explain notations for block matrixes $A \in R^{n \times n}$ divided for the sake of one common partition (cf. [7]).

We denote by $\pi(S) = \{S_1, ..., S_q\}$ a certain fixed partition of a set $S = \{1, ..., n\}$ of indexes in the matrix $A \in R^{n \times n}$ into mutually disjoint non-empty sets. We establish, that the sets S_i $(1 \le i \le q)$ contain consecutive integers and the elements belonging to the set S_i precede elements belonging to the set S_{i+1}. For a short, $nr(S_i)$ $(1 \leq i \leq q)$ we denote by $\underline{i}$ (cf. [7]).

Let us denote by $a(i, S_1)$ (cf. [7]) a sum of elements from i-th row and columns indexed by elements from the set S_1, i.e. $a(i, S_1) = \sum_{j \in S_1} a(i, j)$ for an arbitrary $S_1 \in \pi(S)$ and an arbitrary $i \in S$. In the case, when $a(i, S_1) = a(j, S_1)$ for arbitrary indexes $i, j \in S_k$, $(S_k, S_1 \in \pi(S))$, we denote this sum by $a(\underline{k}, \underline{l})$ (cf. [7]).

Definition 2.1 (This definition is an extension of the definition from [7] for the case, when the matrix is grouped for the sake of two partitions) We say, that *the matrix* $A \in R^{n \times m}$ *is groupable for the sake of two partitions* (a row partition $\pi_w(S_w) = \{S_1, ..., S_{qw}\}$ $(qw \leq n)$ and a column partition $\pi_c(S_c) = \{S_1, ..., S_{qc}\}$ $(qc \leq m)$) if and only if for all couples of (sub)sets S_k, S_1 $(1 \leq k \leq qw, 1 \leq l \leq qc)$ and for each $i \in S_k$ the equality $a(i, S_1) = \underline{a(k, l)}$ is true. The matrix $\underline{A} = [\underline{a(k, l)}]_{1 \leq k \leq qw, 1 \leq l \leq qc}$ we call *a grouped matrix* of the matrix A (for the sake of two partitions $\pi_w(S_w)$, $\pi_c(S_c)$).

$\square$

3. The Reduction of States by Grouping in the Probabilistic Algorithms

Here we give results from [2] i.e. we cite conditions, which must be fulfilled, in order to we may use the method of a reduction by grouping in the case of the probabilistic programs. The technique of grouping relies on the algebraic method of determining of transitive matrixes for probabilistic programs (cf. [3]). Below, we cite briefly a sketch of this technique.

3.1 The Sketch of the Method for Determining of the Transitive Matrix (cf. [3])

Here, we understand the probabilistic algorithms (cf. [3]) as the iterative programs with two additional probabilistic instructions `v:=random` and `either_p` M_1 or M_2. We recall briefly more important facts connected with the considered method.

Let $\Im = < A \cup R; \{\varphi_\Im\}_{\varphi \in \Phi}, \{\psi_\Im\}_{\psi \in \Psi} >$ be a structure for the language L_P, where $A = \{a_1, ..., a_u\}$ is a finite universe. $\Im_\rho$ denotes a probabilistic structure in which the program $K(v_1, ..., v_h)$ is interpreted. ρ is a probability distribution defined on A for a random assignment $v := random$. The algebraic method relies on the following fact.

Fact 3.1 [3] The working of each program $K(v_1, ..., v_h)$ can be represented by a matrix $K = [k_{ij}]_{i, j=1, ..., n}$ $(n = u^h)$, where k_{ij} of K corresponds to the probability that

w_j is the output valuation (after a computation of K), provided that the valuation w_i appears as the input valuation with the probability 1. The matrix formed in this way can be used to determining a vector $\mu' = K_{\mathfrak{I}_\rho}(\mu)$, (an output (sub)distribution) of variables, if μ is an input (sub)distribution. Then $\mu' = \mu \circ K$. □

3.2 The Conditions of Grouping of the Transitive Matrixes

Let $\pi(W^h) = \{W_1,..., W_s\}$ signify a certain fixed partition of the set $W^h = \{w_1,..., w_n\}$ of all possible valuations of variables from $V_h = \{v_1,..., v_h\}$ in universe $A = \{a_1,..., a_u\}$. The following lemmas allow us use the grouping to probabilistic algorithms.

Lemma 3.1 (cf. [2]) Let $I_{[\gamma ?]}$, M be matrixes for a condition and a (sub)program M of a program construction while γ do M and let $W^h = \{w_1,..., w_n\}$ be a set of all possible valuations of this program, (We denote by $W_{1,q} = \{w_1,..., w_q\}$ a set of non-looping valuations, by $W_{q,r} = \{w_{q+1},..., w_r\}$ a set of looping valuations and by $W_{r,n} = \{w_{r+1},..., w_n\}$ a set of final valuations (cf. [3], [8])). Let us assume that $I_{[\gamma ?]}$, M are groupable for the sake of the same partition $\pi(W^h) = \{W_1,..., W_s\}$. Then each of the sets W_i $(i = 1,...,s)$ is a subset of exactly one of sets $W_{1,q}$, $W_{q,r}$, $W_{r,n}$.

We denote the partitions of the sets $W_{1,q}$, $W_{q,r}$, W_{rn} resulting from $\pi(W^h)$ by $\pi(W_{1,q}) = \{W_1,..., W_{q1}\}$, $\pi(W_{q,r}) = \{W_{q1+1},..., W_{r1}\}$, $\pi(W_{r,n}) = \{W_{r1+1},..., W_s\}$. □

Lemma 3.2 (cf. [2]) Let $\mathfrak{I}_\rho$ be a structure (for a language L_P) with universe $A = \{a_1,...,a_u\}$ and let $K(v_1,..., v_h)$ be an arbitrary program realized in A. We say that, if all matrixes corresponding to (sub)programs (of the form v:=τ, v:=random) of K are groupable for the sake of $\pi(W^h)$ and if we can describe all conditions in constructions of the form if γ then M_1 else M_2, while γ do M (in (sub)programs of K) by matrixes $I_{[\gamma ?]}$ which are also groupable for the sake of this partition, then the matrix corresponding to K is groupable for the sake of the common partition. □

4. The Comparison of Methods for the Reduction of States in Probabilistic Algorithms

In this section we quote two lemmas in which we compare two methods of a reduction of valuations in probabilistic programs (by "identifying" and by "grouping"). To the formal proofing the first lemma (cf. [2]) we used the following observation. If we can define congruence on the structure $\mathfrak{I}_\rho$, in which program K is interpreted, then this relation determines in a quotient structure $\mathfrak{I}_{\approx\rho_\approx}$ a set of valuations, which is a partition of the set of valuations in a primary structure. Here, as an extension, we justify the second lemma. First, we recall the method by "identifying" which is exactly described in [8].

4.1   The sketch of the method of "identifying of valuations (cf. [8])

Let $\mathfrak{I} =< A; \{\varphi_\mathfrak{I}\}_{\varphi\in\Phi}, \{\psi_\mathfrak{I}\}_{\psi\in\Psi} >$ denotes a fixed structure (for the language with L_P) with a finite universe $A = \{a_1, a_2, ..., a_u\}$. Let $\mathfrak{I}_\rho$ be a probabilistic structure in which we interpret the program $K(v_1, ... v_h)$. Let us assume, that on $\mathfrak{I}$ is defined congruence $\approx$, which determines the partition of the set A into following equivalence classes $[a_{1_1}] = ... = [a_{1_{i1}}] = \{a_{1_1}, ..., a_{1_{i1}}\}$, ..., $[a_{b_1}] = ... = [a_{b_{ib}}] = \{a_{b_1}, ..., a_{b_{ib}}\}$.

Let $\mathfrak{I}_\approx$ denotes a standard quotient structure of $\mathfrak{I}$ determined by $\approx$. The universe of $\mathfrak{I}_\approx$ is represented by a set $A_\approx = \{[a_{1_1}], [a_{2_1}], ..., [a_{b_1}]\}$. Let W^h be a set of all possible valuations of variables from V_h in A. Then congruence $\approx$ determines a set $W_\approx^h = \{[w_1], ..., [w_{n_\approx}]\}$ of possible valuations of variables from V_h in structure $\mathfrak{I}_\approx$.

$$([w_i] \overset{df}{=} \{w' \in W^h : \forall_{v\in V_l} w'(v) \approx w_i(v)\} \text{ for } i = 1, ..., n_\approx).$$

Theorem 4.1 [8] Let M be a probabilistic program interpreted in a structure $\mathfrak{I}_\rho$. Let us assume, that relation $\approx$ is congruence on $\mathfrak{I}_\rho$. By $\mathfrak{I}_{\approx\rho_\approx}$ we denote a standard quotient structure of $\mathfrak{I}_\rho$ determined by $\approx$. Then for every initial probability distribution μ we have $(M_{\mathfrak{I}_\rho}(\mu))_\approx = M_{\mathfrak{I}_{\approx\rho_\approx}}(\mu_\approx)$, where

$\mu_\approx$ is an initial probability distribution on the set $W_\approx^h$. $\mu_\approx([w]) = \sum_{w'\in[w]}\mu(w')$,

$\rho_\approx$ is a probability distribution, realized in structure $\mathfrak{I}_\approx$, corresponding to a probability distribution ρ for an instruction $v:=random$. $\rho_\approx([a]) = \sum_{a'\in[a]}\rho(a')$.   □

4.2   The Comparison of Two Methods for a Reduction of Valuations

Let $\pi_\approx(W^h)$ denotes a partition of the set W^h determined by congruence $\approx$.

Lemma 4.1 (cf. [2]) Let $K(v_1,...,v_h)$ be a program interpreted in structure $\Im_\rho$ with universe A and let us assume that there exists congruence $\approx$ defined on the structure $\Im$. This congruence determines in $\Im_\approx$ following set of possible valuations of variables $W_\approx^h = \{[w_1],...,[w_{n_\approx}]\}$. Then, the matrix K of a program $K(v_1,...,v_h)$ is groupable for the sake of the partition $\pi_\approx(W^h) = \{[w_1],...,[w_{n_\approx}]\}$. □

Lemma 4.2 Let us assume that $K(v_1,...,v_h)$ is a program interpreted in structure $\Im_\rho$ with universe A. The groupability of the matrix K of the program $K(v_1,...,v_h)$ interpreted in the structure $\Im_\rho$ for the sake of the partition $\pi(W^h) = \{W_1,..., W_s\}$ does not imply the fact, that there exists congruence $\approx$ on $\Im$ such that $\approx$ determines in structure $\Im_{\approx\rho_\approx}$ the set of possible valuations $W_\approx^h = \{[w_1],...,[w_{n_\approx}]\}$ which satisfies for certain permutation $i_1,...,i_s$ of indexes $1,...,s$ the following equalities $W_{i_1} = [w_1],..., W_{i_s} = [w_{n_\approx}]$. □

Sketch of the proof of the lemma 4.2
    In order to justify the thesis given in the lemma 4.2, we shall present an easy example of the program, for which the matrix indexed by valuations from the set W^h is groupable for the sake of the certain partition $\pi(W^h) = \{W_1,..., W_s\}$ and does not exist any congruence $\approx$ on the structure $\Im_\rho$, which determines in $\Im_{\approx\rho_\approx}$ the set of possible valuations $W_\approx^h = \{[w_1],...,[w_{n_\approx}]\}$ such that $W_{i_1} = [w_1],..., W_{i_s} = [w_{n_\approx}]$ for a certain permutation $i_1,...,i_s$ of indexes $1,...,s$.
    Let us consider the program

```
K:   while x<>y do
         if (x=3 ∨ x=4) then y:=random;
```

interpreted in the structure $\Im_\rho$, in which individual variables x, y take the valuations from universe A = $\{1,2,3,4\}$. We define the probability distribution for a random instruction as $\rho = [1/3, 1/4, 1/6, 1/4]$. We establish the following numbering of valuation of variables x, y in the universe A. w_1=(3,1), w_2=(3,2), w_3=(3,4), w_4=(4,1), w_5=(4,2), w_6=(4,3), w_7=(1,1), w_8=(1,2), w_9=(2,1), w_{10}=(2,2), w_{11}=(1,3), w_{12}=(3,2), w_{13}=(4,1), w_{14}=(4,2), w_{15}=(3,3), w_{16}=(4,4). We distinguish three subsets in the set of valuations of the variables: the set of non-looping valuations $W_{1,q} = \{w_1, w_2, w_3, w_4, w_5, w_6\}$, the set of looping valuations $W_{q,r} = \{w_7, w_8, w_9, w_{10}, w_{11}, w_{12}, w_{13}, w_{14}\}$ and the set of final valuations $W_{r,n} = \{w_{15}, w_{16}\}$.

The matrix K_γ^1 (after the first step of the program) is groupable for the sake of the partition $\pi(W^h) = \{W_1, ..., W_9\}$. Both matrixes (the matrix K_γ^1 and the matrix $\underline{K}_\gamma^1$ grouped for the sake of the partition $\pi(W^h) = \{W_1, ..., W_9\}$) are showed below.

$$
\begin{bmatrix}
1/3 & 1/4 & 1/4 & 0 & 0 & 0 & 0 & 0 & 0 & 0 & 0 & 0 & 0 & 1/6 & 0 \\
1/3 & 1/4 & 1/4 & 0 & 0 & 0 & 0 & 0 & 0 & 0 & 0 & 0 & 0 & 1/6 & 0 \\
1/3 & 1/4 & 1/4 & 0 & 0 & 0 & 0 & 0 & 0 & 0 & 0 & 0 & 0 & 1/6 & 0 \\
0 & 0 & 0 & 1/3 & 1/4 & 1/6 & 0 & 0 & 0 & 0 & 0 & 0 & 0 & 0 & 1/4 \\
0 & 0 & 0 & 1/3 & 1/4 & 1/6 & 0 & 0 & 0 & 0 & 0 & 0 & 0 & 0 & 1/4 \\
0 & 0 & 0 & 1/3 & 1/4 & 1/6 & 0 & 0 & 0 & 0 & 0 & 0 & 0 & 0 & 1/4 \\
0 & 0 & 0 & 0 & 0 & 0 & 1 & 0 & 0 & 0 & 0 & 0 & 0 & 0 & 0 \\
0 & 0 & 0 & 0 & 0 & 0 & 0 & 1 & 0 & 0 & 0 & 0 & 0 & 0 & 0 \\
0 & 0 & 0 & 0 & 0 & 0 & 0 & 0 & 1 & 0 & 0 & 0 & 0 & 0 & 0 \\
0 & 0 & 0 & 0 & 0 & 0 & 0 & 0 & 0 & 1 & 0 & 0 & 0 & 0 & 0 \\
0 & 0 & 0 & 0 & 0 & 0 & 0 & 0 & 0 & 0 & 1 & 0 & 0 & 0 & 0 \\
0 & 0 & 0 & 0 & 0 & 0 & 0 & 0 & 0 & 0 & 0 & 1 & 0 & 0 & 0 \\
0 & 0 & 0 & 0 & 0 & 0 & 0 & 0 & 0 & 0 & 0 & 0 & 1 & 0 & 0 \\
0 & 0 & 0 & 0 & 0 & 0 & 0 & 0 & 0 & 0 & 0 & 0 & 0 & 1 & 0 \\
0 & 0 & 0 & 0 & 0 & 0 & 0 & 0 & 0 & 0 & 0 & 0 & 0 & 0 & 1 \\
\end{bmatrix}
$$

$$K_\gamma^1$$

$$
\begin{bmatrix}
7/12 & 1/4 & 0 & 0 & 0 & 0 & 0 & 1/6 & 0 \\
7/12 & 1/4 & 0 & 0 & 0 & 0 & 0 & 1/6 & 0 \\
0 & 0 & 7/12 & 1/6 & 0 & 0 & 0 & 0 & 1/4 \\
0 & 0 & 7/12 & 1/6 & 0 & 0 & 0 & 0 & 1/4 \\
0 & 0 & 0 & 0 & 1 & 0 & 0 & 0 & 0 \\
0 & 0 & 0 & 0 & 0 & 1 & 0 & 0 & 0 \\
0 & 0 & 0 & 0 & 0 & 0 & 1 & 0 & 0 \\
0 & 0 & 0 & 0 & 0 & 0 & 0 & 1 & 0 \\
0 & 0 & 0 & 0 & 0 & 0 & 0 & 0 & 1 \\
\end{bmatrix}
$$

$$\underline{K}_\gamma^1$$

Let us check whether there exists such congruence $\approx$ on $\Im_\rho$, which determines in the structure $\Im_{\approx\rho_\approx}$ the set of possible valuations $W_\approx^h = \{[w_1], ..., [w_{n_\approx}]\}$ fulfilling for a certain permutation $i_1, ..., i_9$ of indexes $1, ..., 9$ the following equalities $W_{i_1} = [w_1], ..., W_{i_9} = [w_{n_\approx}]$.

$W_1 = \{(3,1),(3,2)\}$
$W_2 = \{(3,4)\}$
$W_3 = \{(4,1),(4,2)\}$
$W_4 = \{(4,3)\}$
$W_5 = \{(1,1),(1,2),(2,1),(2,2)\}$
$W_6 = \{(1,3),(3,2)\}$
$W_7 = \{(4,1),(4,2)\}$
$W_8 = \{(3,3)\}$
$W_9 = \{(4,4)\}$

From the form of the partition $\pi(W^h)$ we can notice, that a unique possible congruence $\approx$ on the structure $\Im_\rho$ can identify elements 1 and 2 from a universe A only (different identifications aren't possible).

$[w_1]=W_1=\{(3,1),(3,2)\}$
$[w_3]=W_2=\{(3,4)\}$
$[w_4]=W_3=\{(4,1),(4,2)\}$
$[w_6]=W_4=\{(4,3)\}$
$[w_7]=W_5=\{(1,1),(1,2),(2,1),(2,2)\}$
$[w_{11}]=W_6=\{(1,3),(3,2)\}$
$[w_{13}]=W_7=\{(4,1),(4,2)\}$
$[w_{15}]=W_8=\{(3,3)\}$
$[w_{16}]=W_9=\{(4,4)\}$

Therefore, let us assume, that on the structure $\Im_\rho$ is defined congruence, which determine in the set A following equivalence classes $[1]=[2]=\{1,2\}$, $[3]=\{3\}$, $[4]=\{4\}$. Then $\approx$ determines a following set of possible valuations of variables x, y in the structure $\Im_{\approx\rho_\approx}$

$$W_\approx^h = \{[w_1], [w_3], [w_4], [w_6], [w_7], [w_{11}], [w_{13}], [w_{15}], [w_{16}]\}$$ (a table showed above).

Let us notice, that for valuations $(1,1), (1,2) \in [w_7]$ we have

$\Im, (1,2) \not\models (x \neq y)$ and $\Im, (1,1) \models (x \neq y)$.

From this reason, we obtain that does not exist any congruence $\approx$, which justifies for a certain permutation $i_1,...,i_9$ of indexes $1,...,9$ following equalities $W_{i_1} = [w_1],..., W_{i_9} = [w_{n_\approx}]$.

■

5. Examples of Statistics which we can move from Markov Chains to Probabilistic Algorithms

Since we can represent a certain class of absorbing Markov chains by probabilistic programs, so we can move from theory of Markov chains to theory of probabilistic algorithms statistics listed below. The lemmas marked by [7] are translations of facts given in [7] for Markov chains into the language of probabilistic algorithms. Remaining lemmas we derived on the base well-known facts.

Lemma 5.1 Assumptions:

K - a probabilistic program of the form while γ do M;

$\pi(W^h) = \{W_1,...,W_s\}$ - a fixed partition of the set W^h of all possible valuations in K;

matrixes M, $I_{[\gamma?]}$ are groupable for the sake of the partition $\pi(W^h) = \{W_1,...,W_s\}$.

J_T - the matrix in which submatrixes J_i ($1 \le i \le q$) are columns of values equal to 1 corresponding to indexes belonging to the set $W_i \in \pi(W_{1,q})$.

$$J_T = \begin{bmatrix} J_1 & & 0 \\ & \ddots & \\ 0 & & J_q \end{bmatrix}$$

If the assumptions given above are fulfilled, then

(A)   [7] We can calculate an average number of program steps from the equation:
$$[E_i(v)]_{i \in T} = J_T \underline{N} e_T, \text{ where}$$

$\underline{N}$ - a grouped matrix of the fundamental matrix N,

e_T - a $1 \times \overline{\overline{T}}$ matrix of 1's;

(B)   [7] We determine the canonical matrix $K^1_{A_r}$ of conditional probabilities (on condition that K ends in state r) from the equation

$$K^1_{A_r} = \begin{array}{c} T \\ r \end{array} \begin{bmatrix} T_{A_r} & R_{A_r} \\ 0 & 1 \end{bmatrix}, \text{ where}$$

$$T_{A_r} = \Lambda^{-1}_{rdg} T' \Lambda_{rdg}, \qquad R_{A_r} = \Lambda^{-1}_{rdg} R'_r \Lambda_{rdg}, \qquad A_r = N R_r,$$

(C)   [7] We determine an average number of program steps in the set of non-looping states on condition that program ends (or loops) in state r from the equation

$$E_{iA_r}(v)_{i \in T} = \begin{cases} A^{-1}_{rdg} N' A_{rdg} e = N_{A_r} e & \text{for non} - \text{zero positions in vector } A_r \\ 0 & \text{otherwise} \end{cases}$$

(D)   [7] We determine an average number of different temporary states visited by program from the equation

$$[E_i(v')]_{i \in T} = NN_{dg}^{-1}e.$$

(E)   We calculate an average number of different temporary states visited by program on condition that program ends in state r from the equation

$$E_{iA_r}(v')_{i \in T} = \begin{cases} N_{A_r} N_{A_r dg}^{-1} e & \text{for non} - \text{zero positions in vector } A_r \\ 0 & \text{otherwise} \end{cases}$$

(F)   We calculate an average number of program steps in the set of non-looping states on condition that program ends (or loops) in state r from

$$[E_{iA_r}(v)]_{i \in T} = J_T \underline{N}_{Ar} e_T$$

Example 5.1 We carry out the simulation of an experiment. We assume, that we have the population of people in which each blood group in AB0 blood group system is represented by the same number of men and women. From among members of this population we choose randomly a couple of parents (e. g. with blood group X, Y). We draw for them two children (e.g. with blood groups V, Z). Next, in place of chosen parents, we take a new couple of parents (with blood groups X, Y) from outside of population. In next step, we choose a new couple of children (with blood groups V, Z) and this process repeats until at least one of children will be have a blood group A.

We can realize this problem by following probabilistic program

```
while (x<=6) do begin
    if (x=1 or x=3) then either_1/2 x:=1 or either_1/2 x:=3 or x:=10;
    if (x=2 or x=3) then either_1/2 x:=2 or either_1/2 x:=3 or x:=10;
    if (x=5) then either_1/3 [either_1/3 x:=3 or either_1/2 x:=4 or x:=10] or
                            [either_1/3 x:=1 or either_1/2 x:=2 or x:=6];
    if (x=6) then either_1/4 [either_1/4 x:=3 or either_1/3 x:=4 or
        either_1/2 x:=9 or x:=10] or [either_1/6 x:=1 or either_1/5 x:=2 or
        either_1/4 x:=5 or either_1/3 x:=6 or either_1/2 x:=7 or x:=8];
    if (7<=x<=9) then either_1/3 [either_1/3 x:=3 or either_1/2 x:=4 or x:=9] or
                            [either_1/3 x:=6 or either_1/2 x:=7 or x:=8];
end;
```

We determine following statistics on the base of this program

(A) $[E_i(v)]_{i \in T} = [4 \quad 4 \quad 5 \quad 13/6 \quad 13/6]$

The number 13/6 denotes an average number of generations to obtaining at least one child, which have a blood group A on condition that the first parents have groups B and AB (or AB and AB).

(B) $[E_{iA6}(v)]_{i \in T} = [4 \quad 4 \quad 5 \quad 11/2 \quad 11/2]$

(C) $[E_{iA8}(v)]_{i \in T} = [0 \quad 0 \quad 1 \quad 3/2 \quad 3/2]$

The number 3/2 denotes an average number of generations to obtaining two children with groups A on condition that the first parents have groups B and AB (or AB and AB).

(D) $[E_i(v')]_{i \in T} = [3/2 \quad 5/3 \quad 41/27 \quad 179/126 \quad 55/66]^T$

(E) $[E_{i\underline{A6}}(v')]_{i \in T} = [1 \quad 1 \quad 7/4 \quad 2 \quad 2]^T$

(F) $[E_{i\underline{A8}}(v')]_{i \in T} = [0 \quad 0 \quad 1 \quad 1 \quad 1]^T$

6. Appendix

(a)   The matrix $K = [k_{ij}]_{i,j=1,\dots,n}$ for an instructions $v_r := \tau_{\mathfrak{I}}$ and $v_r := \texttt{random}$.

$$k_{ij} = \begin{cases} 1 \text{ iff } [v_r := \tau_{\mathfrak{I}}]_{\mathfrak{I}_\rho}(w_i) = w_j \\ 0 \text{ iff } [v_r := \tau_{\mathfrak{I}}]_{\mathfrak{I}_\rho}(w_i) \neq w_j \end{cases}, \quad k_{ij} = \begin{cases} \rho(w_j(v_r)) \text{ iff } \forall_{\substack{s=1,\dots,h \\ s \neq r}} w_i(v_s) = w_j(v_s) \\ 0 \qquad\qquad \text{otherwise} \end{cases}$$

Thanks I would like to thank to my supervisor Professor Wiktor Dańko for numerous hints during writing this paper.

References

[1] Borowska A., *The Reduction of the States by grouping in Probabilistic Programs*, unpublished manuscript,

[2] Borowska A., *Comparing Methods of Reduction of the Number of States in Probabilistic Algorithms*; Advanced Computer System; 13th International Multi-Conference; ACS'2006; Vol.1; Szczecin 2006; s.75-85

[2] Dańko W., *The Set of Probabilistic Algorithmic Formulas Valid in a Finite Structure is Decidable with Respect of its Diagram*, FI 19 (1993) 417-431,

[3] Dańko W., Koszelew J., *Properties of Probabilistic algorithms provable in first-order analysis*, unpublished manuscript,

[4] Feller W., *Introduction to the probability calculus*, PWN, Warsaw 1977

[5] Gelfand I. M., *Lectures on Linear Algebra*, Warsaw 1975,

[6] Iosifescu M., *The finite Markov processes*, PWN, Warsaw 1988,

[7] Koszelew J., *The methods of analysis of properties of probabilistic programs interpreted in finite fields*, doctoral thesis, Warsaw 2000,

[8] *Matiematiczieskaja enciklopedija i.m. Winogradow*, Moscow 1984,

[9] Kubik L. T. Krupowicz A, *Introduction to the probability calculus and its applications*, PWN, Warsaw 1982,

[10] Rasiowa H., *Introduction to modern mathematics*, PWN, Warsaw 1971,

Inverted Lists Compression using Contextual Information

Dariusz Czerski, Krzysztof Ciesielski, Michał Dramiński,
Mieczysław A. Kłopotek, Sławomir T. Wierzchoń

Institute of Computer Sci., Polish Acad. of Sciences, Ordona 21, 01-237 Warsaw, Poland
{dcz, kciesiel, klopotek, stw}@ipipan.waw.pl

Abstract. In this paper we present new approach to compression of inverted lists in indexes of information retrieval systems. The technique exploits contextual information obtained from a non-supervised clustering process run on the document collection. A substantial improvement of compression factor is achieved.

1. Introduction

The growing importance of search engines as information retrieval tools for an ordinary user presses for steady research on increase of their speed and efficiency. Proper organization of indexes of the Web content is a crucial and at the same time a challenging task. In Google, Yahoo and most other search engines, efficient processing of typical Boolean queries is achieved via inverted files (or lists) [16], which are used as indexes of document collections. In the inverted lists technology, the list of documents containing a term from a given collection of terms is kept as a single complex record. An important factor for the search time is the amount of memory needed to store the indexing data structures. To achieve acceptable response time to user queries against collections of millions of medium-sized documents, the respective inverted lists have to fit into the main memory. Technical and technological limitations concerning computer memory constitute a hard barrier. To overcome it, various inverted list compression techniques are being applied, but at the expense of search time, construction time and design and implementation becomes harder [1, 6, 7, 14].

The inverted lists methodology has been developed for speedy word-based search through collections of text documents or other semi-structured objects. In this paper we concentrate on Internet documents to be indexed by a visual search engine [2]. We present a novel approach accelerating search through compressed inverted lists, based on a well-balanced compromise between memory requirements and computational burden. We extend previous research concentrated on reducing the memory requirements needed for encoding document identifiers (in the sequel referred to as IDs) by their reordering. It has been shown that this problem is NP-complete [5]. Experimental results show that a heuristic reassignment of document IDs can reduce significantly the inverted list memory requirements. In our search engine, BEATCA, this is achieved as a side-effect of structured document clustering [8].

In Section 2 we briefly recall the ideas of inverted lists and their compression techniques. In Section 3 we present the novel approach, and the experimental results on its efficiency are shown in Section 4. The last Section 5 provides some ideas on future research topics.

2. Inverted lists and their compression

Inverted lists belong to the most important components of any Internet search engine [16]. The term "inverted" means that instead of storing a list of terms which appear in a document, a list of documents for a given term is built. Inverted list consists of two major parts: (1) a dictionary of all the terms occurring in the documents, and (2) for each term a list of ID numbers of documents in which the term occurs. Inverted lists are most efficient when answering ranked Boolean queries. The query answering process using inverted lists runs as follows:
- Query terms are sought in the term dictionary.
- Inverted lists containing the terms are loaded.
- Depending on the logical operator the common part or the sum of lists is constructed and for each document its closeness to the query is calculated.
- At the end summaries of documents found are constructed and the documents are sorted by the similarity to user query.

To calculate the similarity of the query and the document various measures are applied. A first choice may be the cosine measure. More sophisticated one is Okapi BM25 measure, proposed in [12, 13]. Here we do not consider this issue concentrating instead on compression and search in inverted lists. A single entry on the inverted list[1] is the pair $(f_{d,t}, d)$, where $f_{d,t}$ is the number of occurrences of term t in document d. To allow for searching of phrases, this notation needs to be amended by inserting also the information on positions where a term occurs in the document. An inverted list for a single term would then consist of a number of such entries (e.g. $(2,5)$, $(12,1)$, $(3,12)$). By sorting this list, we obtain a well-compressible inverted list (e.g. $(12,1)$, $(2,5)$, $(3,12)$). The compression is achieved via replacing the document IDs with the gaps between them, like in $(12,1)$, $(2,4)$, $(3,7)$. The document gap representation implies a degree of compression because known methods of variable length number encodings (e.g. unary coding, Gamma coding, Delta code, Golomb code) take less space for smaller numbers. In [11] another approach is proposed, suggesting to sort the inverted list on the term occurrence frequency, like in $(2,5)$, $(3,12)$, $(12,1)$. An argument in favor of such a representation is the acceleration in retrieving documents closer to the query. However, the term frequency does not reflect sufficiently the document relevance; hence the similarity of highly ranked documents to the query may be questionable.

---

[1] We follow here the notion introduced for inverted lists by Zobel and Moffat [17]

2.1 Inverted lists compression techniques

Compressed inverted lists significantly increase the efficiency of information retrieval systems [15,16]. The reason for it is that uncompressed lists, not fitting into the main memory, need to be downloaded from the disk more frequently than compressed lists. The compression of inverted lists is mainly based on the possibility of efficient representation of (small) numbers, hence the popular replacement of document IDs (which are in the range of billions for large search engines) with gaps between them (which are of much smaller value). The popular methods of number encoding can be divided into non-parametric (e.g. Elias Gamma and Delta codes) and parametric (e.g. Golomb codes) ones – consult e.g. [15] for details. The non-parametric methods use fixed (static) code words for numbers. The Gamma code allows representing the integer k using a unary number equal $1+ \log_2 k$, followed by $\log_2 k$ bits representing binarily the number $k-2^{[\log_2 k]}$. The total number of bits necessary to encode the integer k in this code is $1+2(\log_2 k)$. This code is quite efficient if a large number of small integers (below 15) is encoded [15]. Delta code is longer than Gamma for smaller numbers, but shorter for larger ones, hence, it is applied to compress large numbers. For an integer k, the Delta code takes the form of Gamma code for the number $1 + \log_2 k$, followed by $\log_2 k$ bits representing binarily the number $k-2^{[\log_2 k]}$. The Delta code length is $1 + 2(\log_2 \log_2 k) + \log_2 k$. The Golomb coding is a representative of parametric compression methods. It is the most efficient one, compared to the previously mentioned. It results from its adaptive capabilities. For a parameter b and an integer k, we encode unarily the number $q+1$, where $q = (k-1)/b$, and subsequently encode binarily $r = k - q \cdot b - 1$. If p is the probability of occurrence of the 'word' $f/(N \cdot n)$, then the optimal value of the parameter b for this word is $[\log(2-p)/-\log(1-p)]+1$. A disadvantage of this compression method is the necessity of storing the parameter b for each compressed data portion.

3. Context Dependent Inverted List

In the previous section we recalled some inverted list compression techniques based on document ID encoding, where especially the gaps between IDs (numerically smaller than IDs) were exploited as a source of memory requirement reduction. But why not to reduce the memory further by making these gaps deliberately smaller? We argue that this can be achieved as a side-effect (see subsection 3.3) of our special contextual document clustering technique (subsection 3.1) based on modified GNG approach (subsection 3.2).

3.1 Contextual local networks

In our approach to document retrieval – like in many traditional IR systems - documents are mapped into m-dimensional term vector space. The points (documents) in this space are of the form $(w_{1,d}, \ldots, w_{m,d})$ where m stands for the number of terms, and each $w_{t,d}$ is a weight for the term t in document d, so-called term frequency/inverse document frequency (TFIDF) weight:

$$w_{t,d} = w(t, d) = f_{td} \cdot \log(N/f_t) \tag{1}$$

where f_{td} is the number of occurrences of the term t in the document d, f_t is the number of documents containing the term t and N is the total number of documents.

The vector space model has been criticized for some disadvantages, polysemy and synonymy, among others, [3]. To overcome these disadvantages a contextual approach has been proposed relying upon dividing the set of documents into a number of homogenous and disjoint subgroups each of which is described by unique subset of terms [8, 9].

The contextual approach consists of two main stages. At first stage a hierarchical model is built, i.e. a collection D of documents is recurrently divided - by using Fuzzy ISODATA algorithm [4] – into homogenous groups consisting of approximately identical number of elements. Such a procedure results in a hierarchy represented by a tree of clusters. The process of partitioning halts when the number of documents inside each group meets predefined criteria[2]. To compute the distance dist(d, c) of a document d to the centroid c, the following function is used: dist(d,c) = 1 – $<d/\|d\|,c/\|c\|>$, where the symbol $<\cdot,\cdot>$ stands for the dot-product of two vectors. Given m_{dG} the degree of (fuzzy) membership of a document d to a group G, this document is assigned to the group with highest value of m_{dG}.

The second phase of contextual document processing is division of term space (dictionary) into – possibly overlapping – subspaces of terms specific to each context (i.e. the group extracted in previous stage). The fuzzy membership m_{tG}, representing importance of a particular term t in a given context G is computed as:

$$m_{tG} = \frac{\sum_{d \in G} f_{td} m_{dG}}{f_G \sum_{d \in G} m_{dG}} \tag{2}$$

where f_G is the number of documents in the group G, m_{dG} is the degree of membership of the document d to group G, and f_{td} is the number of occurrences of the term t in document d. We assume that a term t is relevant for a given context G if $m_{tG} > \varepsilon$, where ε is a parameter.

Removing non-relevant terms leads to the topic-sensitive reduction of the dimension of the term space. This reduction results in new vector representation of documents, and each component of the vector is computed according to the equation:

$$w_{tdG} = f_{td} \cdot m_{td} \cdot \log[f_G/(f_t m_{tG})] \tag{3}$$

where f_t is the number of documents in the group G containing term t.

---

[2] Currently a single criterion saying that the cardinality c_i of i-th cluster cannot exceed a given boundaries $[c_{min}, c_{max}]$. This way the maps created for each group at the same level of a given hierarchy will contain a similar number of documents.

3.2 Growing Neural Gas for Document Clustering

In our BEATCA search engine [8, 9], for each contextual group a single graph-based clustering model is built. Among other methods, we found Growing Neural Gas (GNG) algorithm proposed in [10] to be particularly efficient. Like Kohonen (SOM) networks, GNG can be viewed as a topology learning algorithm, i.e. its aim is to find a structure (represented by an undirected graph) which reflects the topology of a given collection of high-dimensional data. That is small groups of similar documents are represented by the nodes in the undirected graph, and nodes connected by an edge contain relatively similar documents. Like in SOM, each node is characterized by the vector being a summarization of the group; this vector is called the prototype or simply – the centroid. In typical SOM both the number of units (nodes, or cells) and the topology (rectangular or hexagonal lattice) of the map are predefined. As observed in [10], the choice of the SOM structure is difficult, and the need to define a decay schedule (learning rate) for various features is problematic.

The GNG algorithm clusters the document collection incrementally, adding only one new document at single iteration. It starts with very few randomly initialized units and no edges, and new units are inserted successively every k iterations, while edges are added or removed. In a single iteration, the most similar and the second most similar cluster prototypes are identified for the just presented document. This document is added to the winning cluster, and the prototype vectors of the winner and its neighbors in the graph are adjusted "towards" the new document. At the same time an edge is inserted (if absent) between the winner and the second best node, and the edge is "refreshed" (its "age" is set to zero). With each iteration all edges are aging, and too old edges are removed. To determine where to insert new units, local error measures are gathered during the adaptation process (i.e. the sums of the distance between the centroid and the newly added document to a cluster); new unit is inserted near the unit, which has accumulated maximal error. Interestingly, as the cells of the GNG network are connected and disconnected during the process, possibly a disconnected graph is obtained, and its connected components can be treated as different data clusters. The complete algorithm details can be found in [10].

In BEATCA, for each context (a subset of documents and terms, represented by a term-weighting equation (3), a separate GNG graph is built. To model more general similarity relation between contexts, an additional "global" GNG graph is required. Such a graph becomes the root of the contextual model hierarchy. The main graph is created in analogy to previously created ones, where a single example in training data is a weighted centroid of the referential vectors of the corresponding contextual model: $x_i = \sum_{c \in Mi} (d_c \cdot v_c)$, where M_i is the set of cells in i-th contextual model, d_c is the density of the cell and v_c is its prototype vector.

3.3 Linear Ordering of Document IDs for Lists Compression

One of the main goals of the BEATCA project was to create multidimensional document maps in which geometrical vicinity would reflect conceptual closeness of documents in a given document set.

Still, having built a contextual model described in the previous subsection, with a low additional cost we can construct a linear ordering of identifiers of documents in a given collection and use it later during the construction of the inverted lists. Since a major part of the inverted list code is the information about the gaps, we would like to have an ordering which minimizes the distance of identifiers of documents sharing similar terms, thus making the shortest gaps (having the shortest code) much more frequent.

One of the features of the contextual model hierarchy is the balance in the number of the objects that appear at each level. For instance, we have built such a model for a million of documents: it consisted of 400 contexts (ca. 2500 documents each). A single contextual GNG graph consisted of approximately 20-30 cells, and each cell represented about 100 documents. Thus, starting from individual cells, we can impose an order within such a small cluster of a few dozens of documents. Separate chains of ordered documents can then be linked in one chain on the basis of the GNG structure. Finally, we can merge orders within contexts on the basis of the main GNG graph.

On the lowest level of documents within a cell, the ordering is done by the agglomerative clustering technique [16]. On the level of GNG graph cells, we can restrict agglomeration, and hence the ordering, only to the cells connected by the graph edges. While merging two chains of documents C_1 and C_2, we can order them in one of the four ways: $\mathtt{asc}(C_1) \rightarrow \mathtt{asc}(C_2)$, $\mathtt{asc}(C_1) \rightarrow \mathtt{desc}(C_2)$, $\mathtt{desc}(C_1) \rightarrow \mathtt{desc}(C_2)$ or $\mathtt{desc}\ (C_1) \rightarrow \mathtt{asc}\ (C_2)$, where $\mathtt{asc}(C)$ represents ascending order and $\mathtt{desc}\ (C)$ – reverted order (the other possibilities of ordering are redundant). The decision is made on the basis of the similarity between the four extreme (starting and ending) documents in both chains – the merging variant which maximizes the similarity is chosen.

Finally, we obtain a single chain, which is the linear order on all documents in the collection. To build the *ordered inverted list*, we use the rank within constructed order as a new identifier of the document.

4. Experimental results

To demonstrate the validity of our approach, experiments have been carried out for two document collections: the so-called "20Newsgroups" and our own collection of about 1,000,000 documents crawled from WWW by our spider (called "www" here). We studied cooperation of our approach with the three compression methods: Huffman, Gamma, and Delta. We compared ID assignment using our method to "standard" assignment ("as is") and the random ordering.

As expected (see Fig. 1), a totally random assignment of IDs to documents yields in most cases worse compression rates. On the other hand our ID assignment method performs best independently of the type of the compression method (Huffman, Gamma, Delta) used.

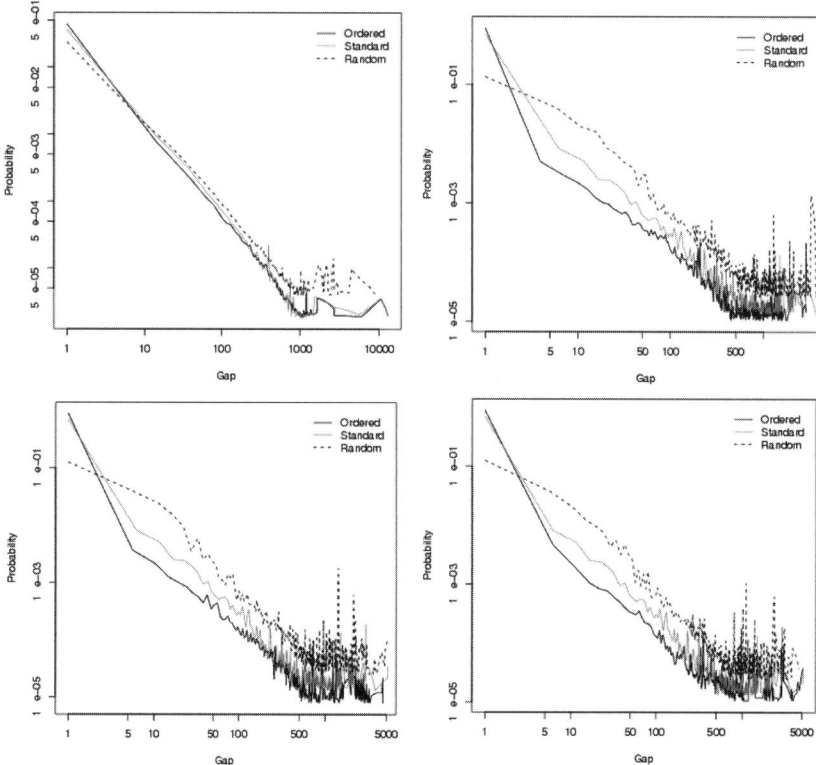

Fig. 1. Occurrence probability vs gap size: (a) 20 News [Gamma] (b) www Huffman
c) www Gamma (d) www Delta

While our ordering of documents' identifiers helps to improve the compression of the inverted lists, the impact of this effect depends on the collection of documents. For example for documents randomly downloaded from the web we obtained a much better result (compression factor) than for 20 NewsGroups (widely used benchmark documents). After contextual ordering of 20 NewsGroups, there is still a room for a better compression, although documents in this collection are naturally ordered. Order of 20 NewsGroups stems from the chronology of messages within topics and on citing previous letters. Our method optimizes only the IDs and gaps parts of inverted lists (has no influence on weights) so the experimental results present both the whole list sizes (with weights overhead) and the optimized part sizes (see Fig. 2). For documents directly crawled (by web spider) from the web, improvement after ordering is significant, because documents are downloaded by many different threads from different sites. Therefore, the documents that have been downloaded at the same time (even if their contents are far from each to other) obtain neighboring IDs. Random ordering of the documents in the database is a cost that we have to pay if we want to use multi threaded web crawler.

The additional cost of calculation of the contextual order for inverted lists is low, because at the same time we build the contextual map model (which is the primary goal). So the new, optimized, ordering of documents is just a by-product of the main process in BEATCA search engine i.e. the creation of hierarchy of clusters. Higher compression of inverted lists has positive influence on the search engine efficiency, i.e. query processing time. Particularly, less memory is used, fewer I/O operations are needed, and smaller amount of information has to be decoded. Similar documents are closely located in the inverted lists what, in case of very large lists, is an additional profit. As, similar documents are returned as a response to similar queries, so to return all relevant documents we have to decode only a short fragment of the inverted list.

The compression factor varies for different types of integer coding techniques used. After contextual ordering of documents, the probability of occurrence of shortest gaps (with length equal 1, what means that documents had subsequent identifiers) increases significantly. However while this probability is similar for the three types of coding used in inverted list (see table 8 and 9), the size of the code (in bits) is different and depends on particular encoding. It is due to the well-known properties of different encoding techniques (e.g. the lowest numbers are encoded best with Gamma code).

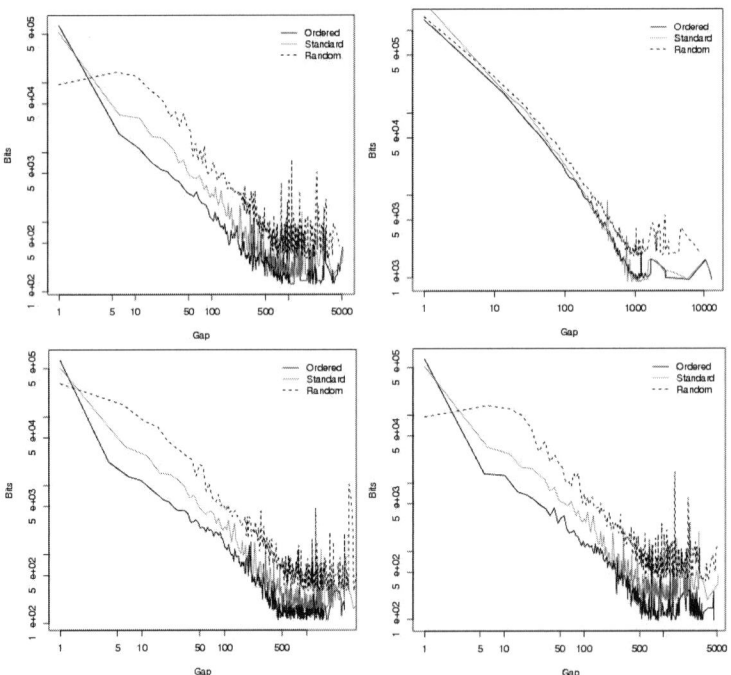

Fig. 2. Code size vs gap size: (a) 20 News [Gamma] (b) www Huffman (c) www Gamma (d) www Delta

Comparing Gamma code with Huffman code, one can see that the Gamma gains more by the ordering of documents than the Huffman code. The latter has the inherent property of adapting itself to particular data which has to be compressed. Concluding, the size of ordered lists under both encodings is similar (Table 5), while Gamma code is significantly less costly during compression and decompression of lists. It's contrary to standard, non-ordered lists where Huffman usually outperforms Gamma.

The probability of small gaps is always higher after the ordering of documents (what is difficult to notice on Figure 1 because of logarithmic scale, but is visible in Table 6). For the ordered set of documents there are also much fewer longest gaps, which have longest codes. For instance, for documents crawled from the web there are almost no gaps longer than 500 (see Figure 1).

It should also be noted, that the probability of a few shortest gaps is almost one (P(gap=1) = 0.87, P(gap < =3) = 0.99), so the ordering is very close to the optimum and not much room is left for improvement of the total code length.

Table 1: Proportion of the total list sizes (starting IDs + gaps + doc weights)

	20 Newsgroups	www Huffman	www Gamma	www Delta
standard / ordered	1.0642	1.2614	1.2869	1.2234
randomized / standard	1.1449	1.6363	1.7107	1.7276

Table 2: Proportion of the list sizes without weight code and starting IDs overhead

	20 Newsgroups	www Huffman	www Gamma	www Delta
standard / ordered	1.0829	1.4063	1.4695	1.3688
randomized / standard	1.1827	1.9034	2.0293	2.0705

Table 3: Total size of the inverted lists (starting IDs + gaps + doc weights), in bits

	20 Newsgroups	www Huffman	www Gamma	www Delta
ordered	23620718	3160578	3439939	3475959
standard	25136488	3986758	4426730	4252418
randomized	28780370	6523371	7572658	7346222

Table 4: List size without weight code overhead, in bits

	20 Newsgroups	www Huffman	www Gamma	www Delta
ordered	19885355	2286453	2472271	2507939
standard	21400956	3112612	3508539	3284473
randomized	25043970	5649158	6654525	6378538

Table 5: List size without weight code and the starting IDs overhead, in bits

	20 Newsgroups	www Huffman	www Gamma	www Delta
ordered	18413019	2002584	2096045	2120690
standard	19938772	2816261	3080227	2902899
randomized	23582508	5360372	6250671	6010514

Table 6: Total probability of the shortest gaps (=1) occurrence

	20 Newsgroups	www Huffman	www Gamma	www Delta
ordered	0.43649	0.87827	0.88023	0.87792
Standard	0.35976	0.68962	0.68962	0.68962
randomized	0.23648	0.13442	0.12604	0.12537

Table 7: Total size of the shortest gaps (=1) code, in bits

	20 Newsgroups	www Huffman	www Gamma	www Delta
ordered	1359004	661447	662925	661185
standard	2240176	519371	519371	519371
randomized	1472568	303705	94926	94421

Table 8: Total probability of the longest gaps (> 1000) occurrence

	20 Newsgroups	www Huffman	www Gamma	www Delta
ordered	0.02750	0.00669	0.00849	0.01163
standard	0.02684	0.00854	0.00854	0.00854
randomized	0.05168	0.01563	0.01603	0.01545

Table 9: Total size of the longest gaps (> 1000) code length, in bits

	20 Newsgroups	www Huffman	www Gamma	www Delta
ordered	4273622	608886	673117	715047
standard	4085485	701505	855340	672629
randomized	5435689	824571	976610	762736

5. Conclusions

Various solutions to the problem of inverted list compression have been proposed in the past. Most research focused on integer number compression techniques [1, 7], but there were also other approaches, based on document reordering idea. For instance, in [6] reordering is based on dedicated hierarchical clustering algorithm. However, contrary to our approach, where clustering scalability and quality is obtained via contextual approach to document clustering for the purpose of map-based search engine creation [9] and the document ordering is just an off-shot of the main process, in the former approach the time and memory scalability is obtained by sub-sampling of data and restricting processing to shortest lists (both effects are controlled by input parameters). Nevertheless, it requires storing the whole clustering model in the main memory, while in our case only individual contextual subgraphs have to be processed.

In this paper we have proposed a novel inverted file clustering technique, targeting at reducing the gaps between documents via ID reassignment based on document clustering. The memory requirement was reduced significantly, especially in cases where the original document IDs are assigned more or less at random (as it is the case for typical crawlers of search engines). The savings stem primarily from the effective reduction of gap sizes: the number of gaps of size 1 grows significantly (P(gap=1) = 0.87 versus P(gap=1) = 0.69 for non-ordered lists and P(gap=1) = 0.13 for random document order), and very large gaps become less frequent. High probability indicates that ordering is very close to the optimal one. Thus, we can even think of further optimization by replacing standard number compression techniques (Huffman, Gamma, Delta, Golomb) with a compression of sequences. For instance, instead of storing long sequence of shortest gaps it can be represented by its length.

The new approach is complementary to known compression techniques, and we have shown that it cooperates well with them. In particular, reordering of documents significantly improves Gamma encoding and makes it reasonable (and computationally less expensive) alternative to the Huffman encoding.

There are also other possibilities to improve inverted lists efficiency. To make query evaluation time shorter, skipping method can be applied [18]. This approach is based on insertion points added to each inverted list evenly after specified number of document IDs. Searching process is accelerated for queries consisting of two or more terms, because by using skips only subparts of the entire list have to by decompressed.

Currently we work on a new idea to accelerate query execution time and new way of distributing inverted lists. Intuitively our new idea is based on the assumption that documents can be split into separable groups (in terms of user queries) and their term spaces are also nearly disjoint. To obtain this decomposition we use modified clustering methods. Results are very promising.

Acknowledgement

This research has been partly funded by the European Commission and by the Swiss Federal Office for Education and Science with the 6th Framework Programme project REWERSE no. 506779 (cf. http://rewerse.net). Krzysztof Ciesielski was partially supported by MNiSW grant no. N516 005 31/0646.

References

[1] Anh, V.N., Moffat, A., Inverted index compression using word-aligned binary codes, *Information Retrieval*, **8**(2004)151-166
[2] Becks, A., *Visual Knowledge Management with Adaptable Document Maps*, Sankt Augustin, GMD 2001
[3] Berry, M.W., Drmac, Z., Jessup, E.R. Matrices, vector spaces and information retrieval, *SIAM Review*, **41**(1999)335-362
[4] Bezdek, J.C., Pal, S.K., *Fuzzy Models for Pattern Recognition: Methods that Search for Structures in Data*, IEEE, New York, 1992
[5] Blanco, R., Barreiro, A., Characterization of a simple case of the reassignment of document identifiers as a pattern sequencing problem, *Proc. of the 28th Annual Internat. ACM SIGIR Conf. on Research and Development in Information Retrieval*, 2005
[6] Blandford, D., Blelloch, G., Index compression through document reordering, in: *Proceesings of Data Compression Conference* (DCC), 2002, pp. 342-351

[7] Cher-Sheng Cheng, Jean Jyh-Jiun Shann, Chung-Ping Chung, Unique-order interpolative coding for fast querying and space-efficient indexing in information retrieval systems, *Information Processing and Management*, **42**(2006)407-428

[8] Ciesielski, K., Kłopotek, M.A., Contextual maps for browsing huge document collections, in: *Proceedings of the 16th International Symposium Methodologies for Intelligent Systems* (ISMIS-2006), LNAI 4203, Springer, 2006

[9] Ciesielski, K. *et al.*, Adaptive document maps, in: *Proceedings. of the Intelligent Information Processing and Web Mining*, Springer, 2006, pp.109-120

[10] Fritzke, B., A growing neural gas network learns topologies, In: G. Tesauro, D.S. Touretzky, and T.K. Leen (eds.) *Advances in Neural Information Processing Systems 7*, MIT Press Cambridge, MA, 1995, pp. 625-632.

[11] Persin, M., Zobel, J., Sacks-Davis, R., Filtered document retrieval with frequency-sorted indexes, *Journal of the American Society for Information Science* **47**(1996)749-764

[12] Robertson, S., Walker, S., Okapi/Keenbow at TREC- 8, In: E. Voorhees and D. Harman, (eds.), *The 8th Text Retrieval Conference* (TREC-8), NIST Special Publication 500-246, Gaithersburg, MD, 2000, pp. 151-161

[13] Robertson, S., Walker, S., Hancock-Beaulieu, M., Gull, A., Lau, M., Okapi at TREC, in D. Harman, ed., *The 1st Text Retrieval Conference* (TREC-1), NIST Special Publication 500-207, Gaithersburg, MD, 1992, pp. 21-30

[14] Silvestri, F., Orlando, S., Perego, R., Assigning identifiers to documents to enhance the clustering property of full text indexes, *Proceedings of the 27th ACM SIGIR Conference*, 2004

[15] Williams H., Zobel J. Compressing integers for fast file access. *Computer Journal*, **2**(1999)193-201

[16] Witten I., Moffat A. and Bell T. *Managing Gigabytes*. Morgan Kaufman Publishers, New York, second edition, 1999

[17] Zobel, J. and Moffat, A., Exploring the similarity space, *ACM SIGIR Forum* **32**(1), 1998, 18-34

[18] Moffat, A. und Zobel, J. Self-indexing inverted files for fast text retrieval, *ACM Transactions on Information Systems*, **14**(1996)349-379.

Hybrid Intelligent Diagnosis Approaches: Analysis and Comparison under a Biomedicine Application

Amine Chohra, Nadia Kanaoui, and Kurosh Madani

Images, Signals, and Intelligent Systems Laboratory (LISSI / EA 3956), Paris-XII University, Senart Institute of Technology, Avenue Pierre Point, 77127 Lieusaint, France
{chohra, kanaoui, madani}@univ-paris12.fr

Abstract. Computer Aided Diagnosis (CAD) is one of the most interesting and most difficult dilemma dealing on one hand with expert (human) knowledge consideration. On the other hand, fault diagnosis is a complex and fuzzy cognitive process and multiple model approaches with soft computing approaches as modular neural networks and fuzzy logic, have shown great potential in the development of decision support. Among difficulties contributing to challenging nature of this problem, one can mention the need of fine classification and decision-making. In this paper, a brief survey on fault diagnosis systems is given. From the classification and decision-making problem analysis, two hybrid intelligent diagnosis approaches are suggested based on image representation. Then, the suggested approaches are applied, analyzed, and compared in biomedicine for CAD, from Auditory Brainstem Response (ABR) test, and the prototype design and experimental results are presented. Finally, a discussion is given with regard to the reliability and large application field of the suggested approaches.

1. Introduction

A *diagnosis system* is basically one which is capable of identifying the nature of a problem by examining the observed symptoms. The output of such a system is a diagnosis (and possibly an explanation or justification) [1]. In many applications of interest, it is desirable for the system to not only identify the possible causes of the problem, but also to suggest suitable remedies (systems capable of advising) or to give a reliability rate of the identification of possible causes. Recently, several decision support systems and intelligent systems have been developed [2], [3] and the diagnosis approaches based on such intelligent systems have been developed for industrial applications [1], [4], [5], and biomedicine applications [6], [7], [8], [9], [10], [11]. Currently, one of the most used approaches to feature identification, classification, and decision-making problems inherent to fault detection and diagnosis, is multiple model approaches with soft computing implying mainly neural networks and fuzzy logic [1], [3], [4], [5], [6], [9], [10], [11], [12], [13].

Over the past decades, new approaches based on artificial neural networks have been developed aiming to solve real life problems as modeling, decision-making, classification, and nonlinear functions approximation [14], [15], [16].

Another aspect of increasing importance, and strongly linked to data processing and the amount of data available concerning processes or devices (due to the high level of sensors and monitoring), is the extraction of knowledge from data to discover the information structure hidden in it. Several approaches have been developed to analyze and classify biomedicine signals: electroencephalography signals [7], electrocardiogram signals [8], and particularly signals based on Auditory Brainstem Response (ABR) test, which is a test for hearing and brain (neurological) functioning, [6], [17], [18], [19]. Traditionally, biomedicine signals are processed using signal processing approaches, mainly based on peak and wave identification from pattern recognition approaches, such as in [6], [7], [8], [17], [18], [19]. In fact, the time (or frequency) is not always the variable that points up the studied phenomena's features leading then to a necessity of multiple knowledge representations (signal, image, …).

This paper deals with pattern recognition (classification) and decision-making based on AI using multiple model approaches with soft computing implying neural networks and fuzzy logic applied to a biomedicine problem. The aim of this paper is absolutely not to replace specialized human but to suggest a decision support tool with a satisfactory reliability degree for Computer Aided Diagnosis (CAD) systems. Thus, a brief survey on fault diagnosis systems is given in Section 2. Afterwards, two hybrid intelligent diagnosis approaches are suggested in Section 3. In Section 4 and Section 5, the suggested approaches are applied to a computer aided auditory diagnosis, from image representation, in order to achieve a diagnosis tool able to assert auditory pathologies based on Auditory Brainstem Response (ABR) test which provides an effective measure of the integrity of the auditory pathway. Then, prototype design, experimental results and their analysis and comparison are given.

2. Fault Diagnosis Systems

Globally, the main goals of fault diagnosis systems for Computer Aided Diagnosis (CAD) [5], [11] are: to detect if a fault is in progress as soon as possible, to classify the fault in progress, to be able to suggest suitable remedies (systems able of advising) or to give a reliability rate of the identified fault through a Confidence Index (CI). CAD is an attractive area leading to future promising fault diagnosis applications. However, dealing with expert (human) knowledge consideration, the computer aided diagnosis dilemma is one of most interesting, but also one of the most difficult problems. The fault diagnosis help is often related to the classification of several information sources implying different representations. Fault diagnosis can be obtained from the classification of only one kind of information (knowledge) representation. However, experts use several information to emit their diagnosis. Then, an interesting way to built efficient fault diagnosis system can be deduced from this concept in order to take advantage from several information. More, experts can use several information sources, in various forms; qualitative or quantitative data, signals, images, to emit their diagnosis. Thus, these information could be issued from different information sources and/or from different representations of a same test. For instance, in case of diagnosis of the same fault classes set, one can consider that these information are independently, in parallel, classified and after the decision-making of their results gives then final results. Final results gives the fault classes set and suitable remedies or a reliability rate of the possible identified fault class.

3. Two Hybrid Intelligent Diagnosis Approaches

The suggested approaches are mainly based on two different knowledge representations (global image representation and sub-divided image representation) and two different classifications (MLP classification and RBF classification) from only one information source. In fact, two interesting configurations appears: global image representation with two different classifications (MLP and RBF), and sub-divided image representations with two different classifications (MLP and RBF). Each configuration in the case of diagnosis of the same fault classes set leads to two different classification results. More, if such classifications are handled by neural networks, which are known to be appropriate for classification [14], [15], [16], [20] the decision-making appears to be difficult particularly in CAD which can be useful and efficient only if the results are given with a reliability parameter, e.g., a CI.

Nature of neural classification results (neural outputs) of the neural architectures used for classification are, in general, not binary values. In fact, for instance, typical MultiLayer feedforward Perceptron networks (MLP) used for classification with sigmoïdal outputs give output class values between [0, 1]. This makes difficult the problem of decision-making from two neural networks. Another neural architecture is based on Radial Basis Function networks (RBF). The analysis of neural classifier outputs shows that, in case of MLP, more the output is close to 1 and more this output will be close to be the identified fault class. Contrarily, more the output is close to 0 and more this output will be far to be the identified fault class. In case of RBF, the outputs are distances from RBF centers. In this case with a new scale of outputs it is easily to make output class values varying between [0, c], where c is a constant to be determined (e.g., see Section 5.1 Fig. 4 (b)). Then, more the output which is a distance is close to c and more this output will be far to be identified as fault class. Contrarily, more the output is close to 0 and more this output will be close to be the identified fault class. From this purpose, one interesting way to built efficient decision-making from two neural networks is fuzzy logic [21]. Thus, the results of the two neural classifications, for each configuration, can be then efficiently exploited in a fuzzy system to ensure a satisfactory reliability. Fuzzy decision-making system can be exploited to capture expert (human) knowledge [2], [22]. Then, decision-making system allows to decide fault classes diagnosis among: Class 1, Class 2, …, and Class M, and its usefulness and efficiency are better traduced with the associated CI.

4. Biomedicine Application: Computer Aided Auditory Diagnosis

The ABR test involves attaching electrodes to the head to record electrical activity from the auditory nerve (the hearing nerve) and other parts of the brain. This recorded electrical activity is known as Brainstem Auditory Evoked Potentials (BAEP).

4.1 Brainstem Auditory Evoked Potentials (BAEP) Clinical Test

When a sense organ is stimulated, it generates a string of complex neurophysiology processes. BAEP are electrical response caused by the brief stimulation of a sense system. The stimulus gives rise to the start of a string of action's potentials that can be recorded on the nerve's course, or from a distance of the activated structures. BAEP are generated as follows (see Fig. 1 (a)): the patient hears clicking noise or tone bursts through earphones. The use of auditory stimuli evokes an electrical response. In fact, the stimulus triggers a number of neurophysiology responses along the auditory pathway. An action potential is conducted along the eight nerve, the brainstem, and finally to the brain. A few times after the initial stimulation, the signal evokes a response in the area of brain where sounds are interpreted.

4.2 Extraction of the Knowledge Representation (Image from Signal)

A technique of extraction [18] allows us, following 800 acquisitions such as described before, the visualization of the BAEP estimation on averages of 16 acquisitions. Thus, a surface of 50 estimations called Temporal Dynamic of the Cerebral trunk (TDC) can be visualized. Average signal, which corresponds to average of 800 acquisitions, and TDC surface could be obtained. Those are then processed into a signal representation as shown in Fig. 1 (b). In this figure, an example of TDC surface for a patient is shown. The average signal (named signal representation) is presented in front of TDC surface which is better shown in Fig. 1 (c). The signal to image conversion (named image representation) is obtained after a processing of TDC surface signal and image processing [9], [10], [23]. Three patient classes are studied: Retro-cochlear auditory disorder's patients (Retro-cochlear Class: RC), Endo-cochlear auditory disorder's patients (Endo-cochlear Class: EC), healthy patients (Normal Class: NC).

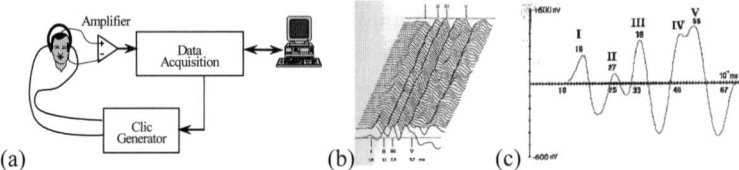

Fig. 1. (a) BAEP clinical test. (b) TDC surface. (c) Average signal processing.

4.3 Suggested Hybrid Intelligent Diagnosis Systems

The hybrid intelligent diagnosis systems suggested in Fig. 2 and Fig. 3 are built of data processing stage, classification stage, primary fuzzy decision-making stage leading to a primary diagnosis, and final fuzzy decision-making stage leading to the final diagnosis. The data processing stage consists of extracting image representations from data source (signals: TDC surface) and deducing the image data. The classification stage consists of the global (and sub-divided) image classifications which are based on MLP and RBF networks. In fact, MLP are *neural global* approximators, whereas RBF are *neural local* approximators [14].

Primary and final fuzzy decision-making stages consists of the Fuzzy System 1 (FS_1) and Fuzzy System 2 (FS_2), respectively, see Fig. 2. These fuzzy decision-making systems are used to capture the decision-making behavior of a human expert while giving the appropriate diagnosis [2], [20]. Note that the two fuzzy inferences of FS_1 and FS_2, based on Mamdani's fuzzy inference, are developed as detailed in the diagnosis approach using only image representation described in [9], [10], with the simplification detailed in [24]. From this simplification, the fuzzy rule base of FS_1 which is built of $3^6 = 729$ rules will make in use only $2^6 = 64$ rules in each inference, while the fuzzy rule base of FS_2 which is built of $3^4 = 81$ rules will make in use only $2^4 = 16$ rules in each inference. Thus, the double classification, from global image representation, is exploited in FS_1 to ensure a satisfactory reliability for a computer aided auditory. Input parameters, obtained from the two neural networks, of FS_1 are RC_MLP, EC_MLP, NC_MLP, RC_RBF, EC_RBF, and NC_RBF. Thus, for each input, FS_1 is able to decide of appropriate diagnosis among Primary Outputs PO_{RC}, PO_{EC}, and PO_{NC}. The diagnosis reliability obtained from the FS_1 is reinforced (enhanced) using the obtained diagnosis result with an Auditory Threshold (AT) parameter of patients, used as a confidence parameter, exploited in FS_2 in order to generate the final diagnosis result. Input parameters, issued from FS_1, of FS_2 are AT, PO_{RC}, PO_{EC}, and PO_{NC}. Thus, for each input, FS_2 is able to decide of the appropriate diagnosis among Final Outputs: FO_{RC}, FO_{EC}, and FO_{NC} with their Confidence Index (CI). Note that same reasoning is developed for Fuzzy System 3 (FS_3) and Fuzzy System 4 (FS_4), see Fig. 3, for sub-divided image representation.

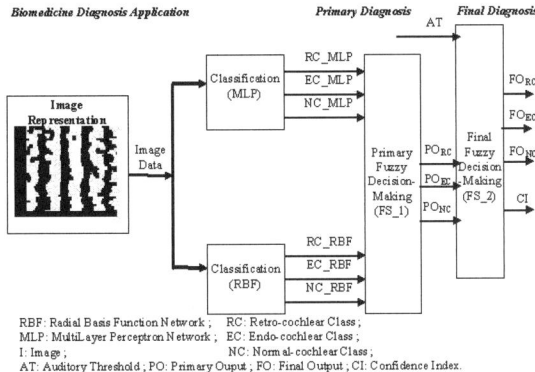

Fig. 2. Hybrid intelligent diagnosis system synopsis (MLP and RBF global images).

5. Prototype Design, Experimental Results, Analysis and Comparison

For the validation of the suggested intelligent system, in the case of auditory diagnosis help, the used data base is issued from a specialized center in functional explorations in oto-neurology CEFON[1] [18]. From the signal to image conversion, the obtained

---

[1] ''Centre d'Explorations Fonctionnelles Oto-Neurologiques'' (CEFON), Paris, France.

database is built of 206 images such as: 38 images represent Retro-Cochlear-Patients, 77 images represent Endo-Cochlear-Patients, and 91 images represent Normal-Cochlear-Patients. From this database, 104 images (around 50 % of the database) are used as learning base (19 Retro-Cochlear-Patients, 39 Endo-Cochlear-Patients, 46 Normal-Cochlear-Patients) while 102 (around 50 % of the database) are used as generalization test base (19 Retro-Cochlear-Patients, 38 Endo-Cochlear-Patients, 45 Normal-Cochlear-Patients).

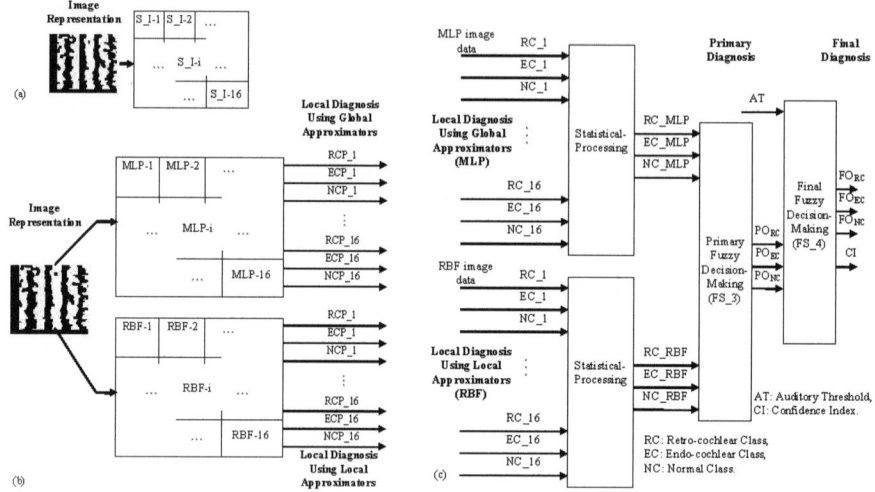

Fig. 3. Hybrid intelligent diagnosis system synopsis (MLP sub-images and RBF sub-images).

Table 1. Image neural classification results (MLP and RBF).

Results	Learning	Generalization	Learning	Generalization
RC	MLP 100 %	MLP 21.05 %	RBF 100 %	RBF 10.52 %
EC	MLP 97.43 %	MLP 42.10 %	RBF 100 %	RBF 36.84 %
NC	MLP 100 %	MLP 51.11 %	RBF 100 %	RBF 51.11 %

Table 2. Image neural classification results (MLP and RBF).

Results	Learning	Generalization	Learning	Generalization
RC	MLP 100 %	MLP 10.52 %	RBF 100 %	RBF 21.05 %
EC	MLP 100 %	MLP 31.57 %	RBF 100 %	RBF 13.15 %
NC	MLP 100 %	MLP 66.66 %	RBF 100 %	RBF 88.88 %

5.1 Prototype Design

First suggested approach illustrated in Fig. 2 is mainly based on a global image representation with MLP classification and RBF classification. Learning and generalization test results of MLP and RBF networks gives the MLP global indicator see Table 1 and RBF global indicator see Table 1. Note that results of the two neural classifications, from MLP and RBF networks give RC_MLP, EC_MLP, NC_MLP and RC_RBF, EC_RBF, NC_RBF which are exploited in FS_1 shown in Fig. 2.

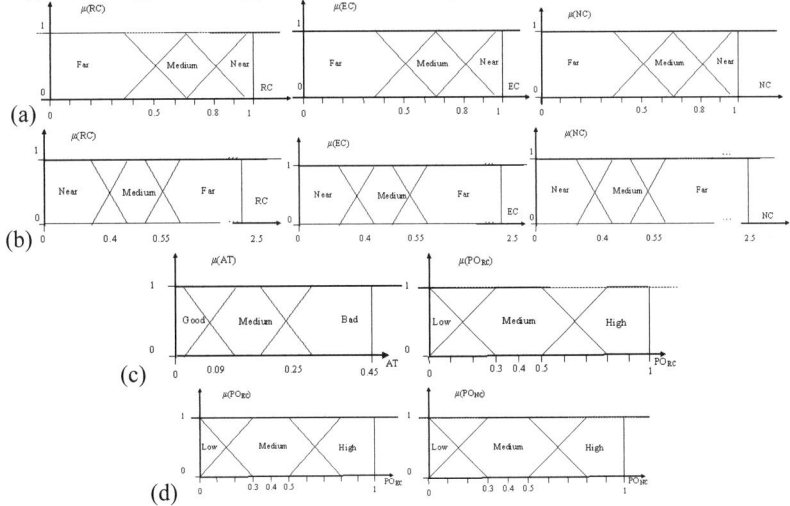

(a)

(b)

(c)

(d)

Fig. 4. Membership functions of: (a) RC, EC, and NC from MLP. (b) RC, EC, and NC from RBF. (c) AT and PO_{RC}. (d) PO_{EC} and PO_{NC}.

Second suggested approach illustrated in Fig. 3 is mainly based on a subdivided image representation: a subdivision of the image in several sub-images as illustrated in Fig. 3 (a), in order to process each pixel in each sub-image [25], avoiding thus some approximations such as mean of a set of pixels. The idea here is to process the original information (pixels), without any kind of approximation, in local sub-images (local indicators). The implemented classification strategy takes advantage from a multiple neural networks based structure. It includes two kind of neural classifiers operating in an independent way: MLP and RBF, as shown in Fig. 3 (b). The obtained images from BAEP's signal to image conversion leaded to divide each image into 16 sub-images (12 areas of 10x20 pixels and 4 areas of 10x10 pixels). So, 16 local diagnosis (aiming to obtain 16 local indicators) are done on the 16 sub-images (S_I-1, ..., S_I-i, ..., S_I-16) using 16 global approximators (MLP-1, ..., MLP-i, ..., MLP-16), while 16 others local diagnosis (16 others local indicators) are done in the same way using 16 local approximators (RBF-1, ..., RBF-i, ..., RBF-16). Indeed, MLP and RBF classifiers operate on basis of a local pattern recognition using local indicators in image, leading to a first diagnosis (local diagnosis). Learning and generalization test results after statistical processing of MLP networks and RBF networks gives two global indicators: MLP and RBF global indicators see Table 2. Note that the results of the two neural classifications, from MLP networks MLP-1 (RC_1, EC_1, NC_1), ..., MLP-16 (RC_16, EC_16, NC_16) and RBF networks RBF-1 (RC_1, EC_1, NC_1), ..., RBF-16 (RC_16, EC_16, NC_16), are processed statistically to give RC_MLP, EC_MLP, NC_MLP and RC_RBF, EC_RBF, NC_RBF and normalized between [0, 1] and exploited in FS_3 shown in Fig. 3 (c).

Thus, the input vector of FS_1, see Fig. 2, is then **I** = [RC_MLP, EC_MLP, NC_MLP, RC_RBF, EC_RBF, NC_RBF]. The membership functions of RC_MLP,

EC_MLP, NC_MLP have been defined in Fig. 4 (a) and those of RC_RBF, EC_RBF, NC_RBF have been defined in Fig. 4 (b). Also, input vector of FS_3, see Fig. 3 (c), is then $\mathbf{I}$ = [RC_MLP, EC_MLP, NC_MLP, RC_RBF, EC_RBF, NC_RBF]. Note that, in this case, membership functions of RC_MLP, EC_MLP, NC_MLP are the same that those of RC_RBF, EC_RBF, NC_RBF (because of statistical processing and normalization between [0, 1]) defined in Fig. 4 (a). Then, for FS_2 and FS_4, the membership functions of AT and PO_{RC} have been defined in Fig. 4 (c) and those of PO_{EC}, and PO_{NC} have been defined in Fig. 4 (d).

5.2 Auditory Diagnosis Results

Results of primary FS_1 and final FS_2 are given in Table 3, while those of primary FS_3 and final FS_4 are given in Table 4. Note that the particularity of the suggested fuzzy decision system is to give for each patient the final diagnosis FO_{RC}, FO_{EC}, FO_{NC} and a Confidence Index (CI) on its decision, e.g., the fuzzy output result $\mathbf{O}$ = {μFO_{RC}, μFO_{EC}, μFO_{NC}, μCI}. Then, the final result is given by: $\mathbf{O}$ = (Max{μFO_{RC}, μFO_{EC}, μFO_{NC}}, μCI). The generalization rate of NC is clearly higher for FS_1 and FS_2 (and FS_3 and FS_4) than for the two classifications. An important contribution of the final fuzzy system FS_2 (and FS_4) is that it gives each fault diagnosis associated with a CI. More, from the analysis and comparison of these results, two main interesting conclusions which make the suggested approaches very promising are deduced. First, correct classifications from FS_2 and FS_4 are not necessarily corresponding to same generalization example patients implying a complementary feature of FS_2 and FS_4. Second, FS_2 and FS_4 take advantage from way to process given information to classify (from global images as global indicators for FS_2 and from sub-divided images as local indicators for FS_4) and from different neural classifications (MLP global approximators and RBF local approximators).

Table 3. Fuzzy decision-making system FS_1 and FS_2 results.

	Learning	Generalization (FS_1)	Learning	Generalization (FS_2)
RC	FS_1 100 %	21.05 % (21.05 %)	FS_2 100 %	15.78 % (21.05 %)
EC	FS_1 97.43 %	39.47 % (52.63 %)	FS_2 89.74 %	39.47 % (47.36 %)
NC	FS_1 100 %	46.66 % (51.11 %)	FS_2 100 %	57.77 % (64.44 %)

Table 4. Fuzzy decision-making system FS_3 and FS_4 results.

	Learning	Generalization (FS_3)	Learning	Generalization (FS_4)
RC	FS_3 100 %	10.52 % (31.57 %)	FS_4 100 %	21.05 % (21.05 %)
EC	FS_3 100 %	15.78 % (34.21 %)	FS_4 94.87 %	57.89 % (65.78 %)
NC	FS_3 100 %	77.77 % (91.11 %)	FS_4 100 %	82.22 % (86.66 %)

6. Discussion and Conclusion

In this paper, two hybrid intelligent diagnosis approaches based on image representation for computer aided auditory diagnosis, based on neural classifications (modular neural networks) and fuzzy decision-making systems has been suggested. It is pertinent to notice that a large number of signal issued representations could be converted in image representations. In fact, such approaches take advantage from features which are unreachable from one-dimensional signal (time dependent waveform). More, it allows to use image-like representation and processing, which offers benefit of a richer information representation (than the signal related one), i.e., features which are unreachable from one-dimensional signal.

In fact, the double classification suggested in this work is exploited in FS_1 (and FS_3), for a primary diagnosis, to ensure a satisfactory reliability. Second, this reliability is reinforced using a confidence parameter Auditory Threshold (AT) with the primary diagnosis result, exploited in FS_2 (and FS_4), in order to generate the final diagnosis giving the appropriate diagnosis with a Confidence Index (CI). In fact, the aim is then to achieve an efficient and reliable CAD system for three classes: two auditory pathologies RC and EC and normal auditory NC. Note that the redundancy inherent in this scheme acts to the benefit of the overall system. Another important point concerns the number of classes in the suggested approaches, i.e., only three output classes. In fact, these approaches could be generalized to many output classes exploiting concept of modular neural networks [3], [13]. Such concept allows to avoid to deal with a huge number of fuzzy rules in case of a great number of output classes.

An interesting alternative for future works could be, the investigation in aspects related to different ways to fuse neural classifiers issued information [26], [27], such as fuzzy neural networks or fuzzy artmap neural networks [20], and in generalization of the suggested approaches to a larger field of applications such as other diagnosis problem in biomedicine, and fault detection and diagnosis in industrial plants [1], [4]. However, number of current system's aspects could be enhanced with a fine tuning of fuzzy rules, and with finer statistical features which could be investigated (higher order statistical features) in statistical processing stage [28].

References

[1] Balakrishnan, K., and Honavar, V., 'Intelligent Diagnosis Systems', Technical Report, Iowa State University, Ames, Iowa 50011-1040, U.S.A., 1997.

[2] Turban, E., and Aronson, J. E., 'Decision Support Systems and Intelligent Systems', Int. Edition, Sixth Edition, Prentice-Hall, 2001.

[3] Karray, F. O., and De Silva, C., 'Soft Computing and Intelligent Systems Design, Theory, Tools and Applications', Addison Wesley, ISBN 0-321-11617-8, 2004.

[4] Meneganti, M., Saviello, F.S., Tagliaferri, R.: Fuzzy Neural Networks for Classification and Detection of Anomalies. IEEE Transactions on Neural Networks, 9, No. 5, (1998) 848-861.

[5] Palmero, G.I.S., Santamaria, J.J., de la Torre, E.J.M., Gonzalez, J.R.P.: Fault Detection and Fuzzy Rule Extraction in AC Motors by a Neuro-Fuzzy ART-Based System. Engineering Applications of AI, 18, Elsevier, 867-874, 2005.

[6] Piater, J. H., Stuchlik, F., von Specht, H., Mühler, R.: Fuzzy Sets for Feature Identification in Biomedical Signals with Self-Assessment of Reliability: An Adaptable Algorithm Modeling Human Procedure in BAEP Analysis. Comput. and Biomedical Resear., 28, (1995) 335-353.

[7] Vuckovic, A., Radivojevic, V., Chen, A.C.N., Popovic, D.: Automatic Recognition of Alertness and Drowsiness from EEG by an Artificial Neural Network. Medical Engineering & Physics, 24 (5), (June 2002) 349-360.

[8] Wolf, A., Barbosa, C.H., Monteiro, E.C., Vellasco, M.: Multiple MLP Neural Networks Applied on the Determination of Segment Limits in ECG Signals. LNCS 2687, Springer-Verlag Berlin Heidelberg, (2003) 607-614.

[9] Chohra, A., Kanaoui, N., Amarger, V.: A Soft Computing Based Approach Using Signal-To-Image Conversion for Computer Aided Medical Diagnosis (CAMD). Information Processing and Security Systems, Edited by K. Saeed and J. Pejas, Springer, (2005) 365-374.

[10] Chohra, A., Kanaoui, N., Madani, K.: Hybrid Intelligent Classification for Computer Aided Diagnosis (CAD) Systems Using Image Representation. Int. Journal Image Processing and Communications, Edited by R. S. Choras, Vol. 10, No. 2, ISSN 1425-140x, pp. 07-15, 2005.

[11] Yan, H., Jiang, Y., Zheng, J., Peng, C., Li, Q.: A Multilayer Perceptron-Based Medical Support System for Heart Disease Diagnosis. Expert Systems with Applications, Elsevier, (2005).

[12] Murray-Smith R. and Johansen T. A., 'Multiple Model Approaches to Modelling and Control', Taylor & Francis Publishers, 1997.

[13] Kittler, J., M. Hatef, R. P. W. Duin, and J. Matas, "On Combining Classifiers", IEEE Trans. Pattern Analysis and Machine Int., Vol. 20, No. 3, pp. 226-239, 1998.

[14] Haykin, S.: Neural Networks: A Comprehensive Foundation,2Ed.Prentice-Hall, 1999.

[15] Zhang, G.P.: Neural Networks for Classification: A Survey. IEEE Trans. on Systems, Man, and Cybernetics – Part C: Applicat. and Reviews, vol. 30, no. 4, 451-462, 2000.

[16] Egmont-Petersen, M., De Ridder, D., Handels, H.: Image Processing with Neural Networks – A Review. Pattern Recognition, 35, pp. 2279-2301, 2002.

[17] Don, M., Masuda, A., Nelson, R., Brackmann, D.: Successful Detection of Small Acoustic Tumors using the Stacked Derived-Band Auditory Brain Stem Response Amplitude. The American Journal of Otology 18, 5, pp. 608-621, 1997.

[18] Vannier, E., Adam, O., Motsch, J. F., 'Objective Detection of Brainstem Auditory Evoked Potentials with a Priori Information from Higher Presentation Levels', Artificial Intelligence in Medicine, 25, pp. 283-301, 2002.

[19] Bradley, A.P., Wilson W.J.: On Wavelet Analysis of Auditory Evoked Potentials. Clinical Neurophysiology, 115, pp. 1114-1128, 2004.

[20] Azouaoui, O., Chohra, A.: Soft Computing Based Pattern Classifiers for the Obstacle Avoidance Behavior of Intelligent Autonomous Vehicles (IAV). Int. J. of Applied Intelligence, Kluwer Academic Publishers, 16, no. 3, pp. 249-271, 2002.

[21] Zadeh, L.A.: The Calculus of Fuzzy If / Then Rules. AI Expert, (1992) 23-27.

[22] Lee, C.C.: Fuzzy Logic in Control Systems: Fuzzy Logic Controller – Part I & Part II. IEEE Trans. On Systems, Man, and Cybernetics, 20, no. 2, pp. 404-435, 1990.

[23] Gonzalez, R. C., Woods, R.E., 'Digital Image Processing', 2 Ed. Prentice-Hall, 2002.

[24] Farreny, H., and Prade, H., 'Tackling Uncertainty and Imprecision in Robotics', 3rd Int. Symposium on Robotics Research, pp. 85-91, 1985.

[25] Piater, J. H., Edward M. Riseman and Paul E. Utgoff (1999), "Interactively Training Pixel Classifiers", International Journal of Pattern Recognition and Artificial Intelligence 13 (2), pp. 171-194.

[26] Wanas, N., Kamel, M. S., Auda, G., and Karray, F., 'Feature-based decision aggregation in modular neural network classifiers', Pattern Recognition Letters 20, Elsevier, pp. 1353-1359, 1999.

[27] Lai, C., D. M. J. Tax, R. P. W. Duin, E. Pekalska, and P. Paclik, "A Study on Combining Image Representations for Image Classification and Retrieval", Int. J. of Pattern Recognition and AI, Vol. 18, No. 5, pp. 867-890, WSPC, 2004.

[28] Kuncheva, L. I., C. J. Whitaker, C. A. Shipp, "Limits on the Majority Vote Accuracy in Classifier Fusion", Pattern Analysis and Applications", 6, pp. 22-31, 2003.

Predicting Incomplete Data on the Basis
of Non Symmetric Similarity Relation

Ewa Adamus, Andrzej Piegat

Faculty of Computer Science and Information Technology, Szczecin University of Technology, Żołnierska 49, 71-210 Szczecin, Poland, eadamus@wi.ps.pl, apiegat@wi.ps.pl

Abstract. The rough set theory was meant as a tool for imprecise and inconsistent information systems. Incomplete information can be also considered as a particular case of imprecise information. Because the rough set theory makes the assumption of completeness of all attributes of input vector, many modifications of this theory were developed describing how to use the incomplete data. This article presents the basic approaches: tolerance relation and non symmetric similarity relation. Furthermore, a new method of supplementing some incomplete objects from an information table has been proposed.

Introduction

Rough set theory operates on the assumption that every considered object is connected with some kind of information. The objects with the same description (the same information) are indiscernible in the aspect of accessible information. The indiscernibility relation, defined in this way, is the mathematic base of rough set theory.

The set of the indiscernible objects is called the *elementary class*. The set that is an union of the elementary classes is a reference to precise set or an inexact one – a rough set. Each rough set has a boundary area, an area that contains objects that don't entirely belong to the class or to its complement. The objects which certainly belong to the class are its *lower approximation* and these which belong to the class only probably are its *boundary area* (the difference between *upper* and *lower approximation*).

Because the original definition of indiscernibility relation makes the assumption of completeness of input vectors of compared objects x and y in the input vector, the problem appears when at least one of the attributes doesn't have its defined value. This is the cause of creating modifications of indiscernibility relation. Some of the basics are described below. Additionally, a proposition of filling in certain incomplete objects based on non-symmetric similarity relation will be presented.

Incomplete data and rough set theory

Generally in the case when missing data occur, we can use either symmetric tolerance relation or non symmetric similarity relation. Basing on these relations we are going to make a comparative analysis.

The reason of introducing the tolerance relation to the "incomplete" input vector is treating incomplete objects inconsistently in the conventional indiscernibility relation. The indiscernibility relation treats an object which doesn't have a value for attribute $a \in A$ as an equivalent, although the real values for this attribute can be different [3]. In the case, when one of the objects has a value for the mentioned attribute a, the objects are treated as different, although the real value for attribute a may be identical with another object's value. We can acquire a consistent treatment of incomplete data by using the tolerance relation defined in [5, 6].

An information system is a pair $S = (U, A)$, where U is a non-empty set of objects called the universe, and A is a set of attributes. For attributes subset $B \subseteq A$, the tolerance relation is defined as follows:

$$TOL(B) = \{(x, y) \in U \times U : \forall \, a \in B, f(a, x) = f(a, y) \text{ or } f(a, x) = * \text{ or } f(a, y) = *\}, \quad (1)$$

the relation is reflexive, symmetric but not necessarily transitive.

$T_B(x)$ is a set of objects that are indiscernible with x in regard to B:

$$T_B(x) = \{y \in U : (x, y) \in TOL(B)\}. \quad (2)$$

The similarity relation is an alternative for the indiscernibility relation for imprecise data or for precise data, which differ insignificantly for the whole analysis ([8]).

Based on definitions in [8, 2] Stefanowski gives a definition of similarity relation that regards incomplete data with definitions of sets approximations [9, 10].

We say that object y is similar to x ($yS_b x$), when:

$$\forall a \in B \text{ such that } f(a, y) \neq *, f(a, x) = f(a, y). \quad (3)$$

The relation isn't similar and reflexive. Additionally, two classes of similarity relations were defined:

- a set of objects similar to x :

$$S_B(x) = \{y \in U : yS_B x\}, \quad (4)$$

- a set of objects, where x is similar to:

$$S_B^{-1}(x) = \{y \in U : xS_B y\}. \quad (5)$$

Based on classes of similarity definitions, the lower and upper approximation for $X \subseteq U$ can be defined as:

$$\underline{B}_S(X) = \{x \in U : S_B^{-1}(x) \subseteq X\}, \quad (6)$$

$$\overline{B}_S(X) = \bigcup \{S_B(x) : x \subseteq X\}. \tag{7}$$

Predicting incomplete data by the use of non symmetric similarity relation

The literature distinguishes the following methods of dealing with the problem of incomplete data:

1. Data with missing values are not taken into consideration.
2. Estimating of the missing data – usually during the data preprocessing.
3. The methods are chosen accordingly to the possibilities of the missing value in some attributes of the input vector. Only the defined values of the incomplete input vector are taken into consideration in that case.

If the problem is applied to the rough set theory, an explicit classification of this theory to one of the mentioned methods cannot be done. In this aspect the theory is the most distinguishable one if compared to all the other methods (see [1]). The incomplete sample, dependently on the context (of reciprocal relations with other objects in the base of knowledge) will certainly be accepted for the further analysis (it will belong to the lower approximation of the given decision concept), or it will not be accepted as it will be found in the boundary area. Thus, when applying the rough set theory to solve the problem of incomplete data it is possible to divide incomplete data into two groups of objects: *certain* and *doubtful*. The first group deals with the data which contain additional information – they are either incomplete unique objects or objects which are similar to their own decision class only (in this case the incomplete sample may be treated as a simplified decision rule). In the case of the doubtful objects those elements will be taken into consideration with some probability in the further analysis. The aim of this work is to establish yet another scenario of dealing with incomplete data, i.e. supplementing the missing data.

On the basis of the interpretation of the approximations of set $X \subseteq U$ (def. 6., 8.) for an incomplete object $x \subseteq U$ one of the following scenarios can be adopted:

For the decision table $DT = (U, A \cup \{d\})$ where $d \notin A$ is the decision attribute and the subset of input attributes $B \subseteq A$ and object $x \subseteq U$ there is a defined class of objects and to which x is similar $S_B^{-1}(x)$ (def. 5.) in order to simplify the recording of the further formulas, index B will be omitted assuming that the whole analysis is done for the subset of attributes $B \subseteq A$. Then:

1. If $S^{-1}(x) \subseteq X$ then the incomplete object x makes the lower approximation of set X. It is an equivalent of the third method for the dealing with incomplete data i.e. **the acceptance of only the defined information in the incomplete sample**.

2. If $S^{-1}(x) \cap X \neq \varnothing$ and $S^{-1}(x) \cap -X \neq \varnothing$ then **the incomplete object x will not be a lower approximation of set X** i.e. it will be found in the boundary area of the decision classes. It is impossible to classify it implicitly. The further part of the article will be devoted to this aspect.

Assuming that $S_r^{-1}(x) = S^{-1}(x) \setminus \{x\}$ i.e. we are interested in the class of objects to which x is similar without the very object (i.e. x is not similar to itself). Let us analyse the situation when set $S_r^{-1}(x)$ represents an opposite decision class, that is $S_r^{-1}(x) \subseteq -X$. If we possess information which is opposite to x, we know what values the incomplete object should not take, then we know the area of permitted values for x, which will comprise of the complementation of set $S_r^{-1}(x)$. Following case 2. for the incomplete object $x \subseteq U$ for which condition: $S^{-1}(x) \cap X \neq \varnothing$ and $S^{-1}(x) \cap -X \neq \varnothing$ is fulfilled we can take one of the following scenarios:

1. If $S_r^{-1}(x) \subseteq -X$, **then incomplete object x is filled with the complement of the similarity class** (see equation (10))
2. Otherwise, if $S_r^{-1}(x) \cap X \neq \varnothing$ and $S_r^{-1}(x) \cap -X \neq \varnothing$ then in order to check whether we possess coherent opposite information we make an analysis of the so-called **directional classes of similarity**.

Similarity relations can be interpreted as representatives of inclusion relations as the similarity of y to x is equivalent to the notion that the description of object y is comprised in the description of object x [10]. However the relation of similarity is a relation of a partial order of set $S^{-1}(x)$ as not each two elements of this set are comparable. For instance the figure 1. objects 8. and 9. are not comparable as they possess different values for the third attribute. In such a case we refer to set $S_r^{-1}(x)$ as **partially ordered**. In relation to this set $S_r^{-1}(x)$ can be presented as a family of disjointed pairs of sets and completely ordered by the inclusion relations (see fig. 1.). The authors of the present article have termed those sets as **directional classes of similarity** and marked with the symbol $S_{rK}^{-1}(y)$ where y fulfills the condition: $y \in S_r^{-1}(x) \wedge S^{-1}(y) = \{y\}$ that belongs to a set of objects between which it is impossible to define the mutual inclusion relation of the objects' description.

$$S_{rK}^{-1}(y) = S_r^{-1}(x) \cap S(y), \tag{8}$$

Eventually set $S_r^{-1}(x)$ can be presented as a sum of the family of directional similarity sets of disjoint pairs:

$$S_r^{-1}(x) = \bigcup S_{rK}^{-1}(y). \tag{9}$$

Within the single directional set of similarity ($S_{rK}^{-1}(y)$) we can define mutual inclusion relations between each two elements of this set. The direction of these relations is determined by the level of incompleteness of the objects.

The exemplary division of set $S^{-1}(x)$ into directional sets of similarity has been presented in a figure 1. as set is a partially ordered set, a convenient form of graphic presentation of this type of the set is a Hasse's diagram.

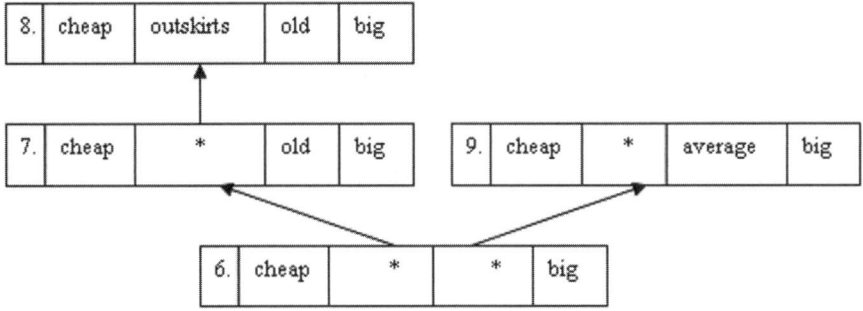

Fig. 1. The exemplary division of set $S^{-1}(x)$ into directional sets of similarity.

The particular branches of the diagram are of course directional sets of similarity, that is completely ordered subsets of a partially ordered set.

The analysis of directional sets of similarity allows to present the case $(S_r^{-1}(x) \cap X \neq \varnothing) \wedge (S_r^{-1}(x) \cap -X \neq \varnothing)$ as two instances:

1. If $\exists (S_{rK}^{-1}(y) \subseteq S^{-1}(x)) \wedge (S_{rK}^{-1}(y) \cap X) \wedge (S_{rK}^{-1}(y) \cap -X)$ - within a single directional set of similarity there is no unity as to the belonging to the decision concept. According to the classic definitions **object x will not be the lower approximation both for set X and -X.**

2. If $\forall (S_{rK}^{-1}(y) \subseteq S^{-1}(x)) \wedge ((S_{rK}^{-1}(y) \subseteq X) \vee (S_{rK}^{-1}(y) \subseteq -X)) \wedge (\left| S^{-1}(y) \right| = 1)$,

   where $\left| S^{-1}(y) \right|$ is the cardinality of the set $S^{-1}(y)$ - in all the directional sets of similarity there is unity as to the belonging to the decision concept and there is at least one set $S_{rK}^{-1}(y)$ representing the opposite decision concept: $S_{rK}^{-1}(y) \subseteq -X$ - in that case the incomplete object is **filled with a complement of a similarity class** (see equation (10)).

To sum up the above considerations an algorithm of dealing with an incomplete object x will be presented, with the assumption that for the decision table $DT = (U, A \cup \{d\})$ and object $x \subseteq U$ there is a defined class of objects, to which x is similar: $S^{-1}(x)$ (def. 5.). Additionally $S_r^{-1}(x) = S^{-1}(x) \setminus \{x\}$ and $S_{rK}^{-1}(y)$ is a directional set of similarity for $y \in S_r^{-1}(x)$. Then:

1. If $S^{-1}(x) \subseteq X$ - **the acceptance of only the defined information in the incomplete sample.**

2. If $S^{-1}(x) \cap X \neq \varnothing$ and $S^{-1}(x) \cap -X \neq \varnothing$ then:

- If $S_r^{-1}(x) \subseteq -X$, then **the incomplete object x is filled with the complement of the similarity class** (see equation (10))
- Otherwise, if $S_r^{-1}(x) \cap X \neq \varnothing$ and $S_r^{-1}(x) \cap -X \neq \varnothing$ then in order to check whether we possess coherent opposite information we make an analysis of the **directional classes of similarity:**
  - If $\exists(S_{rK}^{-1}(y) \subseteq S^{-1}(x)) \wedge (S_{rK}^{-1}(y) \cap X) \wedge (S_{rK}^{-1}(y) \cap -X)$ - **object x will not be the lower approximation both for set X and -X.**
  - If $\forall(S_{rK}^{-1}(y) \subseteq S^{-1}(x)) \wedge ((S_{rK}^{-1}(y) \subseteq X) \vee (S_{rK}^{-1}(y) \subseteq -X)) \wedge (\left|S^{-1}(y)\right| = 1)$ - **the incomplete object x is filled with a complement of a similarity class** (see equation (10)).

The supplementation of the incomplete object x, which qualifies to be supplemented, consists of complement of the class of objects to which the incomplete one is similar: $C(S^{-1}(x))$ except for such objects which belong to tolerance relation class $T(x)$ on the basis of which we can make an explicit classification: $S^{-1}(y) \subseteq X \vee S^{-1}(y) \subseteq -X$:

$$C(S^{-1}(x)) \setminus \{y : y \in T(x) \wedge (S^{-1}(y) \subseteq X \vee S^{-1}(y) \subseteq -X)\}. \tag{10}$$

Experiments

The presented method has been verified on the basis of a set with real measurement data. The experiments were made with the use of the diabetes set (for diagnosing diabetes of Pima Indians) from the popular benchmark dataset [7]. Each sample has 8 inputs and 1 output which takes the value 0 or 1. The whole dataset includes 768 complete samples. The data set was modified by introducing various degrees of incompleteness for the following basic kinds of incompleteness [4]:

- MCAR (*missing completely at random*);
- MAR (*missing at random*);
- NI *(non ignorable)*.

Fig. 2. presents the dependence of the incompleteness degree of the data on the average number of rules making a proper classification (*the number of proper rules/ the number of all the rules*). In order to generate the set of rules, the LEM2 algorithm [3] was used. The similarity relation makes the basis for the method of conditioned supplementing; when there are no samples qualifying to be completed the method comes down to the non-symmetric similarity relation. That is why fig. 2. presents the results of testing for the decision rules generated on the basis of the similarity relation with and without the conditional supplementation. The verification of the rules was made with the use of the *k-fold validation* technique. Fig.2. presents the results of the calculations for the testing stage.

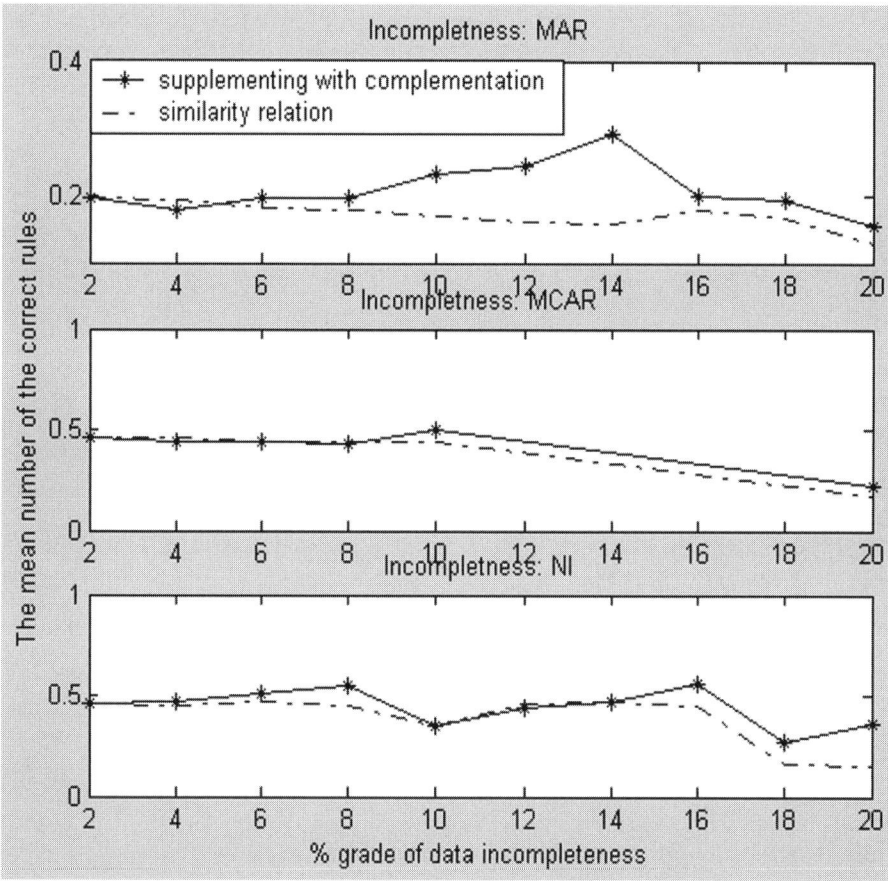

Fig. 2. The relationship between the level of incompleteness of the mean number of the correct rules for testing samples.

The presented results imply that the application of the conditioned supplementation for the induction of rules for incomplete data improves the quality of modeling. Completing certain samples on the basis of the information provided by the non-symmetric similarity relation can bring some beneficial effects for the application of the similarity relation itself.

Conclusions

The authors of the article have attempted to prove that supplementing incomplete data (especially in the cases when this prediction brings into the analysis additional information) has some benefits.

1. Using this method, a consistent decision table isn't converted into an inconsistent one. However, in the case of the RS theory, we have a good tool to deal with the inconsistencies, but the supplemented new objects may bring inconsistencies and be indiscernible with the existing objects.
2. In consequence of such supplementing, we don't lose significant information included in the unique, incomplete objects.
3. Supplementing on the basis of the non-symmetric similarity relation increases the accuracy approximation of the decision class. This is because the set of the newly supplemented objects is entirely included in the lower approximation of the current set.

References

[1] E. Adamus Przegląd metod stosowanych do badań nad niekompletnymi danymi pomiarowymi. VIII *Sesja Informatyki*, II:387-395, Szczecin, 2003.
[2] Greco S., Matarazzo B., Słowiński R. Dealing with missing data In rough sets analysis of multi-attribute and multi-criteria decision problems. *Kluwer Academic Publisher*, p. 295-316, 2002.
[3] J. Grzymala-Busse and A. Y. Wang. Modified algorithms lem1 and lem2 for rule induction from with missing attribute values. Proc.of theFifth International Workshop on Rough Sets and Soft Computing (RSSC'97) at the Third Join Conference on Information Sciences (JCIS'97), Research Triangle Park, NC, pages 69-72, March 2-5 1997.
[4] G. King, J. Honaker and A. Joseph Analyzing Incomplete Political Science Data: An Alternative Algorithm for multiple imputation. *American Political Science Review*, (95) p. 49-69, 2001.
[5] M. Kryszkiewicz. Rough set approach to rules generation from incomplete information systems. *ICS Research Report 55/95, Warsaw University of Technology; also in: International Journal of Information Sciences, 1995.*
[6] M. Kryszkiewicz Rough set approach to incomplete information system. *International Journal of Information Sciences*, (112): p. 39-49, 1998.
[7] Prechelt L.: Proben1 – A set of neural network benchmark problems and bench-marking rules, *Technical Report*, 1994
[8] R. Słowiński and D. Vanderpooten. A generalized definition of rough Approximations based on similarity. *IEEE Transactions on Knowledge and Data Engineering*, 12: 331-336, march/april 2000.
[9] J. Stefanowski and A. Tsoukias. On the extension of rough sets under incomplete information. *New Directions in Rough Sets, Data Mining and Granular-Soft Computing, LNAI 1711, Springer-Verlag, Berlin, 1999.*
[10] J. Stefanowski and A. Tsoukias. Incomplete information tables and rough classification. *Int. Journal of Computational Intelligence.* 2001.

Methods of Designing and System Analysis of Fast Neural Networks and Linear Tunable Transformations

A.Yu. Dorogov

Saint Petersburg State Electrotechnical University "LETI",
5, Prof. Popov st., Saint Petersburg, 197376, Russia,
dorogov@lens.spb.ru

Abstract. This paper discusses the paradigm of fast neural networks (FNN). System invariants of fast transformations are represented. Formal linguistic methods of structure and topologies designing of FNN and linear tunable transformations are developed. The methods of tuning FNN for realization of spectral transformations, regular fractal, optimum filters are considered. The questions of using FNN in quantum calculations are investigated. The method of separating capacity estimation for weakly-connected feed-forward neural networks is offered. The dependence of amount of recognized patterns on neural network freedom degrees is obtained. The experimental results are represented.

1. Introduction

It is well known, what a huge role in processing of signals the discovery of algorithm of fast Fourier transformation (FFT) has played. The use of FFT has let cardinally to decrease amount of computing operations for carrying out of spectral transformations, which considerably has expanded the application of the spectral analysis for data processing area. The FFT realization in technology of the large integrated circuits has resulted in essential decreasing of square of crystals for spectral analyzers, and accordingly has decreased their energy consumption.

For neural networks the problem of decreasing of computing operations amount is actual not less. For large dimensionalities of treated data the neural networks with a multilayer structure require significant volume of computing operations, both for data processing, and for learning of the networks. It restricts application of the large neural networks of given class in real – time systems and essentially complicates hardware realization.

The FFT algorithms have an expressed multilayer structure such as structure of multilayer perceptions; therefore, a natural decision arises to use philosophy of FFT for construction neural networks. It is enough for it in operations "butterfly" of FFT to replace conversion coefficients by variable synapse weights and to add nonlinear activation functions [1]. It is necessary to mention that the first step in this direction was made a long time ago. Since then historical Good's paper [2] (1958) analytical description of fast algorithms for generalized spectral transformations was indicated. From of today view point the generalized spectral transformation is possible to be considered as a neural network with linear functions of activation. In the next years the subject of generalized spectral transformations has been developed in papers of H.Andrews, A.Solodovnikov, G.Labunetc and other authors [3-5].

1.1 Main ideas and methods of decision

The algorithm of FFT has two system restrictions: at first, dimensionality of a vector of treated data for all layers should be identical and, secondly, the significance of this dimensionality should be a composite number, i.e. to be decomposed in a product of all factors. The first restriction is stipulated by an orthogonality of FFT matrix, and the second by regularity of the algorithm that, apparently, is the inevitable pay for speed of processing. Paradigm of fast neural networks inherits a regularity of algorithm of FFT, but expands its possibility by means of rejection of orthogonality and rigid scheme of topological realization. For neural networks with regular structure both regular and irregular topology can be constructed. The choice of topology type can be influenced by two circumstances: data structure and the simplicity of technical realization. For large and super large neural networks (potential area of FNN application) the simplicity of technical realization is the main condition. Therefore, regularity of topology is considered as a composite component of FNN paradigm.

1.2 Obtained outcomes

FNN represents a variant of multilayer feed-forward networks, therefore for their learning the gradient methods like Error Back Propagation can be used, however structural features of FNN allow to simplify the procedure of learning, as well. Special types of FNN are the fast adjustable linear transformations. From FNN they differ by linear functions of activation and absence of biases. The orthogonal adjustable transformations with various topologies were traditionally used for construction of spectral transformations. In terms of adjustable transformations the procedure of learning is usually named as tuning. Typical problem for adjustable transformation is the tuning at a specific system of basis functions, for example it may be Fourier base, Hadamard-Walsh base, etc. The classical systems of basis functions, have, as a rule, the analytical form; therefore, tuning of transformation also is executed in an analytical way. As the structure FNN has fractal properties, the regular fractal sequences can be realized as multilayer FNN. Fractalness generates also special methods of FNN tuning for optimum filters realization. The similarity of FNN structure with the structure of tensor products of vector spaces, allows to use FNN for construction of algorithms of quantum calculations. Above listed items form the main contents of the present paper. The purpose of the paper is to give a representation about system methods of construction FNN and to evaluate their performances as well as to show the potential areas of application.

The rest of the paper is organized as follows: in Section 2 structural analyses of FFT algorithms is fulfilled and system invariants of fast transformations are represented, in Section 3 the concept of fast neural networks is discussed, in Section 4 the realization of fast spectral transformation is represented, in Section 5 the neural network realization of regular fractals is shown, in Section 6 the adapted fast transformations are considered, in Section 7 the application of adapted fast transformations for synthesis quantum algorithms is shown, in Section 8 system performances of weakly-connected neural networks are investigated, in Section 9 the conclusion discussion is presented.

2. Structure analyses of FFT

Analyses of invariant features of fast algorithms we will demonstrate on example of fast Fourier Transformation (FFT). With that end in view we will consider FFT on structure level. Fig.1 depicts a structure model of FFT with 8 dimensionality. Here each graph node corresponds to base operation of "butterfly" type. All connections between the nodes are one-to-one maps and have unit rank. Denote as i the number of node in input layer and as j the number of node in output layer. Then represent the numbers in number system with radix 2

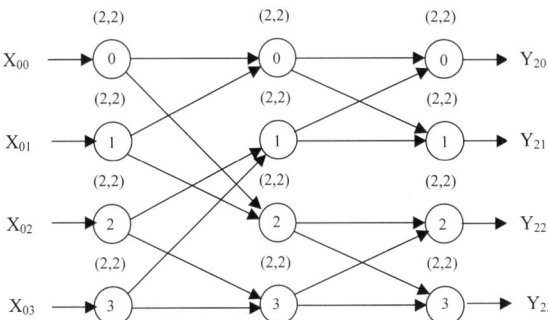

Fig. 1. Structure model of FFT

$$i = \langle i_2 i_1 \rangle = i_2 2 + i_1, \quad j = \langle j_0 j_1 \rangle = j_0 2 + j_1.$$

where $i_\lambda, j_\lambda \in [0,1]$ are bit sites. By means of direct checking we can see that for the structure model the numbering of intermediate layer nodes should be defined by the expression $i^1 = \langle j_0 i_2 \rangle = j_0 2 + i_2$. Fig. 2 depicts one step of construction the structure model. The model is constructed using the following rule: an arc connects nodes of adjacent layers if the order numbers of these nodes have identical digit representations.

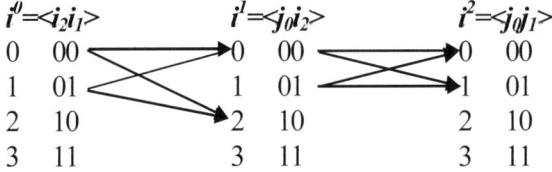

Fig. 2. The rule of structure model building

Symbols i_λ, j_λ we can consider as letters of an alphabet and expression $\langle i_2 i_1 \rangle$, $\langle j_0 i_2 \rangle$, $\langle j_0 j_1 \rangle$ as words of a formal language and expression $\left[\langle i_2 i_1 \rangle \langle j_0 i_2 \rangle \langle j_0 j_1 \rangle \right]$ as sentence of the language. In result we have linguistic description for the structure model which we will name as linguistic model. On base of the example we can draw a following conclusion:

- Only two letter kinds i and j are used for word construction;
- In linguistic sentence all reliable words are constructed from non-recurring letters and have length with unit less than number of layers;
- The words in the sentence are linear ordered according to amount of each letter kind.

2.1 Structure invariant of fast algorithms

Now FFT linguistic model we expand for fast transformation in general. Define the alphabet of formal language as a linear ordered set of non-recurring letters with two kinds of gender names:

$$A = \left\langle \langle i \rangle_I \oplus \langle j \rangle_J \right\rangle$$

where I and J are the ordered sets of «i» and «j» letter gender kinds, respectively. The amount of letters for each set equals to $\kappa - 1$. From the alphabet we will construct words with a length equal to $\kappa - 1$ consisting of non-recurring letters. From the word set we construct a sentence according to the following rule:

- All words in the sentence are ordered according to amount of letters with gender name j;
- The first word in the sentence is formed from I letter set and, therefore, includes zero amount of letters with gender name j.

According to the rule the number of words in any sentence is equal to κ. Let λ and $\lambda + 1$ define the order numbers for a pair of adjacent words in the sentence. Denote through I_λ and J_λ gender subsets of letters for word with order number equal to λ. Then the grammatical rule for permissible sentence may be formulated as follows:

$$I_\lambda \supset I_{\lambda+1}, \qquad J_\lambda \subset J_{\lambda+1}, \tag{1}$$

where $I_0 = I$, $\qquad I_{\kappa-1} = \varnothing$, $\qquad J_{\kappa-1} = J$, $\qquad J_0 = \varnothing$.

The grammar is not connected with transformation kind, not connected with transformation dimensionality, not connected with its structure parameters and it represents a system invariant for any fast algorithms.

2.2 Topological invariants of fast algorithms

Each base operation has input and output field of terminal contacts. The contacts are locally numbered within base operation and globally within a layer. Correspondence between local and global number defines the topology of base operation. Topology of input and output fields may be defined by the following linguistic expressions:

$$U^\lambda = \left\langle \left\langle i^\lambda \right\rangle \oplus u_\lambda \right\rangle, \qquad V^\lambda = \left\langle \left\langle i^\lambda \right\rangle \oplus v_\lambda \right\rangle.$$

The expressions include the number of base operation i^λ in a position numerical system and additional digits u_λ and v_λ which are local number terminal contacts for input and output fields of base operation. In general, the digits may be placed in any position of each linguistic word, but additional condition of topological regularity may establish some restrictions. Since all interlayer connections are one-to-one maps, there is one-to-one map between contacts of adjacent layers, which is defined by the following expression:

$$\left\langle \left\langle i \right\rangle_{I_\lambda} \oplus \left\langle j \right\rangle_{J_\lambda} \oplus v_\lambda \right\rangle * q^\lambda = \left\langle \left\langle i \right\rangle_{I_{\lambda+1}} \oplus \left\langle j \right\rangle_{J_{\lambda+1}} \oplus u_{\lambda+1} \right\rangle,$$

where q^λ is a permutation for letters. As a rule, q^λ is identity. The above expressions establish also one-to-one correspondences between letters: $i \leftrightarrow u, j \leftrightarrow v$. It allows us to use in a transformation design only alphabet with letters u and v gender kinds. Besides, two additional letters u_0 and $v_{\kappa-1}$ have to be included in the alphabet. These two letters are not connected by any whatsoever expressions with other layers and define local contact number for base operation of terminal fields of multilayer network. Upon changing the alphabet, the structure invariant (1) may be expressed as:

$$S_{\lambda+1} \subset S_\lambda, \qquad C_{\lambda+1} \supset C_\lambda,$$

where $S_{-1} = S$, $S_{\kappa-1} = \varnothing$, $C_{-1} = \varnothing$, $C_{\kappa-1} = C$. Here $S = \{u_0 u_1 \ldots u_{\kappa-1}\}$, $C = \{v_0 v_1 \ldots v_{\kappa-1}\}$ are gender letter sets. In result, the structure linguistic sentence goes into two topological linguistic sentences for input and output fields. It may be proved that in fixed alphabet any structure model has the same set of topologies.

2.3 Examples of topological designing of fast algorithm

Let's assume that a structural model is defined by the following sentence:

$$\left[\left\langle i_1 i_2 i_3 \right\rangle \left\langle i_1 i_2 j_0 \right\rangle \left\langle i_1 j_1 j_0 \right\rangle \left\langle j_2 j_1 j_0 \right\rangle \right].$$

For the structure linguistic model, the alphabet is defined as $A_S = \left\langle i_1 i_2 i_3 j_2 j_1 j_0 \right\rangle$. Fig. 3 depicts a graph of the structure linguistic model. For topological linguistic model the alphabet is defined as $A_T = \left\langle u_0 u_1 u_2 u_3 v_0 v_1 v_2 v_3 \right\rangle$. There are many variants of topological realization for the same structure model. Let us consider designing of regular topology.

The following rule may be used for designing of regular topology. Beginning with left position of the alphabet cortege we will step-by-step move 4-place interval limited by a pair of angle brackets along the alphabet cortege. On each step the interval selects a word consisting of 4 letters. In result we obtain the linguistic sentence:

$$\left[\left\langle u_0 u_1 u_2 u_3 \right\rangle \left\langle u_1 u_2 u_3 v_0 \right\rangle \left\langle u_2 u_3 v_0 v_1 \right\rangle \left\langle u_3 v_0 v_1 v_2 \right\rangle\right],$$

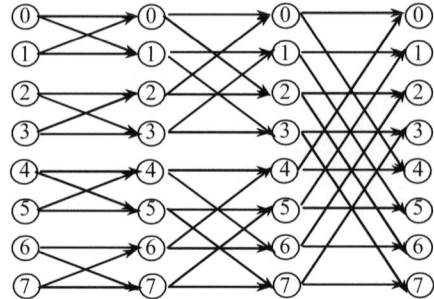

Fig. 3. Graph of structure linguistic model

which defines topology of input fields. Inverse motion of the interval from right position of the alphabet cortege to its left position creates linguistic sentence:

$$\left[\left\langle u_1 u_2 u_3 v_0 \right\rangle \left\langle u_2 u_3 v_0 v_1 \right\rangle \left\langle u_3 v_0 v_1 v_2 \right\rangle \left\langle v_0 v_1 v_2 v_3 \right\rangle\right],$$

which defines topology of output fields. It is easy to check that the sentences satisfy to topological invariant. These sentences may be used for drawing topological graph. Toward this end it is necessary to define radices for digits. Let us define the radices for example by the following correspondence:

$$\binom{A_T}{p} = \begin{pmatrix} u_0 & u_1 & u_2 & u_3 & v_0 & v_1 & v_2 & v_3 \\ 2 & 2 & 2 & 2 & 2 & 2 & 2 & 2 \end{pmatrix}.$$

The topological graph is built with the same rule as a structure model graph. Fig. 4 depicts the topological graph. Each node of the graph is a contact of a base operation and each arc corresponds to multiplication of input magnitude by a coefficient, convergence of arcs to a node means the summing of results.

This topology is known as Good's topology. The regular rule may be expressed analytically. Let us denote as t^λ the topological word selected by the interval on step λ ($\lambda = 0, 1, \ldots, \kappa - 1$), then we get $t^\lambda = \left\langle u_\lambda u_{\lambda+1} \ldots u_{\kappa-1} v_0 v_1 \ldots v_{\lambda-1} \right\rangle$. It is obvious that for input field the topology is defined by condition $U^\lambda = t^\lambda$ and for output field – by condition $V^\lambda = t^{\lambda+1}$.

For each layer of the graph we can build a topological matrix shown in Fig 5. It is a sparse matrix, where units mark non-zero values of coefficients. In matrix form the fast algorithm may be represented as multiplication of the sparse matrices:

$$H = H_0 H_1, \ldots, H_{\kappa-1}.$$

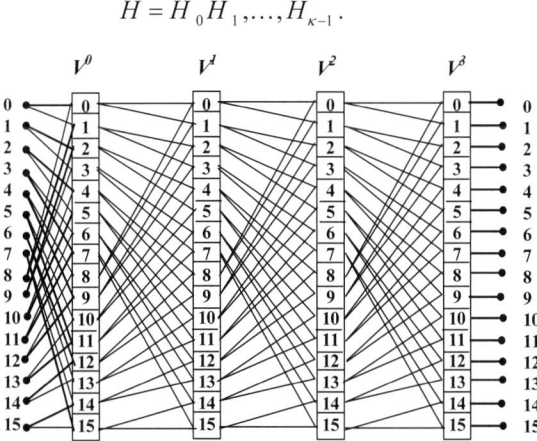

Fig. 4. Realization of Good's topology

Correspondence between digits U_m, V_m and u_λ, v_λ for each sparse matrix is defined by the topological sentences. For example, for the second layer it is

$$\left\langle U_3^1 U_2^1 U_1^1 U_0^1 \right\rangle = \left\langle u_1 u_2 u_3 v_0 \right\rangle, \qquad \left\langle V_3^1 V_2^1 V_1^1 V_0^1 \right\rangle = \left\langle u_2 u_3 v_0 v_1 \right\rangle.$$

(here, and in what follows, the layers are numbered beginning from zero index). The set of the correspondences we name as a topology trajectory and correspondence for terminal fields as boundary conditions. The following expressions are examples of boundary conditions:

V_3	0	0	0	0	0	0	0	0	1	1	1	1	1	1	1	1
V_2	0	0	0	0	1	1	1	1	0	0	0	0	1	1	1	1
V_1	0	0	1	1	0	0	1	1	0	0	1	1	0	0	1	1
V_0	0	1	0	1	0	1	0	1	0	1	0	1	0	1	0	1
$U_3 U_2 U_1 U_0$																
0000	1	1														
0001			1	1												
0010					1	1										
0011							1	1								
0100									1	1						
0101											1	1				
0110													1	1		
0111															1	1
1000	1	1														
1001			1	1												
1010					1	1										
1011							1	1								
1100									1	1						
1101											1	1				
1110													1	1		
1111															1	1

Fig. 5. Good' topological matrix

$$U = \langle U_{\kappa-1}U_{\kappa-2}...U_0 \rangle = \langle u_{\kappa-1}u_{\kappa-2}...u_0 \rangle, \qquad V = \langle V_{\kappa-1}V_{\kappa-2}...V_0 \rangle = \langle v_0 v_1 ... v_{\kappa-1} \rangle. \qquad (2)$$

In FFT algorithms by J.W. Cooley и J.W. Tukey [6] the other rules were used for topology construction. Fig. 6 depicts a topology named as "time-subsampling". Analytical form for the topology is:

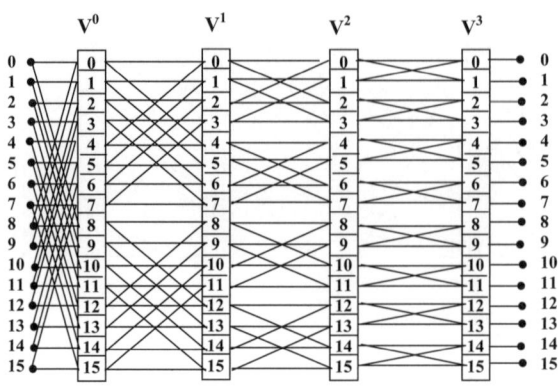

Fig. 6. "Frequency-subsampling" topology

$$U^\lambda = t^\lambda \quad = \langle u_{\kappa-1}u_{\kappa-2}...u_{\lambda+1}u_\lambda v_{\lambda-1}v_{\lambda-2}...v_1 v_0 \rangle,$$
$$V^\lambda = t^{\lambda+1} = \langle u_{\kappa-1}u_{\kappa-2}...u_{\lambda+1}v_\lambda v_{\lambda-1}v_{\lambda-2}...v_1 v_0 \rangle.$$

Fig. 7 depicts a topology named as "frequency-subsampling". Analytical form for the topology is:

$$U^\lambda = t^\lambda \quad = \langle v_0 v_1 ... v_{\lambda-1}u_\lambda u_{\lambda+1}...u_{\kappa-2}u_{\kappa-1} \rangle,$$
$$V^\lambda = t^{\lambda+1} = \langle v_0 v_1 ... v_{\lambda-1}v_\lambda u_{\lambda+1}...u_{\kappa-2}u_{\kappa-1} \rangle.$$

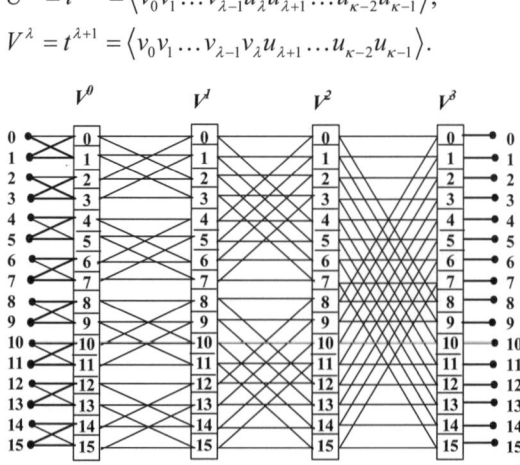

Fig. 7. "Time-subsampling" topology

3. Fast neural networks

FNN is a feed-forward multilayer neural network with structure and topology satisfying to system invariants of fast algorithm. In terms of neural networks each node of structure model is called a neuron kernel and determines a base operation for a vector component. Input field is named as receptor field and output field as axon field. For example, the neuron kernel size is equal to 2×2, the base operation of the neuron kernel for this network is given by the following transformation:

$$\left(s_0 \ s_1 \right) = \left(x_0 \ x_1 \right) \begin{pmatrix} w_{00} & w_{01} \\ w_{10} & w_{11} \end{pmatrix} + \begin{pmatrix} w_0 \\ w_1 \end{pmatrix}$$

and a pair of neuron activation functions $y_0 = f\left(s_0 \right)$ and $y_1 = f\left(s_1 \right)$ (here, and in what follows, the vector is written from the left side of the matrix). The coefficients w_{ij} are named synapse weights and coefficients w_i - bias weights. In the general case, the neural kernel base operation is given by a matrix of size $p_i \times g_i$ (neuron kernel synapse card). It allows us to realize different dimensionalities in terminal fields of neural network. Fast neural network may be taught with a help of well known Error Back Propagation algorithms, however specific features of FNN allow us to use special methods. The typical example is fast tunable transformation.

3.1 Fast tunable transformation

Fast tunable transformation is a linear variant of FNN. Such networks have linear activation function and zero bias weights for all base operations. Denote elements of the synapse card of the kernel i^{λ} by $w_{i^{\lambda}}^{\lambda}\left(u_{\lambda}, v_{\lambda} \right)$, where $u_{\lambda}, v_{\lambda} \in 0, 1, \ldots, \left(p_{\lambda} - 1 \right)$ are indices of the elements in the neuron kernel matrix. The base operation for tunable networks can be written as

$$y_{i^{\lambda}}^{\lambda}\left(v_{\lambda} \right) = \sum_{u_{\lambda}} x_{i^{\lambda}}^{\lambda}\left(u_{\lambda} \right) w_{i^{\lambda}}^{\lambda}\left(u_{\lambda}, v_{\lambda} \right). \tag{3}$$

Let $i^0, i^1, \ldots, i^{K-1}$ be a sequence of nodes determining a path between the terminal layers. We assume that the kernel i^{λ} belongs to the selected path and consider equation (3) as a sequence of equations describing the transformations of the signal along the path. Following the common terminology of neural networks, the inputs and outputs of neuron kernels are referred to as receptor and axon fields, respectively. Coordinates of the receptors and axons are $x_{i^{\lambda}}^{\lambda}\left(u_{\lambda} \right)$ and $v_{i^{\lambda}}^{\lambda}\left(v_{\lambda} \right)$, respectively. All connections between the kernels in the FNN are described by exact single–valued operators of rank one, which identify the coordinates $y_{i^{\lambda}}^{\lambda}\left(v_{\lambda} \right)$ and $x_{i^{\lambda+1}}^{\lambda+1}\left(u_{\lambda+1} \right)$ of the adjacent layers.

The signal receptor–axon transfer between the terminal layers can be defined by the partial derivative:

$$h(U,V) = \frac{\partial y_{j^{\kappa-1}}^{\kappa-1}(v_{\kappa-1})}{\partial x_{j^0}^0(u_0)}.$$

The set of elements $h(U,V)$ determines the transfer matrix H. Successively differentiating equations (3) along the selected path, we obtain:

$$h(U,V) = w_{j^0}^0(u_0,v_0) w_{j^1}^1(u_1,v_1)\dots w_{j^{\kappa-1}}^{\kappa-1}(u_{\kappa-1},v_{\kappa-1}). \tag{4}$$

If the boundary conditions (2) are fulfilled, the last expression takes the form of:

$$h(U,V) = w_{j^0}^0(U_0,V_0) w_{j^1}^1(U_1,V_1)\dots w_{j^{\kappa-1}}^{\kappa-1}(U_{\kappa-1},V_{\kappa-1}),$$

where number of neural kernel i^λ is defined by the chosen topology.

The expressions obtained establish relationship between the entries of the neural network operator matrix H and the kernel elements. Since the network is assumed to be linear, the matrix equation $Y = XH$ completely determines the data transformation in the neural network.

4. Realization of spectral transformations

Now we consider application of fast tunable transformation for realization of fast algorithms of typical spectral transformations.

4.1 Tuning to Walsh-Hadamard basis

The functions from Walsh basis in the Hadamard ordering are defined on an interval of length $N = 2^\kappa$ as follows [7]:

$$had(U,V) = \prod_{\lambda=0}^{\kappa-1}(-1)^{U_\lambda V_\lambda}, \tag{5}$$

where $U = \langle U_{\kappa-1} U_{\kappa-2} \dots U_0 \rangle$ and $V = \langle V_{\kappa-1} V_{\kappa-2} \dots V_0 \rangle$. All digits in the number representation may take only two values: 0 or 1. The variable is the discrete time, and V is the running function number. Let us construct a neural network implementation of the Walsh fast spectral transformation, such that the basis functions are ordered by the columns of the resulting matrix. In the course of the tuning process, it is required to determine parameters of the neuron kernels. We assume that the topology is "time-subsampling" with the boundary conditions (2).

Elements of the resulting spectral transformation matrix are given by (5). Comparing (4) with the definition of the Walsh basis, we obtain:

$$w_{i^\lambda}^\lambda(u_\lambda,v_\lambda) = (-1)^{u_\lambda v_\lambda}, \qquad u_\lambda = U_\lambda, \quad v_\lambda = V_\lambda.$$

The above equation is associated with the following matrix of the neuron kernel:

$$W = \begin{pmatrix} 1 & 1 \\ 1 & -1 \end{pmatrix}.$$

Clearly, all network layers have identical kernels. The matrix representation of the Walsh–Hadamard spectral algorithm for $N = 2^3$ is shown in Fig. 8. The figure also shows the positional representations of the matrix row and column numbers. All empty elements of the matrix are assumed to be zero.

		V_2	0	0	0	0	1	1	1	1	0	0	0	0	1	1	1	1	0	0	0	0	1	1	1	1
		V_1	0	0	1	1	0	0	1	1	0	0	1	1	0	0	1	1	0	0	1	1	0	0	1	1
		V_0	0	1	0	1	0	1	0	1	0	1	0	1	0	1	0	1	0	1	0	1	0	1	0	1
U_2	U_1	U_0																								
0	0	0	1	1							1		1						1				1			
0	0	1	1	−1								1		1						1				1		
0	1	0			1	1					1		−1								1				1	
0	1	1			1	−1						1		−1								1				1
1	0	0					1	1							1		1		1				−1			
1	0	1					1	−1								1		1		1				−1		
1	1	0							1	1					1		−1				1				−1	
1	1	1							1	−1						1		−1				1				−1

Fig. 8. Factored representation of Walsh-Hadamard fast transformation

The transformation matrix is represented in the factored form as $H = H_0 H_1 H_2$. The resulting matrix H has the view:

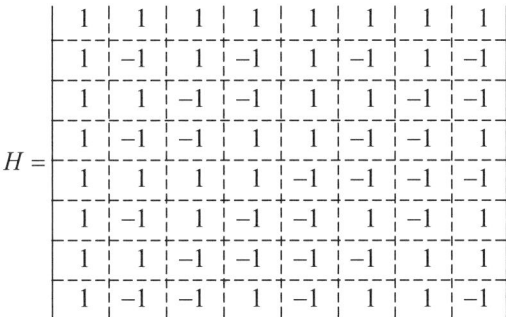

4.2 Tuning to the Vilenkin-Christiansen basis

The generalized system of nonnormalized Vilenkin–Christiansen functions in the Paley ordering [8] is given by:

$$vcf(U,V) = \prod_{\lambda=0}^{\kappa-1} (\omega_\lambda)^{U_\lambda V_\lambda}, \qquad \omega_\lambda = e^{j\frac{2\pi}{p_\lambda}}, \tag{6}$$

where $U = \langle U_{\kappa-1} U_{\kappa-2} \ldots U_0 \rangle$, $V = \langle V_0 V_1 \ldots V_{\kappa-1} \rangle$, $U_\lambda, V_\lambda \in 0,1,\ldots p_\lambda - 1$ .. The functions are defined on an interval of length $N = p_0 p_1 \ldots p_{\kappa-1}$.   The rotation multiplier ω_λ is a complex number represented in the exponential form. The variable U is the discrete time, and V is the running function number. Let us construct a neural network implementation of the fast spectral transformation, such that the basis functions are ordered by the columns of the resulting matrix. We assume that the topology trajectory is given by the following expression:

$$U^\lambda = V^{\lambda-1} = \langle v_0 v_1 \ldots v_{\lambda-2} v_{\lambda-1} u_{\kappa-1} u_{\kappa-2} \ldots u_\lambda \rangle$$

and the boundary conditions by (2). It is a "frequency-subsampling" topology. Comparing (4) with the definition of the basis functions (6), we obtain

$$w_{j^\lambda}^\lambda (u_\lambda, v_\lambda) = (\omega_\lambda)^{u_\lambda v_\lambda}, \qquad u_\lambda = U_\lambda, \quad v_\lambda = V_\lambda .$$

Example. Let $N = 3^2$. The transformation matrix is represented as the product of two matrices, $H = H_0 H_1$. The positional representation of rows and columns of the matrix H is written as $U = \langle U_1 U_0 \rangle$, $V = \langle V_0 V_1 \rangle$

In the considered example, the rotation multipliers are the same for both layers; therefore, all network neuron kernels are identical and given by matrix:

$$W = \begin{pmatrix} 1 & 1 & 1 \\ 1 & \omega & \omega^2 \\ 1 & \omega^2 & \omega \end{pmatrix}$$

where $\omega = e^{j\frac{2\pi}{3}}$. Fig. 9 shows the factored representation of the constructed spectral transformation.

V_0		0	0	0	1	1	1	2	2	2	0	0	0	1	1	1	2	2	2
V_1		0	1	2	0	1	2	0	1	2	0	1	2	0	1	2	0	1	2
U_1	U_0																		
0	0	1			1			1			1	1	1						
0	1	1			ω			ω^2			1	ω	ω^2						
0	2	1			ω^2			ω			1	ω^2	ω						
1	0		1			1			1					1	1	1			
1	1		1			ω			ω^2					1	ω	ω^2			
1	2		1			ω^2			ω					1	ω^2	ω			
2	0			1			1			1							1	1	1
2	1			1			ω			ω^2							1	ω	ω^2
2	2			1			ω^2			ω							1	ω^2	ω

Fig. 9. Factored representation of the Vilenkin–Christiansen fast transformation

4.3 Implementation of the fast wavelet transformation

A discrete packet wavelet basis on the interval of length $N = p_0 p_1 \ldots p_{K-1}$ can be defined by the expression:

$$h(U,V) = \varphi_m \left(U_{K-m}, V_{K-m} \right) \delta \left(\tau_m, \left\langle U_{K-1} U_{K-2} \ldots U_{K-m+1} \right\rangle \right), \tag{7}$$

where $U = \left\langle U_{K-1} U_{K-2} \ldots U_0 \right\rangle$ is the discrete time, $V = \left\langle V_0 V_1 \ldots V_{K-1} \right\rangle$ is the wavelet function number (the wavelet functions are assumed to be columns of the basis matrix), $\varphi_m \left(U_{K-m}, V_{K-m} \right)$ is a set of generating pulses in the frequency localization of the number m, $\delta(,)$ is the Kronecker delta, τ_m is the running number of the wavelet function in the frequency localization m.

A set of wavelet basis functions belonging to one frequency localization is referred as a packet. Functions belonging to one packet possess the same frequency properties but differ from each other by the positions of the generating pulses. The number of functions in a packet (for $m > 0$) is equal to $\left(p_{K-m} - 1 \right) p_{K-m+1} p_{K-m+2} \ldots p_{K-1}$. The zero packet ($m = 0$) consists of only one function identically equal to one on the entire time interval.

The idea of tuning lies in decomposition of Kroneker delta in expression (7). Let us order the functions in each packet by means of the rule $\tau_m = \left\langle V_{K-1} V_{K-2} \ldots V_{K-m+1} \right\rangle$. For such ordering, the Kronecker delta in (7) can be represented as the product of the Kronecker deltas:

$$h(U,V) = \varphi_m \left(U_{K-m}, V_{K-m} \right) \delta \left(U_{K-m+1}, V_{K-m+1} \right) \ldots \delta \left(U_{K-2}, V_{K-2} \right) \delta \left(U_{K-1}, V_{K-1} \right).$$

Comparing this expression with expression (4) for the FNN transfer, we arrive at rules for tuning the neuron kernels. In detail the method of tuning is conceded in [10].

4.4 Tuning to Haar basis

Haar transformation [9] is the simplest wavelet basis defined on the interval with length 2^K. A single two-polarized pulse with the time base equal to two generates the basis. In terms of frequency localization, the basis functions are divided into octaves. The matrix of generating pulses for each octave has the form:

$$\varphi = \begin{pmatrix} 1 & 1 \\ 1 & -1 \end{pmatrix}.$$

As an example, consider the construction of the Haar basis of dimension $N = 2^3$. The basis functions are divided into three octaves, and its transformation matrix is factored in the product of three matrices: $H = H_0 H_1 H_2$. The positional representation of rows and columns of H has the following form: $U = \left\langle U_2 U_1 U_0 \right\rangle$, $V = \left\langle V_0 V_1 V_2 \right\rangle$

In the layer 0 all neuron kernel matrices are equal to the matrix of the generating pulses. In the layer 1 the kernels with the generating pulse matrix occupy positions $i^1 = \langle 0 U_1^1 \rangle$, the other kernels are the identity matrices. In the layer 2 only zero kernel is equal to the generating pulse matrix, all other kernels are equal to the identity matrix. Fig. 10 shows all three matrices of the layer transformations constructed according to the above rules.

U_2	U_1	U_0																									
V_0			0	0	0	0	1	1	1	1	0	0	0	0	1	1	1	1	0	0	0	0	1	1	1	1
V_1			0	0	1	1	0	0	1	1	0	0	1	1	0	0	1	1	0	0	1	1	0	0	1	1
V_2			0	1	0	1	0	1	0	1	0	1	0	1	0	1	0	1	0	1	0	1	0	1	0	1
0	0	0	1			1					1		1						1	1						
0	0	1	1			−1					1		−1						1	−1						
0	1	0		1			1					1		1							1	0				
0	1	1		1			−1					1		−1							0	1				
1	0	0			1			1							1	0							1	0		
1	0	1			1			−1							0	1							0	1		
1	1	0				1			1								1	0							1	0
1	1	1				1				−1							0	1							0	1

Fig. 10. Factored representation of fast Haar transformation

The resulting transformation matrix is given by (8). It is easy to see that the Haar functions are columns of the matrix H.

$$H = \begin{pmatrix}
1 & 1 & 1 & & 1 & & & \\
1 & 1 & 1 & & -1 & & & \\
1 & 1 & -1 & & & 1 & & \\
1 & 1 & -1 & & & -1 & & \\
1 & -1 & & 1 & & & 1 & \\
1 & -1 & & 1 & & & -1 & \\
1 & -1 & & -1 & & & & 1 \\
1 & -1 & & -1 & & & & -1
\end{pmatrix}. \tag{8}$$

The same way may be used for tuning to Fourier basis [10] and other spectral transformations.

5. Neural network approximation of regular fractal

The term "fractal" was introduced into practice by Mandelbrot for description of special class of multidimensional functions which possess the feature of self-similarity and fractional dimensionality. In paper [11] it was shown that neural networks might be used for generation of fractal structures. The kind of fractal imposes some restrictions on neural network structure and topology. In this Section we consider the use of FFN for fractal generation.

5.1 Analytical form of regular fractal

Fig. 11 depicts three consecutive iterations for Cantor's fractal. On each iteration one third of continuous interval is moved off. It is equivalent to the scale deformation in the ratio 1:3. First we will build analytical form for Cantor's fractal and then generalize it for a more wide class of regular fractals. Assume that Cantor's fractal is defined on continuous interval $U = [0,1)$. Any point of the interval we can represent as a fraction in number system with radix 3.

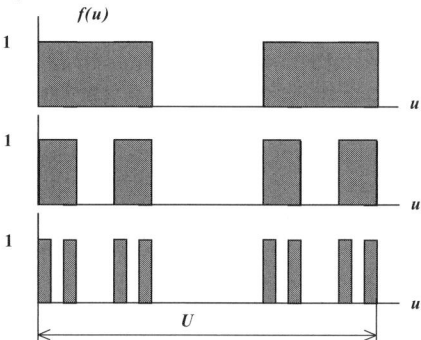

Fig. 11. Cantor's fractal iterations

$$u = 0,u_1 u_2 \ldots u_n \ldots = 3^{-1}u_1 + 3^{-2}u_2 + \ldots + 3^{-n}u_n \ldots \tag{9}$$

where digits $u_i \in \{0,1,2\}$ should be considered as whole arguments, which define a point position on the interval. Let's introduce also continuous arguments $\tilde{u}_i \in [0,3)$. Now the whole digits u_i we consider as result of action of some operator on continuous arguments. It is obvious that the infinite sequence (1) may be broken off in any place and finished by continuous argument. In result, the point of interval is represented as:

$$u = 0,u_1 u_2 \ldots u_{n-1}\tilde{u}_n.$$

Define function:

$$\varphi(\tilde{u}) = \begin{cases} 1 & \textit{для} \quad \tilde{u} \in [0,1), \\ 0 & \textit{для} \quad \tilde{u} \in [1,2), \\ 1 & \textit{для} \quad \tilde{u} \in [2,3). \end{cases}$$

It is easy to see that Cantor's fractal may be represented in analytical form as infinite product:

$$f(u) = \varphi(\tilde{u}_1)\varphi(\tilde{u}_2)\varphi(\tilde{u}_3)\ldots\varphi(\tilde{u}_n)\ldots$$

In general, analytical form of fractal has view:

$$f(u) = \varphi_{i^1}(\tilde{u}_1)\varphi_{i^2}(\tilde{u}_2)\varphi_{i^3}(\tilde{u}_3)\ldots\varphi_{i^n}(\tilde{u}_n)\ldots,$$

where the indexes $i^1, i^2, i^3 \ldots i^n \ldots$ define a permissible set of functions for each iteration.

5.2 Discrete approximation for fractals

In discrete variant the fractal is constructed on sequence of booming discrete intervals:

$$U_i = \{0,1,2,\ldots,N_i-1\}, \quad i=0,1,2,\ldots\kappa-1.$$

The points of the fractal are defined in a position number system as:

$$u = \langle u_{\kappa-1} u_{\kappa-2} \ldots u_0 \rangle.$$

In general, the digits have different ranges of variables: $u_i \in \{0,1,\ldots,p_i-1\}$. The fractal approximation may be expressed as finite product:

$$f(u) \approx \varphi_{i^0}(u_0)\varphi_{i^1}(u_1)\ldots\varphi_{i^{\kappa-1}}(u_{\kappa-1}),$$

where $\varphi_i(u_i)$ are discrete functions. For example, for Cantor's fractal the functions have the following form:

$$\varphi(u) = \begin{cases} 1 & \text{для} \quad u=0, \\ 0 & \text{для} \quad u=1, \\ 1 & \text{для} \quad u=2. \end{cases}$$

5.3.1 Cantor's carpet fractal

Cantor's carpet is a plain geometrical figure defined on two continuous intervals $U=[0,1)$, $V=[0,1)$. Fig 12 depicts one iteration of the fractal.

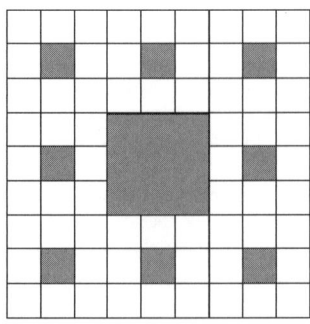

Fig. 12. Cantor's carpet fractal iteration

The point coordinates on the plain are defined as infinite fractions:

$$u = 0, u_1 u_2 \ldots u_n \ldots, \quad u_i \in \{0,1,2\},$$
$$v = 0, v_1 v_2 \ldots v_n \ldots, \quad v_i \in \{0,1,2\}.$$

Discrete approximation for Cantor's carpet is defined as finite product:

$$f(u,v) \approx \varphi(u_0, v_0) \varphi(u_1, v_1) \varphi(u_2, v_2) \ldots \varphi(u_{\kappa-1}, v_{\kappa-1}) \qquad (10)$$

where all functions have the view:

$$\varphi(u_i, v_i) = \begin{pmatrix} 1 & 1 & 1 \\ 1 & 0 & 1 \\ 1 & 1 & 1 \end{pmatrix}.$$

It is easy to see that expression for the fractal coincide with expression for the element of matrix H of tunable fast transformation. Comparing (4) and (10) we get the following rules for defining elements of neural kernels:

$$w_{i^\lambda}^\lambda (u_\lambda, v_\lambda) = \varphi(u_\lambda, v_\lambda).$$

Fig. 13 demonstrates the approximations for Cantor's carpet on intervals with a length equal to $N = 3^2$.

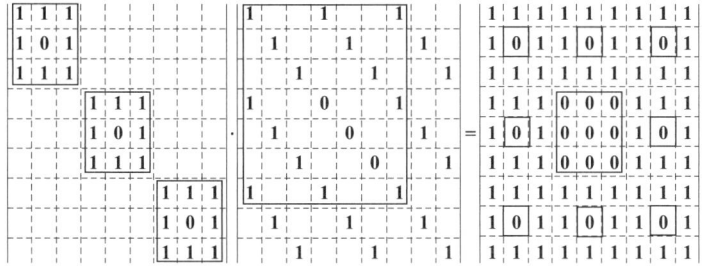

Fig. 13. Neural network approximation for Cantor's carpet fractal iteration

5.3.2 Sierpinski's fractal

Fig. 14 depicts one iteration of two- dimensional fractal named Sierpinski's serviette. The fractal is defined on continuous intervals $U = [0,1)$, $V = [0,1)$. For discrete approximation we change the continuous interval for discrete intervals with a length $N = 2^\kappa$. The forming function of the fractal is defined as:

$$\varphi(u_i, v_i) = \begin{pmatrix} 1 & 1 \\ 1 & 0 \end{pmatrix}.$$

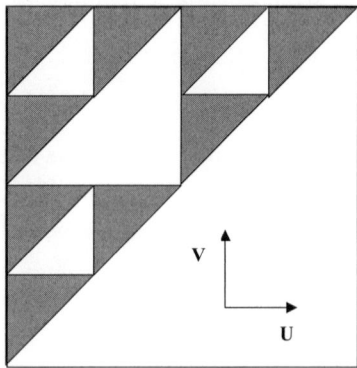

Fig. 14. Sierpinski's serviette

Fig. 15 depicts neural net approximation for Sierpinski's serviette on intervals with a length $N = 2^3$. The approximating neural network has three layers.

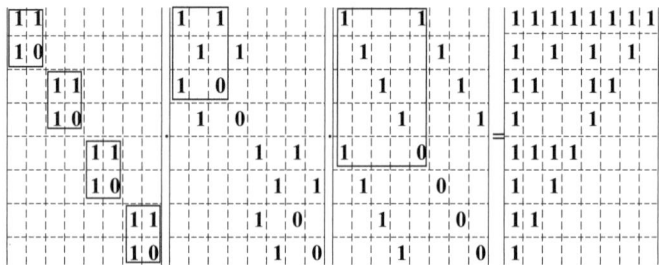

Fig. 15. Neural network approximation for Sierpinski's serviette fractal iteration

5.3.3 Lebesgue's carpet fractal

Fig. 16 depicts two iterations for three-dimensional Lebesgue's fractal. The base of the volume geometrical figure is a square defined on continuous intervals $U = [0,1)$, $V = [0,1)$. Analytical expression for Lebesgue's carpet is represented by infinite logical product:

$$f(u,v) = \phi_1(\tilde{u}_1, \tilde{v}_1) \circ \phi_2(\tilde{u}_2, \tilde{v}_2) \circ \ldots \circ \phi_n(\tilde{u}_n, \tilde{v}_n) \circ \ldots .$$

where logical operation "$\circ$" for two number a and b is defined as $\min(a,b)$.

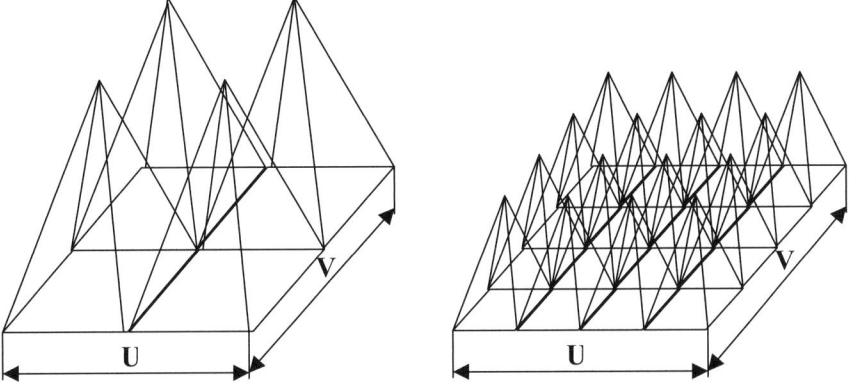

Fig. 16. Lebesgue's carpet fractal iterations

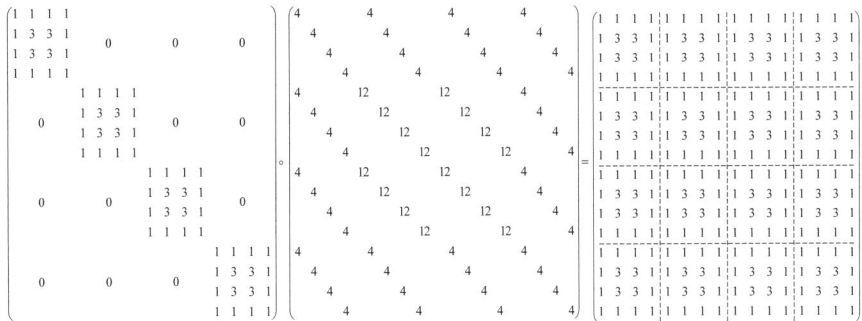

Fig. 17. Neural network approximation of Lebesgue's carpet fractal iteration

The topological realization of neural network which approximates the second iteration of Lebesgue's carpet is shown on Fig. 17. Here fuzzy neural network has two layers and is defined on intervals with a length N=16. Neural kernels for the first and the second layer are

$$W_0 = \begin{pmatrix} 1 & 1 & 1 & 1 \\ 1 & 3 & 3 & 1 \\ 1 & 3 & 3 & 1 \\ 1 & 1 & 1 & 1 \end{pmatrix}, \quad W_1 = \begin{pmatrix} 4 & 4 & 4 & 4 \\ 4 & 12 & 12 & 4 \\ 4 & 12 & 12 & 4 \\ 4 & 4 & 4 & 4 \end{pmatrix}.$$

6. Adapted fast transformations

The methods of digital adapted filtering use a priori information about signal or noise for tuning coefficients of a filter. It permits to get a high ratio of signal to noise. In this Section we consider how it is possible to use fast tunable transformation for realization of plural adaptive filter.

We call a linear transformation adapted to a function if one of the columns of the transformation matrix coincides with the function. Similar to one we can define adaptation to a few functions. The idea of tuning method is based on representation of the function as a product of multiscale factors. Let's assume that the function $f(u)$ is defined on discrete interval with a length $N = p_0 p_1 \ldots p_{\kappa-1}$. It is needed to find representation in the form:

$$f(u) = \varphi_{i^0}(u_0) \varphi_{i^1}(u_1) \ldots \varphi_{i^{\kappa-1}}(u_{\kappa-1}), \tag{11}$$

where $i^m = \langle u_{\kappa-1} u_{\kappa-2} \ldots u_{m+1} \rangle$. Since the matrix elements of fast tunable transformation are calculated as

$$h(U,V) = w_{i^0}^0(u_0, v_0) w_{i^1}^1(u_1, v_1) \ldots w_{i^{\kappa-1}}^{\kappa-1}(u_{\kappa-1}, v_{\kappa-1}), \tag{12}$$

where $i^m = \langle u_{\kappa-1} u_{\kappa-2} \ldots u_{m+1} v_{m-1} v_{m-2} \ldots v_0 \rangle$, therefore the column $v = \langle v_{\kappa-1} v_{\kappa-2} \ldots v_0 \rangle$ of the matrix coincides with the goal if the elements of neural kernels coincide with factors of decomposition (11).

Since the kernel numbers $i^0 = \langle u_{\kappa-1} u_{\kappa-2} \ldots u_1 \rangle$ for zero layer don't depend on variables v, so it is possible to adapt the fast transformation to p_0 functions at the same time.

For construction of decomposition (11) we introduce the sequence of auxiliary functions $f_0, f_1, \ldots, f_{\kappa-1}$ defining them by the recurrent rule:

$$f(u) = f_0 \langle u_{\kappa-1} u_{\kappa-2} \ldots u_0 \rangle, \tag{13}$$

$$f_0 \langle u_{\kappa-1} u_{\kappa-2} \ldots u_0 \rangle = f_1 \langle u_{\kappa-1} u_{\kappa-2} \ldots u_1 \rangle \varphi_{i^0}(u_0),$$

$$f_1 \langle u_{\kappa-1} u_{\kappa-2} \ldots u_1 \rangle = f_2 \langle u_{\kappa-1} u_{\kappa-2} \ldots u_2 \rangle \varphi_{i^1}(u_1),$$

$$\vdots$$

$$f_{\kappa-2} \langle u_{\kappa-1} u_{\kappa-2} \rangle = f_{\kappa-1} \langle u_{\kappa-1} \rangle \varphi_{i^{\kappa-2}}(u_{\kappa-2}),$$

$$f_{\kappa-1} \langle u_{\kappa-1} \rangle = \varphi_{i^{\kappa-1}}(u_{\kappa-1}).$$

From the above expressions follows:

$$\varphi_{i^m}(u_m) = \frac{f_m \langle u_{\kappa-1} u_{\kappa-2} \ldots u_m \rangle}{f_{m+1} \langle u_{\kappa-1} u_{\kappa-2} \ldots u_{m+1} \rangle}, \qquad m = 0, 1, \ldots \kappa - 2.$$

For defining the auxiliary functions we introduce a concept of fractal filter.

6.1 Fractal filtering

Let's represent argument function $f(u)$ in position number system with radices $p_0, p_1, \ldots, p_{\kappa-1}$. The transition formula has view:

$$u = \langle u_{\kappa-1} u_{\kappa-2} \ldots u_0 \rangle = u_{\kappa-1} p_{\kappa-2} p_{\kappa-3} \cdots p_0 + u_{\kappa-2} p_{\kappa-3} p_{\kappa-4} \cdots p_0 + \ldots + u_1 p_0 + u_0$$

where $u_i \in [0, 1, \ldots p_i - 1]$ are digits. In result, the initial function of one argument converts to function of a few arguments. Each argument of the function defines a level of scale description for the function. Fix all arguments apart from u_m. Varying the free argument we obtain an extract S_m with a length p_m. Fractal filter with localization m we name arbitrary functional defined on the extract. It may be expressed as:

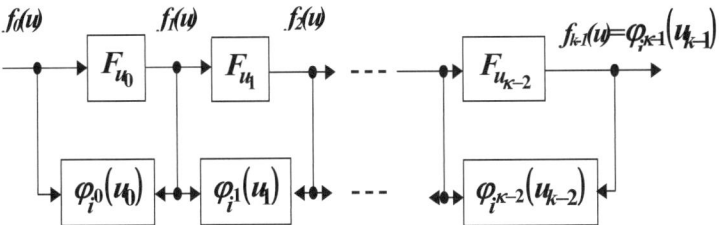

Fig. 18. Schema of calculation of auxiliary functions for tuning adapted fast transformation

$$f_{out} \langle u_{\kappa-1} u_{\kappa-2} \ldots u_{m+1} u_{m-1} \ldots u_0 \rangle = \underset{u_m}{F} \left(f_{inp} \langle u_{\kappa-1} u_{\kappa-2} \ldots u_0 \rangle \right).$$

For example, linear fractal filter with localization m may be defined as:

$$f_{out} \langle u_{\kappa-1} u_{\kappa-2} \ldots u_{m+1} u_{m-1} \ldots u_0 \rangle = \frac{1}{p_m} \sum_{u_m} f_{inp} \langle u_{\kappa-1} u_{\kappa-2} \ldots u_0 \rangle.$$

Analyzing (13) it is easy to see that the sequence of auxiliary functions may be generated by means of a chain of fractal filters as it is depicted in Fig. 18. For the construction any fractal filter may be used, therefore the task has plural decisions.

6.2 Adapted fast transform in fuzzy space

Geometry fuzzy space is defined by operations min and max which act within interval $[0,1]$. Assume $f(u)$ to be arbitrary function defined on interval with a length $N = p_0 p_1 \ldots p_{\kappa-1}$. In fuzzy space the value range of the function belongs to interval $[0,1]$. Here, and in what follows we use notation «∘» и «⊕» for operations min and max, respectively. The task of tuning is reduced to construction of a multiplicative decomposition:

$$f(u) = f\langle u_{\kappa-1} u_{\kappa-2} \ldots u_0 \rangle = \varphi_{i^0}(u_0) \circ \varphi_{i^1}(u_1) \circ \ldots \circ \varphi_{i^{\kappa-1}}(u_{\kappa-1}).$$

The multiplicative factors we can find recurrently, decomposing the initial function in a sequence of logical multiplications:

$$f(u) = f_0 \langle u_{\kappa-1} u_{\kappa-2} \ldots u_0 \rangle,$$
$$f_0 \langle u_{\kappa-1} u_{\kappa-2} \ldots u_0 \rangle = f_1 \langle u_{\kappa-1} u_{\kappa-2} \ldots u_1 \rangle \circ \varphi_{i^0}(u_0),$$
$$f_1 \langle u_{\kappa-1} u_{\kappa-2} \ldots u_1 \rangle = f_2 \langle u_{\kappa-1} u_{\kappa-2} \ldots u_2 \rangle \circ \varphi_{i^1}(u_1),$$
$$\vdots$$
$$f_{\kappa-2} \langle u_{\kappa-1} u_{\kappa-2} \rangle = f_{\kappa-1} \langle u_{\kappa-1} \rangle \circ \varphi_{i^{\kappa-2}}(u_{\kappa-2}),$$
$$f_{\kappa-1} \langle u_{\kappa-1} \rangle = \varphi_{i^{\kappa-1}}(u_{\kappa-1}).$$

There is some freedom in choice of auxiliary functions $f_1, \ldots, f_{\kappa-1}$, which is depending on the being used fractal filter. If we use fractal filter:

$$f_{m+1} \langle u_{\kappa-1} u_{\kappa-2} \ldots u_{m+1} \rangle = \max_{u_m} \left(f_m \langle u_{\kappa-1} u_{\kappa-2} \ldots u_m \rangle \right).$$

Then the multiplicative factors may be found as:

$$\varphi_{i^m}(u_m) = f_{m+1} \langle u_{\kappa-1} u_{\kappa-2} \ldots u_{m+1} \rangle \circ f_m \langle u_{\kappa-1} u_{\kappa-2} \ldots u_m \rangle.$$

The main advantage of fuzzy transformations is a high calculating effectiveness because logical operations are carried out faster than arithmetic operations.

6.3 Spectral adapted fast transformations

The task of compressing is very important in such areas as image processing and telecommunications. It is well known that the maximal decreasing of redundancy is provided by Karhunen-Loeve orthogonal transformations [12,13]. However the transformation doesn't have a fast algorithm and, therefore, it is not used for processing data of high dimensionality. Karhunen-Loeve transformation is formed by eigenvectors of covariation matrix. In practice we can often limit the amount of used eigenvectors to the main component. In this case we can use fast tunable orthogonal transformation for its realization. Synthesis of such transformations we consider in this Section.

For orthogonal case the conditions of adaptation may be expressed as:

$$\begin{cases} \sum_u h(u,v) f(u) = 1 & \text{when } v = x, \\ \sum_u h(u,v) f(u) = 0 & \text{when } v \neq x. \end{cases} \tag{14}$$

where $f(u)$ is normalized to unit ($\sum_u f^2(u)=1.$) function of main components and $h(u,v)$ are elements of transformation matrix. Putting expressions (11) and (12) into the left part of (14) we obtain:

$$\sum_u h(u,v) f(u) = \sum_{u_0} w_{i^0}(u_0,v_0)\varphi_{i^0}(u_0) \sum_{u_1} w_{i^1}(u_1,v_1)\varphi_{i^1}(u_1) \times \ldots$$
$$\ldots \times \sum_{u_{\kappa-1}} w_{i^{\kappa-1}}(u_{\kappa-1},v_{\kappa-1})\varphi_{i^{\kappa-1}}(u_{\kappa-1}).$$

It is obvious that the above conditions of adaptation are fulfilled when:

$$\begin{cases} \sum_{u_m} w_{i^m}(u_m,v_m)\varphi_{i^m}(u_m) = 1 \;\; if \;\; v_m = x_m, \\ \sum_{u_m} w_{i^m}(u_m,v_m)\varphi_{i^m}(u_m) = 0 \;\; if \;\; v_m \neq x_m. \end{cases}$$

Thus, the task of adaptation is reduced to construction of orthogonal neural kernels. For the aim the algorithm of Gram-Schmidt may be used in general case.

7. Quantum algorithms

Of interest may be the application of fast adapted transformation in the field of quantum calculations [14,15]. Classical computers work with states consisting of finite amount of bits. For example, a register with a length n has 2^n different states. In quantum computers q-bit is the minimal informational unit. Q-bit is associated with two-dimensional complex space. Two base vectors $|0\rangle$ and $|1\rangle$ are selected in the space. Q-bit states are any linear combinations of the base vectors: $|\phi\rangle = \alpha|0\rangle + \beta|1\rangle$, where coefficients are normalized by the following condition $\alpha^2 + \beta^2 = 1$. Quantum register is a finite aggregate of q-bits. The base state for the quantum register is a tensor product of base states of its q-bits. The following notations are used for tensor product:

$$|x_{n-1}\rangle \otimes |x_{n-2}\rangle \otimes \ldots \otimes |x_0\rangle = |x_{n-1}x_{n-2}\ldots x_0\rangle.$$

According to general principals of quantum mechanic the state of quantum register with a length n may be any unit length vector in complex space with dimensionality 2^n. The quantum state may be expressed as:

$$|\varphi\rangle = \sum_{|x\rangle \in |x_{n-1}x_{n-2}\ldots x_0\rangle} a_x|x\rangle,$$

where the summing is fulfilled on all base states.

The simplest quantum operation on the register is a two-dimensionality unitary transformation in space of one q-bit. The transformation (named also single qubit gate) is defined by the following matrix:

$$W = \begin{array}{c|cc} & |0\rangle & |1\rangle \\ \hline |0\rangle & w_{00} & w_{01} \\ |1\rangle & w_{10} & w_{11} \end{array}.$$

In the canonical form any unitary matrix may be expressed as:

$$W = \begin{pmatrix} e^{j\gamma_{00}} Cos\theta & e^{j\gamma_{01}} Sin\theta \\ e^{j\gamma_{10}} Sin\theta & -e^{j\gamma_{11}} Cos\theta \end{pmatrix}, \tag{15}$$

where $\gamma_{00} - \gamma_{01} = \gamma_{10} - \gamma_{11}$.

Neural technology deals with the image recognition. In the quantum variant the concept of image is equal to quantum state of register. The fast adapted spectral transformation may be used for construction of quantum state recognition algorithms. The way of solving this task was in essence conceded in the above Section. Some distinctive features are connected with using complex values. For example, the multiplication factor represents as $\dot{\varphi}_{im}(u_m) = \varphi_{im}(u_m)e^{j\alpha_{um}}$ and neural kernel (15) the condition of adaptation to first column are

$$\varphi_{im}(0)e^{j(\gamma_{00}-\alpha_0)}Cos\theta + \varphi_{im}(1)e^{j(\gamma_{10}-\alpha_1)}Sin\theta = 1,$$

$$\varphi_{im}(0)e^{j(\gamma_{01}-\alpha_0)}Sin\theta - \varphi_{im}(1)e^{j(\gamma_{11}-\alpha_1)}Cos\theta = 0.$$

Whence we obtain the calculated formulae for defining neural kernel parameters:

$$tg\theta = \varphi_{im}(1)/\varphi_{im}(0), \quad \gamma_{00} = \alpha_0, \quad \gamma_{10} = \alpha_1, \quad \gamma_{01} - \alpha_0 = \gamma_{11} - \alpha_1.$$

8. Weakly-connected networks

Fast neural networks represent a particular case of more general weakly-connected module neural networks. For the first time a morphological concept of weakly-connectivity was entered in papers [16,17]. Let's consider the concept in more detail.

8.1 System invariants

Denote an oriented graph of structure model as $H(A,\Gamma)$, where the set of nodes A constitutes a set of neural modules and the set of arcs Γ constitutes the inter-module connections. Let's enter the necessary definitions.

The set of nodes getting external input vector will be named as network afferent set. The set of nodes forming of external output vector will be named as network efferent set. Afferent and efferent sets will be called also the terminal sets, and will be denoted as $Afr(H)$ and $Efr(H)$, correspondingly.

Let B be a node of network. One will name as afferent the set of node B (hereinafter it is denoted as $Afr(B)$) the network afferent subset connected by arcs with node B. Similarly we will name as efferent set of node B (hereinafter it is denoted as $Efr(B)$) the network efferent subset connected by arcs with node B. Afferent and efferent subsets will be called the terminal projections, as well.

Definition. Module network is named the weakly-connected one, if for any node the terminal projections of its neighborhood nodes don't intersect. Morphological invariant of weakly-connected neural network may be expressed by the following pair of formulae:

$$Afr(B) = \sum_{A \in \Gamma^{-1}(B)} Afr(A), \tag{16}$$

$$Efr(B) = \sum_{C \in \Gamma(B)} Efr(C),$$

where $\Gamma^{-1}(B)$ - is receptor neighborhood for node B, $\Gamma(B)$ - is its axon neighborhood, symbol $\sum$ denotes a direct sum of correspondent sets. The first expression defines that for any node B the afferent projections of its receptor neighborhood nodes do not intersect. The second expression defines similar condition for efferent projections. It may be shown, that the both expressions are dual and if one of them is true, than the other is also true.

It may be proved that the system invariants of FNN are the consequence of weakly-connected network invariant. The distinctive feature of the weakly-connected networks is absence of parallel paths between their graph nodes. The example of weakly-connected neural network is shown in Fig. 19. The graph nodes correspond to neural modules. In limit case (for FNN) any neural module is a small dimensionality one-layer perceptron (neural kernel).

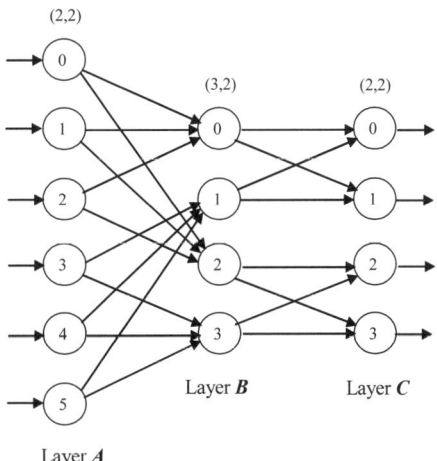

Fig. 19. Weakly-connected multilayer neural network

In Fig. 20, the module presentation of a multilayer topologically fully-connected neural network is shown. In this structure each node corresponds to one neural layer. In these models, the neural module dimensionalities and operator ranks of connections are represented. It is obvious that the module neural network satisfies to system invariants (16) and, therefore, it belongs to a class of structurally weakly-connected neural networks.

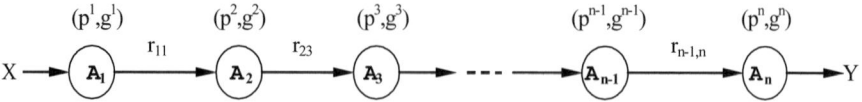

Fig. 20. Structure model topologically fully connected neural network

8.2 Separating capacity for weakly-connected neural networks

The main quality characteristic estimation for feed-forward neural networks is their ability to pattern recognition. Any recognition system has a limit of information capacity, therefore dependence of recognition error on the number of recognized patterns, as a rule, has an emphasized threshold level. The number of patterns corresponding to the threshold level is named as separating capacity [18,19].

There is a problem of choice of a test pattern set for estimation of quality of the pattern recognition systems. When patterns are represented by points of a vector space, the patterns consisting of «general position» points are usually used. According to the definition, a set consisting from N of n - space points is named as the set in the "general position", if any subsets consisting from $n+1$ - space points do not belong to $(n-1)$-space hyperplane. Or otherwise: any subset from $n+1$ - space points forms n - dimensional frame. If $N < n$, the point set in the general position will form a $(N-1)$ - dimensional frame.

Let us say, that the recognize system has separating capacity with level k, if it is capable to recognize any k-dimensional frame. The fact of k-dimensional frame recognition is that the frame can be one-to-one corresponded to any k-dimensional frame of output space in result of system learning. For the total set of indicator linear functions, the estimation coincides with VC-dimension by Vapnik and Chervonenkis [20].

The frame's vectors are often interpreted as ridges of volumetric solid with planer sides (simplex). Sizes of the simplex may by so small as possible, because in the end the set of neural network operators may be locally represented by means of the set of linear affine maps:

$$f(x) - f(x_0) = (x - x_0)W,$$

where vector x_0 defines a frame position in input affine space. Under the condition of arbitrary choice of the input and output k – dimensional frames, the set of linear maps W is isomorphically to tensor multiplication of vector k – spaces. Consequently, the neural network operator set with separating capacity k has to cover operator k^2-space and, therefore, freedom degrees (denoted as S_w) of the neural network have to satisfy the inequality $S_W \geq k^2$. And moreover, if the transform $w \in W$ maps a k – dimensional frame in k – dimensional frame, then $rank(w) \geq k$. In result, one may obtain the following estimation for separating capacity of neural network:

$$k \leq \min\left(\sqrt{S_W}, rank(W)\right).$$

Accuracy of the estimation is defined by degree of sufficient conditions realization for operator covering.   The necessary condition of applicability of the estimation is connectedness of the operator set. For neural network it means that each input layer receptor has to connect with output layer axon. For one layer perceptron with full connections, this condition is fulfilled automatically. Moreover, in one layer perceptron, all synapse weights are independent and their amount one-to-one determinates neural network freedom degrees. In multilayer networks, the situation is different. Due to serial principle of data processing, the synapse weights of different neural layers are mutually dependent and their amount does not define   uniquely the separating capacity of the neural network.

8.3 Parametrical plasticity of neural networks

Now we consider how to calculate degrees of freedom for weakly-connected neural network. Denote E as indication space and D as image space. The defined on vector spaces E, D neural network fulfills map $E \rightarrow D$. The created by means of variation of its synapse weights, neural network operator class forms multidimensional surface in operator space. Dimensionality of the surface is determined by dimensionality of its tangent space. The degree of parametrical plasticity is explicit mathematic equivalent of material point "degrees of freedom" concept known from mechanics.

   In small neighborhood of the tangent space all neural network operators can be conceded as the linear, therefore original nonlinear problem is reduced to investigation of linear tunable operators.

   Module factor. A module network operator manifold consists of connected operator connected manifolds of neural modules. Single out a dual rank r module A and assume that its parameters are varied while parameters of all the rest modules are constantly fixed "in general position" that is with such assembly of parameters that provide maximum dimensionality for module A environment spaces. Denote as $s^A, \overline{c}^A$ dimensionality of signal environment spaces in inputs of direct and dual module A . Actual acting number of freedom degrees of the linear module is equal to $S(A) = s^A \widehat{r} + \overline{c}^A \widehat{r} - \widehat{r}^2$ [21,22], where $\widehat{r} = s^A \circ \overline{c}^A \circ r$ is the acting operator rank (hereinafter symbol «$\circ$» denotes operation of minimum). In a similar manner, singling out modules and individually varying their parameters we obtain that contribution of all modules in total number of freedom degrees is defined by the sum $\sum S(A)$.

Connection factor. In contrast to modules the connection's parameters are fixed in constant and don't change in training process. Joining module operator manifolds, each connection decreases the full number of neural network freedom degrees. Without loss of generality it can be considered that all neural network inter-module connections are linear and injective. Injective connections install exact and one-to-one map between terminal clips of neural modules. Single out a rank r^{AB} connection acting between modules A and B. Denote as s^B and $\overline{c}^A$ dimensionalities of signal output spaces in direct and dual connection. As in mapping image space dimensionality is not more than connection rank so it is rightly $s^B = c^A \circ r^{AB}$ and $\overline{c}^A = \overline{s}^B \circ r^{AB}$. Each of the fix inter-module connection decreases a number of freedom degrees by value

$$s^B \overline{c}^A = \left(c^A \circ r^{AB} \right)\left(\overline{s}^B \circ r^{AB} \right).$$

As all connections are independent so general freedom degrees decreasing will be summed on all connections. Thus, the final freedom degrees calculation formula for the module neural network has the view:

$$S(H) = \sum_A S(A) - \sum_{A \Rightarrow B} \sum \left(c^A \circ r^{AB} \right)\left(\overline{s}^B \circ r^{AB} \right).$$

Weakly-connectionisms factor. Obtained expression shows that calculation of neural network plasticity degree is reduced to calculation of neural module environment signal spaces. In weakly-connected neural network the parallel paths between nodes are absent, therefore for any module the environment signal spaces (which are formed by connection cone) are independent and they form direct space sum. Whence it follows that equivalent dimensionality of any environment space is equal to sum of signal subspace dimensionalities in the connection cone. This condition allows to determinate the environment space dimensionalities for any neural network module. The plasticity calculation method for weakly-connected networks with different structure was represented in paper [23].

8.4 Experimental results

Actual estimation of the neural network separating capacity may be obtained by means of experiment on recognition of an input space k-dimensional frame. A real neural network defines compact operator manifold. Therefore, the test frames have to be restricted by a multidimensional cube. The best variant is to use orthonormal frames. The orthogonal condition is not obligatory but its presence accelerates the neural network learning process. Below the results of experimental investigation for two kinds of neural networks are presented.

1) The topology fully-connected two layers neural network with input and output dimensionalities equal to 8 was trained to the learning set shown in the table. Each row of the table (learning example) comprises input and output data vectors. The assembly of input vectors forms orthogonal Hadamard basis and the assembly of output vectors forms orthogonal unit code. Origin points of the frames correspondent to zero vectors and they define additional learning example. For the neural network

the freedom degrees calculation formulae views as: $S = ND + DM - D^2$, where N, M are neural network dimensionalities (in our case $N = M = 8$), D - is amount of neurons in the first layer. Neural network operator rank is equal to D also.

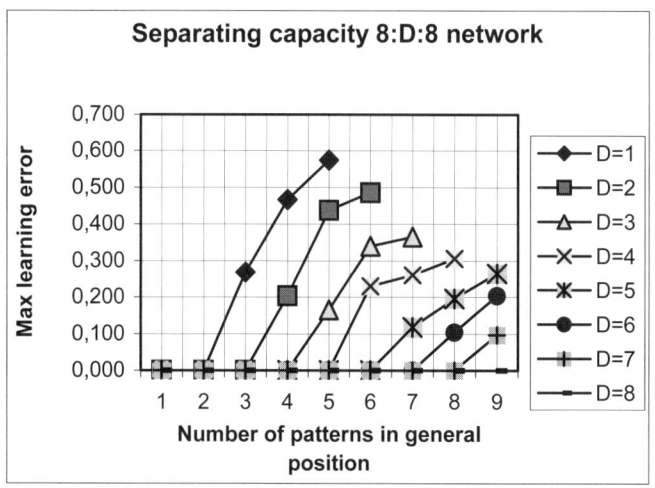

Fig. 21. Experimental estimation of separating capacity of fully-connected neural network

In the experiment the neural network with sigmoid activation function in the first layer and linear activation function in the second layer was used. In the experiment for each value D, the sharp raise position of learning error was defined. The experimental results shown in Fig. 21 demonstrate a good agreement with our theory.

Table. Example of neural network learning set in experimental separating capacity estimating

Input vector								Output vector							
1	1	1	1	1	1	1	1	1	0	0	0	0	0	0	0
1	-1	1	-1	1	-1	1	-1	0	1	0	0	0	0	0	0
1	1	-1	-1	1	1	-1	-1	0	0	1	0	0	0	0	0
1	-1	-1	1	1	-1	-1	1	0	0	0	1	0	0	0	0
1	1	1	1	-1	-1	-1	-1	0	0	0	0	1	0	0	0
1	-1	1	-1	-1	1	-1	1	0	0	0	0	0	1	0	0
1	1	-1	-1	-1	-1	1	1	0	0	0	0	0	0	1	0
1	-1	-1	1	-1	1	1	-1	0	0	0	0	0	0	0	1

2) In Fig. 22 the separating capacity estimation experimental results for fast neural networks [24] with dimensionalities $N = 4, 8, 16$ (and with neural kernel size 2×2) are shown. The FNN structure model for dimensionality $N = 8$ is shown in Fig. 1. The experimental estimations are correspondingly equal to $3, 5, 8$. The freedom degrees calculation formulae for FNN obtained in [23] looks like:

$$S = \sum_{m=0}^{\kappa-1} p_m g_m k_m - \sum_{m=0}^{\kappa-2} D_m \; ,$$

where p_m, g_m are the neural kernel structure characteristics, k_m is the number of the kernels in layer m, D_m - is the amount of connections between the layers m and $m+1$. Operator rank of the networks is equal to their dimensionality. Therefore, its separating capacity was calculated as maximum integer for which $k \le \sqrt{S}$. Theoretical estimations are correspondingly equal to $3,5,8$ and in the present case they coincide with the experimental.

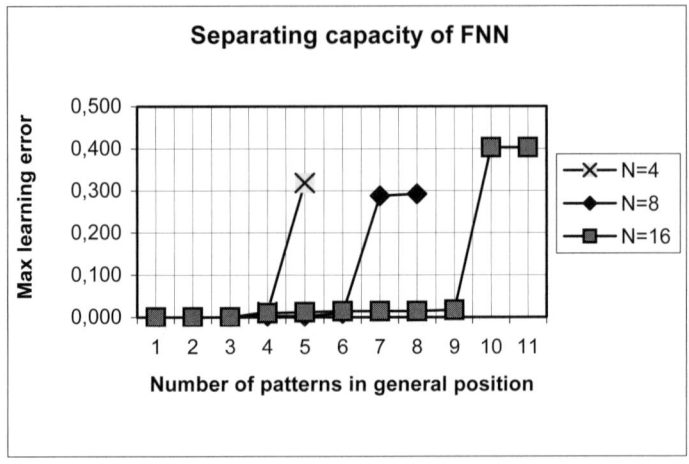

Fig. 22. Experimental estimation of separating capacity of FNN

9. Conclusion

In utilization of neural networks for recognition of large-scale patterns there is a problem of effective use of the calculation resources. The use of fast neural networks makes it possible to solve simultaneously two important practical tasks: (1) to extend the application domain of multilayer neural networks to high-dimensional and real-time systems, and (2) to combine efficient methods for spectral data processing with neural network technology on the basis of a homogeneous software. The fast spectral transformations are particular, but still important, practical applications of the fast neural networks. It has been shown in the paper (see also [24]) that the FNN methodology generalizes the fast algorithms of linear and nonlinear transformations. In addition, the incorporation of the fast spectral transformations into the FNN class helps to understand better their nature and inherent structure, as well as to develop new methodology of their synthesis.

Structure and topological invariants reveal the inside principles of fast transformation creating. It allows to develop the methods structure and topological designing of fast algorithms and to find optimal decisions which to the best degree satisfy the technological base.

The separating capacity characterizes the neural network ability to recognize patterns in general position. The proposed methods for the separating capacity estimation allow to choose the neural network structure which is adequate to formulated task in minimal calculate spending.

10. References

[1] Dorogov, A.Yu., Structure Synthesis of Fast Neural Networks, in *Neurocomputers Design and Application*, New York, 2000, vol. 1, no. 1, pp. 1–18.

[2] Good I.J. The Interaction Algorithm and Practical Fourier Analysis // Journal of Royal Statistical Society. Ser.B.- 1958.- Vol.20.- No.2.- P.361-372.

[3] Andrews, H.C. and Caspari, K.L., A General Technique for Spectral Analysis, *IEEE Trans. Comput.*, 1970, vol. C-19, no. 1, pp. 16–25.

[4] Labunets, V.G., A Unified Approach to Fast Transformation Algorithms, in *Primenenie ortogonal'nykh metodov pri obrabotke signalov i analize sistem* (Application of Orthogonal Methods to Signal Processing and Systems Analysis), Sverdlovsk: UPI, 1980, pp. 4–14. (in Russian).

[5] Solodovnikov, A.I., Kanatov, I.I., and Spivakovskiy, A.M., Orthogonal Bases Synthesis Based on the Generalized Spectral Kernel, in *Voprosy teorii sistem avtomaticheskogo upravleniya* (Theoretical Issues of Automatic Control Systems), Leningrad: LGU, 1976, vol. 2, pp. 99-112. (in Russian).

[6] Cooley J.W., and J.W. Tukey, An Algorithm for the Machine Computation of Complex Fourier Series // Math.Comp. – 1965. – N.19. – P.297-301.

[7] Walsh J.I., A closed set of normal orthogonal functions,- "Amer. J. Math." 1923, v. 45, p. 5-24.

[8] Trakhtman, A.M. and Trakhtman, V.A., *Osnovy teorii diskretnykh signalov na konechnykh intervalakh* (Theory of Discrete Signals on Finite Intervals), Moscow: Sovetskoe Radio, 1975. (in Russian).

[9] Yaroslavskii, L.P., *Vvedenie v tsifrovuyu obrabotku izobrazhenii* (Introduction to Image Processing), Moscow: Sovetskoe Radio, 1979. (in Russian).

[10] Dorogov A.Yu. Implementation of Spectral Transformation in the Class of Fast Neural Networks Programming and Computer Software. Kluwer Academic / Plenum Publishers.- Vol. 29, No 4, 2003.- 13-26p.

[11] Stark J. Iterated function systems as neural networks // Neural Networks.- 1991.-V.4.- pp. 679-690.

[12] Karhunen N. 1947, English translation by Selin I., On Linear Methods in Probability Theory, The Rand Corporation, Doc, T-13, August 1960.

[13] Loeve M. Fonctions Aleatories de Seconde Ordre, Hermann, Paris, 1948.

[14] Feynman R. Quantum mechanical computers. Optics News 11, 1985. Also in Foundations of Physics, 16(6) : 507--531, 1986.

[15] Shor P. W. Algorithms for quantum computation: Discrete log and factoring. In Proceedings of the 35th Annual Symposium on Foundations of Computer Science (Nov. 1994). pp. 124--134, 1994. Institute of Electrical and Electronic Engineers Computer Society Press, ftp://netlib.att.com/netlib/att/math/shor/quantum.algorithms.ps.Z.

[16] Dorogov A.Yu. Structural Synthesis of Modular Weakly Connected Neural Networks. I. Methodology of Structural Synthesis of Modular Neural Networks // Cybernetics and Systems Analysis 37 (2): March - April, 2001.- pp.175-181.

[17] Dorogov A.Yu. Structural Synthesis of Modular Weakly Connected Neural Networks. II. Nuclear Neural Networks // Cybernetics and Systems Analysis 37 (4): July - August, 2001.- pp.470-477.

[18] Cover T.M. Geometrical and Statistical Properties of System of Liner Inequalities with Applications in Pattern Recognition // IEEE Trans. Electronic Computers, 1965, EC-14, 3, pp. 326-334.

[19] Tou .J.T, Gonzaleez R.C. Pattern Recognition Principles.- Addison-Wesley Publishing Company Inc., London, Amsterdam.- 1974.- 411p.

[20] Vapnik V.N. The Nature of Statistic Learning Theory.- Springer-Verlag, New York Inc. 1995.- 188p.

[21] Borisovich U.G., Bliznyakov U.G., Izrailevich Y.A., Fomenko T.N. Introduction in Topology.- Moscow, Nauka Fizmatlit 1995.-416p. (in Russian).

[22] Dorogov A. Yu, Shestopalov M.Yu Separating Capacity of Weakly-Connected Module Neural Networks, Optical Memory & Neural Networks (Information Optics), Vol. 13, No. 3, 2004, p.145-152.

[23] Dorogov A.Yu., Alekseev A.A. Plasticity of Multilayer Weakly-Connected Neural Networks // Neurocomputers Design and Application (Moscow).- No 11, 2001.- pp.22-40. (in Russian).

[24] Dorogov A.Yu. Fast Neural Networks.- Saint Petersburg: Publishing of Saint Petersburg State University.- 2002.- 80p. (in Russian).

Minimal Coverage of Investigated Object when Seeking for its Fractal Dimension

Adam Szustalewicz

Institute of Computer Science, Wrocław University, ul. Joliot-Curie 15, PL-50-383 Wrocław
asz@ii.uni.wroc.pl

Abstract. The measuring of the complexity of river shapes is very important in erosion problems. A perfectly useful way for it is calculating the fractal dimension of curves representing rivers on maps. The shapes of rivers vary in form from smooth to very complicated and algorithm for calculating their fractal dimension should be universal and give good results for both. The paper considers the essence of fulfilling the very difficult and numerically very expensive assumption of the fractal theory about the minimal coverage of the measured objects. The actual version of the algorithm taking care to fulfill the assumption is compared, using 59 objects of different kinds and known fractal dimensions, with four easier and cheaper algorithms of covering. For some objects the obtained results are similar, but generally the elaborated algorithm is the best.

1. Introduction

Everybody knows that line is an one-dimensional object and plane is a two-dimensional object in Euclidean or topological sense.

Patterns of points, lines or other shapes, which neither lie entirely on a line, nor completely fulfill the plane, may be thought as having the dimensionality between one and two. This number is called the pattern's *fractal dimension*. It says much more about the complexity of the pattern than its geometrical features like a length of a curve or the area of the figure. For instance, the length of the Koch-curve equals to infinity, and the plane of the Sierpinski-triangle equals to zero. The fractal dimensions of the both patterns equal to 1.2619 and 1.585 respectively.

In 1977 B. Mandelbrot [6] introduced the term *fractal* to describe *a class of sets with some interesting properties as e. g. self-similarity, underivability at every point and infinite length in a finite space.*

In 1983 Mandelbrot [6] says *a fractal is by definition a set for which the Hausdorff dimension D strictly exceeds the topological dimension. (...) Every set with non-integer D is a fractal.* ☐

Note, that the definition of fractal says nothing about self-similarity – even though the most commonly known mathematical fractals are self-similar.

Mandelbrot said *clouds are not spheres, mountains are not cones, coastlines are not circles and bark is not smooth nor does lightning in a straight line.*

Barnsley wrote in [1] *fractal dimensions (...) are attempts to quantify a subjective feeling which we have about how densely the fractal occupies the metric space in which it lies. Fractal dimensions provide an objective means for comparing fractals. (...) Fractal dimensions are important because they can be defined in connection with real-world data (...) can be attached to clouds, trees, coastlines,...* ☐

In our time, the term *fractal* is applied to description both of artificial objects like Koch-curve or Sierpinski-triangle, and of natural objects as clouds, coastlines, trees,... Fractal dimension of natural objects strictly exceeds their topological dimension, and because of this – fractals are used as models for the growth of bacteria, woody plants and trees [12], [3], for distinguish healthy cells from cancerous cells [2].

Many fractals appear in a variety of physical problems. For example, the Henon map and Lozi map are fractal maps on the plane that describe astronomical orbits. Lorenz attractor is a three-dimensional structure derived from fluid mechanics [8].

It was proved mathematically that for an antenna to work equally well at all frequencies, it must satisfy two criteria. It must be symmetrical about a point. And it must be self-similar, having the same basic appearance at every scale – that is, it has to be fractal. Antennae with special fractal constitution offer better reliability and lower cost than traditional antennas [13].

Each fractal or graphical object possesses a fractal dimension but basically the Hausdorff dimension can be easily calculated only for mathematical fractals. For estimating the real Hausdorff dimension of arbitrary fractal other methods must be applied. These methods or the computed fractal dimensions are called *effective dimensions* (by Mandelbrot).

For calculating the fractal dimension of mathematical fractals the most helpful are: the original *Hausdorff dimension* and the *self-similarity dimension* [9]. For natural objects are at present mostly used: the *box-counting dimension*, the *correlation dimension* and the *mass dimension* [4], [7].

Box-counting method was applied for calculating the fractal dimensions of rivers presented on geographical maps in different scales [9], [10].

Section 2 contains the present knowledge about the box-counting method. The theoretical backgrounds of the method and problems connected with its numerical realization are presented.

Section 3 contains description of six constructed algorithms, which secure better and better minimal covering of considered objects. The results obtained by algorithms are compared.

2. Box-counting method

The current information on the box-counting method – the theoretical assumptions and numerical problems connected with computer realization of the method – are presented in this section. The results obtained in [10] are remind as well.

2.1 Theoretical backgrounds of the method

The theoretical assumptions of the method *Box-counting* are the following:

1. for given $\varepsilon > 0$ the investigated object is covered by sets of diameter at most ε,
2. every such overlapping is the *minimal covering*, it means, the number $N(\varepsilon)$ of sets needed for covering the whole object is the smallest one.

Then
Definition. ([4], [10]) the value d of the limit (if the limit exists)

$$d = \lim_{\varepsilon \to 0} \frac{\log N(\varepsilon)}{\log(1/\varepsilon)} \tag{1}$$

is the *fractal dimension* (FD) of the measured object, or its *box-counting dimension*.□

The theorem proved in [4] says
Theorem. $N(\varepsilon)$ used in the definition above can be defined in equivalent ways as:
1. the smallest number of closed balls of radius ε that cover the object;
2. the smallest number of squares of side equal to ε that cover the object;
3. the number of ε-mesh squares that intersect the object;
4. the largest number of disjoint balls of radius ε with centers in object.   □

In practice, the measured object is usually given in form of an array (a photo or a graphical map) without the possibilities of arbitrary growing the resolution of data. Problems that appear in this connection are presented in the next point.

2.2 Problems connected with practical realization of the box-counting method

Considered data – the measured object – is usually given in form of its bitmap (a photo or a graphical map) with finite resolution and there are no possibilities to growing up the resolution.
   There exist three, the most important problems
1. There are no possibilities to apply *arbitrary small* covering sets; the graphical resolution of images is limited to one pixel only. Thus the set of diameters of covering sets is finite.
2. Is the assumption about the minimal overlapping really essential? If yes, then how to compose the minimal covering?
3. The numerical approximation of the formula (1) uses
   • the construction of a set of coverings of the measured object (for instance with squares with sides equal to ε for a finite sequence of values $\{\varepsilon_j\}$), and next
   • the estimation of the best value of slope b of linear regression $y = a + bx$, constructed for the finite sequence of points

$$\{(x_j, y_j)\} = \{(\log(1/\varepsilon_j), \log N(\varepsilon_j))\}.$$

An example of construction of such regression line is in the Fig. 1. The problem is how, basing on the set of obtained points $\{(x_j, y_j)\}$, to approach values b close to the true dimensions d for a large enough set of objects with known dimensions.

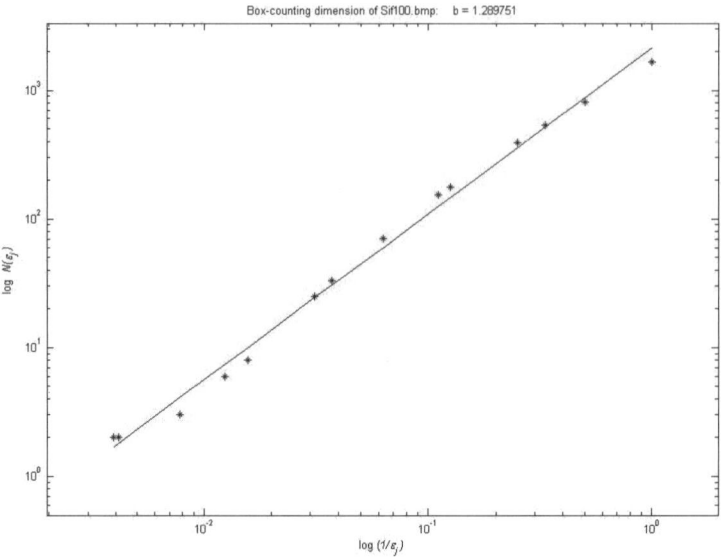

Fig. 1. Square linear regression $y = a + bx$ obtained for the given set of points $\{(x_j, y_j)\} = \{(\log(1/\varepsilon_j), \log N(\varepsilon_j))\}$ for a map of the river Sifnos

The next section contains description of more and more accurate algorithms of covering the measured object with minimal set of covering squares. We try to check the essence of the minimal overlapping assumption formulated in backgrounds of the box-counting method.

3. Looking for a minimal set of covering squares

Algorithms published in literature or in internet cover the measured object with regular, rectangular or square grids with side-length equal to ε. The second theoretical assumption (in Subsection 2.1) of the box-counting method about the minimal covering is not fulfilled. It is impossible to apply arbitrary small covering sets as well, because the resolution of images is bounded to one pixel only.

The aim of the paper is to examine the essence of the assumption about the minimal overlapping onto the accuracy of the obtained fractal dimensions of the measured objects. A sequence of constructed different covering algorithms will be checked if they secure better and better minimal covering of the considered object.

There is considered a set of given 59 objects with known theoretical fractal dimensions. The set contains circles, lines, rectangles and fractals like Koch-Curves, Sierpinski-Triangles, and Sierpinski-Gasket. These objects are different in magnitude and lines form different angles with axes of the coordinate system.

3.1 Variants of coverage of the object

We assume *the measured object lies in a minimal rectangular graphical bitmap.* Such assumption was denoted as essential for instance in [5].

The object is covered with squares of sides equal to ε pixels. The squares can be placed in various ways. The methods of covering the object may be different from very simple to more complicated. The simplest method relies on putting the grid onto the rectangle with the object, fitting the grid-lines with the left-up corner of the rectangle. There exist more complicated variants of this method. The put squares, or whole parts of the created grid can be moved. Of course the mentioned variants differ with their computation complexity.

In the next part we consider the following more and more complicated variants:

G1. *Simplest Grid Covering* is the simplest algorithm. It relies on putting the square grid onto the rectangle with object in agreement with the left-up corner of the rectangle.

G2. *Covering the Rotated Rectangle.* The grid can be put four times successively in agreement with every corner of the rectangle with object. The coverage with the smallest number of grid-squares obtained this way is the result. Such version is equivalent to the rotation of the rectangle with object by a multiple of right angles (it makes no deformations of the object) and fitting the grid with the left-up corner of the rotated rectangle.

G3. *Covering with the Horizontally Moved Grid.* It is not difficult to find the optimal position of covering squares when their movement is restricted to one direction only – for instance horizontal. Such algorithm works very well with filled objects like filled ellipse.

G4. *Rotated Rectangle and Horizontally Moved Grid.* Now the horizontal movement of grid squares (**G3**) is applied to four grids – which, accordingly to the algorithm **G2** agree sequentially with four corners of the object's rectangle. The minimal number of needed squares is the result.

G5. *Shifted Grid.* This is the most complicated algorithm. Succeeding squares can move in both directions before their best position will be designated. The more precise describing is too long and will be located in [11]. The actual version – not the final yet – works very well with objects in form of curves like maps of rivers. The algorithm consists of three main parts:

- *First Part – the coverage of the most external parts of the rectangle.* If some elements of the object lie in the corner, then a square covering this corner is applied. Next, two sequences of mutually tangential squares, adjacent to the put square, may be created along the sides of the rectangle (comp. Figs. 2, 3).

- *Second Part – the coverage of internal parts of succeeding columns of the rectangle.* The covering squares are moved in both directions and algorithm looks for their optimal positions. After the complete coverage of each column the *first part* is repeated.

- *Third Part – applied when the number of uncovered columns of the rectangle is not greater than* ε. The minimal coverage of such strip is obtained without problems. This part finishes the algorithm.

G6. Shifted or Horizontally Moved Grid. If the covered object is full of elements like filled ellipse, then algorithm **G4** may sometimes work better than **G5**. So, the algorithm **G6** applies the set of covering squares which contains the smaller number of squares from sets obtained by **G4** and **G5**.

The first four and the last algorithm are simple and sufficiently described above. The fifth algorithm **G5** is the most complicated, therefore it is described in more details in [11].

Next subsection contains description of results obtained for some representatives of considered objects by all the methods. The figures illustrate different coverage of the Koch-Curve fractal. The fractal is not a filled object and results of algorithms **G5** and **G6** are the same. Because of this we omit results of **G6**.

3.2. The coverage of the Koch-Curve fractal using the methods G1 – G5

Koch-Curve lies in a rectangle of 794×229 pixels. We construct a grid of squares of sides equal to 64 pixels and this grid will cover the fractal. Koch-Curve is a line (not a filled object). Because of this the results of **G5** and **G6** are the same, and we omit results of **G6**.

Pictures with the coverage of Koch-Curve

In the following we show how different ways of manipulating with strips achieve better coverage of the fractal. Five successive exhibits in Fig. 1 show different ways of coverage of the Koch-Curve with squares:

G1. the grid is fitted to the left-up corner of the rectangle and the grid-stripping was not applied; the attained coverage consists of 27 squares.

G2. Fitting the grid to the third corner of the rectangle is equivalent to the applying **G1** to the rectangle rotated for the angle of 270°; the attained coverage consists of 24 squares.

G3. At the beginning the grid is fitted to the left-up corner of the rectangle, then squares can move horizontally, taking their best positions; the attained coverage consists of 22 squares.

G4. The method **G3** is applied to the rectangle rotated for multiples of right angle looking for the minimal number of needed squares; the attained coverage consists of 20 squares.

G5. The algorithm starts with its first part – the coverage of elements lying in corners of the rectangle and forming sequences along the both sides of the rectangle, adjacent to the put square. All squares, used in this part of the algorithm, are marked with filled triangles in Figs. 2, 3. Next the rest of the object is covered. The attained coverage consists of 17 squares.

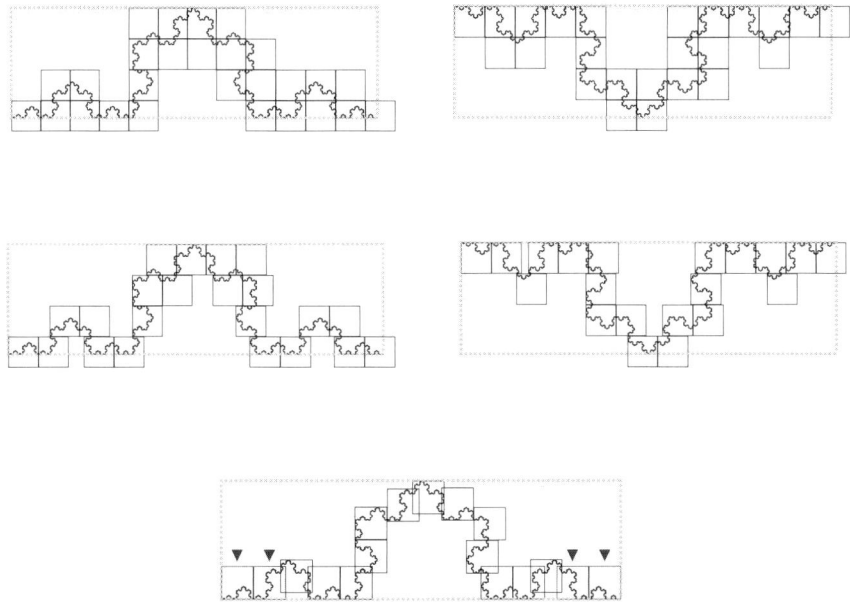

Fig. 2. Different ways **G1**,...,**G5** of manipulating with squares result in different numbers of squares needed for coverage of the Koch-Curve. **G1** (left-up) none grid-stripping – 27 squares. **G2** (right-up) is equivalent **G1** applied to the rectangle rotated for multiples of right angle – 24 squares. **G3** (left-down) equals to **G1** with horizontally moved squares – 22 squares. **G4** (right-down) is equivalent to **G3** applied to the rotated rectangle – 20 squares. **G5** (bottom) – 17 squares. The elements of the object which lie in the rectangle's corners and their boundary neighbours are covered in the first part of the algorithm. They are marked with filled triangles

Any algorithms of **G1**-**G4** can be preceded by the first part of the algorithm **G5** performing the coverage of object's elements located in corners of the rectangle with the object and their boundary neighbours:

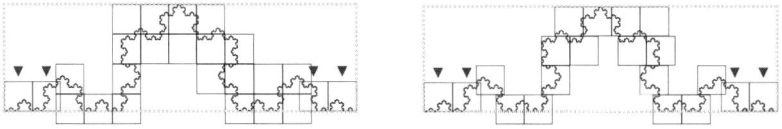

Fig. 3. The coverage of Koch-Curve by algorithms **G1** (left) and **G3** (right) was preceded by the first part of **G5**. The four squares, indicated by filled triangles, cover the object's elements lying in corners of the rectangle and their boundary neighbours. Algorithms with such preceding need 25 (**G1**) and 20 (**G3**) squares instead of 27 and 22 needed in Fig. 2 exhibit **G1** and **G3**

Some considerations on the accuracy of algorithms described above, when applied to some other objects, are presented in next subsection.

3.3 Accuracy of the algorithms G1 – G6 for various objects

Considering 59 objects

We consider 59 objects with known theoretical fractal dimensions: 4 Circles (FD=1), 3 Rectangles (FD=1), 4 Squares (FD=1), 13 Segments (FD=1) forming different angles with axes of the coordinate system, 26 Koch-Curves (FD=1.262), 8 Sierpinski-Triangles (FD=1.585) and 1 Sierpinski-Gasket (FD=1.893).

After the use of algorithms **G1,...,G6** every object, lying in its smallest rectangle $N_{vertical} \times N_{horizontal}$ pixels, is covered by squares of side-lengths ε pixels for ε in form $\varepsilon = 2^k$ or $\varepsilon = 3^l$ and such that

$$\varepsilon \leq \max(N_{vertical}, N_{horizontal}).$$

A sequence of points $\{(x_j, y_j)\} = \{(\log(1/\varepsilon_j), \log N(\varepsilon_j))\}$ is constructed for every variant of algorithms. This set may serve for obtaining the slope of regression line approximating the fractal dimension of the considered object.

Taking all the points $\{(x_j, y_j)\}$ from the sequence, the fractal dimension will be usually approximated inaccurately, because we do not know precisely how many and which points should be taken to estimate most accurately the fractal dimension.

Would it be possible for every algorithm to select automatically some subset of the points, which gives a good approximation of fractal dimensions for most of considered objects?

The easiest way for automatic construction of such subsets for every algorithm is omitting some extreme points (lying at the ends of the constructed regression line – see e.g. Fig. 1). We consider three situations leading to construction of the modified linear regression line:

- retaining **all** constructed points,
- retaining only points obtained for all **squares with side-lengths in form of powers 2**, and
- retaining **special subsets of points**, obtained by removing 1, 2, 3 or more points from either side of the graph displaying the regression line – see Fig. 1 – to obtain the required accuracy for most of the objects.

The obtained results are presented in Table 1. For given errors and chosen subsets of constructed points $\{(x_j, y_j)\}$ we show numbers of objects for which FD was calculated successively.

Table 1. For given errors and chosen subsets of constructed points $\{(x_j, y_j)\}$ the table shows results of calculating FD for 59 considered objects. The numbers say for how many objects their dimension was calculated successively

Errors	Subset	G1	G2	G3	G4	G5	G6
< 1%	all points	9	5	10	10	8	8
	$\varepsilon = 2^k$	7	8	16	16	15	15
	special	20	26	22	22	25	25
< 5%	all points	39	43	39	39	40	40
	$\varepsilon = 2^k$	40	41	43	43	41	41
	special	54	55	57	57	57	57

Experiment was done with 59 objects. The results obtained for special subsets are the best. They are similar for error less than 5%. More interesting are distributions of objects for which the error of calculated FD was less than one percent.

Table 2. Distributions of objects with fractal dimension calculated with **error less than 1%**. The table presents three kinds of selected subsets of constructed points $\{(x_j, y_j)\}$: all of them, the points constructed for $\varepsilon = 2^k$ and their special subsets. The results obtained for special subsets are the best. Geometrical objects, containing straight parts are very difficult for the box-counting method with so rigorous accuracy condition

Subsets	Methods	Numbers of objects						
		4 Circ	3 Rect	4 Squa	13 Segm	26 Koch-C	8 S-Tr	1 S-Gas
all points	G1	0	0	0	0	8	1	0
	G2	0	0	0	0	3	2	0
	G3, G4	1	0	0	0	9	0	0
	G5, G6	2	0	0	0	6	0	0
$\varepsilon = 2^k$	G1	1	0	0	1	4	1	0
	G2	1	0	0	1	5	1	0
	G3, G4	3	0	0	1	11	1	0
	G5, G6	2	0	0	1	12	0	0
special	G1	2	1	2	3	8	4	0
	G2	0	3	2	4	10	6	1
	G3, G4	4	0	1	0	12	5	0
	G5, G6	4	1	2	5	7	5	1

In the case of error less than 1% the worst results are obtained for all points. Two kinds of objects appear in each line only. A little better result is in case of squares with side-length in form of powers 2, we see 3-4 kinds. The best results are obtained for special subsets of points, but only the line for algorithms **G5** and **G6** contains all numbers greater than zero.

Considering 7 selected objects

Table 3 shows the accuracy in calculation the fractal dimension of particular seven objects with known fractal dimensions. The measured objects are: Circle (FD=1), Rectangle (FD=1), Square (FD=1), Line45 (FD=1) – segment creating the angle 45° with axes, Koch-Curve (FD=1.262), Sierpinski-Triangle (FD=1.585) and Sierpinski-Gasket (FD=1.893).

For each combination method×object the analysis of evaluation of FD was based on the subsets of data points for which the investigations presented in Tab. 1 proved to the best.

The accuracy of each method is measured by the relative error evaluated as the ratio of the difference between the calculated and true dimension of the object divided by the true fractal dimension of that object. For further comparisons we take the absolute value of this relative error and express it as percentage.

Let e be the percentage of relative error. The symbols ● and O appearing in the table denote respectively that ● – $e < 1\%$, O – $1\% \le e < 5\%$, otherwise, if $5\% \le e$, we show the calculated FD.

Table 3. Comparison of results of algorithms G1,...,G6 obtained basing on their *special* subsets (the same as in Table 1) for the selected seven objects with known true fractal dimensions: Circle, Rectangle, Line45, Square, Koch-Curve, Sierpinski-Triangle and Sierpinski-Gasket. Denoting by e the percentage of relative error, the applied symbols denote: ● – $e < 1\%$, O – $1\% \le e < 5\%$. Otherwise ($5\% \le e$) the calculated FD is shown

OBJECTS	FD	Calculated FD					
Circle	1.000	●	0.922	●	●	●	●
Rectangle	1.000	●	●	O	O	O	O
Square	1.000	●	●	O	O	●	●
Line45	1.000	0.832	●	O	O	●	●
Koch-Curve	1.262	●	O	O	O	●	●
Sierp-Triangle	1.585	O	●	O	O	●	●
Sierp-Gasket	1.893	O	●	O	O	●	●
ALGORITHMS		G1	G2	G3	G4	G5	G6

One may see – the last two algorithms give the best results, i.e. very small errors for all but one of the objects. It can be proved that Rectangle or Square – because of their corners – are the objects very difficult for box-counting method. For obtaining their fractal dimension with error small enough the rectangle must be covered with squares of really very short side-length.

Looking at the Table 3 we see, that fractal dimensions of considered objects are calculated with errors less than 1% or 5% except of two cases, for which we show directly the calculated fractal dimensions. These cases (written in bold) really differ from the true dimension of the objects.

A statistical characterization of the calculated FDs is presented in form of box-plots in next subsection.

Illustration of calculated FDs by box-plots
The values of fractal dimensions, presented in the Table 3 are calculated for every object by six considered algorithms **G1-G6**.

The Box-Plot is a graph in form of the box with notch, illustrating five statistical measures of data groups:

- The line within the box is the *median* of the group.
- The lower and upper edges of the box are the 25th and 75th percentiles of the group. The distance between them is the *inter-quartile range*.
- The lines extending above and below the box (the whiskers) show the extent of the rest of the group (without outliers).
- The plus signs at the top or at the bottom of the plot show the outliers in the data.
- The notches in the box represent a robust estimate of the uncertainty about the medians for box-to-box comparison.

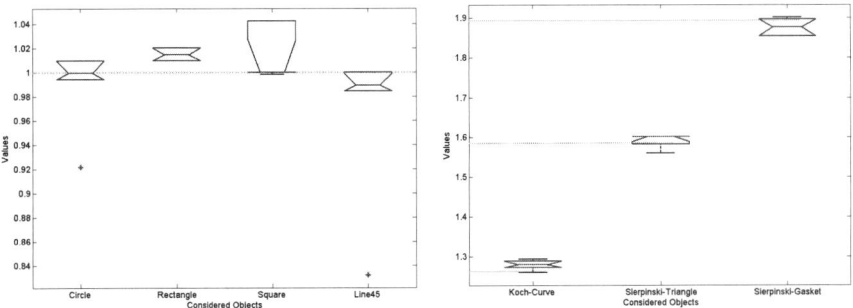

Fig. 4. Box-plot presentation of fractal dimensions calculated for selected objects by the methods **G1-G6**. Left – for geometrical objects: Circle, Rectangle, Square, Line45 (FD=1.000). Two outliers (symbols +) are placed in columns of Circle and Line45 (bold values in Table \ref{tab2}). Right – for fractals: Koch-Curve (FD=1.262), Sierpinski-Triangle (FD=1.585) and Sierpinski-Gasket (FD=1.893).   Horizontal lines are located on values of true fractal dimensions

Every box-plot has been obtained on the basis of six observations chosen by six algorithms **G1-G6** only. The horizontal lines on both pictures are placed on values of true fractal dimensions for particular objects.

4. Conclusions

In Subsection 3.3 the *special subsets* of considered points $\{(x_j, y_j)\}$ were introduced as obtained by removing one, two or more points from either side in the graph exhibiting regression curve $\overline{y} = \overline{y}(\overline{x})$ where $\overline{y} = \log(y)$, $\overline{x} = \log(x)$.

We observe that:

- The computation complexity of **G5** is much higher in comparison with other algorithms,

- **G5** posses better possibilities for constructing special subsets of points $\{(x_j, y_j)\}$:
  - sometimes there exist more than one special subset,
  - usually there exist some other subsets, where the numbers of objects with fractal dimension calculated in desired accuracy are only a little less than the numbers obtained for special subsets.

References

[1] M. Barnsley, *Fractals everywhere*, Boston, Academical Press, Inc. 1988.

[2] W. Bauer, C. D. Mackenzie, *Cancer Detection via Determination of Fractal Cell Dimension*, presented at the Workshop on Computational and Theoretical Biology, Michigan State University, April 24, 1999, see also
http://www.pa.msu.edu/~/bauer/cancer/cancer.pdf.

[3] L. E. Da Costa, J.A. Landry, *Synthesis of Fractal Models for Plants and Trees: First Results*, Fractal 2004, Complexity and Fractals in Nature, Vancouver, Canada, April 4-7, 2004.

[4] K. Falconer, *Fractal geometry, Mathematical Foundations and Applications*, John Wiley \& Sons, New York 1990.

[5] G. Gonzato, F. Mulargia, M. Ciccotti, *Measuring the fractal dimensions of ideal and actual objects: implications for application in geology and geophysics*, Geophys. J. Int. 142, 2000, 108-116.

[6] B. B. Mandelbrot, *The Fractal Geometry of Nature*, W. H. Freeman and Company, New York 1977, 1983.

[7] V. Nordmeier, *Fractals in Physics – From Low-Cost Experiments to Fractal Geometry*, University of Essen, Germany,
http://appserv01.uni-duisburg.de/hands-on/files/autoren/nordm/nordm.htm.

[8] H.-O. Peitgen, H Jurgens, D. Saupe, *Fractals for the Classroom* Part 1, 2, Springer-Verlag, New York 1992 (polish edition by PWN, Warszawa 2002).

[9] A. Szustalewicz, *Numerical problems with evaluating the fractal dimension of real data*, in *Enhanced Methods in Computer Security, Biometric and Artificial Intelligence Systems*, ed. J. Pejas, A. Piegat, by Kluwer Academic Publishers, Springer, New York 2005, 273-283.

[10] A. Szustalewicz, A.Vassilopoulos, *Calculating the fractal dimension of river basins, comparison of several methods*, in *Biometrics, Computer Security Systems and Artificial Intelligence Applications*, ed. Khalid Saeed, Jerzy Pejas, Romuald Mosdorf, by Springer, 2006, pp. 299-309.

[11] A. Szustalewicz, *Choosing best subsets for calculation of fractal dimension by the box-counting method*, manuscript (in preparation).

[12] R. P. Taylor, B. Spehar, C. W. Clifford, B. R. Newell, *The Visual Complexity of Pollock's Dripped Fractals* in Proceedings of the International Conference of Complex Systems, 2002, see also
http://materialscience.uoregon.edu/taylor/art/Taylor/CCS2002.pdf.

[13] K. J. Vinoy, K. A. Jose, V. K. Varadan, V. V. Varadan, *Hilbert Curve Fractal Antenna: A Small Resonant Antenna for VHF/UHF Applications*, Microwave & Opt. Technol. Lett. 29 No. 4, 215-219 (2001).

Networked Robots Personal Tastes Acquisition and Sharing

Yoshiharu Yoshida, Toru Yamaguchi, Eri Sato, and Toshihiro Shibano

Tokyo Metropolitan University 6-6 Asahigaoka, Hino, Tokyo 191-0065 Japan
yoshiharu@fml.ec.tmit.ac.jp yamachan@fml.ec.tmit.ac.jp esato@fml.ec.tmit.ac.jp
shibano.to@shinryo.com

Abstract. Architectonics of systems and communities are becoming more complicated everyday. Communities help one another by riding on their own strength. Similarly, each matured technology needs help mutually to develop. In particular, the wide development that covers not only 'Robot Technology (RT)', but also 'Automotive Technology (AT)' and 'Information Technology (IT)' is expected in nowadays. They are growing in a spiral by interacting one another. We introduce systems in which these technologies collaborate and our approach for intelligent systems. Finally, we show an experiment of Networked Robots and ontological network.

1. Information

Architectonics of systems and communities are becoming more complicated everyday. It is very difficult for a community to grow by itself. In case of disaster, lots of countries will send relief supplies to affected area. In order to live comfortably, people tend to ask for things which they are not able to get locally. That is, as the society becomes matured, it is essential to communicate and obtain from others.

Communities help one another by riding on their own strength. Similarly, each matured technology needs help mutually to develop. In particular, the wide development that covers not only 'Robot Technology (RT)', but also 'Automotive Technology (AT)' and 'Information Technology (IT)' is expected in nowadays. They are growing in a spiral by interacting one another as in Fig 1.

There are many links among electric appliances. We live with personalized appliances, which are achieved by links. AIBO is well known for representing example of personalized robots. Also, personalized robotic cleaners are becoming popular. In the meantime, IT made remarkable progress especially in personalizing-related technology; authentication technology, animation on web page, and web camera. Users who are not familiar with computers can use IT through friendly personal robots.

Also, collaboration with Network Technology is popular in RT field. A new car, PM, i-unit is designed for people to get on easily. When it stands, it looks like a robot, when you get in the car, it looks as if you are getting in the robot, just like a scene from animation. Its design concept is "meeting, linking and hanging out together". It is a symbol of future vehicles. There is a movement of Ubiquitous Network so that networking function is tapped into various systems. A lot of attention has given to Networked Robotics recently. We introduce efforts for networked robots [1].

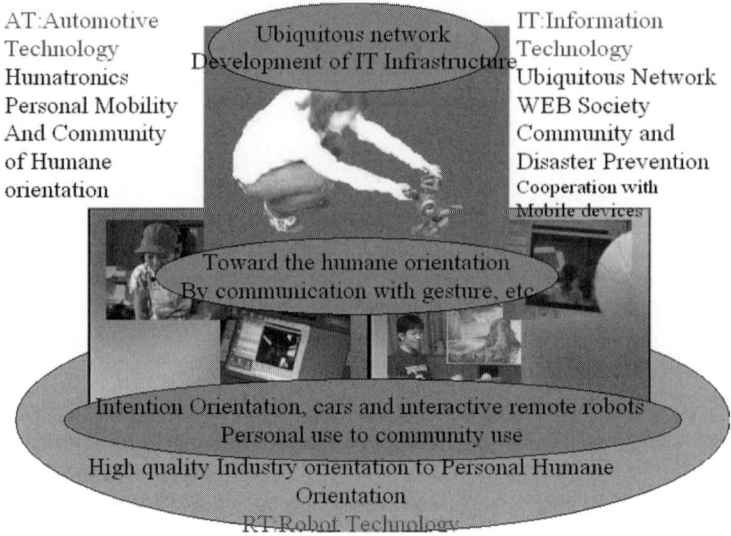

Fig. 1. Technologies glowing in a spiral

2. The study of networked intelligence and robots

Fig 2 shows major efforts led by the government agencies. A lot of efforts are being made. Ministry of Public Management, Home Affairs, Posts and Telecommunications held workshop headed by Prof. Tokuda for networked robots technology, which aims to build an open platform.

On the other hand, the policy of developments of robotics depends on each group or laboratory, but there is a movement that carries on the standardization. NEDO [2] is leading with the standardization of robot elements as 21century robot challenging program. Recently, the committee has decided on groups to be commissioned. The group that headed by Prof. Tanie is going to develop a middle ware for modularity and an open architecture specification.

In IT field, Microsoft plans the next generation natural interface to recognize hands by a stereo vision. In RT field, the interactions between users and robots by gesture recognition are focused.

As the progress of networked robots technology, the gap between human and system is known. There are a huge number of systems in the world and that have become popular, but they don't understand people. Only people could understand them. Humatronics can be a true interface Technology for human and system.

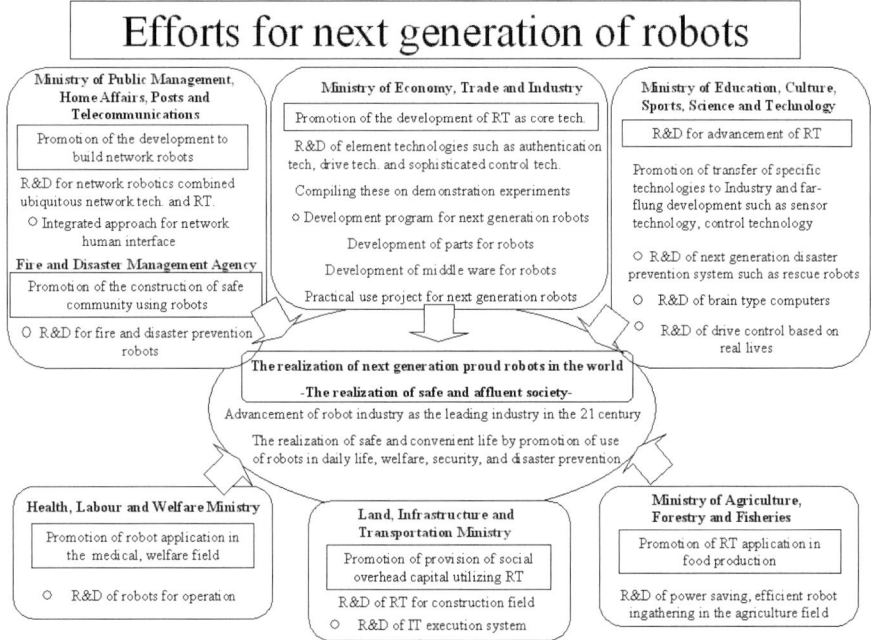

Fig. 2. Efforts for next generation of robots

3. Humatronics

In recent years various systems based on electronics Including cars, computers, mobile phones, and even robots, have been getting into our daily lives. However, currently, an unsymmetrical relationship exists between human and systems, which imposes burdens especially on elderly or handicapped persons. There are various problems to be solved for balancing asymmetry of the relationship between humanand systems. We name the electronics for solving these problems "Humatronics". There is Humatronics on background of our proposed Networked Intelligence.Main purpose of humatronics is to establish the symmetric interaction between human and electronics systems, by giving the systems the capability of understanding humans. Not only the systems but also humans will be sensible through the interaction with such intelligent systems. Another important factor is computer networks, over which the systems can share knowledge, information, and experiences. Intelligent systems connected via networks will bring us seamless support throughout our daily lives. Fig 3,4 shows outline of Humatronics. As show in Fig 5, humatoronics is divided into two stages.

At first, we keep ability to understand and to observe a human being in a system by the first step. Now a person understands a system and uses it. However a system by understanding a person build human being center model that judges the situation and to help.And it establishes the relation that we got of harmony between systems with a human being.

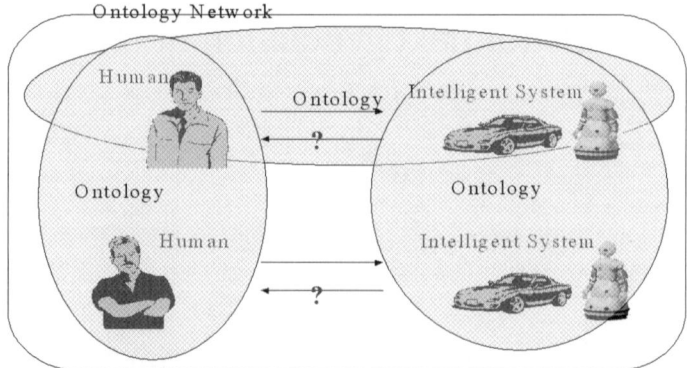

Fig. 3. Humatronics and Ontology

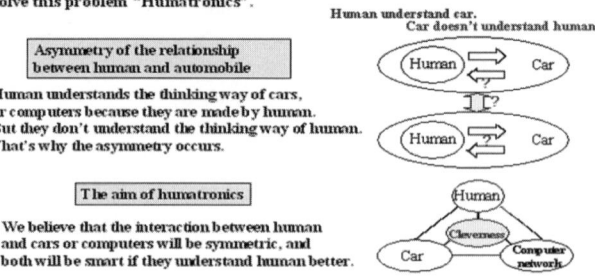

Fig. 4. Humatronics

The second step establishes a network sharing knowledge, experience. We can support human life by it to every corner.

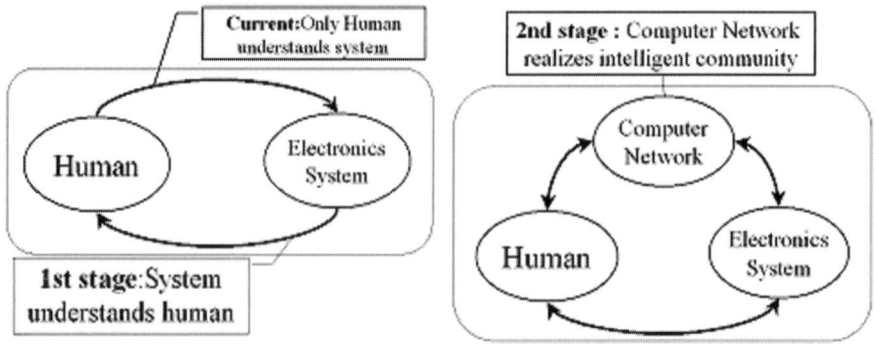

Fig. 5. Step of humatronics

4. Soft-computing oriented ontological network

A. About ontology

The term "Ontology" means a "systematic theory of existence" in the study of philosophy. Philosophically aiming to arrange everything in the systematic world, it is called Ontology [3][4]. We show the ontological concept and the proposal model in Fig 6. Human can communicate by gesture and so on, with whom has different culture and language. Because human has common basis, such as mirror neuron, which 'own' action neuron activates by observing other human motion like a mirror. There is ontology on that extension line. The research into ontology has been performed to study the problem of "Share of knowledge" and "Construction of the knowledge base" in the field of the knowledge processing. The knowledge processing system constructs the knowledge base of the targeted world by using ontology. By studying the targeted concept, a contribution to knowledge sharing can be expected as a result. The ontology which proposed here is the knowledge construction type and it is used for communication between the human and the system. This ontology is called a bottom-up ontology. Ontology is composed of Conceptual Fuzzy Sets (CFS) that has the dispersive expression of concepts. Fig 7 shows Conceptual Fuzzy Sets.

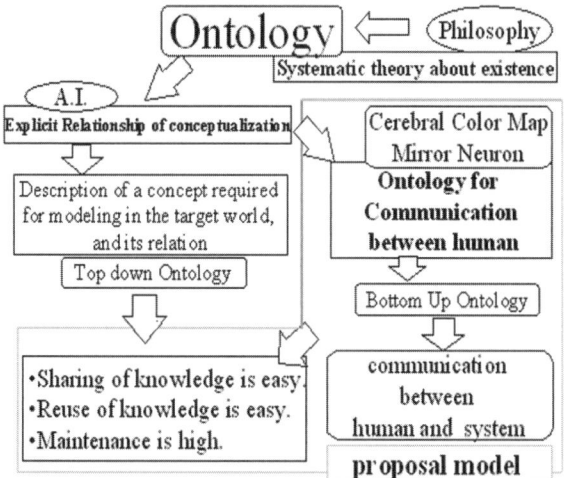

Fig. 6. Ontology and proposal model

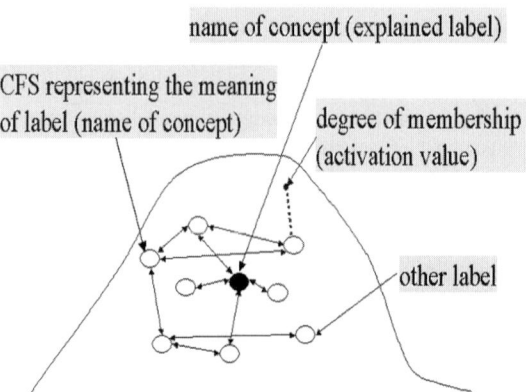

Fig. 7. Conceptual Fuzzy Sets

B. Ontological Network

Ontological Network is a network where agents share ontology. There are many difficulties such as how to share it and how to activate appropriate ontology on the network. Also, we have to consider the problem when the size of ontology is huge. Now, how do we humans handle enormous knowledge? The process of memorizing is almost same among humans and systems; encode, storage, and search when memory is used.

There is a little difference in stages. First, code must be different. When you remember an object, you don't remember the object with explanation, or you would image the vague object with image of words that are used in the sentence when you describe the object. Therefore, we try to encode data that describe by connected data. Ontology shared on Ontological Network is described in this way.

Also, we have to consider the way of storage carefully. Humans can ignore things that have no relation to the object. However search on systems is basically checking every datum. People don't actually ignore them, but they don't mind. Namely, we believe that the reason why people can remember the appropriate object quickly is the ability to concentrate and finding an appropriate data cluster fast. In order to build this ability in systems, we have to store ontology with clustering or tree index structure on Ontological Network. However, these ways are not fundamental solutions because as the volume of data increases, clusters or indexes are also increasing. Namely, it is obvious that it would not able to handle overflown too many clusters or indexes.

To decrease the load when searching, there are lots of efforts such as data squashing. The most promise for ontology can be demonstrated by the use of Graph-based Substructure Pattern Mining because ontology is described by using CFS and mainly a set of more specific instances.

5. Networked robots

RT has been evolving to make a robot that has same ability as human, but there is another future direction of RT to create networked robots. An engineer watched a bird beating the air with its wings, but he succeeded in building an airplane without flapping wings. The next generation robots will have advantage of networking ability that transcends the bounds of astro-boy orientation so that robots and IT devices will collaborate to support users.

In these years, the word "robot" has been used for broader meaning than it used to. "Robot" is defined as "Intelligent System including functions that effect the real world" ATR [5]-centered group that researches networked robots separated robots into 3 types. This idea is very similar as our image of networked robots. So, we use the names here, but concept could be different from the group. First, it is called virtual type robot, which is inside cell phones and so on. These are unconscious type of robots that works to collect information and recognize situations. Also, there are Robots called visible type. They talk to people based on the situation.

Due to build this system, the system needs to know not only the situation but also

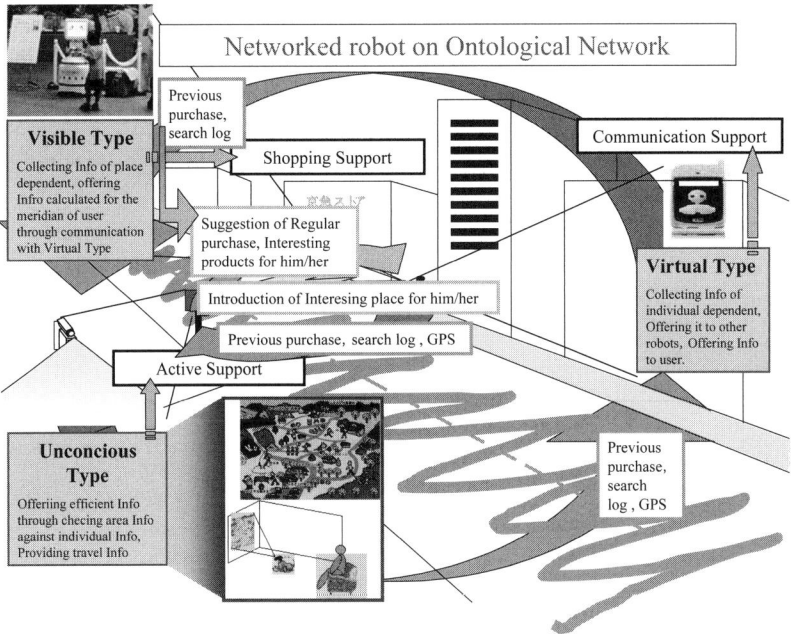

Fig. 8. Networked robots

people's intention through the interaction. Therefore, we suggest Ontological network. We have shown approaches to obtain ontology from human motion. In the meantime, we are trying to acquire ontology from data in social life by using network robots. Fig 8 shows the planed experimental scene.

Data on Ontological Network may be similar as on Semantic-Web. For example, there is a man who buys a bike every two years, and Honda will hold an event near his company when 24 months have passed since he bought a bike last. A networked robot must introduce him this event because system associates the time, bike and purchase preview with Honda. Ontology layer has not decided in detail yet, but you would get information about Honda by searching "bike" through ontology layer.

6. Acquisition of taste information

Asymmetric relation exists between human and system. To solve this problem we decided to create system that has ability to understand human. Our approach is to estimate users inclination from the data such as search log, purchase history, and GPS log.

Although we used the way watching human throw unconscious type robot to extract user's personality and characteristic, we developed system that can pickup more permanent personality.

We take that system can acquire taste information if it collect data such as search, purchase history, and GPS log. We designed the system that virtual type robot collects purchase history and search log, visible type robot inference taste information.

Virtual type robot makes a list of products based on a category, price, and frequency.

7. Experiment

We used fuzzy inference to guess products that a customer would buy.

A visible type robot inputs the data which were provided by a virtual type robot. A visible type robot offers group of products from it by the fuzzy inference. A visible robot shows the products that match recommended products of a shop.

Fig 9 shows the fuzzy rules that we used it this time.

We performed an experiment of networked robots for stores. Fig 10 shows for a whole system this experiment.

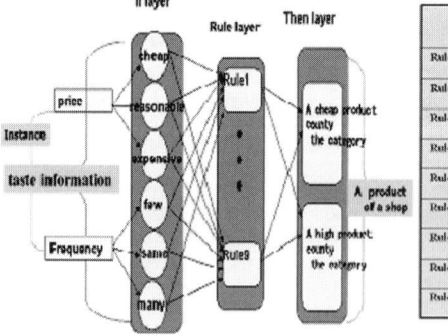

	The price that is used for one shopping	Frequency in a category	A fuzzy reasoning result
Rule1	cheap	few	A group of recommended cheap product
Rule2	cheap	same	A group of recommended cheap product
Rule3	cheap	many	A group of cheap product of the category
Rule4	reasonable	few	A group of recommended reasonable product
Rule5	reasonable	same	A group of reasonable product of the category
Rule6	reasonable	many	A group of reasonable product of the category
Rule7	expensive	few	A group of recommended expensive product
Rule8	expensive	same	A group of expensive product of the category
Rule9	expensive	many	A group of expensive product of the category

Fig. 9. Fuzzy rules

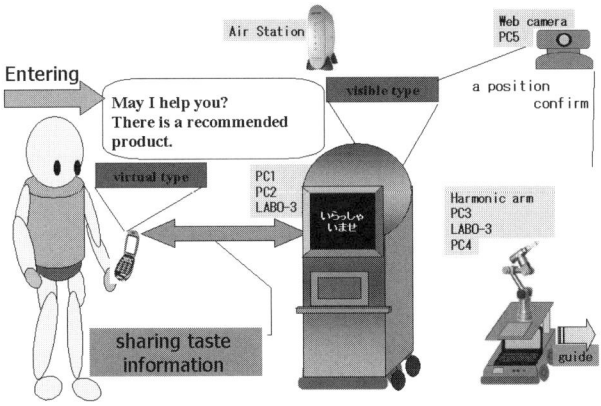

Fig. 10. A system summary

A. Experiment

In this experiments, we aimed to establish networked robots that share taste information and reuse those information to support customer shopping.

The taste information that acquired by the cellular phone which is as a virtual type robot is shared with a visible type robot in a shop. A robot inference a purchase pattern of a user from his or her taste information. A visible type robot compares it with assortment of goods and then shows and suggests products that a customer seem to purchase. By the reasoning, a name of a recommended article, a price, information of a shop were showed by a visible type robot.

And we installed a small PC with a touch panel in the robot which as a human interface. A customer can know store's layout and information of products by touching a panel.

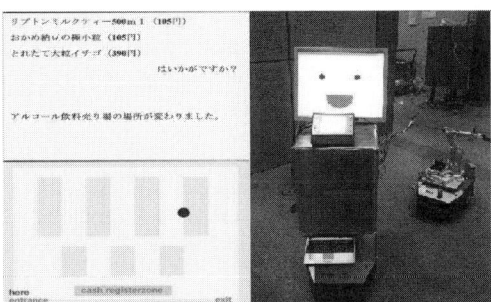

Fig. 11. Experiment picture

Fig 11 shows an examples of a display.

B. Result

We succeed to customer by using the fuzzy inference this experiment.

Different types robot such as virtual type robot and visible type robot, shared taste information. Because of, they cooperated and worked together.

However, analysis of taste information is not prefect namely, the list of products the visible type robot showed didn't much a user's taste completely.

C. Evaluation

We carried out questionnaire. Number of subject is seven the questionnaire consists of four question listed in Fig 12.

Each subject answers one to five for each quest.

item	Average evaluation
Were you useful for one's shopping?	4.5
Was the convenience good?	3.7
Was the article which visible type robots showed a thing to want?	3.8
Do you use this system?	4.0

Fig. 12. Questionnaire result

8. Conclusion

In this paper we showed the method to add the ability of understand human. The algorithm of acquiring and sharing taste information is not just information sharing but also the taste information is reuse depending on the environment believe that acquire in taste information is essential to build a system understanding human.

We plans to collect information that can be extracted from devices among as and develops inference with high accuracy to suggest more appropriate information.

Reference

[1] E. Sato, J. Kawakatsu, T. Yamaguchi, "Networked Intelligent Robots by Ontological Neural Networks", Knowledge-Based Intelligent Information & Engineering Systems, Pp1100-1106 (2004 9/20-9/25)
[2] NEDO, "NEDO:New Energy and Industrial Technology Development Organization," http://www.nedo.go.jp/english/index.html
[3] R.Mizoguchi, "Ontology:foundations and applications," Journal of Japanese Society for Artificial Intelligence, vol. 14, no. 6, 11 1999
[4] Toru Yamaguchi, "Networked Intelligence and Ontology", The 4th IEEE International Workshop WSTST'05 Muroran, Japan, Pp8-10 (2005 5/25-5/27).
[5] T. Yamaguchi, H. Murakami, D. Chen, "Human Centered Support System Using Intelligent Space and Ontological Network", Proc. Of Euro Symposium on CI(2002.6)
[6] T. Yamaguchi, E. Sato, Y. Takama: Intelligent Space and Human Centered Robotics, IEEE Transactions on Industrial Electronics, Vol.50, NO.5 pp.881-889 (2003)

Reduction of Rules of a Fuzzy Model with a Chain Model

Izabela Rejer

University of Szczecin, Faculty of Economics and Management
Mickiewicza 64/66, 71-101 Szczecin, Poland
i_rejer@uoo.univ.szczecin.pl

The aim of this article is to present a method which can be used for eliminating unnecessary rules from a rule base of a fuzzy model. Since the proposed method is based on a chain model of an analyzed system, it is dedicated specially for systems of a chain data distribution. The article presents both – the theoretical background of the method and its application in a real economic system – system of an unemployment rate in Poland in years 1992-1999.

Introduction

A large number of models built via soft-computing techniques are regarded as black-box models, it is as models which internal processes are hardly understandable for a human. Very often the only criterion which is taken into consideration in the process of building such models is an accuracy criterion. In situations when a model is built for automatic performing repeatable actions or calculations, such approach is often justifiable. However, when a model is built in order to support a human in the decision process or in order to explain the behavior of a real system, the accuracy criterion is not sufficient. A model which is constructed in order to support a human in his work should be not only precise but also highly intelligible. Since the interpretation difficulties increase with the model complexity, the model created to support a human should be as simple as possible.

Fuzzy and neuro-fuzzy models are very useful when a real system is to be described in the form of rules understandable for a human. Unfortunately both types of models in their classic form are very prone to the problem known as *curse of dimensionality*, which causes that even when a very small number of input variables described by a very small number of membership functions are used in the model, the resulting rule base can be too complex to be understandable for a human [6].

The *curse of dimensionality* problem is a very serious one but it does not discriminate the fuzzy and neuro-fuzzy models as useful tools for a decision process. The fact is that very often the rule base of a fuzzy model contains a lot of unnecessary rules which can be eliminated without the loss of the model precision. Obviously the problem is how to find out which rules of a fuzzy model are unnecessary ones. Theoretically the solution is simple – it should be enough to reveal which rules are not covered by any data point. In practice, however, such straightforward approach can have sometimes a very serious negative consequence – it can result in a non-continuous fuzzy model (in case of the outliers problem). Since a well design fuzzy model should be a continuous one, another approaches to eliminate unnecessary rules from a fuzzy model rule base should be applied.

The aim of this article is to introduce a method which can be used for identifying unnecessary rules of a fuzzy model but which does not leave the empty regions inside the model and hence, which can be used in case of the outliers problem. The method in its classic form is dedicated for a specific class of systems - chain systems.

A chain system is a system which is characterized by a chain data distribution in a whole domain. Due to this feature the chain system can be described not only by a surface model (e.g. fuzzy model) but also by a parametric curve which shows the very centre of the data distribution and which can be the base for determining the most dense region of data points. The knowledge of the region containing the vast majority of data points can be used to eliminate rules which are placed outside this region. With this approach it is impossible to obtain a non-continuous model because the chain model is always a continuous one.

The application of the method proposed in this article will be illustrated via a real economic system of an unemployment rate in Poland in years 1992-1999. The output variable of this system is *unemployment rate* and the input variables are: *money supply*, *number of inhabitants* and *dollar's rate of exchange*. The data for the survey was provided by the Polish Statistic Department.

The article consists of three main sections. First section addresses the issue of creating a parametric curve model. Second section presents the way of establishing the width of a region surrounding a parametric curve model containing the vast majority of training data. The last section explains the basis of the proposed method of rule reduction and presents its application in a real system.

Parametric curve model

As it was stated in introduction the proposed method of rule reduction is designed for chain systems. Hence, the first issue which should be addressed here is how to find out whether a system has a chain or a surface nature.

The main feature of a multi-dimensional chain system is that its decomposition into one-dimensional subspaces (showing the behavior of each system variable in regard to a parameter t - indicating the approximated data sequence) gives a set of tight chain dependences. Therefore, in order to verify whether a system is of a chain profile, the reverse analysis should be performed. Tight chain dependencies, visible on all two-dimensional graphs presenting the behavior of system variables in regard to t parameter, will indicate the chain profile of the whole system. Sometimes there can be a problem with establishing the approximated data sequence. This problem, however, does not exist when time series systems are under consideration. In this class of systems the parameter t can be interpreted as time variable, explicitly or implicitly given in the data set.

Figure 1 presents data distributions of four variables of the unemployment rate system, described in introduction, in regard to parameter t (which in this case can be interpreted as time). As it can be observed in the figure, all four variables are of a strict chain distribution which indicates that the whole system has also a chain profile.

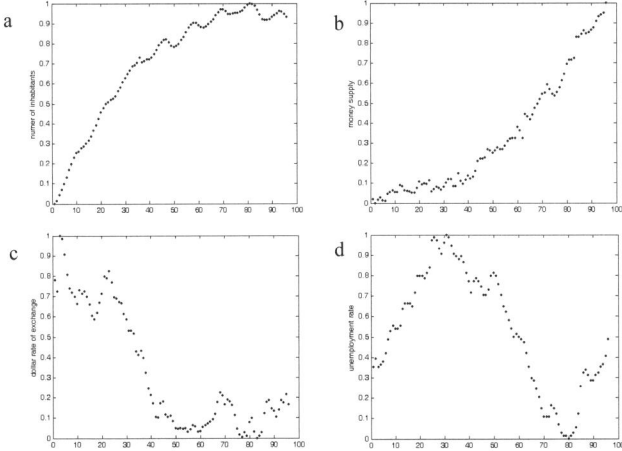

Fig. 1. Time series of the variables of the system of unemployment rate in Poland in years 1992-1999: a) money supply, b) number of inhabitants, c) dollar's rate of exchange, d) unemployment rate

The main benefit of the chain system is that it can be described not only by a surface model but also by a parametric curve [7]. The main idea of the parametric curve modeling method is to build a set of two-dimensional models, where each model describes the behavior of one variable (input or output) in regard to the known parameter *t*. These two-dimensional models can be created with many different mathematic techniques e.g. non-linear neural networks, polynomial regression, splines, etc. Two-dimensional models, built with one of the mentioned techniques, are then assembled together in order to create a multi-dimensional model describing the input-output mapping in the whole space (eq. 1) [2].

$$\begin{cases} x_1 = f_1(t) \\ x_2 = f_2(t) \\ \dots\dots\dots\dots \\ x_n = f_n(t) \end{cases} \quad (1)$$

In order to illustrate the process of parametric curve modeling, the 3D chain model of the unemployment rate was created (input variables: *money supply* and *number of inhabitants*). The neural networks of following parameters were used to build two-dimensional time series models of all system variables [3][5]:

– flow of signals: one-way,
– architecture of connections between layers: all to all,
– hidden layers: 1 hidden layer with suitable number of sigmoid neurons (5 for variable *number of inhabitants*, 3 for variable *money supply*, 4 *for variable unemployment rate*),
– output layer: 1 linear neuron,

- training method: backpropagation algorithm with momentum and changing learning rates,
- training aim: minimize mean absolute error (MAE),
- training time: 20000 epoch,
- testing method: visual control.

Models built with neural networks described above are shown in Fig. 2 (a, b, c). By assembling together all three models, the parametric curve model was created (fig. 2d). The approximated accuracy of this model was calculated using MAE (eq. 2) [1] and was equal to 2.28% [8].

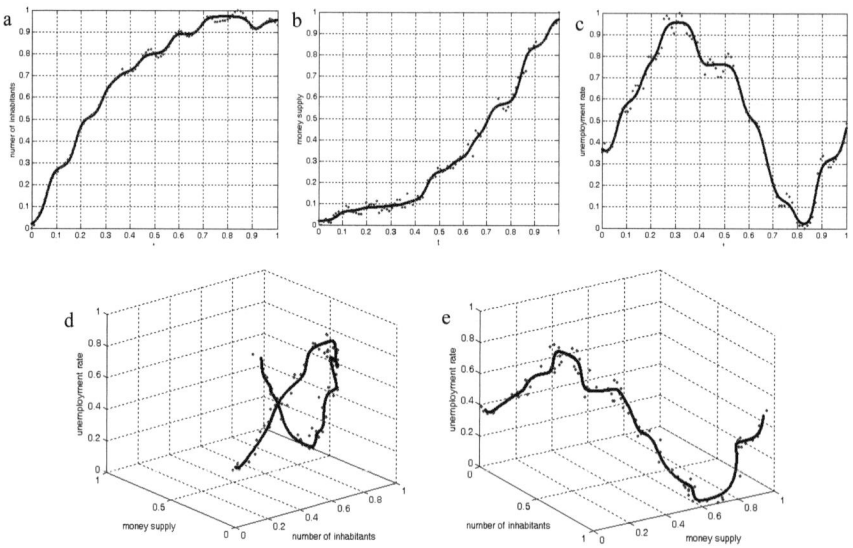

Fig. 2. Unemployment rate system: a, b, c) Two-dimensional time series models; d, e) Three-dimensional parametric curve model

$$MAE = \frac{\sum_{i=1}^{n} z_i^* - z_i}{n}, \tag{2}$$

where: z_i^* – empirical values, z_i – theoretical values, n – number of data points.

Interpolation region of a chain system

Two facts concerning systems of a chain data distribution are very helpful in a process of establishing the region covering most data points of the analyzed system:
1. The parametric curve model shows the very center of the data distribution in a multi-dimensional space.
2. Most data points of the analyzed system lay in a very close distance from the chain model.

Obviously, the knowledge of the center of data points is not sufficient to establish the region covering most data points of the analyzed system. The second point which has to be addressed is a width of this region in a multi-dimensional space. Assuming that the width of this region is the same in each direction, it can be calculated as a radius of a hypertube surrounding the chain model in a multi-dimensional space. In order to establish the radius of this hypertube, the distribution of the absolute distances between each training data point and the chain model, calculated in a multi-dimensional space, are considered. The radius is calculated on the base of three quartiles of this distribution (first, second and third) (eq. 3) [8].

$$R_h = Q3 + \min(Q1; Q2-Q1; Q3-Q2), \tag{3}$$

where: $Q1$ - first quartile (which indicates the region surrounding the chain model covered by 25% of data points), $Q2$ - second quartile (which indicates the region surrounding the chain model covered by 50% of data points), $Q3$ – third quartile (which indicates the region surrounding the chain model covered by 75% of data points), R_h - radius of the hypertube.

Figure 3 presents a hypertube surrounding the chain model of unemployment rate built earlier in this section. The radius of the hypertube, calculated on the basis of eq. 3, was equal to 0.0387. Figure 3a presents the hypertube in the whole system space and fig. 3b – presents its projection on the input space. Obviously for rule reduction algorithm the shape of the hypertube in the input space will be essential.

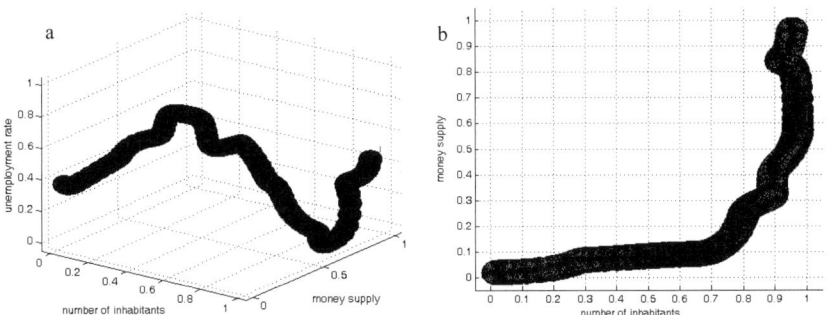

Fig. 3. Hypertube surrounding the chain model of an unemployment rate: a) in the whole system space, b) in the input space

Rule reduction algorithm

The basic idea of the proposed algorithm for rule reduction is to identify rules overlapping the hypertube in the input space. That means all rules which cover data points lying inside the hypertube have to be revealed. It is of no importance whether a rule covers a large number of data points or only one data point – it is essential to find out all appropriate rules. At the end of the search process the chosen rules are left in the model and the remaining ones are discarded.

In order to find out whether a rule overlaps a hypertube, the absolute distances between the boundaries of a rule hypercube and the chain model (which shows the center of the hypertube) in all input dimensions have to be calculated. If all distances are smaller than the hypertube radius, that means the rule overlaps the hypertube and should be left in the model. Obviously, only one of the two possible hypercube boundaries (this placed closer to the hypertube) is taken into account in each input dimension.

There seems to be more than one possibility of determining the rules which should be left in the model on the basis of the hypertube radius. The proposition of the author of this paper is as follows:
1. The chain model is equally sampled in a large number of points.
2. For each sample and for each input dimension:
   - two points are calculated – by adding and subtracting a hypertube radius to/from the sample,
   - the universe of membership functions is searched and two membership functions are chosen - these which intervals contain one of the two previously calculated points,
   - all membership functions situated between the two previously established functions are chosen,
3. The whole universe of rules is searched and the rules which all premises contain any of the membership functions chosen for succeeding dimensions are selected.

The application of the proposed method of rule reduction will be presented on the example of two neuro-fuzzy models of unemployment rate in Poland in years 1992-1999. The models parameters are as follows:
- input membership functions – asymmetrical triangular functions, 5 functions per each input variable (first model) 6 functions per each input variable (second model),
- output membership functions – singletons, 25 (first model) and 216 (second model),
- inference method – MIN-MAX,
- deffuzification method – height method,
- training method – backpropagation algorithm with momentum,
- training time: 10000 epochs.

Experiment one

The fuzzy model used in the first experiment contained two input variables: *number of inhabitants* and *money supply*. Figure 4 illustrates the surface of this model (fig. 4a) and its rule net in an input space (fig. 4b). The MAE of the model was equal to 3.90%.

As it can be noticed in fig. 4b, the rule base of the model was composed of 25 rules. In order to reduce this number, a chain model was built over the input space of the fuzzy model (fig. 5a) and an appropriate hypertube was created (fig. 5b). The hypertube radius was equal to 0.0387.

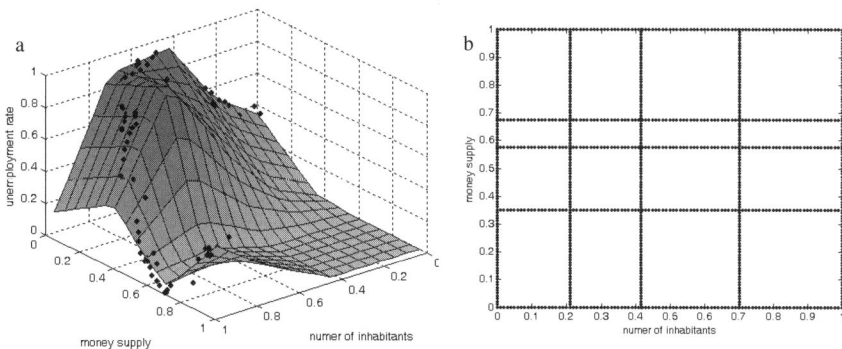

Fig. 4. Two-input fuzzy model of the unemployment rate: a) model surface; b) rule net

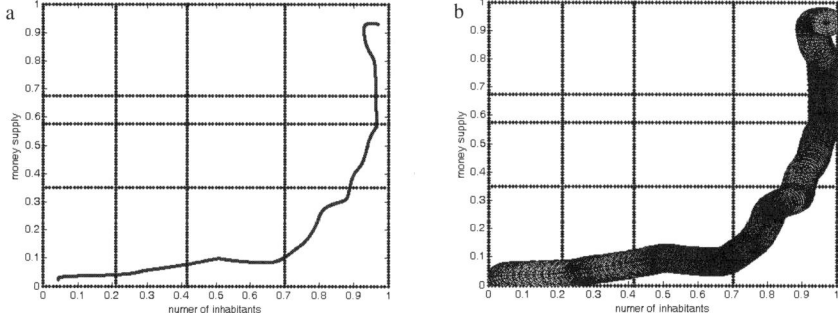

Fig. 5. Chain model (a) and the hypertube (b) over the rule net

According to the algorithm presented earlier in this section, the chain model was equally sampled in 1000 points. Then the hypertube radius was added and subtracted to and from all samples in all dimensions and appropriate set of border membership functions for each dimension was established. Numbers of the chosen membership functions are presented in tab. 1. Next, the set of chosen membership functions was expanded by adding (for each input dimension) membership functions situated between the border ones. And finally, the universe of rules was searched and the rules which premises (in all dimensions) contain any of the membership functions chosen for succeeding dimensions were determined. Figure 6 presents the set of rules which were left in the model after applying the proposed algorithm and tab. 2 presents the numbers of membership functions used in both rule premises in succeeding rules.

The MAE of the fuzzy model containing the reduced rule base was equal to 3.90%. This error value (equal to the value of the original model – 3.90%) proves that all important rules were left in the rule base and that the whole model can be regarded as a complete one. Since one of the most important features of the proposed algorithm is that it discards rules supported by remote outliers, in some applications a very slight difference in both models errors can appear. This difference is a result of leaving some data points (possible outliers) outside the hypertube boundaries.

Table 1. Numbers of border membership functions in both input dimensions

Number of inhabitants		Money supply	
1st border function	2nd border function	1st border function	2nd border function
1	5	1	2
4	5	1	5

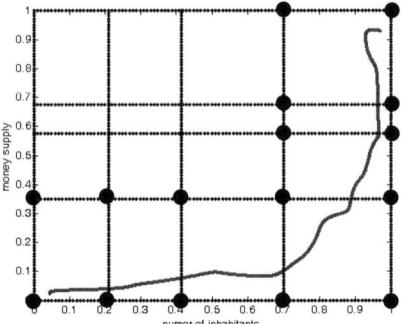

Fig. 6. Rules left in the rule base of the two-input fuzzy model

Table 2. Numbers of membership functions used in the premises of rules left in the two-input fuzzy model

Rule number	Premise 1 Number of inhabitants	Premise 2 Money supply
1	1	1
2	1	2
3	2	1
4	2	2
5	3	1
6	3	2
7	4	1
8	4	2
9	4	3
10	4	4
11	4	5
12	5	1
13	5	2
14	5	3
15	5	4
16	5	5

The application of the proposed method for rule reduction allowed to eliminate 9 out of 25 rules contained in the rule base of the unemployment rate model. That means 36% of rules were identified as unnecessary ones and eliminated from the model. This result is a significant one but far more spectaculars results can be achieved when systems of more input variables are regarded.

Experiment two

The fuzzy model used in the second experiment contained three input variables: *number of inhabitants*, *money supply* and *dollar's rate of exchange*. The parameters of the model were almost the same as described in previous section. The only difference was in the number of input membership functions which was equal to 6 (per each input), and the number of output membership functions which was equal to 216. The model error, after completing the learning process, was equal to 2.63%.

Before starting the algorithm of rule reduction, a chain model of input variables of the analyzed system was constructed and the hypertube radius was established (R_h = 0.097). Then the succeeding steps of the proposed algorithm were applied. After completing the algorithm, the rule base of the original fuzzy model was reduced from 216 to 78 rules. That means the proposed method for rule reduction allowed to identify 138 rules (64%) as unnecessary ones. The MAE of the fuzzy model containing the reduced rule base was exactly the same as the MAE of the base model – it was equal to 2.63%.

Conclusion

The aim of this article was to present a method which can be used for rule reduction of a fuzzy model. The main advantages of the proposed method are as follows:

- The reduction rate is a significant one (in presented applications it was equal to 36% and 64%) which is very important not only when a model is used in its software version as a tool supporting a human but also when a model is a base for hardware implementation.
- The resulting models have the same rate of precision as the non-reduced ones. That means the algorithm eliminates rules which are really unnecessary and do not take part in the inference process.
- The models obtained after applying the proposed method are continuous ones.
- The method allows the researcher to identify and discard rules which are supported by data points situated outside the main data stream (possible outliers).

Although, the practical application of the proposed method was illustrated via a time series system, it is absolutely not limited to them. This is due to the fact that chain models, used in the method, can be constructed not only for time series systems but also for any kind of systems of a chain data distribution in which the data sequence can be established.

References

[1] Aczel, A. D.: Complete Business Statistics, Richard D. Irwin Inc., Sydney (1993)
[2] Bronsztejn I.N., Siemiendiajew K.A., Musiol G., Mühlig H.: Modern Compendium of Mathematic, Polish Science Publisher Warsaw (2004)
[3] Demuth, H., Beale, M.: Neural Network Toolbox User's Guide, The Math Works Inc., Natick MA USA (2000)
[4] Klesk P.: The method of setting suitable extrapolation capabilities for neuro–fuzzy models of multi–dimensional systems", PhD Thesis, Technical University of Szczecin, 2005.
[5] Masters, T.: Practical Neural Networks Recipes in C++, Academic Press Inc (1993)
[6] Piegat, A.: Fuzzy Modeling and Control, Physica-Verlag, New York (1999)
[7] Piegat A., Rejer I. Mikołajczyk M.: Application of Neural Networks in Chain Curve Modelling, Artificial Intelligence and Soft Computing ICAISC 2006 - Lectures Notes in Artificial Intelligence, Springer-Verlag, Berlin (2006) (in publishing)
[8] Rejer I, Mikołajczyk M.: A Hypertube as a Possible Interpolation Region of a Neural Model, Artificial Intelligence and Soft Computing ICAISC 2006 - Lectures Notes in Artificial Intelligence, Springer-Verlag, Berlin (2006) (in publishing)

Singleton Representation of Fuzzy Set for Computing Fuzzy Model Response for Fuzzy Inputs

Karina Murawko-Wiśniewska[1], Andrzej Piegat[1]

[1] Szczecin University of Technology, Żołnierska 49, 71-210 Szczecin, Poland
{KMurawko, APiegat}@wi.ps.pl

Abstract. Classical fuzzy model computes a crisp response for crisp inputs. This paper presents a method for computing fuzzy model response for fuzzy inputs. The method is based on singleton representation of a fuzzy set and it enables to obtain fuzzy response for fuzzy inputs. The presented method is compared with alternative approaches: Zadeh's possibilistic method and method based on similarity measure. The validity of the proposed method is illustrated with experimental results (in comparison with extension principle results).

1. Introduction

There are different types of data in the real world: precise (numerical) data and uncertain data. Numerical data, collected with precise measuring instruments, can be analysed and processed by numerical mathematical methods. Uncertainty of the data can be caused by e.g. imprecision of sensor (human notions) or an attribute that is not quantifiable. Fuzzy set concept, introduced by Zadeh in 1965 [14], is a useful tool for a formal representation of uncertain information. Fuzzy set models the value of a linguistic variable. In [17] Zadeh distinguishes four cases which underlie the use of linguistic variables: bounded ability of sensory organs to resolve and store detail information (e.g. brain), numerical information may not be available, an attribute is not quantifiable, there is a tolerance for imprecision.

Table 1. Illustrative example: a mixed data set which describes flats for sale

x_1 – price [€]	x_2 – total area [m^2]	x_3 – building age [years]	x_4 – flat standard	x_5 – location attractiveness
140000	31	26	high	average
265000	87	76	low	high
160000	42	23	average	low
205000	63	7	very high	average

Illustrative example (Table 1): a data set describes flats for sale, each row contains values of five attributes. Three of them are numerical variables (price, total area, building age); others are linguistic variables (flat standard, location attractiveness). Values of the linguistic variables (x_4, x_5) can not be measured precisely. Assigning each of those linguistic values to one precise (numerical) value or removing variables x_4, x_5 would be an oversimplification which would cause loss of information. Developing methods which process mixed data (precise and uncertain) would enable the use of the whole available data.

Major applications of fuzzy set theory are fuzzy modeling and control, their development started with papers of Zadeh [15], Mamdani and Assilian [6]. Classical fuzzy model [11], [12] consists of three main blocks: fuzzification, inference and defuzzification (Fig. 1). It computes a crisp (numerical) output of the model for crisp inputs. Therefore it is not possible to compute an output of classical fuzzy model when any input is uncertain (fuzzy). Despite the dynamic development of fuzzy modeling research field, only a few papers concerning fuzzy models and controllers with fuzzy inputs have been published. In [1], the design of inverse controller for fuzzy interval systems is exploited. In [10], a linguistic approach to the design of fuzzy granular models is concerned. In [5], the theory and design of interval type-2 fuzzy logic systems are presented.

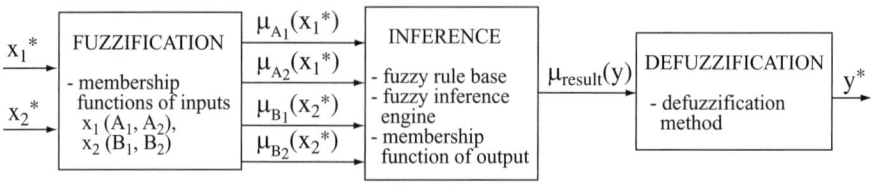

Fig. 1. Structure of an exemplary fuzzy model with two inputs and a single output [11]

The purpose of this study is to develop a method for computing fuzzy model response for fuzzy inputs based on singleton representation of a fuzzy set. The key idea of our approach is to compute fuzzy model output for each singleton representing input fuzzy set and combine the results into an output fuzzy set. The main advantage of this approach is to enable computing the output of fuzzy model both for fuzzy inputs and mixed (numerical and fuzzy) inputs (using the classical fuzzy model without modification). The paper is organized as follows. In section 2, alternative approaches to the problem are presented. In section 3, we apply the singleton representation to computing fuzzy model response for fuzzy inputs. Section 4 shows results of experiments. Finally, conclusions are given in section 5.

2. A review of methods for computing fuzzy model output for fuzzy input

In the approach proposed in [16]: Zadeh's possibilistic method, used for computing with linguistic variables, fuzzy set A is compared with fuzzy sets describing the linguistic variable (A_i) and for each set μ_i is given by

$$\mu_i = \sup(A_i \cap A).$$

(1)

This method describes with a single crisp value (maximal possibility) how much set A is similar to set A_i. The use of the method to compute fuzzy model output for fuzzy inputs results in the crisp output to be received.

The next approach involves similarity measures. Many similarity measures of fuzzy sets have been proposed in the literature [9], [2], [13], [3]. The commonly used similarity measure, proposed by Pappis and Karacapilidis [9], for two fuzzy sets A and B (with continuous membership functions) is defined by

$$S(A,B) = \frac{|A \cap B|}{|A \cup B|} = \frac{\displaystyle\int_{x\,min}^{x\,max} \min(\mu_A(x), \mu_B(x))dx}{\displaystyle\int_{x\,min}^{x\,max} \max(\mu_A(x), \mu_B(x))dx}, \tag{2}$$

where $|A|$ – denotes cardinality of fuzzy set A; $xmin$, $xmax$ are the boundaries of universe of discourse X. The use of similarity measures of fuzzy sets for computing fuzzy model response has been presented in [7]. Similarity measure is used in fuzzification to specify similarity between fuzzy value of input and fuzzy sets describing the fuzzy variable. The model response is non-fuzzy (crisp) value and it depends on the chosen similarity measure.

In the presented approaches fuzzy model response for fuzzy inputs is a crisp value. It is not what one would expect: though input value is fuzzy (uncertain), the output is non-fuzzy.

3. Using Singleton Representation of Fuzzy Set for Computing Fuzzy Model Response for Fuzzy Input

There are different representations of fuzzy set in the literature. For example, in discrete universe of discourse $X=\{x_1,...,x_n\}$ fuzzy set $A \subseteq X$ can be represented by

$$A = \frac{\mu_A(x_1)}{x_1} + \frac{\mu_A(x_2)}{x_2} + ... + \frac{\mu_A(x_n)}{x_n} = \sum_{i=1}^{n} \frac{\mu_A(x_i)}{x_i}. \tag{3}$$

It is the singleton (vertical) representation of a fuzzy set [11], [12,] [4]. Fuzzy set with continuous membership function (X – continuous universe of discourse) is given by

$$A = \int_X \frac{\mu_A(x)}{x}. \tag{4}$$

For any input fuzzy set the fuzzy model response can be computed using the singleton representation. First, fuzzy set is represented by set of singletons (3), therefore fuzzy set with continuous membership functions is discretized. The idea of discretizing the continuous membership functions of fuzzy sets and the use of discrete representation of fuzzy sets in fuzzy arithmetical operations is presented in [4]. The range of singletons for exemplary fuzzy set A is shown in Fig. 2. The singleton s_3, $\mu(s_3)=1$, has the widest representation range, whereas boundary singletons s_1 and s_5 ($\mu(s_1)= \mu(s_5)=0$) have the range reduced to a point.

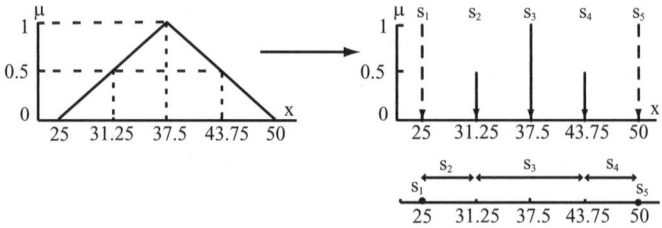

Fig. 2. Fuzzy set A="about 37.5" in continuous and singleton representation

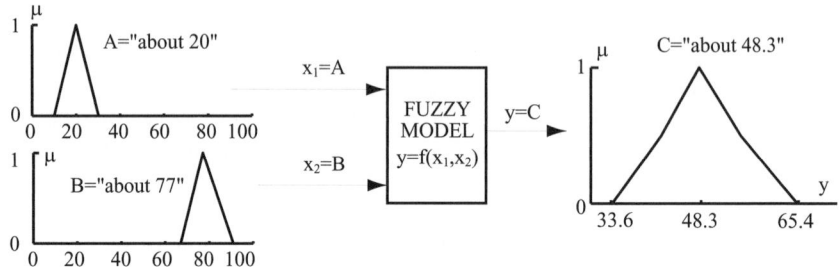

Fig. 3. Computing fuzzy model response for two input fuzzy values

For each singleton of input fuzzy set the model response is computed. Then the output fuzzy set is created with the use of extension principle: the fuzzy model is represented by a mapping $f: X \rightarrow Y$ and for any fuzzy set $A \subseteq X$ fuzzy set $B = f(A)$ is defined by

$$B = f(A) = \{(y, \mu_B(y)) | y = f(x), x \in X\}, \tag{5}$$

where

$$\mu_B(y) = \begin{cases} \sup_{x \in X, y=f(x)} \mu_A(x) \\ 0, \quad \text{else} \end{cases}. \tag{6}$$

If X is the Cartesian product $X_1 \times X_2 \times ... \times X_n$, the fuzzy model is represented by a mapping $f: X_1 \times X_2 \times ... \times X_n \rightarrow Y$, for any fuzzy sets $A_1 \subseteq X_1$, $A_2 \subseteq X_2$, ..., $A_n \subseteq X_n$, fuzzy set $B = f(A_1, A_2 ..., A_n)$ is defined by

$$B = f(A_1, ..., A_n) = \{(y, \mu_B(y)) | y = f(x_1, ..., x_n), (x_1, ..., x_n) \in X\}, \tag{7}$$

where

$$\mu_B(y) = \begin{cases} \sup_{(x_1, ..., x_n) \in X, y=f(x_1, ..., x_n)} \min\{\mu_{A_1}(x_1), ..., \mu_{A_n}(x_n)\} \\ 0, \quad \text{else} \end{cases}. \tag{8}$$

In (8) minimum operation can be replaced by other t-norm (e.g. algebraic product).

Example: fuzzy model with two inputs x_1 and x_2 is given. The values of inputs can not be measured precisely, though the expert describes them with fuzzy sets: A="about 20" and B="about 77". To compute fuzzy model response, input fuzzy sets $x_1=A$ and $x_2=B$ with continuous membership functions are replaced by singleton representation. Next, for each pair of singletons of A and B an output of the model is computed. For each output singleton its membership function value μ_C is computed (where fuzzy set $C=f(A,B)$), and if the output singletons for two pairs of input singletons are the same the maximum membership is chosen according to (9). The result of the computation is fuzzy set C="about 48.3" (Fig. 3)

4. Experiments

In this section we present the results of using proposed method to compute fuzzy model response for fuzzy inputs. The synthetic data set that contains fuzzy sets (Fig. 7) is used as inputs in 10 experiments. The computations are done with two classical fuzzy models designed for functions f_1 (9) and f_2 (10). The known functions are used to enable comparison of the proposed method with other approaches. The models have two inputs (x_1, x_2) and an output (y). Fuzzy sets of inputs and output of both models: A_i, B_j, C_k $(i,j, =1,..,5;$ model 1: $k=1,...,10;$ model 2: $k=1,...,16)$, are shown at Fig. 5 (A_i for x_1 and B_j for x_2). The rules used in the models are given in the following form: "IF $x_1=A_i$ AND $x_2=B_j$ THEN $y=C_k$". The rule bases of model 1 and model 2 are given in Table 1. The inference engines are MAX-MIN type and defuzzification is done by height method.

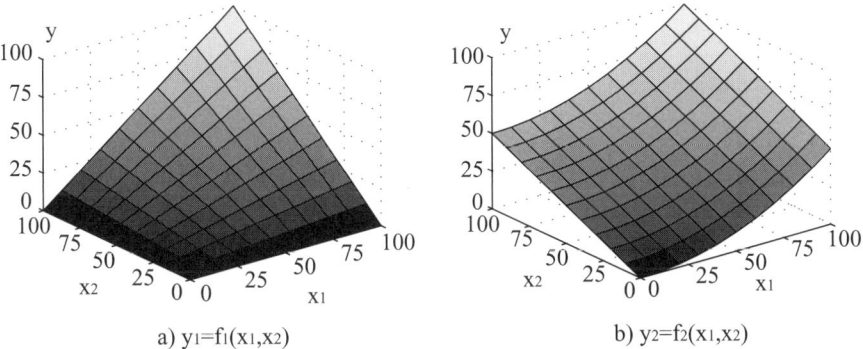

a) $y_1=f_1(x_1,x_2)$ b) $y_2=f_2(x_1,x_2)$

Fig. 4. The surfaces of the mappings used in experiments

Fig. 4 shows the surfaces of the functions used in experiments, function f_1 is used in experiments no. 1-7 and 9. Function f_2 is used in experiments no. 8 and 10. The functions f_1 and f_2 are defined as follows

$$y_1 = f_1(x_1,x_2) = \frac{x_1 \cdot x_2}{100} \qquad (9)$$

and

$$y_2 = f_2(x_1, x_2) = \left(\frac{x_1^2}{100} + x_2\right) / 2 . \tag{10}$$

Based on functions f_1 and f_2 two fuzzy models are designed, their surfaces are shown in Fig. 6. The values of variables x_1, x_2, y_1, y_2 belong to the interval <0;100>.

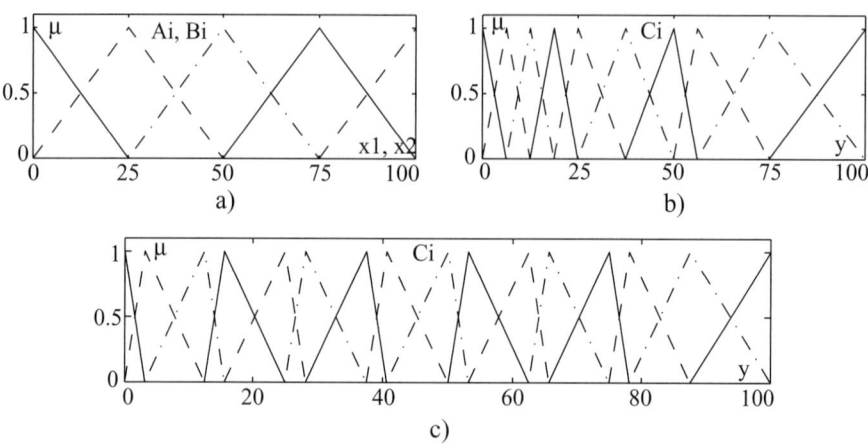

Fig. 5. Fuzzy sets of inputs (a), output of model 1 (b) and output of model 2 (c)

Table 2. The rule bases of model 1 and model 2

MODEL 1					
x_2 \ x_1	A_1	A_2	A_3	A_4	A_5
B_1	C_1	C_1	C_1	C_1	C_1
B_2	C_1	C_2	C_3	C_4	C_5
B_3	C_1	C_3	C_5	C_6	C_7
B_4	C_1	C_4	C_6	C_8	C_9
B_5	C_1	C_5	C_7	C_9	C_{10}

MODEL 2					
x_2 \ x_1	A_1	A_2	A_3	A_4	A_5
B_1	C_1	C_2	C_3	C_6	C_9
B_2	C_3	C_4	C_5	C_8	C_{11}
B_3	C_5	C_6	C_7	C_{10}	C_{13}
B_4	C_7	C_8	C_9	C_{12}	C_{15}
B_5	C_9	C_{10}	C_{11}	C_{14}	C_{16}

In each experiment the input values are two fuzzy sets: $x_1=F_1$ and $x_2=F_2$ (Fig. 7), their singleton representations are given in Table 2. Firstly extension principle is used for computing fuzzy sets $F_3=f_1(F_1,F_2)$, $F_4=f_2(F_1,F_2)$, which are reference results (results of other methods are compared with them). Then the singleton representations of input fuzzy sets F_1 and F_2 are used for computing fuzzy model response (model 1 and 2): Y_1, Y_2 (fuzzy values). Finally Zadeh's possibilistic method and similarity measure method are used for computing fuzzy model response in form of a singleton (crisp value, accordingly z and s).

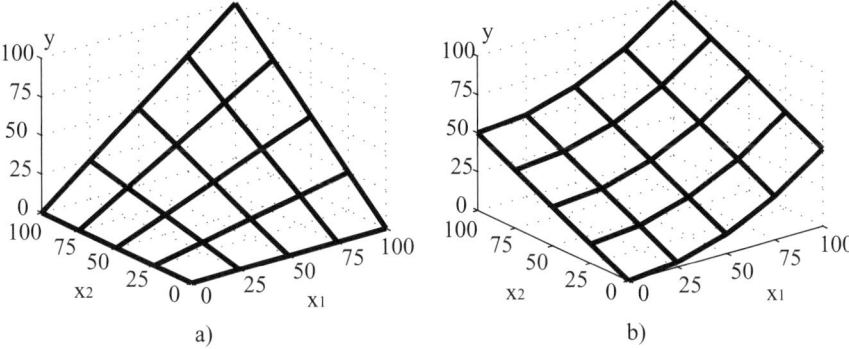

Fig. 6. The surfaces of fuzzy models: (a) – model 1, (b) – model 2

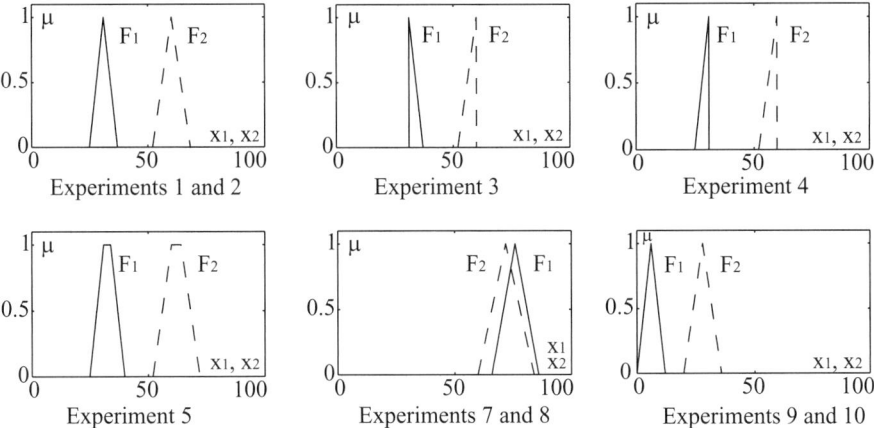

Fig. 7. Input fuzzy sets x_1–F_1 and x_2=F_2; in experiment no. 6: x_1=A_3 and x_2=B_2

Table 3. Singleton representations of input fuzzy sets F_1 and F_2

Experiment No.	Singleton Representation	
	F_1	F_2
1	$F_1 = \frac{0}{25} + \frac{0.5}{28} + \frac{1}{31} + \frac{0.5}{34} + \frac{0}{37}$	$F_2 = \frac{0}{52} + \frac{0.5}{56} + \frac{1}{60} + \frac{0.5}{64} + \frac{0}{68}$
2	$F_1 = \frac{0}{25} + \frac{1}{31} + \frac{0}{37}$	$F_2 = \frac{0}{52} + \frac{1}{60} + \frac{0}{68}$
3	$F_1 = \frac{1}{31} + \frac{0.5}{34} + \frac{0}{37}$	$F_2 = \frac{0}{52} + \frac{0.5}{56} + \frac{1}{60}$
4	$F_1 = \frac{0}{25} + \frac{0.5}{28} + \frac{1}{31}$	$F_2 = \frac{0}{52} + \frac{0.5}{56} + \frac{1}{60}$
5	$F_1 = \frac{0}{25} + \frac{0.5}{28} + \frac{1}{31} + \frac{1}{34} + \frac{0.5}{37} + \frac{0}{40}$	$F_2 = \frac{0}{52} + \frac{0.5}{56} + \frac{1}{60} + \frac{1}{64} + \frac{0.5}{68} + \frac{0}{72}$
6	$F_1 = \frac{0}{25} + \frac{0.5}{37.5} + \frac{1}{50} + \frac{0.5}{62.5} + \frac{0}{75}$	$F_2 = \frac{0}{0} + \frac{0.5}{12.5} + \frac{1}{25} + \frac{0.5}{37.5} + \frac{0}{50}$
7, 8	$F_1 = \frac{0}{66} + \frac{0.5}{71} + \frac{1}{76} + \frac{0.5}{81} + \frac{0}{86}$	$F_2 = \frac{0}{60} + \frac{0.5}{66} + \frac{1}{72} + \frac{0.5}{78} + \frac{0}{84}$
9, 10	$F_1 = \frac{0}{0} + \frac{0.5}{3} + \frac{1}{6} + \frac{0.5}{9} + \frac{0}{12}$	$F_2 = \frac{0}{20} + \frac{0.5}{24} + \frac{1}{28} + \frac{0.5}{32} + \frac{0}{36}$

Table 4. Comparison of the results: modal values of fuzzy sets computed with extension principle (EP) and computed by fuzzy models with singleton representation (SFM); crisp values of fuzzy model response computed using possibilistic method (MP) and similarity measure method (SM)

No.	EP (F_3, F_4)	SFM (Y_1, Y_2)	MP (z)	SM (s)
1	18.6	20.3	21.4	19.9
2	18.6	20.3	21.4	19.9
3	18.6	20.3	21.7	21.5
4	18.6	20.3	19.8	18.5
5	20.2	21.34	22.1	20.53
6	12.5	12.5	8.9	12.2
7	54.7	54.6	55.3	56.7
8	64.9	65.4	66.9	68.1
9	1.7	2.4	3.0	2.3
10	14.2	15.8	15.9	15.2

Singleton values computed with the use of similarity measure method in most of the experiments are proximal to the modal values of fuzzy sets computed with extension principle then singleton values computed with the use of Zadeh's possibilistic method. Both methods' results are crisp values: the information about uncertainty is lost in computations.

On the contrary, computing fuzzy model response with singleton representation preserves data uncertainty. The shapes of resulting fuzzy sets F_3/F_4 and Y_1/Y_2 are also similar (Fig. 8). Results of the proposed method depend on the number of singletons in the representation and precision of the model. The best performance (experiment no. 6) is obtained for input fuzzy sets with modal values in the nodes of the model (in nodes the error of both fuzzy models used in experiments is zero).

5. Conclusions

In this paper we proposed a method for computing fuzzy model response for fuzzy inputs. The method is consistent with extension principle, where the model is represented by a mapping f. It can be used for computing fuzzy model response for any number of input fuzzy sets and also for mixed input data (fuzzy and crisp) and no modification of the model is necessary. If any input is a fuzzy value the model response is a fuzzy set. The experimental results demonstrated that usage of this method provides fuzzy output for fuzzy inputs, analogical to results of computing fuzzy values using extension principle. The shapes of resulting fuzzy sets for both computing methods are also similar. In real world, when data are often mixed types, the proposed method can be useful for computing fuzzy model response for mixed inputs. In the future, we plan to focus on fuzzy model design based on mixed input-output data (crisp and fuzzy).

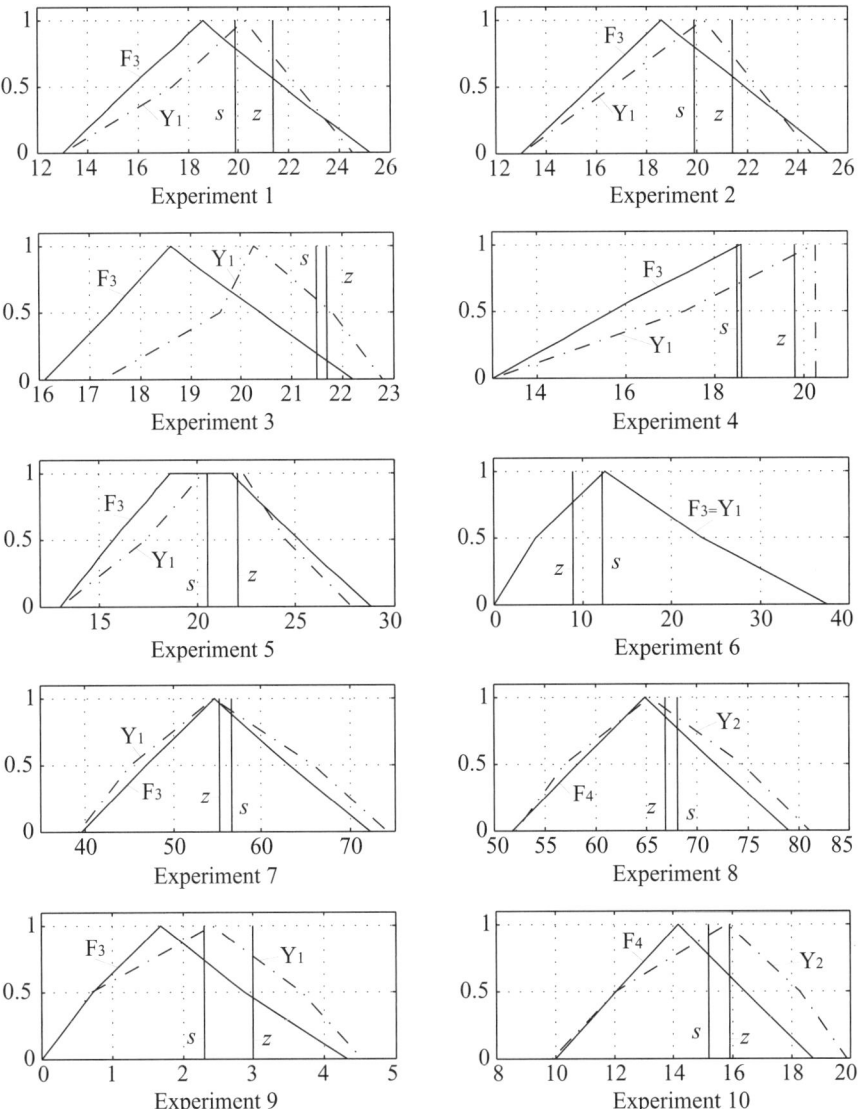

Fig. 8. The graphical presentation of the results: (F_3, F_4) – extension principle result, (Y_1, Y_2) – fuzzy model response, s – the result of method based on similarity, z – the result of possibilistic method

References

[1] Boukezzoula, R., Foulloy, L., Galichet, S.: Inverse Controller Design for Fuzzy Interval Systems. IEEE Trans. Fuzzy Syst. 14 (2006) 111- 124

[2] Chen, S.-M., Yeh, M.-S., Hsiao, P.-Y.: A comparison of similarity measures of fuzzy values. Fuzzy Sets Syst. 72 (1995) 79-89

[3] Fan, J., Xie, W.: Some notes on similarity measure and proximity measure. Fuzzy Sets Syst. 101 (1999) 403-412

[4] Hanss, M.: Applied Fuzzy Arithmetic - An Introduction with Engineering Applications, Springer-Verlag, Berlin Heidelberg New York (2005)

[5] Liang, Q., Mendel, J.M.: Interval type-2 fuzzy logic systems: Theory and design. IEEE Trans. Fuzzy Syst. 8 (2000) 535-550

[6] Mamdani, E.H., Assilian, S.: An Experiment in Linguistic Synthesis with a Fuzzy Logic Controller. Int. J. Man-Machine Stud. 7 (1975) 1-13

[7] Murawko-Wiśniewska, K., Piegat, A.: The Structure of fuzzy model based on mixed data (In Polish). Roczniki Informatyki Stosowanej WI PS Nr 9 (2005) 107-113

[8] Palm, R., Driankov, D.: Fuzzy inputs. Fuzzy Sets Syst. 70 (1995) 315-335

[9] Pappis, C.P., Karacapilidis, N.I.: A comparative assessment of measures of similarity of fuzzy values. Fuzzy Sets Syst. 56 (1993) 171-174

[10] Pedrycz, W., Vasilakos, A.V.: Linguistic models and linguistic modeling. IEEE Trans. Syst., Man, Cybern. B. 29 (1999) 745-757

[11] Piegat, A.: Fuzzy modeling and control (In Polish). Akademicka Oficyna Wydawnicza EXIT, Warsaw, Poland (1999)

[12] Rutkowski, L.: Methods and techniques of artificial intelligence (In Polish). Wydawnictwo Naukowe PWN, Warsaw, Poland (2005)

[13] Wang, W.-J.: New similarity measures on fuzzy sets and on elements. Fuzzy Sets Syst. 85 (1997) 305-309

[14] Zadeh, L.A.: Fuzzy Sets. Inform. Control. 8 (1965) 338-353

[15] Zadeh, L.A.: Outline of a New Approach to the Analysis of Complex Systems and Decision Processes. IEEE Trans. Syst., Man and Cybern. 3 (1973) 28-44

[16] Zadeh, L.A.: From computing with numbers to computing with words - from manipulation of measurements to manipulation of perceptions. IEEE Trans. Circuits Syst. 45 (1999) 105-119

[17] Zadeh, L.A.: Toward a generalized theory of uncertainty (GTU) – an outline. Information Sciences 172 (2005) 1-40

Tuning of Parameters Backstepping Ship Course Controller by Genetic Algorithm

Anna Witkowska[**], Roman Smierzchalski[*]

[*]Gdynia Maritime University, Marine Electrical Engineering Faculty
ul. Morska 83, 81-225 Gdynia,
[**]Gdansk University of Technology, Electrical and Control Engineering Faculty
ul. Narutowicza 11/12, 80-952 Gdansk
e-mail: apuszcz@ely.pg.gda.pl, roms@am.gdynia.pl

Abstract. A ship, as an object for course control, is characterised by a nonlinear function describing the static maneuvering characteristics. One of the methods which can be used for designing a nonlinear course controller for ships is the backstepping method. It was used here for designing the configurations of nonlinear controllers, which were then applied for ship course control. The parameters of the obtained nonlinear control structures were tuned to optimise the operation of the control system. The optimisation was performed using genetic algorithms. The quality of operation of the designed control algorithms was checked in simulation tests performed on the mathematical model of the tanker completed by steering gear.

1. Introduction

In recent ten to twenty years a number of new methods were developed for designing controllers to control nonlinear dynamic systems. These are usually recursive methods, such as backstepping, forwarding, and methods being the mixture of these two. A common concept in these two recursive methods is the design of a globally stable control system, revealing a cascade structure, for a class of nonlinear dynamic systems. In particular, the backstepping method is bases on the Lapunov function theory [La_Salle 1966] but its origin can be found in some theories of linear control, such as the feedback linearisation method, or the LQR method.

The beginning of development of the backstepping method oriented on the design of a nonlinear control systems can be dated on the turn of Eighties and Nineties of the last century, a list and discussion of publications issued in that time can be found in an overview by Kokotović and Arcak [Kokotovic 2001], and also in Fossen [Fossen 2002] and in fundamentally book of backstepping methods [Krstic 1995].The backstepping method directly bases on the mathematical model of the examined system, introducing to it new variables in the form depending of the state variables, controlling parameters, and stabilising functions. The task of a stabilising function is to compensate non-linearities that occur in the system and affect the stability of its operation. The linearisation methods used in the feedback-based systems usually aim at eliminating the non-linearities in the system. The use of the backstepping method makes it possible to form, in an arbitrary way, additional nonlinearities and introduce them to the control system. However, only the undesirable nonlinearities are eliminated from the system [Fossen 1998]. The backstepping method allows to obtain a global stability in cases when the feedback linearisation method only secures local stability.

In marine technology, the presented backstepping method was used in systems steering a ship on its course [Do 2004, Pettersen 2004], to secure course stabilisation. In 1999, Fossen published a work [Fossen 1999], which focuses on practical use of the backstepping method in mechanical systems and its application to ship steering. However, attempts to apply this method in real marine systems revealed numerous problems which needed solving. One of them is the structure and selection of stabilisation functions and identification of their parameters. In order to obtain optimal quality of control of the designed nonlinear course controller, its parameters need tuning. The presented in the literature design systems that make use of the beckstepping method are optimised using classical methods, usually based on the solution of the Riccati equation [Ezal 2000; Krstic 1999].

The article presents the method of automatic optimisation of ship course controller parameters, performed with the aid of a genetic algorithm. So far, this technique has not been employed to solve such kind of problems. The operation of the genetic algorithm bases on generating solutions by imitating the evolutionary process [Goldberg 1989], [Michalewicz 1996].

2. Model of the ship

The geometry of the ship motion is defined in the coordinate system X_o, Y_o, while the motion of the ship itself is described in the relative coordinate system (x,y), fixed to the ship. Motion of the ship is shown in Fig. 1. The control system discussed in the article was designed for steering a ship on the course. In the system, the controlled parameter is the ship course, $\psi(t)$, while the controlling parameter is the rudder angle, $\delta(t)$. The equations describing dynamical characteristics of the ship were derived from Newtonian dynamics laws. It was assumed that for large displacement ships, tankers for instance, transverse movements can be neglected. In the presented investigations, the mathematical model of dynamical characteristics of the ship was assumed that of a model tanker described by Astrom and Wittenmark in „Adaptive Control" [Astrom 1989, Amerongen 1982] and modelled by a nonlinear second-order differential equation, referred to as the Norrbin model [Amerongen1982].

The obtained model is given by the following equation

$$T \cdot \ddot{\psi}(t) + H_N(\dot{\psi}(t)) = K\delta(t). \tag{1}$$

Function $H_N(\dot{\psi}(t)) = \dfrac{\alpha}{\beta}\dot{\psi}^3(t) + \beta\dot{\psi}(t)$ expresses the steady-state relation between

$\delta(t)$ and $\dot{\psi}(t)$. The parameters α and β are real constants and determined from the "spiral test", taking values $\alpha = \beta = 1$ in the model. The parameters $T = T_0(L/u)$, where $T_0 = T_{10} + T_{20} - T_{30}$ and K was determined from relation (2).

$$K = K_0 \left(\frac{u}{L} \right), \; T_i = T_{i0} \left(\frac{L}{u} \right), \quad i = 1,2,3 \, . \tag{2}$$

The model parameters were determined at speed $u = 5$ [m/s]. The length of the examined tanker is $L = 350$ [m]. In the article, the tanker in two loading states is examined. The first state is the ship without cargo (liquid), in this case ballast tanks are filled with water and it is a so called the ballasting state. For the examined tanker in this loading state the model parameters take the values:

$$K_0 = 5.88, \qquad T_{10} = -16.91, \qquad T_{20} = 0.45, \qquad T_{30} = 1.43.$$

The second state of operation refers to the tanks fully laden with the transported liquid and bears the name of the full load state. In this case the model parameters take the values:

$$K_0 = 0.83, \qquad T_{10} = -2.88, \qquad T_{20} = 0.38, \qquad T_{30} = 1.07.$$

The model of dynamic characteristics of the ship was completed by the model of the steering gear, described by [Velagić 2003] and schematically shown in Fig. 2. In this article it was assumed that the rate of rudder motion is approximately limited to $\dot{\delta}_{max} = 6$ [deg/s] until $|\delta_z - \delta| \le 3$ [deg], when the rudder operates in the linear region of the characteristic. The maximum rudder angle is $\delta_{max} = 35$ [deg]. For this assumption the steering gear dynamical characteristic was given by the following equation (3), in which $T_R = 156$ [s] and $K_R = 96$ [deg].

$$\dot{\delta}(t) = \frac{K_R}{T_R} \delta_z(t) - \frac{1}{T_R} \delta(t) \cdot \tag{3}$$

The discussed model of dynamic characteristics of the tanker, and the model of the steering gear, were modelled in Matlab/Simulink.

3. Designing nonlinear controllers

As mentioned before, the controller was designed using the backstepping method. When designing the steering rules with the aid of this method, new state variables z_i and stabilising functions α_i are introduced, in a recurrence way, in i-th step. The number of steps depends on the number of state variables used in the mathematical model of the examined object.

In the present article, the backstepping method was used for developing two algorithms of nonlinear ship course control (nonlinear controllers), denoted as version A and version B. The form of dynamical characteristics of the ship used in version A and B for deriving control rules for the nonlinear controllers is given by formula (1). When deriving the rules of the nonlinear control in version A, dynamical characteristics of the steering gear described by equation (3) was neglected and the control rule were obtained in two steps of backstepping procedure.In version B dynamical characteristics of the steering gear were taken into account and control rule were obtained in three steps.

The nonlinear differential equation (1) can be written in the form of the state equation system where $x_1(t) = \psi(t)$, $x_2(t) = \dot{\psi}(t)$, $u(t) = \delta(t)$ is the controlling input.

$$\dot{x}_1(t) = x_2(t), \quad \dot{x}_2(t) = -\frac{1}{T} H_N(x_2(t)) + u(t), \quad H_N(x_2(t)) = \frac{\alpha}{\beta} x_2^3(t) + x_2(t). \tag{4}$$

Version A Step 1: In the first step new variables are introduced. The first virtual variable z_1 is the control error defined as :

$$z_1 = \Delta\psi(t) = \psi(t) - \psi_z(t) = x_1(t) - \psi_z(t), \tag{5}$$

while the second variable z_2 is the virtual variable determined from the relation

$$z_2 = x_2(t) - \alpha_1(z_1), \tag{6}$$

where $\alpha_1(z_1)$ is the virtual control introduced in the first step. After differentiating Eq. (5) with respect to time and placing relation (4) and (6) we arrive at

$$\dot{z}_1 = \dot{x}_1(t) - \dot{\psi}_z(t) = x_2(t) - \dot{\psi}_z(t) = z_2 + \alpha_1(z_1) - \dot{\psi}_z(t). \tag{7}$$

Then the first Lapunov function is defined as

$$V_1(z_1) = \frac{1}{2} z_1^2. \tag{8}$$

The derivative of the first Lapunov function along the solusion (7) takes the form

$$\dot{V}_1(z_1) = z_1 \dot{z}_1 = z_1 [z_2 + \alpha_1(z_1) - \dot{\psi}_z(t)]. \tag{9}$$

From relation (9) the virtual control $\alpha_1(z_1)$ is derived as

$$-k_1 z_1 = \alpha_1(z_1) - \dot{\psi}_z(t). \tag{10}$$

Transforming Eq. (10) leads to

$$\alpha_1(z_1) = -k_1 z_1 + \dot{\psi}_z(t). \tag{11}$$

After placing the derived relation (11) in Eq. (9) we get the formula for the first derivative of the Lapunov function in this step

$$\dot{V}_1(z_1) = -k_1 z_1^2 + z_1 z_2. \tag{12}$$

Comparing equations (7) and (11) gives us the formula for the first derivative of the newly introduced variable z_1

$$\dot{z}_1 = -k_1 z_1 + z_2. \tag{13}$$

Based on relation (11) and (13) the derivative $\dot{\alpha}_1(z_1)$ for the next design step is also derived, as

$$\dot{\alpha}_1(z_1) = -k_1(-k_1 z_1 + z_2) + \ddot{\psi}_z(t), \tag{14}$$

which is the virtual control derivative in step 1.

Step 2:

The derivative of the second variable is determined from Eq. (6) and (4)

$$\dot{z}_2 = \dot{x}_2(t) - \dot{\alpha}_1(z_1) = -\frac{1}{T}H_N(x_2(t)) + u(t) - \dot{\alpha}_1(z_1).$$ (15)

The second Lapunov function and its derivative takes the form

$$V_2(z_1, z_2) = V_1(z_1) + \frac{1}{2}z_2^2,$$ (16)

$$\dot{V}_2(z_1, z_2) = -k_1 z_1^2 + z_1 z_2 + z_2 \dot{z}_2.$$ (17)

After placing relation (15) into Eq. (17), we get

$$\dot{V}_2(z_1, z_2) = -k_1 z_1^2 + z_2 \left[z_1 - \frac{1}{T}H_N(x_2(t)) + u(t) - \dot{\alpha}_1(z_1) \right]$$ (18)

Form the second derivative given by formula (18) the control is determined as

$$u(t) = -k_2 z_2 - z_1 + \frac{1}{T}H_N(x_2(t)) + \dot{\alpha}_1(z_1)$$ (19)

By substitution the obtained control rule (19) into relation (18), we arrive at the final form of the Lapunov function derivative

$$\dot{V}_2(z_1, z_2) = -k_1 z_1^2 - k_2 z_2^2$$ (20)

which is negatively determined for k_1, $k_2 > 0$. Tuning parameters k_1 and k_2 of the control rule derived with the aid of the backstepping method and given by Eq. (19) is performed using the genetic algorithm described in Chapter 4.

Version B

The mathematical model of the ship was complemented by the equation of the steering machine (3), which can describe by state equation in form of

$$\dot{x}_3(t) = -\frac{1}{T_R}x_3(t) + \frac{K_R}{T_R}u(t),$$ (21)

where $x_3(t)$ is the rudder angle and $u(t)$ is the controlling input. For an object described by state equations (4) and (21) the procedure to design the nonlinear control rule was introduced similarly like in the version A but in three steps. The different was in third step, where we introduced third new state variable $z_3(t) = x_3(t) - \alpha_2(z_1, z_2)$, where α_2 is the second stabilizing function. Then the control rule for the ship and the steering gear as an object is determined as

$$u(t) = \frac{T_R}{K_R}(-k_3 z_3 + \frac{1}{T_R} x_3(t) + \dot{\alpha}_2(z_1,z_2) - z_2), \tag{22}$$

where the time derivative $\dot{\alpha}_2(z_1,z_2)$ is described by equations

$$\dot{\alpha}_2(z_1,z_2) = -k_2\dot{z}_2 - \dot{z}_1 + \frac{1}{T}\dot{H}_N(x_2(t)) - k_1(-k_1\dot{z}_1 + \dot{z}_2) + \ddot{\psi}_z(t), \tag{23}$$

$$\dot{H}_N(x_2(t)) = 3\frac{\alpha}{\beta}x_2^2\dot{x}_2 + \dot{x}_2, \tag{24}$$

for $k_1, k_2, k_3 > 0$.

4. Parameters of nonlinear controllers

The optimisation of the parameters for the derived control rules of the nonlinear controllers given by the formula (19) and (22) were performed using genetic algorithm. Figure 3 shows, in a block schematic form, the structure of the genetic algorithm used in the present analysis for tuning parameters of the examined ship course controller. The tuning programme works until conditions for its stop are met. Two types of algorithm stop conditions are possible. The first condition consists in limiting the maximum number of generations in the optimisation process, while in the second condition the algorithm checks whether the newly generated populations improve considerably the previously obtained solutions. The entire process is repeated until the maximum number of generations is reached. In the examined case, the maximum number of generations was equal to 100, which on the basis of previous investigations was assumed satisfactory. The final solution was the best solution in the most recent population. Below described are particular steps of operation of a genetic algorithm.

Creating the initial population. In order to initiate the initial population the chromosomes are generated randomly using the bit-by-bit method. The length of the chromosome depends on the number of parameters to be coded, and their accuracy n, according to the formula

$$(k_{max} - k_{min}) \cdot 10^{n_i} \leq 2^{m_i} - 1 \tag{25}$$

where: n_i – number of meaningful decimal places defining the accuracy of the parameter, m_i – length of the code sequence for the coded parameter.

Decoding parameters of the controller. From the chromosome extracted are the successive sequences of bits that correspond to the coded parameters. The decimal value for each parameter is calculated using the following formula where: decimal(1010...0112) is equal to the decimal value of the binary chain.

$$k = k_{min} + decimal(1010...011_2)\frac{(k_{max} - k_{min})}{2^{m_i} - 1}$$ (26)

Simulations and evaluation cost. The quality of control of the ship course controller was evaluated here with the aid of a digitised version of the integral quality coefficient, having the form:

$$J_E = \frac{1}{N}\sum_{i=1}^{N}(\Delta\psi_i(t))^2 + \lambda\frac{1}{N}\sum_{i=1}^{N}\delta_i^2(t)$$ (27)

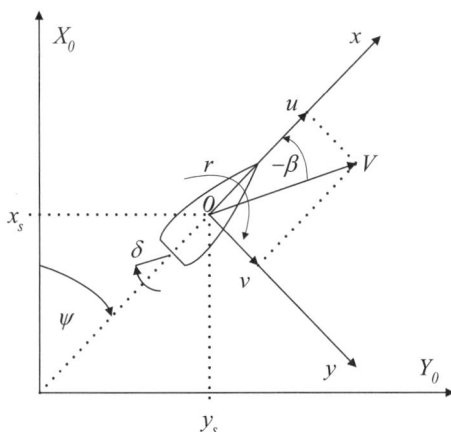

Fig. 1. Ship motion co-ordinate system

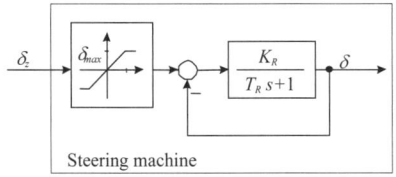

Fig. 3. Steering gear system block diagram

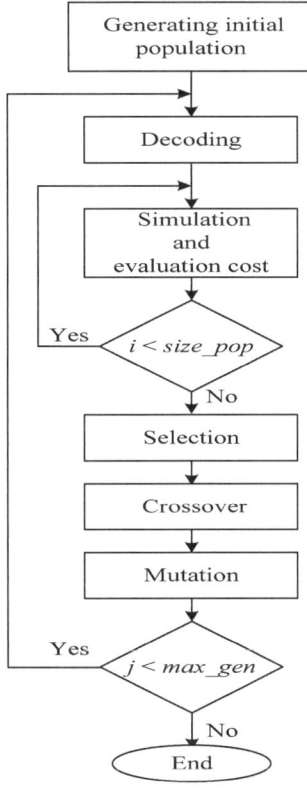

Fig. 2. Block diagram of operations performed by a genetic algorithm

where N is an integer number of iterations in control simulations, λ is the scale factor, in the examined case $\lambda = 0.1$, $\Delta\psi_i(t)$ is the i-th course error determined by subtracting the obtained course from its set value, $\delta_i(t)$ is the i-th angle of the rudder deflection. The genetic algorithm minimises the value of the function (27), by minimising both the course error $\Delta\psi$ and the rudder angle $\delta(t)$. The component connected with the rudder angle is scaled to have a similar amplitude to that of the course error.

Genetic operations. Genetic operations comprise selection, crossover, and mutation. More information about used genetic operation can find [Tomera 2005].

5. Simulation tests

In order to evaluate the quality of the derived algorithm of nonlinear control, simulation tests were performed using the programme package Matlab/Simulink.

Tuning the course controllers parameters with the aid of the genetic algorithm made use of the ship dynamic characteristic equations with the parameters set for the ballasting state. The set course was rapidly changed by 40 [deg]. The quality coefficient, given by formula (27), was determined from the tests trials performed within 500 [s] with sampling period 0.01 [s]. The parameters of the genetic algorithm were: the probability of crossover was $p_c = 0.60$, while the probability of mutation was $p_m = 0.01$.

The best values of the tuned parameters for the examined controller in version A were $k_1=0.0152$, $k_2=335.8$. The best values of the tuned parameters for the examined controller in version B were $k_1=436.07$, $k_2=1973.3$, $k_3=0,0196$. These are the parameter values at which the minimum values of the quality coefficient were obtained at the stage of tuning with the aid of the genetic algorithm. The example results of tuning the parameters of the nonlinear controller with two tuned parameters (version A) are collected in Table 1. In this case the identical minimum values of the quality coefficient were obtained in as many as three tests. The example process of tuning parameters for the nonlinear controller with two parameters is shown in Fig. 4.

Table 1. Results of tuning settings for nonlinear controller with two parameters with the aid of genetic algorithm.

Test no.	N	k_1	k_2	J_E
1	16	0.0156	375.3	12 204 599
2	57	0.0151	337.3	12 202 863
3	**52**	**0.0152**	**335.8**	**12 202 858**
4	33	0.0151	337.5	12 202 912
5	100	0.0151	334.4	12 202 886
6	**53**	**0.0152**	**335.8**	**12 202 858**
7	100	0.0156	375.7	12 204 557
8	48	0.0155	375.6	12 204 457
9	100	0.0152	332.8	12 202 913
10	**96**	**0.0152**	**335.8**	**12 202 858**

The investigations were focused on the effect of changes of object parameters on the quality of control. The controller were tuned for the ship dynamic characteristic equations corresponding to the ballasting state, but in this part of analysis they were used for controlling the ship motion with two different states of load: ballasting and full load. Figure 5a) compare results of the simulation tests performed nonlinear controllers with two parameters (19), marked with solid line and with three parameters (22), marked with a dashed line. In the first 1000 [s] of the tests, the mathematical model of the ship made use of the parameters corresponding to the ballasting state, while during the remaining time the full load parameters were used.

a)

b)

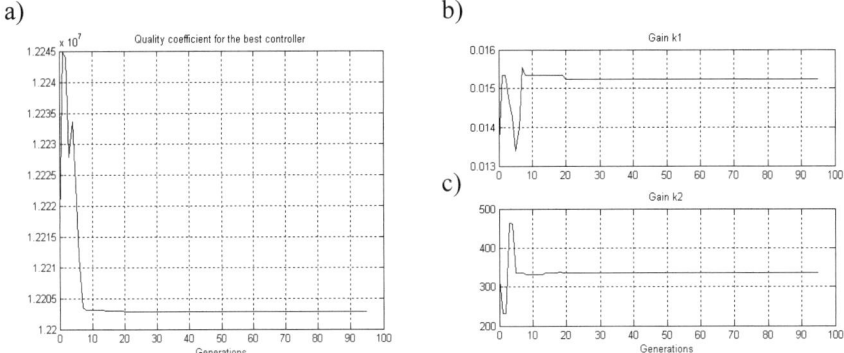

c)

Fig. 4. The process of tuning parameters for the nonlinear controller with two parameters. (a) quality coefficient for the best controller, (b) parameter k_1, (c) parameter k_2

a)

b)

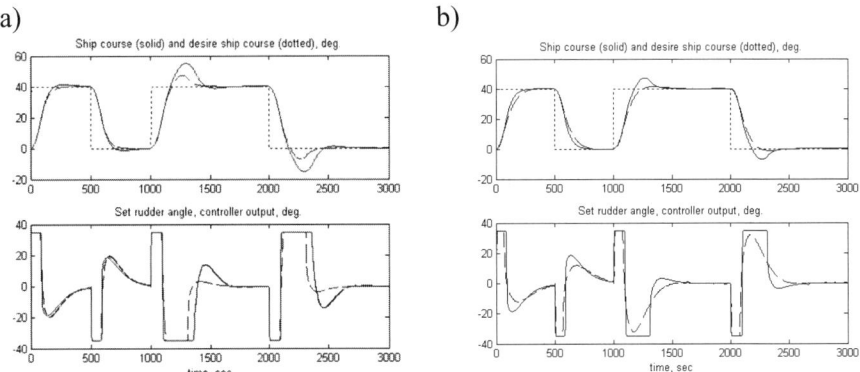

Fig. 5. Comparing results of simulation with tuned controllers: a nonlinear controller with two parameters (solid line), nonlinear controller with three parameters (dashed line), b) nonlinear controller with two parameters (solid line), PD controller (dashed line),

6. Conclusions

The article discusses the two control rules derived for nonlinear controllers designed with the aid of the backstepping method and used for controlling the ship motion on the course. The first control rule with two parameters (version A) were design by neglected the steering gear, the second control rule with three parameters (version B) were taken into account the steering gear in aim of improvement of quality controlled, as shown in Figure 5a. Nonlinear controllers designed with the aid of the backstepping method require tuning of their parameters to the optimal values. The use of genetic algorithms for this purpose produced excellent results. Sample results illustrating the process of tuning the parameters for the nonlinear controller were shown in Fig. 4. The tuned nonlinear controller with backstepping procedure (version

B) were compared with PD controller.The results were shown in Figure 5b. When the ship was in the full load state better results were produced by the PD controller than by the nonlinear controllers designed using the backstepping method. The reason of this regularity lies in the fact that the parameters of the controllers were only tuned for the ballasting state and then were used unaltered for the full load state, which was the source of some error. It turned out that the backstepping method is more sensitive to changes of parameters than the PD controller, which seems to be more robust. Therefore it is necessary to perform the analysis of the model parameters using adaptation techniques, which will be examined in the nearest future.

References

[Amerongen 1982] Amerongen J. (1982). Adaptive steering of ship. A model reference approach to improved manoeuvering and economical course keeping, PhD Thesis, Delft University of Technology, Netherlands.

[Astrom 1989] Astrom K.J, Wittenmark B., (1989). Adaptive Control, Addison Wesley, Reading MA.

[Fossen 1998] Fossen T.I., Strand J.P. (1998). Nonlinear Ship Control (Tutorial Paper), In Proceedings of the IFAC Conference on Control Application in Marine Systems CAMS'98. Fukuoka,Japan.pp. 1–75.

[Fossen 1999] Fossen, T. I. and J. P. Strand (1999). A Tutorial on Nonlinear Backstepping: Applications to Ship Control, Modelling, Identification and Control, MIC-20(2), 83-135.

[Fossen 2002] Fossen T. I. (2002). Marine Control Systems. Guidance, Navigation, and Control of Ships, Rigs and Underwater Vehicles. Marine Cybernetics, Trondheim, Norway.

[Goldberg 1989] Goldberg D. E. (1989). Genetic algorithms in serching, optimisation and machine learning, Reading, MA: Addison Wesley.

[He 1998] He S., Reif K., Unbehauen R. (1998). A neural approach for control of nonlinear systems with feedback linearization, IEEE Trans. Neural Networks, 9(6), 1409–1421.

[Kokotovic 2001] Kokotović P., Arcak M. (2001). Constructive nonlinear control: a historical perspective, *Automatica 37*(5), 637–662.

[Krstic 1995] Krstić M., Kanellakopulos I., Kokotović P.V. (1995). *Nonlinear and Adaptive Control Design*, John Willey&Sons Ltd., New York.

[Krstic 1999] Krstić M., Tsiotras P., (1999) Inverse Optimal Stabilization of a Rigid Spacecraft, *IEEE Transactions on Automatic Control, 44*(5), 1042-1049.

[La_Salle 1966] La Salle J., Lefschetz S. (1966). *Zarys teorii stabilności Lapunowa i jego metody bezpośredniej*, BNI. Warszawa.

[Michalewicz 1996] Michalewicz Z. (1996). *Genetic algorithms + data structures = evolution programs*, Berlin: Springer.

[Pettersen 2004] Pettersen K.Y., Nijmeijer H. (2004). Global practical stabilization and tracking for an underactuated ship – a combined averaging and backstepping approach, *Modelling, Identification and Control, 20*(4), 189–199.

[Skjetne 2005] Skjetne R., Fossen T.I., Kokotović P.V. (2005). Adaptive maneuvering, with experiments, for a model ship in a marine control laboratory, *Automatica 41*(2), 289 – 298.

[Tomera 2005] Tomera M., Witkowska A., Śmierzchalski R., (2005). A Nonlinear Ship Course Controller Optimised Using a Genetic Method. *Materiały VIII Krajowej Konferencji nt. Algorytmy Ewolucyjne i Optymalizacja Globalna,* Korbielów, 30 maja - 01 czerwca 2005 r., ss. 255–262.

[Velagić 2003] Velagić J., Vukić Z., Omerdić E. (2003). Adaptive fuzzy ship autopilot for track-keeping, *Control Engineering Practice, 11*(4), 433–443.

Visualization of Five Erosion Risk Classes using Kernel Discriminants

Anna Bartkowiak, Niki Evelpidou and Andreas Vasilopoulos

Institute of Computer Science, University of Wroclaw, Joliot-Curie 15, Wroclaw 50-383, Poland, aba@ii.uni.wroc.pl
Remote Sensing Laboratory, GeologyDepartment, University of Athens, Panepistimio Zoografou 15784, Greece, {evelpidou,vassilopoulos}@geol.uoa.gr

Abstract. Kernel discriminants are greatly appreciated because 1) they permit to establish nonlinear boundaries between classes and 2) they offer the possibility of visualizing graphically the data vectors belonging to different classes. One such method, called Generalized Discriminant analysis (GDA) was proposed by Baudat and Anouar (2000). GDA operates on a kernel matrix of size N x N, (N denotes the sample size) and is for large N prohibitive. Our aim was to find out how this method works in a real situation, when dealing with relatively large data. We considered a set of predictors of erosion risk in the Kefallinia island categorized into five classes of erosion risk (together N=3422 data items). Direct evaluation of the discriminants, using entire data, was computationally demanding. Therefore, we sought for a representative sample. We found it by a kind of sieve algorithm. It appeared that using the representative sample, we could greatly speed up the evaluations and obtain discriminative functions with good generalization properties. We have worked with Gaussian kernels which need one declared parameter SIGMA called kernel width. We found that for a large range of parameters the GDA algorithm gave visualization with a good separation of the considered risk classes.

1. Introduction

Kernel discriminant analysis (KDA) becomes a more and more popular tool for discriminant analysis [17, 14, 15, 16, [6]. In comparative studies, depending on the data sets, KDA gets the first or second rank; its rival is only SVM, the Support Vector Machine ([14, 15, [16]. Additional advantage of the method is that it may be used for effective graphical visualization of the subclasses of the data.

KDA uses kernels, speaking more precisely: a kernel matrix composed from kernels. The KDA calculations are computer intensive, because they operate on the full kernel matrix $\mathbf{K}$ of size $N \times N$ (N denotes here the number of analyzed data vectors), which may be cumbersome or even prohibitive for large data, see e.g., [1]. A representative sample of data could be a remedy for the lengthy calculations: Instead of performing the calculations using the full kernel matrix $\mathbf{K}_{NxN}$, we seek for a representative sub-matrix $\mathbf{K}_{MxM}$, with $M<<N$, from which we might construct the desired discriminant functions. We may find such a sub-matrix using a kind of sieve

algorithm for the analyzed data. The main principles for finding such a representative subset are: a) apply an operation called *epsilon-sieve* for removing doublets and nearly doublets (epsilon-doublets), choose in each class good representatives, c) balance the learning sample with respect to class sizes.

In our evaluations, we use kernel matrices constructed from Gaussian kernels. They depend from one parameter, SIGMA, called kernel width. We investigate what is the impact of SIGMA on the discriminative power of the constructed discriminant functions.

Section 2 presents shortly the provenance of the data and the rules from which the classes of erosion risk were established. In section 3 we present our proposal of reducing the full matrix $\mathbf{K}_{N \times N}$ to a representative sub-matrix of much smaller size – by using the epsilon-doublets sieve. In Section 4 the essentials of the Generalized Discriminant Analysis (GDA) are presented. Section 5 shows the results obtained for the Kefallinia data when applying Gaussian kernels of various widths SIGMA. In particular, we show in that section the displays of data vectors (belonging to different erosion risk classes) in the coordinate system of the first two canonical discriminant variates found by the GDA algorithm. Section 6 contains some closing remarks.

2. The Erosion Data

The data were gathered by a team from the Remote Sensing Laboratory (RSL), University of Athens (UOA) – during investigations conducted in the Greek island Kefallinia. The entire island was covered by a grid, which contained 3422 cells. The area covered by each cell of the grid was characterized by several variables. More detailed information on the island and collection of the data and importance of establishing erosion risk may be found in ([20, 21, 7, 8, 9, 10, 3]). For our purpose, to illustrate the visualization concepts, we will consider only three variables: drainage density, slope and vulnerability of the soil (rocks). These variables will serve as predictor variables for erosion risk. The values of the variables were rescaled (normalized) to belong to the interval [0, 1]. Next, the values of each predictor variable were subdivided into four categories, as shown in the Table 1 below:

Table 1. Values subdividing each variable into four categories (symbol (*a-b*] means that we account to the given interval all values *x* satisfying $a < x \leq b$; symbol [*a-b*] means that $a \leq x \leq b$)

	[Low]	(Medium]	(High]	(Very High]
Vulnerability	0.298–0.474	0.474–0.650	0.65–0.826	0.826–1.0
Slope	0–0.2	0.2–0.4	0.4–0.6	0.6–1.0
Drainage Density	0–0.01	0.01–0.02	0.02–0.08	0.08–1.0

Thus, for our analysis, we got a data set containing *N=3422* data vectors, each vector characterized by *d=3* categorical variables. An expert GIS system, installed in UOA, was used for assigning each data vector to one of *c=5* erosion risk classes, named in the following: 1.Very High, 2. High, 3. Medium, 4. Low, 5. Very Low.

The assignment to erosion risk classes was done using 13 logical rules established by the experts. The rules are shown in Fig. 1; they permit to classify each data vector from Kefallinia into five classes of erosion risk. For example, Rule 1 reads: **If** Vulnerability is *very high* **and** Slope is *very high*, **then** Erosion risk is very high.

Rule No.	If			then
	VULN	SLOPE	DR DENS →	EROSION RISK
		is		is
1	very High	very High		very High
2	very High	High		very High
3	very High	Medium		very High
4	very High	Low		High
5	High	High		High
6	High	Medium	High	High
7	High	Low		Medium
8	Medium	High		Medium
9	Medium	Medium	High	Medium
10	Medium	Low	High	Low
11	Low	High	High	Low
12	Low	Medium	High	Low
13	Low	Low		very Low

Fig. 1. Logical rules for determination of Erosion Risk. Abbreviations: VULN – Vulnerability; DR_DENS – Drainage Density. Each rule is based on the categories (derived according to principles shown in Table 2) of the considered risk variables. E.g., rule 13 reads: **If** VULNERABILITY is *Low* **and** SLOPE is *Low* **then** EROSION RISK is *Very Low*

3. Finding representative sample – the epsilon doublets sieve

As was noted previously [1], the computational complexity of the GDA algorithm depends on the number of data items and is high when dealing with data size containing several thousands of data items. In such a case, it is preferable to work only with a set of representatives. How may we obtain such a set?

One way is to find the representatives either by selecting a random sample or by finding some prototypes using e.g., Kohonen's SOM [3] or/and Neural Gas [13], [3]. However, the SOM does not yield good representatives [3] and the Neural Gas method needs lengthy calculations [4].

Another way is to apply a kind of sieve to the data.

We decided to use the second alternative. Firstly we found data vectors with values of all the three variables either identical (we call them 'doublets'), or exhibiting only minuscule difference (we call them 'epsilon-doublets').

We have applied the sieve in each class separately. After removal of the found 'doublets' and 'epsilon-doublets', the counts of the classes decreased to: 219,   434, 211,   990,   216, respectively, totaling $N= 2070$, as shown in Table 2 below:

Table 2. Class counts: original and after removal of doublets and epsilon-doublets

Erosion Class	1	2	3	4	5	Total N
Name	vHigh	High	Med	Low	vLow	
Original	240	637	218	1804	523	3422
Reduced	219	434	211	990	216	2070

The applied procedure reduced the data by one third.

Next, we attempted to reduce more the data. It was noted in some other experiments that estimators obtained from a balanced training sample had also good properties in reproducing more accurately external test samples. Therefore, after some considerations, we decided to choose for each class the same number $h=160$ of representatives. This gave us the number n=800 for the total representative sample (balanced with respect to the 5 classes). We found these representatives – in each class of erosion risk –by the neural gas method [13], [22].

Let us say clearly that the established representative sample was obtained by taking into account only the geometrical location of the data vectors; however it does not accounts for their density distribution – which may be undesirable in some analyses.

4. The Concept of Generalized Discriminant Analysis (GDA)

We present here the concept of a generalized discriminant analysis as considered by Baudat and Anouar [5]. The method provides nonlinear discriminant functions living in an extended feature space obtained by kernel transformation of the observed data ([15, 16, 17]). Some other nonlinear discriminant functions are described, e.g., in ([11, 6, 14, 16]).

4.1 Fundamentals of kernel functions

Let x_j, $j=1,...,$ N, denote a (column) data vector, containing observations in d variables ($x_j \in R^d$). The main idea of the kernel method is to transform the observed data – using the transformation Φ – and put them into an extended space F (Hilbert space) usually of much higher dimension:

$$\Phi: x \in R^d \rightarrow \Phi(x) \in F.$$

F is called the feature space; the column vector $\Phi(x)$ is called the image of x in F.

In the following, we will use two important notations: that of a dot product and that of a kernel function. For two vectors x and y with the same number (say d) of components, the **dot product** denotes the inner product between these vectors:

$$(x \bullet y) = \bullet_i x_i y_i, \quad i = 1,...,d$$

A **kernel** k(.,.) is a function that for all x and y belonging to X (the observed space) computes the dot product of the correspondent images

$$k(x, y) = (\Phi(x) \bullet \Phi(y)). \tag{1}$$

The **kernel matrix K** is defined as

$$\mathbf{K}_{NxN} = \{k(\mathbf{x}_i, \mathbf{x}_j)\}, \qquad i,j=1, \dots ,N. \tag{2}$$

For some transformations it is possible to evaluate the inner product between the images (of two inputs) without explicitly computing their coordinates. Thus, we can apply pattern analysis algorithms to the images of the training data in the feature space through indirect evaluation of the inner products (see e.g., Shave-Taylor and Christianini, [18], p. 48, or Mika et al. [14]). Possible choices for k are Gaussian RBF, $k(\mathbf{x}, \mathbf{y}) = \exp\{-\|\mathbf{x} - \mathbf{y}\|^2 /c\}$, or polynomial kernels $k(\mathbf{x}, \mathbf{y}) = (\mathbf{x} \cdot \mathbf{y})^d$, for some positive constants c and d respectively.

In the following, we will use **Gaussian kernels** computed as

$$k(\mathbf{x}, \mathbf{y}) = \exp\{-(\mathbf{x} - \mathbf{y})^T (\mathbf{x} - \mathbf{y})/\sigma\} = \exp\{-(\mathbf{d} \cdot \mathbf{d})/\sigma\}, \tag{3}$$

where $\mathbf{d} = \mathbf{x} - \mathbf{y}$; and $\sigma > 0$ (denoted also **as** SIGMA) is called **kernel width**. When using a larger σ we look at the data globally; taking smaller values of σ we account more for local information [19].

4.2 Discriminant analysis in the feature space (GDA)

We assume that the data vectors $\mathbf{x}$ belong to c classes with cardinalities $n_1, \dots , n_c$. Let M denote the sum $M = \bullet_j n_j$, $j=1, \dots , c$. The input data vector $\mathbf{x}$ may be indexed either by a general index i ($i=1,...,M$) or by a double index kl, $k=1,...,c$; $l=1,...,n_k$. Let $\mathbf{x}_{kl}$ denote the l-th data vector in the k-th class. Assume further that the data vectors – taken as an entire data set – are centered.

Let $\Phi(\mathbf{x})$ denote the transformed data vector $\mathbf{x}$ located in the feature space F. The GDA (Generalized Discriminant Analysis) is nothing else as ordinary Fisherian linear discriminant analysis performed in F. The specificity of the GDA is that it may be performed using only the dot products of the data vectors - without evaluating explicitly the values $\Phi(\mathbf{x})$. The algorithm working that way, elaborated by Baudat and Anouar [5], proceeds as follows:

Let $\underline{\Phi}_k$, $k=1, \dots , c$, denote the class centers in F calculated as

$\quad \underline{\Phi}_k = (1/n_k) \bullet_l \Phi(\mathbf{x}_{kl})$ $l=1, \dots , n_k$.

Define the matrices **T** and **B** (called total inertia **T** and between class inertia **B** [5]) as

$\quad \mathbf{T} = (1/M) \bullet_i \Phi(\mathbf{x}_i) \Phi(\mathbf{x}_i)^T$, $i=1, \dots , M$,

$\quad \mathbf{B} = (1/M) \bullet_k n_k \underline{\Phi}_k(\mathbf{x}_k) \underline{\Phi}_k(\mathbf{x}_k)^T$, $k=1, \dots , c$.

It holds: $\mathbf{T} = \mathbf{B} + \mathbf{W}$, where **W** denotes the within class inertia ($\mathbf{W} = \mathbf{T} - \mathbf{B}$).

4.3 The GDA algorithm

The GDA algorithm proposed by Baudat and Anouar [5] seeks for a vector $\mathbf{v} \in F$ that constructs a new discriminator $u = \Phi(\mathbf{x})^T \mathbf{v}$ being a linear combination of the transformed data vector $\mathbf{x}$. This new discriminant variate u is called the **GDA discriminant variate**. The vector $\mathbf{v}$ is chosen in such a way that it maximizes the ratio of the between class to the total inertia. Let us denote this ratio as η (eta). It may be shown that:

$$\eta = \mathbf{v}^T \mathbf{B} \mathbf{v} / \mathbf{v}^T \mathbf{T} \mathbf{v}, \tag{4}$$

with **B** and **T** defined above.

Because **T** = **B** + **W**, the criterion η takes values from the range $0 \le \eta \le 1$. Big (close to 1) values of η indicate for a good separation of the classes.

So far, the criterion η was formulated in terms of **B** and **T** derived from the transformed values $\Phi(\mathbf{x})$. Baudat and Anouar reformulated the criterion η in such a way, that it appears expressed in terms of the kernel matrix **K**. Then we do not need evaluate explicitly the transformed values $\Phi(\mathbf{x})$.

The GDA variates may be obtained directly from the kernel matrix **K**, without calculating explicitly **T** and **B** (see Baudat and Anouar, [5]). We have used that algorithm for analysis of our data. The results are shown in next section.

5. GDA performed for the erosion data

The training of the system was carried out using 800 representatives (5 classes x 160 representatives) obtained using the neural gas algorithm (see Section 3 and [13, 21]). We have used Gaussian kernels characterized by one parameter: the kernel width σ. There is no clear indication, how to find the proper value of the kernel width. Here we have tried from quite a large range of values: σ (SIGMA) = 49.0, 25.0, 14.0, 10.0, 5.0, 1.0, 3.0, 0.4, 0.0225, 0.09, 0.0081 and 0.0004.

Surprisingly, for all of them we got reasonable (good) results, which may be seen in Table 3 and Figs 2–3. In particular, the first two derived discriminators have a high discriminative power, which increases up to $\eta = 1.0$ – when using the very small kernel width $\sigma = 0.0004$. Figures 2 and 3 show projections of the data vectors to the coordinate system designated by the first two derived GDA variates, obtained when using kernel width $\sigma = 3.0$ and $\sigma = 0.0004$. Upper exhibits show only the projections of the 800 representatives, bottom exhibits – the entire data counting n=3422 data vectors. One may notice the striking similarity between the top and bottom exhibits.

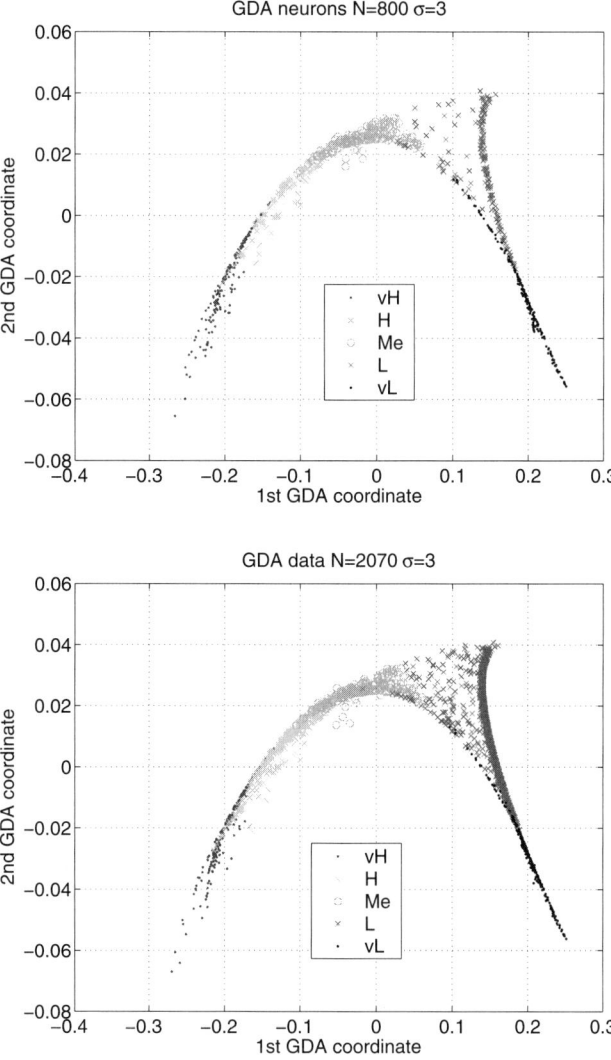

Fig. 2. Visualization of the data in the coordinate system designated by the first two GDA variates obtained using Gaussian kernels with σ=3. Upper exhibit: projection of 800 representatives used for training; bottom exhibit: projection of the entire data set containing 3422 data vectors. High erosion left, low erosion right

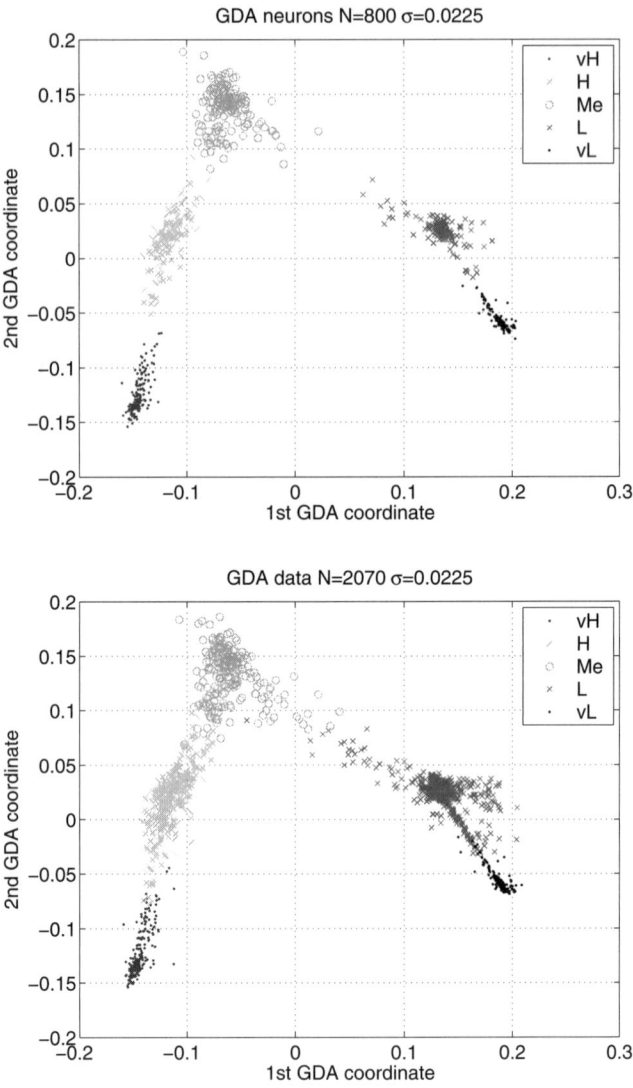

Fig. 3. Visualization as in Fig. 2, however using kernel width σ = 0.0225

Closing remarks

We have considered in detail the algorithm GDA (Generalized Discriminant Analysis) and tested its behavior using a relatively large data set (N=3422). We reduced greatly the time of calculation by finding a representative sample. This consisted in a) removing doublets and epsilon-doublets; b) constructing a learning sample balanced with respect to class sizes; c) choosing representatives in each class by by the neural gas method. The derived GDA variates show good abilities of visualizing graphically both the training and the entire data set. Thus, the method of 'epsilon sieve' proved to be very helpful in reducing computational time and yielding at the same time good results.

The kernel transformation to the new feature space permitted in a sharpened way to visualize the erosion data: we see more clearly the transition (ordering) of the data items with very low, low, through medium, to high and very high erosion risk.

Table 3. Discriminative power η (eta) of GDA variates obtained for 12 values of kernel width SIGMA. The statistics η is shown for the first four discriminant variates – with the largest discriminative power. The row 'rank ($\mathbf{K}$)' shows ranks of kernel matrices for indicated SIGMA.

SIGMA:	49	25	14	10	5	3
eta1	0.9507	0.9512	0.9527	0.9529	0.9535	0.9543
eta2	0.4843	0.6588	0.7113	0.7122	0.7218	0.7254
eta3	0.2191	0.2427	0.5100	0.5100	0.5103	0.5104
eta4	0.0334	0.0892	0.1835	0.1832	0.1849	0.1835
rank($\mathbf{K}$):	5	6	8	8	9	9
SIGMA:	1	0.4	0.09	0.0225	0.0081	0.0004
eta1	0.9584	0.9683	0.9791	0.9912	0.9986	1.0000
eta2	0.7750	0.8045	0.9124	0.9638	0.9919	1.0000
eta3	0.6534	0.6947	0.8294	0.9378	0.9740	1.0000
eta4	0.2339	0.2999	0.6278	0.9059	0.9716	0.9982
rank($\mathbf{K}$):	13	19	52	171	400	799

References

[1] Bartkowiak, A., Evelpidou, N.: Visualizing some multi-class erosion data using kernel methods. In: A. Rizzi, M. Vichi, Eds., Compstat 2006, Proceedings in Computational Statistics, Physica-Verlag, A Springer Company, pp. 805–812, 2006.

[2] Bartkowiak, A., Evelpidou, N.: Visualization of multivariate data with additional class information. In: K. Saeed et al., Image Analysis, Computer Graphics, Security Systems and Artificial Intelligence Applications. WSFiZ Bialystok, 307–320, 2005.

[3] Bartkowiak A., Vassilopoulos A., Evelpidou N.: Choosing data vectors representing a huge data set: Kohonen's SOM applied to the Kefallinia erosion data. Proc. First Int. Conf. on Environmental Research and Assessment, Bucharest, March 23-27, 2003. Ars Docendi P. H., Bucharest, Romania, pp. 505–521, 2003.

[4] Bartkowiak A., Szustalewicz A., Evelpidou N., Vassilopoulos A.: Choosing data vectors representing a huge data set: a comparison of Kohonen's maps and the neural gas method. Proc. First Int. Conf. on Environmental Research and Assessment, Bucharest, March 23–27, 2003. Ars Docendi P. H., Bucharest, Romania, pp. 561–572, 2003.

[5] Baudat, G., Anouar, F.: Generalized discriminant analysis using a kernel approach. Neural Computation 12 (2000), pp. 2385–2404.

[6] Duda, R.O., Hart, P.E., Stork, D.G.: Pattern Classification, 2nd Edition, Wiley. 2001.

[7] Gournelos, Th., Vassilopoulos, A., Evelpidou, N., Giotitsas, Il.: Modelling slop erosional processes. COST Action 634 conference: 'Soil conservation management, perception and policy', Mont Saint Aignan, France, 5-7 June 2005, under edition.

[8] Gournelos, Th., Vassilopoulos, A., Evelpidou, N.: Examples of erosion risk maps using Boolean and fuzzy logical rules in GIS web platforms, Proceedings of 20th International cartographic conference, Beijing China 2001,, Vol. 4. pp. 2472–2479.

[9] Gournelos, Th., Vassilopoulos, A., Evelpidou, N.: An erosion risk map on Samos island, based on fuzzy models, taking into consideration landuse situation after the fire of July 2000, Proceedings of the 7th Conference of Environmental Science and Technology, Syros 2001, pp. 284–290.

[10] Gournelos, Th., Vassilopoulos, A. Evelpidou, N.: Fire danger index using soft computing approach in GIS web platform – a case study from Greece. Proc. First Int. Conf. on Environmental Research and Assessment, Bucharest, March 23-27, 2003. Ars Docendi, Bucharest Romania 2003, pp. 586–595.

[11] Hastie T., Tibshirani R., Friedman J.,: The Elements of Statistical Learning. Springer 2001.

[12] Lachenbruch, P.: Discriminant Analysis. Hafner Press 1975.

[13] Martinetz, M., Berkovich, S., Schulten, K.: 'Neural-gas' network for vector quantization and its application to time series prediction. IEEE Trans. Neural Networks, 4 (1993), pp. 558–569.

[14] Mika S., Rätsch G., Weston J., Schölkopf B., Müller K.R.: Fisher Discriminant Analysis with Kernels. Neural Networks for Signal Processing IX, IEEE 1999, pp. 41–48.

[15] Müller, K-R., Mika, S., Rätsch, G., Tsuda, K., Schölkopf, B.: An introduction to kernel-based learning algorithms. IEEE Trans. on Neural Networks 12(2), 2001, pp. 181–202.

[16] Roth V., Steinhage V.: Nonlinear discriminant analysis using kernel functions. NIPS, Advances in Neural Information Processing Systems 12, Proceedings of the 1999 Conference, MIT Press Cambridge, MA, London, England 2000, pp. 568–574.

[17] Schölkopf, B., Mika S., Burges Ch.J.C, Knirsch, P.H., Müller, K.R., Rätsch G., Smola, A.: Input space versus feature space in kernel-based methods. IEEE Trans. on Neural Networks 10 (1999), No. 5, pp. 1000–1017.

[18] Shawe-Taylor, J., Christianini, N.: Kernel Methods for Pattern Analysis. Cambridge University Press UK. 2004.

[19] Szustalewicz, A.: A practice in applying radial basis functions (RBF) in real situation. J. Soldek, J. Pejas (Eds), ACS'2000, Advanced Computer Systems, Proceedings. Fac. of Computer Science, Technical University of Szczecin. Informa, 2000, pp. 294–299.

[20] Vassilopoulos, A., Gournelos, Th., Evelpidou, N., Land use – Land cover classification for the island of Cephalonia, Proceedings of the VI International conference 'Protection and Restoration of the Environment", 1-5 July, Skiathos, 2002, pp. 1761–1768.

[21] Vassilopoulos, A.: Coastal geomorphological classification in GIS environment of Kefallinia Island. Proc. 6th Pan-Hellenic Geographical Congress of the Hellenic Geographical Society. Thessaloniki 3-5.10.2002. V.1 388–394.

[22] Vesanto, J., Himberg J., Alhoniemi, E., Parhankangas J.: SOM Toolbox for Matlab 5. Som Toolbox team, Helsinki University of Technology, Finland, Libella Oy, Espoo 2000, pp. 1–54. Version 0beta 2.0, November 2001, actualized 2005.
http://www.cis.hut.fi/projects/somtoolbox/

PART II

COMPUTER SECURITY AND SAFETY

Multiple Error Detection in Substitution Blocks for Block Ciphers

Krzysztof Bucholc, Ewa Idzikowska

Poznań University of Technology
Krzysztof.Bucholc@put.poznan.pl, Ewa.Idzikowska@put.poznan.pl

Abstract. In this paper we will describe parity code based approach to multiple error detection in substitution blocks in symmetric block ciphers. We focus on even number error detection. Probability of error detection is analyzed for random and correlated data. The method is demonstrated on an 8-input, 8-output substitution block.

1. Introduction

A substitution box (S-box) is a basic component of block ciphers. Substitution boxes are used to obscure the relationship between the plaintext and the ciphertext. There are m inputs and n outputs in such a box.

Error detection in cryptographic hardware is the subject of many research efforts [1,2].

Cryptographic devices are often objects of deliberated error insertion which rarely is the case in other sort of circuits. Errors cause hazard for the cipher safety. Therefore error detection in cryptographic circuits is of great importance.

There are many techniques which can be used for error detection in digital circuits. All are based on adding redundancy to the circuit. The required extra hardware varies greatly. It can be relatively small, adding a few percent to the circuit area, but it may also lead to doubling of the hardware.

Parity code based solutions require relatively small increase of the hardware complexity. Examples of solutions can be found in [1]. The drawback of the parity code methods is that they can only detect single errors and any odd number of errors.

In this paper we will show how the parity code based approach can be used for even number error detection in a S-box.

2. Errors in substitution blocks

Let us consider a substitution block shown in Fig.1. There are m inputs and n outputs. The number of inputs and outputs may be equal – for example in AES cipher $m=n=8$, or $m>n$ (e.g. DES 6x4) or $m<n$ (e.g. MARS 9x32). Each m-bit input vector is substituted with n-bit output vector as in a mapping function f, which maps m-bit input strings X to n-bit output strings Y, where:

$$Y=f(X) \text{ and } f:\{0,1\}^m \to \{0,1\}^n. \qquad (1)$$

S-boxes are carefully designed to make differential cryptanalysis and linear cryptanalysis as difficult as possible.

Fig. 1. The $m \times n$ S-box

Let us consider the model of erroneous S-box shown in fig. 2.

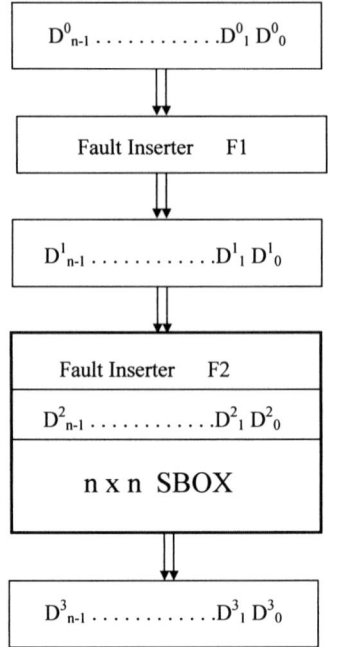

Fig. 2. The model of faulty S-box

There are two fault inserters F1 and F2. Inserters corrupt data by changing one ore more bit.

Let $D^0_{n-1},\ldots,D^0_1,D^0_0$, be an error-free input vector, and $D^3_{n-1},\ldots,D^3_1,D^3_0$ be an output vector. Let $E^1_{n-1},\ldots,E^1_1,E^1_0$ be an error vector used by inserter F1, where $E^1_i \in \{0,1\}$; $E^1_i = 1$ indicates that bit i is faulty. The number of ones in this vector is equal the number of inserted faults. As a result, vector $D^1_{n-1},\ldots,D^1_1,D^1_0$ is the erroneous vector, where $D^1_i = D^0_i \oplus E^1_i$. Similarly $E^2_{n-1},\ldots,E^2_1,E^2_0$ denotes error vector in fault inserter F2. Vector $D^2_{n-1}, \ldots, D^2_1, D^2_0$ is the erroneous vector where $D^2_i = D^1_i \oplus E^2_i$. $\oplus$ denotes exclusive-or operation.

Errors induced by inserter F1 are visible on the S-box inputs and outputs whereas errors induced by F2 are visible only on the S-box outputs. Therefore detection of F2 errors is more complex than detection of F1 errors.

3. Error detection in S-box

3.1 Single error detection

To detect errors visible on S-box inputs, error detection codes can be used. The best known such code is parity code. One additional data line is needed to perform parity checking.

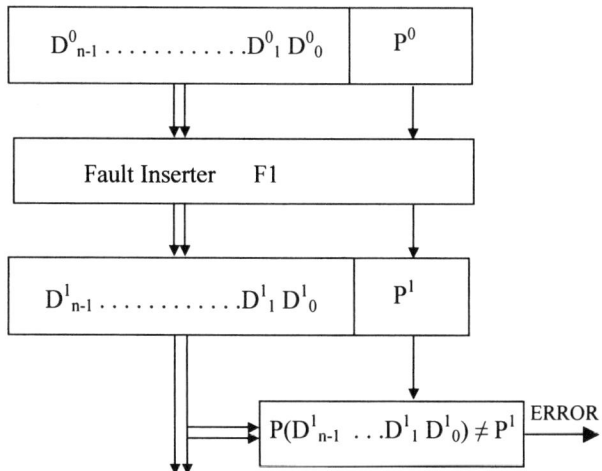

Fig. 3. Detection of errors visible on the S-box inputs

The error detection scheme is shown in fig. 3. P^0 denotes parity bit of the vector $D^0_{n-1} \ldots D^0_1 D^0_0$.

$$P^0 = D^0_{n-1} \oplus D^0_{n-2} \oplus \ldots \oplus D^0_1 \oplus D^0_0 \qquad (2)$$

The fault inserter F1 is very similar to those shown in fig. 2. The only difference is that there is one bit more in error vector. Bit P^0 may also be erroneous.

Parity code detects single errors and any odd number of errors. The circuit overhead is relatively small – one additional data line and parity checking circuit. If stronger detection capability is required, a code with more check bits can be used.

Now let us consider faults induced by fault inserter F2 in fig.2. Such errors are visible only on the S-box outputs.

First of all let us check whether the transformation in S-box preserves parity. It can be accomplished by comparing parities of input and output vectors for all possible input vectors.

It turns out that, for all practically used S-boxes, transformation in the S-box does not preserve parity. As an example the parity preserving properties of the AES S-box are shown in table 1. As it can be seen in table 1, for even input vectors nearly half of the output vectors are also even, whereas the rest are odd. The same is true for odd input vectors.

Table 1. Parity distribution in fault-free AES S-box

Input		Output	
		Even	Odd
Even	128	65	63
Odd	128	63	65

Parity preserving version of S-box is shown in fig. 4.

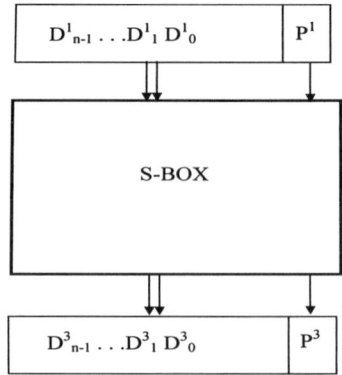

Fig. 4. Parity preserving version of the $n*n$ S-box

There is one extra input line and one extra output line. It means that the $n*n$ S-box is replaced by $(n+1)*(n+1)$ S-box. The drawback of this solution is however the big circuit redundancy. To implement the $(n+1)*(n+1)$ S-box $(n+1)*2^{n+1}$ bits are required whereas $n*2^n$ suffice for the n*n S-box. For example for $8*8$ AES S-Box the parity preserving version requires 4608 bits of memory. Basic version needs only 2048 bits.

3.2 Multiple error detection using $n+k$ error detection codes

Parity code detects single errors and any odd number of errors. Detection of multiple errors (odd and even) requires more than one check bits. There are many error detecting codes available. Methods presented in section 3.1 can be extended to detect multiple errors. In this case more than one extra line is needed for check bits. The main problem is the circuit complexity. To implement the $n*n$ S-box with k check lines for input and output $(n+k)*2^{n+k}$ bits are needed. As an example the redundancy of error detecting versions of the AES (8*8) S-box is shown in table 2.

Table 2. Redundancy in error-detecting version of the AES S-box

Number of check bits	Bits in S-box implementation	Overhead %
0	2048	0
1	4608	125
2	10240	400
3	22528	1000
4	49152	2300

As it can be seen 2 check bits requires 400 % overhead, whereas 3 check bits lead to 1000% overhead. Therefore this approach is impractical. However Bertoni and al. proposed usage of this method for $k=1$ [1].

3.3 Parity based multiple error detection

In this section we will focus on F2 errors (fig. 2). Let us suppose that there is a method which detects error in S-box with probability $p>0$ for single substitution in the S-box. If this procedure is repeated r times using statistically independent input vectors we will achieve probability of the error detection equal to:

$$Pd = 1 - (1 - p)^r \tag{3}$$

Where Pd denotes probability of error detection and r denotes the length of the sequence of vectors.

It means that for any $p>0$ errors can be detected with required accuracy. The higher accuracy the longer sequence of vectors is needed. This is illustrated in fig. 5 for several values of p.

In the method described below single input vector detects error with probability close to ½.

Let $D^0_{n-1} D^0_{n-2} ... D^0_1 D^0_0$ be the input data of the $n*n$ S-box shown in fig.6.
Let us denote the parity of this vector by P^0

$$P^0 = D^0_{n-1} \oplus D^0_{n-2} \oplus ... \oplus D^0_1 \oplus D^0_0 \tag{4}$$

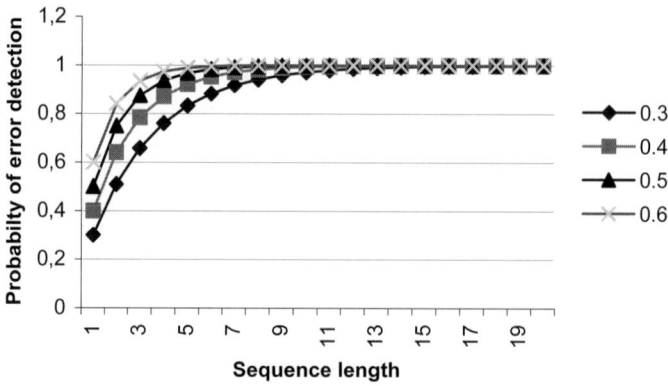

Fig. 5. Probability of error detection for p=0.3, 0.4, 0.5 and 0.6

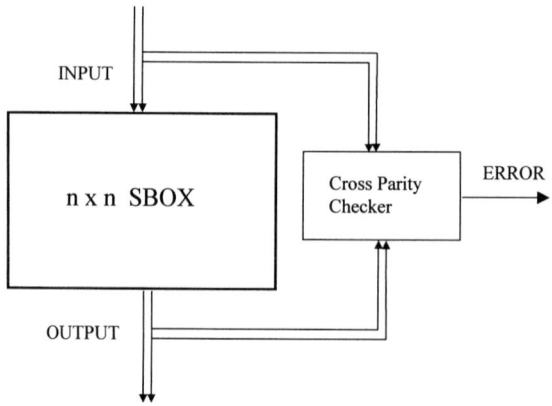

Fig. 6. Cross-parity based error detection

Similarly $D^3_{n-1} D^3_{n-2} ... D^3_1 D^3_0$ denotes output vector and P^3 denotes parity of the output vector.

$$P^3 = D^3_{n-1} \oplus D^3_{n-2} \oplus ... \oplus D^3_1 \oplus D^3_0 \qquad (5)$$

Cross-parity of vectors $D^0_{n-1} D^0_{n-2} ... D^0_1 D^0_0$ and $D^3_{n-1} D^3_{n-2} ... D^3_1 D^3_0$ is defined as

$$CP = P^0 \oplus P^3 \qquad (6)$$

Where *CP* denotes cross-parity.

The circuit shown in fig. 6 contains memory which stores the cross-parity pattern for error free S-box. It requires 2^n bits of memory for $n*n$ S-box.

During the encryption circuit operation, for each pair (input vector, output vector), the cross-parity is derived and compared against the stored good value. If an error occurs (single or multiple) the derived cross-parity can be either proper or faulty.

Probability that in presence of error the derived cross parity does not match the stored pattern depends on the properties of the S-box. For well designed S-box the probability that even input gives even output is close to that even input gives odd output. For example for AES S-box these values are 0.5078125 and 0.4921875 respectively.

It means that single input vector detects error with probability close to ½. Therefore the sequence of r independent vectors detects error with probability

$$Pd \approx 1 - (1/2)^r \tag{7}$$

In fact the data processed in S-box during encryption/decryption may not be independent. Data in consecutive rounds are derived by processing the output data of previous round. Furthermore is possible that the whole block consists of the same values of data.

It turns out, however, that in modern block ciphers dependencies between data in consecutive rounds are quickly obscured. Therefore, despite the fact that the input data in given round are obtained by processing the input data for the previous round, for testing purposes, they can be treated as statistically independent.

We will use the AES cipher as an example of block cipher with single $8*8$ S-box to analyze the data dependencies. There are 3 versions of AES – with 128-bit key, 192-bit key and 256-bit key. We will use the 128-bit data block, 128-bit key version of AES.

The process of encryption consists of 10 rounds [3]. It means that for each round 16 substitutions are required. It makes 160 substitutions for 16-byte (128-bit) block encryption. All rounds consists of the same operations except for the initial round and the final round. There is *AddRoundKey* operation in initial round which sums modulo 2 the plaintext and the key.

To obtain highly correlated sequence of bytes we used the following values of the plaintext and the key:

Plaintext : 00 01 02 03 04 05 06 07 08 09 0A 0B 0C 0D 0D (hexadecimal)

Key: 00 01 02 03 04 05 06 07 08 09 0A 0B 0C 0D 0D (hexadecimal).

The modulo 2 sum gives the following block for substitution in round 1:

00 00 00 00 00 00 00 00 00 00 00 00 00 00 00 00.

Such a sequence possesses the weakest possible error detection property. The error detection power of the whole sequence is equal to the error detection power of one data vector. Therefore, in this case, error detection power of the proposed method depends mainly on the next rounds. All rounds are shown in fig. 7. The correlation among consecutive rounds is shown in table 3.

Data in round 2 and next rounds can be treated as independent from the data in previous round.

```
PT=000102030405060708090A0B0C0D0E0F
KEY=000102030405060708090A0B0C0D0E0F

Round
1     00000000000000000000000000000000
2     B5C9179EB1CC1199B9C51B92B5C8159D
3     2B65F6374C427C5B2FE3A9256896755B
4     D1015FCBB4EF65679688462076B9D6AD
5     8E17064A2A35A183729FE59FF3A591F1
6     D7557DD55999DB3259E2183D558DCDD2
7     73A96A5D7799A5F3111D2B63684B1F7F
8     1B6B853069EEFC749AFEFD7B57A04CD1
9     107EEADFB6F77933B5457A6F08F046B2
10    8EC166481A677AA96A14FF6ECE88C010
```

Fig. 7. AES S-box input data in rounds 1-10

Table 3. Correlation among data in rounds 1-10

Round	1	2	3	4	5	6	7	8	9	10
1	1,00									
2	0,16	1,00								
3	-0,26	-0,42	1,00							
4	0,30	0,19	-0,22	1,00						
5	0,32	0,10	0,00	-0,01	1,00					
6	0,42	-0,04	0,08	0,58	0,03	1,00				
7	0,10	0,12	-0,24	-0,21	-0,24	-0,14	1,00			
8	-0,15	-0,18	0,44	-0,14	0,27	0,03	-0,08	1,00		
9	-0,19	0,04	0,08	0,24	-0,48	0,04	-0,06	0,25	1,00	
10	-0,25	-0,33	0,03	-0,36	0,22	-0,49	0,04	-0,16	-0,41	1,00

Therefore the probability of even error detection for a cipher with n-byte block can be estimated as follows:

$$Pd \approx 0.5 \quad for \ k \le n \tag{8}$$

$$Pd \approx 1 - 2^{-(k-n+1)} \quad for \ k > n \tag{9}$$

where k is the length of the sequence.

Probabilities of error detection using cross-parity based method for random input data and correlated input data are compared in Table 4.

Table 4. Probability of error detection for random and correlated data

Sequence length	Random input data	Correlated input data
1	0,500000000000000	0,500000000000000
2	0,750000000000000	0,500000000000000
3	0,875000000000000	0,500000000000000
4	0,937500000000000	0,500000000000000
8	0,996093750000000	0,500000000000000
10	0,999023437500000	0,500000000000000
16	0,999984741210937	0,500000000000000
17	0,999992370605468	0,750000000000000
20	0,999999046325683	0,968750000000000
24	0,999999940395355	0,998046875000000
32	0,999999999767169	0,999992370605468
40	0,999999999999091	0,999999970197677
48	0,999999999999996	0,999999999883585

To detect error with probability 0.99999, 32 input vectors are required, if input data are correlated, whereas 17 vectors suffice for random data.

4. Concluding remarks

The main advantage of the proposed method is that it requires small overhead. For $n*n$ S-box 2^n bits of memory for cross-parity patterns and 2 n-input parity checkers are needed. It means that for $8*8$ S-box the memory overhead is 12.5%.

The probability of error detection depends on the length of the sequence of input vectors and on the data correlation. Random input data give better results. But even for correlated input data errors can be detected with high probability. For example detection of even errors in the AES S-box with probability 99.999% requires 32 vectors. It means that 2 out of 10 rounds suffice to detect error with this probability.

Acknowledgment

This research was supported by the Polish Ministry of Education and Science as a 2005–2008 research project.

References

[1] Bertoni G., Bregeveglieri L., Koren I., Maistri P., Piuri V., *Error Analysis and Detection Procedures for a Hardware Implementation of the Advanced Encryption Statandard*, IEEE Trans. On Computers Vol. 52 No 4, April 2003, pp.492-505.

[2] Karri R., Kuznetsov G., Goessel M., *Parity Based Concurrent Error Detection in Symmetric Block Cyphers*, proc. of International Test Conference 2003, pp.919-926.

[3] National Inst. Of Standards and Technology, *Federal Information Processing Standard 197, The advanced Encryption Standard(AES)*, November 2001, http://csrc.nist.gov/publications/fips/fips197/fips-197.pdf.

Parallelization Method of Encryption Algorithms

Włodzimierz Bielecki, Dariusz Burak

Szczecin University of Technology, Faculty of Computer Science and Information Systems
Żołnierska St. 71-210 Szczecin, Poland, tel.+48 91 449 55 61
email: wbielecki@wi.ps.pl, dburak@wi.ps.pl

Abstract. An automatic parallelization method of cryptographic algorithms such as DES, Triple DES, IDEA, AES, RC5, Blowfish, LOKI91, GOST, RSA, and data encryption standard modes of operation: CTR, CBC, CFB is presented. The method is based on the data dependency analysis of loops and well-known loop parallelization techniques. The OpenMP standard was chosen for representing the parallelism of algorithms.

1. Introduction

The second most important feature of encryption algorithms after the security level is the cipher speed. In the Internet era, there is extremely important to decrease the time of data encryption and decryption processes in view of a great deal of data to be encrypted and decrypted for each net user. There are various ways to increase the speed of data enciphering and deciphering. The method, presented in this paper, relies on parallelization of sequential source codes of cryptographic algorithms. There are the two different approaches to parallelize sequential algorithms: manual and automatic parallelization. The first one has serious disadvantages such as high costs and considerable time-consuming, because, in this case, there is the necessity to provide a detailed analysis of an algorithm or source code. Automatic parallelization relies on parallelization at source code compilation. Therefore, this method is fast, inexpensive and easy to use. The proposed method is a basis for creating a parallel complier devoted to parallelization of encryption algorithms.

The major purpose of this paper is to present an automatic parallelization method of encryption algorithms. The paper is organized as follows. In section 2, we briefly describe encryption algorithms. Section 3 discusses an automatic parallelization method of encryption algorithms along with a parallelization process for the Blowfish algorithm, parallelization tools and a brief description of data dependences blocking the parallelization process. Section 4 contains speed-up measurements of the most time-consuming loops of encryption algorithms parallelized by means of the automatic method described in Section 3.

2. Encryption Algorithms

Encryption algorithms also known as ciphers are mathematical methods (based on arithmetical, logical and binary operations) to convert a cleartext into a ciphertext (or a ciphertext into a cleartext, in the case of decryption process).

There exist symmetric and asymmetric key encryption algorithms.

Symmetric key encryption algorithms, known also as secret-key algorithms, use the same key for both encryption and decryption processes. The most popular symmetric-key algorithms are the following block ciphers: Data Encryption Standard (DES), Triple DES, International Data Encryption Algorithm (IDEA), and Advanced Encryption Standard (AES). A block cipher is a symmetric key encryption algorithm that transforms a fixed-length block of plaintext data into a block of ciphertext data of the same length.

There are several modes of operations for symmetric key encryption algorithms. Standard modes of operation are the following: ECB, CBC, CFB, OFB and CTR.

Asymmetric key encryption algorithms (also known as public key algorithms) use a different key for encryption and decryption processes and the decryption key cannot (practically) be derived from the encryption key. The most popular asymmetric-key encryption algorithm is RSA [1], [2].

3. Automatic Parallelization Method of Encryption Algorithms

In the previous research works [3], [4], [5], [6], [7], [8], the authors presents manual parallelization of some cryptographic algorithms. We have finally come to the conclusion that it is possible to automatize a parallelization process of cryptographic algorithms.

3.1 Analyzed source codes

Considering the fact that the most time-consuming elements of source code of cryptographic algorithms (including no I/O functions) are loops directly responsible for encryption and decryption processes, we study only such loops. Among many well-known cryptographic algorithms, we selected the most popular ones (both symmetric and asymmetric): DES, Triple DES, IDEA, AES, RC5, Blowfish, GOST, LOKI91, RSA and the standard modes of operation: ECB, CBC, CFB and CTR. The sources of these codes are presented in Appendix A.

3.2 Data Dependences

There are the following basic types of the data dependences that occur in loops:
- Data Flow Dependence,
- Data Antidependence,
- Output Dependence.

A Data Flow Dependence indicates that write-before-read ordering must be satisfied for parallel computing. The following loop yields such dependences:

```
for(int i=0;i<max,i++) a[i] = a[i-1];
```

A Data Antidependence indicates that read-before-write ordering should not be violted when performing computations in parallel. The loop below produces such dependences:

```
for(int i=0;i<max,i++) a[i] = a[i+1];
```

An Output Dependence indicates a write-before-write ordering. The following loop produces such dependences:

```
for(int i=0;i<max,i++) a[0] = a[i];.
```

All of above loops cannot be executed in parallel, because results generated by the loops would be other than that yielded with the serial ones. To execute the loops in parallel, we can eliminate Data Antidependences and Output Dependences. However Data Flow Dependences cannot be removed and limit parallelism [9], [10].

3.3 Parallelization Tools

In order to parallelize encryption algorithms, we have applied the OpenMP API to present parallelized source code and the Petit program in order to find data dependences blocking parallelism.

3.3.1 OpenMP

The OpenMP Application Program Interface supports multiplatform shared memory parallel programming in C/C++ and Fortran on all architectures including Unix and Windows NT platforms. OpenMP is a collection of complier directives, library routines and environment variables that can be used to specify shared memory parallelism. OpenMP directives extend a sequential programming language with SPMD, work-sharing and synchronization constructs and make possible to operate with shared and private data. It is necessary to forecast all problems connected with programming restrictions on parallel processing to build a valid parallel code [11].

3.3.2 Petit

Petit was developed at the University of Maryland as a part of the Omega Project. It is a research tool for analyzing array data dependences that provides indispensable information about data dependences existing in analyzing loops [12].

3.4 Automatic Parallelization Method

Analyzed ciphers source codes are written in the C language. Most of them (DES, Triple DES, LOKI91, IDEA, GOST, RC5) are taken from the monograph [1]. All of them are selected in view of advantageous features such as clarity and a high efficiency. An automatic parallelization method is applicable for loops responsible for encryption and decryption processes of data blocks. Considering the differences in the construction of these loops important for the parallelization process, the proposed method is divided in three procedures. The first one refers to the loops included in symmetric ciphers working in the ECB mode of operation. The second one concerns the loops enclosed in standard modes of operation except from the ECB mode. The third procedure deals with the loops comprised in asymmetric ciphers.

3.4.1 Automatic Parallelization Method- First Procedure

The general form of the loop analyzed in this case was created basing on the detailed analysis of the loop constructions included in the following algorithms: DES, Triple DES, IDEA, AES, RC5, Blowfish, GOST, LOKI91 and is as follows:

```
#define BLOCK_LENGTH (value_1¹)
#define NUBYTY (value_2²)
(type of variables³)*size_1_block_in, *size_1_block_out;
for (i=0; i<NUMBER_OF_BLOCKS; i++) {
    function_1⁴(par_1_1, par_1_2,   ... ,par_1_n);
    function_2⁴ (par_2_1, par_2_2,   ... ,par_2_n);
    ...
    function_n⁴ (par_n_1, par_n_2,   ... ,par_n_n);
    size_1_block_in⁵ += BLOCK_LENGTH / (NUBYTY);
    size_1_block_out⁶ += BLOCK_LENGTH / (NUBYTY);
}
```

[1-] value_1 equals to 8 or 16 (depending on the feature of analyzing block cipher);

[2-] value_2 is the number of bytes for size_1_block_in and size_1_block_out type;

[3-] type of variables is unsigned char or unsigned long;

[4-] function_1, function_2, ..., function_n – functions being elements of the main loop;

when there is the only one function (function_1)- at least one parameter of function_1 is equal to size_1_block_in and size_1_block_out;

when there are two or more functions- at least one parameter of function_1 and function_n is equal to size_1_block_in and size_1_block_out;

[5-] size_1_block_in – variable for an input file;

[6-] size_1_block_out – variable for an output file.

First of all, a parallel compiler finds such loops in examining cipher source code.
To obtain parallelized code, we apply three groups of transformations.
The first one enables for a data dependence analysis.
It consists of the following transformations that have to be executed in turn:

a) the replacement of the functions calls included in the main loop (`function_1`, `function_2`, …, `function_n`) for an equivalent code that contains the bodies of these functions;
b) the replacement of nested *do-while* loops for equivalent *for* loops;
c) the replacement of nested *while* loops for equivalent *for* loops;
d) the substitution of references for equivalent data tables.

These transformations are indispensable, because a proper parallelization process has to enclose a data dependency analysis in order to apply effective dependences removal and parallelization transformations.

The second one permits for antidependences and output dependences removal.

It is made up of the following transformations that have to be executed in succession:

a) the substitution of references for equivalent data tables (indexing by the main loop variable) using the ampersand symbol (&);
b) the privatization of suitable variables (except for variables with the ampersand symbol).

The data dependences removal transformations are indispensable because data dependences limit parallelism available in loops.

The third one is to parallelize source code.

It consists of the following transformations:

a) creating a parallel region of computation applying the directive *#pragma omp parallel* along with with correspondent clauses;
b) the specification of a loop whose iterations should be executed in parallel using the directive *#pragma omp for*.

These transformations are indispensable because they enable multithreaded working.

The general form of a parallelized loop analyzed in this case is the following:

```
#define BLOCK_LENGTH (value_1)
#define NUBYTY (value_2)
local variables declaration;
unsigned char * size_1_block_in, * size_1_block_out;
#pragma    omp    parallel    private    (i,    j,    …,    z,
                  par_local_1_1,      …,       par_local_n_n,
                  par_1_2, …, par_n_n)
#pragma omp for
for (i=0; i< NUMBER_OF_BLOCKS; i++) {
//        function_1(par_1_1, par_1_2,   … ,par_1_n);
par_local_1_1 = &size_1_block_in [BLOCK_LENGTH * i];
par_local_1_2 =   &size_1_block_out [BLOCK_LENGTH * i];
par_local_1_3 =   par_1_3;
. . . . . . . . . . . . . . . . . . . . .
par_local_1_n =   par_1_n;
(body of function_1)
//        function_2(par_2_1, par_2_2,   … ,par_2_n);
par_local_2_1 =   par_2_1;
par_local_2_2 =   par_2_2;
. . . . . . . . . . . . . . . . . . . . .
par_local_2_n =   par_2_n;
```

```
(body of function_2)
 .   .   .   .   .   .   .   .   .   .   .   .   .   .   .   .   .   .   .
//           function_n(par_n_1, par_n_2,   ... ,par_n_n);
par_local_n_1 =   &size_1_block_in [BLOCK_LENGTH * i];
par_local_n_2 =   par_n_2;
 .   .   .   .   .   .   .   .   .   .   .   .   .   .   .   .   .   .   .
par_local_n_n =   par_n_n;
(body of function_n)
//           size_1_block_in += BLOCK_LENGTH / (NUBYTY);
//           size_1_block_out += BLOCK_LENGTH / (NUBYTY);
}.
```

3.4.2 Automatic Parallelization Method- Second Procedure

The general form of the loop analyzed in this case was created basing on the detailed analysis of the loop constructions included in the following modes of operation: ECB, CBC, CFB, OFB and CTR and is as follows

```
for  (i=INIT_VALUE¹;i<NUMBER_OF_CHARS²;i+= BLOCK_) {
     function(par1³, block⁴+i, 1);
     for (j=0; j< BLOCK_LENGTH⁵; j++)
       result[i+j] = block[i+j]^input[i+j- INIT_VALUE];
}
```

1-   0 or BLOCK_LENGTH (depending on a mode of operation);
2-   the number of characters for enciphering (or deciphering);
3-   parameter regarding the key enciphering (or key deciphering);
4-   parameter regarding the data enciphering (or data deciphering);
5-   8 or 16 (depending on type of the cipher).

First of all, a parallel compiler finds loops in such a form in examining cipher source code.

Similarly as in the previous case (subsection 3.4.1), the same three transformations groups can be used to transform sequential source code into parallel one.

The transformation group that enables for a data dependence analysis consists only of a transformation that put the function outside of the most outer loop.

An antidependences and output dependences removal transformations group is made up of the following transformations executed in succession:
a)   the replacement of the outer loop for an equivalent single loop;
b)   the privatization of indexing variables.

The parallelization technique is the same as in the previous case and consists of the following transformations:
a)   creating a parallel region of computation applying the directive *#pragma omp parallel* along with correspondent clauses;
b)   the specification of a loop whose iterations should be executed in parallel using the directive *#pragma omp for*.

The general form of the parallelized loop is the following:

```
function(par1,block,
          NUMBER_OF_BLOCKS-(INIT_VALUE/BLOCK_LENGTH));
#pragma omp parallel private (i)
#pragma omp
for (i= INIT_VALUE; i< NUMBER_OF_CHARS; i++)
    result[i] = block[i] ^ input[i-INIT_VALUE];.
```

3.4.3 Automatic Parallelization Method- Third Procedure

In this case, the general form of the loop is based on the RSA algorithm and is the following:

```
for (i= 0; i< NUMBER_OF_BLOCKS; i++)
    output[i] = (input[i] ^ exponent) % (p*q);.
```

There are only two groups of transformations to transform sequential source code into parallel one.

The antidependences and output dependences removal transformations group is made up of only the privatization of indexing variables.

The parallelization technique is the same as in the previous cases and consists of the following transformations:

a) creating a parallel region of computation applying the directive *#pragma omp parallel* along with with correspondent clauses;

b) the specification of a loop whose iterations should be executed in parallel using the directive *#pragma omp for*.

In this case, the general form of the parallelized loop looks like this:

```
#pragma omp parallel private (i)
#pragma omp
for (i= 0; i< NUMBER_OF_BLOCKS; i++)
    output[i] = (input[i] ^ exponent) % (p*q);.
```

3.5 An Example of the Method Application for the Blowfish Algorithm

Let us to parallelize the following loop that is responsible for the encryption of data blocks (in the case of decryption the parallelization process is the same, and thus we do not describe it) [13]:

```
void blf_enc(blf_ctx *c, unsigned long *data, unsigned
             int blocks){
          unsigned long *d;
          unsigned int i;
          d = data;
          for (i = 0; i < blocks; i++) {
               Blowfish_encipher(c, d, d + 1);
               d += 2;
          }
}
```

Considering this loop, we first have to apply the first procedure of the proposed method.

In accordance with this procedure, we have to replace the call of the Blowfish_encipher() function for equivalent code that contains the body of this function. The transformed form of the blf enc() function is the following:

```
void blf_enc(blf_ctx *c, unsigned long *data, unsigned
             int blocks)
{
        unsigned int i;
        unsigned long *d,*xl,*xr,Xl,Xr,*s=c->S[0],*p= c->P;
        d = data;
        for (i = 0; i < blocks; i++) {
//      Blowfish_encipher(c, d, d + 1);
        xl = d;
        xr = d+1;
        Xl = *xl;
        Xr = *xr;
        Xl ^= p[0];
        BLFRND(s, p, Xr, Xl, 1);
        BLFRND(s, p, Xl, Xr, 2);
        . . . . . . . . . . . . . . . . . . . . .
        BLFRND(s, p, Xr, Xl, 15);
        BLFRND(s, p, Xl, Xr, 16);
        *xl = Xr ^ p[17];
        *xr = Xl;
        d += 2;
        }
}
```

The next transformation is the substitution of the references with equivalent data tables. Therefore the following four expressions: Xl = *xl; Xr = *xr; *xl = Xr ^ p[17]; *xr = Xl; have to be replaced for the suitable four expressions: Xl = xl[0]; Xr = xr[0]; xl[0] = Xr ^ p[17]; xr[0] = Xl;.

The second group of transformations contains the conversion of the references for equivalent data tables using the ampersand symbol (&). The following three expressions: xl = d; xr = d+1; d += 2; have to be replaced by the suitable two expressions: xl = &d[2*i]; xr = &d[2*i+1];.

The second transformation of the second group is the privatization of the following variables: i, xl,xr, Xl, Xr, s, p.

The parallelization technique comprises the two OpenMP directives: #pragma omp parallel and #pragma omp for.

The parallelized loop responsible for the encryption of data blocks is the following:

```
#pragma omp parallel private(i,xl,xr,Xl,Xr,s,p)
#pragma omp for
        for (i = 0; i < blocks; i++) {
        xl = &d[2*i];
        xr = &d[2*i+1];
```

```
    Xl = xl[0];
    Xr = xr[0];
    Xl ^= p[0];
    BLFRND(s, p, Xr, Xl, 1);
    BLFRND(s, p, Xl, Xr, 2);
    . . . . . . . . . . . . . . . . . . . . . .
    BLFRND(s, p, Xr, Xl, 15);
    BLFRND(s, p, Xl, Xr, 16);
    xl[0] = Xr ^ p[17];
    xr[0] = Xl;
    }
}
```

4. Experiments

In order to study the speed-ups of the parallelized loops, we used the computer with the following features:

- 64 x Itanium2 1.5GHz (SGI Altix 3700) (we use up to sixteen processors for the program execution),
- the Intel® C++ Compiler ver.9.0 (that supports the OpenMP 2.5 API).

The results received for the plaintext of the size about 10 megabytes and four independent threads executed in parallel are shown in Table 1.

Table 1. Speed-up measurements of the most time-consuming functions of selected encryption algorithms and modes of operation

Encryption algorithm	Mode of Operation	Encryption process	Decryption process
DES	ECB	3,3	3,4
Triple DES	ECB	3,5	3,6
IDEA	ECB	3,8	3,8
AES (Rijndael))	ECB	3,1	3,3
RC5	ECB	3,4	3,5
Blowfish	ECB	3,6	3,7
LOKI91	ECB	3,8	3,9
GOST	ECB	3,1	3,2
RSA		3,5	3,5
IDEA	CTR	3,5	3,5
IDEA	CBC	1,0	3,4
IDEA	CFB	1,0	3,4

5. Conclusions

The proposed automatic parallelization method of the selected encryption algorithms composes the basis for designing a parallel compiler specialized on encryption algorithms. This method is based on some well-known methods of sequential loops parallelization and the data dependency analysis of loops. All the encryption algorithms analyzed in this paper were successfully parallelized in accordance with the proposed method. Speed-up measurements confirm that the loops parallelized in accordance with the automatic parallelization method have sufficient efficiencies. The use of symmetric shared-memory multiprocessors (SMPs) along with such parallelized encryption algorithms decreases the encryption and decryption time in the case of large amounts of data to be encrypted and decrypted.

References

[1] Schneier, B., Applied Cryptography: Protocols, Algorithms, and Source Code in C, Second Edition, John Wiley & Sons, 2 edition, 1995
[2] Menezes, A.J, van Oorschot, P.C., Vanstone, S.A., Handbook of Applied Cryptography, CRC Press, 1996
[3] Bielecki, W., Burak, D., Exploiting Loop-Level Parallelism in the AES Algorithm, WSEAS Transactions on Computers, Issue 1, Volume 5, January 2006
[4] Beletskyy, V., Burak, D., Parallelization of the Data Encryption Standard (DES) Algorithm, Enhanced Methods in Computer Security, Biometric and Artificial Intelligence Systems, pp.23-33, Kluwer Academic Publishers 2005
[5] Beletskyy, V., Burak, D., Parallelization of the IDEA Algorithm, Lecture Notes in Computer Science, Computational Science- ICCS 2004: 4th International Conference, Kraków, Poland, June 6-9, 2004, Proceedings, Part I, pp.635-638, Springer-Verlag Heidelberg 2004
[6] Bielecki, W., Burak, D., Parallelization of Standard Modes of Operation for Symmetric Key Block Ciphers, Image Analysis, Computer Graphics, Security Systems and Artificial Intelligence Applications Vol.I (ACS-CISIM 2005), Białystok 2005
[7] Bielecki, W., Burak, D., Parallelization of Symmetric Block Ciphers, Computing, Multimedia and Intelligent Techniques special issue on Live Biometrics and Security, Volume 1 (2005) No.1 Published June 2005, Czestochowa University of Technology
[8] Burak, D., Automatyczne zrównoleglenie algorytmu Triple DES, Materiały VIII Sesji Naukowej Informatyki PS, Szczecin 2003 (in polish)
[9] Allen, R., Kennedy, K., Optimizing compilers for modern architectures: A Dependence-based Approach, Morgan Kaufmann Publishers, Inc., 2001
[10] Moldovan, D.I., Parallel Processing. From Applications to Systems, Morgan Kaufmann Publishers, Inc., 1993
[11] OpenMP Application Program Interface, Version 2.5, May 2005
[12] Kelly, W., Maslov, V., Pugh, W., Rosser, E., Shpeisman, T., Wonnacott, D., New User Interface for Petit and Other Extensions. User Guide. 1996
[13] http://mirrors.isc.org/pub/DragonFly/dragonfly-current/src/secure/lib/libcrypt/blowfish.c

Appendix A

1. DES

```
void  des_enc(des_ctx  *dc,  unsigned  char  *data,  int
            blocks) {
        unsigned long work[2];
        int i;
        unsigned char *cp;
        cp = data;
        for(i=0;i<blocks;i++) {
                scrunch(cp,work);
                desfunc(work,dc->ek);
                unscrun(work,cp);
                cp+=8;
        }
}
```

2. Triple DES

```
void  Ddes_encdec(des_ctx  *dc,  unsigned  char  *data,  int
            blocks) {
        unsigned long work[2];
        int i;
        unsigned char *cp;
        cp = data;
        for(i=0;i<blocks;i++) {
                scrunch(cp,work);
                desfunc(work, KnL);
                desfunc(work, KnR);
                desfunc(work, Kn3);
                unscrun(work,cp);
                cp+=8;
        }
}
```

3. IDEA

```
void  idea_enc(idea_ctx  *c,  unsigned  char  *data,  int
            blocks){
        int i;
        unsigned char *d = data;
        for(i=0;i<blocks;i++){
                ideaCipher(d,d,c->ek);
                d+=8;
        }
}
```

4. AES

```
void block_encrypt(RIJNDAEL_context *ctx, UINT8 *input,
                   int inputlen,UINT8 *output) {
         int i, nblocks;
         nblocks = inputlen / RIJNDAEL_BLOCKSIZE;
         for (i = 0; i<nblocks; i++) {
                 rijndael_encrypt(ctx, input, output);
                 input += RIJNDAEL_BLOCKSIZE;
                 output += RIJNDAEL_BLOCKSIZE;
         }
     }
```

5. RC5

```
void rc5_encrypt(rc5_ctx *c, u4 *data, int blocks) {
         u4 *d, *sk;
         int h, i, rc;
         d = data;
         sk = (c->xk) + 2;
         for (h = 0; h < blocks; h++){
                 d[0] += c->xk[0];
                 d[1] += c->xk[1];
                 for (i = 0; i < c->nr * 2; i+=2 ) {
                         d[0] ^= d[1];
                         rc = d[1] & 31;
                         d[0] = ROTL32(d[0], rc);
                         d[0] += sk[i];
                         d[1] ^= d[0];
                         rc = d[0] & 31;
                         d[1] = ROTL32(d[1],rc);
                         d[1] += sk[i+1];
                 }
                 d += 2;
         }
     }
```

6. Blowfish

```
void blf_enc(blf_ctx *c, unsigned long *data, unsigned
             int blocks){
         unsigned long *d;
         unsigned int i;
         d = data;
         for (i = 0; i < blocks; i++) {
                 Blowfish_encipher(c, d, d + 1);
                 d += 2;
         }
     }
```

7. GOST

```
void gost_enc(gost_ctx *c, u4 * d,int blocks) {
            int i;
            for(i=0;i<blocks;i++){
                 gostcrypt(c,d);
                 d+=2;
            }
      }
```

8. LOKI91

```
void  loki_enc(loki_ctx  *c,  unsigned  char  *data,  int
                 blocks){
            unsigned char *cp;
            int i;
            cp = data;
            for(i=0;i<blocks;i++){
                 enloki(c,cp);
                 cp+=8;
            }
      }
```

9. RSA

```
for (i= 0; i< blocks; i++)
      output[i] = (input[i] ^ exponent) % (p*q);
```

10. ECB

Encryption process:
```
ecb_encryption(&c,data,total);
```

Decryption process:
```
ecb_decryption(&c,data,total);
```

11. CBC

Encryption process:
```
for(int i=0;  i<8;  i++)
      data_iv[i] = data[i] ^ iv[i];
ecb_encryption(&c data_iv,1);
for(i=0;  i<8;  i++)
            data_enc[i] = data_iv[i];
for(i=8;  i<total;  i+=8) {
      for (int j=0;  j<8;  j++)
            data_iv[i+j] = data[i+j] ^ data_enc[i+j-8];
      ecb_encryption(&c,data_iv+i,1);
      for(int k=0;  k<8;  k++)
            data_enc[i+k] = data_iv[i+k];
}
```

Decryption process:
```
for(int i=0;  i<8;  i++)
```

```
        data_iv[i] = data_enc[i];
ecb_decryption(&c data_iv,1);
for(int i=0; i<8; i++)
        data_dec[i] = data_iv[i] ^ iv[i];
for(i=8; i<total; i+=8) {
        ecb_decryption(&c,data_iv+i,1);
        for (int j=0; j<8; j++)
            data_dec[i+j] = data_iv[i+j] ^ data_enc[i+j-8];
}
```

12. CFB

Encryption process:
```
for(int i=0; i<8; i++)
        data_xored[i] = iv[i];
ecb_encryption(&c, data_xored,1);
for(i=8; i<total; i+=8) {
  for(int j=0; j<8; j++)
        data_xored[i+j] = data[i+j-8] ^ data_xored[i+j-8];
        for(int k=0; k<8; k++)
                data_enc[i+k-8] = data_xored[i+k];
        ecb_encryption(&c, data_xored+i,1);
}
```

Decryption process:
```
ecb_encryption(&c, iv,1);
for(int i=0; i<8; i++)
  data_dec[i] = iv[i] ^ data_enc[i];
for(i=8; i<total; i+=8) {
  ecb_encryption(&c, data_xored+i,1);
  for(int j=0; j<8; j++)
        data_dec[i+j] = data_enc[i+j] ^ data_xored[i+j-8];
}
```

13. CTR

Encryption process:
```
for(int i=0;i<total;i+=8) {
        ecb_encryption(&c,counter+i,1);
        for(int j=0;j<8;j++)
                data_enc[i+j] = data[i+j] ^ counter[i+j];
}
```

Decryption process:
```
for(int i=0;i<total;i+=8) {
        ecb_encryption(&c,counter+i,1);
        for(int j=0;j<8;j++)
                data_dec[i+j] = data_enc[i+j] ^ counter[i+j];
}
```

When a Family of Iris Flower is Normal, Then are Others Abnormal?

Akira Imada

Brest State Technical University
Moskowskaja 267, Brest 224017 Republic of Belarus
akira@bsty.by

Abstract. This article is not a report of success but rather a challenge to those who claim to have successfully designed a network intrusion detection system by means of a machine learning technique using artificial dataset to train and to test the system.

1 Introduction

Those highly qualified hackers who provide security services to companies during the daytime and then go home at night to conduct totally illegal hacking are the ones who are the most dangerous. — by Enis Senerdem from Turkish Daily News on 29 March 2006.

Designing a network intrusion detection system is one of the hottest issues in our computer network society. Designing such a system with so-called a soft-computing seems to become a sort of fashion these days. When we try one of these approaches, we need a dataset to *train* the system if our strategy is a supervised learning, and also need it to *test* the system afterwards. Usually we employ an artificial dataset for the purpose. In fact we could find a lot of such datasets in public domain. *Spearman's iris-flower* dataset[1] is an example and probably one of the most frequently used ones. Yet another most frequently used is *KDD-cup-99* dataset.[2] We doubt, however, these datasets cannot necessarily reflect data of computer network connections in real world. We don't know what does a coming intrusion look like until it has completed the illegal connection when actually it is too late.

Previously we posed a doubt about using KDD-cup-99 dataset in designing an intrusion detection system [1]. In this paper, on the other hand, we concentrate on the iris flower dataset among others and give it a consideration on how an intrusion can be reflected by a family of iris flowers and how an intrusion can be detected by an intelligent way, if any.

---

[1] This can be obtained from University of California Urvine Machine Learning Repository. ftp://ics.uci.edu: pub/machine-learning-databases.

[2] See http://kdd.ics.uci.edu/databases/kddcup99/kddcup99.html.

2   What does iris flower dataset look like?

The iris flower dataset is made up of 150 samples consists of three species of iris flower, that is, *setosa, versicolor* and *virginica*. Each of these three families includes 50 samples. Each sample is a four-dimensional vector representing four attributes of iris flower, that is, *sepal-length, sepal-width, petal-length*, and *petal-width*.

This iris flower dataset is perhaps one of the most often used datasets in research works concerning pattern recognition/classification, machine learning, data mining, etc. As such, there have been a fair amount of studies in which this iris flower dataset is employed as a dataset to train and to test an intrusion detection system.

Quite naturally, all of these papers report their success in designing a system. Let us take an example from among many others. Castellano et al. [2] assumed one family of this iris flower to be abnormal whilst the other two to be normal. The whole dataset was divided into 10 parts each of which has 15 samples and are uniformly drawn from the three classes. The system is trained by the remaining 135 samples. The originally picked up 15 samples are used to test the results. After this 10-fold cross validation, the authors concluded that their system with fuzzy neural network using Takagi-Sugeno model shows the invasion detection rate is 96% while the false alarm rate is 0.6%.

In reality, however, it is not so simple. Just imagine that it would be quite easy for a hacker to explore an unlearned region to invade the network. Or worse, we should know hacker is a person who is very good at locating attack just behind a normal.

2.1   A visualization by Sammon mapping

We now take a look at how those iris data are distributed in the whole search space. We tried a *Sammon mapping* to get a bird's eye view of those data in a fictitious 2-dimensional space.

Sammon mapping maps a set of points in a high-dimensional space to the 2-dimensional space with the distance relation being preserved as much as possible, or equivalently, the distances in the n-dimensional space are approximated by distances in the 2-dimensional space with a minimal error.

One of our results of Sammon mapping of iris flower dataset is shown in Fig. 1. Just a brief look at the figure reveals us that there remains an enormously big region of unlearned.

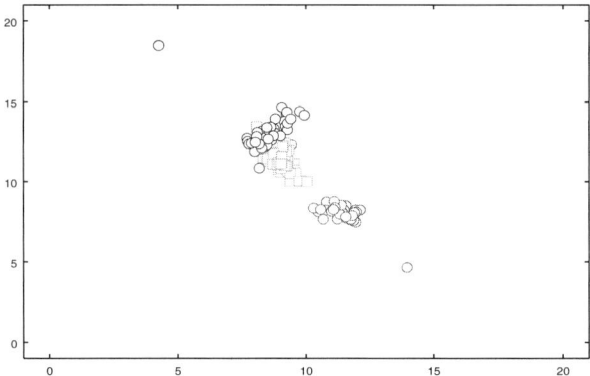

Fig. 1. A two dimensional visualization of the iris flower data by Sammon Mapping. The 150 data of three families, 50 data each, are plotted.

3 Five challenges

In this section we challenge readers of this article with five problems.

Standard settings. We now start by formalizing the standard way of using iris dataset to design a network intrusion detection system.

Standard Experiment (One is attack while the others are normal)
Assuming one out of three families of iris flower to represent illegal transactions while the remaining two families represent legal ones. Is it possible then to simulate a system for network intrusion detection by using part of this dataset to train and the remaining data to test the system?

We have so many candidate techniques to design such a system with. Sabhnani et al. [3] might be a good summary in which we can overview such techniques applied to design intrusion detection system.³ Those applied in their paper are (i) *Multi-layer Perceptron*, (ii) *Gaussian Classifier*, (iii) *K-mean Clustering*, (iv) *Nearest Cluster Algorithm*, (v) *Radial Basis Function*, (vi) *Leader Algorithm*, (vii) *Hypersphere Algorithm*, (viii) *Fuzzy Art Map*, and (ix) *C4.5 Decision Tree*. Our experiment here was made with a two-layer perceptron, as an example, whose implementation for the iris dataset is shown in Fig. 2.

First of all, in order to see how it works, we apply this two-layer perceptron to the iris dataset under a standard situation where one family assumed to be attack and the other two to be normal. We determined the configuration of synaptic

---

³ Target in their paper was not the iris dataset but to the KDD-cup-99 dataset which is more demanding than the iris dataset.

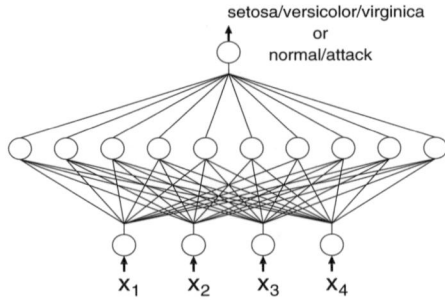

Fig. 2. A possible implementation by two layer perceptron to detect one family as attack while the other two as normal.

weight values of the perceptron by a Genetic Algorithm with chromosomes being made up of all the synaptic weights of the perceptron. One of the results of the evolution is shown in Fig. 3 which suggests that the task is quite easy.

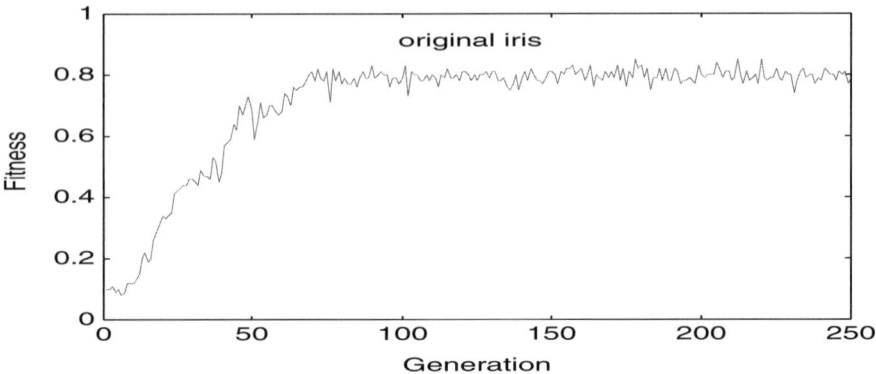

Fig. 3. A result of our experiment to evolve neural network attack detector under a standard setting.

3.1 What if both normals and attacks are not well clustered?

It is too simplified or too optimistic assuming both normal and attack data are well clustered such as the iris dataset. We now look at what will happen if both normal and attack data are distributed at random as an extreme case, such as those shown in Fig. 4.

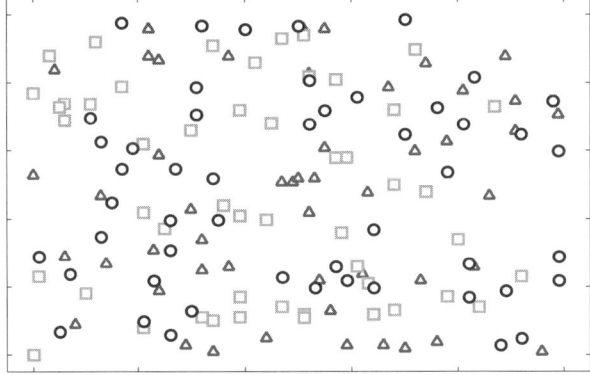

Fig. 4. An example of randomly distributed 100 normals and 50 attacks shown in a fictitious 2-dimensional search space.

Now our first challenge is:

Challenge 1 (Randomly located normals and attacks) *(1) Create 100 normal samples and 50 attack samples all at random. (2) Then train the system using half of these samples of normal and attack. (3) Test the system with remaining half of the samples of normal and attack.*

This might be reminiscent of the experiment by Ayara et al. [4] who created, in the context of network intrusion detection, a set of 8-bit binary random strings as training samples of normal patterns assuming other comparable amount of 8-bit binary patterns as abnormal with their results being very successful in recognizing both normal and abnormal.

Yes, still this is not so difficult because the data used were fixed ones. How about, however, if we create a *mutant from a normal* each time as an attack, and as such, attacks are not *a priori* known fixed data any more?

3.2 Can a system recognize a mutant as mutant?

When we use the iris dataset as artificial dataset of normal and abnormal access to a computer network, our assumption is that attacks are apart enough from normal data. However this does not necessarily reflect a reality. Skillful hackers attack a network so that their transaction being as similar as normal, wishing network administrator wouldn't notice. We simulate this situation by mutating normal data and considering them as attacks.

Mutation. We now introduce a mutation which is to be applied to the data in order to avoid for the data to be deterministic since real data are never expected to be deterministic. Each of the iris dataset is given as the form of

$$(x_1, x_2, x_3, x_4).$$

Then with a small probability called *mutation rate* we modify records by

$$x_i^{\text{new}} = x_i^{\text{old}} + r\sigma_i \quad (i = 1, 2, 3, 4)$$

where σ_i is standard deviation of 150 values of x_i, and r is a small random number which is created anew each time when mutation occurs. Then our problem might turn into as follows.

Challenge 2 (Mutant of normal as attack) *(1) Create 100 normal samples all at random. (2) Then 50 out of those samples are mutated as attack. (3) Train with half of the normal and mutants behind them. (4) Test with the remaining half.*

The situation might be too demanding since we assume all normal samples are distributed at random. In order to reduce the requirement, let us go back to the iris dataset.

3.3 What if outlier hides behind normals?

It would be more realistic that normal data are well clustered in the whole universe of possible data, and the attack data are mutants of those normals as the previous subsection. A fictitious 2-dimensional plots are shown in Fig. 5.

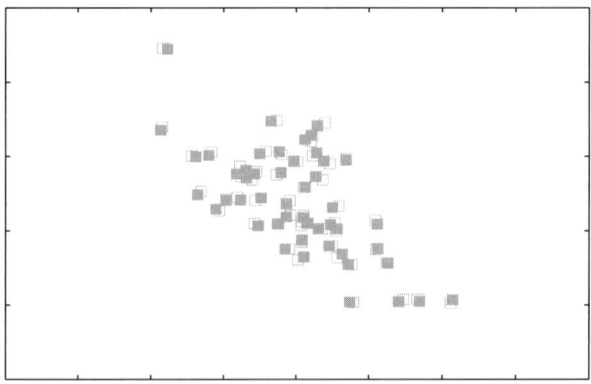

Fig. 5. An example of 50 attacks who try to hide behind the normals of the iris family which is one of the three shown in Fig. 1.

Then the challenge here is:

Challenge 3 (Attacks who hide behind normals) *(1) Assume one family of iris flower as normal (2) Then all of the family member are mutated as attack. (3) Train with half of normal and mutated attacks. (4) Test with the remaining half of normals and newly created mutants of attack.*

Is the system which was trained by a given deterministic attack samples still immune to attacks by new mutants from normals? It seems hard to believe.

3.4 Previous attack data work as training sample?

Then how about an idea of not using attack data in training the system? Can we train a system only with normal samples? How the system can learn only from normal data to detect attacks? This is further difficult issue but actually is our must, since we usually have enormous amount of normal data while we have no information about coming attacks until it's too late.

In their articles, Gomez et al. [5] claimed, *"A new technique for generating a set of fuzzy rules can characterize the abnormal space using only normal samples."*[4] Gomez et al. designed the detector they call an *evolving-fuzzy-rule-detector* with what they call an *immuno-fuzzy approach*.

Let's be a little more specific and apply the method to the iris flower dataset.[5] First of all, we define five linguistic terms:

$$\{Low,\ Medium\text{-}low,\ Medium,\ Medium\text{-}high,\ High\}$$

where *Medium* and its both neighbors are specified using triangle membership functions while *Low* and *High* are using trapezoidal membership functions. Then an example of a set of rules is

---

IF
x_1 *is Law or Medium-law;*
x_2 *is High;*
x_3 *is Medium or Medium-high or High; and*
x_4 *is Medium-low or Medium.*

THEN
$\mathbf{x} = (x_1, x_2, x_3, x_4)$ *is Attack.*

Assuming k such rules, Gomez et al. defined a *degree of membership of $\mathbf{x}$ to be an attack* as

$$\mu_{\text{attack}}(\mathbf{x}) = \max_{i=1,\ldots,k} \{\text{Eval}_{R_i}(\mathbf{x})\}$$

---

[4] This is not the original expression in their paper, but paraphrased by the author of this article.

[5] Gomez et al. used the KDD-cup-99 dataset instead of the iris flower dataset.

where $\text{Eval}_{R_i}(\mathbf{x})$ is the fuzzy true value evaluated by the *IF*-part of the rule R_i, and thus $\mu_{\text{attack}}(\mathbf{x})$ closer to zero means that $\mathbf{x}$ is more likely to be a normal and closer to one is more likely to be an attack.

Then our chromosome comprises four genes corresponding to $x_1, \cdots, x_4$, and each of those genes is 5-digit binary string corresponding to five fuzzy linguistic terms. For example, $((11001)(01001)(10000)(11100))$ implies:

---

x_1 *is Low or Medium-Low or High*

x_2 *is Medium-Low or High*

x_3 *is Low*

x_4 *is Low or Medium-Low or Medium*

---

where fitness is essentially the evaluation of *how few a rule covers a set of given N normal training samples.*[6]

Thus the authors claimed, *"It detects attacks with the detection rate 98.30% and false alarm rate 2.0%."* It would be terrific if the report was really successful, but we think it fishy more or less.

Though this *training-only-with-normal* is our ultimate goal, it is not so simple to be realized. To study how this is difficult, why not give it a try the following?

Challenge 4 (Can a sommelier be trained without bootlegs?)
(1) Assume one family of iris as normal while the other two abnormal. (2) In addition, create an attack dataset at random and call them dummy attacks. (3) Train your intrusion detection system only with the normal set. (4) Then, try two tests, one with only abnormal, and the other with only dummy, avoiding any a priori prediction.

This issue is something like we require a wine-taster to recognize a bootleg champagne or a not-champagne-but-sparkling-wine by only providing him/her a plenty of real champagne to learn with.[7] Can a sommelier be trained without bootlegs?

3.5   Is an intelligent decision better than random one?

Moreover, we have to be careful, because we sometimes have a tendency to *unconsciously* pick up only a set of data that will be suitable to draw our *a priori* expected conclusion, if not *intentionally* at all.

---

[6] A volume of the subspace represented by the rule is also taken into account.

[7] Or, in an opposite way. I usually enjoy Georgian sparkling wine like once a week, but still a real champagne would be able to pretend to be a Georgian one to me.

Drugs to ... are no more effective than placebos for most patients ... found no significant difference than the placebos or at increased risk of death compared to placebo.

This is from an article of a newspaper.[8] A *harmless dummy pill* or even *powder-from-sugar* sometimes has an effect as, or more efficient than, a medicine under developing enough to cure a disease for a group of innocent volunteers. Why don't we try the following question?

Challenge 5 (A placebo experiment) *(1) Create a simple device which randomly returns either one of normal or attack regardless of the input. (2) Prepare a test dataset including enough amount of records uniformly from normal and attack. (3) Compare the performances of the detector you designed with the random-reply-machine created in step 1, feeding the same dataset prepared in step 2.*

See Fig. 6.

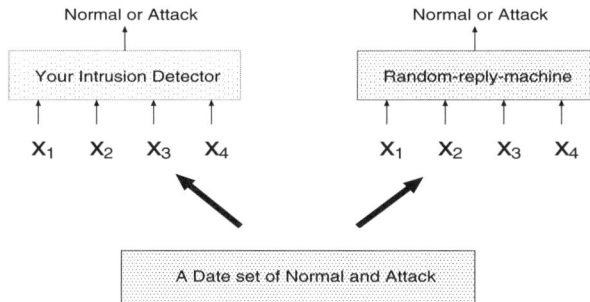

Fig. 6. Intelligently designed attack detector versus randomly reply machine.

4 A result — Still seems to be an easy task?

We tried to evolve a configuration of weights for the two-layer perceptron mentioned above with fitness evaluation being *how the perceptron detects the samples of normal and attack data correctly.* When we used (i) a set of random data as normal and attack such as those in Fig. 4, and (ii) one family of iris as normal and their mutants as attack, such as the ones in Fig. 5, the evolution never reached to a satisfactory level while, as already mentioned, it evolved fairly easy when we gave two families of iris as normal and the other family as attack such as the ones in Fig. 1. The fitness versus generation of these three cases are shown in Fig. 7.

---

[8] By Benedict Carey in the New York Times on 12 October 2006.

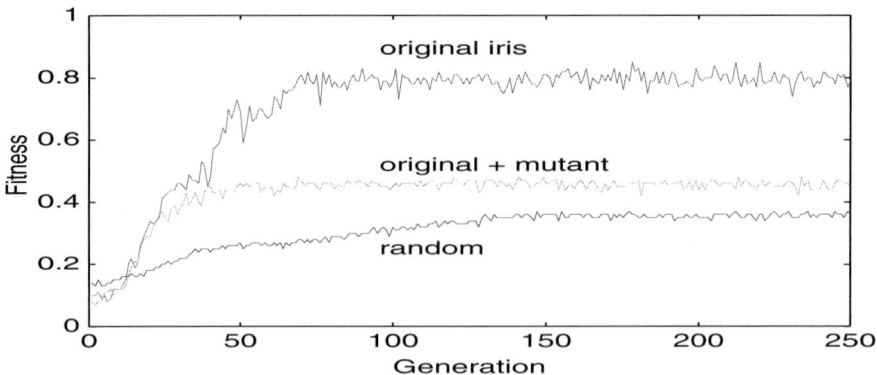

Fig. 7. The results of three of our Genetic Algorithm experiments: under a standard setting (original iris), with attack hidden behind normal (original + mutant), and with random dataset (random).

5   Concluding Remarks

We feel sorry that we have described the above not so optimistically. However, we should be careful to draw a conclusion from our experiment or simulation. We sometimes tend to overestimate our results so that we like it. Needles to say, however, this article is not to deny the possibility, but instead we hope it to be a challenge for real new innovative approaches to be emerged.

References

1. A. Imada (2006) *"How Many Parachutists will be Needed to Find a Needle in a Pastoral? — Who is a lucky one?"* Proceedings of the International Conference on Neural Networks and Artificial Intelligence, pp. 53–60.
2. G. Castellano, and A. M. Fanelli(2000) *"Fuzzy Inference and Rule Extraction using a Neural Network."* Neural Network World Journal Vol. 3, pp. 361–371.
3. M. Sabhnani, and G. Serpen (2003) *"Application of Machine Learning Algorithms to KDD Intrusion Detection Dataset within Misuse Detection Context."* Proceedings of the International Conference on Machine Learning: Models, Technologies and Applications, pp. 209–215.
4. M. Ayara, J. Timmis, R. D. Lemos, L. N. D. Castro, and R. Duncan (2002) *"Negative Selection: How to Generate Detectors."* Proceedings of 1st International Conference on Artificial Immune Systems, pp. 89–98.
5. J. Gomez, F. Gonzalez, and D. Dasgupta (2003) *"An Immuno-Fuzzy Approach to Anomaly Detection."* Proceedings of IEEE International Conference on Fuzzy Systems, Vol. 2, pp. 1219–1224.

This article was processed using the LaTeX macro package with LLNCS style

Strong Boolean Functions with Compact ANF Representation

Anna Grocholewska Czurylo

Institute of Control and Information Engineering, Poznan University of Technology,
pl. Marii Sklodowskiej-Curie 5, Poznan, Poland
czurylo@sk-kari.put.poznan.pl

Abstract. Boolean functions are basic building blocks of virtually any cipher. Tremendous amount of research is devoted to finding Boolean functions that would be best suited for the job. A number of cryptographic criteria have been proposed that a Boolean function should fulfill to be considered for use in a cipher system. Most of these criteria in one way or another are correlated with function's nonlinearity. Also a number of specific algebraic constructions and algorithms have been developed that allow us to obtain such Boolean functions with those desirable properties. Efficient representation and implementation of such cipher systems is another challenge faced by today's cryptologists. This article presents a simple algorithm that is able to randomly generate Boolean functions with surprisingly good cryptographic properties, which at the same time have extremely short ANF representation, which could lead to efficient implementations.

Introduction

Ever since Shannon proposed the use of two basic transformations, confusion and diffusion to form a product cipher, most modern cryptographic algorithms rely (in some way) on the use of so called S-boxes (that provide confusion) and P-boxes (that provide diffusion of bits) While P-boxes play an important role in block ciphers, the cryptographic strength (resistance to cryptanalysis) of a cipher comes from carefully designed S-boxes.

One may argue that a secure cipher can also be made using random S-boxes, providing they are large enough (such as 12 input bits). Another way to make a cipher more secure even while using not optimized S-boxes is to use more rounds. The example of this approach is FEAL algorithm, which becomes immune against linear cryptanalysis when the number of rounds is bigger then 32. However, if a cryptographic algorithm should be strong and fast at the same time then its careful design is a must.

Since the creation of DES, plenty of research has gone into finding better S-boxes and better techniques to break them. The most basic method of cryptanalysis is the exhaustive search method, also known as the brute force and known plaintext attack. This method uses merely one block of known plaintext and the resultant ciphertext to find the secret key.

Linear cryptanalysis was first openly published as a means for attacking DES by Mitsuru Matsui at EUROCRYPT'93. His method attempts to find a linear relation among the plaintext, ciphertext, and keys as they pass through the S-boxes. Eli Biham and Adi Shamir published their new method of cryptanalysis in 1990 called Differential Cryptanalysis. They define this as a method which analyses the effect of particular differences in plaintext pairs on the differences of the resultant ciphertext pairs. These differences can be used to assign probabilities to the possible keys and to locate the most probable key. The idea behind differential cryptanalysis is to throw out key choices that are unlikely, and keep choices that are very likely. From this reduced subset, a cryptanalyst can run an exhaustive search to find the correct key. Other attacks also exist, but ones mentioned above are most widely described in the literature and commonly used for testing ciphers' strength.

Each attack that is better then exhaustive search explores some weakness in S-boxes. After some new attack is published a new design criteria for S-boxes can be introduced which makes the cryptographic algorithm immune against that particular attack. Researchers can also examine how S-box design matches up against those cryptanalysis techniques. Because of the continuous progress in the development of cryptanalysis techniques careful design of S-boxes becomes more and more important. Large random S-boxes, increased number of rounds or long keys may become irrelevant if cryptographic attack exploits some inherent flaw in S-boxes.

The basic building blocks of virtually any cipher are Boolean functions. Tremendous amount of research is devoted to finding Boolean functions that would be best suited for the job. A number of cryptographic criteria have been proposed that a Boolean function should fulfill to be considered for use in a cipher system. Most of these criteria in one way or another are correlated with function's nonlinearity. A number of specific algebraic constructions and algorithms have been developed that allow us to obtain Boolean functions with those desirable properties. Efficient representation and implementation of such cipher systems is another challenge faced by today's cryptologists. This article presents a simple algorithm that is able to randomly generate Boolean functions with surprisingly good cryptographic properties which at the same time have extremely short ANF representation, which could lead to efficient implementations.

The paper is organized as follows. Section Preliminaries provides some basic definitions and notations that are used throughout the remainder of the article. In the next section an algorithm is described that generates cryptographically strong Boolean functions. Experimental results and comparisons to other research are given in section Experimental Results. Then conclusions follow.

Preliminaries

We use square brackets to denote vectors like $[a_1, ..., a_n]$ and round brackets to denote functions like $f(x_1, ..., x_n)$.

Boolean function

Let $GF(2) = <\Sigma, \oplus, \bullet>$ be two-element Galois field, where $\Sigma = \{0, 1\}$, $\oplus$ and $\bullet$ denotes the sum and multiplication mod 2, respectively. A function $f: \Sigma^n \rightarrow \Sigma$ is an n-argument Boolean function. Let $z = x_1 \cdot 2^{n-1} + x_2 \cdot 2^{n-2} + \dots + x_n \cdot 2^0$ be the decimal representation of arguments $(x_1, x_2, \dots, x_n)$ of the function f. Let us denote $f(x_1, x_2, \dots, x_n)$ as y_z. Then $[y_0, y_1, \dots, y_{2^n-1}]$ is called a truth table of the function f. Alternatively, a Boolean function may be represented over $\{-1, 1\}$ in what is known as the polarity truth table, distinguished using the "hat" notation: $\hat{f}(x)$.

Linear and nonlinear Boolean functions

An n-argument Boolean function f is linear if it can be represented in the following form: $f(x_1, x_2, \dots, x_n) = a_1 x_1 \oplus a_2 x_2 \oplus \dots \oplus a_n x_n$. Let L_n be a set of all n-argument linear Boolean functions. Let $M_n = \{g: \Sigma^n \rightarrow \Sigma \mid g(x_1, x_2, \dots, x_n) = 1 \oplus f(x_1, x_2, \dots, x_n)$ and $f \in L_n\}$. A set $A_n = L_n \cup M_n$ is called a set of n-argument affine Boolean functions. A Boolean function $f: \Sigma^n \rightarrow \Sigma$ that is not affine is called a nonlinear Boolean function.

Balance

Let $N_0[y_0, y_1, \dots, y_{2^n-1}]$ be a number of zeros (0's) in the truth table $[y_0, y_1, \dots, y_{2^n-1}]$ of function f, and $N_1[y_0, y_1, \dots, y_{2^n-1}]$ be number of ones (1's). A Boolean function is balanced if $N_0[y_0, y_1, \dots, y_{2^n-1}] = N_1[y_0, y_1, \dots, y_{2^n-1}]$.

Algebraic Normal Form

A Boolean function can also be represented as a maximum of 2^n coefficients of the Algebraic Normal Form. These coefficients provide a formula for the evaluation of the function for any given input $x = [x_1, x_2, \dots, x_n]$:

$$f(x) = a_0 \oplus \sum_{i=1}^{n} a_i x_i \oplus \sum_{1 \le i < j \le n} a_{ij} x_i x_j \oplus \dots \oplus a_{12\dots n} x_1 x_2 \dots x_n$$

where $\sum$, $\oplus$ denote the modulo 2 summation.

The order of nonlinearity of a Boolean function $f(x)$ is a maximum number of variables in a product term with non-zero coefficient a_J, where J is a subset of $\{1, 2, 3, \dots, n\}$. In the case where J is an empty set the coefficient is denoted as a_0 and is called a zero order coefficient. Coefficients of order 1 are $a_1, a_2, \dots, a_n$, coefficients of order 2 are $a_{12}, a_{13}, \dots, a_{(n-1)n}$, coefficient of order n is $a_{12\dots n}$. The number of all ANF coefficients equals 2^n.

Let us denote the number of all (zero and non-zero) coefficients of order i of function f as $\sigma_i(f)$. For n-argument function f there are as many coefficients of a given order as there are i-element combinations in n-element set, i.e. $\sigma_i(f) = \binom{n}{i}$.

Hamming distance

Hamming weight of a binary vector $x \in \Sigma^n$, denoted as $hwt(x)$, is the number of ones in that vector.

Hamming distance between two Boolean functions $f, g: \Sigma^n \rightarrow \Sigma$ is denoted by $d(f, g)$ and is defined as follows:

$$d(f,g) = \sum_{x \in \Sigma^n} f(x) \oplus g(x)$$

The distance of a Boolean function f from a set of n-argument Boolean functions X_n is defined as follows:

$$\delta(f) = \min_{g \in X_n} d(f,g)$$

where $d(f, g)$ is the Hamming distance between functions f and g. The distance of a function f from a set of affine functions A_n is the distance of function f from the nearest function $g \in A_n$.

The distance of function f from a set of all affine functions is called the nonlinearity of function f and is denoted by N_f.

Bent functions

A Boolean function $f: \Sigma^n \rightarrow \Sigma$ is perfectly nonlinear if and only if $f(x) \oplus f(x \oplus \alpha)$ is balanced for any $\alpha \in \Sigma^n$ such that $1 \leq hwt(\alpha) \leq n$.

For a perfectly nonlinear Boolean function, any change of inputs causes the change of the output with probability of 1/2.

Meier and Staffelbach [12] proved that the set of perfectly nonlinear Boolean functions is the same as the set of Boolean bent functions defined by Rothaus [15]. Perfectly nonlinear functions (or bent functions) have the same, and the maximum possible distance to all affine functions.

Bent functions are not balanced. Hamming weight of a bent function equals $2^{n-1} \pm 2^{n/2-1}$.

Walsh transform (WHT)

Let $x = (x_1, x_2, ...,x_n)$ and $\omega = (\omega_1, \omega_2, ...,\omega_n)$ both belong to $\{0,1\}^n$ and $x\omega = (x_1\omega_1, x_2\omega_2, ..., x_n\omega_n)$. Let $f(x)$ be a Boolean functions on n variables. Then the Walsh transform of $f(x)$ is a real valued function over $\{0,1\}^n$ that can be defined as:

$$W_f(\omega) = \sum_{x \in \{0,1\}^n} (-1)^{f(x) \oplus x\omega}$$

The Walsh transform is sometimes called the spectral distribution or simply the spectra of a Boolean function. It is an important tool for the analysis of Boolean function.

Autocorrelation (AC)

The autocorrelation function (AC) is a vector $R_f(s)$ of 2^n integers similar to WHT. It gives an indication of the imbalance of all first order derivatives of a Boolean function. The derivative of a Boolean function $\hat{f}$, taken with respect to vector s is defined as $D_s f(x) = f(x) \oplus f(x \oplus s)$. The autocorrelation values are proportional to the correlation that $f(x)$ has with $f(x \oplus s)$. The autocorrelation function is defined by

$$\hat{R}_f(s) = \sum_x \hat{f}(x) \cdot \hat{f}(x \oplus s).$$

Affine transform and Equivalence classes

An affine transform of a Boolean function is a transformation defined in terms of a linear transform and a dyadic shift. A linear transform involves the multiplication of the input vector of a Boolean function by a non-singular binary matrix. A dyadic shift (a translation) involves the complement of a subset of input bits.   An affine transformation is defined as combination of a linear transform and dyadic shift. The addition if an affine function to the output of a Boolean function is also an affine transformation. An equivalence class is a group of Boolean functions related by affine transforms.

Correlation immunity and resilience

Xiao and Massey [5] have provided a spectral characterisation of correlation immune functions using Walsh transform. We can use that as a definition of correlation immunity:
  A function $f(x_1, x_2, ...,x_n)$ is m-order correlation immune (CI) iff its Walsh transform W_f satisfies $W_f(\omega) = 0$, for $1 \leq hwt(\omega) \leq m$. Note that balanced m-order correlation immune functions are called m-resilient functions and if f is balanced then $W_f(0) = 0$. Thus, a function $f(x_1, x_2, ...,x_n)$ is m-resilient iff its Walsh transform W_f satisfies $W_f(\omega) = 0$, for $0 \leq hwt(\omega) \leq m$.
  By an (n,m,d,x) function we mean an n-variable, m-resilient (balanced m-order CI) function with degree d and nonlinearity x. In the above notation the degree component is replaced by a '-' (i.e. $(n,m,-,x)$), if we do not want to specify a degree.

Generating strong Boolean functions

A lot of research in cryptography concentrates on constructing strong Boolean functions for application in ciphers. Most of these constructions are deterministic in nature - they use a defined formula to obtain a cryptographically sound Boolean function, usually by transforming other Boolean functions, often of lower number of arguments [1, 7, 8, 11]. Another approach is to use some sort of evolutionary heuristic algorithms [2, 10].

Both of these techniques have proven themselves very useful in generating function being among the best know examples for cryptographical qualities. They have however, also some potential drawbacks. Deterministic nature of algebraic constructions could in theory lead to designing a new attack that would exploit the particularities of a given construction. Both approaches, i.e. constructions and genetic algorithms give Boolean functions that have roughly half of total number of coefficients in their ANF representations. That in turn translates to big storage requirements and less efficient hardware implementations. For example, in case of 16-argument functions, half of ANF coefficients mean more then 32000.

The algorithm presented in this paragraph is able to randomly generate either bent functions or highly nonlinear balanced functions, of up to 16 arguments, with very good cryptographic properties that can have ANF representation as short as under a hundred coefficients.

We start off by describing an algorithm that generates bent Boolean functions. These functions, as described earlier, have the best achievable nonlinearity. They exist only for even number of arguments and are not balanced, but they are clearly defined and in any case, such functions are of interest in cryptography as they can provide a good starting point for modifications that lead to highly nonlinear balanced functions. Best nonlinearity for balanced functions or functions on even number of arguments is not known.

It is impossible to find all bent functions by a pure random search for 6-argument Boolean functions. ANF representation of Boolean functions opens up some possibilities for random search. We have used that representation to generate successfully random bent functions of up to 16-argument functions.

Operating on ANF representation gives a great control over the nonlinear characteristics of generated functions, namely the number of ANF coefficients of every order. Basic properties of bent functions can then be used to tremendously narrow search space which makes generation of bent functions feasible for n up to 16 on a standard PC machine.

The algorithm for the generation of bent functions in ANF domain takes as its input the minimum and maximum number of ANF coefficients of every order that the resulting functions are allowed to have. Since the nonlinear order of bent functions is less or equal to $n/2$, clearly in ANF of a bent function there can not be any ANF coefficient of order higher then $n/2$. This restriction is the major reason for random generation feasibility, since it considerably reduces the possible search space.

The number of ANF coefficients of orders less or equal to $n/2$ can be fixed or randomly selected within allowed range. If the number of coefficients for a given order i is fixed then all generated functions will have the same number of coefficients of that order, but the coefficients themselves will be different in each generated function. If the number of coefficients for a given order i is randomly selected then all generated functions will not only have different coefficients but also the number of coefficients of order i will vary from function to function. It is of course possible to fix the number of coefficients for some orders and obtain varied number of coefficients for other orders.

A drawback of the method results from the fact that it does not guarantee the generation of bent functions without repetitions, although the chance of generating two identical bent functions is minimal with any reasonably selected ranges of number of ANF coefficients. Moreover, the algorithm can not generate all bent functions, and is in fact heavily restricted by feasibility limit that prohibits generation of functions with high number of ANF coefficients. Total number of possible Boolean functions grows with the number of coefficients of higher orders and generating a bent function quickly becomes infeasible. So the algorithm works good with the low number of higher order coefficients. Due to the above limitation, this method does not generate all possible bent functions with equal probability. In principle, it would be possible but is not feasible for the reason described above. One has to limit the number of higher order coefficients and at the same time prohibit the generation of some bent functions.

Algorithm 1 Random generation of bent functions.
INPUT:
- the number n of arguments such that n is even,
- for each order ord such that $0 \leq$ ord $\leq n/2$ define minimum (denoted as $cmin_{ord}$) and maximum (denoted as $cmax_{ord}$) number of coefficients of ANF such that $0 \leq cmin_{ord} \leq cmax_{ord} \leq \binom{n}{ord}$.

OUTPUT:
- randomly generated perfect nonlinear function f_{ANF} in ANF,
- randomly generated perfect nonlinear function f_{TT} in the form of the truth table.

METHOD:
1. Repeat steps (1a) and (1b) for each order ord such that $0 \leq ord \leq n/2$:
    a) generate randomly the number of coefficients c_{ord} of ANF for a given order ord such that $cmin_{ord} \leq c_{ord} \leq cmax_{ord}$,
    b) for f_{ANF} fix randomly the value 1 for coefficients of order ord.
2. Transform f_{ANF} to f_{TT}.
3. Calculate the distance of f_{TT} from the set of affine functions.
4. If the distance calculated in the step (3) is equal to $2^{n-1} - 2^{n/2-1}$, then f_{TT} (and f_{ANF}) is perfect nonlinear - stop; otherwise go to (1).

If the first input of Algorithm 1 is dropped (allowing n to be even or odd) then the algorithm can be used to obtain highly nonlinear functions even for odd number of arguments (in the remainder of this paper we will refer to it as to Algorithm 1'). These functions are not bent (as these do not exist for odd argument number) so step (4) of the algorithm is not performed - the algorithm should be used in a loop that generates random functions, many of which are highly nonlinear.

Algorithm 1' can be used to generate highly nonlinear balanced Boolean functions. It just should be run until a resulting function is balanced. Also, the requirement of $0 \leq ord \leq n/2$ is no longer necessary, as we are not expecting a bent function.

In the next section we look at the properties of functions generated in the above described way.

Experimental results

Nonlinearity

Table 1 summarizes the results obtained related to the nonlinearity of balanced Boolean functions. The table shows nonlinearity of balanced Boolean functions achieved by the best currently known techniques along with best theoretical upper bounds and the best currently known examples. Table gives values for Boolean functions of 8 up to 12 arguments. Results for lower number of arguments are the same for all methods and are in fact maximum achievable.

Table 1. Conjectured upper bounds and attained values for nonlinearity of balanced functions

n	8	9	10	11	12
LUB	118	244	494	1000	2014
BK	116	240	492	992	2010
BC	112	240	480	992	1984
R	112	230	472	962	1955
RHC	114	236	476	968	1961
GA	116	236	484	980	1976
DNL	114	236	480	974	1972
NLT	116	238	486	984	1992
ACT	116	238	484	982	1986
GEN	**116**	**240**	**488**	**992**	**2002**

Abbreviations used in Table 1 are: LUB - Lowest Upper Bound, BK - Best Known [6], BC - Bent Concatenation, R - Random, RHC - Random + Hill-Climb [2], GA - Genetic Algorithms [10], DNL - Direct Non-Linearity [2], NLT - Non-Linearity Targeted [2], ACT - Auto-Correlation Targeted [2], and finally GEN - Balanced Randomly Generated functions (results presented in this paper).

Resilience

The maximum nonlinearity is known for all Boolean functions on even number of variables - it is achieved by bent functions. The maximum nonlinearity for odd variable Boolean functions is known for $n \leq 7$. Also, maximum nonlinearity question is solved for balanced and resilient functions on n variables for $n \leq 5$ (which is easy to do by exhaustive computer search). Let's consider cases for $6 \leq n \leq 10$.

For $n=6$ the random generation algorithm achieves the best possible results, that is, it can generate 1, 2, and 3-resilient Boolean functions with nonlinearities of 24, 24 and 16 respectively. Also for $n=7$ the algorithm generates functions with best known nonlinearities and resilience degrees (i.e. 1, 3, 4-resilient for nonlinearities 56, 48 and 32). 2-resilient function with nonlinearity of 56 is not known. In 8-arguments the algorithm did not find (8,3,-,112) function which is known. All other resilient functions for their respective nonlinearities have been found. For $n=9$ the algorithm found following good functions: (9,1,-,240), (9,2,-,224), (9,5,-,192) and (9,6,-,128). And for n=10: (10,1,-,480), (10,3,-,448), (10,5,-,384), (10,7,-,256).

Affine equivalence

Recently a subject of affine equivalence has received a lot of attention after discovery of linear redundancy in AES S-box [3]. It has been shown that all the output functions of the AES S-box can be mapped to each other using affine transformations, and hence they are all in the same equivalence class. As AES S-box is the only nonlinear element in the cipher, any weakness can lead to possible future attacks.

A new criterion for designing S-boxes has been proposed by Fuller and Millan [4] stating that a S-box should not have any linear redundancy, i.e. all functions constituting a S-box should be from different affine equivalence classes.

AES S-box is a 8x8 S-box with nonlinearity of 112. Authors of [3,4] propose to use modified 8x8 S-box that eliminates this linear redundancy. Proposed S-box has nonlinearity of 106 and is currently best known non-redundant 8x8 S-box. It has been constructed by modifying an AES S-box.

Many properties of Boolean functions covered by various cryptographic criteria remain unchanged by affine transform, such as algebraic degree and nonlinearity. Absolute values of Walsh transform and autocorrelation function are both rearranged by affine transforms. The frequency distribution of the absolute values in these transforms is invariant under affine transform. To prove that two functions are from different equivalence classes it is then sufficient to show that either of their respective Walsh transform and autocorrelation function frequency distributions are different. If these distributions are the same functions still can be from different classes though. For the purpose of this paper it was sufficient however to test only the distributions.

The algorithm presented in this paper has been tested to see if it can produce highly non-linear, non-redundant 8x8 S-box. It turns out that it can easily generate such S-boxes with nonlinearity of 104. So far that's the highest nonlinearity achieved by this algorithm. However, the advantage of the algorithm lies in the fact that it can be successfully used to generate highly nonlinear, non-redundant S-boxes of sizes up to 16x16.

Conclusions

The algorithm presented in this paper is able to randomly generate either bent functions or highly nonlinear balanced functions, of up to 16 arguments, with very good cryptographic properties that can have ANF representation as short as under a hundred coefficients. Of course such short ANF representation also presents some risk as far as designing a potential attack on a cipher. Still, these functions might prove useful not only in the design of cryptographic systems, but as an interesting research tool. Having such a short ANF representation they might provide an insight into key properties and internal workings of highly nonlinear Boolean functions, leading to designing new more efficient constructions or design criteria.

References

[1] C. M. Adams, S. E. Tavares. *Generating and Counting Binary Bent Sequences*. In *IEEE Transactions on Information Theory* , IT-36:1170--1173, 1990.

[2] J. A. Clark, J. L. Jacob, S. Stepney. *Searching for cost functions*. In *CEC 2004: International Conference on Evolutionary Computation, Portland OR, USA, June 2004*, pages 1517--1524, IEEE 2004.

[3] J. Fuller, W. Millan. *On Linear Redundancy in the AES S-box*. In *Cryptology ePrint Archive, report 2002/111* , eprint.iacr.org, Aug 2002.

[4] J. Fuller, W. Millan. *Linear Redundancy in S-Boxes*. In *T. Johansson, editor, February 24-26, 2003. Revised Papers, volume 2887 of Lecture Notes in Computer Science* , pages 74--86, 2003.

[5] X. Guo-Zhen, J. Massey. *A spectral characterization of correlation immune combining functions*. In *IEEE Transactions on Information Theory* , 34(3):569--571, May 1988.

[6] X. D. Hou. *On the norm and covering radius of first-order Reed-Muller codes*. In *IEEE Transactions on Information Theory* , 43(3):1025--1027, May 1997.

[7] J. B. Kam, G. Davida. *Structured Design of Substitution-Permutation Encryption Networks*. In *IEEE Transactions on Computers*, C-28:747--753, 1979.

[8] J. A. Maiorana *A Class of Bent Functions*. In *R41 Technical Paper*, 1971.

[9] W. Meier, O. Staffelbach.. *Nonlinearity criteria for cryptographic functions*. In J. J. Quisquater, J. Vandewalle, editors, *Advances in Cryptology: EUROCRYPT 1989*, pages 549--562, LNCS 434, Springer, 1989.

[10] W. Millan, A. Clark, E. Dawson. *Heuristic design of cryptographically strong balanced Boolean functions*. In *Advances in Cryptology: EUROCRYPT 1998*, pages 489--499, LNCS 1403, Springer, 1998.

[11] O. S. Rothaus. *On bent functions*. In *Journal of Combinatorial Theory: Series A*, 20:300--305, 1976.

Visual Cryptography Methods as a Source of Trustworthiness for the Signature Creation and Verification Systems

Jerzy Pejaś, Michał Zawalich

Szczecin University of Technology, Poland, {jpejas, mzawalich}@wi.ps.pl

Abstract. The trusted presentation of the signed or being signed data is one of the key problem, which should be solved in so called secure signature creation and verification devices. Such presentation (in literature respectively known as a *What You See Is What You Sign* (*WYSIWYS*) and *What You See Was Signed* (*WYSWS*) problems) is the crucial issue especially in distributed environment. The trust assigned to various elements of such environment is limited so the participation of the commonly accepted Trusted Party (TP) operating on-line is the solution of that problem [1, 2]. The paper contains proposal of some modification of the secure signature creation and verification protocol, which was presented by W. Chocianowicz, *et al.* [1, 2]. The modification is made in the part related to the trusted presentation of the data, which should be signed by the signer or validated by the verifier. The modification is based on the visual cryptography methods allowing the human to verify the authenticity of the data being signed or signed, without any knowledge of cryptography, cryptographic computations, or computational devices.

1. Introduction

Legally binding of the electronic document with the adequate electronic signature requires using of the secure signature-creation device. Secure signature-creation devices (SSCD), by appropriate technical and procedural means, must ensure at least that (Annex III of 93/1999/EC [12]):

a) the signature-creation-data used for signature generation can practically occur only once and its secrecy is reasonably assured;
b) the signature-creation-data used for signature generation, with reasonable assurance, cannot be derived and the signature is protected against forgery using currently available technology;
c) the signature-creation-data used for signature generation can be reliably protected by the legitimate signatory against the use of others.

Annex III further requires that secure signature-creation devices must not alter the data to be signed or must prevent such data from being presented to the signatory prior to the signing process.

When the signer signs an electronic document, he/she commits the virtual piece of paper she/he sees when she/he views the electronic document.

The main electronic signature and verification problem is to achieve such assurance level, that electronic objects generate semantically equivalent virtual documents each time they are both opened for signature and verification processes. It is obvious, that if the document presented to the signer is substantially different from this one presented to the verifier, then the verifier's conclusion about what the signer signed will differ from what signer thought he or she signed.

In general we could state that the application of digital signatures to electronic documents lacks an important feature: are you sure that what you see is what you sign (WYSIWYS) and what you see was signed (WYSWS)? If you manually sign a paper document, you will see what you sign. But what can we say in an electronic environment? Is it possible to forge electronic documents and fool someone into signing something he did not intend to sign?

The answer for stated question is very important, especially in the context of the signing and verifying processes. The process of signing an electronic document consists of three stages at least: (a) the preparation of the source document to be signed, (b) preview of the document and sending it (as a whole, as a part or the hash value only) by signing application to the technical component (for example some smart card with the cryptoprocessor), (c) signature creation by the technical component and sending it back to the signing application. Next, the verification process consists of two stages: (a) the formal verification of the electronic signature validity and (b) the presentation of the document to be verified.

It is obvious that weak protection of the information, which is being sent between the system components (the signing application, the technical component, the presentation module) can lead to the situation when every of these elements may receive input data different from the intended data which finally the user was going to sign. Such situation can be dangerous for the signer or the verifier during the explicitly review the data being signed or verified, particularly in the distributed signature creation and verification systems (see Figure 1).

As shown in Figure 1, the three corner functional scheme of the distributed signature creation and verification system forms the environment containing the following elements:

- signature creation system (SCS): the system, consisting of the signature creation application (SCA) and the technical component that creates an electronic signature,
- application provider (AP): the subject (usually, person or organization who develops and/or sells and/or supports a service used by a citizen) which needs to prepare a transaction instruction and an associated signature request containing the text being signed by the signer; from the signer's point of view the application provider plays a role of a trusted party;
- signature service provider (SSP): it makes the electronic signature service available to the signer and the verifier; this service, in the cooperation with application provider (AP) and the signer equipped with the technical component (SSCD) or the verifier, as well, authorizes and authenticates every signing or verification process;
- end-entity (EE): the signer or the verifier making or validating the electronic signature with the application software, delivered by the signature service provider (SSP),

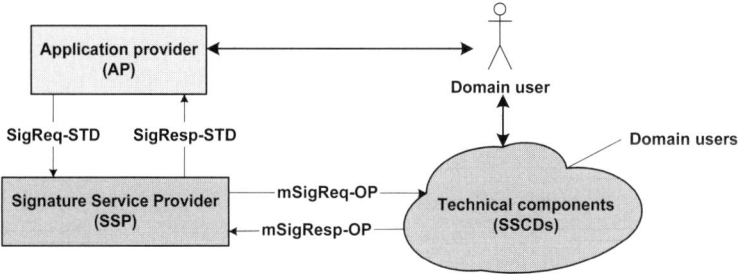

Fig. 1. Three corner functional scheme of the distributed signature creation and verification system (source: TR 102 203 [11])

It is assumed a signer uses a computer with standard equipment (its own or available at some public place) connected to a network and equipped with a standard interface device (IFD) for communication with integrated circuit(s) cards (ICCs). The role of SSCD can be played by ICC with crypto-processor. It is also assumed signer's environment among which he/she acts is wholly untrustworthy.

2. Previous and related works

In the paper of A. Spalka, et. al. [3] three different approaches are presented to facilitate the usage of digital signatures in insecure environments. The authors refer to those approaches as *secure hardware, secure software* and *mental arithmetic*. They stated also that *all three existing approaches force the signatory to explicitly review the data that is going to be signed before it is processed. The user must do this even if she just finished working with it in her application software. This sharply reduces the ease-of-use.*

Two first approaches need to use the trusted hardware or software modules. In opposite to this the third approach is a simple consequences of the limited (or even lack of) trust to the hardware and software: if the user (the signer or verifier) does not trust neither the hardware nor the software being under his sole control, then the system should be able to force the signatory or the verifier to compute simple cryptographic operations by mental arithmetic. In this approach (A.Spalka, et.al. [3]) *a signature computed by the smart card is sent to the (trusted) Online Verification Service. This service verifies that the signature matches the data for which it has been computed. It then encrypts the data by applying the substitution table and the One-Time-Pad and transmits this encrypted information through the insecure computer to the user. The signatory applies the One-Time-Pad and the substitution table to the encrypted information and retrieves the decrypted data. She compares if the decrypted data matches the data she wanted to sign. Decryption is done without the untrusted computer.*

Another approach to the solution of a secure signature creation problem in distribute environment was presented by J. Pejaś, et.al. [2]. This solution is based on the cumulative trust to the parties involved in a signature or verification process, and a write-once-read-multiple mechanism.

In opposite to the approach based on a *mental arithmetic* the cumulative trust method requires a signer or verifier to send the document to be signed or verified to the application provider (AP) first and then AP forwards its to a signature service provider (SSP). The SSP prepares the document for visualization and then allows the user to view it many times (also from different stations). The data presented to a user are the graphic representation of a document which is signed or is going to be signed, together with built-in random challenge (a random number). The signer or verifier should read this challenge carefully and sent it back to SSP (the answer is typed directly on the keypad of PIN-pad and sent to SSP over a secure channel). The correct user's answer means giving his consent to make the electronic signature or the acceptance of a document content being verified.

Proposed method of building a challenge explicitly into an electronic document has two disadvantages. Firstly an intended recipient of the data is not obligate to make independently any others operations (for example by mental arithmetic), besides of sending back the confirmation of the received challenge. Secondly, the data presented to the user for confirmation should be sent to his computer securely. Unfortunately, a decryption process is realized on the user's computer which can be wholly untrustworthy. It may disclose this challenge to unintended subjects, attempting to forge electronic signatures (for example, it can occur when SSP is in possession of the data to be signed or signed, which have been forged before the document leaves a user's computer or during the data transmission over the Internet to SSP server. Thirdly, the response on the challenge must be sent to SSP confidentially too. And finally, the data can be falsely presented by a card graphic driver – the driver may modify original image sent by SSP in such a way that the signer or verifier will get a presentation of the data different than these which the user will intend to sign or accept.

Our main goal is to prove that usage of visual cryptography methods allows to remove disadvantages mentioned above. To achieve this aim, the paper is organized into the following sections. In Section 3 we introduce visual cryptography and give details of the visual authentication approach. We also give details of our approach to the trusted visualization of the electronic document which is signed or was signed, present a simple example, and discuss how this can be used in distributed signing or verifying system. Section 4 provides some preliminary results regarding mixed authentication schemes used in distributed signing and verification system. We conclude with section 4, in which we highlight our contributions and overview future extensions planned

3. Visual Cryptography

In 1994, Naor and Shamir [4] presented a new cryptographic paradigm based on the pixel level. They termed this *visual cryptography* and introduced it as a method for encrypting such things as handwritten notes, pictures, graphical images, as well as typed text stored as a graphic image. We assume that this technique's characteristics make it appropriate for trust document presentation.

3.1 Definition of visual sharing schemes

Assume that the given n users and some secret information which is a collection of black and white pixels. In k-out-of-n secret sharing schemes a sender wishing to transmit a secret message distributes n transparencies among n recipients, where the transparencies contain random picture. Next, the encryption of the secret information should be done in such way that k or more users can see the secret information by stacking their transparencies, while $k - 1$ or less users gain no information.

Each original pixel of a secret information appears in n modified versions (called shares) - one for each transparency. Each share is a collection of m black and white subpixels.

We formalize these requirements in the following definition of a visual cryptograpy scheme, which is equivalent to that given in [4], and is adopted from P. A. Eisen, D. R. Stinson [8]and M.Krause and H. U. Simon [5]. For binary vector v, let $H(v)$ denote the Hamming weight of v, i.e. the number of ones in v. Then:

Definition 1. *A k out of n visual secret sharing scheme consists of two collections of Boolean $n \times m$ matrices C0 and C1. This scheme has threshold d and relative contrast α if the following three conditions are met:*

(i)   *for any $S \in C0$ the Boolean OR V of any k of the n rows satisfies $H(V) \leq d\text{-}\alpha m$,*

(ii) *for any $S \in C1$ the Boolean OR V of any k of the n rows satisfies $H(V) \geq d$,*

(iii) *for any $j < k$ chosen rows the submatrices of the matrices from C0 and C1 occur with the same frequencies.*

Properties (i) and (ii) are called the *contrast conditions*, and property (iii) is called the *security condition*. Contrast level, related to the grey level is interpreted by the visual system of the users as black if $H(V) \geq d$ and as white if $H(V) \leq d - \alpha m$, for some fixed threshold $1 \leq d \leq m$ and relative contrast α. We say, that the image should be recognizable, if the gray level of a black pixel (in k superimposed shares) is darker that the gray of a white pixel.

To guarantee security we should insure that if there are less than k shares, no information is leaked. Assume that there are j shares available and $j < k$, and the rows from matrices C0 and C1 occur with equal probability. When these cases are considered, the Hamming weight follows a uniform distribution $H(V) = f(q)$.

The basic 2 out of 2 visual cryptography scheme (see M. Naor, A. Shamir [4]) consists of a secret message encoded into two transparencies, one transparency representing the ciphertext and the other acting as a secret key. Both transparencies appear to be random dots when inspected individually and provide no information about the original plaintext. However, by carefully aligning the transparencies, the original secret message is reproduced. The actual decoding is accomplished by the human visual system.

3.2 Document authentication based on visual cryptography

Authentication can be supported by 2-out-of-2 visual secret sharing. A shadow in visual cryptography is not the whole generated share, but a single collection of subpixels generated from a given pixel. It can be said, that a share consists of the same number of shadows as the amount of pixels in a secret image. In case of (2,2) sharing, the shadows, which consist of 2x2 subpixels are used. This allows keeping right proportions of the image. For shadows 2x2 following cases are possible:

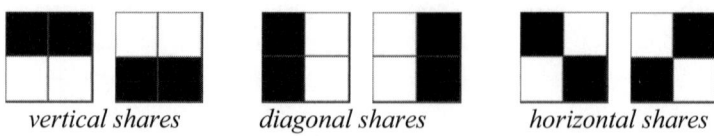

vertical shares   *diagonal shares*   *horizontal shares*

Fig. 2. Visual forms of shares, 2x2 subpixels (source: M. Naor, A. Shamir [4])

Assume that there are given entities in visual authentication process: end entity (EE), who is a subject which signs or verifies the message, electronic signature service provider (SSP) and adversary (A). Assume also that a subject that authenticates signing process (SSP) has received signed or being signed document, transmitted earlier by end entity.

Then, after M. Naor, B. Pinkas [9] following definition of document visual authentication scenario can be accepted. It is adjusted to needs of distributed signature creation and verification systems.

Definition 2 *(visual authentication scenario). Assume that the end entity (EE) has following abilities:*
  (i)   he can identify an image built on basis of pattern given on Fig.3; this image is a result of stacking two shares, received in a 2-out-of-2 visual sharing scheme,
  (ii) he can verify control areas: EXTERNAL PATTERN, TEXT, INTERNAL PATTERN and CONTENTS on black and grey background, received as a result of stacking 2 shares (transparencies),
  (iii) he can check if two images are similar.

In a phase of initiation or on every demand of signing or verifying subject, SSP generates image G_r which consists of white and black pixels located randomly and areas marked with white thin line: TEXT, INTERNAL PATTERN and CONTENTS. On this ground, based on 2-out-of-2 visual sharing scheme, SSP creates transparency T_r (EE share) and additional information A_r (e.g. transparency identification code) and confidentially transmits to end entity (EE).

We say that polynomial attack to break given authentication scenario is a function of security parameters P_{r} of TEXT area sizes (r_1, c_1), INTERNAL PATTERN (r_2, c_2), and CONTENTS (r_3, c_3).

End entity (EE) can use transparency T_r to authenticate only one document (it is one time authentication method). If the document consists of many pages, then security parameters P_r for each page have to vary, which means, that EE has to use separate dedicated transparency to authenticate each page.

Of course, more desirable methods are those, which are safe for multiple authentications. General construction of multiple authentication scheme resolves into placing on transparency more than one collection of areas TEXT, INTERNAL PATTERN and CONTENTS (one of each on every page). The number of these collections set in single share (shadow) depends on security parameters, which define area sizes used by every collection and also depends on transparency size (for details see M. Naor, B. Pinkas [9]). Another difficulty of this solution lies in the fact that in case of many pages, user EE might have problems with appropriate placing his share onto SSP's share.

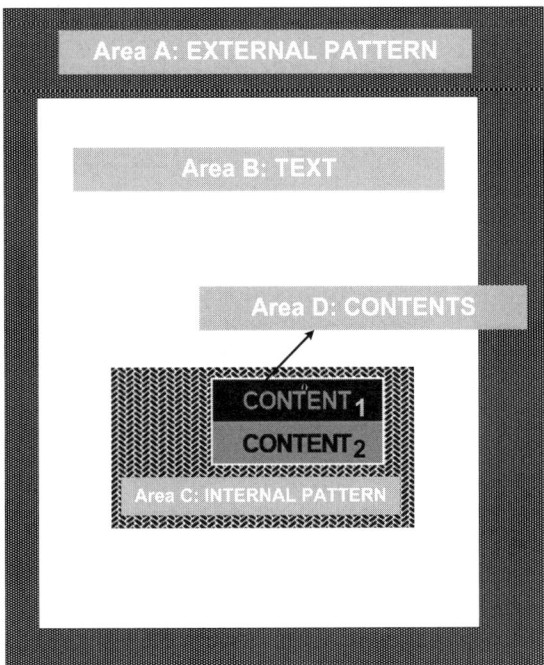

Fig. 3. The proposition of a image template for visual document authentication

Next step to create visual authentication system is defining the right authentication protocol. Assume that signature service provider (SSP) prepares document for presentation on every demand of signing or verifying subject. The document contains 4 distinguished areas: EXTERNAL PATTERN (area A), TEXT (area B), INTERNAL PATTERN (area C) and CONTENTS (area D). EXTERNAL PATTERN area contains randomly generated black, white and grey bits[1]. Within TEXT area the contents of presented document is placed and in $CONTENT_1$ and $CONTENT_2$ random value (challenge) and particularly relevant data, respectively, which occurs in signed or verified document[2] (e.g. bill value). This information composes message m. INTERNAL PATTERN area can be in text wrapped mode.

---

[1] Grey bit is received from a matrix 2x2, which contains three black subpixels and one white subpixel

[2] That kind of data should be pointed by subject which signs or verifies the document. If such data is not pointed, then signature service provider SSP copies CONTENT to this area.

Definition 3 *(visual authentication protocol, see M. Naor, B. Pinkas [9]).*

SSP wants to present to EE signed or being signed document (message m), where the context of the message is also known to adversary A.

(i)   *SSP sends message c to EE, which is a function of m and image G_r generated in phase of initiation (see Definition 2),*

(ii) *Before message c gets to end entity EE it can be modified by adversary and take shape of c',*

(iii) *Upon receiving message c' end entity EE outputs FALSE or <ACCEPT, $CONTENT_2$> visually reconstructed by EE using function parameters: c', possessed T_r transparency and additional information A_r. EE acceptance of presented document requires sending to SSP reconstructed request ($CONTENT_1$ area).*

Authentication scenario (Definition 2) and authentication protocol (Definition 3) compose visual authentication system. We say, that the visual authentication system is *(1-p)-authentic* (see M. Naor, B. Pinkas [9]), if for any message m communicated from SSP to EE the probability that EE outputs (*ACCEPT, m'*) is at most *p* (where *m'* is different from *m*).

It is certain, that probability value of false message acceptance should be the lowest (at most, equal to zero) and is dependant on used authentication scheme. In next chapter, two methods of visual authentication will be presented: *position on screen* and *black and gray* and further, the proposal of merging those methods is presented. It provides higher level of resistance to tampering message and lower probability of accepting forged message.

3.3 One time authentication – *position on screen* method with conjunction with black and grey method

Observe that in 2-out-of-2 visual secret sharing scheme shadows containing 2x2 subpixels are used. Adversary can freely change the message sent from SSP to EE. However legal sharing of visual secret according to 2x2 sharing method should contain exactly two black subpixels in every square 2x2 representing pixel.

In distributed signature creation and verification system, the main aim of adversary's attack is to modify TEXT contents and $CONTENT_2$, but only when $CONTENT_1$ contains particularly relevant data ($CONTENT_2$ area is different than $CONTENT_1$).

In reference to above, three types of modifications can be distinguished, which adversary can perform on the document presented to signing or verifying subject (first two are identical with types distinguished by M. Naor, B.Pinkas [9]):

1. he can change the position of the two black subpixels inside the squares representing pixel; such change might not be noticed by EE,
2. he can put more or less than two black subpixles inside a square; this produces an illegal share which will probably go unnoticed by EE unless it is done in many pixels at one time,
3. he can copy the whole INTERNAL PATTERN area and paste it to tampered document.

First two types of modifications allow adversary changing the content of image, yet the third type allows authenticating it. Appliance of combination of both visual authentication methods (*position on screen* and *black and gray*) and bonding INTERNAL PATTERN area with the document is aimed to detect changes of type 1, 2 or 3 within an image.

   Position on screen scheme assumes that image consists of r ×c pixels. In a phase of initiation signature service provider (SSP) transmits to signing or verifying subject (EE) the location within bounding box of size r' ×c' pixels, in which message should be placed. Bounding box is marked on transparency with thin line so that EE can easily check if the message is located within it. In case of attack there are (r-r') × (c-c') equally probable different collections of pixels to reverse (assuming that EE can notice single bit change in an image). If adversary chooses wrong collection, the attack will be detected. Probability of success is at most (M. Naor, B. Pinkas [9]):

$$\frac{1}{(r-r')(c-c')} \tag{1}$$

In *black and gray* scheme security is exponential in the Hamming distance between the message that SSP sends to EE and the message that adversary wishes to display. The weakness of this method is a reduction in the contrast of the presented image. This method incorporates gray and black pixels, where black pixel contains 4 black subpixels and gray pixel contains three black subpixels and one white subpixel. Probability of success is:

$$p = 2e^{-2\frac{\varepsilon^2}{1+\varepsilon}t} \tag{2}$$

where t is an upper bound on $t_{m'}$ (the maximum Hamming distance of a displayed message from m' such that a user may accept the displayed message as m') over all messages m'.

   Both presented schemes can be combined into one method so that there is a bounding area CONTENTS marked on the share, which location is known only to EE and SSP. Within this area "black and grey" scheme is performed. Thanks to introducing such scheme combination adversary is not capable of changing contents of secret message just by inverting pixels and every attack attempt is easily detected. It is very difficult even after revealing bounding box location.

4. Trusted document presentation

Assume the following scenario of the data authentication process conducted by SSP that is responsible for reliable presentation to signer or verifier signed or being signed data:
1. electronic signature provider (SSP) generates the share (a symmetric key equivalent) and sends it confidentially to the EE,
2. EE sends to SSP the request for the document authentication being transferred early to SSP through AP (see Fig.1)

3. SSP generates own share related to the contents of presented document, the challenge and particularly relevant data indicated by EE,
4. EE aligns his share on SSP share carefully, reads the decrypted areas and then, if the verification is positive, sends the contents of *CONTENT₁* area (the challenge) to SSP confidentially.

4.1 End entity (EE) share generation

The SSP creates image size of $r_1 \times c_1$ pixels using the pseudorandom number generator (PRNG). Each image pixel is translated into randomly selected matrices of 2x2 subpixels as shown on Fig. 2.

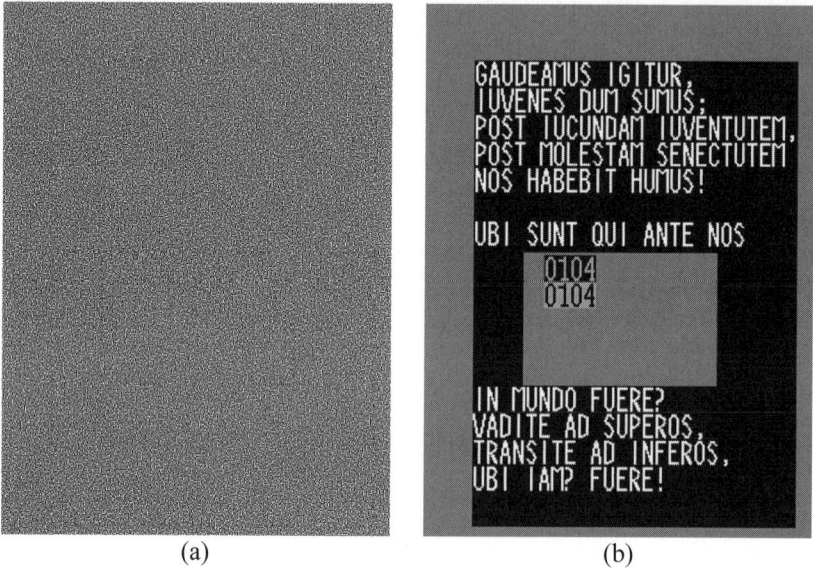

(a)   (b)

Fig. 4. EE share (a) and auxiliary image being used to generate the SSP share only (b)

The image contains four marked areas A, B, C i D (Fig. 4 (a)). The SSP splits this image in accordance with 2-out-of-2 secret sharing scheme and one of two resulting share sends confidentially to EE. The transferred share is one time secret key known to SSS and EE only; this share cannot be disclosed to any unauthorized subjects.

4.2 Share generation with secret

When receiving the document from EE for signing or verification, the signature service provider (SSP) puts the contents of this document into template from Fig. 3 (some example of filled template is shown on Fig. 4 (b)). Next, basing on prepared image and the share transferred early to EE, subject SSP generates his own share. The share generation process can be made in four steps.

First step concerns the C area, which is located outside the window bounding D area. The SSP randomly chooses the matrices of 2x2 subpixels and one after one puts into generated share.

In second step SSP creates the bounding D box. The bounding D area is split into two parts. SSP for one of these parts (*CONTENT₁* area) generates random challenge (secret) and writes it into image in gray (when all shares are stocked together each pixel of this area has three black subpixels) on a black background (the shares stacked together have the black subpixels only); the second part (*CONTENT₂* area) contains particularly relevant data (indicated by EE), but this time the information is written in black on a gray background.

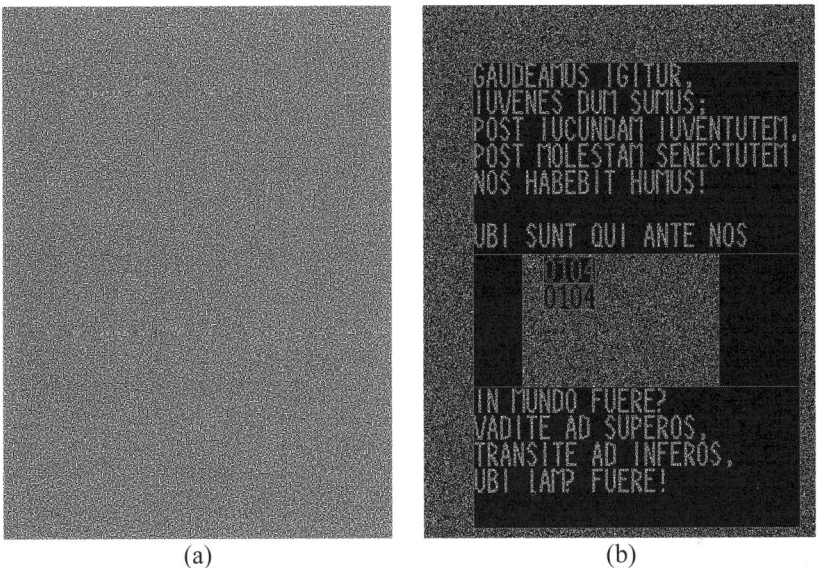

Fig. 5. The SSP transparency (a) and the image after aligning the EE and SSP transparencies (b)

The text area B is filled in third step; the text from this area is the same as text which was sent by EE to SSP. This area is prepared by SSP in such way that when we stack on it the EE transparency then the original text is visible.

Finally the SSP generates A area, which contains randomly located pixels in randomly chosen black, white or gray colors.

For the EE transparency from Fig. 4 (a) and auxiliary image shown on Fig. 4(b) the created SSP share has the form as on Fig. 5 (a). This share is sent to EE (not necessarily in the confidential way).

4.3 Image decryption

To decrypt the secret message received form the SSP, the EE should photocopy each pattern on a separate transparency, align them carefully, and additionally project the result with an overhead projector. It is also possible to align the EE transparency directly on the screen image, which contains the SSP share. The decryption should give the result like on Fig. 5(b).

4.4 Security considerations

The contents document presentation is trustworthy only if an adversary is able to fulfil two following necessary and sufficient conditions simultaneously: (a) guess a location of B, C and D areas and (b) change information in B and *CONTENT₂* areas into such information, which is expected by a signer or verifier (of course, only if an adversary has tampered this information during sending it by EE to SSP).

Assume that the aim of an adversary attack is to guess the location of CONTENS area and the modification of the data placed into $CONTENT_2$ area. It is assumed also that the following definitions and symbols are used:

(a) $r \times c$ – the A area size in pixels; we assume that an adversary knows a size of this area;

(b) $r_1 \times c_1$ – the B area size in pixels, where $r_1 = r - r'$, $c_1 = c - c'$ and $r' \in [1, t_{11}]$, $t_{11} < r$, $c' \in [1, t_{12}]$, $t_{12} < c$;

(c) $r_2 \times c_2$ – the C area size in pixels, where $r_2 = r_1 - r_1'$, $c_2 = c_1 - c_1'$ and $r_1' \in [1, t_{21}]$, $t_{21} < r_1$, $c_1' \in [1, t_{22}]$, $t_{22} < c_1$;

(d) $r_3 \times c_3$ – the D area size in pixels, where $r_3 = r_2 - r_2'$, $c_3 = c_2 - c_2'$ and $r_2' \in [1, t_{31}]$, $t_{31} < r_2$, $c_2' \in [1, t_{32}]$, $t_{32} < c_2$;

(e) $P(B_1)$ and $P(B_2|B_1)$ – respectively, the probability that an adversary succeeds in guessing the B area size and the conditional probability that an adversary succeeds in guessing the location of the B area, given that its size is known;

(f) $P(C_1|B_1 \cap B_2)$ and $P(C_2|C_1 \cap B_1 \cap B_2)$ – respectively, the conditional probability that an adversary succeeds in guessing the C area size, given that the B area size and its location is known and in guessing the location of the C area, given that the B area size and its location as well as the C area size are known;

(g) $P(D_1|B_1 \cap B_2 \cap C_1 \cap C_2)$ and $P(D_2|D_1 \cap B_1 \cap B_2 \cap C_1 \cap C_2)$ – respectively, the conditional probability that an adversary succeeds in guessing the D area size, given that the B and C areas sizes and their locations are known and in guessing the location of the D area, given that the B and C areas sizes and their locations as well as the D area size are known;

(h) $P(E|B \cap C \cap D)$ – the conditional probability that the end entity (EE) falsely accepts the information from area D, which was modified by an adversary, assuming that an adversary knows all parameters of areas B, C and D (the B, C and D are the joint events $B_1 \cap B_2$, $C_1 \cap C_2$ and $D_1 \cap D_2$, respectively).

Then, the following lemma can be formulated:

Lemma 1: If the adversary is able to guess the D area size and its location and the end entity (EE) falsely accepts the information from area D, which was modified by an adversary, assuming that an adversary knows all parameters of areas B, C and D, then the average conditional probability of success of this attack is

$$P_{avg}\left(D\cap E|B\cap C\right)=\frac{1}{t_{31}^{2}t_{32}^{2}}H\left(t_{31}\right)H\left(t_{32}\right)*2e^{-2\frac{\varepsilon^{2}}{1+\varepsilon}t} \tag{3}$$

where $B = B_1\cap B_2$, $C = C_1\cap C_2$ i $D = D_1\cap D_2$, t is an upper bound on t_m (the maximum Hamming distance of a displayed message in area CONTENT from m' such that a user may accept the displayed message as m') over all messages m', hamming distance between any two semantically different messages m and m' in area D is at least $2(t'+4(1+\varepsilon)t/3)$ and t' is an upper bound on number of pixels of share sent by the adversary, in which the number of black subpixels is different from two.

Proof: By the property of conditional probability follows that, when two events, D and E, are dependent, the probability of both occurring is:

$$P_{avg}\left(D\cap E|B\cap C\right)=P_{avg}\left(D|B\cap C\right)P_{avg}\left(E|B\cap C\cap D\right) \tag{4}$$

On the other hand, the components shown in equation (4), are equal, respectively:

$$P_{avg}\left(D|B\cap C\right)=P_{avg}\left(D_{1}|B\cap C\right)P_{avg}\left(D_{2}|B\cap C\cap D_{1}\right)$$
$$=\frac{1}{t_{31}^{2}t_{32}^{2}}H\left(t_{31}\right)H\left(t_{32}\right) \tag{5}$$

where:

$$H\left(t_{i1}\right)=\sum_{r_{i-1}=1}^{t_{i1}}\frac{1}{r_{i-1}'}$$
$$H\left(t_{i2}\right)=\sum_{c_{i-1}=1}^{t_{i2}}\frac{1}{c_{i-1}'} \tag{6}$$

and

$$P_{avg}\left(E|B\cap C\cap D\right)=2e^{-2\frac{\varepsilon^{2}}{1+\varepsilon}t} \tag{7}$$

The evaluation of (7) has been proved by A. Naor, B. Pinkas [9] (see also the section 3.3). From the equations (4), (5) and (7) it follows that the evaluation given in equation (3) is correct. □

If the values of t_{31} and t_{32} are sufficiently big (of course, this could result in small D area size), then the average conditional probability of success $P_{avg}(D\cap E|B\cap C)$ is small enough to conclude that the presented document is trusted. This fact is more obvious if an adversary doesn't know also the sizes and locations of B and C areas (see the evaluation given in Lemma 2).

Lemma 2: For assumption and symbols from Lemma 1, the average conditional probability of the adversary's success in guessing the sizes and locations of B, C and D areas, and in tampering the information from area D is

$$P_{avg}(B \cap C \cap D \cap E) = \frac{1}{t_{11}^2 t_{12}^2} H(t_{11})H(t_{32}) * \frac{1}{t_{21}^2 t_{22}^2} H(t_{21})H(t_{22}) *$$
$$\frac{1}{t_{31}^2 t_{32}^2} H(t_{31})H(t_{32}) * 2e^{-2\frac{\varepsilon^2}{1+\varepsilon}t} \tag{8}$$

Proof: Like for the proof of Lemma 1 we apply the property of the conditional probability firstly, and then calculate the average probability value for each component of the joint probability P(B∩C∩D∩E):

$$P_{avg}(B \cap C \cap D \cap E) = P_{avg}(B)P_{avg}(C|B)P_{avg}(D|B \cap C)P_{avg}(E|B \cap C \cap D) \tag{9}$$

$$P_{avg}(B) = P_{avg}(B_1 \cap B_2) = P_{avg}(B_1)P_{avg}(B_2|B_1)$$
$$= \frac{1}{t_{11}^2 t_{12}^2} H(t_{11})H(t_{12}) \tag{10}$$

$$P_{avg}(C|B) = P_{avg}(C_1|B)P_{avg}(C_2|B \cap C_1)$$
$$= \frac{1}{t_{21}^2 t_{22}^2} H(t_{21})H(t_{22}) \tag{11}$$

Finally, the evaluation of (8) follows from equation (5), (7), (10) and (11). □

The evaluations of average conditional probabilities of adversary's guessing the sizes and locations of B, C and D areas are correct if the EE is able to recognize even one pixel changed in any of areas built-into image presented to him. In practice, the EE can be able to detect the change only if the Hamming distance between image that SSP sends to EE and the image that the adversary wishes to display to him exceeds some limited number of pixels. However, this number of pixels don't increase essentially the probabilities, which are given by equations (5), (10) and (11) (compare also M. Naor, B. Pinkas [9]).

5. Conclusions and further works

The article proposes the utilization for visual authentication methods in distributed signature creation and verification systems. It is shown that combination of two authentication methods: "position on screen" and "black and gray" enables credible presentation of signed or being signed documents even by untrustworthy computer. Such scheme of data presentation characterizes with high resistance to adversary attacks.

Trustworthy data presentation method is presented on exemplary data with respondent monochromatic images. User can verify authenticity of data directly on the computer screen by printing SSP share on transparency or combining images from two projectors.

Proposed method has two disadvantages. Firstly, user EE can authenticate only one image (one page) with one share. In case of document containing many pages, authentication of such paper would require using many shares. Secondly, visual authentication scheme is effective only for monochromatic images. However, colourful images can be authenticated as well, e.g. when digital photography is signed.

Further work on improving this method will lead to connecting only one share with one or group of presented documents (single- or multi-page documents and colourful documents). The solution of the defined problem would extend the practical use of this method, assuming that the problem of generating shares for colourful images, has been solved (e.g. M. Nakajima, Y. Yamaguchi[10]).

References

1. W. Chocianowicz, J. Pejaś, A. Ruciński *The Proposal of Protocol for Electronic Signature Creation in Public Environment*, in Enhanced Methods in Computer Security, Biometric and Artificial Intelligence Systems, Springer New York 2005
2. W. Chocianowicz, J. Pejaś, A. Ruciński *Problems of trusted presentation the data to be signed and verified* (in polish), VII Krajowa Konferencja Zastosowań Kryptografii ENIGMA'2004, Warszawa, May 2004
3. A. Spalka, A.B. Cremers, H. Langweg *Trojan Horse Attacks on Software for Electronic Signatures*, Informatica 26 (2002) 191-203 pp.191-204
4. M. Naor, A. Shamir *Visual Cryptography*, in Advances in Cryptology - Eurocrypt '94, A. De Santis ed., Lecture Notes in Computer Science, Springer-Verlag Berlin, 1994, pp. 1-12
5. M. Krause, H. U. Simon *Determining the Optimal Contrast for Secret Sharing Schemes in Visual Cryptography*, Electronic Colloquium on Computational Complexity, ECCC Reports 2000, Report TR00-003, ISSN 1433-8092
6. G. Ateniese, C. Blundo, A. De Santis, D. R. Stinson Visual *Cryptography for General Access Structures*, Electronic Colloquium on Computational Complexity (ECCC), 1996
7. L. W. Hawkes, Alec Yasinsac, C. Cline *An Application of Visual Cryptography To Financial Documents*, The Florida State University, College of Arts and Sciences Department of Computer Science Research, TR-001001, 2000
8. P. A. Eisen, D. R. Stinson *Threshold Visual Cryptography Schemes With Specified Whiteness Levels of Reconstructed Pixels*, Designs, Codes and Cryptography, Springer Netherlands, vol. 25, No 1, January 2002
9. M. Naor, B. Pinkas *Visual Authentication and Identification*, in Advances in Cryptology - CRYPTO '97, 17th Annual International Cryptology Conference, Santa Barbara, California, USA, August 1997, Lecture Notes in Computer Science, Springer-Verlag Berlin, 1997
10. M. Nakajima, Y. Yamaguchi *Extended Visual Cryptography for Natural Images*, Journal of WSCG, Vol.10, No.2, 2002
11. ETSI TR 102 203 *Mobile Commerce (M-COMM) - Mobile Signatures - Business and Functional Requirements*, V1.1.1 (2003-05), Technical Report
12. Directive 1999/93/EC of the European Parliament and of the Council of 13 December 1999 on a Community framework for electronic signatures, Official Journal of the European Communities, 19.1.2000

Neural Network as a Programmable Block Cipher

Piotr Kotlarz[1], Zbigniew Kotulski[2]

[1] Kazimierz Wielki University, Bydgoszcz, piotrk@ukw.edu.pl
[2] Institute of Fundamental Technological Research, PAS
and Institute of Telecommunications, WUT, zkotulsk@ippt.gov.pl

Abstract. A model of Boolean neural network is proposed as a substitute of a bock cipher. Such a network has functionality of the block cipher and one additional advantage: it can change its cryptographic properties without reprogramming, by training the network with a new training set. The constriction of the network is presented with an analysis of the applied binary transformations. Also three methods of training the network (what corresponds to the re-keying of a block cipher) are presented. Their security and effectiveness are analyzed and compared.

1. Introduction

In popular cryptographic communication protocols, like SSL, IPSec, SCP, etc., the designers provide several encryption algorithms, with an option of extending their list. Among the reasons of such a solution one could give the permanent progress of cryptanalytic attacks that can compromise a cipher. The possibility of changing the cipher makes that even if some algorithm is broken, the whole protocol remains valid. For example, development of linear and differential cryptanalysis shaken DES security, protocols with additional cryptosystems (e.g. 3DES, AES) implemented preserved their functionality for secure communication.

The DES case shows that the problem of breaking protocols due to breaking component cryptographic algorithms is crucial in a case of the expected long life of communication devices with the security protocols built-in. The designers and producers of the information infrastructure must take this problem into account.

For several years one can find in the literature results concerning application of programmable logic arrays for implementation of cryptographic algorithms. This fact is especially important for hardware implementations of cryptosystems. Any change in hardware is very complicated, so application of programmable (and, therefore, reconfigurable) element in the hardware seems to be a remedy in a case when we must modernize an algorithm. Such solutions already exist, e.g., in the paper [1] a cryptographic accelerator realizing IDEA block cipher is presented. A proposal of application of the processor RipeRench for cryptographic algorithms is given in [2]. Further, the authors realize algorithms CRYPTON [3] and RC6 [4] using the reconfigurable RipeRench. Another implementation of CRYPTON in reconfigurable logical chips is presented in [5]. More information about application of the programmable devices to ciphers implementation and, more general, signal processing, can be found in [6].

In spite of the application of the programmable logical chips could be a solution of the problem of updating cryptographic algorithms built-in the network security components, in this paper we propose an alternative solution. In our opinion (based on earlier studies) the proposed solution of application of neural networks as universal updatable encryption algorithms could be a good alternative. After an appropriate design of such a network the implementing a new block cipher in the network and, then, the training process with adequate training sets should do periodic update of the algorithm.

In the papers [7-9] we proposed an idea of realization of the elementary operations of block ciphers (permutations and non-linear substitutions, S-boxes) by neural networks. We considered problems of efficiency of training of such networks and possibility of composing complete block ciphers of the elementary component neural networks. Now it is time to study the security of functioning of such neural network-based cryptosystems at each phase of its life: training and regular work as a cipher. Let us concentrate on the training process. We assume that the encrypting neural network is installed at a remote server (servers). At the client side we have the owner of the system, who can modify (from his location) the properties of the network and chose the transformation performed by it. For the sake of clarity, we consider now the neural network that realizes some permutation. So, the changes of the cryptosystem are the changes of permutation performed by the neural network. In spite of such a solution is not a general encrypting neural network; we can build the cipher as a composition of traditional S-boxes and permutations realized by neural networks. The included neural networks play a role of the switching elements in the cipher that make possible to change the cryptographic properties.

2. Neural network realizing elementary permutations

The concept of application of the neural network realizing permutations for cryptographic algorithms was proposed and presented in details in the paper [7]. For the purposes of this presentation we give here the outline of this method. Generally, the idea of application of a neural network as a universal cryptographic algorithm is based on constructing any complicated structure transforming block of bits onto blocks of bits as a combination of small blocks (neural networks) realizing elementary permutations (and, if needed, substitutions). In Fig. 1 are presented two examples of the networks realizing permutations that will be used in this paper. In each case, the left picture presents symbolically the transformation of bits, which is the permutation while the right one is the scheme of neural network realizing this permutation.

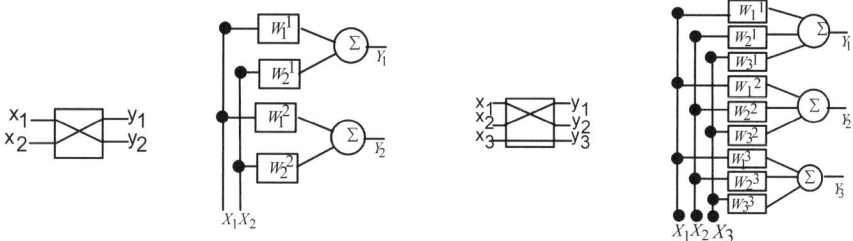

Fig. 1 Sample neural network blocks realizing elementary permutations

3. Modification of permutation realized by a neural network

Assume that we have the neural network that is trained to realize some transformation of the block of bits of a fixed length into the block of bits of the same length and playing a role of the block cipher. The problem considered in this paper is: how to change the neural network to make it realizing some other block cipher (or the block cipher with different cryptographic properties). We assume that the structure of neural network remain constant during the lifetime of the system. The changing permutation is made by appropriate changes of the weight coefficients of neurons in the network. Thus, the replacement of one algorithm (old cryptosystem) by another (the new one) is by a certain training process, with the earlier designed training set. For this purpose we propose the supervised training method. For the user the network is considered as a black box located at a distant server. Thus, there is a need of preparing a method of remote modifying the algorithm realized by the neural network. Since we assumed that the security protocol applying our cryptographic algorithm works in the client-server architecture, we assign the role of client to system's administrator. Playing his role, he should be able to modify the algorithm at the remote server, performing some well-defined training process. This process can be made in two ways. One possibility is to train the network at the server using the adequate training set. In this case the training data must be transmitted from client to server. Another possibility is to train an identical copy of the neural network at the client side. Now, the resultant weights must be transmitted to the server and substituted at the network site. The two proposed methods of training should be extensively analyzed with respect to efficiency and required bandwidth occupation at data transmission, quality of training process, necessary resources at the client and server side and the security and reliability of the obtained cryptographic algorithm. **Training at a server side**. As we mentioned above, one of the possible ways of changing cryptographic algorithm realized by the neural network is performing the training process at the server (S). To do this we must transmit to the server the appropriate training data, which was earlier prepared at the client (C) side, to put into action the training program. In Fig. 2 is presented the architecture of the C-S system responsible for the training data exchange and the training procedure. The party S can work in two modes: the training mode (T1) and the operation mode (T2). In T1, operating just after the training data is supplied, the training process is performed and, as a result, the cryptographic algorithm realized by the neural network is changed. In T2 the neural network works as a black box realizing the cryptographic algorithm, in our case a block encryption. To complete the notation used in the picture, the open channel denotes some insecure communication channel, e.g., Internet. By cryptogram we understand the secured information being exchanged between the parties C and S of the communication protocol.

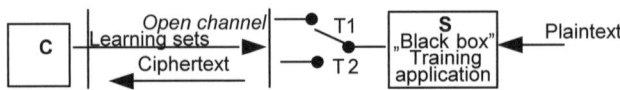

Fig. 2 Training at the server S side

Since this paper we concentrate on the security of the process of dynamical changes of the cryptographic algorithm inserted in the neural network, for the sake of clarity of presentation we restrict our consideration to a binary transformation of the block of 16 bits onto the block of 16 bits. More precisely, the transformation realizes a permutation of the block of 16 bits. The scheme of the permutation is presented in Fig.3. For the construction of the complete 16-bit permutation we used blocks of elementary neural networks that realize 2-bit and 3-bit permutations. The details of such blocks and their properties were discussed in details in the paper [7]. Let us remark that using analogous blocks it is possible to build also non-linear substitutions, which can be used for building S-boxes, the supplementary component elements of many present-day block ciphers. The examples of such structures are also presented in the papers [7], [8], and [9]. However, now we concentrate on permutations. The detailed description of the 16-bit permutation build of some number of elementary neural network blocks is presented in the diagram below. In Fig.3 a network built of two layers of blocks of smaller neural networks is presented. Each of the layers realizes different permutation, what is symbolically denoted as σ1, σ3. The additional permutation σ2 reflects the connections between the outputs of one layer of the blocks and the inputs of the blocks of the other layer. In the right hand side of the Fig. 3 the permutation realized by the network is presented.

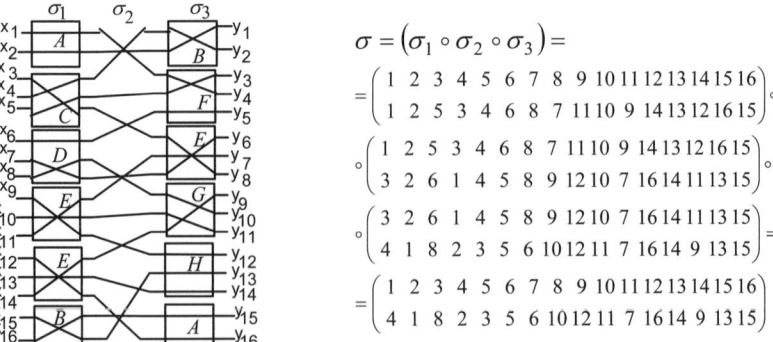

Fig. 3 Neural network realizing a permutation

To summarize the diagram, the permutation realized by the resultant neural network is a composition of three 16-bit permutations, realized by individual layers, what is expressed by Eq. (1).

$$\sigma = \left(\sigma_1 \circ \sigma_2 \circ \sigma_3\right) \qquad (1)$$

In the above scheme, the permutations σ_1, σ_2 are these, which are being changed during the training procedure, while the permutation σ_2 remains unchangeable. In the methodology, which is implemented and verified at the moment we propose the training procedure independent for each of the permutations σ_1 and σ_3. Thus, we need two training sets for the two permutations. In further studies we plan to propose an effective procedure of training the three-layer network with a single training set. Such a procedure would be more convenient and more confidential, because it would not need knowledge of the internal structure of the neural network by the training procedure. The preparation of a security protocol with the neural network-supported encryption algorithm runs in several steps. First, the network is implemented at the server; its structure is presented in Fig.3. Next, random values of weights are inserted to it. Finally, using some training set (earlier prepared at the client side, individually for each requires permutation, and transmitted to the server) the training program at the server side performs the training of the network. In this paper we present some selected sample fragments of the training sets for the permutations σ_1, σ_3.

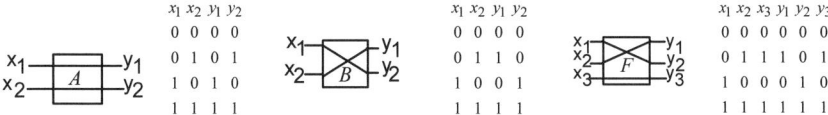

Fig. 4 Selected sample blocks of the network with the fragmentary training sets

In Fig. 4 are presented fragments of the training sets for several chosen sample elementary modules, but not the complete training set. One, having the full knowledge about the complete neural network and the content of the training sets for individual blocks, can reconstruct the training set for the complete network. How to construct a general training set, can be found in our earlier papers [7, 8]. However, making the methods effective needs additional studies.

As we remarked, the training set must be delivered to the server to the program training the network. The transmission of this set is through an insecure communication channel. Asking about the security of the algorithm update procedure, we must assume that an adversary can have the content of the training set. If the complete training set is transmitted, the adversary has the complete information about the permutation (cryptographic algorithm). He simply obtains this information by some analysis, because the training set corresponds to a unique permutation. The essential information for the adversary is the topological structure of the network. Certainly, we could assume that this structure is secret, but such a solution seems to be inefficient. First, it contradicts the presently valid rule of knowledge the algorithm (the secret algorithm cannot be analysed and its security is never sufficiently sure). Moreover, the adversary can always train a similar network (e.g., with the same number of inputs and outputs) and obtain very similar algorithm, what together with other cryptanalytic techniques would completely break the cipher. So, the remedy could be transmission of not the complete training set, but only of some partial information, which together with some trapdoor information would make possible the reconstruction of the complete training set at the server side and performing the training procedure. In Fig. 3 the elementary blocks of the neural network are denoted as A, B, F. Using these notations (reflecting the network internal structure) we can transmit the fragmentary training sets for each blocks, as it is presented in Fig. 4. Using these components one can construct, at the server side, the complete training set for the whole neural network realizing the cryptographic algorithm. Such a solution gives some security for the algorithm update process provided the internal structure of the complete network (its topology) remains secret.

The problem of security of the algorithm update process at the server side is strictly connected to the efficiency of such a training process. First, the server must be equipped with the training software, which must be secure during learning the network and during the storage in inter-learning period. Then, the process of training is server resources- and time-consuming, what is especially important in a case of large number of servers located over the network and serviced by the training systems. Finally, the servers are often located in an un-trusted environment, so such attacks, as sniffing/spoofing and analysis of electronic discharge are possible. For this reasons, one should look for alternative solutions of dynamic changing encryption algorithms built-in the remote network security devices equipped with neural networks.

Training at a client side. A natural alternative for training neural network at the server side is training the identical copy of the network at the client side and transmission of the obtained result to the server. As we know, the neural network is completely defined (in the model we apply for encryption) by the architecture of the functional blocks (being certain neural networks), the structure of neurons inside the blocks and the weights of these neurons. Thus, information sufficient to change the algorithm is contained in the weights (we assume that the structure of neural network remains unchangeable in the server). The result of the training is the vector of weights. Such a vector must be transmitted form a client to the server to update the cryptographic algorithm.

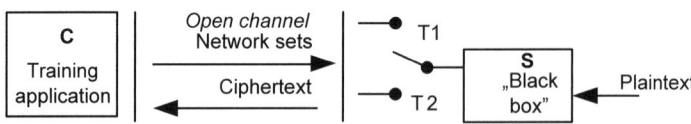

Fig. 5 Training at the client C side

The communication scheme for training the neural network at the client side is presented in Fig. 5. Now, the server S again works in two modes. Mode T1 is the update of the weights in the neural network blocks, what corresponds to inserting a new cryptographic algorithm into the server's "black box". Mode T2 is the operation mode, where a plaintext inputs the "black box" and the corresponding ciphertext outputs it. Certainly, the "black box" performs also the inverse operation.

The presented solution is especially effective (less server time consuming, smaller volume of information transmitted) in the case of updating several servers. Also the neural network update program at the server side is less complicated. It works without the observer's supervision, what is required in the case of the neural network training at the server side. It is possible the automatic update of the weights with some self-check algorithm afterwards.

The neural network weights update can be performed in two ways. In the following two sections of the papers we show the outline how the two methods can be performed.

Transmission of updated weights. In Fig. 5 we present the transmission of parameters of a neural network. In this case the parameters are new values of weights. The basic assumption to make such a procedure effective is that both parties of the protocol, client C and server S are equipped with the neural networks with identical internal architecture. After the training stage, the weights of neurons obtained at the client side are transmitted to the server. The server is switched to the mode T1 and the weights are introduced into the neural network, overwriting the previous values. Then, the server is switched to the mode T2 and starts realizing a new encryption algorithm. For the neural network presented in Fig. 3 we have 64 weights and such a number of coefficients must be sent through the communication channel, see Eq. (2).

$$w = [w_1 ... w_{64}] \tag{2}$$

The information sent must contain the assignment of the weights to neurons. Since some functionally identical blocks in the network architecture repeat (as it is seen in Fig. 3), the weights for identical blocks can be sent only once. Next, they must be substituted as many times as needed. This property reduces the amount of information transmitted during the update process. Eq. (3) presents the sample weight vectors for the defined blocks $A, B,..., H$ of the neural network presented in Fig. 3.

$$W_A = [w_{A1} ... w_{A4}], W_B = [w_{B1} ... w_{B4}], W_C = [w_{C1} ... w_{C6}], W_D = [w_{D1} ... w_{B6}] \tag{3}$$

$$W_E = [w_{E1} ... w_{E6}], W_F = [w_{F1} ... w_{F6}], W_G = [w_{G1} ... w_{G6}], W_H = [w_{H1} ... w_{H6}]$$

Consider now the security of the weights updating process. Assume at the beginning that the transmission of the weights is by an open communication channel (that is, an adversary knows the weights). Trying to answer the question, what information about the cryptographic algorithm is contained in the weights we must say, that even if the weights together with the architecture of the neural network completely describe the cryptographic algorithm, then the weights alone give no information about it. For a successful attack an adversary should know the structure of blocks, their internal connections and assignment of weights to particular neurons. Thus, the algorithm remains secure provided the adversary does not know the neural network (our "black box") architecture, even if the weights are transmitted by an open communication channel. The last sentence, in fact, contradicts the widely used rule of the public knowledge of the applied cryptographic algorithm. In the following sections we propose two methods of solving this problem.

Before we go further, let us remark, that the proposed solution of application of the neural network for implementation of cryptographic algorithms slightly differs form analogous application of the programmable logical circuits. To update the algorithm, in the first case, we can send only a sequence of numbers (the weights), while in the second one we need the complete code of the cipher.

Transmission of differences of weights. Assume now that we wish to protect the transmitted weights against interception by an adversary. The method proposed in this section does not apply cryptography for increasing security of the update procedure. The adversary, to attack successfully the weights values should permanently trace traffic between client and server to collect all transmitted updates of weights. This effect can be obtained, if instead of the complete set of new weights W' we will transmit to the server their differences R to the previous values of weights W. The updating program at the server, knowing the old weights W and differences R can easily restore the new weights W', what symbolically is presented in Eq. (4). Here we present only the updating procedure for two weights; the others are completely analogous.

$$R = W \pm W', \qquad W'_A = [W_{A1} \pm W_{R1},...,W_{A4} \pm W_{R4}], W'_B = [W_{B1} \pm W_{R1},...,W_{B4} \pm W_{R4}],... \qquad (4)$$

In the proposed method, the effective updating the neural network is possible under two conditions. First, both networks: at the client side and at the server side must be initiated with the same values of weights. Then, the update must be synchronous, what means that no update of weights can be neglected at the server side. This forces the server to monitor continuously signals about the weights updates (remembering the present state of weights and the prompt receiving the differences of weights by the network updating program). If we additionally assume that the initial state of the neural network is a secret (the adversary cannot restore the initial values of weights), then both the internal structure of the neural network and the updates of weights (the transmitted differences of weights) need not be confidential to keep confidentiality of the communication protected by the neural network.

4. A unified solution for update of a permutation

The methods presented in Chapter 3 assumed that the updating data (the training set, the weights, or the differences of weights) was transmitted by an open communication channel. However, we can assume a possibility of using a secure (encrypted) channel for transmission of the critical updating data. Fig. 6 presents this situation.

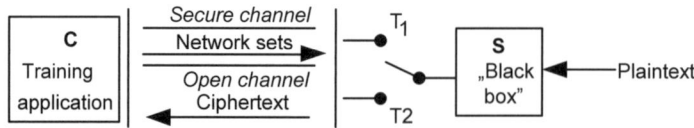

Fig. 6 Data transmission through the secure communication channel

The amount of the required data is relatively small (especially in the case of weights), so we can use asymmetric cryptography to deliver the data in a secure way. This method should not introduce a significant delay in operating the system. An alternative could be application of some popular secure tunneling method, e.g., SSL.

The data exchange scheme presented in Fig. 6 shows that the secure channel is used only in the updating T1 mode. After the update the "black box" is switched to the operating T2 mode and the server starts regular work, which is the cryptographic algorithm implemented in the neural network starts encryption communication.

To conclude, if the pair client-server has no secure communication channel (the asymmetric secure communication is too absorbing for the parties and the parties do not have a symmetric secure channel), then can be used the simplest solution. After calculating the new weights the operator of the communication protocol can update the weights manually, moving the required data in some mobile device.

5. Simulations

To verify usability of particular neural networks for implementing permutations of bits in blocks of various lengths, we made a number of simulations. The obtained results are presented in Table 1.

Table 1. Results of simulations for different neural networks

Neurons	No. of neurons within a network	Plaintext length (in bits)	Average training time (sec.)	Time of the brute-force plaintext attack (sec.)
Perceptrons	4	4	0.03	1099.20
Perceptrons	16	8	0.32	6306.60
Perceptrons	36	16	1.21	More than 168000
Boolean neurons	10	4	0.02	4.09
Boolean neurons	24	8	0.1	136.12
Boolean neurons	36	16	0.8	739.23

The estimation of training time for, both, perceptrons and Boolean neurons, enables the comparison of the efficiency of the two networks. Moreover, the last column of Tab. 1 contains estimation of time of brute-force attack for the known plaintext-ciphertext pairs. In the attack the space of possible weights values has been searched to obtain the agreement of the texts. The conclusion of the simulations (Tab. 1) is that the Boolean network in more effective but also more vulnerable to attacks. Thus, more experiments are needed to construct an optimal neural network realizing a complete encryption algorithm (not only a permutation).

6. Summary

In this paper we considered possible difficulties and threats during the process of updating cryptographic algorithm working at a remote server. We postulated the secure process of modifying the cipher. For the sake of clarity, we restricted our considerations to the neural networks realizing permutations. However, using methods of representing S-boxes in neural networks, proposed in [7], we could first represent any substitution-permutation block cipher as a neural network and then extend the update method to such a cipher.

We showed that the transmission of the training set by an open channel is not a good solution. An adversary who obtains the training set can reconstruct the cryptographic algorithm realized by the neural network. Updating the weights of neurons of the neural network is a much more secure solution. The supplementary application of asymmetric cryptography solves the problem of secure update of the neural network algorithm. However, not always such a method can be applied, because the asymmetric cryptography requires relatively strong computational resources of the server and significantly complicates the procedure of the update.

The results presented in this paper are mostly demonstrative. They show that it is possible a secure mechanism of dynamic updating the cryptographic algorithms realized by appropriately designed neural networks. However, to study practical effectiveness and exploitation efficiency of such algorithms, one must define the procedure for the complete cipher, containing both linear (permutations) and nonlinear (S-box) blocks, and perform its practical Internet tests.

To summarise, lest us remark that our proposal is in some sense more general than so-called neural cryptography, which utilizes neural networks for a secret key agreement through a public communication channel (see [10]). The proposed solution agrees a complete cryptographic algorithm, in spite of it is still not perfect.

References

[1] E. Mosanya, Ch. Teuscher, H.F. Restrepo, P. Galley, E. Sanchez, CryptoBooster: A Reconfigurable and Modular Cryptographic Coprocessor, in: Cryptographic Hardware and Embedded Systems: Proc. CHES'99, LNCS 1717, Springer Berlin 1999.

[2] R. Taylor, S. Goldstein, A High-Performance Flexible Architecture for Cryptography, Proceedings of the Workshop on Cryptographic Hardware and Embedded Systems, Worcester August 1999.

[3] C.H. Lim, CRYPTON: A New 128-bit Block Cipher, Proceedings of the First Advanced Encryption Standard Candidate Conference, Ventura, California, NIST, 1998.

[4] L.R. Knudsen, Correlations in RC6, Department of Informatics, University of Bergen, N 5020 Bergen:, July 29, 1999.

[5] W. Laskowski, Programmable logical circuits as tools supporting cryptographic data protection, Przegląd Telekomunikacyjny, Vol. LXXIV, no. 3/2001. (In Polish)

[6] T. Łuba, K. Jasiński, B. Zwierzchowski, Programmable logical circuits processing signals and information – digital circuit engineering in multimedia and cryptography, Przegląd Telekomunikacyjny Vol. LXXVI no. 8–9/2003. (In Polish)

[7] P. Kotlarz, Z. Kotulski, Application of neural networks for implementation of cryptographic functions, in:Multimedia in Business and Education, ISBN83-9182218-7-0

[8] P.Kotlarz, Z.Kotulski, On application of neural networks for S-boxes design, in: P. S. Szczepaniak, J.Kacprzyk, A. Niewiadomski, ed. Advances in Web Intelligence, AWIC 2005, LNCS 3528, pp. 243-248, Springer, Berlin 2005.

[9] P. Kotlarz, Z. Kotulski, Artificial intelligence methods in the present-day cryptography, Proceedings of Ploug'05, Zakopane 2005. (In Polish)

[10] I. Kanter, W. Kinzel, E. Kanter, Secure exchange of information by synchronization of neural networks, Europhys. Lett. 57, 141, 2002.

On Intermediate Evaluation of Block Ciphers [1]

Krzysztof Chmiel

Poznań University of Technology, pl. Skłodowskiej-Curie 5,
60-965 Poznań, Poland, Chmiel@sk-kari.put.poznan.pl

Abstract. In the paper an intermediate evaluation of block ciphers method is presented. As a criterion of quality, probability of the best nonzero linear approximation is taken. The main idea of the method is to restrict considerations to only two types of approximations: zero and nonzero. For a cipher graph G of zero-nonzero approximations is constructed. Algorithm SP calculates the shortest path of a specified length in graph G. This path determines the best zero-nonzero approximation of the cipher, that fulfils approximation conditions. The method is quite general but it is not independent of the structure of a cipher. In the paper the method is presented for DES.

1. Introduction

Well constructed block cipher should be resistant to any kinds of cryptographic attacks. To the most important general methods of cryptanalysis belong differential cryptanalysis [1], [6] and linear cryptanalysis [2], [3], [4], [5], [6], [8]. Both methods were successfully applied to the Data Encryption Standard, where S-boxes with six input bits are used. In paper [6] it is shown, that with increase of the number of bits, the linear approximation becomes more effective than the differential one. Therefore, the presented evaluation of block ciphers is restricted to the linear approximation.

We distinguish the following three methods of block cipher evaluation. In the first, *exact* method, the best nonzero linear approximation of a cipher is determined. In the second, *rough* method, the best nonzero linear approximation of a cipher is assumed to be a composition of the best nonzero linear approximations of a single iteration. In the third, *intermediate* method, we find the best zero-nonzero approximation of a cipher, that fulfils approximation conditions. The first method should be applied to existing ciphers. The remaining methods, that omit the details of a cipher, are useful at the stage of construction.

The basic idea of linear cryptanalysis is to describe a given cipher algorithm by a linear approximate expression, so-called linear approximation. In general, the *linear approximation* of function $y = f(x)$: $\{0, 1\}^n \rightarrow \{0, 1\}^m$ is defined as an arbitrary equation of the form:

---

[1] This research was supported by the Polish Ministry of Education and Science as a 2005–2008 research project.

252   Advances in Information Processing and Protection

$$\bigoplus_{i\in y'} y_i = \bigoplus_{j\in x'} x_j, \tag{1}$$

which is fulfilled with approximation probability $p = N(x',y')/2^n$, where $x' \subseteq \{1, 2, ..., n\}$, $y' \subseteq \{1, 2, ..., m\}$ and $N(x',y')$ denotes the number of pairs (x, y) for which the equation holds. For simplicity the above equation is written in the following form:

$$y[y'] = x[x']. \tag{2}$$

The sets of indexes x', y' are called input and output *mask* respectively and the function $N(x',y')$ is called the *counting function* of the approximation. The *effectiveness* of the approximation is represented by magnitude of $|\Delta p| = |p - 1/2|$. By the *zero linear approximation* we mean approximation with $x' = y' = \Phi$, which probability p is equal to 1 for arbitrary function f. Masks x', y' are often denoted by numbers, corresponding to the zero-one representation of sets.

2. Approximation Conditions

Let us consider iteration function h_2 which is composed of two rounds of *DES* (fig.1).

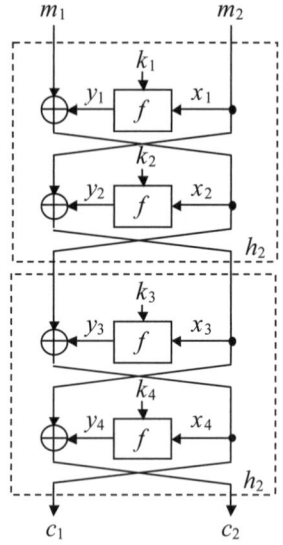

Fig. 1. Composition of iteration functions h_2 of *DES* (function h_4)

The best nonzero approximation of function h_2 is obtained for one zero and one best nonzero approximation of function f. According to the rough method, the best nonzero approximation of *DES* is assumed to be a composition of the best nonzero approximations of a single iteration. Therefore, it contains eight zero and eight best nonzero approximations of f. In fact, the number of zero approximations is less because of approximation conditions.

The general form of the approximation of function $c_1\|c_2 = h_4(m_1\|m_2, k_1, ..., k_4)$, which is realized as a presented in figure 1 composition of iteration functions h_2, is as follows:

$$c_1[c_1'] \oplus c_2[c_2'] = m_1[m_1'] \oplus m_2[m_2'] \oplus k_1[k_1'] \oplus ... \oplus k_4[k_4']. \tag{3}$$

To compute the linear approximation of function h_4, for given linear approximations of all functions f, the following set of equations can be written, that describe the linear approximations of functions f and XOR of consecutive rounds:

$$y_1[y_1'] = x_1[x_1'] \oplus k_1[k_1'], \tag{4}$$
$$x_2[y_1'] = y_1[y_1'] \oplus m_1[y_1'], \tag{5}$$
$$y_2[y_2'] = x_2[x_2'] \oplus k_2[k_2'], \tag{6}$$
$$x_3[y_2'] = y_2[y_2'] \oplus x_1[y_2'], \tag{7}$$
$$y_3[y_3'] = x_3[x_3'] \oplus k_3[k_3'], \tag{8}$$
$$x_4[y_3'] = y_3[y_3'] \oplus x_2[y_3'], \tag{9}$$
$$y_4[y_4'] = x_4[x_4'] \oplus k_4[k_4'], \tag{10}$$
$$c_2[y_4'] = y_4[y_4'] \oplus x_3[y_4']. \tag{11}$$

After addition of the above equations modulo 2, we obtain:

$$\begin{aligned} x_4[y_3'] \oplus x_4[x_4'] \oplus c_2[y_4'] = m_1[y_1'] \oplus x_1[y_2'] \oplus x_1[x_1'] \oplus \\ \oplus x_2[y_1'] \oplus x_2[x_2'] \oplus x_2[y_3'] \oplus \\ \oplus x_3[y_2'] \oplus x_3[x_3'] \oplus x_3[y_4'] \oplus \\ \oplus k_1[k_1'] \oplus ... \oplus k_4[k_4']. \end{aligned} \tag{12}$$

Considering that $x_4 = c_1$ and $x_1 = m_2$, we have:

$$\begin{aligned} c_1[y_3' \oplus x_4'] \oplus c_2[y_4'] = m_1[y_1'] \oplus m_2[y_2' \oplus x_1'] \oplus \\ \oplus x_2[y_1' \oplus x_2' \oplus y_3'] \oplus \\ \oplus x_3[y_2' \oplus x_3' \oplus y_4'] \oplus \\ \oplus k_1[k_1'] \oplus ... \oplus k_4[k_4']. \end{aligned} \tag{13}$$

Comparing the above approximation with the general form of the approximation of function h_4, for input masks we obtain:

$$m_1' = y_1', \; m_2' = y_2' \oplus x_1'. \tag{14}$$

Similarly, for output masks we have:

$$c_1' = y_3' \oplus x_4', \; c_2' = y_4'. \tag{15}$$

The *approximation conditions* of function h_4, that eliminate internal variables x_2 and x_3, are as follows:

$$y_1' \oplus x_2' \oplus y_3' = 0, \; y_2' \oplus x_3' \oplus y_4' = 0. \tag{16}$$

3. Zero-Nonzero Approximations

In the intermediate method with respect to *DES* we assume, that the best nonzero approximation of the block cipher corresponds to maximal possible number of zero approximations of function f and to the best nonzero approximations of the remaining functions f. Thus, we restrict our considerations to zero and nonzero approximations of function f. In table 1 are shown zero-nonzero approximations of iteration function h_2. Symbol 0 denotes zero approximation and symbol 1 nonzero approximation of function f_j, i.e. of j-th function f, where $j = 1, 2$.

Table 1. Zero-nonzero approximations of function h_2

No	f_1	f_2
0	0	0
1	1	0
2	0	1
3	1	1

In the composition of two iteration functions h_2 (fig. 1), the approximations of both iterations must fulfil approximation conditions of function h_4. Considering the zero-nonzero approximations we assume, that the approximation condition is fulfilled whenever it can be fulfilled. In table 2 are shown sequences of masks that fulfil the first of the two approximation conditions. Symbol 0 denotes zero mask and symbol 1 nonzero mask. The approximation condition is fulfilled in all cases apart from the case of two zero masks and one nonzero mask.

Table 2. Sequences of masks that fulfil approximation condition $y_1' \oplus x_2' \oplus y_3' = 0$

y_1'	x_2'	y_3'
0	0	0
1	0	1
0	1	1
1	1	0
1	1	1

For any effective approximation of an arbitrary function $y_j = f(x_j)$, the following implication is fulfilled:

$$y_j' = 0 \Rightarrow x_j' = 0. \tag{17}$$

It means, that the only effective approximation with zero output mask is the zero approximation. Function f of *DES* is *properly constructed*, i.e. the only effective approximation with zero input mask is the zero approximation. For properly constructed function f holds:

$$x_j' = 0 \Rightarrow y_j' = 0. \tag{18}$$

Considering that f is properly constructed, the first approximation condition is fulfilled for sequences of approximations of functions f_j shown in table 3. Symbol 0 denotes zero and symbol 1 nonzero approximation of function f_j.

Table 3. Sequences of approximations of functions f_j that fulfil approximation condition $y_1' \oplus x_2' \oplus y_3' = 0$

f_1	f_2	f_3
0	0	0
1	0	1
0	1	1
1	1	0
1	1	1

To obtain sequences of approximations of functions f_j, that fulfil both approximation conditions of function h_4, it is sufficient to compose the sequences of approximations of functions f_1, f_2, f_3 with the sequences of approximations of functions f_2, f_3, f_4. The result is shown in table 4.

Table 4. Zero-nonzero approximations of function h_4 that fulfil approximation conditions

No	f_1	f_2	f_3	f_4
0	0	0	0	0
6	0	1	1	0
7	1	1	1	0
11	1	1	0	1
13	1	0	1	1
14	0	1	1	1
15	1	1	1	1

Thus, seven from among sixteen zero-nonzero approximations of function h_4, fulfil approximation conditions. Approximation number **0** corresponds to the zero approximation of function h_4. To the best nonzero approximation of function h_4, in the intermediate quality evaluation method, corresponds approximation number **6** with two zero and two nonzero approximations of function f.

4. Graph of Zero-Nonzero Approximations

An equivalent description of the zero-nonzero approximations of function h_4 from table 4, is the oriented graph $G = (V, E)$ of zero-nonzero approximations of *DES*, presented in table 5. The elements of set V of vertices are the zero-nonzero approximations of iteration function h_2. A pair of approximations (A_i, A_{i+1}) belongs to E, if approximations A_i and A_{i+1} fulfil the approximation conditions of the composition of functions h_2.

From graph G it follows, that approximation number **0** of the first function h_2 implies approximation number **0** of the second function h_2 of the composition. Taking into account the formulas for input and output masks, in effect we obtain the zero approximation of the composition. For approximation number **1** of the first function h_2, the only approximation of the second function h_2 is approximation number **3**. Approximation number **2** of the first function h_2, can be followed by approximation number **1** or **3** of the second function h_2. In the case of approximation number **3** of the first function h_2, there is possible any approximation of the second function h_2, apart from approximation number **0**.

Table 5. Graph G of zero-nonzero approximations of *DES*

Approximation A_i		Approximation A_{i+1}	
No	$f_1 f_2$	$f_3 f_4$	**No**
0	00	00	**0**
1	10	11	**3**
2	01	10, 11	**1, 3**
3	11	10, 01, 11	**1, 2, 3**

Graph G will be used to determine the maximal possible number of zero approximations of function f in nonzero approximation of *DES*. Let $w: V \rightarrow R$ be the cost function, that assigns to vertices the number of ones in their zero-one representation. Thus, the value of function w, for approximation A_i of function h_2, is equal to the number of nonzero approximations of function f in A_i. Graph G with the cost function w is presented in figure 2.

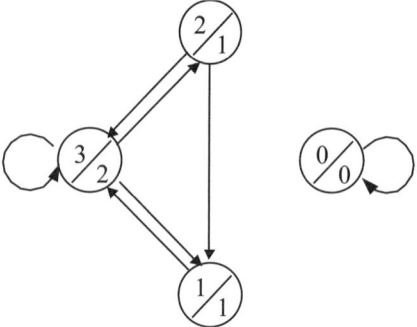

Fig. 2. Graph G with cost function w

The maximal number of zero approximations of function f in nonzero approximation of *DES* exists in the sequence with minimal summarized cost, of eight nonzero vertices of graph G. The presented in the next chapter algorithm *SP* calculates such a sequence of vertices.

5. Algorithm *SP*

Let $G = (V, E)$ be a directed graph with cost function $w: V \rightarrow R$, that assigns to vertices cost from the set of real numbers. Sequence of vertices $p = (v^{(1)}, v^{(2)}, ..., v^{(r)})$ such, that $(v^{(m)}, v^{(m+1)}) \in E$ for $m = 1, 2, ..., r-1$, will be called a path of length r from vertex $v^{(1)}$ to vertex $v^{(r)}$. The cost of path p is equal to the sum of costs of its vertices:

$$w(p) = \sum_{m=1}^{r} w(v^{(m)}).\tag{19}$$

Let notation $p^{(r)}: v_i \Rightarrow v_j$ denote, that $p^{(r)}$ is a path of length r from vertex v_i to vertex v_j. The path $s^{(r)}: v_i \Rightarrow v_j$ is the shortest path from vertex v_i to vertex v_j, i.e. it fulfils condition:

$$w(s^{(r)}) = \min\{w(p^{(r)})| \, p^{(r)}: v_i \Rightarrow v_j\}.\tag{20}$$

The shortest path of length r in graph G is the path $o^{(r)}$ such, that:

$$w(o^{(r)}) = \min\{w(s^{(r)})| \, v_i, v_j \in V \}.\tag{21}$$

The presented in this chapter algorithm SP, calculates the path $o^{(r)}$, i.e. the shortest path of length r in graph G, without any restrictions on the graph and the cost function. In particular there can be loops in the graph, negative costs of vertices and cycles with negative costs. Algorithm SP is based on the following property.

Property 1.
Let in directed graph $G = (V, E)$ with cost function $w: V \to R$, $s^{(m+1)}: v_i \Rightarrow v_j$ be the shortest path of length $m + 1$ from vertex v_i to vertex v_j. Furthermore let $s^{(m)}: v_i \Rightarrow v_k$ denote the shortest path of length m from vertex v_i to some vertex v_k such, that $(v_k, v_j) \in E$. Then:

$$w(s^{(m+1)}) = \min\{w(s^{(m)})+ w(v_j) \mid v_k \in V \}.\tag{22}$$

Proof.
Let us assume, that the shortest path $s^{(m+1)}: v_i \Rightarrow v_j$ is composed of the path $p^{(m)}: v_i \Rightarrow v_k$, which is not the shortest, and of vertex v_j. Obviously $(v_k, v_j) \in E$. Then, considering that $w(p^{(m)}) > w(s^{(m)})$ where $s^{(m)}: v_i \Rightarrow v_k$, holds:

$$w(s^{(m+1)}) = w(p^{(m)}) + w(v_j) > w(s^{(m)}) + w(v_j),\tag{23}$$

which is in contradiction to the assumption, that path $s^{(m+1)}$ is the shortest.

$\blacklozenge$

From property 1 it follows, that the cost of the shortest path of length $m + 1$, for arbitrary pair of vertices (v_i, v_j), can be calculated with use of costs of the shortest paths of length m from initial vertex v_i to remaining vertices. Taking into account, that the shortest path of length $m + 1$ in graph G, i.e. path $o^{(m+1)}$, can start at any vertex v_i, the cost $w(o^{(m+1)})$ will be calculated with use of costs of the shortest paths of length m between any pair of vertices [7].

Without loss of generality, algorithm SP is presented for the graph of zero-nonzero approximations $G = (V, E)$, where $V = \{0, 1, ..., 2^n-1\}$ and cost $w(v)$ is equal to the number of ones in binary representation of vertex v. In the calculations is used cost matrix C, which holds costs of addition of vertex j to the path from vertex i to vertex k, defined as follows:

$$C(k, j) = \begin{cases} w(j) & for \quad (k, j) \in E \\ \infty & for \quad (k, j) \notin E. \end{cases}\tag{24}$$

Cost matrix C for graph G of algorithm DES is presented in table 6.

Table 6. Cost matrix C for graph G of algorithm DES

k	j			
	0	**1**	**2**	**3**
0	0	∞	∞	∞
1	∞	∞	∞	2
2	∞	1	∞	2
3	∞	1	1	2

C

In order to calculate cost $w(o^{(r)})$ of the shortest path of length r in graph G, are successively calculated matrices $C^{(m)}$ of costs of the shortest paths of length m between any pair of vertices, where $1 \leq m \leq r$. The cost matrix of the first iteration $C^{(1)}$, is defined in the following way:

$$C^{(1)}(i, j) = \begin{cases} w(j) & for \quad i = j \\ \infty & for \quad i \neq j. \end{cases} \tag{25}$$

Cost matrices $C^{(m)}$ for graph G of algorithm DES are shown in table 7. Matrix $C^{(8)}$ corresponds to the number of rounds of algorithm DES equal to 16.

Table 7. Cost matrices $C^{(m)}$ for graph G of algorithm DES

i	j			
	0	**1**	**2**	**3**
0	0	∞	∞	∞
1	∞	1	∞	∞
2	∞	∞	1	∞
3	∞	∞	∞	2

$C^{(1)}$

i	j			
	0	**1**	**2**	**3**
0	0	∞	∞	∞
1	∞	∞	∞	3
2	∞	2	∞	3
3	∞	3	3	4

$C^{(2)}$

i	j			
	0	**1**	**2**	**3**
0	0	∞	∞	∞
1	∞	4	4	5
2	∞	4	4	4
3	∞	4	5	5

$C^{(3)}$

i	j			
	0	**1**	**2**	**3**
0	0	∞	∞	∞
1	∞	5	6	6
2	∞	5	5	6
3	∞	6	6	6

$C^{(4)}$

i	j			
	0	**1**	**2**	**3**
0	0	∞	∞	∞
1	∞	7	7	7
2	∞	6	7	7
3	∞	7	7	8

$C^{(5)}$

i	j			
	0	**1**	**2**	**3**
0	0	∞	∞	∞
1	∞	8	8	9
2	∞	8	8	8
3	∞	8	9	9

$C^{(6)}$

i	j			
	0	**1**	**2**	**3**
0	0	∞	∞	∞
1	∞	9	10	10
2	∞	9	9	10
3	∞	10	10	10

$C^{(7)}$

i	j			
	0	**1**	**2**	**3**
0	0	∞	∞	∞
1	∞	11	11	11
2	∞	10	11	11
3	∞	11	11	12

$C^{(8)}$

Cost matrix of the next iteration $C^{(m+1)}$ is calculated with use of matrix $C^{(m)}$ and matrix C in the following way:

$$C^{(m+1)}[i, j] = \min\{C^{(m)}[i, k] + C[k, j] \mid 0 \leq k \leq 2^n - 1\}. \tag{26}$$

Calculation of matrix $C^{(m+1)}$ is realized by procedure NEXT-$C^{(m)}$, of time complexity $O(|V|^3)$, presented in figure 3.

NEXT-$C^{(m)}(C^{(m)}, C, n, C^{(m+1)})$
1. **for** $i \leftarrow 0$ **to** $2^n{-}1$ **do**
2.   **for** $j \leftarrow 0$ **to** $2^n{-}1$ **do**
3. $C^{(m+1)}[i, j] \leftarrow \infty$
4.   **for** $k \leftarrow 0$ **to** $2^n{-}1$ **do**
5. $C^{(m+1)}[i, j] \leftarrow \min(C^{(m+1)}[i, j], \ C^{(m)}[i, k] + C[k, j])$
6. **return**

Fig. 3. Procedure calculating cost matrix $C^{(m+1)}$

The shortest path $o^{(r)}$ of length r in graph G it is a path with the minimal cost in matrix $C^{(r)}$, defined as follows:

$$w(o^{(r)}) = \min\{ \ C^{(r)}[i, j] \mid 0 \leq \ i, j \leq 2^n{-}1 \ \}. \tag{27}$$

PRINT-PATH$(C, C^{(1)}, ..., C^{(r)}, n, r, i, j)$
1. write(j)
2. **for** $m \leftarrow r{-}1$ **downto** 2 **do**
3. $min \leftarrow \infty, \ mink \leftarrow 0$
4.   **for** $k \leftarrow 0$ **to** $2^n{-}1$ **do**
5.   **if** $C^{(m)}[i, k] + C[k, j] < min$
6.   **then** $min \leftarrow C^{(m)}[i, k] + C[k, j], \ mink \leftarrow k$
7.   write('$\leftarrow$', $mink$), $j \leftarrow mink$
8. **if** $r > 1$ **then** write('$\leftarrow$', i)
9. **return**

Fig. 4. Procedure writing the shortest path of length r from vertex i to vertex j

Procedure PRINT-PATH, of time complexity $\mathrm{O}(r \cdot |V|)$, writing the shortest path of length r from vertex i to vertex j, is presented in figure 4. The shortest path is written in the reverse order. In particular this procedure is used to write the path $o^{(r)}$.

SP(G, n, r)
1. INI-C(G, n, C)
2. INI-$C^{(1)}(G, n, C^{(1)})$
3. **for** $m \leftarrow 1$ **to** $r - 1$ **do**
4.   NEXT-$C^{(m)}(C^{(m)}, C, n, C^{(m+1)})$
5. $wo^{(r)} \leftarrow \min\{ \ C^{(r)}[i, j] \mid 0 \leq \ i, j \leq 2^n{-}1\}$
6. **for** $i \leftarrow 0$ **to** $2^n{-}1$ **do**
7.   **for** $j \leftarrow 0$ **to** $2^n{-}1$ **do**
8.   **if** $C^{(r)}[i, j] = wo^{(r)}$ **then** PRINT-PATH$(C, C^{(1)}, ..., C^{(r)}, n, r, i, j)$
9. **return**

Fig. 5. Algorithm SP to calculate the shortest path of length r in graph G

Algorithm SP to calculate the shortest path of length r in directed graph $G = (V, E)$ with cost function $w: V \rightarrow R$, where $V = \{0, 1, ..., 2^n{-}1\}$, is presented in figure 5. In steps 1-4 are calculated cost matrices C and $C^{(1)}, \ldots, C^{(r)}$. In step 5 is determined the minimal value of matrix $C^{(r)}$. Then, in steps 6-8, for each pair of vertices (i, j) with minimal value in matrix $C^{(r)}$ is written the shortest path from i to j. Thus, in general are written many shortest paths of length r in graph G, but a single one of more possible for a pair of vertices. The time complexity of algorithm SP is $O(r \cdot |V|^3)$ and the space complexity is $O(r \cdot |V|^2)$.

In the case of graph G of zero-nonzero approximations of DES, algorithm SP should write the shortest nonzero paths of length r in graph G. To this end, suffices the following modification of step 5 of algorithm SP:

$$5'. \quad wo^{(r)} \leftarrow \min\{ \ C^{(r)}[i, j] \mid 1 \le i, j \le 2^n-1 \ \}. \tag{28}$$

6. Evaluation of *DES* Quality

In the intermediate method with respect to DES we assume, that the best nonzero approximation corresponds to maximal possible number of zero approximations of function f and to the best nonzero approximations of the remaining functions f. Maximal number of zero approximations of f in nonzero approximation of 16-round DES, is determined by the shortest nonzero path of length $r = 8$ in graph G of zero-nonzero approximations. The shortest path, calculated by algorithm SP, is:

$$2 \rightarrow 1 \rightarrow 3 \rightarrow 2 \rightarrow 1 \rightarrow 3 \rightarrow 2 \rightarrow 1. \tag{29}$$

The cost of this path is equal to 10 and therefore the maximal number of zero approximations of f in nonzero approximation of DES is equal to 6.

The best nonzero approximation of f has probability $|\Delta p^+| = 20/64$ and corresponds to the best nonzero approximation of S-box $S5$ [2]. For probability $|\Delta p_a^+|$ of the best nonzero approximation of DES, which contains 10 best nonzero approximations of function f, we obtain:

$$| \Delta p_a^{\ +} \ | = 2^9 \prod_{j=1}^{10} (20/64) \le 1/2^7. \tag{30}$$

Algorithm DES with 16 rounds seems to be too easy to approximate. Let us consider 48-round DES. The shortest nonzero path of length $r = 24$ in graph G is:

$$\begin{aligned} 2 \rightarrow 1 \rightarrow 3 \rightarrow 2 \rightarrow 1 \rightarrow 3 \rightarrow 2 \rightarrow 1 \rightarrow \\ 3 \rightarrow 2 \rightarrow 1 \rightarrow 3 \rightarrow 2 \rightarrow 1 \rightarrow 3 \rightarrow 2 \rightarrow \\ 1 \rightarrow 3 \rightarrow 2 \rightarrow 1 \rightarrow 3 \rightarrow 2 \rightarrow 1 \rightarrow 3. \end{aligned} \tag{31}$$

The cost of this path is equal to 32 and therefore it corresponds to 32 nonzero and 16 zero approximations of function f. For probability of the best nonzero approximation of 48-round variant of DES we have:

$$| \Delta p_a^{\ +} \ | = 2^{31} \prod_{j=1}^{32} (20/64) \le 1/2^{22}. \tag{32}$$

This value of probability is closer to the adequate value for a 64-bit block cipher, which in author's opinion is:

$$|\Delta p_a^+| \leq 1/2^{33}. \tag{33}$$

The adequate value could be obtained by improvement of S-boxes $S1$, $S5$ and $S7$ to probability of their best nonzero approximation $|\Delta p^+| \leq 16/64$.

7. Conclusion

The intermediate evaluation method of block ciphers is useful at the stage of construction. The main idea of the method is to omit the details of a cipher and to restrict considerations to only two types of linear approximations: zero and nonzero. With use of algorithm SP in graph G of zero-nonzero approximations is determined the best zero-nonzero approximation of a cipher, that fulfils approximation conditions. Effectiveness of this approximation is used to evaluate the cipher. In the paper the method is presented for DES. The adequate effectiveness, for a 64-bit block cipher, is obtained by 48-round variant of DES with improved S-boxes.

References

[1] Biham, E., Shamir, A.: Differential Cryptanalysis of the Data Encryption Standard. Springer-Verlag, Berlin Heidelberg New York (1993)
[2] Chmiel K.: Linear Cryptanalysis of the Reduced DES Algorithms. Proceedings of the Regional Conference on Military Communication and Information Systems 2000. WIŁ, (Zegrze 2000) vol. 1, 111-118
[3] Chmiel, K.: Linear Approximation of Arithmetic Sum Function. In: Sołdek, J., Drobiazgiewicz, L. (eds.): Artificial Intelligence and Security in Computing Systems. Kluwer Academic Publishers, Boston Dordrecht London (2003) 293–302
[4] Chmiel, K.: Fast Computation of Approximation Tables. In: Saeed, K., Pejaś, J. (eds.): Information Processing and Security Systems. Springer-Verlag, Berlin Heidelberg New York (2005) 125–134
[5] Chmiel, K.: On Arithmetic Subtraction Linear Approximation. In: Pejaś, J., Piegat, A. (eds.): Enhanced Methods in Computer Security, Biometric and Artificial Intelligence Systems. Kluwer Academic Publishers, New York (2005) 125–134
[6] Chmiel, K.: Differential and Linear Approximation of S-box Functions. In: Saeed, K. et al. (eds.): Image Analysis, Computer Graphics, Security Systems and Artificial Intelligence Applications. Białystok (2005) vol.1, 191-200
[7] Cormen, T.H., Leiserson, C.E., Rivest, L.R.: Introduction to Algorithms. MIT (1994)
[8] Matsui, M.: Linear Cryptanalysis Method for DES Cipher. In: Helleseth, T. (ed.): Advances in Cryptology Eurocrypt'93 (1993) 386–397

Development of Concealing the Purpose of Processing for Programs in a Distributed Computing Environment

Yuji Kinoshita, Koichi Kashiwagi, Yoshinobu Higami, Shin-Ya Kobayashi

Ehime University, 3 Bunkyo, Matsuyama, Ehime 7908577 Japan

Abstract. Recently, distributed computing systems are popular among network security researchers. Distributed computing systems have the problem of required programs being analyzed by malicious computers and people. That is to say, in the four senses of a program, the purpose of processing can be analyzed. The easiest solution to this problem is constructed of only trustworthy computers. However, not all computers on the Internet can be considered trustworthy. There are presently no effective security solutions for this problem. We are developing systems to conceal the purpose of processing. In this paper, we prove that the proposed method conceals the purpose of processing. The proposed method is adaptability with the mobile code systems and grid of the distributed computing systems. We are planning on a method of interleaving multiple fragments, and making an effective dummy code and segments.

Key words: Obfuscation, Distributed Computing System, Security

1. Introduction

Recently, distributed computing systems are popular among network security researchers. If a program has mobility, it is daunting to think that malicious network users could analyze the programs. Therefore, classified information might let the secret out. The easiest solution of this problem is constructing systems of only trustworthy computers. There is presently no effective security solution. There are various techniques to hinder analysis and encryption techniques for these restrictions. It is not a guarantee that these methods could absolutely prevent malicious computers and people from analyzing the programs. Consequently, we are developing a new method whose strength of concealment can be guaranteed quantitatively. We assume that code migration is used to execute multiple programs on multiple computers. Presently, we are qualitatively indicating the difficulty of analyzing a program.

2. Proposal technique

2.1 Difficult Program Analysis

A program with mobility to prevent malicious analysis uses program obfuscation and cryptographic methods. However, it is not guaranteed that these methods prevent malicious analyzing of programs. For instance, when programs are transmitted encryption methods are used, and programs are received after decryption. The program analysis becomes difficult by this method. However, there is still a possibility of analyzing by checking the memory of the computer after the program is received, and using the incircuit emulator. The program obfuscation is a method of complicating the program, and making the analysis difficult. The program obfuscation has a condition in which obfuscated data must be corresponding to the input data. The program obfuscations are variable. For instance, there is the permutation and modification of a variable name, etc. However, the program obfuscation is not complete because there is a possibility that the program is analyzed for relation between input data and output data. In addition, there is the Mobile Cryptography. This method can be executed for encrypted data. The program analysis can be made difficult, because there is no decryption. However, there is a problem with the restriction to the special polynomial and rational function. Then, we propose the concealment method of the purpose of processing corresponding to the distributed computer environment.

2.2 Concealment Method of Purpose of Processing

The program has data and processing. There are existing purposes for each. The program analysis is difficult because it conceals the purpose of processing. 'The Concealment Method of the Purpose of Processing' is shown as a method of concealing the purpose of processing. Proposal methods are as follows:
1. The preparation of one or more trustworthy computers.
2. Each program to be executed is divided respectively into fragments by the trustworthy computer.
3. Several fragments from different programs are interleaved and conjoined, producing segments.
4. Dummy codes are inserted into the segment, called dummy segments. The dummy codes don't influence results of the original program execution.
5. Make the dummy segments. It is not necessary for getting the results, but used only to mislead other computers.
6. Trustworthy computers distribute most of the segments to other computers. The trustworthy computer executes the several segments as well.
7. Trustworthy computers handle data transfer between segments.

It can be difficult for an analytical person to analyze the segments of 2, 3, and 4. If two or more analytical people conspire with each other, the analytical group has the segments of 1, 5, 6, and 7, making the analysis difficult.

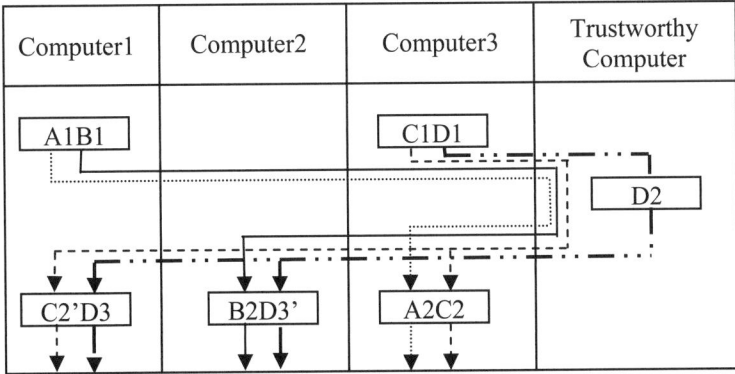

Fig. 1. Example of connecting fragments that use the proposed technique

Figure 1 shows one example of the program execution that uses the proposed technique. The interleaving and the made segments are distributed to computers, and they are executed by dividing D from program A. The fragment that is attached with " ' " such as C2' is a dummy fragment, and the arrow shows the flow of the I/O data. Even if an analytical person who owns computer (1), (2), and (3) in Figure 1 conspire with each other, analysis of program D becomes difficult because computer (1), (2), and (3) cannot obtain fragment D2. In program C, the analysis becomes difficult because there are two connections of the fragment (route) by the dummy fragment.

3. Evaluation method for difficult of analysis

To difficulty of discovering fragment's route quantitatively evaluates. When fragment is connection to other stage's fragment, there are three connection with fragments. The stage is execution phase where each computers could be execution and trustworthy computer gradually distributes two or more fragments. We explain three connection with fragments.

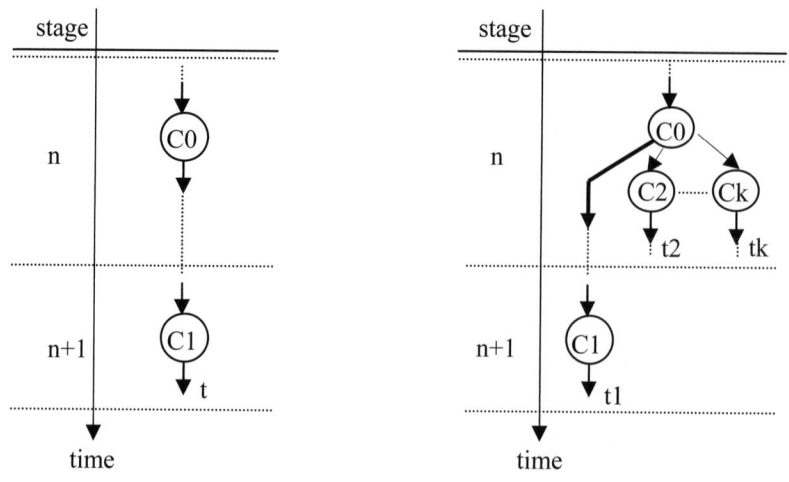

(1) Not branch and there have an immediate dependence of stepped over stages.

(2) At least one route steps over stages and branch part

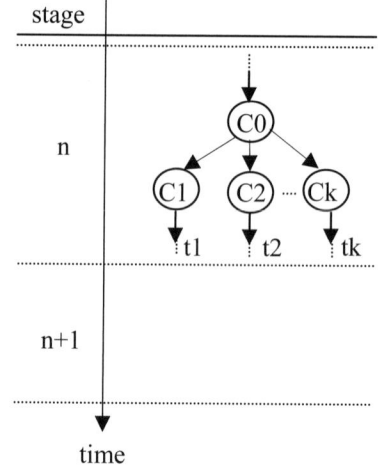

(3) Branch part without stepping over stages

Fig. 1A. A part of connection with fragments

1. Not branch and there have an immediate dependence of stepped over stages.
C_1 is correct, and it is assumed that the number of routes thought about from C_1 back
is t. Then, If C_0 is correct, there is a pattern of including the route after C_1 or a pattern
of NOT including the route after C_1. It is (1), C_0 is correct, the number of routes after
C_0 solutes by the following expression.

$$\text{The following number of routes from } C_0 \ = \ t+1$$
$$(\text{t: number of routes thought about from } C_1 \text{ back})$$

2. At least one route steps over stages and branch part.
C_i (i=1...k) is correct, and it is assumed that the number of routes thought about since
C_i is t_i. Then, If C_0 is correct, there is a pattern of the including number of routes after
C_1 or a pattern of NOT including the route after C_1. It is (2), C_0 is corrected fragment,
because if all route after Ci doesn't include route after C_0, trustworthry computer
sends output data by C_0. It is (2), C_0 is correct, the number of routes after C_0 solutes
by the following expression.

$$\text{The following number of routes from } C_0 \ = \ \prod_{i=1}^{m}(t_i+1)$$

$$(\text{t : Number of routes thought about from } C_{i(i=1,2,\cdots,k)} \text{ back})$$

3. Branch part without stepping over stages
C_i(i=1...k) is correct, and the number of routes after C_i are t_i. Then, If C_0 is correct,
there is a pattern of the including number of routes after C_1 or a pattern of NOT
including the route after C_1. It is (3), When the route after C_0 and it doesn't contain
the route after C_i, C_0 is not correct fragment. Therefore, at least the route after C_i
must include the route after C_0. It is (3), C_0 is correct, the number of routes after C_0
solutes by the following expression.

$$\text{The following number of routes from } C_0 \ = \ \prod_{i=1}^{m}(t_i+1)-1$$

$$(\text{t : Number of routes thought about from } Ci(i=1,2,\cdots,k) \text{ back})$$

The purpose of subtracting one by this expression, it is to omit the case where the
route thought about by C_i is not included in the route thought about since C_0.
Attention of (1),(2),(3), we count the number of routes. We repeat all stages, we count
up all correct routes in all stages.

Execution phase

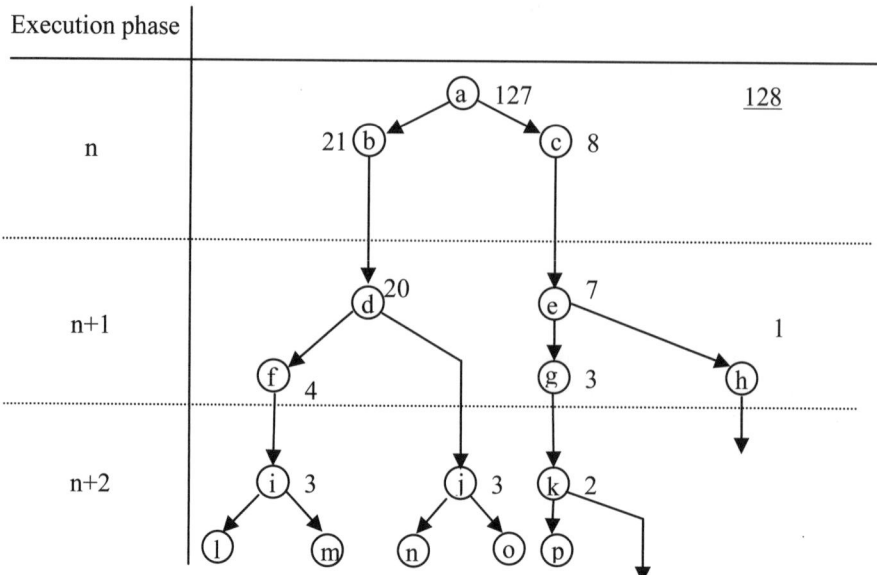

Fig. 2. Route of program fragment without branch

It explains by using figure2. First of all, it pays attention to i, l, and m. Because this is a form of (3), three kinds of routes are thought from a back. Because j, n, and o are the forms of (3), three kinds of routes are thought from j back. Because k and p are the forms of (2), two kinds of routes are thought from k back. Next, because j and i are the forms of (1), four kinds of routes are thought from f back. Because g and k are the forms of (1), three kinds of routes are thought from g back. Because d, f, and i are the forms of (2), 20 kinds of routes are thought from d back. Because e, g, and h are the forms of (3), seven kinds of routes are thought from e back. The route that can be thought to repeat the calculation like this from a back becomes 197 kinds. However, for the code that is not correct to have to think, 128 kinds of routes are finally thought. It becomes a lower bound to which this number of routes quantitatively evaluates the difficulty of the analysis.

Besides this, there is a proposal to analyze difficultly.

1. Method of making synthetic fragment from division of many prepared programs, making program fragment, and doing interleave defending the execution order by program fragment and dummy code

2. The name of the variable and the function is made a meaningless name.

An analytical person or groups become difficult the analysis of the program fragment by these two techniques. An analytical person or groups become difficult the analysis of the program because more programs are divided and interleave. An analytical person requires thought about a lot of codes in inserting the dummy code, and the analysis becomes difficult. Because an analytical person or groups cannot guess the data role and the purpose role from the name of the variable and the function by making the name of the variable and the function a meaningless name, the analysis becomes difficult. Two or more program A, B, and C are prepared. It divides on the computer that can trust of each. The program fragment that divides A is assumed to be A1, A2, and A3. The program fragment that divides B is assumed to be B1, B2, and B3. The program fragment that divides C is assumed to be C1 and C2. The dummy code is assumed to be D1 and D2. There is a variable named a11 and a12 in A1. There is a variable named a21 and a22 in A2. There is a variable named a31 and a32 in A3. There is a variable named b11 and b12 in B1. There is a variable named b21 and b22 in B2. There is a variable named b31 and b32 in B3. There is a variable named c11 and c12 in C1. There is a variable named c21 and c22 in C2. There is a variable named d11 and d12 in D1. It is assumed that there are d21 and d22 in D2. Program fragment A1, B1, and D1 in that are interleaving done, and synthetic fragment A1B1D1 is generated. a11, a12, b11, b12, d11, and d12 are replaced with $\alpha 1$, $\alpha 2$, $\alpha 3$, $\alpha 4$, $\alpha 5$, and $\alpha 6$ on the computer that can trust it at this time.

4. Conclusion

In this paper, we proposed "Concealing the Purpose of Processing for Programs" in a distributed computing environment, and method of quantitatively appreciable of effect of concealment.

We described the problem of the distributed computer environment , and the present described the solution. We enumerated the problem of obfuscation and cryptographic methods. we proposed the Concealment the purpose of processing ,it is effective security by untrustworthy computers on internet. The proposal method is difficult to analyze for malicious computers and people, malicious computers and people are conspiring, it is difficult to analyze. We quantitative evaluated, based on the route that was the connection of fragments of the Concealing purpose of processing.

5. Future research

In this paper, we prove that the proposed method conceals the purpose of processing. Also, showing the proposed method's adaptability with the mobile code systems and grid of the distributed computing systems, including its wide range of adaptability. We feel further research on a method of how to interleave multiple fragments, and how to make an effective dummy code and segments is needed.

6. References

[1] T.Sander, C.F.Tschudin, "Towards Mobile Cryptography", Technical Report 97-049, International Computer Science Institute, Berkeley, Nov. 22, 1997
[2] S.Morigaki, K.Kashiwagi, Y.Higami, S.Kobayashi "Method to Hide a Purpose of Processing for Code Migration", IPSJ, DICOMO2004, pp.357-360, 2004-7
[3] S.Morigaki, K.Kashiwagi, Y.Higami, S.Kobayashi "Hiding a Purpose of Processing for Some Programs in Distributed Computer Environment", SJCIEE, pp.244, 2004-9
[4] Y.Kinoshita, K.Kashiwagi, Y.Higami, S.Kobayashi "Consideration of concealing the Purpose of Processing for Programs in a Distributed Computing Environment", SJCIEE 2005-9

Covert Channel for Improving VoIP Security

Wojciech Mazurczyk, Zbigniew Kotulski

[1] Warsaw University of Technology, Faculty of Electronics and Information Technology, Institute of Telecommunications 15/19 Nowowiejska Str. 00-665 Warszawa, Poland
{W.Mazurczyk Z.Kotulski}@tele.pw.edu.pl
[2] Polish Academy of Sciences, Institute of Fundamental Technological Research zkotulsk@ippt.gov.pl

Abstract. In this paper a new way of exchanging data for Voice over Internet Protocol (VoIP) service is presented. With use of audio watermarking and network steganography techniques we achieve a covert channel which can be used for different purposes e.g. to improve IP Telephony signaling protocol's security or to alternate existing protocols like RTCP (Real-Time Control Protocol). In this paper we focus on improving VoIP security. The main advantage of this solution is that it is lightweight (it does not consume any transmission bandwidth) and the data sent is inseparably bound to the voice content.

1. Introduction

Nowadays VoIP (Voice over Internet Protocol) is one of the most popular communication technology designed for IP networks. Although there are many standards proposed (SIP, H.323) there are two fields in which IP Telephony is lacking. The first one is providing certain Quality of Service (QoS) parameters (e.g. low end-to-end latency, packet loss) and the second are security considerations as described in [3]. The latter causes to seek for a new approaches. In [16] we proposed to improve signalling protocol's and conversation's security with digital watermarking technique, while in [15] to alternate RTCP (Real-Time Control Protocol) [5] functionality for VoIP RTP digital streams with digital watermarking and network steganography. In this paper we would like to present the possibilities that covert channels in IP Telephony can offer. We would like also to focus more on improving VoIP security. As in [15] we will use two information hiding techniques, mentioned above. In this way we gain important advantages such as: verification of the transmission's source and the content sent (both authentication and integrity services). Additionally, this solution is lightweight, and does not consume transmission bandwidth, because the control bits (a header of the new, proposed protocol) are transmitted in a covert (steganographic) channel and appropriate, the protocol data is inseparably bound to the voice content as a digital watermark.

The paper is organized as follows. In Section 2 both techniques, digital watermarking and steganography, are described. Next, we give details about proposed solution in Section 3. Finally, we sum up with conclusions in Section 4.

2. Steganography and Digital Watermarking

Steganography and Digital Watermarking are Information Hiding subdisciplines [9]. The general difference between those two techniques is that the steganography's aim is to keep the existence of the information secret whereas the watermaking aim is to make it imperceptible.

2.1 Steganography: a covert channel

Steganography is a process of hiding secret data inside other, normally transmitted data. Usually it means hiding a secret message within an ordinary message and its extraction at the destination point. In ideal situation, anyone scanning data will fail to know it contains covert data. In modern digital steganography, data is inserted into redundant (provided but often unneeded) data, e.g. fields in communication protocols, graphic image, etc. TCP/IP (or network) steganography utilizes the fact that few headers in the packet are changed during transit ([9], [7], [8], [10]).

In this paper we will exploit a covert channel, which is a method of communication that is not a part of an actual computer system design, but can be used to transfer information to users or system processes that normally would not be allowed to access the information. In TCP/IP stack, there is a number of methods available, whereby covert channels can be established and data can be exchanged secretly between communication parties. An analysis of the headers of typical TCP/IP protocols e.g. IP, UDP, TCP, HTTP, ICMP results in fields that are either unused or optional [8]. This reveals many possibilities where data can be stored and transmitted. As described in [7] the IP header possesses fields that are available to be used as a covert channel. Those fields are marked in Figure 1 with italics. The total capacity of those fields exceeds 60 bits per packet. And there are potentially UDP and RTP protocol's fields left that can be also used for this purpose.

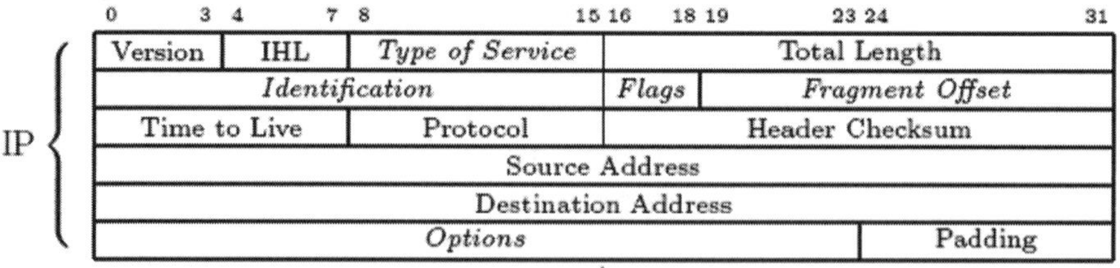

0   3 4   7 8   15 16   18 19   23 24   31
Version	IHL	*Type of Service*	Total Length		
Identification		*Flags*	*Fragment Offset*	
Time to Live	Protocol	Header Checksum		
Source Address				
Destination Address				
Options |||| Padding

IP {

Fig. 1. The IP header with marked fields (italics) available for network steganography [7]

Furthermore, we can distribute those bits that we want to transmit among protocol header's fields in a predetermined fashion (this pattern can be exchanged during a signalling phase of conversation). In those chosen fields we will transmit only the header (control bits) of our protocol. That is how we will use the network steganography technique. The header consists of 6 bits per packet (as will be described in details in Section 3), so such a type of the transmission is potentially hard to discover.

2.2 Watermarking: the imperceptible information

Digital watermarking is a multidisciplinary methodology widely developed in the last decade. It covers a large field of various aspects, from cryptography to signal processing, and is generally used for marking the digital data (images, video, audio or text). There are several applications for the digital watermarks, described in [1] and [2], that include: **fingerprinting** (embedding a distinct watermark into every copy of the author's data), **annotation watermark/content labelling** (embedding information, which describes the digital work that can be later extracted) and **usage control/copy control** (authors can insert a watermark that indicates the number of copies permitted for each user). However, the most important applications for our purposes are: the possibility of embedding the **authentication and integrity watermark** and exchanging additional information inside this watermark.

The audio digital watermark that will be used in the proposed here authentication and integrity solution must possess certain parameters like: robustness, security, transparency, complexity, capacity, verification and invertibility. Those parameters are described in details in [1] and [2]. Their optimization for real-time audio system is crucial. Additionally one has to take into consideration that they are often mutually competitive, so there is always a compromise necessary. That is why the embedded watermark, that we will use, should be characterized by **high robustness**, **high security** and must be **non-perceptual**. Not every audio watermarking technique is applicable for our solution. IP Telephony is a demanding, real-time service. That is why we can apply the watermarking schemes that really work for the real-time conversations. Such algorithms are described e.g. in [2] and [4].

Generally, watermarking algorithm consist of two phases: first is **embedding** of the watermark into the voice at the source and then its **extraction** at the destination. In IP Telephony we can also distinguish those phases: as soon as the conversation begins, certain information is embedded into the voice samples and sent through the communication channel. Then, the digital watermark is extracted from voice stream before it reaches the callee. After that the retrieved information is verified. If the watermark's data sent is correct, the conversation can be continued.

Most digital watermarking algorithms for the real-time communication are designed to survive the typical non-malicious operations like: low bit rate audio compression, codec changes, DA/AD conversion or packet loss. For example, in [2] the watermarking scheme developed at the Fraunhofer IPSI (Institut Integrierte Publikations und Informationssysteme) was tested for different compression methods. Results revealed that the large simultaneous capacity and robustness depend on the scale of the codec compression. When the compression rate is high (1:53), the watermark is robust only when we embed about 1 bit/s. With a lower compression rate we can obtain about 30 bit/s, whereas the highest data rate was 48 bit/s with good robust, transparent and complexity parameters. Moreover for the monophonic audio signal, which is a default type for the IP Telephony the watermark embedding algorithm appeared around 14 times faster and the watermark detector almost 6 times faster than the real-time one.

The next important thing for proposed here scheme is how much information we can embed into the original voice data. This will influence the speed of the authentication and integrity process throughout the conversation. This parameter is expected to be high but it is not crucial in our solution. With low compression rates we propose to add a pre-conversation stage. In this stage there will be few seconds of the RTP packets exchange without the conversation. It will delay the setup of the call but then, during the conversation, the time of the watermark verification will be shorter. However, the lowest payload watermarks (about 1 bit/s) cannot be accepted in our solution because in this case the conversation would have to last enormously long to work correctly.

3. Possible covert channels in VoIP based on Information Hiding

In Section 1 we presented our previous ideas that used Information Hiding techniques to create covert channels to:

I.   Secure media stream along with the signalling protocol's messages exchanged during the initial phase of the call. This mechanism is described in [16] and uses only audio digital watermarking technique.

II.   Secure conversation and to functionally alternate RTCP protocol with use of the steganography and audio digital watermarking as described in [15].

In this paper we will combine those two approaches to achieve conversation and signalling protocol security with use of the both information hiding techniques and a universal, secure channel to exchange additional data (e.g. for RTCP parameters).

So this new, steganographic protocol utilizes covert channel that consists of two subchannels: one created by using digital watermarking, second using network steganography.

For the IP Telephony system the most important security services are: **authentication**, **integrity** and **confidentiality**. We must emphasize that the first two can be provided with the use of our protocol. The third should be guaranteed in a different manner, e.g., with the use of the security mechanisms from a classical security model (the cryptographic mechanisms).

3.1 General protocol overview

The solution presented here requires modifications of the general watermarking system presented with the continuous line in Figure 2. We are proposing to add a new functional block called Pre-processing Stage (**PPS**) which is marked in this figure with the dotted line. It will be responsible for preparing (processing) data before the watermark embedding stage.

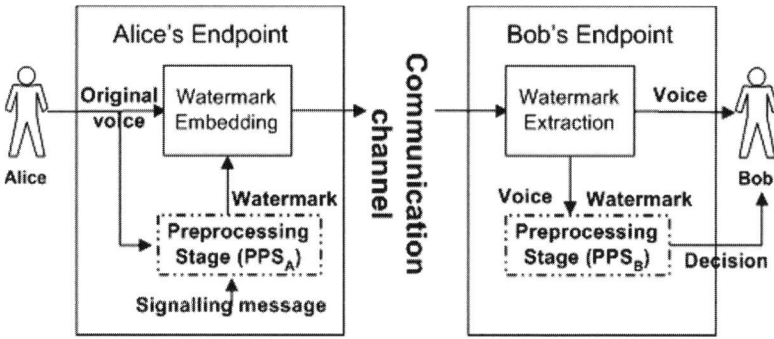

Fig. 2. Modified watermarking scheme with the new Preprocessing Stage (PPS) block for voice transmission from Alice to Bob

The mechanism works as follows: we provide a signalling message and a sample of the caller's original voice at Alice's endpoint as an input to the PPS block in the transmitter. The way the PPS block processes information is covered in [16]. After the digital watermark is embedded and sent through the communication channel, the information in the receiver is retrieved and verified in an analogous block in the other endpoint. If the retrieved information is correct, the connection will continue.

But as we circumscribed earlier we will also use the network steganography technique to create an additional covert channel that will be used to transmit header (control bits). The control bits will be used to distinguish the parameters sent. In this case the digital watermarking will be used only to carry the appropriate parameters (user data, security information and additional parameters).

Additionally, to simplify characterization of the presented solution we assume that our solution will be used in the IP protocol version 4 networks [14].

3.2 Protocol Data Unit description

The protocol we are proposing here possesses PDU (Protocol Data Unit), the size of which must be kept to minimum. It is important, because as we said in the Section 2, the capacity of the watermark is limited (if we want watermark also to posses simultaneously other parameters like robustness or security).

Every PDU consists of a header (control bits) and a certain number of data bits that are embedded into the sender/receiver voice. The header/control fields are transmitted in a covert channel in unused/optional fields of the IP/UDP/RTP protocol's headers. The actual value of the data is embedded into voice as a digital watermark. The header bits are organized in fields as shown in the Table 1.

Table 1. The header fields and their function

Type of field	No. of bits	Function
P (Parameter)	4	Indicates the parameter that is transmitted inside the watermark
S (Side)	1	Indicates the side of the communication (1 - sender, 0 – receiver)
C (Continuity)	1	Indicates if a packet contains the beginning or continuation of the parameter indicated in the field P (1 – beginning of new parameter, 0 – continuation of the last parameter)

As the capacity of the watermark depends greatly on the codec's compression rate, so it is possible that one parameter can be distributed into a number of IP packets. The size (number of bits) of each parameter that will be transmitted with described here protocol should be low. We assume that all the parameters should not exceed 32 bits. This is a totally subjective choice based on average watermark's capacity. However we do not dictate this value. It should depend on the network bandwidth, status and codec's compression rate. The exemplary values of the field P are shown below:

0001 – authentication or integrity parameter (32 bits)
0010 – informational parameter 1 (32 bits)
0011 – informational parameter 2 (32 bits)
0100 – informational parameter 3 (32 bits)
0101 – post authentication and integrity parameter (32 bits)
...

The number of bits used to indicate the parameters (field P) can be changed. In the above proposition each parameter is identified by 4 bits, which allows to define 16 parameters. If there is need for less number of parameters then the number of bits can be decreased.

If we enclose the information of the side of the communication as well (field S) we can exchange information not only about the data we send but also about the data we receive.

The PDU can have one of the two payload types: **security** or **informational**. The security payload means that the PDU contains certain authentication and/or integrity information that should be verified after its extraction. Two kinds of the security payloads are available, the first is used to provide authentication and integrity of the voice, its source and signalling protocol messages. The role of the second one is to authenticate the protocol's parameters that were sent earlier (both the security and the informational ones). Details about the security payload and cryptographic operations in this protocol will be covered in Section 3.3.

Another payload type is the informational one. Each PDU carries one parameter's data (the whole parameter or only part of it). The description of the PDU is also illustrated in Figure 3.

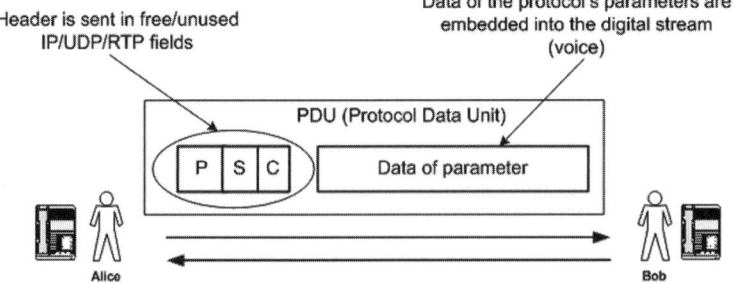

Fig. 3. Description of the Protocol Data Unit

We assume that we want to use suggested solution to improve the conversation and signalling protocol security simultaneously exchange other information too. We will not describe the form of the information parameters here as the exemplary ones based on RTCP protocol are circumscribed in [15]. Generally, we can use this cover channel to exchange any information for the VoIP system that is necessary – it can be connected with QoS or with other aspects of the call. In this paper we will focus only on the security parameters.

Usually, in one IP/UDP/RTP packet there are about 20-30 milliseconds of voice, which is about 20-30 bytes, depending on the type of the codec used. Supposing that we are able to embed on average about 10 bits/s of the watermark into the voice stream, we must send more than 3 packets to achieve those 10 bits. In this protocol we set parameter's value to 32 bits, so it will be transmitted in about 9-12 packets in more than 3 seconds of the voice signal. In the example scenario in Fig. 4, we see how the exemplary parameter is transmitted (for assumption: 10 bits of watermark per packet).

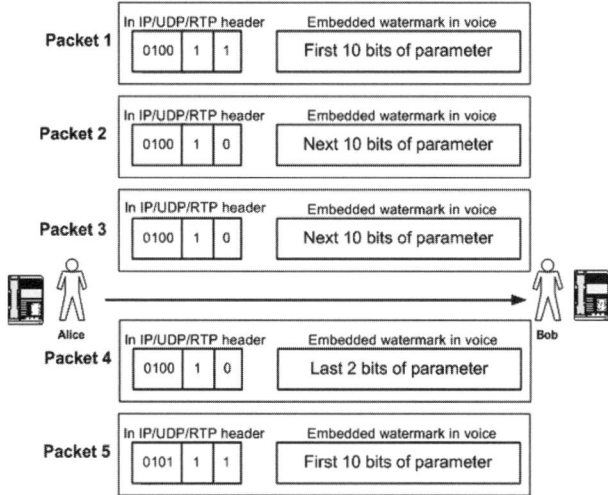

Fig. 4. Exemplary protocol operation (for assumption: 10 bits of watermark per packet)

As we can see in the above figure, the parameter characterized by the code 0100 was sent in four IP/UDP/RTP packets. In the first packet both fields S and C were set to 1. In the next packet field C changed its value to 0 because it is a continuation of the parameter's data that was sent in the last packet. At the destination there must be a buffer to extract all data from each packet. After transmitting all the packets for one parameter, the data is available to be used (if this is informational parameter) or to be verified (for security reasons).

3.3 Authentication and integrity parameter calculation and security payload

In Section 3.2 we mentioned that two security payloads are available:

- One is used to provide the authentication and integrity of the voice, its source and signalling protocol that is used in a particular VoIP system
- Second is to authenticate the protocol parameters (both the security and informational ones) that were sent earlier. The authentication and integrity calculation will be performed similarly as described in [6] but with the watermark specific considerations.

The first security parameter is created in a following way: hash function (H) is performed on the certain voice sample (VF) and on signalling protocol messages stored in a special buffer (inside the PPS block marked in Figure 1). Then this value is concatenated with the global identifier of caller (IDX), a preshared password (PASS), and, eventually, the random value (R) and the time stamp (TS). Using the last parameter is optional, because it requires tightly synchronized clocks. However, it is useful since it can protect against the replay attacks. After that, the hash function is performed again. The result, which we will call a **token,** is embedded as a watermark into the voice content. The token for calling party A is shown below:

$$
TokenA_N = H\left(H(VF_N)) \| H(SM_N) \| \begin{pmatrix} TS \\ PASS \\ ID_A \end{pmatrix} \| R \right) \| R \tag{1}
$$

On the other side of the communication channel, before the caller's voice reaches the callee, the token from the watermark must be retrieved and verified. This can be done because the callee computes analogous token locally, and then the two tokens are being compared.

We assumed earlier that each parameter transmitted will consist of 32 bits. So, if the token exceeds this value, there will be additional hash function performed. Then, only the predetermined, chosen bits will be transmitted as a security parameter.

The second security payload is a special purpose parameter that will be used to improve security of the protocol internally and the transmission. The general idea of its calculation is presented in Figure 5.

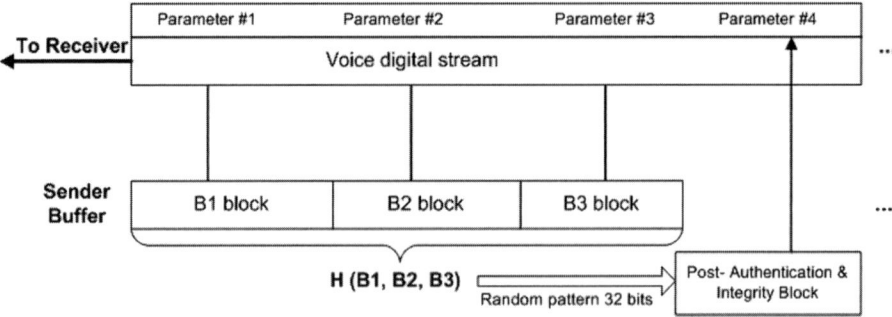

Fig. 5. Example of authentication and integrity mechanism for transmitted parameters

First, we must emphasize that during a conversation (RTP packets flow) there will be constant two-way exchange of a certain sequence of parameters. Those parameters can be susceptible to e.g. modifications or other attacks. To prevent this situation every *n-th* parameter is used to authenticate and provide integrity of n-1 parameters that were transmitted earlier.

For the situation in Fig. 5. n=4, three parameters that contain informational or first kind of the security payload are stored in the sender buffer. After they are all in place (B1, B2 and B3 blocks), the hash function (H) can be calculated, if the result value is too long. Since we assumed certain parameter length, we have to choose only 32 bits from the hash to be transmitted. For every conversation this pattern, in which the bits are chosen, should be changed and its determination should be set and sent in a signalling phase of the connection.

Additionally, we assume that we use the mechanism of LoT (Level of Trust) value described in [15] and [16]. This is because the attacker can disrupt the transmission of the header/controls bits or because the poor network conditions can cause the situation in which the receiver is unable to retrieve any parameters that were transmitted by the sender. That is why both parties of the conversation will update special parameter named LoT (Level of Trust) during the conversation. If a parameter (security or informational) is received and verified, the LoT value increases. In any other situation its value decreases. Additionally, the parameters that are exchanged during the   conversation influence the LoT value differently. The informational parameters add/subtract to the LoT's value 1, the first kind security parameters 2 and the second kind security parameter 5. The breakage of the call (or notification to the calling parties) will take place if the value of the LoT parameter is equal or below the given threshold or if the certain timer expires.

4. Conclusions

The protocol that uses a covert channel for the VoIP transmission was presented. It is based on the information hiding techniques: network steganography which helps to pass the header (control bits) and audio digital watermarking to transmit the actual parameter's data in a voice stream. The most important advantages of our solution are that it does not consume available, transmission bandwidth and that it improves IP Telephony's security.

What we want to emphasize is that the process of sending information for this protocol is continuous in time and, although the bit rate per second offered by the audio digital watermarking and network steganography is usually not very high we are able to exchange quite an amount of the data, if the whole conversation is considered.

The variety of different kinds of the parameters that can be used in our solution is not limited to the security ones. That is why this protocol can be freely extended to other data (informational data) that can be helpful for the VoIP connections. Finally, by using the presented solution one can gain: the signaling protocol and conversation security as well as a secure multipurpose channel for exchanging other parameters.

References

[1] J. Dittmann, A. Mukherjee, M. Steinebach: Media-independent Watermarking Classification and the need for combining digital video and audio watermarking for media authentication", Proceedings of the International Conference on Information Technology: Coding and Computing, IEEE Computer Science Society, Las Vegas, Nevada, USA (2000) 62-67

[2] M. Steinebach, F. Siebenhaar, C. Neubauer, R. Ackermann, U. Roedig, J. Dittmann: Intrusion Detection Systems for IP Telephony Networks, Real time intrusion detection symposium, Estoril, Portugal (2002) (17)1-9

[3] D. Richard Kuhn, Thomas J. Walsh, Steffen Fries: Security Considerations for Voice Over IP Systems, Computer Security Division, Information Technology Laboratory, National Institute of Standards and Technology (2004)

[4] S. Yuan, S. Huss: Audio Watermarking Algorithm for Real-time Speech Integrity and Authentication, International Multimedia Conference Proceedings of the 2004 Multimedia and security workshop on Multimedia and security, Magdeburg, Germany (2004) 220 - 226

[5] H. Schulzrinne, S. Casner, R. Frederick, V. Jacobson: RTP: A Transport Protocol for Real-Time Applications, IETF, RFC 3550, July 2003.

[6] S. Miner and J. Staddon. Graph-based authentication of digital streams. In Proceedings of the IEEE Symposium on Research in Security and Privacy (2001) 232-246

[7] S. J. Murdoch, S. Lewis: Embedding Covert Channels into TCP/IP. Information Hiding (2005) 247-26

[8] K. Ahsan, D. Kundur: Practical Data Hiding in TCP/IP. In: Proceedings of Workshop on Multimedia Security at ACM Multimedia '02, Juan-les-Pins (on the French Riviera), December 2002

[9] Petitcolas, F., Anderson, R., Kuhn, M.: Information Hiding – A Survey: IEEE Special Issue on Protection of Multimedia Content, July 1999

[10] K. Szczypiorski: HICCUPS: Hidden Communication System for Corrupted Networks. In Proc. of: The Tenth International Multi-Conference on Advanced Computer Systems ACS'2003, October 22-24, 2003 Międzyzdroje, Poland, pp.31-40, ISBN 83-87362-61-1

[11] T. Friedman, R. Caceres, A. Clark: RTP Control Protocol Extended Reports (RTCP XR), IETF, RFC 3611, November 2003

[12] V. Korjik, G. Morales-Luna: Information Hiding through Noisy Channels, Proceedings of 4th International Information Hiding Workshop, Pittsburgh, PA, USA, (2001) 42-50

[13] M. K. Mihcak, R. Venkatesan: A Perceptual Audio Hashing Algorithm: A Tool For Robust Audio Identification and Information Hiding, Proceedings of 4th International Information Hiding Workshop, Pittsburgh, PA, April 2001.

[14] Information Sciences Institute University of Southern California: IP (Internet Protocol), IETF, RFC 791, September 1981.

[15] W. Mazurczyk, Z. Kotulski: New security and control protocol for VoIP based on steganography and digital watermarking - Informatyka - Badania i Zastosowania (IBIZA 2006), Kazimierz Dolny 9-11 February 2006

[16] W. Mazurczyk, Z. Kotulski - New VoIP traffic security scheme with digital watermarking - In Proceedings of SafeComp 2006, Lecture Notes in Computer Science 4166, pp. 170 - 181, Springer-Verlag, Heidelberg 2006

Cryptanalysis of Chaotic Product Cipher

Adrian Skrobek, Paweł Sukiennik

(askrobek@wi.ps.pl, psukiennik@wi.ps.pl)
Szczecin University of Technology, 71-210 Szczecin, Poland

Abstract. The central contribution of this paper is a cryptanalysis of chaotic product cipher attempt. We use the method of an approximation of the blurred chaotic orbit as a cryptanalyticall tool. Also, problems concerned with design of chaotic product ciphers are presented in this article. A proposition of algorithm improvement is also made. This improvement makes the algorithm more secure.

1. Introduction

Presentation of weaknesses and an attempt to cryptanalyse chaotic product cipher algorithm based on a couple of logistic maps, proposed by A. Sarkar [17] is the aim of this article. The most common problem concerned with proposed chaotic cipher algorithms is inaccuracy in specification and week cryptanalysis, which makes them susceptible for many kinds of attacks (comp. [4]). An attempt to cryptanalyse cipher algorithm which will allow recreating a key with great probability is presented in this article. There are also design problems related to inaccuracy in specification. It is the reason, why correct implementation of algorithm is so difficult.

1.1 Elementary definitions

Presented in [17] cipher algorithm works on a basis of a pair of discrete dynamical systems. Dynamical system (comp. [27]) is the couple (S, F), where S is a state space, whereas $F : S \rightarrow S$ is a continuous transformation of semi group iterations. Initial state trajectory s_0 is a $\{s_n\}_{n=0}^{\infty} \subset S$, obtained from iteration $s_{n+1} = F(s_n)$, for $n = 0, 1, 2, \dots$. Chaotic systems, are dynamical systems which fulfill following requirements: (1) system contains dense periodic points, (2) system has mixing properties and (3) system is exponentially sensitive to initial conditions. From a cryptography point of view – the chaoticity of dynamical system is very important. To determine the level of chaoticity, the value of Lyapunov exponent needs to be calculated using formula 1:

$$\lambda = \lim_{t \to \infty} \frac{1}{t} \ln \frac{|\delta x(t)|}{|\delta x(0)|} \tag{1}$$

Exponents are the measure of how fast two orbits recede or bring closer with each other. If the system is of k-dimensions, there are at most k Lyapunov exponents. Chaotic system acts in chaotic way if the value of $\lambda > 0$ [7].

1.2 Product cipher

Product ciphers are combination of several simple operations: transpositions and substitutions. Although simple permutation and substitutions ciphers are susceptible to cryptanalysis, their combination allows to create strong cipher [3]. Cipher transformation for product cipher, (a combination of $e^{(s)} \circ e^{(t)}$) can be defined as:

$$E_e(m) = (e^{(s)}(m_1)_{e^{(t)}(1)}, e^{(s)}(m_2)_{e^{(t)}(2)}, ..., e^{(s)}(m_n)_{e^{(t)}(n)}) = c$$

$$m = (m_1, m_2, ..., m_n) \in M$$

$$c = (c_1, c_2, ..., c_n) \in C$$

$$e \in K$$

where: $e^{(s)}$ – substitution operation, $e^{(t)}$ – transposition operation, M – entire set of n length series over some alphabet A_M, C – entire set of n length series over some alphabet A_C, K – set of all keys. Combination of operations $e^{(s)} \circ e^{(t)}$ is called mixing transformation [19]. Product cipher function is often used as a round in a block cipher, compatible with Feistel schema [3].

1.3 Cipher algorithm description

According to description in [17] analyzed cipher is based on a couple of logistic maps defined with formula 2. First logistic map defines a key stream used in substitution cipher, whereas the second one (with different key value, the initial x_0 value is changed) is used to select block in a transposition operation. Combination of transposition and substitution of operations results as product cipher. Combination of two different transformations protects logistic map from disclosing its state variable or key parameter in a proper data sequence [12]. In presented algorithm the key value is an initial value x_0 of logistic map (in cipher specification r = 4.0 is proposed).

$$x_{n+1} = f(x_n, r) = r \cdot x_n (1 - x_n) \tag{2}$$

Assumed symbols over A_M and A_C are 8 bits long. The keys are the initial values of both chaotic systems, defined as $INI1$ and $INI2$. The table of characters c is an input and the table e of ciphered characters is an output. The cipher procedure is described in [17] with algorithms 1 and 2 (N is a length of plain text). Algorithm 3 and 4 describe decipher procedure.

Algorithm 1 *Ciphering, phase I (substitution)*

Input:	$INI1$ – cipher key, c – plain text, N – length of input text
Output:	m – a series of initially encrypted characters

1. $p_0 \leftarrow INI1$
2. $\forall_{i=1,2,...,N}$ do steps from 3 to 5
3. $\quad p_i \leftarrow p_{i-1}\ 4.0\ (1 - p_{i-1})$
4. $\quad y_i \leftarrow \text{int}(p_i \cdot 255.0 + 0.5)$
5. $\quad m_i \leftarrow c_i \oplus y_i$

Algorithm 2 *Ciphering, phase II (transposition)*

Input:	$INI2$ – cipher key, m – a series of initially ciphered characters from phase I, N – length of a plain text
Output:	e – ciphertext

1. Creation of cyclic list containing initially ciphered elements (using algorithm 1) $m = \{m_0, m_1, ..., m_N\}$
2. $q_0 \leftarrow INI2$
3. $\forall_{i=1,2,...,N}$ do steps from 4 to 8
4. $\quad q_i \leftarrow q_{i-1}\ 4.0\ (1 - q_{i-1})$
5. $\quad z_i \leftarrow \text{int}(q_i \cdot N + 0.5)$
6. $\quad$ Iterate through cyclic list $z_i - 1$ times obtaining n_i-th element
7. $\quad e_i = m_{n_i+1}$
8. $\quad$ Remove element $n_i + 1$ from cyclic list

Algorithm 3 *Deciphering, phase I (transposition)*

Input:	$INI2$ – cipher key, e – cipher text, N – length of cipher
Output:	m – a series of initially ciphered chars
Notice:	symbol $\varnothing$ means uninitialized element of cyclic list

1. $q_0 \leftarrow INI2$
2. Creation of cyclic list $m \leftarrow \{ \varnothing_0, \varnothing_1,..., \varnothing_N\}$
3. $z_0 \leftarrow 0$
4. $\forall_{i=1,2,...,N}$ do steps from 5 to 8
5. $\quad q_i \leftarrow q_{i-1} \cdot 4.0 \cdot (1 - q_{i-1})$
6. $\quad z_i \leftarrow \text{int}(q_i \cdot N + 0.5)$
7. $\quad$ Iterate through cyclic list $z_i - 1$ times omitting filled fields, obtaining n_i-th element
8. $\quad m_{n_i+1} \leftarrow e_i$

Algorithm 4 *Deciphering, phase II (substitution)*

Input:	$INI1$, m – a series of initially ciphered characters, N – length of cipher
Output:	c – plain text

1. $p_0 \leftarrow INI1$
2. $\forall_{i=1,2,...,N}$ do steps from 3 to 5
3. $\quad p_i \leftarrow p_{i-1} \cdot 4.0 \cdot (1 - p_{i-1})$
4. $\quad y_i \leftarrow \text{int}(p_i \cdot 255.0 + 0.5)$
5. $\quad c_i \leftarrow m_i \oplus y_i$

2. Cipher algorithm cryptanalysis

During cipher algorithm analysis, cryptanalyst knows all implementation details, variable values range, initial states and so on. The key value is the only unknown value, however the range of that value is known. This approach is acquiescent with Kerckhoffs principle, where the security of the cipher can depend only on the cipher key [3, 25]. Nowadays, the following classical cipher attacks are common: (1) cipher text only attack, (2) known plain text attack, (3) chosen plain text attack and (4) chosen cipher text attack. Attack other than with cipher text only is reasonable, when the cipher algorithm is built in cryptographic device or when for example establishing SSL session. At that time, even though the keys remain hidden, the attacker can send any message to a device or server and acquire return message. Algorithms under analysis were implemented in Java with decimal precision *IEEE*-754 standard [1, 23].

This product cipher encrypts plain text blocks of different sizes. It is a consequence of the second phase of encryption, where the initially encrypted message is transposed with appropriate permutation. The permutation depends on length of encrypted block but is always invariant for the same size of block. Furthermore, blocks of the same length are always encrypted with the same keystream. Having this knowledge, we could collect original keystream of first phase, by performing encryption of blocks of increased sizes. Next we can reconstruct the original key with use of collected keystream.

2.1 Reconstruction of keystream

For a certain key the cipher algorithm always generates the same sequence y_i. In the second cipher phase permutation of elements from phase one occurs. That permutation is different for each length of plain text. Using chosen plain text attack , the sequence y_i can be reconstructed as well as permutation values $P^{(i)}$, $i = 1, 2,..., N$. Authors elaborated algorithm 5, which allows to generate sequence y_i, which is undistributed by the value of permutations calculated in second phase.

Algorithm 5 *Reconstruction of permutations for permutation cipher*

Input:	N – length of series
Output:	y – the sequence of series y generated in the first phase of cipher algorithm for each series length $k \in \{1, 2, ..., N\}$, P – the series of permutation tables generated in the phase two of cipher algorithm for each series length $k \in \{1, 2, ..., N\}$
Notice:	symbol $\varnothing$ in point 1 means table length 0, in point 2 means uninitialized element of table.

---

1. Create empty tables $y^{(0)} \leftarrow \varnothing$, $e^{(0)} \leftarrow \varnothing$
2. $\forall_{i = 1, 2, ..., N} c^{(i)} \leftarrow \{0_1, 0_2, ..., 0_i\}$, $P^{(i)} \leftarrow \{\varnothing_1, \varnothing_2, ..., \varnothing_i\}$ do step 3 to 5
3. $e^{(i)} \leftarrow E_e(c^{(i)})$
4. if $\exists_v, e^{(i)}(v) \notin e^{(i-1)}$ then $y^{(i)} \leftarrow y^{(i-1)} \cup \{e^{(i)}(v)\}$
5. $\forall_{k = 1, 2, ..., i} P_k^{(i)} \leftarrow \eta(y_k^{(i)}, e^{(i)})$, where $\eta(\cdot)$ is a position of k-th element of table $e^{(i)}$ in table $y^{(i)}$.

Series of continuous $y^{(i)}$ values will be obtained as well as permutation values $P^{(i)}$, $i = 1, 2, \ldots, N$ performed in phase two. An example for key of $INI1 = 0.28$ and $N = 5$ is presented in table 1.

Table 1. Recreation the sequence of $y^{(i)}$, $i = 1, 2, \ldots, N$ for $INI1 = 0.28$ and $N = 5$.

I	$e^{(i)}$	$y^{(i)}$	$P^{(i)}$
1	206	206	1
2	206, 159	206, 159	1, 2
3	239, 206, 159	206, 159, 239	3, 1, 2
4	59, 206, 159, 239	206, 159, 239, 59	4, 1, 2, 3
5	59, 182, 206, 159, 239	206, 159, 239, 59, 182	4, 5, 1, 2, 3

2.2 *INI1* key approximation

When having stream y, it is possible to approximate (with some precision) a value of $INI1$. It is known, that $y_i = \lfloor p_i \cdot 255.0 + 0.5 \rfloor$, therefore interval can be calculated. This interval is called a "blurred" orbit. The method of approximation real value of orbit was originally presented in [28]. In our approach we apply this method for the key value approximation. The initial interval for values $y_1 = f(INI1, 4.0)$ can be calculated using formula 3. Using formula 4 it is possible to calculate range for key $INI1 = f^{-1}(y_1, 4.0)$ based on y_1 value.

$$B(i) = \left(\frac{2(i-1)+1}{510}, \frac{2i+1}{510} \right) \ni y_i \tag{3}$$

$$y_{n-1} = f^{-1}(y_n, r) = \begin{cases} \dfrac{1 - \sqrt{1 - 4\dfrac{y_n}{r}}}{2} \\ or \\ \dfrac{1 + \sqrt{1 - 4\dfrac{y_n}{r}}}{2} \end{cases} \tag{4}$$

Formula 4 produces two equivalent values for the previous orbit y_{n-1}. In order to estimate range of key values more precisely it is necessary to narrow the range obtained by calculation of $B(i)$. To do so it is necessary to create initially ciphered stream of y_n elements using permutation table. The next step is to calculate the previous range of orbit value by calculating scopes of following intervals, which narrows previously acquired interval. The formal definition of this procedure is presented in algorithm 6.

2.3 Example of *INI1* value approximation

For given key $p_0 = INI1 = 0.28$ and $N = 8$, sequence $y_8 = (206, 159, 239, 59, 182, 208, 152, 245)$. For value of 206 it is a range $\hat{y}_1 \in (0.805882, 0.809803)$. For analyzed key value $INI1 = 0.28$, value $y_1 = y_0 \cdot 4 \cdot (1 - y_0) = 0.28 \cdot 4 \cdot (1 - 0.28) = 0.8064$. It is approximation of key value, with relative error of 0.2%.

To calculate the value of $INI1$ more precisely it is necessary to use the second element from obtained table y. It is known, that $p_2 = p_4 \cdot 4 \cdot (1 - p_1)$. Using formula 3, the range value of p_2 can be recalculated. This time, the range $p_2 \in (0.621568, 0.625490)$ is calculated. Because of chaotic orbit ergodicity, it can be assumed, that the previous value of p, p_1 must be in range, where each point will hit the p_2 range in the next step. It is possible, that new range p_1 will narrow previous p_1 range. If this happens, the actual p_1 range will come closer to the p_1 value. In order to determine previous orbit value for logistic map it is necessary to use equation 4.

Algorithm 6 *Calculating approximate key value*

Input: N – key length, c – cipher sequence
Output: l_0, h_0 – lower and upper chaotic orbit value interval scope for second
           iteration

---

1. $\forall_{k=1, 2, ..., N}$ do steps 2 to 16
2. $l_k \leftarrow \min(B(c_k))$
3. $h_k \leftarrow \max(B(c_k))$
4. $\forall_{i=k, k-1, ..., 1}$ do step 5 to 16
5. $l^{(1)} \leftarrow \min(f_1^{-1}(l_i), f_1^{-1}(h_i))$
6. $h^{(1)} \leftarrow \max(f_1^{-1}(l_i), f_1^{-1}(h_i))$
7. $m^{(1)} \leftarrow \dfrac{l^{(1)} + h^{(1)}}{2}$
8. $l^{(2)} \leftarrow \min(f_2^{-1}(l_i), f_2^{-1}(h_i))$
9. $h^{(2)} \leftarrow \max(f_2^{-1}(l_i), f_2^{-1}(h_i))$
10. $m^{(2)} \leftarrow \dfrac{l^{(2)} + h^{(2)}}{2}$
11.   if $m^{(1)} \in [l_{i-1}, h_{i-1}]$ then do steps 12 to 13
12. $l_{i-1} \leftarrow \max(l^{(1)}, l_{i-1})$
13. $h_{i-1} \leftarrow \min(h^{(1)}, h_{i-1})$
14.   if $m^{(2)} \in [l_{i-1}, h_{i-1}]$ then do steps 15 to 16
15. $l_{i-1} \leftarrow \max(l^{(2)}, l_{i-1})$
16. $h_{i-1} \leftarrow \min(h^{(2)}, h_{i-1})$

When equation 4 is used the following values are obtained: 0.192416, 0.807583, 0.194013, 0.805986. Only in the second and fourth case, the value of y_1 is 206, therefore we discard other values. New range $p_1 = (0.805986, 0.807583)$ is smaller, therefore it is more precise. The middle value is equal to 0.806784. When equation 4 is used again, the approximate key value of $INI1 = 0.280218$ is obtained.

Next approximations of p_1 values are presented in table 2. The δ_k value is the relative error of the middle value approximation, calculated with formula 5.

The range of the possible key values does not get smaller, starting with seventh iteration. It is a result of decimal digit arithmetic precision, which is compatible with

IEEE-754 standard. Finally, the value of *INI*1 ∈ {0.279980, 0.720020}. These are two equivalent approximate key values. The width of the intervals is presented in figure 1, whereas relative error of p_1 value is presented in figure 2.

$$\delta_k = |0.5 \cdot (l_k + h_k) - p_1| \cdot 100\% / p_1 \tag{5}$$

Table 2. Following approximations of p_1 value (values rounded to 6 and 3 decimal digits)

k	$l_k = \min(B_k)$	$h_k = \max(B_k)$	$\bar{p}_1 = |l_k - h_k|$	$(l_k + k_k)/2$	δ_k
1	0.805882	0.809804	0.003922	0.807843	0.179
2	0.805986	0.807584	0.001598	0.806785	0.048
3	0.805986	0.806891	0.000905	0.806438	0.005
4	0.806308	0.806767	0.000459	0.806537	0.017
5	0.806308	0.806515	0.000207	0.806411	0.001
6	0.806308	0.806419	0.000112	0.806411	0.005
7	0.806308	0.806419	0.000112	0.806411	0.005

2.4 *INI*2 key approximation

To approximate the value of the *INI*2 key it is required to define ranges to which orbit q_i belongs. To specify them, the observation of the following chosen elements from the phase two must be used. The right element to chose depends on range number, to which orbit q_i falls. Unfortunately, all but the first element might be chosen in more than one way. The last element will be chosen for each number from range $1 \le Z_i \le N$. Actually the set of range numbers can be defined, which causes selection of chosen element according to formula 6.

$$Z_i = \{z : 1 \le z \le N, z = l + (N - k + 1) \cdot m, m = 0,1,2,...\} \tag{6}$$

where $l \ge 1$ is the shortest distance between $e_k - e_{k-1}$ elements (first element e_0 is the *HEAD*), $k = 1, 2, ..., N$ – element number, N – number of elements.

After the distance between elements is found, analyzed element is removed from the cyclic list and the next search starts with the element preceding removed element. Operation is repeated until all elements are removed from the list (after N operations). After obtaining following range numbers or following range sets, the initial value can be approximated using formula 5.

3. Improvement suggestions

Generating the same cipher text values for given key and plain text is main weakness of the cipher. This approach may cause the cipher to be susceptible for attacks, where cipher blocks intercepted in transition canal are substituted. It is a good method to send a random number (*IV*) as a first block to the encoder, while all following as a result of *xor* operation of first block and plain text block. When deciphering, it is necessary to decipher the first block to obtain the *IV* value, and then the following blocks. This approach was used in [21].

Reconstruction of the *INI*1 and *INI*2 values would be impossible, if a secret permutation between plaintext letter and portion of attractor had been applied. In this case information about index of reached portion of attractor can't be used to obtain any information about ranges of orbit value. This approach has been applied in [5].

The initial value of each chaotic system is the cipher key. These are two real numbers $x_0 \in (0, 1)$. In the double precision arithmetic representation compatible with [11], each floating point number uses 64 bits. This produces key length of 128 bits, which is a safe length from cryptographic point of view [15]. However some complex number bits are easy to forecast. Double length complex number compatibly with *IEEE*-754 has one bit of sign, 11 bits of exponent and 52 bits of mantissa. Effective bit count of an floating point number can be calculated using Shannon entropy, specified with formula 7:

$$H(n) = -\sum_{i=1}^{n} p(i)\log_2 p(i) \tag{7}$$

where $p(i)$ – is a probability of a given series of symbols length n occurrence. After examining calculations, it occurs that effective bit count of floating point numbers, generated by logistic map for parameter $r = 4.0$ is equal to 54. Because key bit count is effectively equal to 108, the security requirements are not fulfilled.

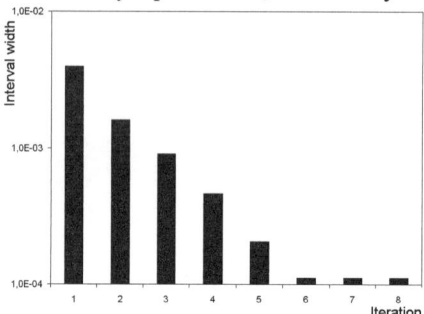

Fig. 1. Width of B interval for p_1 value in iteration count function

Fig. 2. Relative error δ for p_1 value in iteration count function (in %)

Also, the problem of key pair equivality occurs when the keys complement to 1.0 for logistic map. Logistic map returns the value of x_1 for some value of x_0 as well as for $x'_0 = 1 - x_0$. This decreases the keys size making them 2 bits smaller. Use of logistic map in proposed cipher algorithm is also a bad idea, because it meaningly impedes use of control parameter r as a part of the key. Shifting control parameters along the key would allow increasing its length highly and as a result higher level of security would be acquired, thus making key length greater then 128 bits.

Logistic map is chaotic when the value of control parameter $r > s_\infty$, where s_∞ =3.5699.. is a Feigenbaum point [10]. Unfortunately, logistic map contains many areas of non-chaoticity, which causes attacks susceptibility on functions if they use local parameter modulation [1]. Instead of using logistic map, piecewise linear map is proposed as presented in [14]. Piecewise linear map has positive Lyapunov exponents in a range of entire control parameter $p \in (0, 0.5)$. It can be used instead of logistic map, and both control parameters can be transferred into the key, thus making key length approximately 210. Piecewise linear map and logistic maps (square maps) are one of the fastest chaotic functions (only a few arithmetic operations and comparisons). Piecewise linear maps are often proposed to be used in cryptography [8, 14, 18, 20].

As it was mentioned at the beginning, used in the cipher mixing function is often used as a single round in the block cipher. As an example, there are 16 rounds in the DES algorithm [16]. To increase confusion and diffusion of plain text it is possible to redesign analyzed algorithm to work in few rounds. It is also possible to control each chaotic system with its control parameter value in allowed range using another chaotic function. However, it is obvious that each round makes the algorithm work longer. Complexity of cipher algorithm makes testing difficult, therefore some existing errors may not be detected [15].

4. Comparison with other algorithms

Presented in [17] algorithm belongs to a class of discrete chaotic ciphers, which implementation relies on n-times iteration of chaotic function [4]. Algorithms proposed in [5, 13, 22] also belong to discrete chaotic cipher group. Most of this algorithms were effectively cryptanalysed [2, 6, 12] or other algorithms based on them were created [9, 26]. Safety of discrete algorithms is based on chaotic systems ergodicity. In these algorithms multiple iterations of chaotic system method is used for processing a single character of plain text. Partitioning of atractor into ε-intervals, making discovery of internal state difficult, can also be used. Internal state of cipher is in most cases the value of the chaotic system orbit or orbits. Chaotic function and reverse function (which are exponentially sensitive to initial conditions) multiple iteration method is also used in algorithms.

Conclusions

Effective cryptanalysis of the algorithm which allows to reproduce key values of *INI*1 and *INI*2 is presented in this article. Problems concerned cipher designing, like lack of documentation, weaknesses of cryptographic keys and inadequate chaotic function selection are also brought out. To increase security of the cipher, additional mixing transformation in one block of cipher rounds can be performed. Additional CBC or CTR mode of the block cipher can be used resulting in stream cipher [24]. To increase performance of the cipher, parallelism of the algorithm can be implemented. All design changes require to change the way cipher works, therefore more cryptanalysis is required.

Literature

[1]   G. Álvarez, F. Montoya, M. Romera, and G. Pastor. *Cryptanalysis of a discrete chaotic cryptosystem using external key.* Physics Letters A, 319, December 2003.

[2]   G. Álvarez, F. Montoya, M. Romera, and G. Pastor. *Cryptanalysis of an ergodic chaotic cipher.* Physics Letters A, 311, May 2003.

[3]   S. Vanstone A. Menezes, P. van Oorschot. *Handbook of applied Cryptography.* CRC Press, Inc., 1997.

[4]   G. Alvarez and S. Li. *Cryptographic requirements for chaotic secure communications.* ArXiv Nonlinear Sciences e-prints, November 2003.

[5]   M. S. Baptista. *Cryptography with chaos.* Physics Letters A, 240, March 1998.

[6]   Eli Biham. *Cryptanalysis of the chaotic-map cryptosystem suggested at EUROCRYPT '91.* Lect. Notes in Comp. Sci., 547, 1991.

[7]   P. Cvitanović, R. Artuso, R. Mainieri, G. Tanner, and G. Vattay. *Classical and Quantum Chaos,* volume Version 7.0.1. Niels Bohr Institute, August 2000.

[8]   Shujun Li Department. *When chaos meets computers.*

[9]   Z.-H. Guan F. Huang. *A modified method of a class of recently presented cryptosystems.* Chaos, Solitons and Fractals, 2005.

[10]   D. Saupe H.-O. Peitgen, H. Jurgens. *Fractals for the Classroom.* Springer-Verlag New York, Inc., 1992.

[11]   Steve Hollasch. *IEEE standard 754 floating point numbers.* IEEE, 2004.15

[12]   Goce Jakimoski and Ljupco Kocarev. *Analysis of some recently proposed chaos-based encryption algorithms.* Phys. Let. A, 291, 2001.

[13]   Z. Kotulski, J. Szczepański. *Discrete chaotic cryptography* (DCC). NEEDS, 1997.

[14]   Shujun Li, Xuanqin Mou, and Yuanlong Cai. *Improving security of a chaotic encryption approach.* Physics Letters A, 290, 2001.

[15]   B. Schneier, N. Ferguson. *Practical Cryptography.* John Wiley & Sons, Inc., 2003.

[16]   National Institute of Standards and Technology. FIPS PUB 46-3, *Data Encryption Standard* (DES). pub-NIST, October 1999.

[17]   A. Sarkar. *Encryption with chaos.* National Conference on Nonlinear Systems & Dynamics, India, 2003.

[18]   Roland Schmitz. *Use of chaotic dynamical systems in cryptography.* Journal of the Franklin Institute, 2001.

[19]   Claude E. Shannon. *Communication theory of secrecy systems.* Bell Systems Technical Journal, 28(4):656_715, 1949.

[20]   S. Li, X. Mou, Y. Cai *Pseudo-random bit generator based on couple chaotic systems and its application in stream ciphers cryptography.* Indocrypt 2001. Springer-Verlag, 2001.

[21]   J. Pejaś, S. Berczyński, Y. A. Kravtsov and A. Skrobek. *Cryptographic properties of some cryptosystem with modulation of the chaotic sequence parameters.* ACS, 2004.

[22]   I. Sasase S. Mori T. Habatsu, Y. Nishio. *A secret key cryptosystem by iterating a chaotic map. Springer-Verlag,* 1998.

[23]   Frank Yellin Tim Lindholm. *The java virtual machine specification,* 1999.

[24]   A. Renvall T.W. Cusick, C. Ding. *Stream Ciphers and Number Theory.* Elsevier, 1998.

[25]   A. Kerckhoffs. *La cryptographie militaire. Journal des Sciences Militaires,* 1883.

[26]   K. Wong W. Wong, L. Lee. *A modified chaotic cryptographic method. Computer Physics Communications,* 2001.

[27]   J. Szczepański, Z. Kotulski. *On constructive approach to chaotic pseudorandom number generators.* RCMIS, 2000.

[28]   Jiri Fridrich and James F. Geer. *Reconstruction of blurred orbits under finite resolution.* Applied Mathematics and Computation, 71(2–3):227–245, September 1995.

Embedding of Stego–Messages in Monochrome Images on the Base of Rank Filtering

Larisa Dobryakova, Orest Popov

Faculty of computer science Szczecin University of Technology, Zolnierska St. 49, 71–210 Szczecin, Poland
ldobryakova@wi.ps.pl, popov@wi.ps.pl

Abstract. In this article the embedding of stego–messages in media data is analyzed. Least Significant Bits of samples of data are modified on the base of a double rank filtering. The experimental inspection of algorithms correctness and the calculation of magnitude of container distortion are carried out. It is shown, that the average size of deviation decreases twice

Introduction

Steganography is a science about such organization of the hiding data communication at which the fact of data communication disappears. This is difference than cryptography, which hides the meaning of a message but does not hide the message itself [1].

In computer steganodraphy exist two fundamental file types: the stego–message (the secret message) and the container – a file which is used for concealment in it of the message. The initial state of the container without the hidden information is a container–original, and final when it already contains the stego–message is a container–result. An images, sound, video are frequently used as a container–original files. Embedding of the stego–message in the image is accompanied by some distortions, but character of distortions should be minimal. The viewer should not notice deterioration of the container–original dates [2].

Least Significant Bits. One of known methods of the steganography [3, 6] with use Multimedia files is substitution of Least Significant Bits (LSB) of the container by the corresponding stego–message. If the container–original represents the monochromic image as an array $I \times J$ of the integer binary N–digit numbers:

$$D_{i,j} = \sum_{n=0}^{N-1} d_{i,j,n} \cdot 2^n, \quad i = 0,1,...,I-1, \ j = 0,1,...,J-1, \quad \text{where} \quad d_{i,j,n} \in \{0,1\} \quad \text{—} \quad \text{n-th}$$

binary digit for i,j sample of container–original, the number range is equal $0 \leq D_{i,j} \leq (2^N - 1)$ and if the stego–message text may be writing as a bit line of K bits $s_0 s_1 \cdots s_k \cdots s_{K-1}$, $s_k \in \{0,1\}$, $k = 0, 1, ..., K-1$, then the containers–result may be marked as:

$$D_{i,j}^{+} = \sum_{n=0}^{N-1} d_{i,j,n}^{+} \cdot 2^{n}, \quad i = 0,1,...,I-1, j = 0,1,...,J-1, d_{i,j,n}^{+} \in \{0,1\} \quad \text{—} \quad n\text{–th binary digit}$$

for i,j sample of container–result. The method of replacement LSB can be described as follows:

$$
\begin{cases}
k = 0 \ /*k - \text{a sample number of the stego – message} */ \\
\text{for } i = 0,1,...,I-1: \\
\quad \text{for } j = 0,1,...,J-1: \\
\qquad \text{if } k < K \text{ then } D_{i,j}^{+} = s_{k} + \sum_{n=1}^{N-1} d_{i,j,n} \cdot 2^{n} \\
\qquad\qquad \text{else } \{D_{i,j}^{+} = D_{i,j}; k = k+1;\} \\
\text{end; end;} \\
\text{if } k<K \text{ then Goto Error\_The\_Short\_Container}
\end{cases}
\tag{1}
$$

The stego–message changes of LSB $d_{i,j,0}$ the first K samples of a container–original.

Method of a pseudorandom interval. The method of a random interval consists in pseudorandom distribution of bits the confidential message on the container [8]. The interval between consecutive embeddings bits messages is function of coordinates of the previous modified sample: magnitude of a step is defined by an amount of units in binary value of number of an element i of container–original, which was modified preliminary[1]. For the two–dimensional data a array $D_{i,j}$ is decomposed in a vector D_{t}^{*} :

$$
\begin{cases}
t = 0; \\
\text{for } i = 0,1,...,I-1: \\
\quad \text{for } j = 0,1,...,J-1: \\
\qquad D_{t}^{*} = D_{i,j}; t = t+1; \\
\text{end; end;}
\end{cases}
\tag{2}
$$

Let's present i as a L–digit binary number without a sign: $\{i = \sum_{l=0}^{L-1} b_{l} \cdot 2^{n}, b_{l} \in \{0,1\}, l = 0, 1,...,L\}$. Size of change of a step we shall designate as **step**. The stego–message is embed in the container on the basis of the following algorithm:

---

[1]At calculation of a step a multiplication of the sum of an amount of an units in the binary value of the number of an element on some is used S, which represents itself as the elementary key. This coefficient can accept the whole values. In this article S=1.

$$\begin{cases} i = 1 \\[4pt] \text{for } k = 0,1,...,K-1: \\[4pt] D_i^+ = -d_{i,N-1} \cdot 2^{N-1} + s_k + \sum_{n=1}^{N-2} d_{i,n} \cdot 2^n \\[4pt] \text{step} = \sum_{l=0}^{L-1} b_l \\[4pt] i = i + \text{step}; \\[4pt] \text{end}; \end{cases} \qquad (3)$$

After application of algorithm (3) is folding the vector D_t^* in array $D_{i,j}^+$.

Method of a block embedding. The container–original is broken on K not crossed blocks $\Delta_m d_{i,0}$, where $m = 0,1,....,K-1$. For each block calculates the bit of parity

$b(\Delta_m d_{i,0})$: $b(\Delta_m d_{i,0}) = \left(\displaystyle\sum_{i \in \Delta_m d_{i,0}} d_{i,0} \right)_{\bmod 2}$. In each block embeds one bit of the message

s_k . If the bit of parity is not equal to the flowed value the bit of the message $b(\Delta_m d_{i,0}) \neq s_k$, that one of LSB of block $\Delta_m d_{i,0}$ is inverted (the choice is casual) and $b(\Delta_m d_{i,0}) = s_k$. The choice of the block can occur pseudorandom[2] [8].

LSB modification of medial dates on the base of a rank filtering

LSB modification of medial dates on the base of a one–dimensional median filtering[3], experimental inspection of its correctness and calculation of magnitude of container distortion at introduction of the stego–message are described in articles [4, 5, 7].

In these articles an operation of LSB $d_{i,j,0}$ rank filtering in an aperture (2×2) can

be described as follows [7]: $d_{i,j,0}^r = \text{rank}_r \begin{pmatrix} d_{i,j-1,0} & d_{i,j,0} \\ d_{i+1,j-1,0} & d_{i+1,j,0} \end{pmatrix}$, $i = 0, 1, ..., I-1$;

$j = 0,1, ..., J-1$, $1 \le r \le 4$. The filtering is reduced to ranking on increase of the samples values of a container fragment by a size (2×2) $\{d_1' \le d_2' \le d_3' \le d_4'\}$ and replacement of the sample $d_{i,j,0}^r$ by the element d_r' of this ranking sequence. Let's define operation of a double rank filtering of ranks $r = 1$ and $r = 4$ for LSB $d_{i,j,0}$ in the aperture of samples (2×2) :

---

[2] Thus distortion of the container is the variable size of a   which depends on length of the message and from the sizes of the container. They also can differ in size.

[3] The median filtering represents a special case of a rank filtration at $\text{rank}_{R/2}$; R – the upper bound of a rank.

$$d^1_{i,j,0} = \mathrm{rank}_1 \begin{pmatrix} d_{i,j-1,0} & d_{i,j,0} \\ d_{i+1,j-1,0} & d_{i+1,j,0} \end{pmatrix}, \ d^4_{i+1,j,0} = \mathrm{rank}_4 \begin{pmatrix} d_{i,j-1,0} & d_{i,j,0} \\ d_{i+1,j-1,0} & d_{i+1,j,0} \end{pmatrix}, \quad (4)$$

$$i = 0, 2, 4, ..., I-2; \quad j = 1, 2, ..., J-1.$$

Modification function of a signal can be submitted as the table 1.

Table 1. Modification of LSB of the container ($d_{i,j-1,0}, d_{i,j,0}, d_{i+1,j-1,0}, d_{i+1,j,0}$ — the ranked series).

$\begin{pmatrix} d_{i,j-1,0} & d_{i,j,0} \\ d_{i+1,j-1,0} & d_{i+1,j,0} \end{pmatrix}$	$\begin{pmatrix} 0 & 0 \\ 0 & 0 \end{pmatrix}$	$\begin{pmatrix} 0 & 0 \\ 0 & 1 \end{pmatrix}$	$\begin{pmatrix} 0 & 0 \\ 1 & 0 \end{pmatrix}$	$\begin{pmatrix} 0 & 0 \\ 1 & 1 \end{pmatrix}$
$d_{i,j-1,0}, d_{i,j,0}, d_{i+1,j-1,0}, d_{i+1,j,0}$	0000	0001	0001	0011
$d_{i,j,0}$	0	0	0	0
$d^1_{i,j,0}$	0	0	0	0
$d_{i+1,j,0}$	0	1	0	1
$d^4_{i+1,j,0}$	0	1	1	1
$\begin{pmatrix} d_{i,j-1,0} & d_{i,j,0} \\ d_{i+1,j-1,0} & d_{i+1,j,0} \end{pmatrix}$	$\begin{pmatrix} 1 & 0 \\ 0 & 0 \end{pmatrix}$	$\begin{pmatrix} 1 & 0 \\ 0 & 1 \end{pmatrix}$	$\begin{pmatrix} 1 & 0 \\ 1 & 0 \end{pmatrix}$	$\begin{pmatrix} 1 & 0 \\ 1 & 1 \end{pmatrix}$
$d_{i,j-1,0}, d_{i,j,0}, d_{i+1,j-1,0}, d_{i+1,j,0}$	0001	0011	0011	0111
$d_{i,j,0}$	0	0	0	0
$d^1_{i,j,0}$	0	0	0	0
$d_{i+1,j,0}$	0	1	0	1
$d^4_{i+1,j,0}$	1	1	1	1
$\begin{pmatrix} d_{i,j-1,0} & d_{i,j,0} \\ d_{i+1,j-1,0} & d_{i+1,j,0} \end{pmatrix}$	$\begin{pmatrix} 0 & 1 \\ 0 & 0 \end{pmatrix}$	$\begin{pmatrix} 0 & 1 \\ 0 & 1 \end{pmatrix}$	$\begin{pmatrix} 0 & 1 \\ 1 & 0 \end{pmatrix}$	$\begin{pmatrix} 0 & 1 \\ 1 & 1 \end{pmatrix}$
$d_{i,j-1,0}, d_{i,j,0}, d_{i+1,j-1,0}, d_{i+1,j,0}$	0001	0011	0011	0111
$d_{i,j,0}$	1	1	1	1
$d^1_{i,j,0}$	0	0	0	0
$d_{i+1,j,0}$	0	1	0	1
$d^4_{i+1,j,0}$	1	1	1	1
$\begin{pmatrix} d_{i,j-1,0} & d_{i,j,0} \\ d_{i+1,j-1,0} & d_{i+1,j,0} \end{pmatrix}$	$\begin{pmatrix} 1 & 1 \\ 0 & 0 \end{pmatrix}$	$\begin{pmatrix} 1 & 1 \\ 0 & 1 \end{pmatrix}$	$\begin{pmatrix} 1 & 1 \\ 1 & 0 \end{pmatrix}$	$\begin{pmatrix} 1 & 1 \\ 1 & 1 \end{pmatrix}$
$d_{i,j-1,0}, d_{i,j,0}, d_{i+1,j-1,0}, d_{i+1,j,0}$	0011	0111	0111	1111
$d_{i,j,0}$	1	1	1	1
$d^1_{i,j,0}$	0	0	0	1
$d_{i+1,j,0}$	0	1	0	1
$d^4_{i+1,j,0}$	1	1	1	1

The comparisons $d_{i,j,0}$ with $d^1_{i,j,0}$ and $d_{i+1,j,0}$ with $d^4_{i+1,j,0}$ has shown, that the inversion of operands in only four combinations from sixteen. This property can be used for embedding in the container of pair sample of the stego–message, which consists of 0 and 1:

$$\begin{pmatrix} d_{i,j-1,0} & d_{i,j,0} \\ d_{i+1,j-1,0} & d_{i+1,j,0} \end{pmatrix} = \begin{vmatrix} \begin{pmatrix} 0 & 1 \\ 0 & 0 \end{pmatrix} => s_k s_{k+1} = 00; & \begin{pmatrix} 0 & 1 \\ 1 & 0 \end{pmatrix} => s_k s_{k+1} = 01 \\ \begin{pmatrix} 1 & 1 \\ 0 & 0 \end{pmatrix} => s_k s_{k+1} = 10; & \begin{pmatrix} 1 & 1 \\ 1 & 0 \end{pmatrix} => s_k s_{k+1} = 11 \end{vmatrix} \tag{5}$$

The embedding of the stego–message in the container is presented in the table 2.

Table 2. The embedding of stego–message in the container (at all other combinations $s_k s_{k+1}$ and $d_{i,j,0}$, the container does not change and $s_k s_{k+1}$ does not embed into the container).

$s_k s_{k+1}$	$\begin{pmatrix} d_{i,j-1,0} & d_{i,j,0} \\ d_{i+1,j-1,0} & d_{i+1,j,0} \end{pmatrix}$	Modification of the container	The embedding of $s_k s_{k+1}$
00	$\begin{pmatrix} 0 & 1 \\ 0 & 0 \end{pmatrix}$	no	yes
00	$\begin{pmatrix} 0 & 0 \\ 0 & 1 \end{pmatrix}$	$\begin{pmatrix} 0 & 1 \\ 0 & 0 \end{pmatrix}$	yes
00	$\begin{pmatrix} 0 & 1 \\ 1 & 0 \end{pmatrix}, \begin{pmatrix} 1 & 1 \\ 0 & 0 \end{pmatrix}, \begin{pmatrix} 1 & 1 \\ 1 & 0 \end{pmatrix}$	$\begin{pmatrix} 0 & 0 \\ 1 & 1 \end{pmatrix}, \begin{pmatrix} 1 & 0 \\ 0 & 1 \end{pmatrix}, \begin{pmatrix} 1 & 0 \\ 1 & 1 \end{pmatrix}$	no
01	$\begin{pmatrix} 0 & 1 \\ 1 & 0 \end{pmatrix}$	no	yes
01	$\begin{pmatrix} 0 & 0 \\ 1 & 1 \end{pmatrix}$	$\begin{pmatrix} 0 & 1 \\ 1 & 0 \end{pmatrix}$	yes
01	$\begin{pmatrix} 0 & 1 \\ 0 & 0 \end{pmatrix}, \begin{pmatrix} 1 & 1 \\ 0 & 0 \end{pmatrix}, \begin{pmatrix} 1 & 1 \\ 1 & 0 \end{pmatrix}$	$\begin{pmatrix} 0 & 0 \\ 0 & 1 \end{pmatrix}, \begin{pmatrix} 1 & 0 \\ 0 & 1 \end{pmatrix}, \begin{pmatrix} 1 & 0 \\ 1 & 1 \end{pmatrix}$	no
10	$\begin{pmatrix} 1 & 1 \\ 0 & 0 \end{pmatrix}$	no	yes
10	$\begin{pmatrix} 1 & 0 \\ 0 & 1 \end{pmatrix}$	$\begin{pmatrix} 1 & 1 \\ 0 & 0 \end{pmatrix}$	yes
10	$\begin{pmatrix} 0 & 1 \\ 0 & 0 \end{pmatrix}, \begin{pmatrix} 0 & 1 \\ 1 & 0 \end{pmatrix}, \begin{pmatrix} 1 & 1 \\ 1 & 0 \end{pmatrix}$	$\begin{pmatrix} 0 & 0 \\ 0 & 1 \end{pmatrix}, \begin{pmatrix} 0 & 0 \\ 1 & 1 \end{pmatrix}, \begin{pmatrix} 1 & 0 \\ 1 & 1 \end{pmatrix}$	no
11	$\begin{pmatrix} 1 & 1 \\ 1 & 0 \end{pmatrix}$	no	yes
11	$\begin{pmatrix} 1 & 0 \\ 1 & 1 \end{pmatrix}$	$\begin{pmatrix} 1 & 1 \\ 1 & 0 \end{pmatrix}$	yes
11	$\begin{pmatrix} 0 & 1 \\ 0 & 0 \end{pmatrix}, \begin{pmatrix} 0 & 1 \\ 1 & 0 \end{pmatrix}, \begin{pmatrix} 1 & 1 \\ 0 & 0 \end{pmatrix}$	$\begin{pmatrix} 0 & 0 \\ 0 & 1 \end{pmatrix}, \begin{pmatrix} 0 & 0 \\ 1 & 1 \end{pmatrix}, \begin{pmatrix} 1 & 0 \\ 0 & 1 \end{pmatrix}$	no

The embedding of the stego–message into the container can be presented as follows:

$$
\left\{
\begin{array}{l}
k=0 \quad /*\,k - \text{a sample number of the stego} - \text{message} */ \\[4pt]
\text{for } i = 0, 2, 4,..., I-2 : \\[4pt]
\text{for } j = 1, 2, ..., J-1 : \\[4pt]
\quad \text{if } k < K \\[4pt]
\quad \text{then if } (d_{i,j,0} \,\&\, \overline{d_{i+1,j,0}}) \text{ then if}(s_k s_{k+1} = d_{i,j-1,0} d_{i+1,j-1,0}) \\[4pt]
\qquad\qquad\qquad\qquad \text{then } \left\{ D_{i,j}^{+} = D_{i,j}; D_{i+1,j}^{+} = D_{i+1,j}; k = k+2 \right\} \\[4pt]
\qquad\qquad\qquad\qquad \text{else } \left\{
\begin{array}{l}
D_{i,j}^{+} = d_{i,j,N-1} d_{i,j,N-2} \cdots d_{i,j,1} \overline{d_{i,j,0}} \\[4pt]
D_{i+1,j}^{+} = d_{i+1,j,N-1} d_{i+1,j,N-2} \cdots d_{i+1,j,1} \overline{d_{i+1,j,0}}
\end{array}
\right\} \\[10pt]
\quad \text{if } (\overline{d_{i,j,0}} \,\&\, d_{i+1,j,0}) \\[4pt]
\qquad \text{then if } (s_k s_{k+1} = d_{i,j-1,0} d_{i+1,j-1,0}) \text{ then } \left\{
\begin{array}{l}
D_{i,j}^{+} = d_{i,j,N-1} d_{i,j,N-2} \cdots d_{i,j,1} \overline{d_{i,j,0}} \\[4pt]
D_{i+1,j}^{+} = d_{i+1,j,N-1} d_{i+1,j,N-2} \cdots d_{i+1,j,1} \\[4pt]
k = k+2
\end{array}
\right. \\[16pt]
\qquad \text{else if } k = K \text{ then } \left\{
\begin{array}{l}
F_{min} = J(i+1) - 2(J-j) \\[4pt]
D_{i,j}^{+} = D_{i,j} \\[4pt]
k = k+1
\end{array}
\right\} \text{ else } D_{i,j}^{+} = D_{i,j} \\[16pt]
\text{end; end;} \\[4pt]
\text{if } k<K \text{ then Goto Error\_The\_Short\_Container}
\end{array}
\right.
\tag{6}
$$

F_{min} – a minimum of amount of the sample of container, necessary for the embedding of the stego–message. The procedure of errors processing "Error_The_Short_Container" is not considered in this article. Such asynchronous modification of LSB of the container–original are reduced with probability of detection of the stego–message in the container–result. The algorithm of asynchronous regeneration of the stego–message from container–result is below resulted (the method of transfer of parameter K here is not considered):

$$
\left\{
\begin{array}{l}
k = 0 \\[4pt]
\text{for } i=0,2,...,I-2 : \\[4pt]
\text{for } j=1,2,...,J-1 : \\[4pt]
\quad \text{if } (d_{i,j,0}^{+} \,\&\, \overline{d_{i+1,j,0}^{+}}) \text{ then } \left\{ s_k s_{k+1} = d_{i,j-1,0}^{+} d_{i+1,j-1,0}^{+} ; k=k+2 \right\} \\[4pt]
\quad \text{if } k \geq K \text{ then goto End\_of\_destego} \\[4pt]
\text{end; end;} \\[4pt]
\text{End\_of\_destego :}
\end{array}
\right.
\tag{7}
$$

Experimental verification of a precision of LSB modification

For experimental verification of the algorithm precision of a signal embedding in the container we used a two–dimensional array of random binary numbers $d_{i,j,0} \in \{0,1\}$, $i = 0,1,2,...,I-1$, $j = 0,1,2,...,J-1$, as the LSB of the container–original.

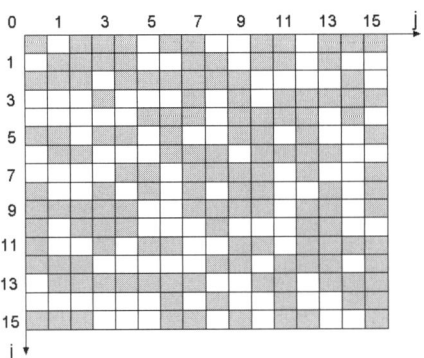

Fig. 1. LSB of the test container–original $d_{i,j,0}$.

Fig. 2. The test stego–message s_k =[0000111111110000]

Fig. 3. The test stego–message s_k =[1010110101010010]

Accordantly to it is modified LSB of container–original samples $d_{i,j,0}$ (fig. 1). As a test of the stego–messages we are used two bit lines: s_k = [0000111111110000] (fig. 2) and random sequence s_k = rand(1,16) (fig. 3). On fig. 4÷5 results of the embedding of test stego–messages s_k in the test container–original $d_{i,j,0}$ are shown.

   On fig. 1÷5 the following designations are accepted: $\square$ $d_{i,j,0} = 0$; $\blacksquare$ $d_{i,j,0} = 1$; $\boxtimes$ $s_k = 0$; $\blacksquare$ $s_k = 1$; $\boxtimes$ – change of values of the container– original with 0 on 1 without embedding s_k; $\boxtimes$ – change of values of the container– original with 1 on 0 without embedding s_k.

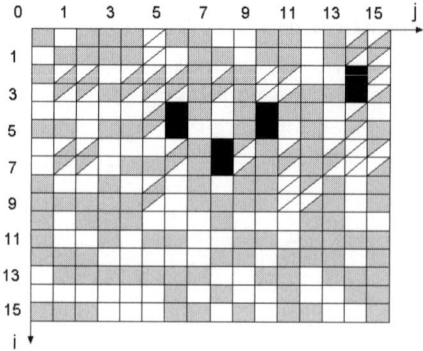

Fig. 4. Embedding of $s_k=[0000111111110000]$ in LSB of container–original $d_{i,j,0}$.

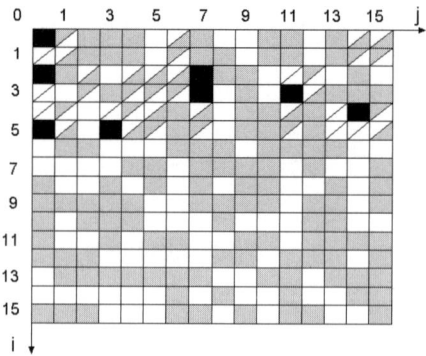

Fig. 5. Embedding of $s_k=[1010110101010010]$ in LSB of container–original $d_{i,j,0}$.

On the basis of the analysis of readout it is possible to allocate some properties of algorithm:

1. Embedding of any two elements of the stego–message in sample $D_{i,j-1}$ and $D_{i+1,j-1}$ is accompanied by replacement of even number $D_{i,j}$ in odd $(D_{i,j}+1)$ and replacement of odd number $D_{i+1,j}$ on even $(D_{i+1,j}+1)$; thus deviation is brought in the container $\varepsilon = \pm 1$.

2. Not all pairs samples $D_{i,j}$, $D_{i+1,j}$ change at embedding of the stego–message.

3. Deviation of the container–original without embedding in the container of the next pair bits stego–messages are possible.

4. Minimally necessary length of the container–original F_{min}, sufficient for embedding of the stego–message depends on contents as container–original, and the stego–message

Deviation of the container at embedding of the stego–message

For distortions of the container–original is frequently used Mean Square Error (MSE):

$$MSE = \frac{1}{F_{min}} \sum_{i=0}^{I_{end}} \sum_{j=0}^{J_{end}} (d_{i,j,0} \oplus d^+_{i,j,0}), \text{ где } I_{end} = [F_{min} / J], \; J_{end} =]F_{min} / J[\tag{8}$$

where F_{min} – a minimum of amount of the sample of container, necessary for the embedding of the stego–message; $\oplus$ – the sum of the module 2.

Operators $[F_{min} / J]$ and $]F_{min} / J[$ mean the whole part of integer division and the whole remainder accordingly.

Size of distortion of the container at updating LSB on the basis of a method the double rank filtering

In table 3 there are various variants of test stego–containers and variants of the test messages introduced into them. A modelling of experiments based on MATLAB. For each variant is counted the Mean Square Error of container–original MSE_{RF} and parameter F_{min} (for embedding of the stego–message by the metod of the double rank filtering). Also sizes of distortion of the container–original are counted at introduction by the method of replacement of the LSB MSE_{LSB}, by the method of a pseudorandom interval MSE_{PRI}, by the method of a block embedding. MSE_{BE} (6).

Table 3. Average size of deviation of a modified part of the container.

Test–container, $d_{i,0}$	Test–message, s_k	Dimen–sion of the contain–ner, $I \times J$	Dimen–sion of the message, K	F_{min}	MSE_{RF}	MSE_{LSB}	MSE_{PRI}	MSE_{BE}
Random process	Random process	256	16	209	0.13	0.41	0.119	0.244
Random process	Random process	512	32	402	0.13	0.48	0.124	**0.288**
Random process	Random process	1024	32	500	0.12	0.41	0.120	0.260
Random process	Random process	1024	64	930	0.13	0.54	**0.128**	0.250
Random process	Random process	2048	128	1735	**0.13**	**0.55**	0.118	0.241

Experiment has shown, that the maximal estimation at modification the container–original on base a rank filtering equal to of 0.13, and at replacement of the first K samples of the container–original of 0.55. At use of an asynchronous method of modification on base a rank filtering the average size of deviation of the container–original MSE_{RF} four times is less, than at a synchronous method of embedding MSE_{LSB}.

Experiment has shown, that the Mean Square Error the container–original on base a rank filtering MSE_{FP} twice is less, than at the method of a block embedding.

Conclusion

Algorithms of steganography constantly are improved, appear new forms and formats of representation of the graphic data. In the following works of authors results of researches of messages embedding in media data on base a rank filtering of the LSB of the container with the aperture (3×3), and also results of researches of embedding of messages at Fourier–images media of the data will be published.

Literature

[1] Matsiu K., Tanaka K., Nakamura Y. Digital signature on a facsimile document by recursive MH coding// Symposium On Cryptography and Information Security, 1989.
[2] Gribunin V.G., Okov I. N., Turintsev I.V. Digital steganography// Moscow. SOLON–PRESS. 2002.(in Russian)
[3] Petitcolas F., Anderson R. Information Hiding – A Survey// Proceedings IEEE, Special Issue on Identification and Protection of Multimedia Information. 1999, #7.
[4] Dobryakova L., Ochin E. Embedding of digital watermarks in media data on base a median filtering// Works of VI International conference „ The Analysis, prediction and management in difficult systems"//Saint Petersburg// Publishing house „System", 2005. (in Russian)
[5] E. Ochin, L. Dobryakova. Architecture of processors a median filtering in steganography systems on a base of media data// Methods of computer science of management // Poland, Szczecin, 2005. (in Polish)
[6] Bender W., Gruhl B., Morimoto N., Lu A. Techniques for data hiding // IBM systems journal. 1996, vol.35, # 3.
[7] Kornatowski E, Kowalski J., Algorithms of digital processing of signals// Electric faculty The Technical University of Szczecin, Szczecin, 2000. (in Polish)
[8] Konahovich G., Puzyrenko A., A komputer steganography. The theory and practice// MK–Press, Kiev, 2006. (in Russian)

PART III

IMAGE ANALYSIS, GRAPHICS AND BIOMETRICS

JPEG 2000 IMAGE CODING STANDARD - A REVIEW AND APPLICATIONS

Ryszard S. Choraś

Faculty of Telecommunications
University of Technology & LS
85-796 Bydgoszcz, S. Kaliskiego 7, POLAND
choras@utp.edu.pl

Abstract. The Joint Photographic Experts Group has recently created a new image coding standard called JPEG 2000, which is to be used in various multimedia applications. JPEG 2000 standard integrates such features as good quality at lossless and lossy compression, embedded lossy to lossless coding, progressive transmission by pixel accuracy and by resolution, robustness to the presence of bit - errors and ROI - region of interest coding which has not been presented in existing compression algorithms so far.

1 INTRODUCTION

The JPEG 2000 standard has been created by the Joint Photographic Experts Group (JPEG), also denominated as ISO/IEC JTC/SC29/WG1. JPEG 2000 is being released in following parts [2], [5]:

Part 1: core technology (+ JP2 file format)
Part 2: extended coding tools (+ JPX)
Part 3 (12 & 13): motion JPEG2000 (MJ2)
Part 4: conformance testing for Part 1
Part 5: reference software (JJ2000+Jasper)
Part 6: compound documents (JPM)
Part 7: Has been abandoned
Part 8: JPSEC (encryption, watermarking)
Part 9: JPIP (interactive protocols)
Part 10: JP3D (hyperspectral/volumetric)
Part 11: JPWL (wireless applications).
Part 12: ISO Base Media File Format (common with MPEG-4)

JPEG 2000 supports lossy and lossless compression of grayscale and color images. In addition to this basic compression functionality, numerous other features are provided, including:

1. progressive recovery of an image by fidelity or resolution;
2. region of interest coding, whereby different parts of an image can be coded with differing fidelity;

3. random access to particular regions of an image without need to decode the entire code stream;
4. a flexible file format with provisions for specifying opacity information and image sequences;
5. good error resilience.

In this paper, we are essentially concerned with the fundamental building blocks of the JPEG 2000 Part 1 standard, as well as a summary of the technologies used in other Parts.

2 THE JPEG 2000 COMPRESSION ENGINE

The JPEG 2000 standard was designed to complement, not replace, the JPEG standard. The basic block diagram of the JPEG 2000 encoder and the decoder is presented in Fig. 1. Main components include preprocessing, DWT (discrete wavelet transform), quantization, tier-1 coding (arithmetic coding), tier-2 coding (bitstream organization).

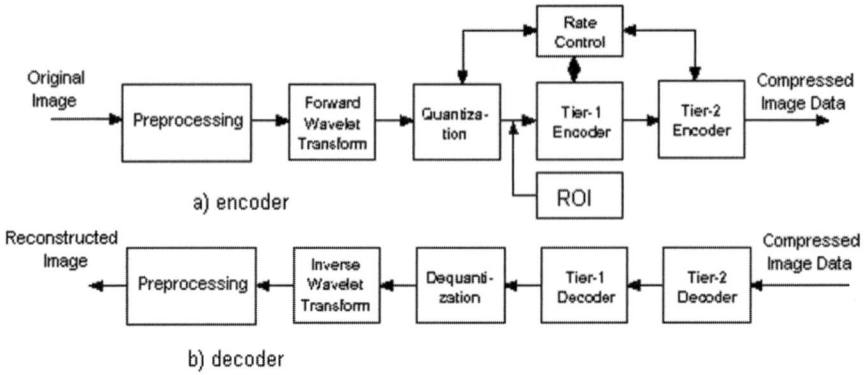

Fig. 1. Block diagram of the JPEG 2000 coder (a) and decoder (b).

The JPEG2000 encoding procedure is as follows:

- The image is decomposed into components.
- The image components can be decomposed (optionally) into rectangular tiles. The tile-component is the basic unit of the original or reconstructed image.
- The wavelet transform is applied to each tile, decomposing it into different resolution levels.
- These decomposition levels are made up of sub-bands of coefficients that describe the frequency characteristics of local areas of the tile-component, rather than across the entire tile-component.

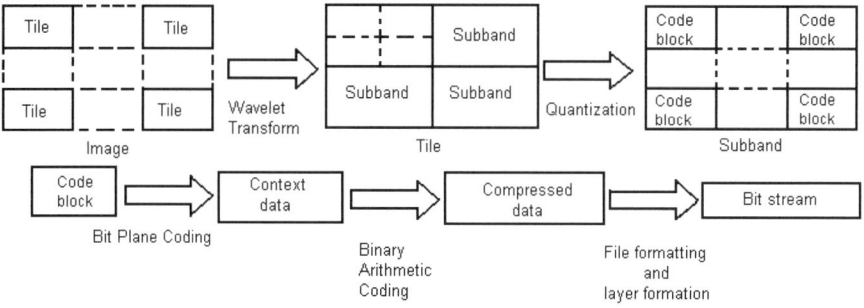

Fig. 2. Partitioning of image into tiles, sub-bands and code blocks.

- Sub-bands of coefficients are quantized and partitioned into rectangular arrays of "code-blocks".
- Bit-planes of the coefficients of a code-block are entropy coded.
- The encoding can be done such that certain ROIs can be coded with higher quality as compared to the background.
- Markers are added to the bitstream to allow error resilience.
- The code-stream has a main header at the beginning that describes the original image and the various decomposition and coding styles that have to be used to locate, extract, decode, and reconstruct the image with the desired resolution, fidelity, region of interest or other characteristics.

2.1   Preprocessing

In the first stage, pre-processing is performed (Fig. 3).
At this point, it is important to understand the image model that JPEG2000 uses. From the standard's point of view, an image is composed of one or more components (up to 2^{14}), and each component consists of a matrix of samples representing the luminosity of the component at that point. The sample values are integer valued, can be either signed or unsigned, and can have between 1 and 38 bits/sample. The source/input image is decomposed into one or several (up to $2^{14} = 16382$) components.The sample values for each component have bit-depth in the range $1 - 38$ bits, and have integer value.

Each component is decomposed into several rectangular non-overlapping tiles. All operations including component mixing, DWT, quantization and entropy coding are performed independently on the images tiles. The tile size are arbitrary allowed with respect that larger tiles perform visually better than smaller tiles and typical size is 512×512, or 256×256, according to the size of the input image (Fig. 4).

JPEG2000 expects its input sample data to have a nominal dynamic range centered about zero. This expectation is necessary since JPEG2000 uses high-

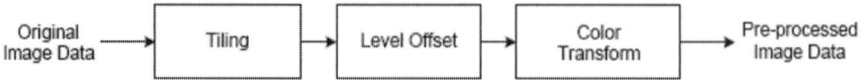

Fig. 3. Pre-processing sub-stages.

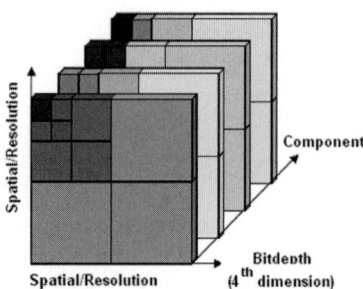

Fig. 4. Wavelet processed components

pass filtering. The level offset pre-processing stage ensures that this expectation is met. If the original B-bit image sample values are unsigned (non-negative) quantities, an offset of -2^{B-1} is added so that the samples have a signed representation in the range $-2^{B-1} \leq x[n] < 2^{B-1}$. If the data is already signed (centered around zero), no adjustment is performed.

Next the DWT is applied on each tile, and an iteration of DWT decomposes a tile-component into a lower resolution and three sub-bands: HL, LH, HH. This process can be repeated recursively on the lower resolution to create additional sub-bands. n-level DWT results in $3n + 1$ sub-bands (Fig. 5).

Further, each sub-band is partitioned into several precincts and each precinct includes several code blocks. The coefficients of each sub-band are quantized. Each code block is entropy coded independently using arithmetic coding in the tier-1 coder. The arithmetic coder is the context-based MQ coder. The last step is packetization (tier-2 coder) which packetizes the final bitstream into data packets.

JPEG 2000 supports multiple - component images and for both lossless and lossy compression uses reversible component transformation (RCT) and only for lossy compression irreversible component transformation (ICT) is used.

In JPEG2000 an irreversible color transform (ICT) is performed to convert RGB data into YCrCb data according to the following (Fig. 6):

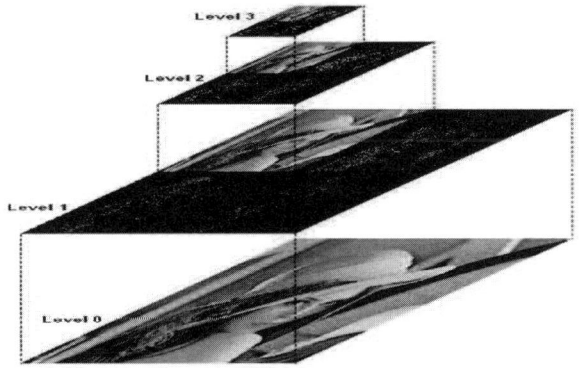

Fig. 5. Wavelet transform - diadic decomposition

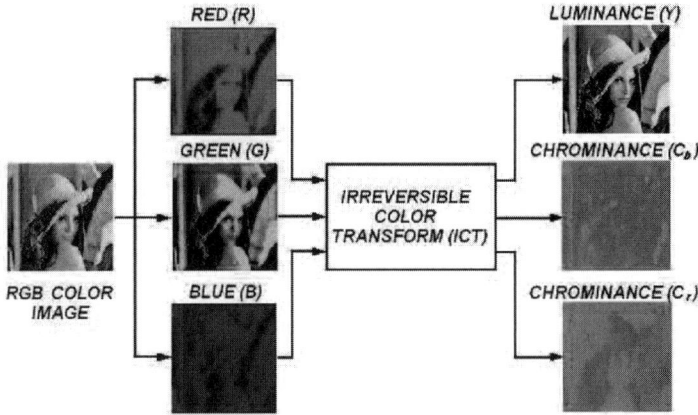

Fig. 6. Irreversible color transform

$$\begin{bmatrix} Y \\ C_r \\ C_b \end{bmatrix} = \begin{bmatrix} 0.299 & 0.587 & 0.114 \\ -0.16875 & -0.33126 & 0.5 \\ 0.5 & -0.41869 & 0.08131 \end{bmatrix} * \begin{bmatrix} R \\ G \\ B \end{bmatrix} \tag{1}$$

The inverse transform can be shown as

$$\begin{bmatrix} R \\ G \\ B \end{bmatrix} = \begin{bmatrix} 1.0 & 0 & 1.402 \\ 1.0 & -0.34413 & -0.71414 \\ 1.0 & 1.772 & 0 \end{bmatrix} * \begin{bmatrix} Y \\ C_r \\ C_b \end{bmatrix} \tag{2}$$

The RCT is simply a reversible integer-to-integer approximation to the ICT. The forward and inverse RCT are performed as

$$Yr = \lfloor \frac{R+2G+B}{4} \rfloor \qquad R = Ur + G$$
$$Ur = R - G \qquad G = Yr - (\frac{Ur+Vr}{4}) \qquad (3)$$
$$Vr = B - G \qquad B = Vr + G$$

2.2   2-D filter banks and sub-band coding

As mentioned earlier, both reversible integer-to-integer and nonreversible real-to-real wavelet transforms can be used. Since lossless compression requires no data to be lost due to rounding, a reversible wavelet transform that uses only rational filter coefficients is used for this type of compression. In contrast, lossy compression allows for some data to be lost in the compression process, and therefore nonreversible wavelet transforms with non-rational filter coefficients can be used. In order to handle filtering at signal boundaries, symmetric extension is used. Symmetric extension adds a mirror image of the signal to the outside of the boundaries so that large errors are not introduced at the boundaries. The default irreversible transform is implemented by means of the biorthogonal Daubechies 9-tap/7-tap filter. The Daubechies wavelet family is one of the most important and widely used wavelet families. The analysis filter coefficients for the Daubechies 9-tap/7-tap filter, which are used for the dyadic decomposition, are given in Table 1, and a graph of the corresponding wavelet is shown in Fig. 7. The default reversible transform is implemented by means of the Le Gall 5-tap/3-tap filter, the coefficients of which are also given in Table 1.

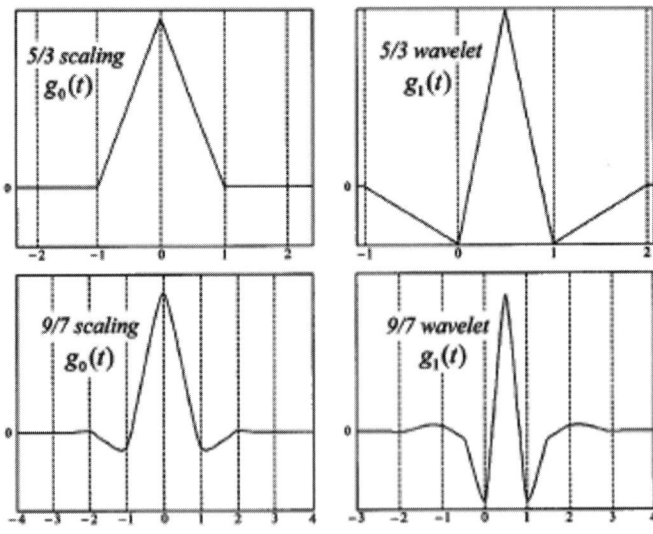

Fig. 7. Synthesis scaling and wavelet functions for the 5/3 and 9/7 subband filter sets.

The processing along rows and columns leads to problem at the image edges. The solution of this problem is to periodically extend the image, but unfortunately as the value of sample (n) can be very different from that of sample (1) edges artefact may be introduced. To alleviate this problem, the image should be extended in a symmetric way (Fig. 8).

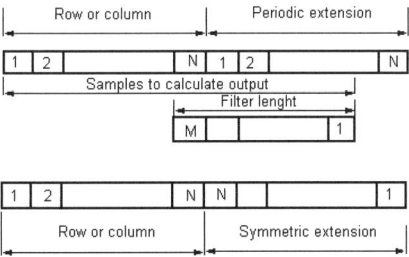

Fig. 8. Periodic and symmetric expansions of row or column of an image.

Table 1. Coefficients of the filters

	The biorthogonal 9/7 filter				The integer 5/3 filter			
	Analysis filters		Synthesis filters		Analysis filters		Synthesis filters	
n	Lowpass h_n	Highpass g_n	Lowpass s_n	Highpass r_n	Lowpass h_n	Highpass g_n	Lowpass s_n	Highpass r_n
0	0,8527	0,7885	0,7885	0,8527	6/8	1	1	6/8
±1	0,3774	-0,4181	0,4181	-0,3774	2/8	-1/2	1/2	-2/8
±2	-0,1106	-0, 0407	-0,0407	-0,1106	-1/8			-1/8
±3	-0,0238	0,0645	-0,0645	0,0238				
±4	0,0378			0,0378				

The standard supports both convolution-based and lifting-based filtering mode. For both modes to be implemented, the signal first needs to be extended periodically. This is done to ensure that for the filtering operations that take place at the boundaries of the signal, one signal sample exists and corresponds to each coefficient of the filter. Thus, how far the signal is extended on each side of the boundary depends on the number of filter coefficients. Convolution-based filtering is done by performing a series of dot products between the high-pass and low-pass filter coefficients and the extended one-dimensional signal. Lifting-based filtering is done by updating odd sample values with a weighted sum of even sample values, and updating even sample with a weighted sum of odd sample values.

Both the irreversible and reversible transformations are described using lifting-based filtering, which is a very efficient implementation of the DWT. The lifting scheme [15] consists of three steps - the split, the predict and the update steps. The split step partitions the data into two disjoint sets - the odd subset and even subset. The even subset is used to predict the odd subset. The prediction errors are usually small since most real-life data exhibit local correlation. The prediction errors are used to update the even set in the update step. The update step is usually chosen in such a way that the resulting coefficients have some nice mathematical properties such as vanishing moments, the same DC component as that of the original signal.

Fig. 9 shows the lifting steps for the data $x[n]$. The data $x[n]$ is split into an even subset $x_e[n] = x[2n]$ and an odd subsets $x_o[n] = x[2n+1]$. The even subset is used to predict the odd subset and the prediction errors $x_o[n] - P(x_e[n])$ are stored as $d[n]$. The prediction errors are used to update the even subset $x_e[n] + U(d[n])$ and the updated coefficients are stored as $s[n]$. Here $d[n]$ and $s[n]$ correspond to wavelet and scaling coefficients respectively. The inverse wavelet transform is obtained by inverting the lifting steps.

For the revertible 5/3 analysis filter, the coefficients of output signal y are computed as

$$y(2n + 1) = x_{ext}(2n + 1) - \lfloor \frac{x_{ext}(2n) + x_{ext}(2n + 2)}{2} \rfloor \tag{4}$$

$$y(2n) = x_{ext}(2n) + \lfloor \frac{y(2n - 1) + y(2n + 1) + 2}{4} \rfloor \tag{5}$$

where x_{ext} is the extended input signal, y is the output signal, and $\lfloor a \rfloor$ indicates the largest integer not exceeding a.

The corresponding inverse transformation for the reversible 5/3 synthesis filter are

$$x(2n + 1) = y_{ext}(2n + 1) - \lfloor \frac{x(2n) + x(2n + 2)}{2} \rfloor \tag{6}$$

$$x(2n) = y_{ext}(2n) + \lfloor \frac{y_{ext}(2n - 1) + y_{ext}(2n + 1) + 2}{4} \rfloor \tag{7}$$

where y_{ext} is the extended input signal, x is the output signal.

For irreversible 9/7 analysis and synthesis filter we have the 4 lifting steps and 2 scaling steps:

- analysis filter

$$
\begin{aligned}
y(2n + 1) &\leftarrow x_{ext}(2n + 1) + (a \times [x_{ext}(2n) + x_{ext}(2n + 2)]) \\
y(2n) &\leftarrow x_{ext}(2n) + (b \times [y(2n - 1) + y(2n + 1)]) \\
y(2n + 1) &\leftarrow y(2n + 1) + (c \times [y(2n) + y(2n + 2)]) \\
y(2n) &\leftarrow y(2n) + (d \times [y(2n - 1) + y(2n + 1)]) \\
y(2n + 1) &\leftarrow -K \times y(2n + 1) \\
y(2n) &\leftarrow \frac{1}{K} \times y(2n)
\end{aligned}
\tag{8}
$$

- synthesis filter

$$x(2n) \leftarrow K \times y_{ext}(2n)$$

$$x(2n+1) \leftarrow -\frac{1}{K} \times y_{ext}(2n+1)$$

$$x(2n) \leftarrow x(2n) - (d \times [x(2n-1) + x(2n+1)])$$

$$x(2n+1) \leftarrow x(2n+1) - (c \times [x(2n) + x(2n+2)]) \tag{9}$$

$$x(2n) \leftarrow x(2n) - (b \times [x(2n-1) + x(2n+1)])$$

$$x(2n+1) \leftarrow x(2n+1) - (a \times [x(2n) + x(2n+2)])$$

where $a = -1.586$, $b = -0.052$, $c = 0.883$, $d = 0.444$ and the scaling factor $K = 1.230174105$.

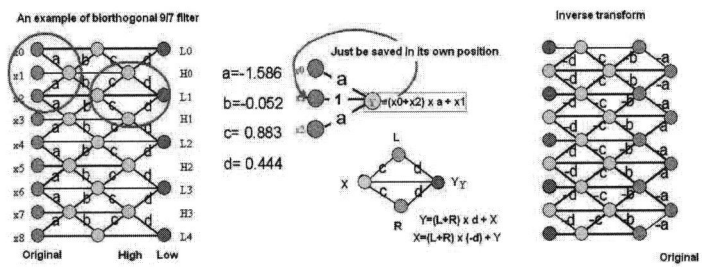

Fig. 9. Wavelet transform using lifting

2.3   Quantization

In JPEG 2000 quantization is performed on each coefficient obtained after wavelet transform. If reversible 5/3 integer filter is used, then no information is lost and quantization is not performed for these coefficients.

If irreversible wavelet transform is used, each wavelet-transformed coefficients $c_b(u, v)$ of the sub-band b are quantized as

$$q_b(u, v) = sign(c_b(u, v)) \left\lfloor \frac{|c_b(u, v)|}{\Delta_b} \right\rfloor \tag{10}$$

where: Δ_b is quantization coefficient defined relatively to dynamic range R_b of subband b, by exponent ε_b and mantissa μ_b as

$$\Delta_b = 2^{R_b - \varepsilon_b} \left(1 + \frac{\mu_b}{2^{11}}\right) \tag{11}$$

The dynamic range R_b depends on the number of bits used to represent the tile component of the input image and on the choice of the wavelet transform. All quantized coefficients are signed values.

Dequantization rule is

$$z = [q_b(u, v) + rsign(q_b(u, v))\Delta_b] \text{ for } q_b(u, v) \neq 0$$
$$z = 0 \qquad\qquad\qquad \text{otherwise} \qquad (12)$$

where:
$q_b(u, v)$ -quantized index,
Δ_b - quantizer step size,
$sign(q_b(u, v)$ - sign of $q_b(u, v)$,
r - reconstruction bias.

In JPEG 2000 quantizer index is encoded on bit at a time starting from the MSB and proceeding to the LSB. The quantized wavelet coefficient is insignificant if quantizer index $q_b(u, v)$ is still zero.
Once the first nonzero bit is encoded, the coefficient becomes significant and its sign is encoded. If the p least significant bits of the quantizer index still remain to be encoded, the reconstructed sample is obtained with step size $\Delta_b 2^p$.
The transform coefficients are quantized with a dead-zone scalar quantizer. A different quantizer is employed for the transform coefficients of each sub-band. In the case of lossless coding, the quantizer step sizes are forced to be one, so that the quantizer indices are nothing more than the transform coefficients themselves.

2.4 EBCOT coding (embedded block coding with optimized truncation)

Embedded coding, which is useful for scalability and efficient rate control, is the main feature of JPEG 2000. The basic idea in EBCOT is to divide each sub-band into blocks of samples which are coded independently. For each block, a separate bitstream is generated without using any information from the other blocks. The bit stream has the property that it can be truncated to a variety of discrete lengths.

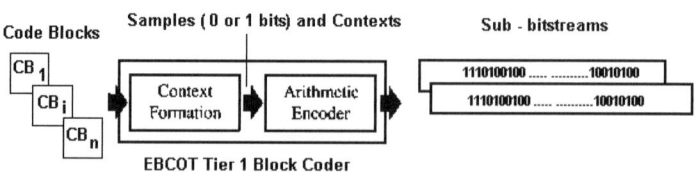

Fig. 1 . EBCOT Tier 1 block coder

EBCOT is a two-tiered coder, where the first tier is a block coder and the second tier is for rate-distortion optimization and bitstream formation. The tier-1 coding is performed on the code blocks where each code block is entropy -

coded using the MQ-coder. Tier 1 of EBCOT is actually a context-based adaptive arithmetic encoder. Code blocks are independently coded by this block coder into sub-bit-streams. According to the functionality, the block coder can be further partitioned into two steps, context formation (CF) and arithmetic encoder (AE), as shown in Fig. 10. Before CF, the quantized (in lossy mode) or non quantized (in lossless mode) wavelet coefficients are converted from two complement representations to sign-magnitude format. Let $s(u, v)$ denote the sign of the quantized wavelet coefficient $sc(u, v)$, and let $mc(u, v)$ denote the quantized magnitude, i.e., $mc(u, v) = |sc(u, v)|$. If the precision of $mc(u, v)$ is P bit, then $0 \leq mc(u, v) \leq 2^P$. We identify the pth bit of $mc(u, v)$ as $mc_p(u, v)$, where $p = P - 1, \ldots, 0$. The pth bit plane of this code block is composed of the pth bit of each sample in this code block. The scanning order in a code block is from the MSB of the magnitude part $(p = P - 1)$ to the LSB $(p = 0)$. A sample is called "significant" after the first "1" bit $(mc_p(u, v) = 1)$ is met while encoding the magnitude part from the MSB to the LSB, and it is called "insignificant" before the first "1" bit appears.

In Tier 1 encoding, code blocks are coded one bit-plane at a time starting from the MSB bit-plane with a non-zero element to the LSB plane.Within a bit plane, every four rows form a "stripe", and the scanning order is stripe by stripe from top to bottom. In every stripe, data are scanned bit by bit from top to bottom and column by column from left to right. Within a bit-plane the data is scanned in stripe fashion, with 4 rows per stripe, column-by-column order from left to right (Fig. 11). Each bit at every location is coded in one of three non-overlapping passes: the Significance Propagation Pass (SP); the Magnitude Refinement Pass (MR); and the Cleanup Pass (CP). A significance state is defined for every bit location which, along with the significance state of the eight neighboring locations in the context window (Fig. 12), governs its pass membership. All locations are assigned insignificant state initially. A location becomes significant immediately after its first non-zero bit has been coded. A sample location belongs to:
- SP pass, if it is currently insignificant but at least one of its neighbors (neighboring locations in the context window) is significant;
- MR pass, if the location is significant and has not been coded in the SP pass; and
- CP pass, if the location has not been coded in either the SP or MR passes.

The individual bit planes of the coefficients in a code-block are coded within three coding passes.
Pass 1 - "significant propagation pass (SP)" - samples that are currently insignificant, but have at least one immediate significant neighbor are coded first. A bit is coded if its location is not significant, but at least one of its eight surrounding neighbors is significant. Nine context bins are generated based both on how many and which ones are significant and on which sub-band this code block belongs to. This context is delivered to the arithmetic decoder (along with the bitstream) and the decoded coefficient bit is returned. If the value of this bit is

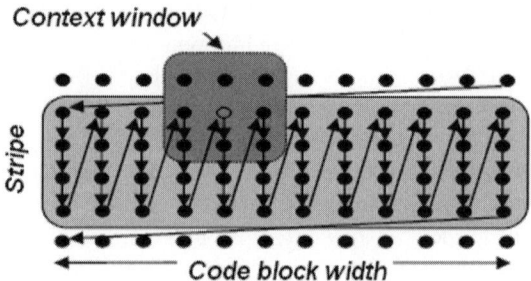

Fig. 11. Stripe Based Scanning Order and Context Window

"1" then the significance state is set to 1 and the next bit to be decoded is the sign bit for the coefficient. Otherwise, the significance state remains "0".

Pass 2 - "magnitude refinement pass (MR)" - codes subsequent bits following the most significant bit for each coefficient. It includes the bits from coefficients that are already significant (except those that just become significant in the prior significance propagation pass). The context is determined by the summation of the significance state of the horizontal, vertical and diagonal neighbors. These are the states as currently known to the decoder, not the states used before the significance decoding pass.

The last pass - "clean-up pass (CP)" - all bits not coded in the first two passes are coded in this pass. The clean-up pass uses the neighbor context and run-length context.

A bit is typically "significant" if it is a 1. However, JPEG2000 utilizes context-significance, which means that a bit at position j which is insignificant (zero) is actually context significant if the context, $K^{sig}[j]$, is greater than zero. The context is determined through a complex relationship between $K^{v}[j]$, $K^{h}[j]$, and $K^{d}[j]$, where $\sigma[]$ is the significance of the bit at position j. It is true that $K^{v}[j] = 0$, $K^{h}[j] = 0$, and $K^{d}[j] = 0$ if and only if all 8 immediate neighbors are insignificant. Also, bits which are outside the boundaries of the current code block are considered to be insignificant for context calculation.

$$K^{h}[j] = \sigma[j_r, j_c - 1] + \sigma[j_r, j_c + 1]$$
$$K^{v}[j] = \sigma[j_r - 1, j_c - 1] + \sigma[j_r + 1, j_c] \tag{13}$$
$$K^{d}[j] = \sum_{k_r = \pm 1} \sum_{k_c = \pm 1} \sigma[j_r + k_r, j_c + k_c]$$

Generally, context of the bit is generated according to the status of its neighbors using four coding primitives: zero coding (ZC), run-length coding (RLC), sign coding (SC) and magnitude refinement (MR). ZC and SC primitives are used in the first and third pass. MR is used in the second pass only, and RLC is

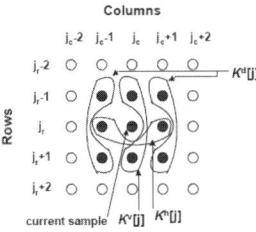

Fig. 12. Calculation of significance coding contexts.

used in the third pass.

The distribution of the number of bits coded in the three passes vary greatly from bit plane to bit plane.

Once the entire image has been compressed, a postprocessing operation passes over all the compressed blocks and determines the extent, to which each block's embedded bit stream should be truncated in order to achieve a particular target bit rate, distortion bound or other quality metrics [1].

Each code-block B_i is coded independently, producing an elementary embedded bitstream C_i. If number of truncation points $z_i + 1$ is finite, bitstream have length L_i^z with

$$0 = L_i \leq L_i^1 \leq \ldots \leq L_i^{2i} \tag{14}$$

The overall reconstruction image distortion can be represented as a sum of distortion contributions from each of the code-blocks D_i^z (e.g. Distortion if its embedded bitstream is truncated to length L_i^z). D_i^z depends upon the sub-band to which block B_i belongs.

The code-blocks are compressed independently, the final compressed bitstream is constrained by L_{max}, the truncation points are selected such that

$$\sum_i L_i^z \leq L_{max} \quad \text{and} \quad D = \sum_i D_i^{z_i} \tag{15}$$

The optimally truncated bitstream $C_i^{z_i}$ is simply concatenated (Fig. 13).

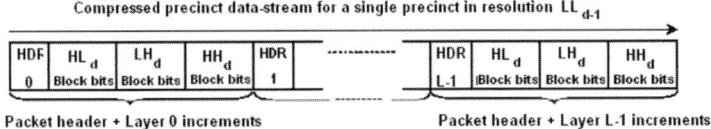

Fig. 13. Bit-stream formed by concatenated truncated code block bit-stream.

More generally, the final bit stream is composed from a collection of so-called "layers", where each layer has an interpretation in terms of overall image quality [6].

There are a total of K quality layers, from Q to Q_{K-}. The first layer Q contains optimized code-block contributions, having lengths $L_i^{z_i^0}$, which minimize the distortion,

$D = \sum_i D_i^{z_i^0}$ and $\sum_i L_i^{z_i^0} \le L_{max}$.

Subsequent layers Q_λ, contain additional contributions from each code block, having lengths $L_i^{z_i^\lambda} - L_i^{z_i^{\lambda-1}}$ which minimize the distortion

$D^\lambda = \sum_i D_i^{z_i^\lambda}$ and $\sum_i L_i^{z_i^\lambda} \le L_{max}^\lambda$.

Although Tier 2 is part of the EBCOT algorithm, the practical implementation detail is not defined in the standard and not restricted in the design of an encoder. The tier-2 coder performs a post-compression rate-distortion allocation using block summary information. The final bit-stream is generated in this stage.

The final JPEG2000 bitstream is organized as follows: A set of different main headers (including a main header (SIZ), a coding style header (COD), a quantization header (QCD), a comments header (COM), a start of a tile parts header (SOT)) is followed by packets of data which are all preceded by a packet header. In each packet appear the codewords of the code-blocks that belong to the same image resolution and layer, the header identifies the data. Depending on the arrangement of the packets, different progression orders may be specified.

2.5 ROI - Region - of - Interest

Region of interest (ROI) coding is important in applications where certain parts of an image are of a higher importance than the rest of the image. In these cases the ROI is decoded with higher quality and/or spatial resolution than the background. During the transmission of the image these regions need to be transmitted first. Example applications are:
- client/server applications where the server initially transmits a low quality resolution version of an image. The client then selects an area of the image as a ROI and the server transmits only the data needed to refine (i.e., improve the spatial resolution/quality) of that ROI [8].
- image databases browsing.

ROI coding is based on the MAXSHIFT method (Fig. 14), which proceeds as a five-step process:

1. Generate ROI Mask: Determine the set of wavelet coefficients that belong to the ROI. The mapping of the ROI from the spatial domain to the wavelet domain is dependent on the used wavelet filters and is simplified for rectangular and circular regions;

2. Find scaling value, s - magnitude of the largest wavelet coefficient in the background (not in the ROI), is found;
3. Scale down Background coefficients by s; all of the wavelet coefficients in the background are scaled down by $(s + d)$, where d is a small constant. This makes all of the wavelet coefficients in the background have a magnitude < 1. Therefore, the decoder just has to scale up (by $s + d$) all coefficients that have a magnitude < 1;
4. Write s to the bit-stream;
5. Apply bit-plane entropy coding as usual.

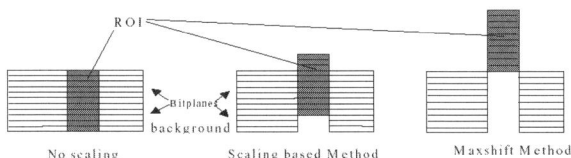

Fig. 14. MAXSHIFT method

Unfortunately, coefficient scaling reduces coding efficiency, as code-blocks that lie on the boundary of the ROI have to be coded twice: once for the ROI with a zero background, and once for the background with a zero ROI. In addition, coefficient scaling also increases the required dynamic range for JP2K. In Fig. 15 Lena image default JPEG 2000 and maxshift ROI coding with 0.125bpp is shown.

JPEG 2000   JPEG 2000 with ROI

Fig. 15. Lena image default JPEG 2000 and maxshift ROI coding

Yet another benefit of JPEG 2000 is its ROI capability, or Region of Interest. The use of wavelets allows one to be able to select a certain area of an image to view at a high quality, while leaving the rest of the image at a lower quality. This allows the user to only view a necessary portion of the image instead of the entire image. This significantly reduces the amount of memory the image requires, and the amount of time required to access the image. Fig. 16 shows the image compression quality (PSNR value) vs. the bit rate (in bits per pixel) for an image that was compressed using both the ROI encoding and the standard encoding method. The quality of the entire image is also shown on the graph. As is seen from Figure 16, the quality of the selected area of the image is significantly improved when the ROI method is used.

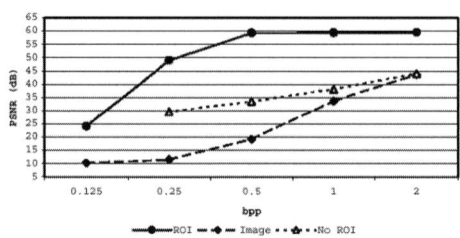

Fig. 16. Comparison between ROI encoding and standard encoding

3   JPIP - JPEG 2000 Internet Protocol

JPEG 2000 Internet Protocol provides a powerful and flexible client-server architecture. It is possible to store only one compressed file at the server and transmit the resolution, quality, ROI specified by the client, without having to transmit or decode the entire code-stream.

JPIP standard defines syntaxes and methods for remote interaction with JPEG code-stream. JPIP specifies interactions between a client and a server whereby meta data, structure and partial or entire image code-steams may be exchanged efficiently. Fig. 17 provides an overview of a JPIP client-server architecture.

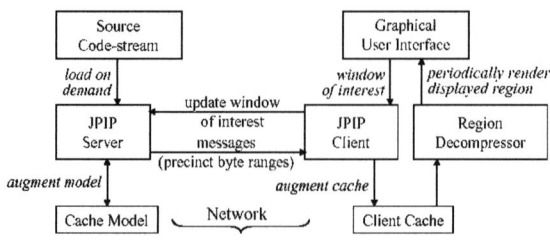

Fig. 17. JPIP architecture

The JPIP standard is primarily concerned with the description of a new protocol for interacting with JPEG 2000 content. With the JPIP protocol, a client does not directly access the compressed file. Rather, it formulates requests using a simple descriptive syntax which identifies the current "window" of the client-side application. JPIP requests identify the client's spatial region of interest, resolution and image components of interest, allowing the server to determine the most appropriate response elements and to optimally sequence them. As we shall see, JPIP allows the server to adjust the sequence in which data is returned, so as to minimize disk thrashing while optimizing the image quality available at the client. A single JPIP request is sufficient to obtain an arbitrary region of an image, at a selected size/resolution, so that JPIP requests can be embedded as static targets within HTML pages.

The data-stream is organized into segments, with one segment for each of the L quality layers. Each segment commences with a header, identifying the contribution made by each codeblock's bit-stream to the corresponding quality layer. This is followed by the block contributions themselves. In a JPEG 2000 code-stream, the segments are called "packets" and the packets from different precincts are interleaved following one of a number of predefined progression orders. For the purposes of JPIP [10], it is convenient to refer to the entire precinct data-stream as a single entity, any leading prefix of which may be delivered by the server.

Fig. 17 illustrates the typical interaction envisaged by JPIP between a client application and a remote server. An important aspect of Fig. 17 is the separation of the image decompression/rendering process from client-server communication.

The inherent scalability of JPEG 2000 means that an image can be meaningfully rendered from almost any subset of the original compressed data. This allows the "window" to be rendered directly from the cache before waiting for new data to arrive. In fact, it is often helpful to render a larger region of the image than just the "window", to provide an interactive user with navigation context. As the client receives more data from the server, the cache contents grow and rendering is repeated to progressively refine the image quality both within and around the focus window. The actual communication between client and server consists of request/response pairs. The request identifies the focus window via its geometric attributes, rather than low-level JPEG2000 constructs. This has several benefits:

1) JPIP requests can be compact and intuitive, facilitating their inclusion as URL's in HTML pages;

2) JPIP requests can be used to extract an appropriate image region from a non-JPEG 2000 file (e.g. a server may offer a transcoding service);

3) the "window" expresses an end-user's ultimate interests, rather than a client's interpretation of those interests in terms of JPEG 2000 elements allowing the server to determine the best way to respond to the request.

The JPIP protocol is designed to be transport-neutral. A primary objective is that JPIP communication can be realized using HTTP/1.1 as the underlying transport, without interfering with existing HTTP infrastructure.

As suggested by Fig. 17, the client typically caches the data-bin contents transferred by the server in response to previous requests. JPIP identifies each request as either stateless or statefull. Statefull requests are made in the context of a communication session, whose state is maintained by the server. Although sessions require the server to allocate some persistent resources, sessions can significantly reduce its computational and I/O load. In the worst case, a stateless server may need to open the image, interpreting, extracting and reordering its contents each time a request arrives. On the other hand, a statefull server can generally minimize its interaction with the original image file, relying on information accumulated while processing previous requests. Perhaps even more significantly, a statefull server may keep track of the number of bytes from each data-bin which it has already sent to the client. In this way, only the missing information need be sent in response to future requests.

The client manages connection establishment, channel transport negotiation, application requests for a ROI, generation of requests to the server and processing the asynchronous data received from the server. The client uses the ROI request to define the resolution size location, component, layers, and other JPEG 2000 parameters of interest.

The server response delivers image and image related data in precinct-based streams, tile-based streams or whole images. JPIP servers store the state of a communication session and maintain a cache model of the client to avoid sending information that the client already has in its cache from previous request. Decomposition and display process at the client can be decoupled from the client-server communication. For efficient communication, the server can transmit only the data that is needed to fully reconstruct the ROI, and for efficient computation the client can use only the data in needs for the ROI.

4 Conclusions

The proposed JPEG 2000 scheme appears to offer similar or improved image quality performance relative to the current JPEG standard for compression of various images, yet has additional features useful for these applications, indicating that it should be included as an additional standard transfer syntax.
The superiority of the JPEG 2000 can be subjectively judged with Fig. 18, where the reconstructed image Lena is shown after compression of 0.25bpp.

JPEG 2000 offers significant improvements over previous image compression standards not only in terms of compression performance, but also coding flexibility. However, to fully utilize the features available in JPEG 2000, understanding of both the encoding algorithm and the parameter set used to control is required.
JPIP has been designed to provide efficient data transfer, responsive perfor-

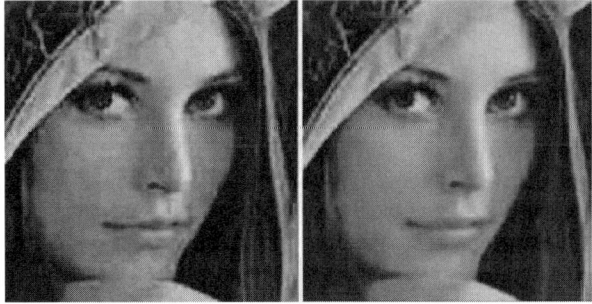

Fig. 18. Reconstructed images compressed at 0.25bpp by means of a) JPEG and b) JPEG 2000

mance, flexibility and effective random access for JPEG 2000 data. Its philosophy is consistent across all data types, including code-stream headers, compressed imagery data, and meta data. This allows JPIP to provide interactive services for all members of the JPEG 2000 family of files, including JP2, JPX, MJP, JPM and later JP3D. Moreover, JPIP servers can be developed to efficiently meet the needs of a wide range of applications, from simple image browsing, to sophisticated multi-channel navigation of massive hyperspectral images overlayed with context-dependent meta data.

References

1. Taubman D. and Marcellin M. (2002) *JPEG 2000: image compression fundamentals, standards and practices*. Kluwer Academic Publishers, 2002.
2. ISO/IEC 15444-1 and ITU-T Recommmendation T.800, Information technology - JPEG 2000 image coding system, 2002.
3. ISO/IEC 14495-1 and ITU-T Recommmendation T.87, Information technology - Lossless and near-lossless compressionn of continuous-tone still images, 2000.
4. Taubman D.(1998). EBCOT: Embedded block coding with optimized truncation. Tech. Tep. N1020R, ISO/IEC JTC 1/SC29/WG 1, Octber 1998.
5. http://www.jpeg.org/jpeg.html.
6. Taubman D.(2000). High performance scalable image compression with EBCOT *IEEE Trans. Image Proc.*, 9(7), pp. 1158- 1170, 2000.
7. Adams M.D. (2001).   The JPEG-2000 Still Image Compression Standard, Tech.Rep. N2412, ISO/IEC JTC 1/SC 29/WG 1 September 2001.
8. Santa-Cruz D., Ebrahimi T., Larsson M., Askelof J. and C. A. Christopoulos C.A. (1999). Region of Interest Coding in JPEG 2000 for Interactive Client/Server Applications, In Proceedings IEEE 3rd Workshop on Multimedia Signal Processing, pp.389-394, September 1999.
9. Christopoulos C.A., Askelof J. and Larsson M. (2000) Efficient Methods for Encoding Regions of Interest in the Upcoming JPEG 2000 Still Image Coding Standard, *IEEE Signal Processing Letters*, Vol. 7, No. 9, pp. 247-249, September 2000.
10. Deshpande S. and Zeng W. (2001) Scalable Streaming of JPEG2000 Images Using Hypertext Transfer Protocol, *Proc. ACM*, MM, 372-281, 2001.

New Experiments on Word Recognition Without Segmentation

Khalid Saeed, Marek Tabedzki

Faculty of Computer Science, Bialystok Technical University
Wiejska 45A, 15-351 Bialystok, Poland[1].
e-mail: {khalids, tabedzki} @wi.pb.edu.pl
http://aragorn.pb.bialystok.pl/~zspinfo/

Abstract. A new hybrid system for word recognition is discussed in this work. The system is based on a modification to the view-based approach presented in authors' previous works. The system does not need thinning or segmentation of the analyzed word. The word is treated as a whole image. The characteristic vectors taken from both top and bottom views of the image are processed with the method of minimal eigenvalues of Töeplitz matrices. The obtained series of minimal eigenvalues are used for classification with Artificial Neural Networks. The results of the experiments on a set of common English words are presented.

1. Introduction

In this paper we present further modification with new experiments on the method of word classification and recognition presented in our previous works [1-2]. The conventional methods and the most known of them need to deal with either separated word letters [3-7] or, the classifying algorithms suppose to separate the word into letters (process of segmentation) in their preprocessing stages [8-10]. In this paper, however, the word is looked at as a single complete object ready for processing without any preprocessing stages (Fig. 1). The approach is not presented for the first time. It was applied to groups of animal names [1-2]. In [1] Neural Networks were used in classification while in [2] the recognition system used Töeplitz matrices for image description and the k-Nearest Neighbor classifier. Here, it is applied to recognize a number of commonly used English words, printed with various fonts.

The main idea in this method is based on a hybrid approach using the idea of fusing the view-based algorithm with the algorithm of minimal eigenvalues of Töeplitz matrices. The essential ideas of the view-based recognition system were presented in [11-12]. Originally, it was used to recognize Latin characters. In case of words only two in four views are analyzed, the upper and lower views. The most significant characteristic points are extracted from each image to form the feature vector describing the tested word. This vector is then used to create Töeplitz matrices,

---

[1] This work was supported by the Rector of Bialystok Technical University – grant no. W/WI/10/07

according to the algorithm of minimal eigenvalues [13-14]. The series of the minimal eigenvalues obtained from these matrices are the basis for further classification.

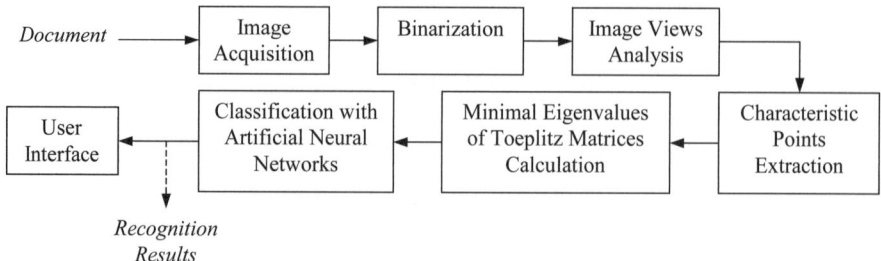

Fig. 1. Block diagram

In [2] words were classified with the Nearest Neighbor method – characteristic vectors of tested words were compared point-to-point to vectors in the learning set to find the most similar one. In former researches concerning character recognition, the method of Töeplitz matrices proved to give very good results and high Success Rate when used together with an ANN-based classifier. This hybrid approach allowed obtaining promising results [12]. That is why the authors used Artificial Neural Networks [15] as classifiers in their experiments. In this case the learning set LS is used to train the neural network NN. The series of minimal eigenvalues calculated for the word under testing is applied as the input to the neural network. At the output we get a class label to which the given word should be categorized.

The method was tested on database of 150 different words – we used a list of most common English words [16]. Each word was printed with 150 different fonts (small caps only), both standard serif or sans-serif fonts as well as fonts imitating handwriting (examples of the used fonts were presented in our previous works [1-2]). One-third of this database was our LS (the part containing knowledge of our system). The effectiveness of the method was tested with the remaining part of the database.

Our goal is to test how our system performs in noticeably different conditions than the typical character recognition system deals with. Thus we introduce a large number of classes already larger than in our previous work and considerably larger than in a typical character recognition system. Many other methods concentrate on finding a large number of characteristic data and a large number of examples for each class. Another way is followed in order to limit unnecessary growth of data and to show how our system performs with the reduced data set dimension.

2. View-Based Approach

This idea was first presented and fully described in our papers in [12], [17]. At first it was used for recognition of single characters. Here it is applied to recognize whole words. Hereafter, for the reader convenience, here we repeat the basic theory introduced in previous works [1-2], [12], [17] as well as its modification.

This method bases on the fact, that for correct image recognition we usually need only partial information about its shape – its silhouette or contour.

Two "views" of each word are examined to extract from them a characteristic vector, which describes the given word. The view is a set of points that plot one of two projections of the object (top or bottom) – it consists of pixels belonging to the contour of a word and having extreme values of y coordinate – maximal for top, and minimal for bottom view (Fig. 2).

Fig. 2. Two views of a sample word

Both of the essential conventional stages of segmentation and thinning in the image processing techniques are unnecessary here. Only the shape of the word is analyzed. The only necessary preprocessing stage is the image binarization to convert the scanned image into a black-and-white one.

Next, characteristic points are marked out on the surface of each view to describe the shape of that view. The method of selecting these points and their amount may vary. In our experiments 12 points are taken for each view (the number of points was 30 in previous works, but without Töeplitz considerations).

To find the characteristic points, one needs to divide the word image vertically into a number of identical segments equal to the number of points we want to obtain. Next, we find the position of the highest and the lowest pixel in each segment – these are the points of top and bottom views (Fig. 3).

Fig. 3. Characteristic points

The next step is the calculation of y coordinates for the selected points. Thus we obtain two 12-element characteristic vectors describing the given word.

Next, these two vectors together with their two values describing the aspect ratio of the picture (width by height) are transformed into a one 26-element vector, which describes the given word to be the base for further analysis. It is also possible to directly use this vector in the classification process. This time we use an additional transformation stage to stress the characteristics of the tested word.

3. Minimal Eigenvalues Algorithm

In the next step the values from the characteristic vector are treated by the method of minimal eigenvalues of Töeplitz matrices [13], [18]. Only values from views are used. The values from each of the two views are processed individually, so we create two series of Töeplitz matrices and obtain two series of their minimal eigenvalues.

This method has proved its feasibility in many of our previous works. It gave good results for many issues related to the recognition of text, voice, signature, etc. This time it is applied to word recognition.

According to Töeplitz algorithm [18], the characteristic vector elements are considered as the coefficients of Taylor series:

$$T(p) = c_0 + c_1 p + c_2 p^2 + ... + c_n p^n + ... \tag{1}$$

which are used to form (Eq.2):

$$[H] = \begin{bmatrix} c_0 & c_1 & c_2 & ... \\ c_{-1} & c_0 & c_1 & ... \\ c_{-2} & c_{-1} & c_0 & ... \\ ... & ... & ... & ... \end{bmatrix} \tag{2}$$

where $[H]$ is an infinite Hermitian matrix, $c_{-i} = c_i$ for all $i = 1 - n$ and is of Töeplitz type. From these matrices, calculate the minimal eigenvalues $\lambda_{min}\{D_i\}$ for $i = 0, 1, 2, ..., n$. Then, the following feature vector is formed:

$$F = \{\lambda_0, \lambda_1, \lambda_2, ..., \lambda_n\} \tag{3}$$

Thus we obtain a monotonically nonincreasing series, which furnishes a good description of the image it represents, even when the image is very complicated [13]. Fig.4 shows the behavior of the λ's for three different words. The curves of the same word are similar, but for different words they differ from each other.

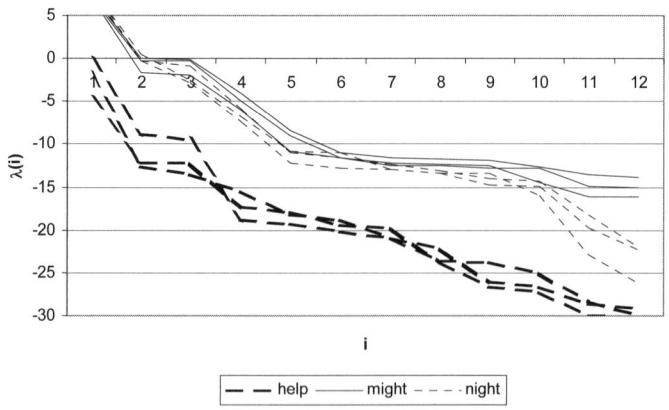

Fig. 4. Series of minimal eigenvalues for different words

For each view we calculate a series of twelve minimal eigenvalues to get two 12-element vectors and one 2-element vector (ratio information) describing the given word, to be the base for the further classification. These three vectors are normalized, according to the formula of Eq. 4 so that their values are in the range <0;1>.

$$y_j \leftarrow \frac{y_j}{\sqrt{y_1^2 + y_2^2 + \ldots + y_N^2}} \tag{4}$$

It is worth noticing that the number of computed eigenvalues is smaller than that in the previous experiments. This is a trial to reduce the calculation time while at the same time improving the performance.

4. Classification with Artificial Neural Networks

For the sake of classification, the computed two series of minimal eigenvalues describing the two views of the tested word together with the aspect ratio values of input image, are combined into one 26-element feature vector.

For classification stage one needs to gather a set of examples, used to train the Neural Network and the base for classification. These examples are already classified words – vectors calculated in the same manner, as described above, each labeled the name (or ID number) of its class. This set of examples forms the Learning Set LS. In the experiments presented in this work we use 1/3 of collected samples as an LS – that is 50 examples out of the 150 words. The rest of our database is used for testing purposes (Test Set - TS).

To classify a given word with the method of Nearest Neighbor [19] we need to compare its characteristic vector point-to-point to the characteristic vectors of all examples contained in the LS and find the most similar word and assume the tested vector belongs to the same class as that of the nearest neighbor.

Despite its advantages this method can be time-consuming, especially in the case of huge data sets. To avoid this, we use Artificial Neural Networks.

In this case a characteristic vector describing the given word, obtained from the series of minimal eigenvalues is an input data for the Network. We used Multi-Layered Perceptron: classic feed-forward neural network with one hidden layer (composed of 125 neurons), trained by the backpropagation method [15]. As a transfer function, we consider the bipolar logistic sigmoid function (Eq. 5).

$$F(n) = \frac{2}{1 + e^{-2n}} - 1 \tag{5}$$

The network has 26 inputs (the input vector describing each word is also built of 26 elements) and 150 outputs (the number of classes in our database). The number of neurons in the hidden layer is determined according to Kolmogorov's Theorem [20].

First, the network is trained with vectors from the TS. The training stage is performed until the recognition rate climbs to 95% (about 300 epochs). Next, the fully trained network is tested with the remaining words (words from the TS) – 26-element vector describing the given word (obtained from view-based algorithm) is fed into the input of the network. In the output we get information about the class of the input vector. Classification with Neural Networks has ended with 82% correctly recognized words. Table 1 presents the detailed results for some selected words.

Table 1. Results of recognition for selected words

Word	Recognition Rate
change	100%
might	96%
night	91%
make	85%
head	76%
house	59%
from	54%

As can be seen, the results for different words differ. For example, all tested samples of the word "change" were correctly recognized. On the other hand, for the word "from" the recognition rate was only 54%. On the whole the results are promising – for over one-half of the tested words, the recognition rate does not drop below 80%. Table 2 presents detailed results for different fonts.

Table 2. Results of recognition for selected fonts

Font Name	Recognition Rate
Arial Bold	96%
Georgia	93%
Goudy Handtooled	92%
Souvenir Light	82%
Comic Sans MS	67%
Dauphin	35%
Bernhard Fashion	22%

As can be seen, some fonts (mainly calligraphic or decorative) have lowered the success rate of the recognition. In fact, with more than half of the used fonts, the obtained recognition rate was over 85% and for some of them the effectiveness was even nearly 100%. The problem with untypical fonts can be solved by further expansion of the TS.

Table 3 presents some of the miss cases. The first column contains tested words, the second shows the false result and the third the percentage of the miss case to the whole number of iterations. For example, the word "cover" was in 17% recognized as "never". As can be seen, shapes of mistaken words are in fact very similar: "house" and "home", "hand" and "head", "down" and "draw" – and therefore, they can easily be classified inaccurately showing false results of classification. A possible solution to such a problem is to add some more characteristic points, and gather more data to distinguish those words more accurately. But because our main goal was to avoid increasing data dimension or characteristic vector size and hence long computations, we would rather add another stage in the system of recognition, to set apart those words of similar shapes. This will be the subject of our future works.

Table 3. Miss cases in the algorithm

Word	Recognized as	Rate
cover	never	17%
house	home	13%
at	of	12%
down	draw	11%
head	hand	11%
hand	head	10%

5. New Experiments

Our last work [25] introduced some modification to the above algorithm. We changed the manner, in which the Neural Networks are employed. Using Neural Networks as in previous experiments has some drawbacks. Because we need one output neuron to represent one class, the size of the Neural Networks (number of neurons and connections) depends not only on the size of input feature vector, but also on the number of classes. In the case of many classes, Neural Network may grow numerously. Even our 150 classes need Network composed of nearly 300 neurons and over 20 thousand neural connections. However, a set of 150 words is rather small – real-life system should operate on thousands of words. Maintaining such a huge network is troublesome. The problem does not lie in using such a network – calculations are performed very quickly and do not slow down the speed of the recognition system. The real problem is in the learning process. Big network means a lot of learning. Of course this is done only once, so it may not seem to have a real difference, but adding new classes is difficult. A big network requires also a much larger Training Set.

Because of this, we tried to accommodate different NN-based classifiers. In [25], instead of using one Network with multiple outputs, we used an array of Neural Networks, each with only one output. The number of networks is equal to the number of classes – one network represents one class and is responsible for detecting if the tested word belongs to its class. In such a case we observe the signal on the output neuron. No signal means that the given word belongs to another class and should be tested with another network.

In these first experiments we use a very simple network – two-layered feed-forward neural network with one neuron in the output layer and two neurons in the hidden layer, trained by the backpropagation method [15]. As a transfer function, we again consider the bipolar logistic sigmoid function (Eq. 5), as in the previously presented experiments.

It should be noted, that each network has only about 50 neural connections, compared with the 20 thousand ones in the previous case. Training even 150 such networks is a much simpler task than training one whole bigger one.

In the case of Neural Network array, one problem can emerge – sometimes more than one network detects the tested word as belonging to its class, and hence the given word is treated as unrecognized. It is a good place, to employ another ("second step") system, which deals with such problematic cases.

Experiments were performed on the same set of data described before. The obtained results are of slightly lower success rate than before – about 77% of correctly recognized words – although for some words the results were improved. This rate can certainly be changed by altering the Neural Network architecture (for example adding some neurons in the hidden layer). However, careful inspection shows that the rate of incorrectly recognized words is actually very low (only about 1% to 3%). The problem is in unrecognized words – over 20% of words cannot be recognized by this system. This is for both cases, when none of the networks in the array could give an answer and when the word is recognized by two of them. More details and results can be found in [25].

6. Conclusions

For the sake of comparison we repeat here some results of our former experiments (fully presented in [1-2]).

It should be mentioned, that the introduced modifications are not only concerning classification method or analysis stage. Some minor tweaks were also introduced in other parts of the recognition process, including altered characteristic points acquisition, different ratio-values inclusion, or the modified characteristic vector normalization. All this has impact on final results. Also the number of characteristic points as well as the number of calculated eigenvalues differs in latest experiments. The obtained results may not always be directly comparable, because of the different data sets – earlier experiments used smaller sets of different words than in the present work. The first experiments [1] with much smaller data set (less than one-half of the current data) led to an 88% recognition rate with classic Nearest Neighbor method, and 80% with Neural Networks (lower effectiveness results from the great number of classes and rather tiny TS).

Experiments with Töeplitz matrices for word recognition [2] were applied on a comparable in size set of different words allowed obtaining quite similar recognition rate – about 80% correctly classified words. In this work, however, the addition of Neural Networks to the Töeplitz approach led to noticeably high success rate.

Word recognition was also compared with the results obtained using Hidden Markov Models [21] by De Oliveira et al. [22]. The HMM classifiers for recognition of month names gave a recognition rate of 75.9%. The same author applied NN classifiers on the same base of words to achieve 81.8% recognition rate. Larger database was used by Lavrenko et al. in his work concerning handwritten words recognition in historical documents [23]. Recognizing words without segmentation was in a 65% classifying rate. Compared with these achievements, our results are more than satisfactory.

The presented in this paper modification combines View-Based method with the method of minimal eigenvalues of Töeplitz matrices and Artificial Neural Networks as a classifier. The hybrid system of Töeplitz matrices and ANN had already proved its high recognition rate in spoken word and speaker recognition [24].

The results of experiments show that this hybrid method is proficient for printed-word recognition. However, the efficiency for some of the words is not so high, although generally the results are promising and encouraging for further work. The problem of miss classification can be resolved by adding another stage to the system of recognition – dealing with problematic pairs of words. Alternatively, the stage of classification can be extended into tree-like process, with separate classes in its leaves. The presented method is elastic and easily accepts further improvements and adjustments. The future work will therefore concentrate on a more effective way of obtaining characteristic values. More experiments are being processed. Authors' next work will focus on adding the mentioned in the paper "second step" to deal with the problematic (unrecognized) cases. Moreover, the dictionary is being expanded while our team is working on testing the presented in this work methods with handwritten words.

Acknowledgements

This work is a revised version with new experiments added to the work published by the authors in the conference proceedings of ACS-CISIM 2007 under the title "A Hybrid Word-Recognition System."

7. References

[1] Tabedzki, M., Saeed, K.: View-Based Word Recognition System. *ICNNAI'2006*. 31 May - 2 June, 2006, Brest, Belarus, pp. 145-148.

[2] Tabedzki, M., Saeed, K.: A View-Based Töeplitz-Matrix-Supported System for Word Recognition without Segmentation. *ISDA'2006*. October 16-18, 2006, China.

[3] Burr, D.J.: Experiments on Neural Net Recognition of Spoken and Written Text. *IEEE Trans. on Acoustic, Speech and Signal Processing,* Vol. 36. 1988, pp. 1162-1168

[4] Cheung, A., Bennamoun, M., Bergman, N. W.: An Arabic Optical Character Recognition System Using Recognition-Based Segmentation. *Pattern Recognition*, Vol. 34, No. 2. 2001, 215-233.

[5] Amin, A.: Off-Line Arabic Character recognition: the-state-of-art. *Pattern Recognition*, Vol. 31, No. 5. 1998, pp. 517-530.

[6] Govindan, V. K., Shivaprasad, A. P.: Character Recognition – Review. *Pattern Recognition*, Vol. 23, No. 7. 1990, pp. 671-683.

[7] Jain, A. K., Duin, R. P. W., Mao, J.: Statistical Pattern Recognition: A Review. *IEEE Trans. on Pattern Analysis and Machine Intelligence*, Vol. 22, No. 1, 2000, pp. 4-37.

[8] Gonzalez, R. C., Woods, R. E.: *Digital Image Processing*. Addison-Wesley Publishing Company, 1992, pp. 7-9, pp. 413-414.

[9] Amin, A., Mari, J.: Machine Recognition and Correction of Printed Arabic Text. *IEEE Trans. on Systems Man, and Cybernetics*, Vol. SMC-19, No. 5. 1989, pp. 1300-1306.

[10] El-Sheikh, T. S., Guindi, R.: Computer recognition of Arabic cursive scripts. *Pattern Recognition*, Vol. 21, No. 4. 1988, pp. 293-302.

[11] Rybnik, M., Chebira, A., Madani, K., Saeed, K., Tabedzki, M., Adamski, M.: A Hybrid Neural-Based Information-Processing Approach Combining a View-Based Feature Extractor and a Treelike Intelligent Classifier. *CISIM – Computer Information Systems and Industrial Management Applications*. WSFiZ Press, Bialystok 2003, pp. 66-73.

[12] Saeed, K., Tabedzki, M.: A New Hybrid System for Recognition of Handwritten-Script. *COMPUTING – International Scientific Journal of Computing*. Institute of Computer Information Technologies, Volume 3, Issue 1, Ternopil 2004, pp. 50-57.

[13] Saeed, K.: A New Approach in Image Classification. *Proc. 5th International Conference on Digital Signal Processing and its Applications – DSPA'03*. Moscow 2003. Vol. 1, pp. 49-52.

[14] Saeed, K., Tabedzki, M.: Cursive-Character Script Recognition using Töeplitz Model and Neural Networks. L. Rutkowski, J. Siekmann, R. Tadeusiewicz, L. Zadeh (Eds), *Lecture Notes in Computer Science – LNCS 3070*. Springer-Verlag, Heidelberg 2004, pp.658-663.

[15] Haykin, S.: *Neural Networks. A Comprehensive Foundation*. Prentice Hall. New Jersey, USA, second edition, 1999.

[16] http://www.world-english.org

[17] Saeed, K., Tabedzki, M., Adamski, M.: A New View-Based Approach for object Recognition. *CONRADI, Research Review*, Vol. 2, No. 1. University of Vaasa, Turku 2003, pp. 80-90.

[18] Saeed, K.: On The Realization of Digital Filters. *Proc. The 1st International Conference on Digital Signal Processing and its Applications – DSPA'98*. Vol. 1, Moscow, 1998, pp. 141-143.

[19] Shakhnarovish, G., Darrell, T., Indyk, P.: *Nearest-Neighbor Methods in Learning and Vision*. The MIT Press, 2005.

[20] Kolmogorov, A. N.: *On the Representation of Continuous Functions of Several Variables by Superposition of Continuous Functions of One Variable and Addition*. Dokl. Akad. Nauk SSSR, 1957, vol. 114, pp. 953-956.

[21] Guillevic, D., Suen, C. Y.: HMM Word Recognition Engine. *Fourth International Conference on Document Analysis and Recognition – ICDAR97*. 1997, pp. 544-547.

[22] De Oliveira, J. J. Jr., De Carvalho, J. M., De A. Freitas, C. O., Sabourin, R.: Evaluating NN and HMM Classifiers for Handwritten Word Recognition. *Computer Graphics and Image Processing*. Elect. Engg Dept., Fed. Univ. of Campina Grande, Brazil, 2002, pp. 210-217.

[23] Lavrenko, V., Rath, T. M., Manmatha, R.: Holistic word recognition for handwritten historical documents. *Document Image Analysis for Libraries*. 2004, pp. 278-287.

[24] Saeed, K., Nammous, M.: A Speech-and-Speaker Identification System – Feature Extraction, Description, and Classification of Speech-Signal Image. Accepted for publication in *IEEE Trans. on Ind. Electronics – Humatronics*. New York, USA, 2006.

[25] Tabedzki, M., Saeed, K.: Modified Word Recognition System – New Performance. Accepted for publication in *IEEE-CISIM*. 2007.

Signature Verification by View-Based Feature Extractor and DTW Classifier

Khalid Saeed, Marcin Adamski

Faculty of Computer Science, Bialystok Technical University
Wiejska 45A, 15-351 Bialystok, Poland
http://aragorn.pb.bialystok.pl/~zspinfo/

Abstract. This paper presents a human identifying system on the basis of their signature image analysis. For feature extraction, the system uses the view-based approach with one of the three versions of Dynamic Time Warping (DTW) method. The experiments are carried out for each of the three versions of DTW and use various combinations of feature vectors. The average percentage of properly classified signatures has achieved 84%.

1. Introduction

Verification of documents authenticity is an important issue in our life. Despite its weakness, handwritten signature is still the most common way for authorizing and consequently assessing documents credibility. From legal contracts to payment bills the signature plays an important role and is used in everyday transactions. It is usually written on paper without any special equipment. Therefore, the only information available, which future verification may be based on, is the static image of the signature. This kind of authorization is obviously far from being perfect. It is not difficult for a skilled person to forge someone's signature. Shape of the signature can be duplicated when someone has an access to the original signatures and enough time to train.

Most of the research in automatic analysis of handwritten signatures is focused on verification and forgery resistance [1-2]. In this work we address another problem which is the identification task. In some cases there is a need to identify a person who initialed a particular form and the authenticity of the initial may be of second importance. Methods focused on forgery resistance may be too restrictive for this task. They require relatively large training set consisting of both genuine and forged samples that may be unavailable [1-2]. The presented method treats a signature as a word-like graphical object classifying it on the basis of its shape characteristics. This approach allows for designing fast and easy to train (only a few or even one sample per class) system.

This human identifying system can also be extended by various verification methods based on both static (signature image) and dynamic (writing time, pen pressure and azimuth) features to check for potential forgery. Dynamic features can be acquired by means of a tablet or a camera device [3-4].

2. Input data

In order to prepare data for classification algorithm, the images of signatures are first stored as Portable Network Graphics files (Fig 1). This particular format for graphical files provides lossless compression that retains all important features without introducing distortions and results in relatively small footprint. Images can be obtained by means of scanning devices from original documents. The segmentation of signatures from acquired scans is not considered in this work, but can be easily implemented by applying certain constraints on the position of the signature inside the analyzed document. Other problems are noise and defects caused by poor quality of documents and the scanning process. In our experiments we used threshold technique to eliminate minor distortions and convert images from grayscale into black-and-white binary map.

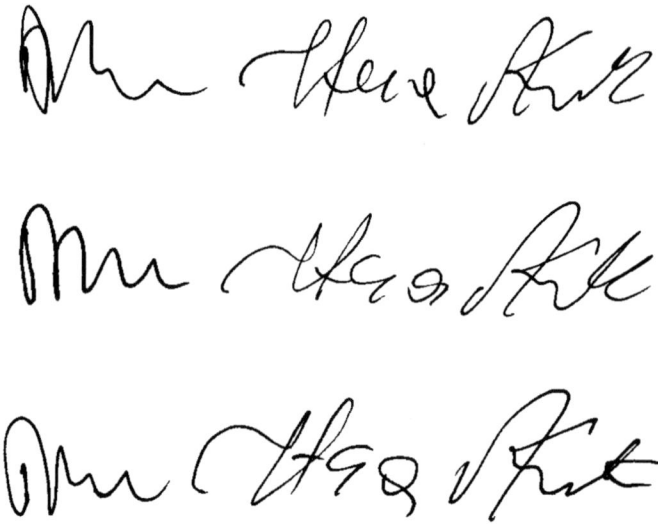

Fig. 1. Examples of signature bitmaps.

3. Feature extraction

The line of a signature in an image consists of a large amount of pixels. Depending on the resolution and thickness of ink trace it can even reach a few dozen thousands of points. Classification of such a complex object may pose a very difficult task. In fact, most of the points do not give additional information and can be safely ignored. There are many techniques for reducing their number whilst preserving the most important features that allow differentiating between signatures. Some of the approaches are: thinning [5], projections [6], view-based approach [7-8], and contour based techniques [9].

In this paper we used view-based approach which gave very good results in recognition of handwritten letters and typed words [7-8]. The view-based algorithm selects only those points with minimal and maximal values of y coordinates. Points with maximal values form what is called the upper view, whilst points with minimal values form the down view. This process is illustrated in Fig 2.

(a)

(b)

(c)

Fig. 2. Signature(b) with its upper(a) and down(c) views.

If a particular view is segmented into distinct parts all of them are concatenated in order to form one continuous object. As a result for each of the views the following feature vector is constructed (1):

$$Y =< y_1, y_2, ..., y_{N-1}, y_N > \tag{1}$$

4. Reduction of data and normalization

In order to further reduce the number of points a simple sampling may be used by selecting every n-th value from the acquired feature vectors. The value of n is chosen in such a way that it preserves the proportions of the analyzed image.

The method used in this system computes n using the following equations (2,3,4). The coefficient m controls the number of the resulted points ($m = 20$ was used during the experiments).

$$\max = \max(y_1, y_2, ..., y_{N-1}, y_N), \ \min = \min(y_1, y_2, ..., y_{N-1}, y_N) \tag{2}$$

$$H = \max - \min \tag{3}$$

$$n = H / m \tag{4}$$

Normalization of the feature vectors is important when the signatures are written in different scales. In this work the feature vectors were normalized to get values ranging in $< 0,1 >$ (5):

$$Y^R = \frac{Y^R - \min}{H} \qquad (5)$$

5. Classification

In order to classify the resulted feature vectors, a measure based on Dynamic Time Warping algorithm [10,11] is used. DTW algorithm defines a measure between two sequences $x_1, x_2, ..., x_{K-1}, x_K$ and $y_1, y_2, ..., y_{L-1}, y_L$ as a recursive function (6):

$$D(i, j) = \min \left\{ \begin{array}{c} D(i, j-1) \\ D(i-1, j) \\ D(i-1, j-1) \end{array} \right\} + d(x_i, y_j) \qquad (6)$$

The distance measure $d(x_i, y_j)$ can be chosen in various ways depending on the application. In our case, the Manhattan distance is used. The calculations are carried out using dynamic programming. The key part of this algorithm is the computation of cumulative distance $g(i, j)$ as the sum of distance $d(x_i, y_j)$ and one of the cumulative distances found in earlier iterations (7):

$$g(i, j) = \qquad (7)$$
$$= d(x_i, y_j) + \min\{g(i-1, j), g(i, j-1), g(i-1, j-1)\}$$

For classification purpose three modifications to the basic algorithm are applied. The first uses a window which constrains possible paths in the matrix of $g(i, j)$.

The second modification compares derivatives of signals. The third uses a slope constraint allowing warping path to follow only particular directions.

5.1 Window constraint

In order to reduce excessive warping of sequences, a constraint is applied that restricts warping paths to a region called window. In this work we calculate the window size dynamically based on the lengths of the sequences that are currently compared (8):

$$w = \min\{K, L\} * p\% \qquad (8)$$

5.2 Comparison of signal derivatives

In this approach we use Derivative Dynamic Time Warping [11] algorithm which compares first derivatives of sequences. For estimation of derivative a simple method based on averaging sequence slope is used (9):

$$y'(i) = \frac{(y(i) - y(i-1)) + (y(i+1) - y(i-1))/2}{2}, 1 < i < N \tag{9}$$

5.3 Slope Constraint

Slope constraint allows warping path to follow only particular directions. The constraint applied in this work is based on studies [10-11] and can be expressed by the following equation (10):

$$g(i, j) = \min \begin{cases} g(i-1, j-2) + 2*d(i, j-1) + d(i, j) \\ g(i-1, j-1) + 2*d(i, j) \\ g(i-2, j-1) + 2*d(i-1, j) + d(i, j) \end{cases} \tag{10}$$

6. Results

The aim of this study is to evaluate the performance of human identification process based on handwritten signatures and compare various modifications of dynamic time warping applied to this task. The database of the signatures consists of 60 signatures written by 20 individuals. Each of the initials was scanned with the resolution of 150dpi. For each person, each of the signature versions was used as a reference pattern to classify the third one. Therefore 120 tests (20 signature types x 3 reference patterns x 2 signatures being classified) were conducted in each variant of the experiment.

Tables 1, 2, 3 and 4 present the percentage of properly classified signatures. The column titles have the following meanings:

- *p* – percentage of maximum window's size,
- **DTW** – basic algorithm with window constraint,
- **DDTW** – dynamic time warping with window constraint,
- **DTWS** – basic algorithm with window and slope constraints.

Table 1. Percentage of properly classified signatures based on down views.

p	DTW	DDTW	DTWS
10%	59.17%	46.67%	70.83%
20%	59.17%	46.67%	70.83%
30%	59.17%	46.67%	70.83%
40%	60.00%	46.67%	70.83%
50%	61.67%	46.67%	70.83%
60%	63.33%	47.50%	70.83%
70%	65.83%	50.00%	70.83%
80%	65.83%	50.83%	70.83%
90%	62.50%	52.50%	**71.67%**
100%	54.17%	42.50%	67.50%

Table. 1 illustrates the results of the classification process using only down views. The classification rate in this case achieved 71% and was the highest in Dynamic Time Warping algorithm with both slope and window constraints.

In the second experiment (Table 2) only upper views were considered when identifying the signature owners. In this case results are better and the best classification rate is 76% of properly classified initials.

Table 2. Percentage of properly classified signatures based on upper views.

p	DTW	DDTW	DTWS
10%	68.33%	61.67%	75.00%
20%	68.33%	61.67%	75.00%
30%	68.33%	61.67%	75.00%
40%	68.33%	61.67%	75.00%
50%	68.33%	61.67%	75.00%
60%	69.17%	62.50%	75.00%
70%	70.00%	63.33%	75.00%
80%	70.83%	67.50%	75.00%
90%	70.83%	73.33%	**76.67%**
100%	50.83%	42.50%	68.33%

Next, both of the views were considered when computing the distance measured between tested and reference vectors. Combining information from upper and down views increased the classification rate to 83%.

Table 3. Percentage of properly classified signatures based on down and upper views.

p	DTW	DDTW	DTWS
10%	74.17%	60.00%	**83.33%**
20%	74.17%	60.83%	**83.33%**
30%	74.17%	60.83%	**83.33%**
40%	74.17%	60.83%	**83.33%**
50%	74.17%	61.67%	**83.33%**
60%	75.00%	62.50%	**83.33%**
70%	75.83%	65.83%	**83.33%**
80%	77.50%	65.00%	**83.33%**
90%	78.33%	68.33%	82.50%
100%	65.00%	50.00%	76.67%

In the last trial we also used both views but we increased the influence of the upper view on the final result by incrementing its weight coefficient in the total distance measure. The percentage of properly identified signatures reached 84%, then.

Table 4. Percentage of properly classified signatures based on down and upper views with weight factor.

p	DTW	DDTW	DTWS
10%	74.17%	60.83%	**84.17%**
20%	74.17%	61.67%	**84.17%**
30%	74.17%	61.67%	**84.17%**
40%	74.17%	61.67%	**84.17%**
50%	74.17%	62.50%	**84.17%**
60%	75.83%	63.33%	**84.17%**
70%	75.00%	65.83%	**84.17%**
80%	77.50%	64.17%	**84.17%**
90%	78.33%	68.33%	82.50%
100%	64.17%	47.50%	76.67%

7. Comparison with other approaches

To illustrate how the results achieved in this study relate to other works on the subject of off-line signature recognition an outcome of the algorithm presented in [12] is shown in Table 5. The researches used five reference signatures per individual and also provided forged examples of genuine signatures.

Table 5. Experimental results obtained in [12]

Type I Error (%)	Type II Error (%)			Total Error (%)
	Random	Simple	Simulated	
10.33	4.41	1.67	15.67	8.02

It is difficult to compare both approaches because the experiment in [12] was focused on signature verification. However, it is worth to mention that despite using five referenced signatures the rejection error (type I error) is still relatively high. In our study we used only one reference signature per subject which made our task very difficult. In some applications, however, where additional reference samples are unavailable it may be an important asset.

8. Conclusions

In this work we presented a human identifying method using handwritten signatures. The method is based on a combination of view-based approach for image classification and the Dynamic Time Warping classifying algorithm. Although the proper recognition rate has achieved 84% it is worth noticing that there is only one reference signature per subject in the training set. Most of the systems use six or more genuine signatures and several forgeries for each subject to prepare the classification algorithm.

This system focuses on identification task but as mentioned earlier it may be also supplemented by the verification process. In our future studies we are planning to build a hybrid system which can both identify and verify signatures using either offline or online information depending on its availability.

Acknowledgements

This work is a revised version of the work published by the authors in the proceedings of ACS-CISIM 2006 Conference. Both this and the previous works were supported by the Rector of Bialystok Technical University – grant no. W/WI/10/07.

8. References

[1] Ferrer M. A., Alonso J. B., Travieso C. M.: Offline Geometric Parameters for Automatic Signature Verification Using Fixed-Point Arithmetic. *IEEE Transactions on Pattern Analysis and Machine Intelligence*, vol. 27, no. 6, 2005, pp. 993-997.

[2] Lee L., Berger T., Aviczer E.: Reliable on-line Human Signature Verification Systems. *IEEE Transactions on Pattern Analysis and Machine Intelligence*, vol. 18, no. 6, 1996, pp. 643-647.

[3] Saeed K.: Efficient Method for On-Line Signature Verification. *Proceedings of the International Conference on Computer Vision and Graphics - ICCVG'02*, vol. 2, Zakopane,
Poland, 2002, pp. 25-29.

[4] Munich M.E., Perona P.: Visual identification by signature tracking. *IEEE Transactions on Pattern Analysis and Machine Intelligence*, vol. 25, no. 2, 2003, pp. 200-217.

[5] Saeed K.: Image Analysis for Object Recognition. *Bialystok Technical University Press*, Bialystok, Poland, 2004.

[6] Saeed K., Predko A., Rybnik M.: A Projection-Based Criterion for Polish Script Identification. *Computing, Multimedia and Intelligent Techniques*, vol. 1, no. 1, 2006.

[7] Saeed K., Adamski M.: Offline signature classification with DTW application. *XIV Conference on Informatics Systems - KBIB'05 (in Polish)*, vol. 1, pp. 455-460.

[8] Tabędzki M., Saeed K.: View-Based Word Recognition System. *International Conference on Neural Networks and Artificial Intelligence*, Brest, Belarus, 2006, pp. 145-148.

[9] Adamski M., Saeed K.: Classification of handwritten signatures based on boundary tracing. *International Conference on Neural Networks and Artificial Intelligence*, Brest, Belarus, 2006, pp. 201-205.

[10] Sakoe H., Chiba S.: Dynamic Programming Algorithm Optimization for Spoken Word Recognition. *IEEE Transactions on Acoustics, Speech, and Signal Processing*, vol. 26, no. 1, 1978, pp. 43-49.

[11] Keogh E. J., Pazzani M. J.: Derivative Dynamic Time Warping. *First SIAM International Conference on Data Mining Proceedings*, Chicago, IL, USA, 2001, pp. 187-194.

[12] Santos C., Justino E. J. R., Bortolozzi F., Sabourin R.: An Off-Line Signature Verification Method Based on the Questioned Document Expert's Approach and a Neural Network Classifier. *Proceedings of the Ninth International Workshop on Frontiers in Handwriting Recognition, IEEE*, USA, Washington DC, 2004, pp. 498-502.

Increasing Performance of Fingerprint Recognition Systems using Reconstruction of Ridge Lines Methods

Georgy Kukharev, Edward Półrolniczak

Szczecin University of Technology, Faculty of Computer Science and Information Technology,
ul. Żołnierska 49, 71-210 Szczecin
gkukharev@wi.ps.pl, epolrolniczak@wi.ps.pl

Abstract. The paper compares methods can be used for increasing recognition rate of fingerprint recognition systems using idea of reconstructing ridgelines. Some of methods useful for that purpose can be found in literature. The paper proposes such methods for increasing recognition rate in connection with image enhancement methods. There is also discussed influence of global image enhancement methods for reconstruction of ridge lines in the digital fingerprint image and the assertion is introduced that performance of recognition of fingerprint ridge lines can't be performed without preceding global image enhancement stage.

Introducing into reconstruction of digital fingerprint image ridge lines idea

Reconstruction of fingerprint ridgelines is a stage that is not clearly separated from other stages of image enhancement steps. In the article is recommended to treat the reconstruction stage as separate stage of fingerprint recognition process. By reconstruction of ridgelines there is meant the situation where every ridge line is analyzed and missing information is recovered basing on some premises in appropriate way.

Many of fingerprint recognition algorithms have been proposed in the literature [1][2][3]. Most of them treat fingerprint as pattern of ridges on the surface of fingertip. This structure is formed in the fetal period and is not changing during human life. There are several well-known properties of fingerprints:

- structure of ridges have different characteristic for different fingerprints,
- configuration of details is an individual characteristic,
- configuration of ridges and details are permanent and don't change with time except of scratches and injuries.

The uniqueness of fingerprints is determined by local ridge characteristic - minutiae. There are many minutiae details identified in ridges lines characteristic. Such characteristics can be for example the ridge ending and the ridge bifurcation. Very important stage of whole process is detection of minutiae. Efficiency of the recognition depends on precision of locating those minutiaes.

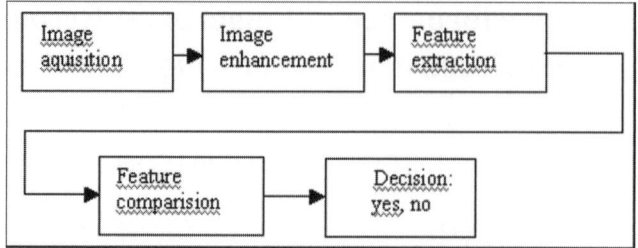

Fig. 1. Typical AFIS (Atomated Fingerprint Recognition System) model

In preprocessing step is very important to clarify visibility of ridge lines – then extraction of features will be more precise and number of extracted false features will be minimized. To achieve this goal many filtration methods have been proposed:
- bandpass filtration,
- contextual/directional filter,
- directional Fourier transform filter [8],
- Gabor filters [7], and other approaches.

Usually on such prepared image it is easy to find minutiaes, which are simply points where lines of ridges connects or ends.

It needs to be stressed that in every method there is present filtration step. Without this step results may strongly vary depending on finger and environment conditions. Filtration is the one method used to increase clarity of ridges but don't "repair" ridges in any way. Filtration methods are not directed to find missing information. Those methods try to remove noise and make more visible previously not visible data. Discussion of difference between filtering and reconstructing is situated in the next chapter.

Continuing review of recognition process it has to be stressed that properly filtered and reconstructed fingerprint image can be strong basis for minutia extraction. After minutiaes are extracted matching can be performed. Also there are many matching algorithms. Usually matching algorithms try to find common minutiaes.

Describing these methods is beyond the scope of this article and can be found in referenced literature.

Noisy and not complete fingerprints and the need of reconstruction stage

Digital fingerprint images are mostly not ideal. Image acquisition process is introducing many unwanted characteristics: noise, low sharpness and bad light balance.

Some other disturbing characteristics depends on the state of fingerprint. It can be injured, to wet, to dry. Some of problems can be illustrated by figure 2.

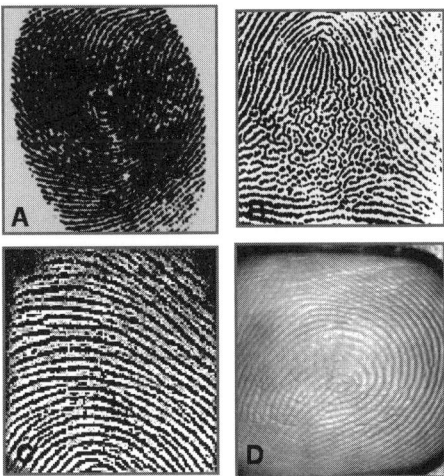

Fig. 2. Illustration of selected problems found in fingerprint images

On figure 2. there are four digital images of fingerprints presented. Source of images differs. Image "A" is taken using traditional ink method. It is clear to see that some ridgelines are not separated. In some places it is not easy to see where are they flowing – there are only black blurs. Image "B" has totally destroyed ridgelines pattern. Image "C" is taken using capacitive scanner – the image is noisy and ridgelines are sometimes not clear. Image "D" is taken using optical scanner – it shows that ridgelines are well visible but light balance of the image needs to be repaired. What does reconstruction method do in such situations? For example in case "A" reconstruction should bring ridgelines through blurs. It should try to connect ridges, which doesn't lie in blur regions using some premises like local ridge direction, distance between ridges and other parameters.

Image enhancement methods and ridgelines reconstruction methods

It is stated that reconstruction of ridgelines methods are not effective if they are not preceded by global image enhancement methods.

Some of image enhancement methods used as entry stage for reconstruction of ridgelines are:
- image histogram equalization,
- histogram stretching methods,
- low-pass filtering,
- median filtering,
- directional filtering,
- set of Gabor filters.

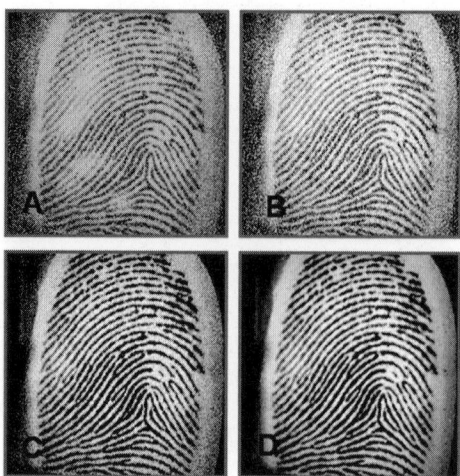

Fig. 3. Original noisy fingerprint image (A), results of image enhancement methods (B)(C)(D)

Figure 3. presents results of using some of image enhancement methods. By letter "A" is depicted original image on which image enhancement is performed then. There was added some distortion like noise, scratches, irregular white balance. After use of methods for histogram stretching the image looks like the one on image "B". Next step was histogram equalization presented on "C" – pattern of ridgelines is well visible now. Finally median filtering was used to remove noise as presented on "D". Median filtering removes impulse noise but is not capable to repair destroyed broken ridgelines.

The goal of image enhancement methods is to gain clarity of ridgelines pattern, remove noise and correct white balance. These methods are not pretended for completing data of ridgelines. One or more of those methods can be used in entry image enhancement block, which prepares for reconstruction stage. In regular fingerprint recognition systems a set of image enhancement methods is used. After that some of binarization methods and thinning methods are used. Usually image prepared for minutiae searching by image enhancement step contains broken ridgelines, which seems not to be true situation and incorporate into minutia pattern some false minutiae. On the other hand ridgelines, which were previously not clear in the image, are false connected now and generate false bifurcation minutiae. The only way is to introduce reconstruction stage in whole process. Some authors propose to use reconstruction-like methods called ridgelines pruning or minutiae pruning but it is performed on binary image where many of information is loosen. Those methods can't derive from rich of information image like gray-scale image. The gray-scale image is the one can give set of logically connected information that gives possibility to "understand" how pattern of ridges behaves. Image enhancement step is necessary as entry step for reconstruction of ridgelines. In some cases it is not possible to reconstruct if there are no clear premises.

On the figure 4. try of use reconstruction step without entry image enhancement stage is presented.

Fig. 4. Result of use of reconstruction methods without prior use of image enhancement

The same reconstruction methods but used for properly prepared image gives noticeably better results (figure 5.).

It has to be clearly said that the reconstruction stage can consists of many various methods can be sometimes found in image enhancement step. Sometimes the difference rely on properly tuned parameters which allows reuse some premises we can find in the image of the ridgelines pattern.

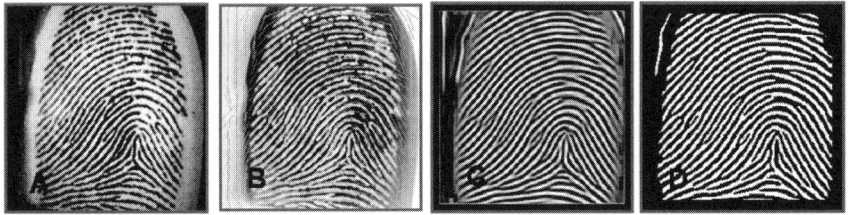

Fig. 5. Image reconstruction steps

Figure 5. shows as follow:
- image produced by image enhancement step (A),
- example of orientation field calculated (B),
- reconstruction effect achieved by appropriate use of Gabor filters (C),
- binarized result (D).

At the last image it can be easily found the ridgelines pattern has filled out missing parts contrary to results presented on figure 4.

Here can be formulated rules describing reconstruction stage:
- saves local direction of ridgeline,
- keeps flow of global orientation field,
- connects corresponding ridgelines – they have to lie on the same "route",
- generates connection points if it is reasonable,
- don't generate false minutiae.

Comparing different combinations of image enhancement and image reconstruction methods

To achieve the goal it is possibly to use plenty of combinations of image enhancement and reconstruction methods. Some propositions will be presented in that section.

First idea that could have capabilities of ridgelines pattern reconstruction is to connect low-pass filtering with gaining of spectrum.

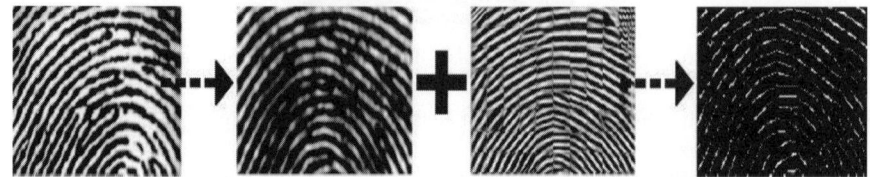

Fig. 6. Reconstruction idea using low-pass filtering and gain of spectrum

Gaining of spectrum can be rewritten as:

$$g(x,y) = F^{-1}\{F(u,v)x \mid F(u,v)\mid^{K}\} \tag{1}$$

,where F denotes spectrum of fingerprint image.

Low-pass filtering is used to remove noise observed in the image. Additional blur effect can make second step more efficient – image looks softer. Second stage gains the spectrum [5]. Taking into account spatial domain it gains local wave characteristics. It gives as a result some ridges repaired according to constructed rules. It is easy to seem the method has weeks – especially it has to be performed for local blocks. It results in discontinuity on block borders.

Another idea is to connect transversal smoothing with Gabor filtration [6]. It gives better results than previously presented method.

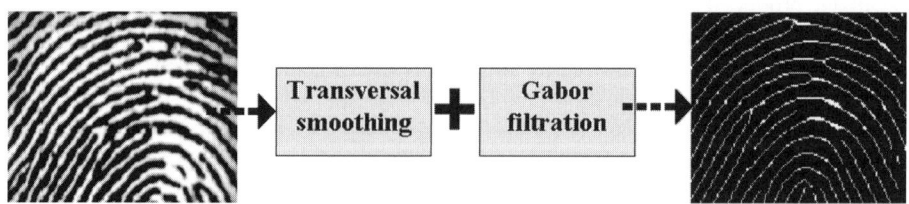

Fig. 7. Connecting transversal smoothing with Gabor filtration

Transversal smoothing [1] is operation performed on ridgelines so it is needed to locate the ridges in the image [4]. After point on the ridge is located the section perpendicular to direction of the ridge is smoothed using some smoothing filters (for example Gaussian filter). The procedure repeats for all points on in the ridge and for all ridges in the image. It results smoothen ridgelines but whole image is not blurred so it saves usable information for next step. In the step of Gabor filtration using properly tuned parameters it is achieved filling of gaps in the ridges. Behavior of

Gabor filtration in spatial domain strongly depends on calculation of orientation parameter in local neighborhood.

Gabor filtration is rewritten and presented below.

$$G(x,y,f,\Theta)=\exp\left\{\frac{-1}{2}\left[\frac{(x\sin\Theta+y\cos\Theta)^2}{\delta_x^2}+\frac{(x\cos\Theta-y\sin\Theta)^2}{\delta_y^2}\right]\cos(2f(x\sin\Theta+y\cos\Theta))\right\} \qquad (2)$$

In the formula (2):
- x,y mean localization of the center of Gabor filter mask,
- ¬ describes orientation of the mask,
- f denotes frequency of the mask.

Results and conclusion

Essential conclusion of the idea of connection enhancement and reconstruction methods is that it is not possibly to decide what combination is better because each combination needs to be tested in full fingerprint recognition process.

First scheme (connection of low-pass filtering and gaining of Fourier spectrum) presented in the article gives results collected in table 1. It leads to conclusion that fingerprint recognition scheme using ridge line reconstruction only is giving worse results than recognition using image enhancement only, but connection of image enhancement methods and reconstruction methods clearly rises results.

Table 1. Results of using first presented scheme

	Db_opt1	Db_opt2	Db_cap	Db_term	Mean
With image enhancement	85,5%	87,2%	90%	79,2%	85,48%
With image reconstr.	80,2%	81,1%	85,1%	72,5%	79,73%
Combination of methods	95%	97,5%	98%	85%	93,86%

In the second case (connection transversal smoothing and Gabor filters) use reconstruction only without using enhancement methods is giving slightly better results than using pure enhancement, but connection of proposed stages gives better results again.

Table 2. Results for second presented scheme

	Db_opt1	Db_opt2	Db_cap	Db_term	Mean
With image enhancement	87,5%	89,9%	92%	82,2%	87,9%
With reconstruction	88,4%	90,1%	93%	82%	88,36%
Combination of methods	96,5%	97,8%	99%	89%	95,56%

Results point to conclusion that using investigated combination gains results of recognition rate.

References

[1] Dario Maio, Davide Maltoni, "Direct Grey-Scale Minutiae Detection In Fingerprints", IEEE Transaction On Pattern Analysis And Machine Intelligence, Vol. 19, No. 1. Jan. 1997.

[2] Nalini K. Ratha, Kalle Karu, Shaoyun Chen, Anil. K. Jain, "A Real - Time Matching System for Large Fingerprint Databases, IEEE Transaction on Pattern Analysis and Machine Intelligence, Vol. 18, No. 8. Jan. 1996.

[3] J.H. Wegstein, "An automated Fingerprint Identification System", US Government Publication, Washington, 1982.

[4] Jeng-Horn Chang, Kuo Chin Fan, "Fingerprint ridge allocation in direct gray-scale domain", Pattern Recognition 34 (2001) 1907-1925.

[5] A.J.Willis, L.Myers, "A cost-effective fingerprint recognition system for use with low-quality prints and damaged fingertips", Pattern Recognition 34 (2001) 255-270.

[6] Tai Sing Lee, "Image Representation Using 2D Gabor Wavelets", IEEE Transaction on Pattern Analysis and Machine Intelligence, Vol. 18, No. 10, Oct 1996.

[7] Lin Hong, Yifei Wan, Anil Jain, "Fingerprint Image Enhancement: Algorithm and Performance Evaluation", IEEE Transaction on Pattern Analysis and Machine Intelligence, Vol. 20, No. 8. Jan. 1998.

[8] Sherlock, Monro, Millard, "Fingerprint enhancement by directional Fourier filtering", IEEE Proc. Visual. Image Signal Process. 141 (2) (1994) 7.

Design and Prototyping of an Industrial Fault Clustering System Combining Image Processing and Artificial Neural Network Based Approaches

Matthieu Voiry [1,2] ,Véronique Amarger [1] ,Kurosh Madani [1] , and François Houbre [2.]

[1] Images, Signals, and Intelligent System Laboratory
(LISSI / EA 3956), Paris-XII-Val de Marne University,
Senart Institute of Technology, Avenue Pierre Point, Lieusaint, 77127, France,
{amarger, or madani}@univ-paris12.fr
[2] SAGEM REOSC
Avenue de la Tour Maury, Saint Pierre du Perray, 91280, France
{mathieu.voiry or francois.houbre}@sagem.com

Abstract. Fault diagnosis of optical devices in industrial environment is a challenging but crucial task, since it ensures products' nominal specification and manufacturing control. Defects detection and issued information processing are among chief phases for succeeding in such diagnosis. A new scratches and digs defects detection and characterization method exploiting Nomarski microscopy issued imaging has been developed. It allows automatic check of optical devices during industrial process. Issued images contain several items which have to be detected and then classified in order to discriminate between "false" defects and "abiding" ones. In this paper, a processing method is proposed for a first step of pattern recognition from Nomarski images. A first phase permits to extract items images and a second phase allows us to cluster them using an unsupervised neural network technique, Self-Organizing Map.

1 Introduction

A major step for high-quality optical devices faults diagnosis concerns scratches and digs defects detection and characterization. These kinds of aesthetic flaws, shaped during different manufacturing steps, could provoke harmful effects on optical devices' functional specificities, as well as on their optical performances by generating undesirable scatter light, which could seriously damage the expected optical features. A reliable diagnosis of these defects becomes therefore a crucial task to ensure products' nominal specification. Moreover, such diagnosis is strongly motivated by manufacturing process correction requirements in order to guarantee mass production quality with the aim of maintaining acceptable production yield.

Unfortunately, detecting and measuring such defects is still a challenging problem in production conditions and the few available automatic control solutions remain ineffective. That's why, in most of cases, the diagnosis is performed on the basis of a human expert based visual inspection of the whole production. However, this conventionally used solution suffers from several acute restrictions related to human operator's intrinsic limitations (reduced sensitivity for very small defects, detection exhaustiveness alteration due to attentiveness shrinkage, operator's tiredness and weariness due to repetitive nature of fault detection and fault diagnosis tasks).

To construct an automatic diagnosis system, we propose an approach based on three main operations: detection, classification and decision. The first operation is based on Nomarski microscopy issued imaging. Three main advantages, distinguishing Nomarski microscopy (known also as "Differential Interference Contrast microscopy" [1] [2]) from other microscopy techniques, have motivated our preference for this imaging technique. The first of them is related to the higher sensitivity of this technique comparing to the other classical microscopy techniques (Dark Field, Bright Field [3]). Furthermore, the DIC microscopy is robust regarding lighting non-homogeneity. Finally, this technology provides information relative to depth (3-th dimension) which could be exploited to typify roughness or defect's depth. This last advantage offers precious additional potentiality to characterize scratches and digs flaws in high-tech optical devices. Therefore, Nomarski microscopy seems to be a suitable technique to detect surface imperfections. Issued images contain several items which have to be detected and then classified in order to discriminate between "false" defects (correctable defects) and "abiding" (permanent) ones. Indeed, because of industrial environment, a number of correctable defects (like dusts or cleaning marks) are usually present beside the potential "abiding" defects.

The present paper is essentially concerned by the second operation for which a new processing method of Nomarski images combining two phases is proposed. A first phase permits to automatically extract items images and a second phase allows us to cluster them using an unsupervised neural network technique, the Self-Organizing Map (SOM) [4].This paper is organized as follows: in the next section, the method used to properly perform detection and extract images of items is presented. Then, the Section 3 deals with the coding and clustering phases processed on these images. In Section 4, optical components automatic checking facilities are described and some investigations on real industrial data are carried out; the obtained results are also presented. Finally, the last section will conclude and give some perspectives.

2 Items Images Extraction

The aim of this first stage is to extract defects images from DIC detector issued digital image. A new method is proposed, which includes four phases:
- Pre-processing: DIC issued digital image transformation in order to reduce lighting heterogeneity influence and to enhance the aimed defects' visibility,
- Adaptive matching: adaptive process to match defects,
- Filtering and segmentation: noise removal and defects' outlines characterization.
- Defect image extraction: correct defect representation construction.

In the pre-processing phase, as presented in [5], the intensity of every pixel in the image is modified according to the relation (1), where P (respectively P') represents pixel's intensity before (respectively after) the transformation. M and σ are the mean and the standard deviation of grey-level in a 5x5 neighborhood of considered pixel.

$$P' = \frac{P}{M + \sigma} \tag{1}$$

The first consequence of the aforementioned transformation is to balance the image dynamic: lighting heterogeneities (due to non-uniform floodlighting) and local contrast modifications (due to focus and material thickness variations, or microscope optics imperfections) are corrected. As shown in Figure 1b, its second consequence is to enhance defects visibility in the processed image.

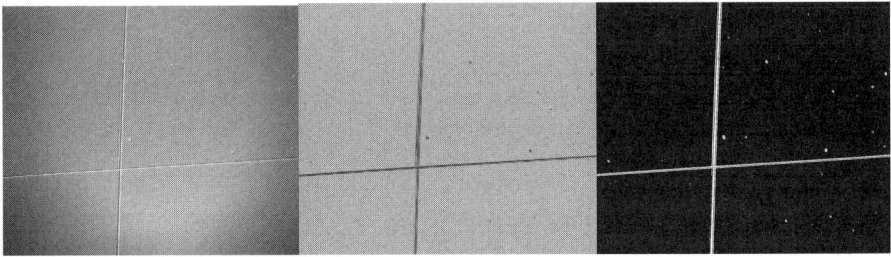

Fig. 1. a) Left: Image obtained from DIC microscopy; b) Middle: The same image after pre-processing phase; c) Right: The same image after adaptive matching phase.

In order to perform defects detection, a thresholding operation is performed, exploiting physical considerations. The choice of threshold is indeed very important: too small, defects can not correctly be detected, and too large, noise (due to surface's roughness) can be taken into account. To establish the threshold, the use of conventional procedures (as isodata or histogram modeling [6]) is ineffective in our case. We propose then to use a technique based on the detection of the roughness appearance to determine the effective threshold. The image is initially divided into squares of 8x8 pixels. Evaluating the number of squares whose the pixel of minimum intensity has the considered grey-level, the curve presented in Figure 2a is obtained. An interesting feature is that the obtained curve is almost the same for any image. The threshold T is experimentally set thanks to relation (2), where Max is the grey-level corresponding to the maximum of the curve, and H the WDMH (width of middle high) of the curve.

$$T = Max - H/2 \tag{2}$$

This approach gives good and repetitive results as shown in Figure 1c presenting the image of Figure 1a after matching phase. Thanks to this matching scheme, sensitivity of DIC microscopy is preserved, since all of the defects deeper than roughness range are detected.

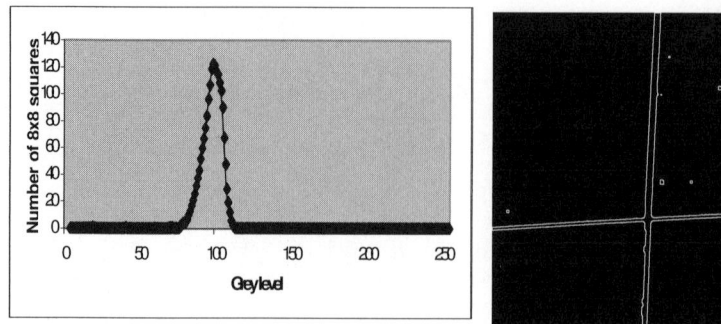

Fig. 2. a) Number of squares (8x8 pixels) whose the pixel of minimum intensity has the grey-level reported in abscissa. b) Image of Figure 1a after whole processing.

Then, classical filter and morphological erosion are applied to define defects outlines. Filtering consists in replacing each pixel P by the nth pixel in the sorted list of all pixels in a m-square neighborhood of P. For little n values, it is almost equivalent to a morphological dilatation but it filters isolated white pixels corresponding to noise. Then, by applying well-sized morphological erosion, we obtain accurate outlines of detected defects. Final result of processing is shown in Figure 2b, representing the image of Figure 1a after contouring phase.

Finally, the image associated to a given detected item is constructed considering a stripe of ten pixels around its pixels. Thus the obtained image gives an isolated (from other items) representation of the defect (e.g. depicts the defect in its immediate environment). Figure 3 gives four examples of detected items images using the aforementioned technique. It shows different characteristic items which could be found on optical device in industrial environment.

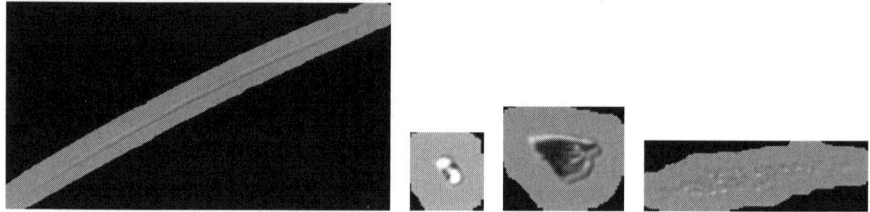

Fig. 3. Images of different characteristic items: a) scratch; b) dig; c) dust; c) cleaning marks.

3 Items Images Clustering

Information contained in generated images is highly redundant and these images don't have necessarily the same dimension (typically this dimension can turn out to be hundred times as high). That is why this raw data cannot be directly processed and has first to be appropriately encoded. This is done using a set of transformations described bellow.

3.1   Relevant Data Extraction

Such transformation must naturally be invariant with regard to geometric transformations (translation, rotation and scaling) and robust regarding different perturbations (noise, luminance variation and background variation). In this paper, Fourier-Mellin transformation is used as it provides invariant descriptors, which are considered to have good coding capacity in classification tasks (see [7]). The Fourier-Mellin transform of a function $f(r;\theta)$, in polar coordinates, is given by relation (2), with $q \in Z$, $s = \sigma + ip \in C$ (see[8]):

$$M_f(q;s) = \int_{r=0}^{\infty} \int_{\theta=0}^{2\pi} r^{s-1} \exp(-iq\theta) f(r;\theta) dr d\theta \qquad (3)$$

In [9], are proposed a set of associated features invariant with regard to geometric transformations:

$$I_f(q;s) = M_f(q;s)\left[M_f(0;\sigma)\right]^{\frac{-s}{\sigma}}\left[M_f(1;\sigma)\right]^{-q}\left|M_f(1;\sigma)\right|^{q} \qquad (4)$$

In order to calculate efficiently Fourier-Mellin transform in discrete Cartesian coordinates, we perform the convolution of the image with an appropriate filters bench proposed in [10]:

$$M_f(q;\sigma+ip) \approx \sum_k \sum_l h_{p,q}(k,l) f(k_0 - k, l_0 - l) \qquad (5)$$
$$\scriptstyle 1 \leq (k^2 + l^2) \leq r_{max}^2$$

where $f(i;j)$ is the grey-level of pixel whose Cartesian coordinates are $(i;j)$, $(k_0;l_0)$ are the Cartesian coordinates of the image's centre of gravity, r_{max} is the maximal radius of the image, and where :

$$h_{p,q}(k,l) = \frac{\exp\left(i\left[\frac{p}{2}\ln(k^2+l^2) - q \cdot \arctan(\frac{l}{k})\right]\right)}{(k^2+l^2)^{1-\frac{\sigma}{2}}} \qquad (6)$$

Finally, the processed features have to be normalized. In this purpose we use the centring-reducing transformation modifying each feature F_i as follows:

$$F_i = \frac{F_i - M}{\sigma} \qquad (7)$$

where M is the mean value of the feature F_i over the database and σ its standard deviation.

3.2   Data Clustering

A clustering operation is then performed using an unsupervised neural network technique, the Self-Organizing Map (SOM) [4]. This algorithm projects multidimensional feature space into a low-dimensional presentation. Typically a SOM consists of a two dimensional grid of neurons. A vector of features is associated with each neuron. During the training phase, these vectors are tuned to represent the training data. Similar data are projected to the same or nearby neurons in the SOM, while different ones are mapped to neurons located further from each other, resulting in a clustering data. Thus, SOM is an efficient tool for quantizing the data space and projecting this space onto a low-dimensional space, while conserving its topology. SOM is often used in industrial engineering [11] [12] to characterize high-dimensional data or to carry out classification tasks.

4   Implementation on industrial data

4.1   Optical device automatic control facilities

In order to validate the above-presented concepts and to provide an industrial prototype, an automatic control system has been realized. It involves an Olympus B52 microscope combined with a Corvus stage, which allows scanning an entire optical component (Figure 4a). 50x magnification is used, that leads to microscopic 1.77mm x 1.33 mm fields and 1.28µm x 1.28µm sized pixels. The proposed image processing method is applied on-line. A post-processing software enables to collect pieces of a defect that are detected in different microscopic fields (for example pieces of a long scratch) to form only one defect, and to compute an overall cartography of checked device (Figure 4b). It gives also some morphological measurements of detected defects and provides operators with a useful interface. This complete system has been successfully used to control quality of a number of SAGEM products.

Fig. 4. a) Automatic Control System. b) Cartography of a 100mm x 65mm optical device (pointed out scratch is 13mm long and therefore is detected in several microscopic field but is interpreted by post-processing software as only one defect).

4.2   Experimental set-up

Aforementioned facilities were used to acquire a great number of defects images. These images were coded using Fourier-Mellin transform with $\sigma = 1$ and $(q, p) \in \{(q, p)/(q = 0; 0 \leq p \leq P) \cup (1 \leq q \leq Q; -P \leq p \leq P)\}$ where $P = 1$ and $Q = 2$ (see Equation 3). Such transform provides a set of 13 features for each item. Then we trained a Self Organized Map with the images database. SOM's neurons are arranged along a rectangular grid and the distance between two neurons is the classical Euclidean distance. Three experiments called A, B, C were carried out, using two optical devices. Table 1 shows the different parameters corresponding to these experiments. It's important to note that, in order to avoid false classes learning, items images depicting microscopic field boundaries or two (or more) different defects are discarded from used database.

Experiment	Optical Device Identifiant	Cleaning	Number of studied microscopic fields	Correspondant studied area	Number of items in the learning database	SOM's grid shape
A	1	No	1178	28 cm²	3865	15x7
B	2	No	605	14 cm²	1910	20x8
C	2	Yes	529	12,5 cm²	1544	10x8

Table 1. Description of the three experiments.

4.2   Results and discussion

Figures 6, 7 and 8 show the lattice of neurons corresponding to the three experiments respectively. In these figures, the depicted defect for each node is chosen randomly among the examples of the database which are projected onto the node under consideration; the size of images is normalized, so the real scale is not respected. In the three cases, the similarities between adjacent nodes are apparent and some clusters of similar data are identified. Moreover, in major cases, database items projected in the same neurons have the same appearance; two examples are presented in the Figure 5. Such defects probably belong to the same class of defects. Thus, the performed clustering operation seems relevant. However, data projected onto neurons which are near "natural" class boundaries, are sometimes inhomogeneous.

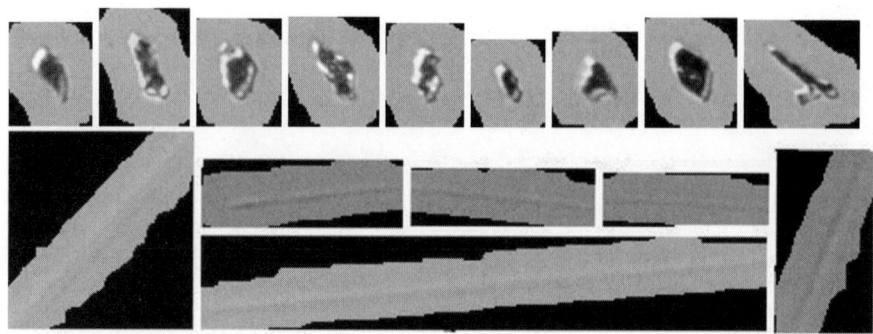

Fig. 5. Some items corresponding to the 28th and to the 93rd neuron of Figure 6 respectively.

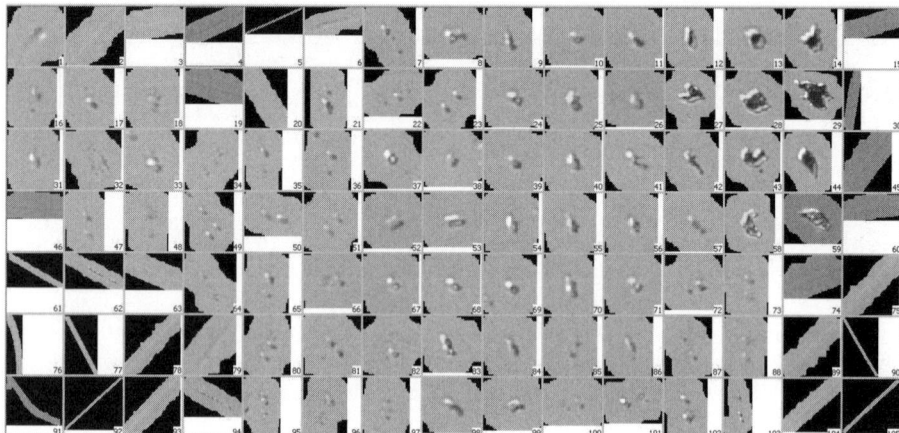

Fig. 6. Representation of the map corresponding to the experiment A.

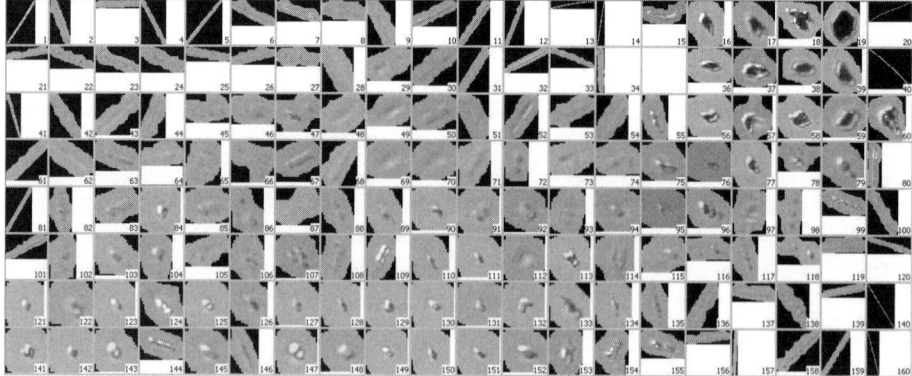

Fig. 7. Representation of the map corresponding to the experiment B.

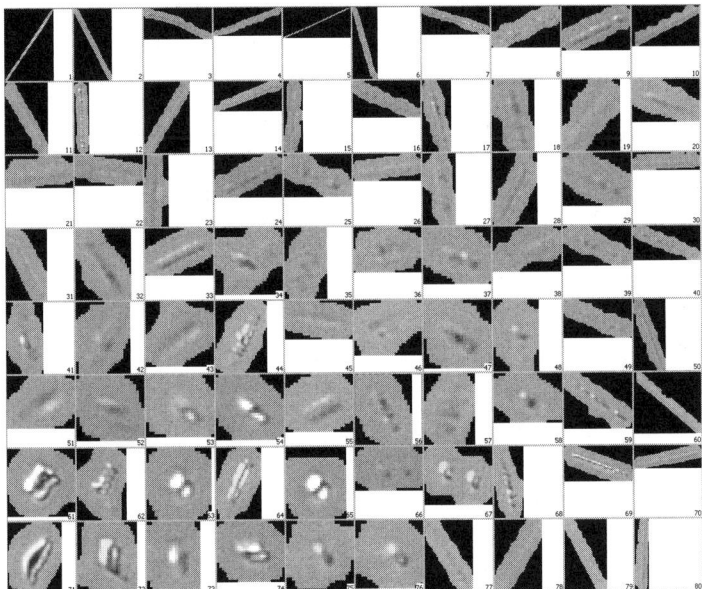

Fig. 8. Representation of the map corresponding to the experiment C.

When observing obtained maps from experiments A and B, we notice the presence of clusters similar in nature. On the contrary, when comparing maps from experiments A and B with the result of the experiment C, we find that classes corresponding to big black items (see nodes 28, 29, 43, 44 from map A and nodes 17, 18, 19, 37, 38, 39 from map B) are absent in the third map. This is coherent with the fact that experiments A and B studied both non cleaned devices and therefore dealt with the same kind of defects, unlike experiment C. On the other hand, it implies that the mentioned defect classes would probably correspond to dusts.

6 Conclusion

A reliable diagnosis of aesthetic flaws in high-quality optical devices is a crucial task to ensure products' nominal specification and to enhance the production quality by studying the impact of the process on such defects. In this paper, we propose an approach based on Nomarski microscopy, which provides robust detection and reliable measurement of outward defects. This approach has been implemented in a full system, which was successfully used to check a number of SAGEM optical components with an excellent reliability and sensitivity. But, to ensure a reliable diagnosis, this process should be completed by an automatic classification system in order to discriminate between "false" defects (correctable defects) and "abiding" (permanent) ones. We first need to extract relevant information from raw Nomarski images, to obtain exploitable data for a classification scheme. This paper has presented an items images extraction method and clustering of these images using an unsupervised neural network technique, SOM. Since well-founded clusters and pretty homogeneous neuron associated data are exhibited, the proposed method is pertinent and robust. A cluster corresponding to dusts has indeed been highlighted and comparable well-defined clusters have been obtained for two different devices. On the other hand, using SOM is in itself attractive, because it allows exploiting non-labelled samples (without expert intervention). However, data projected onto neurons which are near "natural" class boundaries, are sometimes inhomogeneous and we have only considered simple databases without cross-class items. If these limitations are overcome, classification could be directly completed by expert neuron labelling [13]. SOM can also constitute an efficient pre-processing phase for a finer classification.

References

1. P. Bouchareine: Métrologie des Surfaces. Techniques de l'Ingénieur, vol. R1390, 1999.
2. S. Chatterjee: Design Considerations and Fabrication Techniques of Nomarski Reflection Microscope. Optical Engineering, vol. 42, no. 8, pp. 2202-2212, 2003.
3. P. E. J. Flewitt and R. K. Wild: Light Microscopy. in Physical Methods for materials characterisation,1994.
4. T. Kohonen: Self Organizing Maps, 3rd edition, Berlin: Springer, 2001.
5. P. Bourgeat, F. Meriaudeau, K. W. Tobin, and P. Gorria: Patterned Wafer Segmentation. Proceedings of SPIE, vol. 5132, no. Quality Control by Artificial Vision VI, pp. 36-44, 2004.
6. R. C. Gonzalez and R. E. Woods: Digital Image Processing, 2nd edition Addison-Wesley, 2002.
7. A. Choksuriwong, H. Laurent, and B. Emile: Comparison of invariant descriptors for object recognition. IEEE International Conference on Image Processing (ICIP), pp. 377-380, 2005.
8. S. Derrode, "Représentation de Formes Planes à Niveaux de Gris par Différentes Approximations de Fourier-Mellin Analytique en vue d'Indexation de Bases d'Images." Thèse de Doctorat - Université de Rennes I, 1999.
9. F. Ghorbel: A Complete Invariant Description for Gray Level Images by the Harmonic Analysis Approach. Pattern Recognition, vol. 15, pp. 1043-1051, 1994.
10. G. Ravichandran and M. Trivedi: Circular-Mellin features for texture segmentation. IEEE Trans. Image Processing, vol. 4, pp. 1629-1640, 1995.
11. T. Kohonen, E. Oja, O. Simula, A. Visa, and J. Kangas: Engineering Applications of the Self-Organizing Maps. Proceedings of the IEEE, vol. 84, no. 10, pp. 1358-1384, Oct.1996.
12. J. Heikkonen and J. Lampinen: Building Industrial Applications with Neural Networks.,Proc.European Symposium on Intelligent Techniques, ESIT'99, 1999.
13. O. Silvén, M. Niskanen, and H. Kauppinen: Wood Inspection with Non-Supervised Clustering. Machine Vision and Applications, vol. 13, no. 5, pp. 275-285, 2000.

Image Pre-classification for Biometrics Identification Systems

Michał Choraś

Image Processing Group, Institute of Telecommunications
University of Technology & Life Sciences
S. Kaliskiego 7, 85-796 Bydgoszcz, Poland
chorasm@utp.edu.pl

Abstract. In the article we discuss the problem of image pre-classification in biometrics identification systems. In such systems acquired images contain various parts of human body. Specifically, we present fingerprint image classification and we introduce the original method of human ear image pre-classification based on the geometrical approach.

1 Introduction

Biometrics human identification based on features extracted from digital images has recently gained much attention in computer science community. In order to faster database search in the system's identification/decision module, the preliminary classification of images is often performed. It is a common procedure in many computer vision applications and therefore it could be also applied into a biometrics system. Classification of acquired images may be the second image processing stage (after image enhancement).

However, not all of the biometrics images are convenient to be pre-classified. Hereby we consider fingerprint and human ear images which can be pre-classified on the basis of geometrical features of extracted contours topology.

In Section 2 we present the basics of fingerprint image pre-classification. In Section 3 we introduce an original method of human ear images pre-classification. Experiments, discussion and conclusions are given next.

2 Pre-classification of Fingerprints

The first stage in a fingerprint image processing biometrics identification system is usually contour enhancement and extraction. Then on the basis of the extracted contours' topology pre-classification of images may be performed [1][2][3]. One of the most popular contour topology approach to fingerprint classification is based on ridges direction map obtained by Gabor filtering [4][5].

The configuration of ridges within a fingerprint may be classified as Arch, Loop and Whorl [1][6].

An Arch (Fig. 2) has ridges that start at the left edge of the fingerprint and flow relatively continuously and smoothly across the image towards the right

Fig. 1. Acquired fingerprint image (left) and the same image after contour extraction and thinning.

side of the image without any looping back nor circular patterns.
A Loop (Fig. 3) has ridges of high curvature that form a loop from either the left or the right side of the fingerprint. A Whorl (Fig. 4) also has high-curvature ridges forming more circular, concentric or spiral pattern.

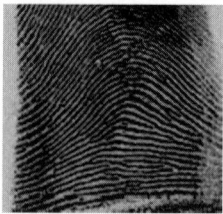

Fig. 2. An example of fingerprint image classified as Arch.

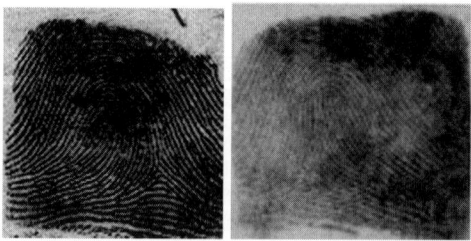

Fig. 3. Fingerprint images classified as Loops: a) right loop, b) left loop.

The two major approaches based on global or local features have been taken to automatic fingerprint identification. In a given fingerprint we may extract global features e.g. cores and deltas, or/and local features such as endings and bifurcations of fingerprint ridges [7][8].

Fig. 4. An example of fingerprint image classified as Whorl.

A core is essentially the centre of the fingerprint, and more accurately is the centre of a high-curvature region of ridges. A delta is a region in the fingerprint where ridges form a triangular configuration. The minutiae points (local features) are points where ridges end - ridge ending and points where ridges split - ridge bifurcation (Fig. 5). Moreover, other types of minutiae points are defined, such as spurs, islands, dots, lakes [8][9].

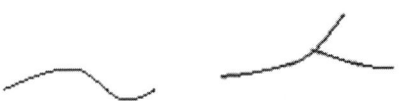

Fig. 5. Ridge ending and bifurcation

3 Pre-classification of Ear Images

Ear biometrics is a relatively novel anatomical method of human identification. But due to its advantages it has gained some attention recently [10].

In our previous work we introduced ear biometrics and some related work [11][12]. We have also developed several original methods of geometrical feature extraction from ear images [13]. Our approach is motivated by actual procedures used by forensic experts and the police [14][15]. Hereby we present an original method of ear images pre-classification in a biometrics system.

3.1 Ear Image Preprocessing

Most methods of biometrics human identification based on image analysis (e.g. face or fingerprint recognition) contain the pre-processing step. It is mainly due to the fact that images acquired in the enrollment step may be of low quality and may contain noise. This will surely happen if the images are acquired by distant cameras or if the environment cannot be controlled.

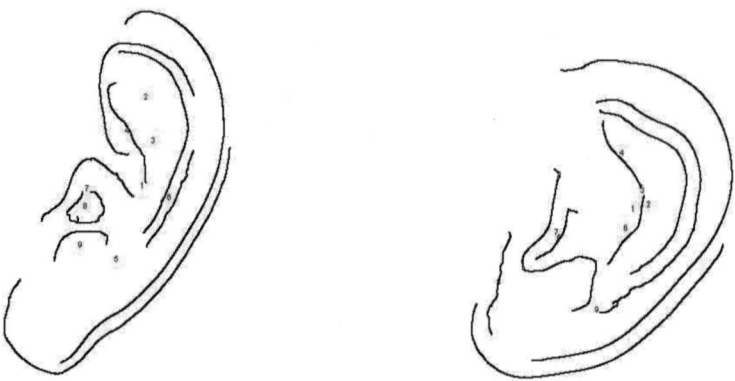

Fig. 6. Selected (longest) contours in the test images 'macfir' and 'szysob'.

Therefore in the proposed ear biometrics methods the following pre-processing operations are first performed:

- contrast enhancement,
- filtration,
- histogram equalization.

Most objects within images may be unambiguously characterized by their contours. It means that contours contain an important information allowing object description, representation and calculation of parameters enabling object recognition [16]. Contours extracted from ear images describe major information included in ear image. Therefore extraction of illumination changes is the first step of the proposed feature extraction methods for ear identification [17].

3.2   Contour detection based on illumination changes

Contours corresponding to earlobes are very diversified and contain enormous amount of information allowing ear identification. The purpose of the proposed method is to extract earlobe contours. We use local method based on pixel illumination values and changes [18][19]. We consider image window of the size of $n \times n$ elements. We usually use 3×3 image window (Table 1).

Let I_H and I_L be defined as:

$$I_H = \max \left\{ \begin{array}{l} g\left(x-1, y-1\right), g\left(x, y-1\right), g\left(x+1, y-1\right), \\ g\left(x-1, y\right), g\left(x, y\right), g\left(x+1, y\right), \\ g\left(x-1, y+1\right), g\left(x, y+1\right), g\left(x+1, y+1\right) \end{array} \right\}, \qquad (1)$$

$$I_L = \min \left\{ \begin{array}{l} g\left(x-1, y-1\right), g\left(x, y-1\right), g\left(x+1, y-1\right), \\ g\left(x-1, y\right), g\left(x, y\right), g\left(x+1, y\right), \\ g\left(x-1, y+1\right), g\left(x, y+1\right), g\left(x+1, y+1\right) \end{array} \right\}. \qquad (2)$$

Table 1. Coordinates of the 3×3 window elements.

Element	x-1	x	x+1
y-1	g(x-1,y-1)	g(x,y-1)	g(x+1,y-1)
y	g(x-1,y)	g(x,y)	g(x+1,y)
y+1	g(x-1,y+1)	g(x,y+1)	g(x+1,y+1)

For each image element $g(x, y)$, the difference in illumination values $S(x, y)$ is calculated: $S(x, y) = I_H - I_L$. Binary contour image $b(x, y)$ is defined as:

$$b(x, y) = \begin{cases} 1 & for \quad S(x,y) \geq T(x,y) \\ 0 & for \quad S(x,y) < T(x,y) \end{cases} \tag{3}$$

where:

– T is a threshold value given by:

$$T(x, y) = \mu - k * \sigma, \tag{4}$$

where:
– μ - mean value:

$$\mu = \frac{1}{n^2} \sum_{x=1}^{n} \sum_{y=1}^{n} g(x, y), \tag{5}$$

– σ - standard deviation:

$$\sigma = \sqrt{\frac{1}{(n^2 - 1)} \sum_{x=1}^{n} \sum_{y=1}^{n} (g(x, y) - \mu)^2}, \tag{6}$$

– k - certain value ($20 < k < 50$) corresponding to the sensivity of the described algorithm.

According to the described algorithm we obtain the binary image $b(x, y)$ with the extracted contours of the earlobe.

3.3 Ear Pre-classification Algorithm

Ears presented in images can be classified into left ear or right ear. Such classification is possible while basing on the longest contour within ear image. Such contour usually corresponds to the outer earlobe.

Its length is computed according to (7):

$$L_c = \sum_{q=1}^{Q-1} \sqrt{(x_{q+1} - x_q)^2 + (y_{q+1} - y_q)^2}, \tag{7}$$

where:

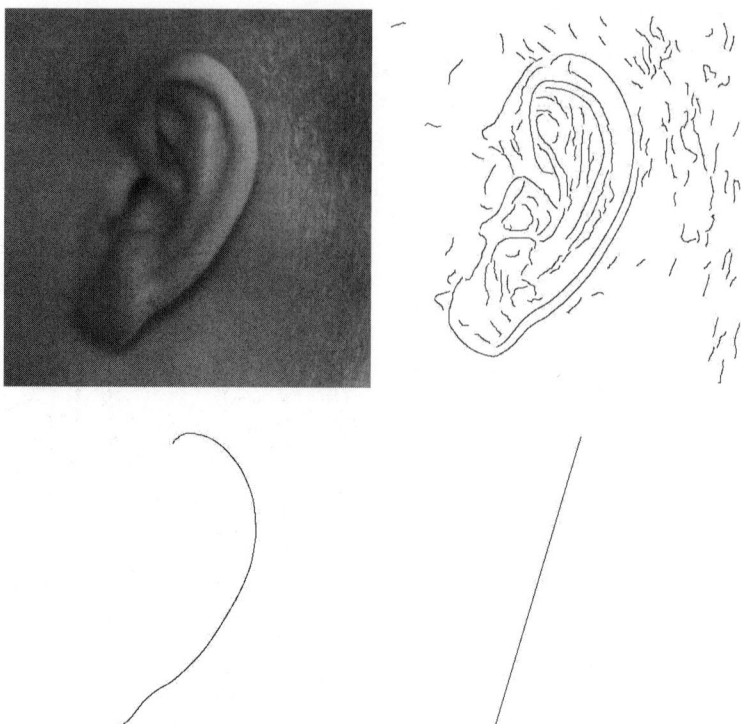

Fig. 7. The result of contour extraction and classification of the image 'macfir'. The maximal chord is tilted with the angle of $\delta = 73.3$. The ear is classified as left ear.

- Q - number of contour points,
- c - number of contours, for $c = 1, \ldots, C$,
- (x, y) - coordinates of contour points,
- q - indexation of the current contour point.

After evaluation of ear images from our database we defined so called *short contours*, which are eliminated. We eliminate the contours for which:

$$L_c \leq t \times L_c max, \tag{8}$$

where t is a parameter chosen empirically. In result of such processing we obtain images with the limited number of contours (Fig. 6).

Then we perform image pre-classification procedure. Firstly, we search for the ending points of the longest chord of the longest contour. We search for the first point of the longest contour l_{cmax} - let it be the point p_c with the coordinates (i_c, j_c). Let (i_b, j_b) be the coordinates of the current contour point p_b. We calculate the distances between the point p_c and the consecutive points p_b.

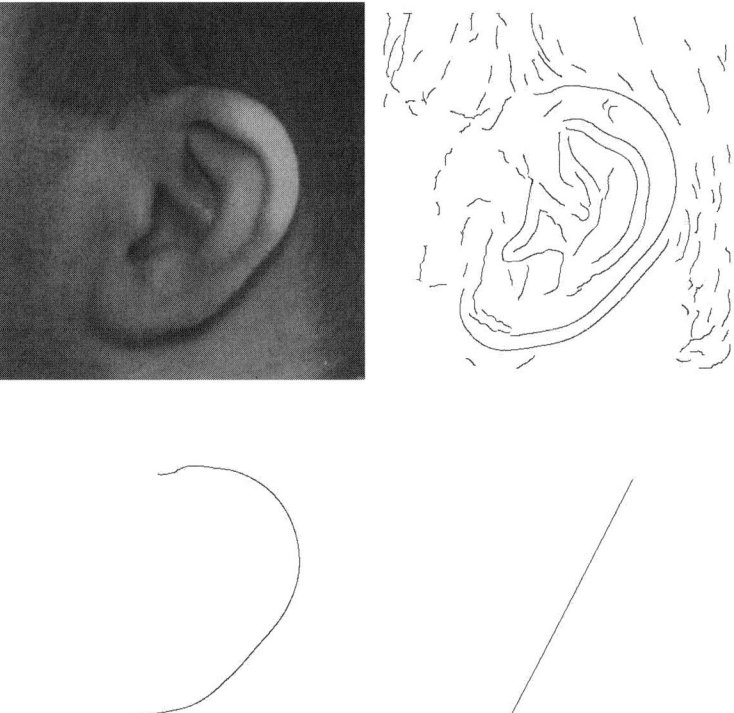

Fig. 8. The result of contour extraction and classification of the image 'szysob'. The maximal chord is tilted with the angle of $\delta = 62.0$. The ear is classified as left ear.

The maximal chord is defined by:

$$Chord_{\max} = \max\left\{\sqrt{(i_c - i_b)^2 + (j_c - j_b)^2}\right\} \qquad (9)$$

for: $b = 1 \ldots N$, where N is the number of contour points.

The coordinates of the current point in the image, for which the computed chord is the maximal chord, are denoted by (i_{bmax}, j_{bmax}). Then the inclination angle between the maximal chord and the horizontal image axis is computed. If the angle value $\delta \leq 90$ the examined ear is classified as left ear. If the angle value $90 \leq \delta \leq 180$ the examined ear is classified as right ear. The pre-classification is performed on the basis of the assumption that in the acquisition stage the ear is placed in the natural vertical position. Otherwise the point of intersection with the contour should be found. Then, we should determine if that point is placed on the left or right side of the maximal chord of the longest ear contour. However, in ear enrolment procedure ears had always been placed in the normal position.

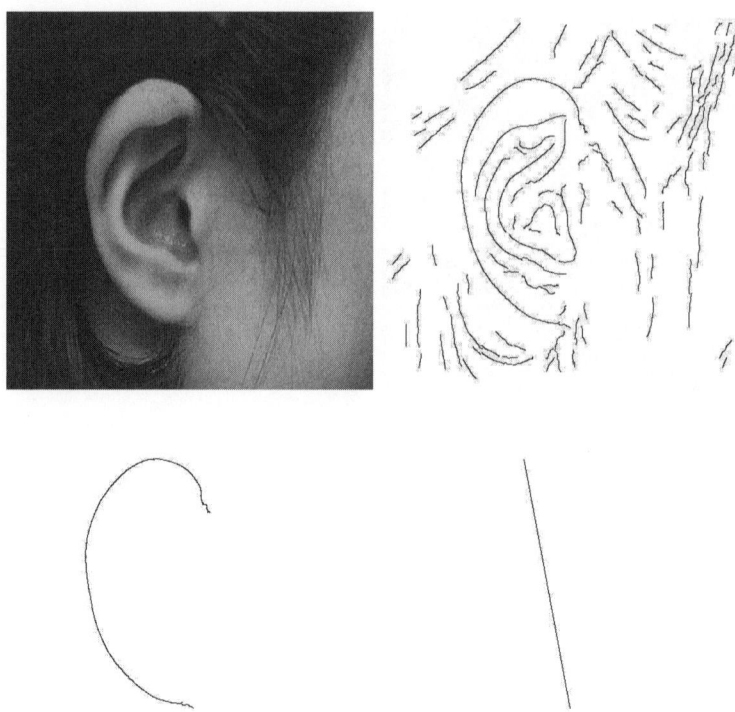

Fig. 9. The result of contour extraction and classification of the image 'prapod'. The maximal chord is tilted with the angle of $\delta = 100.8$. The ear is classified as right ear.

The results of ear classification for test images 'macfir', 'szysob' and 'prapod' from our database are presented in Figures 7-9.

4   Experiments

In order to perform the experiments, our own ear image database was created. The part of our ear database is presented in Fig. 10. In the process of enrolment, by analogy with face recognition methods, we store 10 images for each person (perpendicular to the camera $0°$, $30°$ and $-30°$, $60°$ and $-60°$) for 2 values of illumination in the room. In the process of acquisition we obtain ear images of resolution of 512×512 and 256 graylevels, which are stored in the popular image formats.

We tested ear pre-classification algorithm on images from 80 users stored in our database.

In our experiments we achieved error-free pre-classification for all the images from our test ear database (800 images).

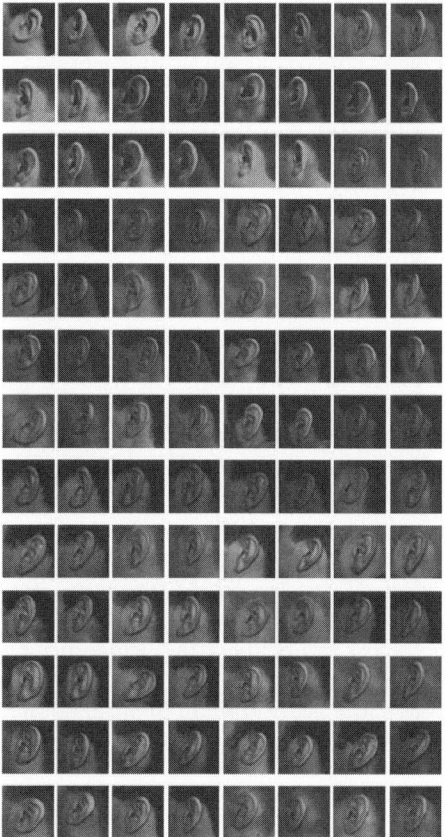

Fig. 10. Part of our ear images database. The images in 2 orientations 0° and 30° for a person are shown.

5   Conclusion

In the article we discussed methods of fingerprint images pre-classification. Moreover, we introduced an original idea of human ear images pre-classification based on geometrical parameters of the earlobe. According to our present knowledge this issue has not been addressed and published so far.

We performed experiments that prove our method to be effective. We achieved error-free ear images pre-classification on our test ear database.

In ear biometrics identification control access systems (and therefore in the pre-classification module) the problem of overcast ears (e.g. by hair) is marginal, since there is always the possibility of a proper ear image acquisition (with the user's cooperation) [10]. Therefore in the experiments we focused on images of the visible ears.

6   References

1. Halici U., Jain L.C., Erol A., "Introduction to Fingerprint Recognition," in: *Jain L.C. et al. (Eds): Intelligent Biometric Techniques in Fingerprint and Face Recognition*, CRC Press, pp. 153-192, 1999.
2. Hong L., Jain A.K., Classification of Fingerprints Images, Proc. of Scandinavian Conf. on Image Analysis, 1999.
3. Jain A.K., Pankanti S., Fingerprint Classification and Matching, in The Image and Video Processing Handbook, 2000.
4. Hamamoto Y., "A Gabor Filter-Based Method for Fingerprint Identification," in: *L.C. Jain et al. (Eds): Intelligent Biometric Techniques in Fingerprint and Face Recognition*, CRC Press, pp. 135-151, 1999.
5. Prabhakar S., Fingerprint Classification and Matching Using a Filterbank, PhD Thesis, Michigan State University, 2001.
6. Maltoni D., Maio D., Jain A.K., Prabhakar S., Handbook of Fingerprint Recognition, Springer, 2003.
7. Pankanti S., Prabhakar S., Jain A.K., On the Individuality of Fingerprints, IEEE Trans. on PAMI, vol. 24, no. 8, 1010-1025, 2002.
8. Maio D., Maltoni D., "Minutiae Extraction and Filtering from Gray-Scale Images," in: *L.C. Jain et al. (Eds): Intelligent Biometric Techniques in Fingerprint and Face Recognition*, CRC Press, pp. 1-34, 1999.
9. Prabhakar S., Jain A.K., Pankanti S., Learning Fingerprint Minutiae Location and Type, Pattern Recognition, vol. 36, no. 8, 1847-1857, 2003.
10. Choraś M., "Ear Biometrics in Passive Human Identification Systems," Proc. of Pattern Recognition in Information Society (ICEIS-PRIS), 169-175, Cyprus, 2006.
11. Choraś M., "Ear Biometrics Based on Geometrical Feature Extraction," Journal ELCVIA (Computer Vision and Image Analysis), vol. 5, no. 3, pp. 84-95, 2005.
12. Choraś M., "Further Developments in Geometrical Algorithms for Ear Biometrics," in F.J Perales and B. Fisher (Eds.): Articulated Motion and Deformable Objects - AMDO 2006, 58-67, LNCS 4069, Springer-Verlag 2006.
13. Choraś M., "Human Identification Based on Ear Image Analysis" (in Polish), Ph.D. Thesis, ATR Bydgoszcz, 2005.
14. Kasprzak J., *Forensic Otoscopy (in Polish)*, University of Warmia and Mazury Press, 2003.
15. Kasprzak J., "Polish Methods of Earprint Identification", The Information Bulletin for Shoeprint/Toolmark Examiners, vol. 9, no. 3, 20-22, 2003.
16. Pellegrino F.A. , Vanzella W., Torre V., "Edge Detection Revisited," IEEE Trans. Sys., Man and Cybern., Part B, vol. 34, no. 3, 1500-1518, 2004.
17. Marr D. , Hildreth E., "Theory of edge detection," Proc. Royal Soc., vol. B207, pp. 187 - 217, 1980.
18. Kim D.S., Lee W.H., Kweon I.S., "Automatic edge detection using 3X3 ideal binary pixel patterns and fuzzy-based edge thresholding," Pattern Recognition Letters, vol. 25, no. 1, pp. 101-106, 2004.
19. Acton S.T. , Mukherjee D.P. , "Area operators for edge detection," Pattern Recognition Letters, vol. 21, no. 6-7, pp. 771-777, 2000.

Application of Improved Projection Method
to Binary Images

Dariusz Frejlichowski, Alji Maow

Faculty of Computer Science, Szczecin University of Technology,
email: dfrejlichowski@wi.ps.pl, amaow@wi.ps.pl

Abstract. In this paper a new method of binary objects representation, based on modification of a widely known and utilized method of projection, is presented. Nowadays, two the most popular ways of combining projections for both coordinates (two vectors for each; horizontal and vertical projection) are: summation of both vectors components and concatenation of those vectors. The most important drawback of mentioned approaches is related to the fact that significant information is lost. The aim of this article is to show the new method of vectors combination – representation in a form of complex vector. The method was explored by using three different groups of binary images. Namely, airplanes and trademarks silhouettes (significantly distorted), and real radar images for comparative navigation.

1. Introduction

Binary representation is a very popular method of depicting objects which are to be recognized. Usually, the black shape on a white background is presented. It is used to different shapes, like digits, letters (for example: extracted from a car license), road signs, trademarks etc. The area of possible applications is almost endless.

In literature one can find two different ways of binary images representation – silhouette (the whole object, with its interior) and boundary (the contour of an object only). The most general classification of binary representation methods is strictly based on the above distinction ([1]).

The method of projection is a very common way of representing objects in aspects of their silhouettes, and more generally – all binary images. This method is so popular that sometimes different names are used for exactly (or almost) the same approach. For example, Fang et al. ([2]) called it *the projection profiles*, and Soltanzadeh ([3]) used *the projection histogram* name.

The projection method was used for example in recognition of signature patterns ([2]), classification of simple patterns ([4]), localization of eyes in face images ([5]), detection of the orientation (portrait/landscape) of a binary image page ([6]), recognition of Arabic signs ([7]) and letters ([8]), Persian digits ([3]) and comparative navigation ([9]). Those are only few examples, mentioned to point out the really widespread application of the method.

Roughly speaking, the projection for binary images relies on two stages. First of all, we perform two separate projections, for X and Y coordinate (so-called vertical and horizontal projections). Few examples of projected binary images (for different classes of shapes) are depicted on *Fig.1*. Sometimes in literature we can find other propositions, e.g. two or more vertical projections or combination of many vertical and horizontal projections for sub-images extracted from an image ([8]).

Let us concentrate our attention on the traditional and most popular way of projecting the image pixels. As it was mentioned, we have two projections, for X and Y axes. That gives us two vectors, so usually a combination of them into one is performed, as an additional stage.

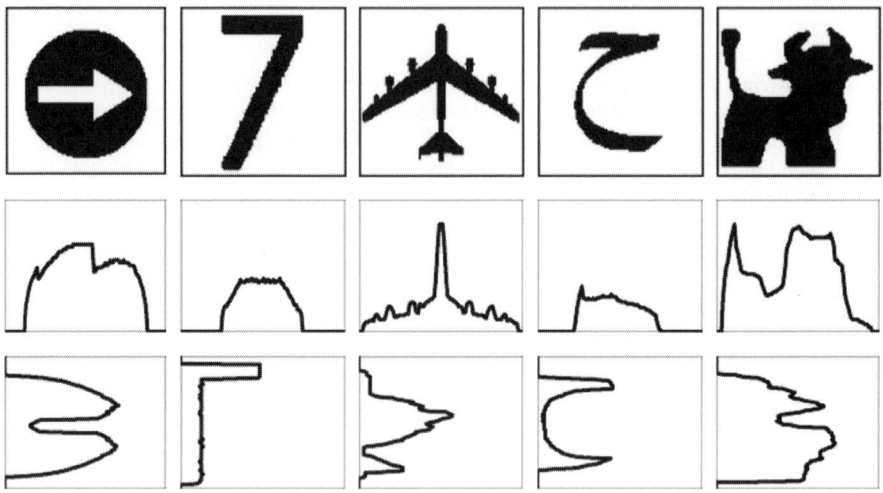

Fig. 1. Binary images (first row), its horizontal (second row) and vertical (third row) projections.

One way of doing this is to sum up those vectors, and another – to concatenate them. In the first case we lose information about differences between each coordinates (see *Fig. 2.* for an example). In the second case, we lose information about spatial positions of points belonging to the object. The additional drawback of the second approach is that every object has to be represented using twice as much memory as using the first one.

A solution to above problems is proposed in this paper. Simply, we are using a vector in a complex form. It occurs when elements from projected vectors for X and Y axes are put into a complex plane. The elements of projected X axis make a real part, and elements of projected Y axis – an imaginary part of a complex vector. Such approach gives us opportunity to enhance the generalization of information in the considered aspect. And, we use the less memory for representing an object as in the case of concatenation.

Remaining part of the paper is organized as follows. In the part 2 traditional approach is depicted. In the part 3 – all the new suggestions are discussed. Section 4 provides some experimental results, for three different experiments, performed separately. Finally, section 5 concludes the paper.

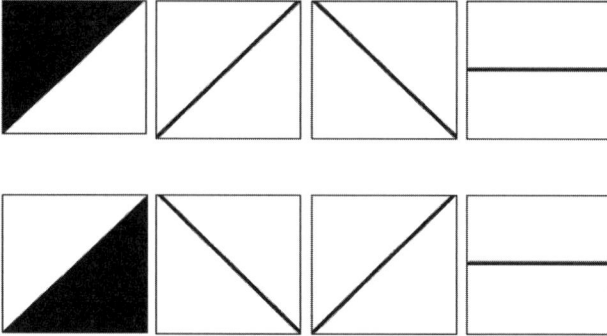

Fig. 2. Simple illustration for ambiguity of vectors summation: two different objects (first column) have different vertical (second column) and horizontal (third column) projections, but the summation (fourth column) is the same.

2. Traditional Approach

The method of projection is very popular among the binary image recognition, mainly because of its simplicity, intuitiveness and speed. It can be computed in real time ([4]). The traditional approach is robust to translation of an object and, thanks to normalization, can be invariant to scaling. It is also robust to some level of noise. Originally it is not invariant to rotation of an object, but in [4] a method for overcoming this problem was proposed. It generates series of projections at different angles and then uses them to match images in database. In some applications this additional work is not obligatory and only the robustness to shifting and scaling is needed and sufficient.

Another popular improvement of the projection method is the partition into sub-images and determining a few separate projections. This approach is usually applied to more complicated images ([8]), where objects belonging to different classes are too similar to each other.

The process of constructing projections can be described as follows.

Let us assume that we have a binary digital image. White color is represented by zeros and black by ones. If we work on a binary object, then we can assume that the white color is reserved for background pixels and the black color for the pixels belonging to the object.

First of all we calculate the amount of ones in each row (we summarize values in rows). That gives us a vector of M values, where M is an amount of rows in an image what gives us the vertical projection of the image. Five examples for various binary images are presented on *Fig 1* - in the second row.

Secondly, we calculate the amount of ones in columns (we summarize the values in columns). That gives us vector of N values, where N is a number of columns. This is a horizontal projection of an image. Examples are shown on *Fig. 1*, in the third row.

It is possible to use binary representations, with object placed on a square image. In such case, the number of columns and rows is the same. It means, that M is equal to N here.

For vertical projection the earlier description can be phrased as follows:

$$V_m = \sum_{n=1}^{N} I_{m,n} \, , \tag{1}$$

where:
$m = 1, ..., M;$
M – number of rows in image I;
N – number of columns in image I;
$I_{m,n}$ – pixel at row m and column n.

And for the vector of horizontal projection:

$$H_n = \sum_{m=1}^{M} I_{m,n} \, , \tag{2}$$

where:
$n = 1, ..., N;$
M – number of rows in image I;
N – number of columns in image I;
$I_{m,n}$ – pixel at row m and column n.

The combination of vectors V and H is the last step of the approach. There are two different methods to be discussed. The first one simply summarizes elements in vectors V and H. The number of elements in vectors has to be equal in such case.

The second method concatenates elements in vectors V and H, so in result we receive a vector with an amount of elements equal to the amount of the elements in vectors V and H together. In this case the condition of identical number of elements in vectors is not necessary.

The first method in some cases can lead to loss of information. For example, for two images, differing from each other by rotation of 90 degrees, the resultant description will be the same.

On the other hand, the concatenation approach leads to loss of spatial information and enforces us to keep more memory space for base elements, because vector representing an object is much more numerous. For example, if we have binary image of equal sides (square), then the description achieved using concatenation will be twice as numerous as when the summation is used. This problem is less critical for small databases, for example letters extracted from car license plates. But often in real applications, we have to use databases with hundreds or even thousands instances, e.g. in the comparative navigation ([9]).

3. Proposed Approach

The main idea presented in this paper is based on usage of complex vectors. This can decrease the undesirable influence of traditional methods of combining projected vectors on binary image representation. Similar observation was done in [10] for the LDA-KL combined method generalization. It can be easily applied here to the two feature vectors.

The idea is simple. We make the complex vector Z to represent the combination of projections V and H (see *Eq. 1* and *2*), where i means imaginary unit:

$$Z = V + iH \tag{3}$$

The above equation can be rewritten for every single element of the vectors:

$$z_m = v_m + ih_m, \tag{4}$$

where:
v_m – element in V;
h_m – element in H;
$m = 1, .., M$.

It sounds obvious that in above case number of elements in both vectors must be the same ($M = N$). On the other hand, it is possible to combine vectors that do not fulfill this requirement. We can simply insert zeros into the vector with a lower dimension.

4. Experimental Results

In order to evaluate the properties of the proposed modification of the projection method and compare it with traditional approach we have performed three separate recognition experiments.

The goal of the first experiment was to compare the behavior of the method with summation approach, when objects are very similar to each other are considered. Very often researchers use silhouettes of airplanes for this task. It is obvious, because shapes of different classes can be very similar in this case. Usually, even for human, the proper classification of airplanes shapes is too difficult.

The second experiment used the binary images of trademarks (*all trademarks presented in this paper have scientific and exemplary merit and belong to their owners*). We again compared the proposed method with summation. The method of concatenation was not explored, because it has the same properties as our approach, except it needs more memory for storage. In this experiment, test objects were less similar than in the previous case. Instead, they were significantly distorted (see *Fig. 4*).

At the end, the proposed method was applied to digital radar images, that are the basis for the comparative navigation ([11]).

4.1 Silhouettes of airplanes

Here, shapes belonging to twenty classes of airplanes were used. They are depicted on *Fig. 3*. The idea of the experiment was simple. We were trying to explore the ability of the two methods to distinguish objects, when they are very similar in shape.

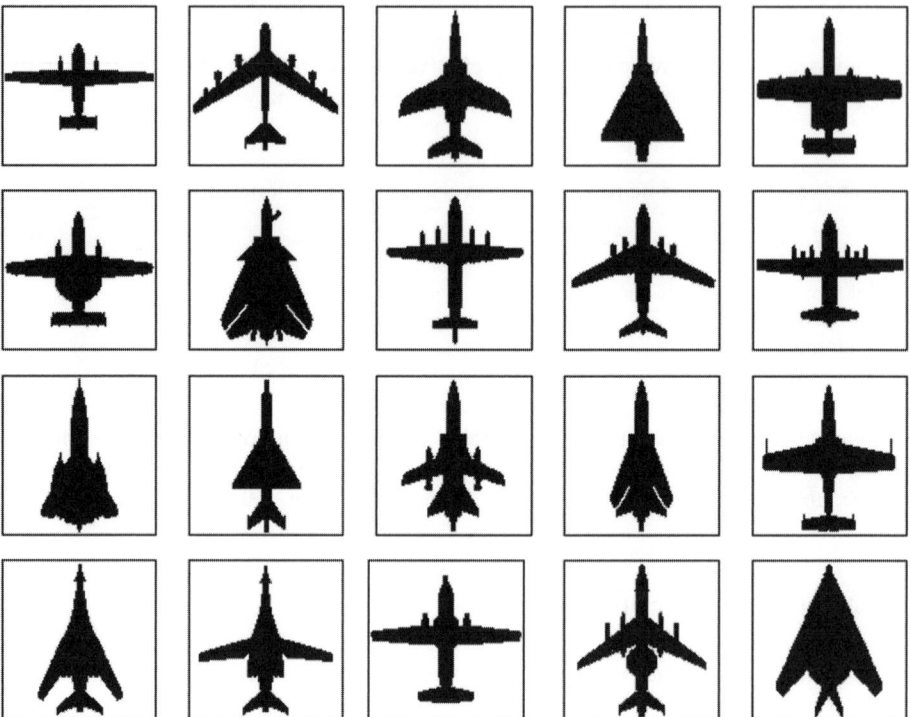

Fig. 3. Shapes used in the first experiment.

The results of the experiment confirmed the expectation, that the most popular and widespread approach, based on summation of the two projected vectors, can sometimes fail, when objects are similar.

Every time the object to recognize was represented using summation method. Those representations were compared with all other transformed objects using simple Euclidean distance. The smallest dissimilarity measure indicated the base object, pointed as the closest by the method.

As it turned out, when the summation is used, the smallest value is achieved for each class, when comparing with the same object. That is definitely the desired result. But unfortunately the same value of dissimilarity (equal to 0) is sometimes achieved for other classes at the same time. For example the values of dissimilarity for classes 4th and 5th were both equal to zero. The approach treats them as the same class.

When analyzing results of the experiment, we found out, that FRR (*False Rejection Rate*) was equal to 0%, but FAR (*False Acceptance Rate*) was 2% here.

Those problems were not present, when the complex vector was used. For all twenty shapes being explored the dissimilarity measure for proper class was 0, and for all other not (FRR = 0% and FAR = 0%).

4.2 Trademarks

The aim of the second experiment was to compare the new approach with the summation in the presence of significant deformations. This time, we have used the binary images of trademarks, which are less similar to each other than the airplanes in the former experiment.

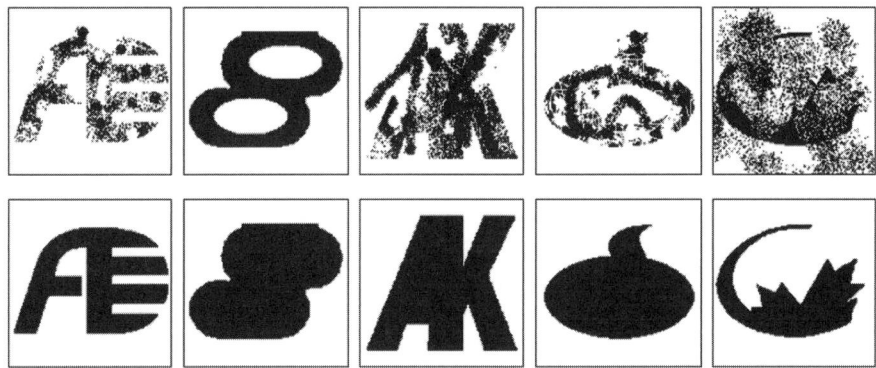

Fig. 4. Few examples of objects used in experiment – test objects (first row) and database elements according to them (second row).

The database contained 50 different logos. For recognition we used 100 strongly deformed versions of them (few examples are presented on *Fig.4*, every time the original, unaffected version of the test object is placed under it). In each single case we were comparing description of the object under recognition with all the database objects. It is obvious that every image was represented in the same way. Firstly using sum of vectors *V* and *H*, then, using the new method.

To select the recognized object we were calculating again the Euclidean distance between the object being recognized and all the database instances. The smallest value of distance between the pattern and the object explored indicated the pattern closest to object being explored.

The whole number of comparisons was 5000. As it turned out, the combination of projected vectors into complex performs better than traditional approach, even in the presence of such significant distortions.

The whole recognition rate for the proposed method was 86%. Such result can be considered as a quite promising; especially when we take the high level of objects distortions into account (see *Fig. 4*). The same objects were tested with usage of the traditional method – the summing up of vertical and horizontal projections. This test gave 78% recognition rate.

4.3 Comparative navigation based on digital radar images

The positioning is a process of determining the certain position of an object on the Earth surface at the particular moment. At sea, that means the establishing not only the place, but also the course of a vessel. The position of a vessel is usually given using polar coordinates (latitude and longitude).

The comparative navigation is one of the methods used in the positioning. Roughly speaking it is the real-time process of comparing the registered image (e.g. radar or sonar image) with an image stored in the database ([9]). This is performed to derive the position of a vessel. One of the possible methods, that can be used here is the utilization of simple pattern recognition algorithms.

The third experiment used the proposed modification of the projection method as a way of representing the radar image. It is possible, because a radar image consist only of two colors – black (water) and white (mainland or other objects reflecting airwaves, e.g. other vessels). That is why it can be treated as simple binary image as in the former two experiments.

For every database image as well as for the being recognized one we have applied the complex projection method to achieve the vector representing image. The real radar images were used. As the method of classification the Generalized Regression Neural Network (GRNN) was used. This method was pointed out as the best and most popular for the task of positioning using radar images ([11]).

The training set was composed of 300 feature vectors. An example of the result (for vector not belonging to training set) achieved during the experiment is presented in *Table 1*. The real coordinates and the result of neural network is presented there, as well as the error in meters. The test set was composed of 150 radar images (it is obvious, that test images were different from those used in the training process).

Table 1. Exemplary result of the Neural Network, proper values corresponding to it and error for one of the 300 test images

	Latitude	Longitude
Output of the NN	53° 58,322' N	14° 18,067' E
The real coordinates	53° 58,320' N	14° 18,082' E
Error in meters	3,78	25,2

As the efficiency criterion the RMS (Root Mean Square) for the whole set was used as well as the difference between real and achieved positions for every individual case (in meters).

The analysis of the experimental results confirmed the possibility of application of the complex projection approach to the problem of positioning using digital radar images. The RMS error was not larger than 0,03, what is equal to 50 meters distance. It is absolutely sufficient for comparative navigation tasks.

5. Conclusions and Future Work

The method of projection (*projection profiles*, *projection histograms*) is a very popular and widespread representation of binary images. Simplicity and fast obtainment are its most important advantages. But it has one important drawback. It doesn't preserve the spatial information about the image pixels. In this article a modification of the method was proposed. Instead of traditional ways of combining vectors of the horizontal and vertical projections, we have proposed to use the complex vector. In this vector the real part contains the vertical projection and the imaginary part is designed for the horizontal one.

The initial study of the method confirmed that it has better properties than traditional approach. Three separate experiments were performed.

Firstly, the shapes of silhouettes were tested. The goal of this experiment was to compare the behavior of the approach proposed in this paper with the traditional method based on summation of projected vectors. Also, we were curious, how those methods works, when objects under recognition are very similar (that is why the airplanes were considered). As it turned out, the new method is slightly better than the older one. Yet, above all, its result is not ambiguous for shapes belonging to different classes. This is the most desirable and important property for every shape descriptor.

Secondly, the trademark images database was explored. The same two methods were explored. However, this time, the test images were significantly distorted, when comparing with the base elements corresponding to them. Again, the complex method was better. The 86% RR achieved is sufficient, especially when having in mind the level of distortions used (see *Fig. 4* in above section).

The last experiment was exploring the possibility of applying the complex projection method in the comparative navigation basing on radar images. The results were very promising. The error smaller or equal to 50 m is satisfactory enough for the task. Especially, when considering large size of typical sea vessels.

Yet, later work can be performed in future. For example it is planned to add Fourier or DCT transform as a next step, mainly to reduce the influence of noise. As well the suggestion of using polar coordinates is promising.

Authors would like to thank prof. Kukharev for the scientific discussion about binary images (both, contour and region representation), what has resulted in the idea of combination of projection vectors "with usage of *i*".

References

[1] Frejlichowski D., Lack of parts in silhouette during recognition of contour objects, Proc. of 8th computer science scientific session, pp. 181 - 188, Szczecin 2003 (in Polish)

[2] Fang, B., Leung, C.H., Tang, Y.Y., Tse, K.W., Kwok, P.C.K., Wong, Y.K, Off-line signature verification by the tracking of feature and stroke positions, Pattern Recognition, Vol. 36, Iss. 1, January, 2003, pp. 91-101

[3] Soltanzadeh, H., Rahmati, M., Recognition of Persian handwritten digits using image profiles of multiple orientations, Pattern Recognition Letters, Vol. 25, Iss. 14, October 15, 2004, pp. 1569-1576

[4] Fuh, C.-S., Liu H.-B., Projection for pattern recognition, Image and Vision Computing, Vol. 16, Iss. 9-10, July, 1998, pp. 677-687

[5] Kukharev G., Kuźmiński A., Biometric Techniques Part 1 - Methods of Face Recognition, Szczecin University of Technology, Faculty of Computer Science, Szczecin, 2003 (in Polish)

[6] Le D.X., Thoma G.R., Automated portrait/landscape mode detection on a binary image, Proc. 1993 SPIE: Symposium on Aerospace and Remote Sensing - Visual Information Processing II, Orlando, FL, April 14-16, 1993, Vol. 1961, pp. 202-212

[7] Ismail M.A., Gad S., Off-line Arabic signature recognition and verification, Pattern Recognition Vol. 33, Iss. 10, pp. 1727-1740, October, 2000

[8] Saeed K., Image Analysis for Object Recognition, Bialystok Technical University Press, 2004

[9] Stateczny A., (red.), Methods of comparative navigation, Scientific Society of Gdansk, 2004 (in Polish)

[10] Yang, J., Ye H., Zhang D., A new LDA-KL combined method for feature extraction and its generalisation, Pattern Analysis and Applications, Vol. 7, Iss.: 2, July, 2004, pp. 40-50

[11] Stateczny A. Maow A., Processing Digital Radar Images in Teaching Artificial Neural Network and Target Positioning Problems, Polish Journal of Environmental Studies, Vol. 15, No. 4B, pp. 171-174

PART IV

COMPUTER SIMULATION AND DATA ANALYSIS

A Consideration of Processor Utilization on Multi-Processor System

Koichi Kashiwagi, Yoshinobu Higami, Shin-Ya Kobayashi

Ehime University, 3 Bunkyo, Matsuyama, Ehime, 7908577 Japan
{kashiwagi, higami, kob}@cs.ehime-u.ac.jp

Abstract. List-scheduling is a key to achieve high performance for multi-processor system. The objective is to minimize a processing time of parallel programs. To this end, a lot of scheduling algorithms are proposed. On the other hand, processor utilization may decrease to aim at the shortest processing time. For improvement of processor utilization, there is the deadline method which we have proposed. In this method, we restrict the number of available processors using limitation. In this paper, we show the improvement of processor utilization by proposed method and the validity of the limitation.

Introduction

List scheduling is one distinguishing features of parallel versus sequential programming. A lot of list scheduling algorithms have been proposed, however, they consider shortening processing time primarily, because scheduling aims at minimizing the overall completion time of parallel programs. As a result, these traditional scheduling algorithms try to use all available processors, and then, processor utilization extremely decreases [1]. The other side, it is also a just claim to use restricted resources effectively.

For example, in CP/MISF [2], when there are ready tasks and idle processors, these tasks are allocated to the idle processors even if this allocation shortens processing time only a little. On the other hand, such processors work only few time intervals to execute the tasks. This situation brings unfortunately decrement of processor utilization.

So, we had proposed 'deadline method' in order to deal with the problem [3] [4]. In this method, available processors are restricted by the limitation that is calculated from property of executed task set. In this paper, we show the improvement of processor utilization by deadline method and the validity of the limitation.

We explain about target multi-processor system. An executed job is divided into several tasks. We call these tasks task set. A Scheduling algorithm allocates task set to processors. Number of processors that are necessary for executing task set is determined by scheduling algorithm. All processors that are allocated task are exclusively reserved while the task set is executed. The processor utilization is shown the following.

$$\frac{\sum_{i=1}^{N} s_i}{u \times pt} \qquad\qquad (1)$$

where, N is a number of tasks, s_i is a task size, u is a number of processor used by scheduling algorithm, and pt is a processing time. Processors utilization is a real number grater than 0 and less than or equal to 1.

Deadline method

Property of task set

Let $T = \{T_1, T_2, ..., T_N\}$ denotes a task set, where N is number of tasks. All tasks have one or more predecessors and successors except for start and end tasks. s_i is a task size of T_i, i.e., it is also amount of computation needed by T_i .

A task set is conveniently represented as a directed acyclic graph called a task graph [5]. When a(i, k) = 1, T_i must be completed before T_k begins. Then, T_i is one of predecessors of T_k and T_k is one of successors of T_i. On the other hand, a(i, k) = 0 indicates that T_i and T_k are independent. Now pl_i denotes the longest path among paths from T_i to end task in the task graph. The critical path (CP) of task set is the longest path among pl_i in the task graph, i.e., it is the maximum of pl_i.

The task can be processed only after all predecessors of the task have been done, and then each task cannot start before certain time. The lower bound of this time when available processors are enough is called 'earliest starting time (EST)'. We refer est_i as the earliest starting time of T_i. On the other hand, task must be done before certain time in order to achieve the shortest processing time of task set. In other words, if task has not finished by the certain time, it takes longer time than CP to complete execution of all tasks. We call the time 'latest completion time (LCT)' and refer lct_i as the latest completion time of T_i [1].

Limitation of available processors

Now we define 'execution probability' of each task as probability if the task is processed or not at any instant [1]. Anyway, if execution probability of T_i is 1 at some point, T_i must be processed in order to achieve the shortest processing time of task set.

We can determine the execution probability of task with its EST and LCT. We let $f_i(t)$ be the task execution probability of a T_i at time t.

$f_i(t)$ is defined zero before est_i or after lct_i, and $f_i(t)$ is not zero between est_i and lct_i. Next, in case of $lct_i - est_i <= 2s_i$, $f_i(t)$ is determined by equation (2) from Fig. 1.

Similarly, in case of $lct_i - est_i > 2s_i$, $f_i(t)$ is determined by equation (3) from Fig.2.

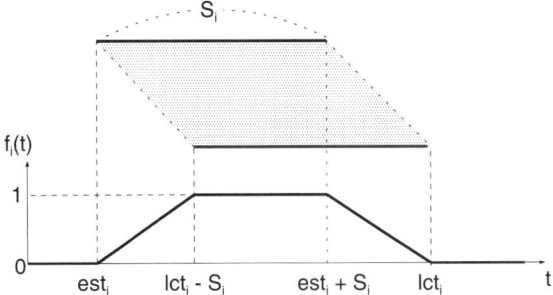

Fig. 1. time vs. execution probability (lcti – esti <= 2si)

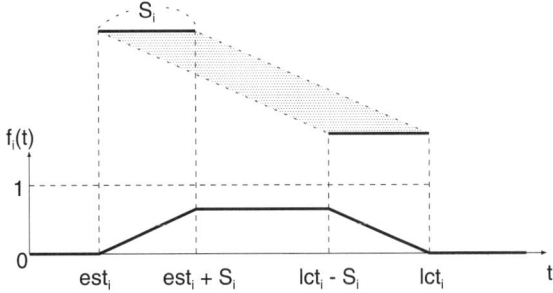

Fig. 2. time vs. execution probability (lcti – esti >2si)

$$f_i(t) \equiv \begin{cases} 0 & : \quad t < est_i, \, lct_i \le t \\ \dfrac{t - est_i}{lct_i - est_i - s_i} & : \quad est_i \le t < est_i + s_i \\ \dfrac{s_i}{lct_i - est_i - s_i} & : \quad est_i + s_i \le t < lct_i - s_i \\ \dfrac{lct_i - t}{lct_i - est_i - s_i} & : \quad lct_i - s_i \le t < lct_i \end{cases} \qquad (2)$$

$$f_i(t) \equiv \begin{cases} 0 & : \quad t < est_i, \, lct_i \le t \\ \dfrac{t - est_i}{lct_i - est_i - s_i} & : \quad est_i \le t < est_i + s_i \\ \dfrac{s_i}{lct_i - est_i - s_i} & : \quad est_i + s_i \le t < lct_i - s_i \\ \dfrac{lct_i - t}{lct_i - est_i - s_i} & : \quad lct_i - s_i \le t < lct_i \end{cases} \qquad (3)$$

So, we can consider the summation of the $f_i(t)$ from i = 1 to N as expectation of required number of processors at time t in order to complete task set for the shortest time. We define F(t) as the following. In other words, at time t, number of tasks that are processed is expected F(t).

$$F(t) = \sum_{i=1}^{N} f_i(t) \tag{4}$$

We have proposed two kinds of the limitations. First, we make the maximum of F(t) from time 0 to time CP the limitation L_m of available processors.

$$L_m = \max(0 \le t \le CP)\, F(t) \tag{5}$$

Second, we make the average of F(t) from time 0 to time CP the limitation L_a of available processors. The average of F(t) is calculated the following.

$$
\begin{aligned}
L_a &= \left(\int_0^{CP} F(t)dt \right)/CP \\
&= \left(\int_0^{CP} \sum_{i=1}^{N} f_i(t)\, dt \right)/CP \\
&= \left(\sum_{i=1}^{N} \int_0^{CP} f_i(t)dt \right)/CP \\
&= \left(\sum_{i=1}^{N} s_i \right)/CP
\end{aligned}
\tag{6}
$$

Release of the limitation

First, we define the time that subtract task size from LCT as 'latest starting time (LST)' and refer to $lct_i - s_i$ as lst_i. All tasks $\{T_1, T_2, ..., T_N\}$ are allocated at each lst_i at the latest when processors exist infinitely and communication time is zero, then processing time should be CP. When available processors are limited to the limitation, some tasks may not be allocated to available processors at each lst_i because of the limitation. When such tasks exist, processing time increases from CP.

So, for task T_i which was not allocated at lst_i, the limitation is canceled temporarily and it allocated to the processor which could not be used because of the limitation, at lst_i. We call these processors temporarily available processors. In this way, since all tasks are allocated by LST at the latest, processing time become CP. This is the fundamental part of the deadline method [3] [4].

On the other hand, the processor that can be used now with this way is not used in time before LST. Consequently, if task T_i can be allocated before lst_i then it can be allocated at its time. As a result, idle time of the processor may be reduced. In scheduling, $availTime_i$ defined by the earliest time which can perform an allocation of T_i. $availTime_i$ satisfies $est_i <= availTime_i <= lst_i$.

For example, when tasks T_i, T_j and T_k with the same LST (i.e. $lst_i = lst_j = lst_k$) are not allocated to the available processors at the LST, at first, T_i is allocated temporarily available processor. If the processor is not used until $availTime_i$, T_i is allocated at $availTime_i$. Next, when $availTime_i + s_i <= lst_j$ and T_j is chosen as a following task for allocation, if $availTime_j <= availTime_i + s_i$ then T_j is allocated at $availTime_i + s_i$. Finally, when $availTime_i + s_i + s_j <= lst_k$, T_k is allocated the same processor. If $availTime_i + s_i + s_j < availTime_k$ then T_k is allocated at $availTime_k$. Fig. 3 shows this allocation.

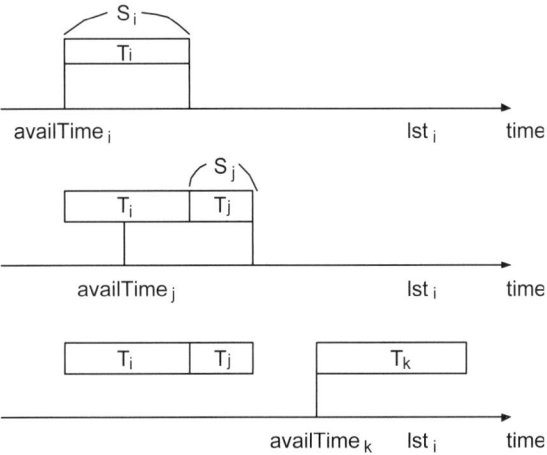

Fig. 3. Example of allocation by the deadline method

Pseudo task sets

We make pseudo task sets generated with random series in order to evaluate proposed method. The pseudo task sets are made based on number of tasks, task size, and dependent relation between tasks. The dependent relation between task T_i and T_k is shown the following.

$$P[a(i, k) = 1] = p \quad \text{for} \ 1 <= i < k <= N$$

$$P[a(i, k) = 0] = 1 - p \quad \text{for} \ 1 <= i < k <= N \tag{7}$$

$$P[a(i, k) = 0] = 1 \quad \text{if} \ i >= k,$$

where N is the number of tasks and p is the probability that T_i and T_k are dependent of each other.

We prepare two types of pseudo task sets. First, n is specified as 100, 200, and 500. p is specified 0.1 and 0.2. Namely, six kinds of task sets are made from the combination of n and p. A task size follows an exponential distribution with an average of 100 unit time. Additionally, each task set is made 10 times. We call these task sets Type 1.

Next, we consider the condition of restricting the number of predecessors, since it increases with the number of tasks in the way of type 1. Consequently, we add average number of predecessors as one of the elements that make pseudo task set. The average number of predecessors (np) is specified 1, 2, and 3. Other elements to make the pseudo task set are the same as Type 1. We call these task sets Type 2.

Table 1 and Table2 show minimum, average, and maximum of CP, L_m, and L_a in Type 1 and Type 2, respectively.

Table 1. minimum, average, and maximum of CP, L_m, and L_a in Type 1

(N, p)	CP			L_m			L_a		
	Min.	Ave.	Max	Min.	Ave.	Max	Min.	Ave.	Max
(100,0.1)	1823	2328.92	3643	5	6.9	8	4	4.8	5
(100,0.2)	2508	3700.27	4824	4	5.3	6	3	3.1	4
(200,01)	3463	4530.68	5718	6	7.4	9	4	4.8	5
(200,0.2)	5202	6636.51	8420	5	5.6	6	3	3.5	4
(500,0.1)	9844	10939	12043	7	8.2	9	5	5.1	6
(500,0.2)	16996	18278.2	20321	5	6.1	7	3	3	3

Table 2. minimum, average, and maximum of CP, L_m, and L_a in Type 2

(N, p, np)	CP			L_m			L_a		
	Min.	Ave.	Max	Min.	Ave.	Max	Min.	Ave.	Max
(100,0.1,1)	595	764.51	1016	14	18.4	21	10	13.2	15
(100,0.1,2)	884	1166.39	1885	8	12.7	17	6	9.6	12
(100,0.1,3)	1382	1735.03	2004	8	9.4	11	6	6.4	8
(100,0.2,1)	709	925.27	1201	11	15.8	20	8	11.4	14
(100,0.2,2)	897	1289.61	1763	7	11.2	14	5	8.3	11
(100,0.2,3)	1051	1749.5	2161	7	8.9	12	5	6.2	9
(200,0.1,1)	794	1079.44	1539	19	28.2	34	14	19.9	24
(200,0.1,2)	1140	1492.5	1810	15	19.8	26	11	14.4	19
(200,0.1,3)	1597	1989.41	2593	11	14.6	17	8	11	13
(200,0.2,1)	821	1019.5	1261	22	29.4	36	16	20.5	25
(200,0.2,2)	1081	1388.46	1790	16	19.9	23	13	14.9	16
(200,0.2,3)	1519	1980.07	2747	12	14.8	16	8	10.8	13
(500,0.1,1)	965	1251.04	1623	47	58	71	33	41	49
(500,0.1,2)	1249	1712.42	2542	26	42.6	52	19	30.8	39
(500,0.1,3)	1660	2250.55	3223	23	31.5	40	18	23.8	29
(500,0.2,1)	1007	1229.9	1439	47	59	75	35	41.6	51
(500,0.2,2)	1350	1661.91	2082	32	41.9	53	23	30.8	38
(500,02,3)	1630	2140.35	2551	27	31.5	38	20	23.8	30

Evaluation

We simulate execution of pseudo task sets by using CP/MISF with deadline method and evaluate processor utilization. We have already known processor utilization is improved by deadline method [3] [4]. However, the optimum limitation that processor utilization becomes the maximum might exist. Thus, to evaluate processor utilization, the limitation is assumed to be the integer between from 1 to L_m. Of course, L_m is different in each task set, and $L_a <= L_m$. We call the optimum limitation L_o.

For example, table 3 shows processor utilization of each limitation for a pseudo task set of Type 1 (N = 100, p = 0.1). In this case, L_o is 5 and 6. And then, L_a is the same as one of the optimum limitations.

Type 1 and Type 2 have 60 and 180 task sets respectively. Table 4 shows averages of processor utilizations of Type 1 and Type 2 to each limitation. Here, processor utilization when deadline method with L_x is used is shown $pu(L_x)$. In general, processor utilization when deadline method is not used is lower than $pu(L_m)$ [3] [4]. Thus, we see from table 4 that processor utilizations are improved by using L_m or L_a as limitation.

71.7% of L_a is the same as L_o in Type 1. 96.1% of L_a is the same as L_o in Type 2. Average and maximum of $pu(Lo) - pu(La)$ are 0.037 and 0.239 in Type 1, respectively. Similarly, they are 0.003 and 0.189 in Type 2, respectively.

As a result, high processor utilization can be obtained by using deadline method with L_a.

Table 3. example of schedling result

limitation	processor utilization
1	0.4876
2	0.5485
3	0.4876
4	0.6269
5	0.7314
6 (L_a)	0.7314
7	0.6269
8 (L_m)	0.5485

Table 4. average of processor utilization

limitation	Type 1	Type 2
L_m	0.5457	0.7017
L_a	0.6756	0.9548
L_o	0.7126	0.9576

Conclusion

We have proposed deadline method to improve processor utilization on multi-processor system. The method restricts available processors by the limitation. The limitation is calculated from property of executed task set. We have proposed maximum and average of expectation of number of tasks executed at the same time as the limitation. In this paper, we simulated execution of pseudo task sets by using CP/MISF with deadline method and evaluated processor utilization. As a result, processor utilizations are improved and almost of them became the maximum. Consequently, we showed the improvement of processor utilization by deadline method and the validity of the limitation.

References

[1] K. Kashiwagi and S. Kobayashi, "Limitation of used processor for task scheduling," Proc. of 19th IASTED International Multi-Conf. Applied Informatics, pp. 122-126, Innsbruck, Austria, Feb. 2001.

[2] H. Kasahara and S. Narita, "Practical multiprocessor scheduling algorithms for efficient parallel processing," IEEE Trans. Computers, no. 33(11), pp.1023-1029, 1984.

[3] K. Kashiwagi and S. Kobayashi, "Consideration of task's deadline for scheduling method with used processors limitation," Proc. of Advanced Computer Systems, no. VII-9, pp. 487-496, Mielno, Poland, Oct. 2001.

[4] K. Kashiwagi, Y. Higami, S. Kobayashi, "Improvement of the processors operating ratio in task scheduling using the deadline method," Proc. of 10th International Multi-Conference, Advanced Computer Systems 2003, Oct. 2003.

[5] V. A. F. Almeida, L. M. M. Vasconcelos, J. N. C. Arabe, D. A. Menasce, "Using random task graphs to investigate the potential benefits of heterogeneity in parallel systems," Supercomputing '92. Proceedings, pp. 683-691, Nov. 1992.

Reliability of Node Information on Autonomous Load Distribution Method

Michihiko Kudo, Koichi Kashiwagi, Yoshinobu Higami, Shin-Ya Kobayashi

Faculty of Engineering, Ehime University 3 Bunkyou-cho, Matsuyama,
Ehime, 790-8577 Japan
kudo@koblab.cs.ehime-u.ac.jp, {kashiwagi, higami, kob}@cs.ehime-u.ac.jp,

Abstract. We have proposed "Autonomous Load Distribution (ALD) Method" as one of the load distribution algorithm for multi-computer system. In ALD Method, a node has other nodes information to request for task processing with making a list of candidate. In this paper, we study reliability of node information. Reliability of node information is important issue because its measure concerns whether the node distributes load effectively or not. To show that point, we simulated under a given set of conditions.

1. Introduction

A multi-computer system consists of a collection of computers, which are under the one control, connected by a network. In the system, each user submits tasks at their host computers for processing. Also, multitasking and multi-user mode are available. In the result, the random arrival of tasks can cause load bias among nodes, some computers are heavily loaded while other computers are idle or lightly loaded.

In the system, it is necessary to distribute tasks for efficient utilization of system resources and fast processing. However, since the number of nodes which consists one system is increasing, it is difficult for each user to grasp all those loads and processing ability, and to distribute tasks appropriately. Therefore, some kinds of method with which a node distributes load automatically are proposed from the former [1]. We have proposed "Autonomous Load Distribution (ALD) Method" as one of the load distribution algorithm for a multi-computer system. It is shown by reference that the method is superior to some methods proposed in the past [2] [3] [4]. To date, we have implemented the method and some other load distribution methods.

2. Autonomous load distribution method

In ALD Method, a node with arrival of a task negotiates with other nodes, and the node which executes the task is determined (Fig.1). An each node decides how to negotiate other nodes to distribute self load by sending a request, and also decides the request from other nodes for executing the task. To decide such things, other nodes information is used by the node. Node information consists of own load state, node

ID, processor speed, and properties of communication path. When the request is accepted, the node which decided acceptance negotiates additionally to find a lower load node. In addition, each node does not need to have all nodes information in the system because negotiations among nodes provide new nodes information to the node exchanging node information.

Node information has a validity period. It means a measure how long loads of the node exists. As time advances, it is considered that reliability of node information is being low. Using a validity period, high reliability one can be used when treating node information.

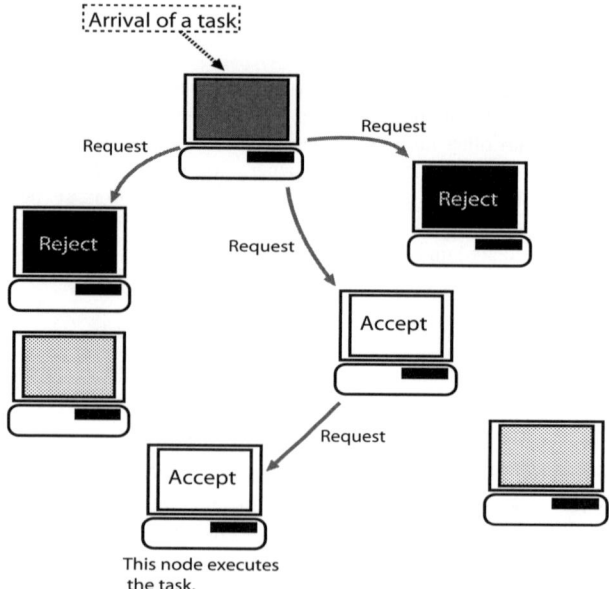

Fig. 1. Negotiation among nodes on ALD method

2.1 The Request Decision Procedure

After a task arrives or a node accepts the request from other nodes, the node determines whether it should request execution of the task to other nodes or not. This procedure is called "The Request Decision Procedure" (Fig. 2 (a)). It consists of "Making a list of candidate" and "Negotiating with other nodes". We call the node which requests "requester".

- Making a list of candidates

A requester estimates the task processing time itself and other nodes using the task size and nodes information. A list of candidates is obtained by sorting the nodes within a validity period in incremental order of task processing time which is estimated. When the requester estimates a node over a validity period, its node load is assumed zero because of low reliability of the information, and they are added to the list.

Finally, the requester is added to the end of the list. When no node with less estimated task processing time than the requester is found, the requester executes the task.

- Negotiating with other nodes

After making a list of candidates, a requester negotiates to the node which is the head of the list. When the node which is the head of the list is the requester, it executes the task without negotiating. When the requester negotiates, it sends the request message to the negotiation partner. Its message includes information of the task, nodes information which concerned the negotiation, and the processing time estimated by the requester. The node which received the request message sends the reply message including a result of the request and own information. When the result is acceptance, the node which accepted does The Request Decision Procedure in the same way. Contrary, the result is rejection; the requester negotiates with the next node of the list. If there is self node in the list, the node executes the task. Moreover, the requester updates the node information database its own based on the node information included in the request result.

2.2 The Reply Decision Procedure

When a node receives the request message from other nodes, the node performs the Reply Decision Procedure (Fig.2 (b)). Here we call the node requested from the requester "requestee". In this procedure, the requestee estimates the task its own processing time (T_l) is based on the task information included in the request message. As compared with its own task processing time (T_l) and the processing time estimated by requester (T_n), if is shorter than T_n ($T_l < T_n$), the request will be accepted and the acceptance message will be transmitted. Otherwise, then the request is rejected and returns the rejection message.

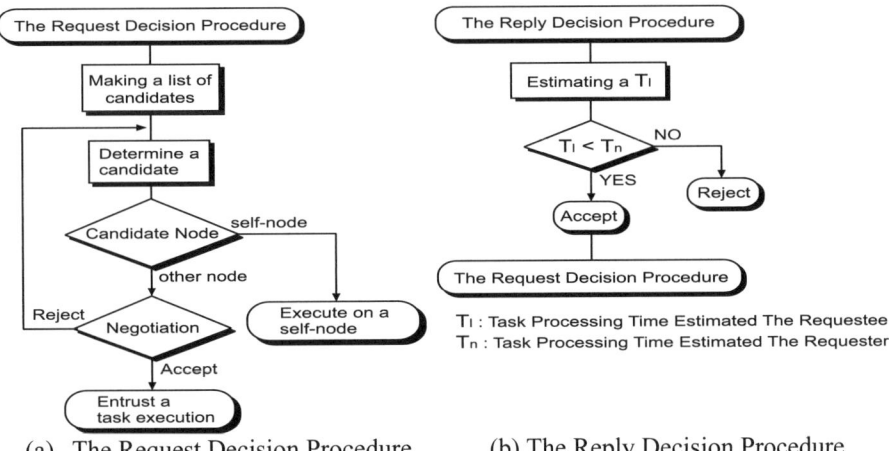

(a) The Request Decision Procedure   (b) The Reply Decision Procedure

Fig. 2. Algorithms of The ALD method

2.3 Management of Node Information

Each node has other nodes information to negotiate others. As a negotiation is done, other nodes information which can be obtained is increasing. In the result, it causes a problem with more memory usage and more overhead resulted from more negotiation. To control the problem, the number of nodes information which one node can have should be limited and unnecessary node information should be deleted.

When unnecessary node information is deleted, conditions to select are shown as follows.

- A load state of node information is higher than a load state of a node which has the information.
- Node information is over the validity period.
- A load state is highest in other nodes information when no load state of nodes information is higher than load state of a node which has information.

2.4 Reliability of Node Information

In ALD method, as a validity period is provided to node information, there are two kind of information, within the period or over the period. If a node negotiates with a node over the period, the request will be rejected because of no using a node within the period. In the result, it may cause load distribution is not effectively. To examine the detail of ALD method, we simulate the method. Main items to examine are as follows.

- The number of negotiation with a node with the period, and over the period
- The rate of average success of negotiation
- Utilization rate of nodes

3. Evaluation

3.1 Simulation Conditions

The system consists of 100 sets of node, equal processing power, properties of communication path, and CPU scheduling on each node is Round-Robin. Also, the number of node information which a node can have sets 10.

- System Load

Task size follows the exponential distribution and the average arrival interval (average introduction interval) of a task also follows an exponential distribution. Average arrival intervals at nodes where tasks are introduced are equal.

Here, the average task size is referred to as $\overline{w}$; the average arrival interval is referred to as $\overline{t}$, and then $\lambda = \overline{w} / \overline{t}$ is a node load. We define an average of a node load in a system as a system load Λ.

$$\Lambda = \frac{1}{N}\sum_{i=1}^{n}\lambda_i \tag{1}$$

In the above equation, n is the number of nodes ($1 \le n \le N$) at which are arrived tasks. When arrival of tasks to partial nodes arises, there are nodes at which are not arrived tasks in the system. They can not negotiate autonomously, so wait for other nodes to negotiate with self. We set n at 50. In order to change system load for evaluation, we change the average task arrival interval $\bar{t}$ (and fix the average task size at 1[sec]).

3.2 Simulation Result

We simulate two kinds of a system load, 0.3 and 0.5.

Firstly, the result of 0.3, the number of node information over the validity period in the node (Fig.3 (b)) is more than with the validity period (Fig.3 (a)). This means that a validity period is tended to over because almost all the nodes are lightly loaded or idle.

And the candidate list made from node information the node has is shown Fig.3 (c), (d). Commonly-observed feature is the number of node information in the candidate list is fewer than the number of node information the node has. This feature results from the same reason. Also, in Fig.3 (c), the floor is 1 because self information is assumed valid.

In the result, almost all the requestees are nodes over the valid period (Fig.3 (e)).

Secondly, the result of 0.5, the number of nodes information in the node is shown Fig.4 (a), (b). As the load of the node higher than when system load 0.3, each validity period is tended to within. But if there are a large number of node information with a validity period in the node (Fig.4 (a)), the number of node information with a validity period in the candidate list decreases (Fig.4 (c)). In contrast, the number of node information between Fig.4 (b) and Fig.4 (d) is nearly equal.

In the result, the sum of requestee within the validity period is near the sum of requestee over the validity period (Fig.4 (e)).

Av. Nego. when S.load is 0.3 is more than when 0.5 but Av. Succ. is fewer than when 0.5 in Table 1. This means that reliability of the nodes information (that is almost all the nodes are over the period) is low in system load 0.3.

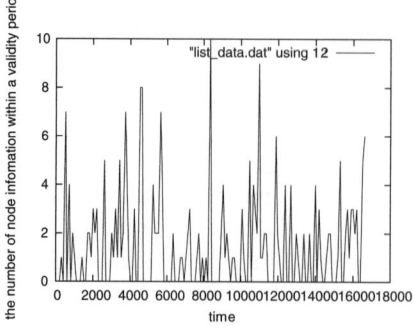

(a) The number of node information within a validity period in the node

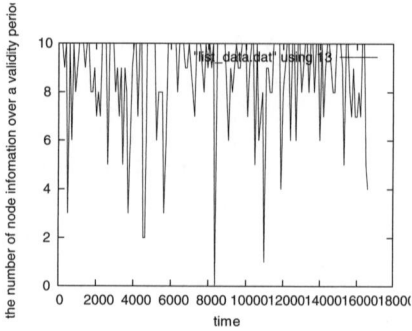

(b) The number of node information over a validity period in the node

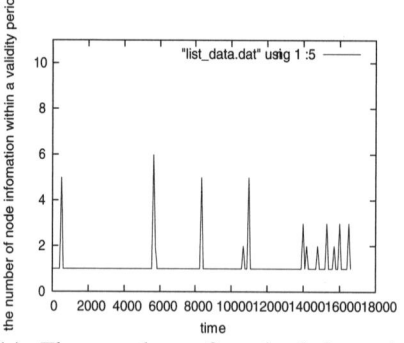

(c) The number of node information within a validity period in the candidate list

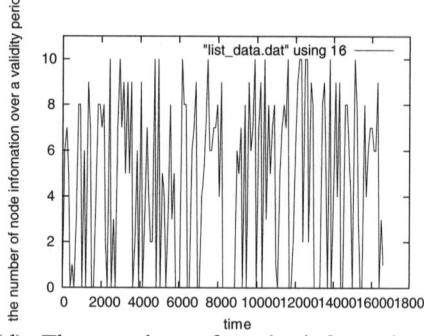

(d) The number of node information over a validity period in the candidate list

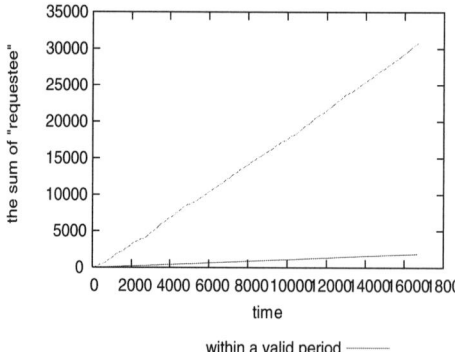

(e) The sum of "requestee" at the node

Fig. 3. The system load 0.3

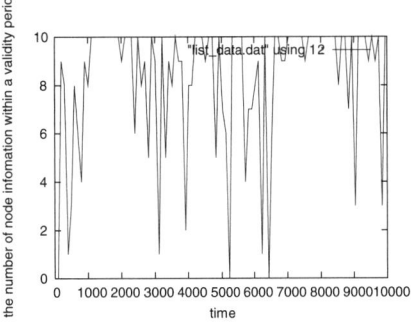

(a) The number of node information
within a validity period in the node

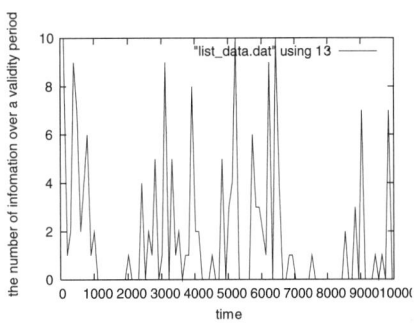

(b) The number of node information
over a validity period in the node

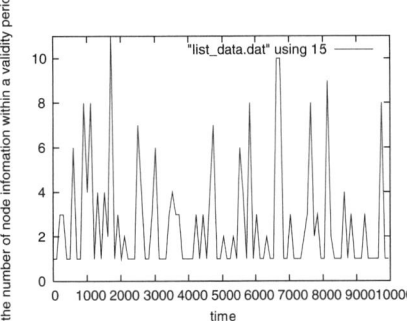

(c) The number of node information
with a validity period in the candidate
list

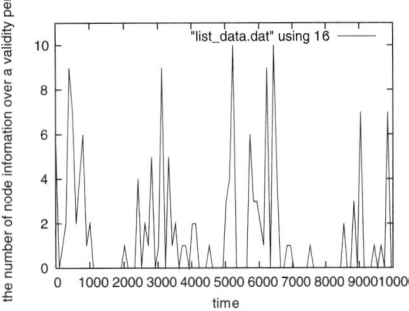

(d) The number of node information
over a validity period in the candidate
list

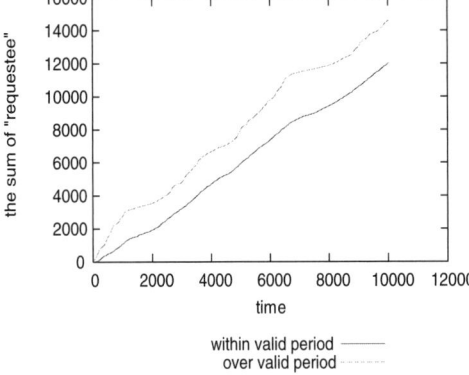

within valid period ———
over valid period ------

(e) The sum of "requestee" at the node

Fig. 4. The system load 0.5

Table 1. Performance of two kinds of system load

S.load	Opp	MRT [sec]	Av. Acc	Self [%]	Av. Nego.	Av. Succ. [%]
0.3	1695077	1.227	0.763	50.175	3.390	44.020
0.5	1319726	6.111	0.803	48.391	2.639	54.836

S.load: System load
Opp.: The number of Opportunity of negotiation at the node
MRT: Mean response time
Av. Acc: The number of Average Acceptance per a task
Self: The rate of Self execution
Av. Nego.: The number of Average Negotiation per a task
Av. Succ.: The rate of Average Success of negotiation

4. Conclusion

A node distributes load automatically by ALD Method through negotiating other nodes to find a lower load node. To negotiate, each node has other nodes information, but information has a validity period. If a candidate list consists of many nodes information such system load 0.3, it causes more negotiation which is low rate of success.

5. References

[1] N.G.Shivaratri, P.Krueger, and M.Singhal. "Load distributing for locally distributed systems". IEEE Computer, 25, No.12, pp. 33-44, Dec.1992.
[2] S.Kobayashi, H.Kimura, and T.Takebe. "A Load Distribution Method for Multicomputer System Based on Inter computer negotiation". Proceeding of 1993 Joint Technical Conference on Circuits/System, July 1993.
[3] S.Kobayashi, T.Ogawa, and T.Watanabe. "Autonomous Load Distribution for Multi Computer Systems(in Japanese). IEICE D-I, VOL.J79-D-I, NO.11, pp.903-915, Nov.1996.
[4] S.Miyazaki and S.Kobayashi. "Improvement of Autonomous Load Distribution Algorithm with Receiver Initiated Mechanism". IPSJSIG Notes, 2001-DPS-102, pp.139-144.

Methodology of Developing Computer-Based Training Systems for Operators of Dynamic Objects

Orest Popov, Tatiana Tretyakova, Anna Barcz, Piotr Piela

Szczecin University of Technology, Faculty of Computer Science and Information Systems
ul. Żołnierska 49, 71 – 210 Szczecin
email: popov@wi.ps.pl, ttretiakowa@wi.ps.pl, abarcz@wi.ps.pl, ppiela@wi.ps.pl

Abstract. Vocational education and training that use a computer technology is an inherent part of training process for operators of dynamic objects. This article presents some methodological rules for creating e-training and e-learning systems belonging to the class of systems with real-time working model of the teaching object. Further, the idea of creating e-training and e-learning systems and a general structure of the teaching process are presented. Within the confines of rules of creating e-training and e-learning systems the ontology is described. It allows to present in a comprehensive way the system's domain. This approach serves for working up the methodological basics of creating the domain knowledge base. The meaning of verified models of the dynamic objects is shown and finally, the mathematical method of model's improvement based on sensitivity theory and singular value decomposition of matrices are described. Subject is consistent with the directions determined in The Bologna Declaration [16] and The Lisbon Strategy [5] concerning the problems of teaching and improving.

Introduction

Among wide variety of categories of the intelligent training systems it could be possible to distinguish a class including simulation systems. Such systems are designed for passing declaration knowledge about the object that is necessary in the teaching process of operator and procedural knowledge that is connected with practical activities and is responsible for developing proper habits and abilities.

There are three fundamental characteristics, which are distinguishing the intelligent training systems with the simulation system among other computer-based training systems.

Firstly, such systems include the dynamics model of the controlled object. Secondly, in any simulation system the cooperation between student and model based on the information model. This model fulfills the role of student's interface. The third characteristic is the teaching model, which includes rules, methods, structure of essential exercises and some other attributes of the teaching process.

Any intelligent training system, which possesses the mentioned above characteristics, will be further defined as the dynamic intelligent tutoring system and any tutoring process – as dynamic tutoring.

All described problems are studied during the international project ASIMIL (Aero user-friendly simulation-based distance learning) within the confines of the 5th Framework Programmee of European Union [1]. The tasks that were realized during the ASIMIL project serve as examples of using the proposed solutions.

Structure of the dynamic intelligent training system

Regardless of the subject domain in the structure of the intelligent training system (figure 1) it could be possible to distinguish: bases of knowledge and data, a deduction mechanism, an user interface and some additional elements (e.g. program for correction and supplement the knowledge base). In case of dynamic intelligent training systems (DITS) it is necessary to complete the structure by a simulation system, which reproduce the behavior and appearance of the dynamic real training object.

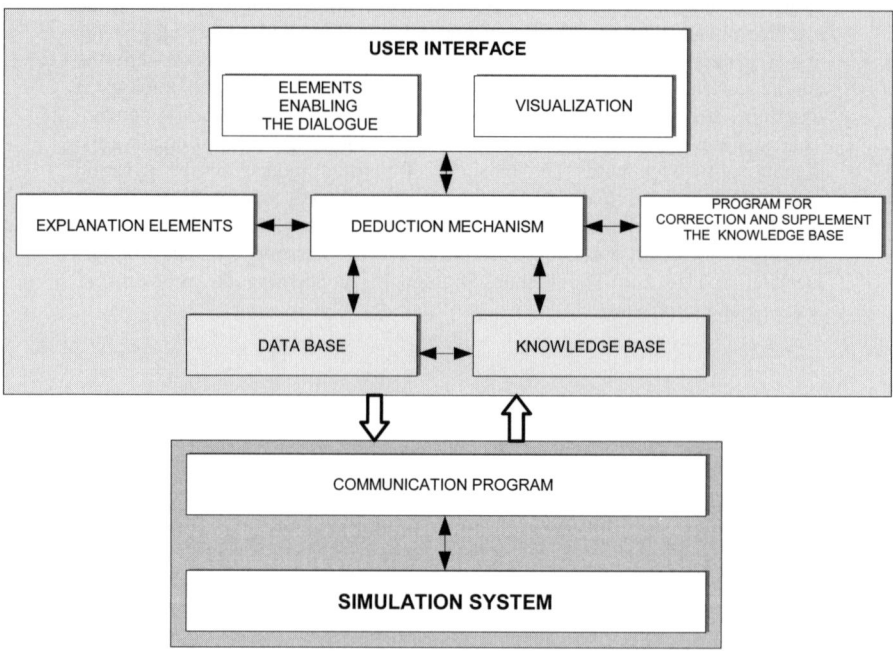

Fig. 1. Dynamic intelligent tutoring system

Methodology of creating the dynamic intelligent training system

Methodology of creating the DITS depends on the subject domain from which the training object comes from. A training object for the given class of the systems is a process of control the dynamic object. There is no one methodology of creating such systems that is established for all subject domains and types of dynamic objects. Nevertheless, a common feature of creating the DITS is that in each case after the structural analysis and analysis of the tutoring system's logic in the specific subject domain the following steps must be taken:

- establish the processes in the DITS,
- describe necessary ontologies concerning the problem/subject domain and some pedagogical aspects,
- create a dynamics model of the control object with visualization.

The crucial issue during the design process of the DITS is creating the knowledge base. A structure of the training system may be done on base of analysis of an usual logic of training process, which consists in a sequence of the connected steps: "trainee's action => measuring the action => analysis => classification of mistakes => evaluation => advice and recommendations for the trainee => repeating the action => increasing the difficulties of the task => etc.". Such analysis of training's process allows representing it as a structure, which is shown on the figure 2 [8, 9].

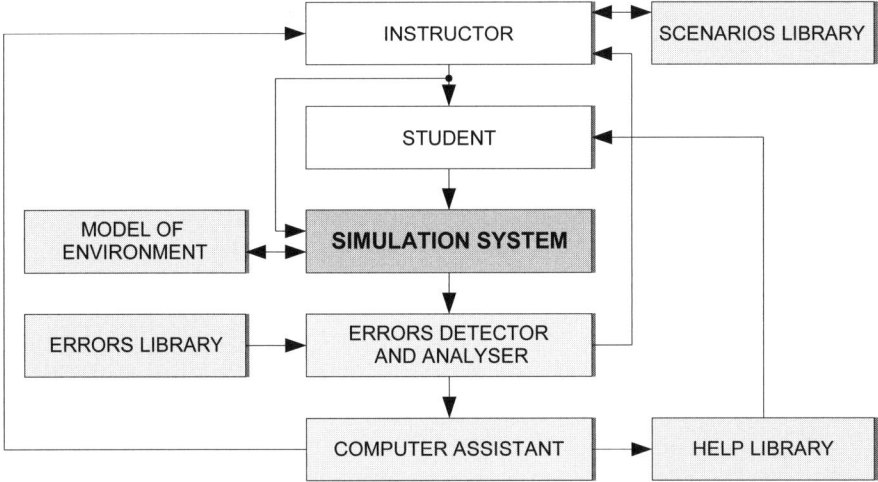

Fig. 2. The structure of DITS for civil aviation pilots [16].

The ontology of the problem/subject domain, which presents the hierarchy of knowledge applying in the tutoring system, can be use in the creating process of the knowledge base.

The concept of ontology has been introduced into the computer science by Thomas Gruber [4]. In terms of computer science ontology is a formal specification of the described area's concepts, defined by means of knowledge representation language [3]. In other words, ontology determines the concepts used for description and representation of concrete areas, and communications between them. The ontology is used in the knowledge's management, it allows simplifying process of the analysis of non-structured and ill-structured problems, allows avoiding occurrence of some contradictions and mistakes during design of knowledge's bases.

For describing the ontology, various languages and systems can be used (e.g. tree). In this case a graph can describe one or several hierarchies with relation "is-a-part-of".

In the formal form, ontology and relations between the concepts of ontology are shown by means of symbols of the set theory. Let us show a model of ontology as set:

$$M=\{C, R, I, A\}$$

where:

M - model of ontology of the subject domain,

C - concepts of the subject domain,

R - relationships between the concepts of the subject domain,

I - mechanism of interpretation the concepts and relationships between the concepts,

A - axioms.

Levels of knowledge representation in the knowledge's base of training dynamic system correspond to hierarchy of ontology, which describes the area of training's process, in view of all features of this process - pedagogical and cognitive.

In the field of creation of dynamic e-learning systems ontology includes:

- the ontology of areas for which the system of training is created,
- the ontology of techniques of training's process, namely pedagogical and cognitive aspects of training, and also
- the ontology of the necessary supplements used in system of training of dynamic processes operators (for example: models of dynamic objects and processes).

Let us consider a formal model of ontology on an example of intelligent computer-based training system of civil aircraft's pilots (figure 3) [14].

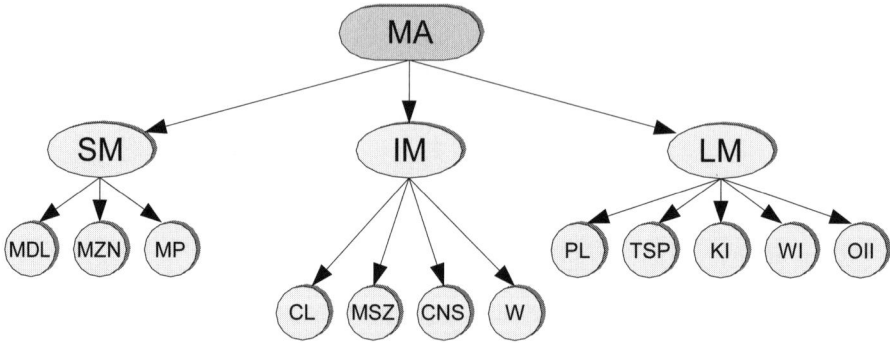

Fig. 3. The model of ontology for the civil aviation pilots.

The conceptual model of a field of knowledge **MA** is specified by a set **MA = {SM, IM, LM}** where the ontology of the domain simulation model **SM** include: model of flight dynamics, model of engines (power-plant) and model of landing gears. The ontology of the domain information model **IM** includes: characteristics of flight, environment's model, characteristics of non-standard situations, visual representations of devices and elements of the cabin in process of virtual flight. Further, the model of training's process **LM** is represented in the following manner: flight procedures, training of standard procedures, coordination of instrumental and non-instrumental information, proposals made by the virtual instructor, operative intervention of the real instructor. Presented sets can be complete by the new concepts and the model of domain knowledge can be detailed by adding new levels of the graph. In the considered example the hierarchies with the relation "is-a-part-of" are included.

Beside the tasks of creating the knowledge base, there is a wide variety of group of tasks concerning the creating of simulation systems, which reproduce in real-time the behavior of the real tutoring object [6, 7]. The mathematical model of the dynamic of the tutoring object is a base of the simulation system. In case of real dynamics objects their behavior is described by sets of nonlinear differential or difference equations. A computer realization of the dynamic model includes some problems connected with the numbers representation, selection of the stable numerical algorithms and problem of errors estimation. One of the most important issues is numerical solving of the differential equations. There exist a number of numerical methods for solving such equations, for example Euler's and Runge-Kutty methods. The Euler methods and Adams-Bashfort method could be applied in case of creating real-time software.

The simulation system reproduce also appearance of the real tutoring object hence the necessity of creating the virtual tutoring environment, like virtual cockpit for example. This topic has been described in [6, 7, 8]. The virtual reality makes possible to immerse student in the virtual environment and doing the activity the same as in the real object (figure 4).

Fig. 4. Virtual cockpit

Generally, the methodology of developing dynamic intelligent training system can be described as a bunch of methods used during solving the tasks such as:

- structural analysis of the tutoring system, where the system's elements, relations and relationships should be described ,
- creating the mathematical models of a number of specific processes that describe the behavior of the object and realization of this models in an interactive manner with a help of effective numerical methods (calculations done in the real-time);
- studying teaching contents, fixing order of the teaching materials and ways of assess the student progress,
- creating the workstation for the student and the teacher (the instructor) which should be equipped with the adequate software and hardware interface.

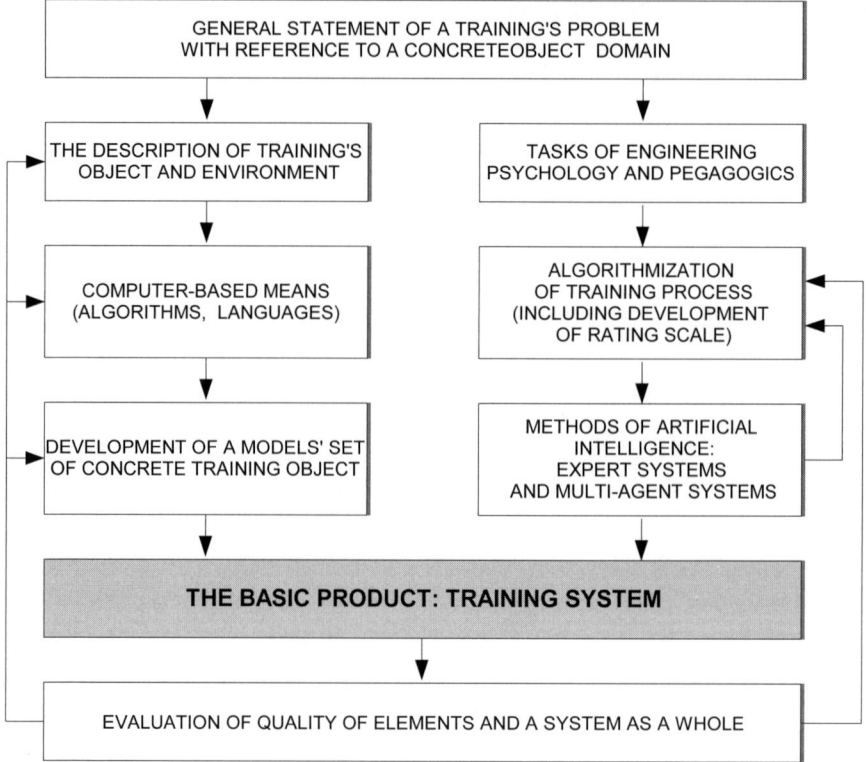

Fig. 5. The stages of creating the dynamic intelligent tutoring system [9].

The mentioned tasks can be divided into two groups: tasks related to the creating of the simulation system and tasks related to the organization of the tutoring process. Both of the groups can be realized simultaneously (figure 5).

A lot of these tasks are described as the standards. One of the first organizations that worked up recommendations for the process of creating the computer-based training systems was the Aviation Industry Computer Based Training Committee (AICC). The AICC published a set of documents concerning (among others):

- equipment of the student and teacher workstation (recommendations for the software and hardware),
- quality of sounds and pictures,
- management of the tutoring process,
- cooperation and communication between the tutoring system and the simulation system.

There exist some recommendations concerning implementation of the procedures and naming conventions for variables to make the cooperation between different scientific centres possible. The Sharable Courseware Object Reference Model (SCORM) is a collection of standards and specifications for web-based e-learning. It defines communications between client-side content and a host system called "run-time environment"(commonly a function of a learning management system).

The evaluation of the quality of the dynamic intelligent training system

The evaluation of the quality of the dynamic intelligent training system is connected to the evaluation of the quality of both the teaching process and the simulation system. In this article the evaluation of quality of the simulation system is considered.

Each mathematical model, even the most accurate, is an approximation of the real object only. The character and level of the simplification depends on the needs and can be a subject of change depending on the aims of modelling. The assumptions and simplifications that have been introduced during the modelling process causing that the model should be verified, validated and tested. The mentioned activities have a continuous nature. In case of unsuccessful validation we can change the model's structure or the values of the model's parameters. Second case is called calibration. For the nonlinear mathematical models of the real dynamics objects the calibration is done by the heuristic methods. It is difficult and time-consuming process. In [2, 10, 11, 13] authors proposed two main approaches to the correction-process: the sensitivity of the non-liner systems and studies of the sets of the linear models with using singular value decomposition of the adequate matrices.

As have been shown in [2, 3, 15, 17] the motion of the system (1)

$$\dot{X} = \Phi(t, U, \mu), \qquad X(0) = X_0 \tag{1}$$

can be described as the following set of equations:

$$\begin{cases} \dot{X}_b = X_b(t, U, \mu_b), & X(0) = X_0 \\ \dot{S} = \dfrac{\partial \Phi}{\partial X} S + \dfrac{\partial \Phi}{\partial \mu}, & S(0) = 0 \\ X(t) = X_b(t) + S\Delta\mu \end{cases} \tag{2}$$

where:

$X_b \in R^n$ –base state vector,

$U \in R^m$ –control vector,

$\mu_b \in R^p$ –vector of parameters,

t - time.

S –matrix of the sensitivity functions,

$$\frac{\partial \Phi}{\partial X} = \begin{pmatrix} \dfrac{\partial \varphi_1}{\partial x_1} & \cdots & \dfrac{\partial \varphi_1}{\partial x_n} \\ \dfrac{\partial \varphi_n}{\partial x_1} & \cdots & \dfrac{\partial \varphi_n}{\partial x_n} \end{pmatrix} \text{ and } \frac{\partial \Phi}{\partial \mu} = \begin{pmatrix} \dfrac{\partial \varphi_1}{\partial \mu_1} & \cdots & \dfrac{\partial \varphi_1}{\partial \mu_p} \\ \dfrac{\partial \varphi_n}{\partial \mu_1} & \cdots & \dfrac{\partial \varphi_n}{\partial \mu_p} \end{pmatrix} \tag{3}$$

First equation of the set (2) describes the based motion of the non-liner system. The second one describes changes in time of the entire multitude of the sensitivity functions. The last equation describes the behaviour of the system with the new value of the parameter (after the calibration). The character of the non-liner relations in the system and his dimension does not influence fundamentally algorithm of solving such a task.

In the second approach the set of the linear models has been used. Applying the linear models to describing the behaviour of the real object considerably simplifies the calibration because the well known mathematical methods (theory of linear differential equations and the linear algebra) can be used.

$$\dot{X} = AX + BU + F(t) \tag{4}$$

where:

$X_b \in R^n$ –base state vector,

$U \in R^m$ –control vector,

$F(t) \in R^n$ –vector of disturbances,

A, B - matrices with the constant coefficients, $\dim A = (n \times n)$, $\dim B = (n \times m)$

The change of the dynamic characteristics of the object that is described by the linear equation (4) can be done on this way:

- the idea of the modal control , which is referred to the changes of the eigenvalues of the matrix A,
- the singular value decomposition that allows changing the efficiency of the control signal (the changes of the elements form the vector B).

Both of the tasks have been described in detail in [10, 11, 12] and the general algorithm was presented.

Conclusion

In this paper a concept of the dynamic intelligent training system for operators of the dynamic systems was introduced. Some characteristics were defined and the main elements were presented. The problems, connected with the creating of the knowledge base and creating of the simulation system, were analyzed. The methodology of creating the dynamic intelligent tutoring system was proposed. All problems mentioned in the presented paper have been applied during the international project ASIMIL.

Reference

[1] Barcz A., Banaś P., Popov O., Tretyakova T., *ASIMIL - Projekt 5 - go ramowego programu Unii Europejskiej (Udział Wydziału Informatyki w projekcie Unii Europejskiej)*, Materiały 5 Sesji Naukowej Informatyki WIPS, Szczecin, 2000;

[2] Barcz A., Popov O., *Verification of the processes' mathematical models in the computer-based tutoring system using the sensitivity analysis*, Materiały 10. Międzynarodowej Konferencji Advanced Computer Systems – ACS 2003, Międzyzdroje, 2003;

[3] Barcz A., Popov O., *Zagadnienia kalibracji modeli obiektów dynamicznych*, Roczniki Informatyki Stosowanej: Metody Informatyki Stosowanej w zarządzaniu, tom 9, redakcja R. Budziński, Wydział Informatyki, Politechnika Szczecińska, Szczecin, 2005;

[4] Gruber T., *The Acquisition of the Strategic Knowledge*, Academic Press, 1989;

[5] Leney T., *Achieving the Lisbon goal:The contribution of VET*, Executive Summary, 2004; http://www.vetconference-maastricht2004.nl

[6] Popov O., Barcz A., Piela P., Sobczak T., *Practical realization of modeling an airplane for an intelligent tutoring system*, Materiały 9. Międzynarodowej Konferencji Advanced Computer Systems – ACS 2002, Międzyzdroje, 2002;

[7] Popov O., Barcz A., Piela P., Sobczak T., *Problem of the flight simulation in computer-based training systems for civil aviation*, Proceedings of the 6th International Conference Intelligent Tutoring Systems, Workshop Simulation Based Training, Biarritz, 2002;

[8] Popov O., Barcz A., Piela P., Tretyakov A., *Some problems of design of computer-based training systems for civil aviation pilots, methods of their solving*, 16th IFAC Symposium on Automatic Control in Aerospace – ACA 2004, St. Petersburg, 2004;

[9] Popov O., Lalanne R., Gouarderes G., Minko A., Tretyakov A., *Structure of Multi-Agent Tutoring System and its Application in Aeronautical Training*, International Journal of Computers, Systems and Signals, Pretoria, RPA, Vol. 3, No. 2, 2002;

[10] Popov O., Piela P., *Korekta parametrów komputerowych modeli dynamiki na przykładzie modelu dynamiki lotu samolotu*, Roczniki Informatyki Stosowanej Wydziału Informatyki Politechniki Szczecińskiej nr. 6, Szczecin, 2004;

[11] Popov O., Piela P., *Structural transformation of dynamic systems' models and their using in a Computer-Based Tutoring System*, Proceedings of the 9th International Conference Advanced Computer Systems; part II, p. 339 – 347, Międzyzdroje 2002, Polska;

[12] Popov O., Piela P., *Metodyka korekcji i weryfikacji modeli dynamiki wykorzystywanych w komputerowych systemach nauczania*, Roczniki Informatyki Stosowanej Wydziału Informatyki Politechniki Szczecińskiej nr. 9, Szczecin, 2005;

[13] Popov O., Tretyakov A., *Quantitative measures of systems structural qualities in control, management and identification problems*, Proceedings of Workshop on European scientific and industrial collaboration WESIC'99, Newport, United Kingdom, 1999;

[14] Popov O., Tretyakova T., *Ontologies as a technique of knowledge management in open e - learning systems for operators of dynamic processes,* Studies & Proceedings of Polish Association for Konwledge Management, Volume Editor: W. Bojar, Bydgoszcz, 2006;

[15] Rosenwasser E., Yosupov R., *Sensitivity of automatic control systems,* CRC Press, Washington, 2000;

[16] *The European Higher Education Area – The Bologna Declaration of 19 June 1999*: Joint Declaration of the European Ministers of Education; www.bologna-bergen2005.no;

[17] Wierzbicki A., *Modele i wrażliwość układów sterowania,* Wydawnictwa Naukowo Techniczne, Warszawa, 1977;

Algorithms of Identification of Multi-connected Boundary Geometry and Material Parameters in Problems Described by Navier-Lame Equation using the PIES

Eugeniusz Zieniuk, Agnieszka Bołtuć, Andrzej Kużelewski

University of Bialystok, Institute of Computer Science
Sosnowa 64, 15-887 Bialystok, Poland
Tel. +48857457671, Fax. +48857457662
{ezieniuk, aboltuc, akuzel}@ii.uwb.edu.pl

1. Introduction

Boundary problems can be divided on two groups: analysis (simple) and synthesis (inverse) problems [1,6]. From a practical point of view the latter group form a very significant category of problems that are more complex than former. Inverse problems are often described as ill-posed [6] because they do not always have a solution or number of solutions can be infinite. Inverse problems are usually divided into three groups: problem of identification of material parameters, boundary conditions or shape of the boundary geometry.

In order to solve these problems various methods can be used. However, the most frequently used methods based on minimization of functional. In practice, it is equivalent to multiple solving of analysis problem with modified boundary geometry. Analysis problems can be solved using well-known numerical methods, such as the Finite Element Method (FEM) [2,11] or the Boundary Element Method (BEM) [3,4]. However, application of both of them are very inconvenient when we should repeat it in iteration process with modified boundary geometry because they require traditional discretization.

In our previous papers we propose a method based on the Parametric Integral Equation System (PIES), which does not require discretization contrary to traditional element methods. The boundary geometry in the PIES is modelled by means of small number of corner points, which define necessary number of linear segments. Modification of such geometry is reduced to changing positions of chosen corner points. For that reason, identification of the boundary geometry is reduced to identification of coordinates of corner points.

Problems of identification of the boundary geometry were successfully considered by authors in the case of 2D [8] and 3D [10] boundary problems described by Laplace's equation. The problem of identification of polygonal boundary geometry described by Navier-Lame equation [9] was successfully examined, as well.

This paper presents solution of problems from two different groups: identification of the shape of the boundary and identification of material parameters. First of all, as a development of our previous work, the problem of identification of a shape of multiply connected boundary geometry described by Navier-Lame equation is considered. The second part of the work is connected with problem of identification of the Poisson's ratio v and shear modulus μ.

2. The PIES, its solution and definition

2.1 Definition of boundary geometry with one and many surfaces

In order to define the boundary geometry in the PIES only corner points are posed [7]. The number of these points is much less than the number of boundary nodes required in the traditional BEM for boundary elements defining. The next great advantage of that way of modelling is the fact, that the number of corner points described domains with identical shapes but different areas is the same. It denote that the number of input data is independent of area of domains with the same shapes.

In distinction to the traditional boundary elements, moving of arbitrary corner points will result in the modification of a considerable part of the boundary geometry. These points are used to modify the shape of the boundary geometry, therefore they are exploited in identification process, as well. Thus, the identification of the shape of the boundary geometry is reduced to the identification of corner points exclusively.

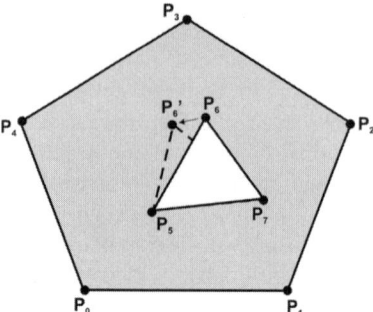

Fig. 1. Definition and modification of multi-connected boundary geometry

Figure 1 presents the way of modelling and modification of multi-connected boundary geometry by means of linear segments and corner points. Presented geometry is built with two boundaries: external with 5 corner points $P_i(i=0,1,...,4)$ and internal with 3 corner points $P_i(i=5,6,7)$. Modification is made by only one corner point P_6.

2.2 Mathematical foundations of the PIES

The Parametric Integral Equation System (PIES) used to solve Navier-Lame equation with arbitrary boundary conditions is presented by the following formula [7]

$$0.5\boldsymbol{u}_p(s_1) = \sum_{r=1}^{n} \boldsymbol{J}_r \int_{s_{r-1}}^{s_r} \left\{ \overline{\boldsymbol{U}}_{pr}^*(s_1,s)\boldsymbol{p}_r(s) - \overline{\boldsymbol{P}}_{pr}^*(s_1,s)\boldsymbol{u}_r(s) \right\} ds, \qquad (1)$$

where $s_{p-1} \le s_1 \le s_p$, $s_{r-1} \le s \le s_r$.

Integrand functions $\overline{U}_{pr}^{*}(s_1,s)$ and $\overline{P}_{pr}^{*}(s_1,s)$ occurred in (1) are presented in the following forms

$$\overline{U}_{pr}^{*}(s_1,s) = -\frac{1}{8\pi(1-v)\mu}\begin{bmatrix} (3-4v)\ln(\eta)-\dfrac{\eta_1^2}{\eta^2} & -\dfrac{\eta_1\eta_2}{\eta^2} \\[2mm] -\dfrac{\eta_1\eta_2}{\eta^2} & (3-4v)\ln(\eta)-\dfrac{\eta_2^2}{\eta^2} \end{bmatrix}, \qquad (2)$$

$$\overline{P}_{pr}^{*}(s_1,s) = -\frac{1}{4\pi(1-v)\eta}\begin{bmatrix} P_{11} & P_{12} \\ P_{21} & P_{22} \end{bmatrix}, \quad p,r = 1,2,.....n, \qquad (3)$$

where

$$P_{11} = \left\{(1-2v)+2\frac{\eta_1^2}{\eta^2}\right\}\frac{\partial\eta}{\partial n}, \qquad P_{12} = \left\{2\frac{\eta_1\eta_2}{\eta^2}\frac{\partial\eta}{\partial n}-(1-2v)\left[\frac{\eta_1}{\eta}n_2+\frac{\eta_2}{\eta}n_1\right]\right\},$$

$$P_{21} = \left\{2\frac{\eta_2\eta_1}{\eta^2}\frac{\partial\eta}{\partial n}-(1-2v)\left[\frac{\eta_2}{\eta}n_1+\frac{\eta_1}{\eta}n_2\right]\right\}, \qquad P_{22} = \left\{(1-2v)+2\frac{\eta_2^2}{\eta^2}\right\}\frac{\partial\eta}{\partial n},$$

$$\frac{\partial\eta}{\partial n} = \frac{\partial\eta_1}{\partial\eta}n_1+\frac{\partial\eta_2}{\partial\eta}n_2, \qquad \eta = [\eta_1^2+\eta_2^2]^{0.5}, \qquad \eta_1 = \Gamma_r^{(1)}(s)-\Gamma_p^{(1)}(s_1) \qquad \text{and}$$

$$\eta_2 = \Gamma_r^{(2)}(s)-\Gamma_p^{(2)}(s_1).$$

Functions $\Gamma_r^{(i)}(s)$, $i=1,2$ occurred in these expressions are parametric linear segments. The boundary geometry defined by means of these functions is included into mathematical formalism of fundamental (2) and singular (3) boundary solutions.

2.3 Numerical solving of the PIES

The PIES (1) can be solved using various numerical methods for solving integral equation systems. One of the simplest methods, which requires only single integration, is the pseudospectral method.

The solving of the PIES is reduced to approximation one of the unknown boundary functions. These functions in the PIES are not directly connected with approximation of boundary geometry. Separation of the approximation of boundary geometry from the approximation of boundary functions gives possibility of more effective approximation of boundary functions and modelling of boundary geometry.

For the approximation of boundary functions $u_r(s)$, $p_r(s)$ on each individual segment r, the following approximation series were applied

$$p_r(s) = \sum_{k=0}^{N} p_r^{(k)} T_r^{(k)}(s), \qquad u_r(s) = \sum_{k=0}^{N} u_r^{(k)} T_r^{(k)}(s), \qquad (4)$$

where $u_r^{(k)}, p_r^{(k)}$ are the unknown coefficients, N is the number of coefficients and $T_r^k(s)$ are global base functions on the segments, e.g. Chebyshev polynomials of any degree.

After substitution (4) into (1) and written down obtained expression for all collocation points we obtain system of algebraic equations with respect to unknown coefficients $u_r^{(k)}$ or $p_r^{(k)}$

$$AX = B \qquad \text{where} \qquad X = \{u_r^{(k)}, p_r^{(k)}\}^T . \qquad (5)$$

Next, after substitution computed coefficients into approximation series (4) we obtain expression which allows to receive solutions at any points on each segment.

3. Algorithm of identification of boundary geometry and material constants

3.1 Identification of unknown part of multi-connected boundary geometry

The problem solved in that paper concerns identification of an unknown part of boundary geometry modelled in the PIES for the Navier-Lame equation. It is assumed that both empirical values at some measurement points on the analyzed part of the boundary geometry and boundary conditions are known. To reconstruct the unknown part of the boundary geometry (based on known empirical values) the PIES is used.

In the PIES for defining the boundary geometry we use only small number of corner points $P_p(p = 0,1,....n)$. Any modification of boundary geometry is also performed by those points. For that reason, identification process is reduced to identification of coordinates of an unknown corner points.

If we have experimental values $\tilde{u}_{ol}(s_i), i = 1,2,..m, o = 1,2$ obtained at m measurement points at the boundary l of the problem, we can use the least square method for solving considered problem

$$S(s,P_p) = 0.5 \sum_{i=1}^{m} \left\{ \sum_{o=1}^{2} \left[\tilde{u}_{ol}(s_i,P_p)^* - u_{ol}(s_i,P_p) \right]^2 \right\}, \qquad (6)$$

where $\tilde{u}_{ol}(s_i,P_p)^*$ are experimental values of measurement points at a given boundary, while $u_{ol}(s_i,P_p)$ are numerical values obtained from the PIES (1).

The shape of the considered domain is included in the kernels (2,3) of the PIES and is defined by corner points. Solutions obtained from the PIES are continuous in each segment. With their help we can easily obtain values of solutions at measurement points, which depend on the shape of the identified boundary. When defining a boundary shape in the continuous way by means of linear segments, they depend on the corner points. Therefore, minimization of formula (6) should be performed with respect to these points. Formula (6), after differentiation, can be written as follows:

$$\frac{\partial S(s,P_p)}{\partial P_p} = \sum_{i=1}^{m} \left\{ \sum_{o=1}^{2} \left[\tilde{u}_{ol}(s_i,P_p)^* - u_{ol}(s_i,P_p) \right] \frac{\partial u_{ol}(s_i,P_p)}{\partial P_p} \right\}, \qquad p = 1,2,....M, \qquad (7)$$

where M is the number of identified corner points.

In that expression computation of the first order derivative of the boundary function $u_{ol}(s_i,P_p)$ with respect to corner points $P_p (p = 1,2,....M)$ is required. This function is defined by means of the PIES (1). Therefore, the derivative can be easily computed numerically.

In order to calculate the derivative, the PIES (1) should be solved twice for two insignificantly different (ΔP_p) corner points. Once the PIES is solved for initial geometry (defined by means of corner points P_p) and then for the geometry modified by displacement of corner points about ΔP_p.

After equating to zero (7), a system of $2M$ algebraic equations with respect to the unknown coordinates of corner points is obtained. It is a non-linear system of algebraic equations with respect to the unknown corner points. Newton's iterative method is used to solve it. That system is presented in the following matrix form

$$\{\nabla_p(P)\}_{(k)}\{\delta P_p\} = -\{F_p(P)\}_{(k)} \tag{8}$$

where matrix $\nabla_p(P)$ is presented in the following form

$$\nabla_p(P) = \begin{bmatrix} \dfrac{\partial F_p(s,P)}{\partial P_p} & \dfrac{\partial F_p(s,P)}{\partial P_{p+1}} & \cdots\cdots & \dfrac{\partial F_p(s,P)}{\partial P_{p+P}} \\[2mm] \dfrac{\partial F_{p+1}(s,P)}{\partial P_p} & \dfrac{\partial F_{p+1}(s,P)}{\partial P_{p+1}} & \cdots\cdots & \dfrac{\partial F_{p+1}(s,P)}{\partial P_{p+P}} \\[2mm] \cdots\cdots & \cdots\cdots & \cdots\cdots & \cdots\cdots \\[2mm] \dfrac{\partial F_{p+P}(s,P)}{\partial P_p} & \dfrac{\partial F_{p+P}(s,P)}{\partial P_{p+1}} & \cdots\cdots & \dfrac{\partial F_{p+P}(s,P)}{\partial P_{p+P}} \end{bmatrix}_{(k)} \tag{9}$$

and $F_p(s,P)$ is the expression found on right-hand side of the formula (7).

Coefficients of matrix (9) are obtained after analytical differentiation of the function $F_p(s_i,P)$ ($p=1,2,....M$) with the respect to all corner points. As the result of the differentiation following formulas are obtained

$$\frac{\partial F_p(s,P)}{\partial P_p} = \sum_{i=1}^{m}\sum_{o=1}^{2}\left\{-\frac{\partial u_{ol}(s_i,P_p)}{\partial P_p}\frac{\partial u_{ol}(s_i,P_p)}{\partial P_p} + [\tilde{u}_{ol}(s_i,P_p)^* - u_{ol}(s_i,P_p)]\frac{\partial^2 u_{ol}(s_i,P_p)}{\partial P_p^2}\right\},$$
$$\frac{\partial F_p(s,P)}{\partial P_{p+1}} = \sum_{i=1}^{m}\sum_{o=1}^{2}\left\{-\frac{\partial u_{ol}(s_i,P_p)}{\partial P_{p+1}}\frac{\partial u_{ol}(s_i,P_p)}{\partial P_{p+1}} + [\tilde{u}_{ol}(s_i,P_p)^* - u_{ol}(s_i,P_p)]\frac{\partial^2 u_{ol}(s_i,P_p)}{\partial P_p \partial P_{p+1}}\right\}, \tag{10}$$

To compute the elements of matrix (9) with formulas (10) it is necessary to compute the second order derivative of the boundary functions with the respect to corner points. For that purpose approximate way of derivatives computation can be used.

Columned matrix $F_p(P)$ found on the right-hand side of system (8) is presented in the following form:

$$\{F_p(P)\} = \begin{Bmatrix} F_p(s,P) \\ F_{p+1}(s,P) \\ \cdots\cdots \\ F_{p+P}(s,P) \end{Bmatrix}_{(k)} \tag{11}$$

where $F_p(s,P)$ is the expression found on right-hand side of the formula (7).

The first order derivative of the boundary function with the respect to corner points is computed numerically by means of formula (10).

New values of corner points $P_p^{(k+1)}$ in the following steps of iteration process are as follows

$$P_p^{(k+1)} = P_p^{(k)} + \delta P_p. \tag{12}$$

We can identified corner points as a result of iteration process assuming any initial corner points $P_p^{(0)}$ $(p=1,2,....M)$ in (12). Iteration process is completed when the last two values of coordinates of corner points are the same or when the difference between empirical and numerical values at measurement points becomes minimal.

3.2 Identification of material constants

For identification of material constants we use the same algorithm as for previous task. If we describe a vector of material parameters as $C = \{v, \mu\}$ and we have experimental values $\tilde{u}_{ol}(s_i)$, $i = 1,2,..m$, $o = 1,2$ obtained at m measurement points at the boundary l of the problem, expression (6) takes the following form

$$S(s,C) = 0.5 \sum_{i=1}^{m} \left\{ \sum_{o=1}^{2} \left[\tilde{u}_{ol}(s_i,C)^* - u_{ol}(s_i,C) \right]^2 \right\}, \tag{13}$$

where $\tilde{u}_{ol}(s_i,C)^*$ are experimental values of measurement points at a given boundary and with given material constants, while $u_{ol}(s_i,C)$ are numerical values obtained from the PIES (1).

Values at measurement points depend on values in C, therefore minimization of above formula should be performed with respect to material parameters. After that we obtained

$$\frac{\partial S(s,C)}{\partial C} = \sum_{i=1}^{m} \left\{ \sum_{o=1}^{2} \left[\tilde{u}_{ol}(s_i,C)^* - u_{ol}(s_i,C) \right] \frac{\partial u_{ol}(s_i,C)}{\partial C} \right\}. \tag{14}$$

First order derivatives from (14) are computed numerically in the same way as before. Then we should equate (14) to zero and after that we obtain system of 2 algebraic equations with respect to the unknown values of material constants

$$\{\nabla(C)\}_{(k)} \{\delta C\} = -\{F(C)\}_{(k)} \tag{15}$$

where matrix $\nabla(C) = \dfrac{\partial F(s,C)}{\partial C}$ and vector $F(C) = F(s,C)$, where $F(s,C)$ is the expression found on right-hand side of the formula (14).

To compute the elements of matrix $\nabla(C)$ it is necessary to compute second order derivative of boundary functions with respect to material constants. An approximate way of derivative computation can be used for this purpose.

Finally, new values of material constants $C^{(k+1)}$ in the following steps of the iteration process are as follows

$$C^{(k+1)} = C^{(k)} + \delta C. \tag{16}$$

4. Testing examples

We take into consideration inverse problem with multi-connected polygonal boundary geometry and boundary conditions presented in Fig. 2. An unknown part of the boundary geometry is described by three corner points P_4, P_5, P_6 (two linear segments).

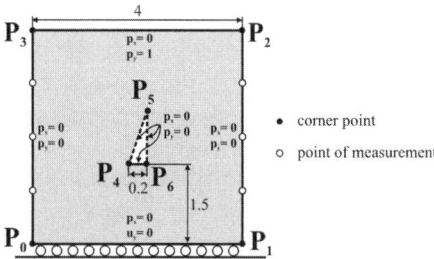

Fig. 2. Definition of multi-connected polygonal boundary geometry

Measurement points are located on a known part of the boundary (such as in Figure 2). Measured values in the points are as follows: $u_{1x}(s=0.25)=-0.59$, $u_{1y}(s=0.25)=0.97$, $u_{2x}(s=0.5)=-0.6$, $u_{2y}(s=0.5)=1.93$, $u_{3x}(s=0.75)=-0.58$, $u_{3y}(s=0.75)=2.89$, $u_{4x}(s=0.25)=0.58$, $u_{4y}(s=0.25)=2.89$, $u_{5x}(s=0.5)=0.6$, $u_{5y}(s=0.5)=1.93$, $u_{6x}(s=0.75)=0.59$, $u_{6y}(s=0.75)=0.97$. The solution of the problem is to find coordinates of the corner point P_5. Expected solution is $x_1=2.0$ and $x_2=2.5$. Solutions obtained in identification process are presented in Table 1.

Table 1. Solutions in identification process of multi-connected polygonal boundary geometry

number of iterations	coordinates of initial point P_5		coordinates of identified point P_5'	
	x_1	x_2	x_1	x_2
11	1.5	2.5	1.996	2.655
20	1.5	3.0	1.997	2.656
5	2.0	2.0	2.0	2.542
3	2.0	3.0	2.0	2.503
16	2.5	2.5	2.002	2.667
23	2.5	3.0	2.001	2.677

Visualization of selected results of identification process is presented in Fig. 3.

As can be seen all obtained results are almost the same independently of initial boundary geometry, but they are a bit different from expected solution. Coordinate x_1 is always the same as expected one, but coordinate x_2 is identified with some error. In our opinion, the error is connected with the shape of internal boundary. We can see that changing position of the point P_5 along coordinate x_2 has smaller influence on the shape of the cavity than along coordinate x_1. It can be connected with assumed level of accuracy of measurements, as well. However, it requires more detailed researches. Despite requirement of several number of iterations in identification process, it can be described as fast.

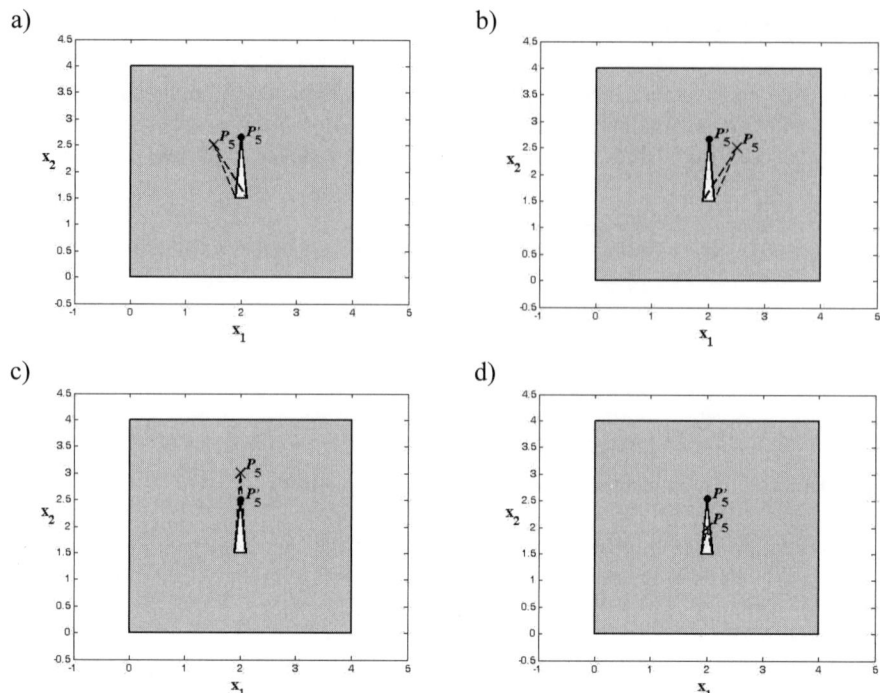

Fig. 3. Selected initial and identified geometries (dashed and solid lines, respectively),
× - initial corner point, ● - identified corner point

The next stage of researches on inverse problems was connected with identification of material constants: the Poisson's ratio υ and shear modulus μ. Two examples with different shape and complexity of boundary geometry and kind of posed boundary conditions were solved and included.

In the first example the boundary problem from Fig.4a was taken into account. Experimental values were taken from 6 boundary points (three on each vertical side of considered square geometry).

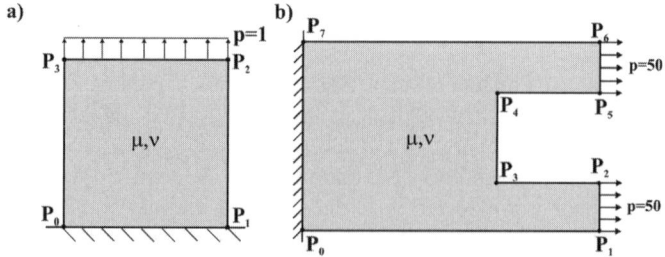

Fig. 4. Identification of material parameters a) first example, b) second example

In order to solve the problem different values of initial material constants were considered. Obtained results are presented in Table 2.

Table 2. Initial and obtained results of identification process

Initial values		Obtained values		Number
ν	μ	ν	μ	of iterations
0.4	1.3	0.400020	1.000100	21
0.5	1	0.400002	0.999989	4
0.1	1	0.400001	0.999994	6
0.4	0.1	0.400001	0.999990	14
0.5	1.2	0.400016	1.000090	8
0.5	0.1	0.400006	1.000010	10
0.1	0.1	0.400001	0.999990	15
0.05	1.2	0.400003	0.999991	6

Analyzing solutions from above table it appears that convergence of the method is excellent. Regardless of initial points obtained material constants are $\mu = 1$ and $\nu = 0.4$.

Second example is concerned with more complex boundary geometry presented in Fig. 4b. Six measurement points are located on boundary $P_7 P_0$ and $P_3 P_4$. Results of performed identifications are presented in Table 3.

Table 3. Initial and obtained results of identification process

Initial values		Obtained values		Number
ν	μ	ν	μ	of iterations
0.03	80	0.300024	79.9978	4
0.43	80	0.300004	79.9958	7
0.3	30	0.300000	79.9999	8
0.3	100	0.300004	79.9955	6
0.1	40	0.300001	79.9996	7
0.05	105	0.300011	79.9987	4
0.4	25	0.300000	79.9999	8
0.45	95	0.300002	79.9983	5

As can be seen from above juxtaposition accuracy of obtained results is very high. The iterative identification process always converges to the same values of material constants $\mu = 80$ and $\nu = 0.3$, which correspond to material constants of rustless steel.

5. Conclusions

Very important stage of boundary geometry identification problems is repeated solving of analysis problems. For that reason, application of effective method for repeated solving of analysis problems is great challenge. Proposed PIES fulfilled that task, because it does not require any discretization, what reduces time and cost of calculations. In identification problems we use combination of the PIES and mean squared criterion. Proposed method was successful in the case of identification of polygonal geometry, therefore it was applied to more complicated cases such as multi-connected domains. The problems risen in that case require more detailed researches. However, it appears to be more effective than methods which require traditional discertization. Examined algorithm was also applied to problems of identification of material parameters. In accordance with expectations, it is very effective, accurate and fast.

Acknowledgments

Research work financed from the science budget for the years 2005-2007 – Polish project number 3T11F01528

References

[1] Beck J. V., Blackwell B, St. Clair, Jr. C. R., Inverse Heat Conduction: Ill-posed Problems, Wiley-Interscience, New York, 1985.
[2] Beer G, Watson J.O., Introduction to finite and boundary element methods for engineers, John Wiley & Sons, New York, 1992.
[3] Beskos D.E., Boundary element methods in mechanics, North-Holand, Amsterdam, 1987.
[4] Brebbia C.A., Telles J.C.F., Wrobel L.C., Boundary element techniques, theory and applications in engineering, Springer-Verlag, New York, 1984.
[5] Liu G.R., Han X., Computational inverse techniques in non-destructive evaluation, CRC Press LLC, 2003.
[6] Tikhonov A.N., Arsenin V.Y., Solution of Ill-posed problems, John Wiley & Sons, New York, 1977.
[7] Zieniuk E., Bołtuć A., Non-element method of solving 2D boundary problems defined on polygonal domains modeled by Navier-Lame equation, International Journal of Solids and Structures, 43, 7939-7958, 2006.
[8] Zieniuk E., Bołtuć A., Identification of polygonal domains using PIES in inverse boundary problems modeled by 2D Laplace's equation, TASK QUARTERLY 9 No 4, 415-426, 2005.
[9] Zieniuk E., Bołtuć A., Kużelewski A.: Identification of polygonal boundary geometry using the PIES in problems described by Navier equation, Advanced Computer Systems Vol. II, 227-236, 2006.
[10] Zieniuk E., Szerszeń K., Bołtuć A., 3D boundary shape identification in boundary-value problems using the Parametric Integral Equation System with the aid of genetic algorithms, Image Analysis, Computer Graphics, Security Systems and Artificial Intelligence Applications Vol. I, 43-51, 2005.
[11] Zienkiewicz O.C., The Finite Element Methods, McGraw-Hill, London, 1977.

Analysis of an Open Linked Series Three-station Network with Blocking

Walenty Oniszczuk

Bialystok University of Technology, Faculty of Computer Science,
ul. Wiejska 45A, 15-351 Bialystok, Poland
walenty@ii.pb.bialystok.pl

Abstract. This paper describes an analytical study on open three-station network models with blocking assuming that there are finite capacity buffers at the front of each server. Tasks arrive from the source station at station A in a Poisson fashion at a rate λ, and the service times at the first and second station are exponentially distributed with a mean of s^A and s^B respectively. Both service stations have buffers with finite capacities. Here, a two-dimensional state graph was constructed and a set of steady-state equations is created. These equations allow for calculating state probabilities for each graph state. In the next part of the paper, the algorithms for calculation of the main measures of effectiveness in an open three-station model are presented. The numerical part of this paper contains examples of an investigation of the three-station models, where there are presented the results of the calculation of the main measures of effectiveness and quality of service (QoS) parameters.

1. Introduction

In mathematical models of discrete flow systems, which are realistic and effective tools for performance analysis of a wide class of systems such as computer systems and networks, telecommunication networks, queuing network models (QNM) with finite capacity queues and blocking are often used [1, 5, 11, 14]. Over the years, many publications related to the analysis and application of QNMs with finite capacity queues and blocking in the field of computer science or operations research have been written [2, 4, 8, 9]. Finite capacity queuing network models are of great value towards effective congestion control and quality of service (QoS) protection of modern discrete flow networks. Blocking in such networks arises because the traffic of jobs through one queue may be momentarily halted if the destination queue has reached its capacity [6, 7, 12, 13]. Exact closed-form solutions for QNMs with blocking are not generally attainable except for some special cases. As a consequence, numerical techniques and analytic approximations have been proposed for the study of arbitrary QNMs under various types of blocking mechanisms. Authoritative expositions of the subject appear in Perros [10] and Balsamo et al. [3]. However, there is still a great interest in the systems with buffer capacity limitations under different blocking mechanisms [2]. A blocking mechanism restricts the total intensity of the input streams by forcing certain limitations on the blocking and synchronization procedures. Such models are in constant demand for the performance evaluation and predication of more complex systems such as high-speed telecommunication networks or flexible manufacturing systems, etc.

Most research in the area of an open network with blocking linked in series (see for example [10]) uses some approximation algorithms. These approximation algorithms are based on the notion of decomposition. That is, the series network configuration is broken up into sub-systems and each sub-system is analyzed separately. In order to analyze a sub-system in isolation, one needs information from other sub-systems. This requirement leads to an iterative scheme whereby the sub-systems are successively analyzed until some criterion of convergence is achieved. The approximation algorithms presented in most of the publications are based on either single-station or two-station decomposition. In single-station decomposition, each sub-system consists of a single station; in a two-station decomposition, each sub-system consists of two adjacent stations. We note one that can construct a decomposition algorithm where each sub-system consists of more than two adjacent stations, say three stations. Such an approximation algorithm will probably be more accurate than a single-station or a two-station decomposition. This kind of approach is presented in this paper. The state of this queuing network can be described by a pair of variables indicating the number of tasks in the first station and the number of tasks in the second station. However, it will be more calculation intensive since it will take longer to analyze each sub-system.

This paper provides the mathematical study of a special type of network configuration (three-station), as shown in Fig. 1.

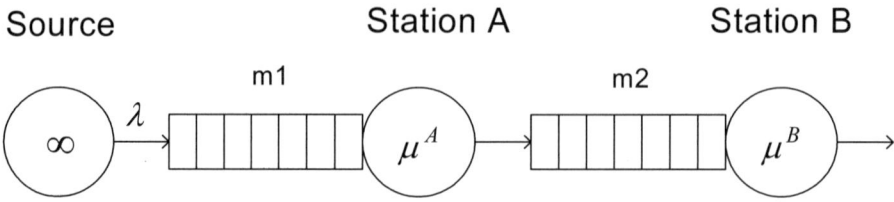

Fig. 1. Three-station network with blocking

This kind of network has a single service line at the first station, and other station the same with a single servicing line. Between these stations is a common waiting buffer with finite capacity, for example equal to $m2$. When this buffer is full, the accumulation of new tasks from the first station is temporarily suspended and a phenomenon called blocking occurs, until the queue empties and allows new inserts. Similarly, if the first buffer (with capacity $m1$) ahead of the first station is full, then the source station is blocked. This is the classical mechanism for controlling the intensity of the arriving tasks stream, which comes from the source station to the servicing two-station.

In this kind of network configuration, no more than $m1+m2+2$ tasks can be processed simultaneously and the three-station network becomes idle, if there are no tasks in both servicing stations. Assuming that the input stream from a source station to the servicing stations represents a Poisson process and the service time in both servicing stations corresponds to a random variable with an exponential distribution, this is a Markovian model of a network with series station blocking. At the beginning of this paper all possible states of the three-station network are defined, then the steady state probabilities and the main tandem measures of effectiveness are calculated. Additionally, algorithms for the calculation of blocking probabilities of the source station, the first station and simultaneously both stations, delay time in the buffers, blocking time in the source and first station, the percentage of buffers filling, etc. are shown.

The structure of the paper is as follows. Section 2 specifies the model of the three-station network and shows procedures for finding the state probabilities in a Markov linked in series three-station model, in Section 3, the procedures for calculating the main measures of effectiveness are given. Model implementation and a numerical example are described in Section 4. Finally, conclusions are drawn in Section 5.

2. Exact numerical analysis

In this paper, we consider open queuing networks consisting of finite capacity queues linked in series. We refer to such an arrangement of queues as a three-station configuration. With the exception of some special cases, a three-station configuration does not have a closed-form solution. One way of analyzing such queuing networks is to solve numerically for the stationary probability vector of the underlying Markov process. This method is feasible when the queuing network is not too large.

Let us consider the three-station network with blocking as shown in Fig.1. The input tasks stream comes from the source station to the station A. This station has a finite capacity buffer and it can accept only $m1+1$ tasks. A new task, which arrives at the full first station buffer, is forced to wait in the source station and blocks it. Each task at the first station is processed on the service line and upon service completion sent to station B. If there is a free servicing line on this station, the service process starts immediately, if not, the task must wait in the buffer. If the buffer is full, any task upon service completion at station A, is forced to wait and blocks this station.

The general assumptions for this three-station model are:

- an external task stream arriving from the source station to station A is assumed to be a Poisson stream, with rate $\lambda=1/a$, where a is mean inter-arrival time,
- single service line is on station A,
- single service line is available on station B,
- in both stations the service time for each task represents an exponentially distributed random variable, with mean $s^A = 1/\mu^A$ and $s^B = 1/\mu^B$, where μ is mean service rate,
- the buffers capacities are finite, for example equal to $m1$ and $m2$.

Under these assumptions, if the first or the second buffer is full, any task upon completion of service at the source station or at station A, is forced to wait in its service line. The transfer process from the source station to station A or from the first station to B station depends only on service process in stations A or B respectively. Physically, blocked tasks stay on the source station or on station A, but the nature of the service process in stations *A* and *B*, allows one to treat them as located in additional places in the buffers and they belong to stations *A* or *B*. In this case, there can be a maximum of *m1+2* tasks assigned to the first servicing station including task in the source that can be blocked. Similarly, there can be a maximum of *m2+2* tasks assigned to station *B* with task blocked in station *A*.

If the numbers of tasks located simultaneously in the network in the first and second servicing stations are denoted by *i* and *j*, then a Markov model with two-dimensional state space and with a unique one path from the state *(0,0)* to any state *(i,j)* and back to the state *(0,0)* is defined in this paper (see Figure 2).

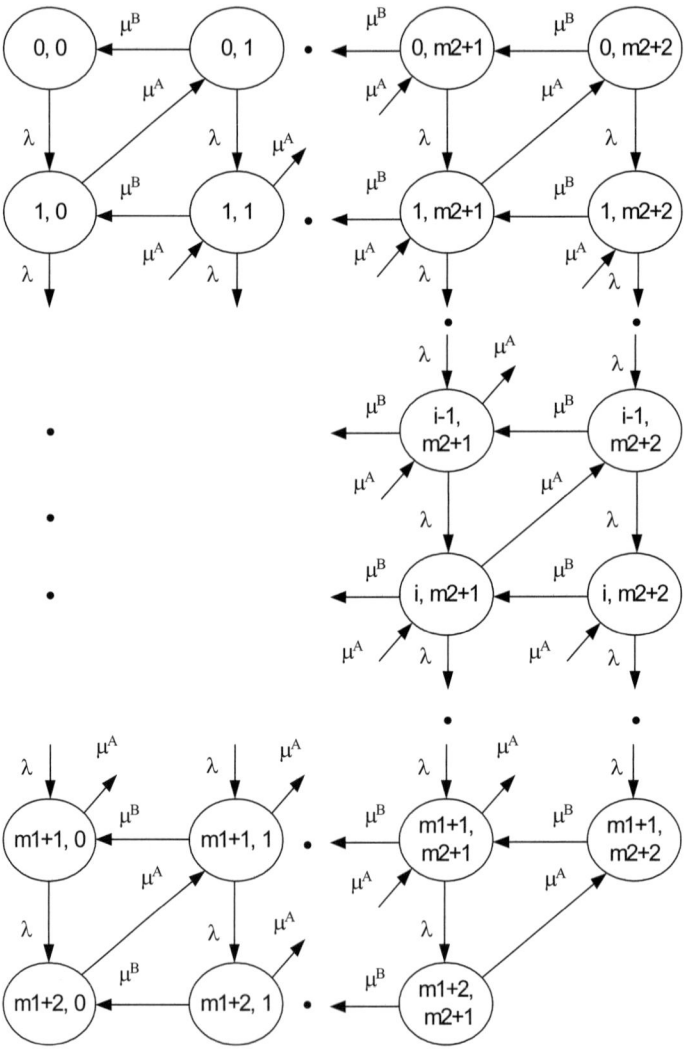

Fig. 2. Two-dimensional network state diagram.

Based on analysis the state space diagrams, the process of constructing the steady-state equations in the Markovian model, can be divided by the several independent steps, which describe some similar, repeatable schemas (see Fig. 2). These steady-state equations are:

$$\lambda \cdot p_{0,0} = \mu^B \cdot p_{0,1} \qquad \text{for } i = 0, \ j = 0$$

$$(\lambda + \mu^B) \cdot p_{0,j} = \mu^A \cdot p_{1,j-1} + \mu^B \cdot p_{0,j+1} \qquad \text{for } i = 0, \ j = 1, \ldots, m2+1$$

$$(\lambda + \mu^A) \cdot p_{i,0} = \lambda \cdot p_{i-1,0} + \mu^B \cdot p_{i,1} \qquad \text{for } i = 1, \ldots, m1+1, \ j = 0 \qquad (1)$$

$$(\lambda + \mu^B + \mu^A) \cdot p_{i,j} = \lambda \cdot p_{i-1,j} + \mu^A \cdot p_{i+1,j-1} + \mu^B \cdot p_{i,j+1}$$

$$\text{for } i = 1, \ldots, m1+1, \ j = 1, \ldots, m2+1$$

And for states with blocking the equations are:

$$(\lambda + \mu^B) \cdot p_{0,m2+2} = \mu^A \cdot p_{1,m2+1} \qquad \text{for } i = 0, \ j = m2+2$$

$$\mu^A \cdot p_{m1+2,0} = \lambda \cdot p_{m1+1,0} + \mu^B \cdot p_{m1+2,1} \qquad \text{for } i = m1+2, \ j = 0$$

$$(\mu^A + \mu^B) \cdot p_{m1+2,j} = \lambda \cdot p_{m1+1,j} + \mu^B \cdot p_{m1+2,j+1} \qquad \text{for } i = m1+2,$$

$$j = 1, \ldots, m2$$

$$(\mu^A + \mu^B) \cdot p_{m1+2,m2+1} = \lambda \cdot p_{m1+1,m2+1} \qquad \text{for } i = m1+2, \ j = m2+1 \qquad (2)$$

$$(\lambda + \mu^B) \cdot p_{i,m2+2} = \lambda \cdot p_{i-1,m2+2} + \mu^A \cdot p_{i+1,m2+1} \qquad \text{for } i = 1, \ldots, m1,$$

$$j = m2+2$$

$$\mu^B \cdot p_{m1+1,m2+2} = \lambda \cdot p_{m1,m2+2} + \mu^A \cdot p_{m1+2,m2+1} \qquad \text{for } i = m1+1, \ j = m2+2$$

Here, a queuing network with blocking linked in series, under appropriate assumptions, is formulated as a Markov process and the stationary probability vector can be obtained using numerical methods for linear systems of equations. If there is a model network with finite number of states, its steady-state probabilities can be found directly from equations (1) and (2) by using some iteration method and the normalizing condition for the sum of state probabilities. From the tandem state graph (see Figure 2) analysis, we can calculate the total number of the tandem states easily:

$$K = (m_1 + 3) \cdot (m_2 + 2) + m_1 + 2 \qquad (3)$$

there are k_1 states without blocking:

$$k_1 = (m_1 + 2) \cdot (m_2 + 2) \qquad (4)$$

and k_2 states with blocking:

$$k_2 = m_1 + 2 + m_2 + 2 \qquad (5)$$

For the first iteration, as an approximation of probability values, we can take that all the values are equal to:

$$p_{i,j} = \frac{1}{K} \qquad (6)$$

To speed up the convergence of the iteration process, during the next iteration step, the value of each probability may be calculated as the mean from its previous result and the result obtained by putting its previous value to the set of equations (1) and (2) etc.

3. Measures of effectiveness

The procedures for calculating quality of service (QoS) parameters and basic measures of effectiveness use the steady-state probabilities in the following manner:
Idle probability p_{idle}:

$$p_{idle} = p_{0,0} \qquad (7)$$

Station A blocking probability p_{blA}:

$$p_{blA} = \sum_{i=0}^{m1+1} p_{i,m2+2} \qquad (8)$$

Source station blocking probability p_{blS}:

$$p_{blS} = \sum_{j=0}^{m2+1} p_{m1+2,j} + p_{m1+1,m2+2} \qquad (9)$$

Both stations (source and station A) simultaneous blocking probability p_{blAS}:

$$p_{blAS} = p_{m1+1,m2+2} \qquad (10)$$

The average number of blocked tasks in station A:

$$n_{blA} = \sum_{i=0}^{m1+1} 1 \cdot p_{i,m2+2} \qquad (11)$$

The average number of active (non-blocked) tasks in station A:

$$l_A = \sum_{i=1}^{m1+2} \sum_{j=0}^{m2+1} 1 \cdot p_{i,j} \qquad (12)$$

The average number of tasks in the first buffer v_A:

$$v_A = \sum_{i=2}^{m1+1} \sum_{j=0}^{m2+1} (i-1) \cdot p_{i,j} + \sum_{i=1}^{m1} i \cdot p_{i,m2+2} + \sum_{j=0}^{m2+1} m1 \cdot p_{m1+2,j} + m1 \cdot p_{m1+1,m2+2} \tag{13}$$

The average number of tasks in station A:

$$n_A = \sum_{i=1}^{m1+1} \sum_{j=0}^{m2+1} i \cdot p_{i,j} + \sum_{i=0}^{m1} (i+1) \cdot p_{i,m2+2} + \sum_{j=0}^{m2+1} (m1+1) \cdot p_{m1+2,j} + (m1+1) \cdot p_{m1+1,} \tag{14}$$

The average number of blocked tasks in source station:

$$n_{blS} = \sum_{j=0}^{m2+1} 1 \cdot p_{m1+2,j} + 1 \cdot p_{m1+1,m2+2} \tag{15}$$

The average number of simultaneous blocked tasks in both stations (source and station A) n_{blAS}:

$$n_{blAS} = 1 \cdot p_{m1+1,m2+2} \tag{16}$$

The average number of tasks on the service line in station B:

$$l_B = \sum_{i=0}^{m1+2} \sum_{j=1}^{m2+1} 1 \cdot p_{i,j} + \sum_{i=0}^{m1+1} 1 \cdot p_{i,m2+2} \tag{17}$$

The average number of tasks in the second buffer v_B:

$$v_B = \sum_{i=0}^{m1+2} \sum_{j=2}^{m2+1} (j-1) \cdot p_{i,j} + \sum_{i=0}^{m1+1} m2 \cdot p_{i,m2+2} \tag{18}$$

The average number of tasks in station B (buffer + server):

$$n_B = \sum_{i=0}^{m1+2} \sum_{j=1}^{m2+1} j \cdot p_{i,j} + \sum_{i=0}^{m1+1} (m2+1) \cdot p_{i,m2+2} \tag{19}$$

The mean blocking time in station A:

$$t_{blA} = \frac{n_{blA}}{\mu^B} \tag{20}$$

The mean blocking time in source station:

$$t_{blS} = n_{blS} \cdot \left(\frac{1}{\mu^A} + t_{blA} \right) \tag{21}$$

The simultaneous mean blocking time in both stations (source and station A):

$$t_{blAS} = n_{blAS} \cdot \left(\frac{1}{\mu^A} + t_{blA} + \frac{1}{\mu^B} \right) \tag{22}$$

The mean waiting time in the buffer A:

$$w_A = v_A \cdot \left(\frac{1}{\mu^A} + t_{blA} \right) \tag{23}$$

The mean response time in station A:

$$q_A = \frac{1}{\mu^A} + t_{blA} + w_A \tag{24}$$

The mean waiting time in the buffer B:

$$w_B = \frac{v_B}{\mu^B} \tag{25}$$

The mean response time in station B:

$$q_B = w_B + \frac{1}{\mu^B} \tag{26}$$

The average network throughput time:

$$t_{thr} = \frac{1}{\lambda} + t_{blS} + q_A + q_B \tag{27}$$

The effective input stream rate (intensity):

$$\lambda_1 = \frac{1}{\frac{1}{\lambda} + t_{blS}} \tag{28}$$

4. Numerical examples

In this section, to demonstrate the analysis of a three-station network with blocking, the following configuration is chosen: $m1 = 10$, $m2 = 6$. The service rates in stations A and B are equal to: $\mu^A = 7.0$ and $\mu^B = 5.0$. The inter-arrival rate to network changes within a range from 1.0 to 10.0 for studying of the model with a different coefficient of the utility. This model has 116 states, 96 states are without blocking and 20 states are with blocking.

For the model above, the following results were obtained, majority of which are presented in Figure 3, Figure 4 and Table 1.

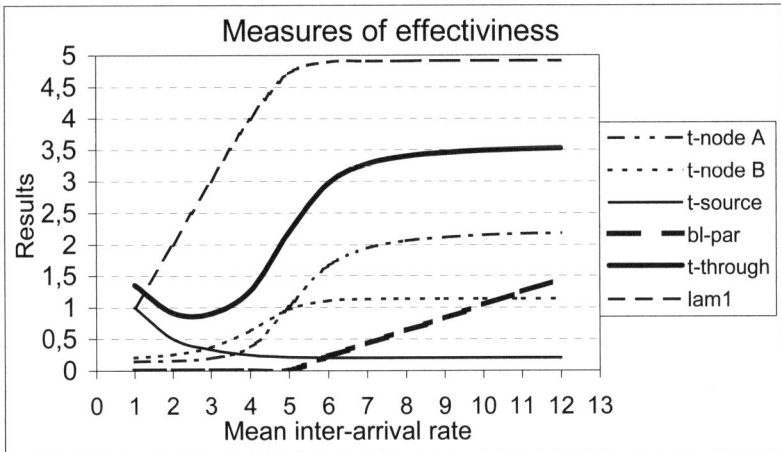

Fig. 3. The measures related to the mean time: *t-node A* is the mean response time in station *A*, *t-node B* is the mean response time in station *B*, *t-source* is the effective source mean inter-arrival time, *bl-par* is the relation of the source mean blocking time to the mean inter-arrival time, *t-through* is the average network throughput time, *lam1* is the effective input stream rate.

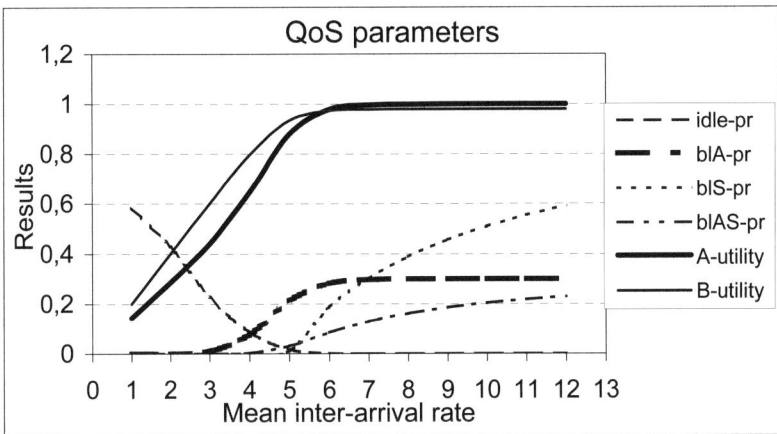

Fig. 4. Graphs of QoS parameters, where *idle-pr* is the idle network probability *blA-pr* is the station *A* blocking probability, *blS-pr* is the source station blocking probability, *blAS-pr* is the both stations simultaneous probability *A-utility* is the station *A* utilization factor, *B-utility* is the station *B* utilization factor.

Table 1. The comparison of the average number of tasks in both stations

λ	The average number of tasks						Station A utility	Station B utility
	n_{blA}	n_{blS}	v_A	v_B	n_A	n_B		
1.0	0.000	0.000	0.024	0.050	0.167	0.250	0.143	0.200
2.0	0.001	0.000	0.115	0.265	0.401	0.665	0.286	0.400
3.0	0.011	0.000	0.360	0.850	0.800	1.450	0.439	0.600
4.0	0.077	0.006	1.374	2.175	2.019	2.970	0.645	0.795
5.0	0.212	0.066	4.466	3.856	5.345	4.790	0.879	0.934
6.0	0.282	0.189	7.314	4.536	8.291	5.509	0.978	0.973
7.0	0.297	0.301	8.593	4.656	9.589	5.635	0.996	0.979
8.0	0.300	0.388	9.149	4.674	10.148	5.654	0.999	0.980
9.0	0.300	0.456	9.429	4.677	10.429	5.657	1.000	0.980
10.0	0.300	0.510	9.589	4.678	10.589	5.657	1.000	0.980
11.0	0.300	0.555	9.690	4.678	10.690	5.657	1.000	0.980
12.0	0.300	0.592	9.757	4.678	10.757	5.657	1.000	0.980

The results of experiment show that effect of blocking appears when the utilities of stations A and B are greater than *0.70*. Here, the network throughput time and the blocking time quickly increases (the bad quality service parameters). In the moderate utility interval, the network works properly and most of the quality of service (QoS) parameters are easy to keep at the appropriate level.

5. Conclusion

In this paper, the mathematical model of an open linked series three-station stochastic transition network with blocking is presented. In this network model a phenomenon of blocking appears simultaneously in the source station and in the first service station. Here, the mathematical procedures allows for calculating the network main measures of effectiveness including the blocking probabilities. These measures may be calculated for any given service rates in both stations and when the inter-arrival rates from a source station is given.

The results of experiments presented in Section 4 show that depending on the model parameters the mathematical modelling allows for finding the proper rate range for an input stream that guarantees congestion avoidance in the network. In the opposite case if given an input stream rate, the analysis allows taking another model characteristic, which guarantees that blocking probabilities should be in the proper range.

This work is supported by the Bialystok University of Technology W/WI/7/03 grant.

References

[1] Akyildiz I.F. Mean Value Analysis for Blocking Queuing Networks, IEEE Transaction on Software Engineering, Vol. 14(4), pp. 418-428, 1988.

[2] Balsamo S., de Nitto Persone V. A survey of product form queueing networks with blocking and their equivalences, Annals of Operations research, Vol. 48(1/4), pp. 31-61, 1994.

[3] Balsamo S., de Nito Persone V., Onvural R. Analysis of Queueing Networks with Blocking, Kluwer Academic Publishers, Boston, 2001.

[4] Clo M.C. MVA for product-form cyclic queueing networks with blocking, Annals of Operations Research, Vol. 79, pp. 83-96, 1998.

[5] Economou A., Fakinos D. Product form stationary distributions for queueing networks with blocking and rerouting, Queueing Systems, Vol. 30(3/4), pp. 251-260, 1998.

[6] Gomez-Corral A. A Tandem Queue with Blocking and Markovian Arrival Process, Queueing Systems, Vol. 41(4), pp. 343-370, 2002.

[7] Martin J.B. Large Tandem Queueing Networks with Blocking, Queueing Systems, Vol. 41(1/2), pp. 45-72, 2002.

[8] Morrison J.A. Blocking probabilities for multiple class batched arrivals to a shared resource, Performance Evaluation, Vol. 25, pp. 131-150, 1996.

[9] Onvural R. Survey of closed queuing networks with blocking, Computer Survey, Vol. 22(2), pp. 83-121, 1990.

[10] Perros H.G. Queuing Networks with Blocking. Exact and Approximate Solution, Oxford University Press, New York, 1994.

[11] Sereno M. Mean value analysis of product form solution queueing networks with repetitive service blocking, Performance Evaluation, Vol. 36-37, pp. 19-33, 1999.

[12] Strelen J.Ch., et al. Analysis of queueing networks with blocking using a new aggregation technique, Annals of Operations Research, Vol. 79, pp. 121-142, 1998.

[13] Tolio T., Gershwin S.B. Throughput estimation in cyclic queueing networks with blocking, Annals of Operations Research, Vol. 79, pp. 207-229, 1998.

[14] Zhuang L., Buzacott J.A., Liu X-G. Approximate mean value performance analysis of cyclic queueing networks with production blocking, Queueing Systems, Vol. 16, pp. 139-165, 1994.

Hyperplane Method Implementation for Loops Parallelization in the .NET Environment

Włodzimierz Bielecki, Maciej Poliwoda

Computer Science Departament, Technical University of Szczecin
Zolnierska str.,49, 71-210 Szczecin, Poland
wbielecki@wi.ps.pl, mpoliwoda@wi.ps.pl

Abstract. An implementation of the hyperplane method for perfectly nested loops parallelization is described. A tool developed enables parallelizing and running C sources in the .Net environment. This tool finds loops declared by the user to be parallelized, parses them, and builds correspondent parallel programs when possible. The .NET Framework functionality to support multithreaded programming is used to generate parallel programs by means of the developed tool. Limitations of the tool and plans for future work are attached.
Keywords: Loop Parallelization, Hyperplane Method, .Net environment.

Introduction

Parallel programming is a basic approach for achieving concurrency with a piece of software. Parallel programming techniques permit us to run a program on two or more processors within a single physical or a single virtual computer. Manual writing the efficient parallel program is typically a difficult and error-prone task. Parallelizing compilers are needed to generate quickly efficient parallel programs. Many techniques for parallelizing compilers have been developed to expose loop parallelism, minimize synchronization, and improve memory locality in the past [2]. The hyperplane method for loop parallelization is one of effective techniques to be implemented in parallelizing compilers [6].

In this paper, we present an implementation of the hyperplane method in the .Net environment. Multithreading is used to generate parallel programs representing loops paralelism. A thread is a stream of executable code within a process that has the ability to be scheduled. A process can have multiple threads and therefore has as many flows of control as there are threads. Each thread will execute independently and concurrently with its own sequence of instructions. All threads within the same process exist in the same address space. All of the resources belonging to the process are shared among the threads. Threads do not own any resources. Any resources owned by the process are sharable among all of the threads of that process. In a multiprocessor system, threads within the same process can execute simultaneously on different processors. Synchronization mechanisms such as mutexes are needed to protect share memory in order to control race conditions. There are several models that can be used to delegate work among threads and manage when threads are created and canceled [5]. In our implementation, we have chosen the master-worker model where a single thread (master) creates the threads (workers) and assigns each a task. The master thread delegates the task each worker thread is to perform by specifying a function.

We have used the .NET Framework functionality to support multithreaded programming to generate parallel programs by means of the developed tool.

The rest of the paper is organized as follows. Section 2 presents background. The hyperplane method is described in Section 3. In Section 4, we consider how our tool is organized. Experiments with the tool are discussed in Section 5. Finally, we conclude and present future work on the tool.

Background

In this paper, we consider the following generic perfectly nested loop

$$\textit{for } I_1 = S_1, E_1$$

$$\quad \textit{for } I_2 = S_2(I_1), E_2(I_1)$$

$$\quad \dots$$

$$\quad\quad \textit{for } I_n = S_n(I_1, \dots I_{n-1}), E_n(I_1, \dots I_{n-1})$$

$$\quad\quad\quad H(I_1, \dots I_n)$$

$$\quad\quad \textit{endfor}$$

$$\quad \dots$$

$$\quad \textit{endfor}$$

$$\textit{endfor}$$

where $I_1, \dots, I_n$ are the iteration indices; S_i and E_i are the lower and upper loop bounds that are affine functions of the iteration indices $I_1, \dots, I_{i-1}$; implicitly a stride of one is assumed; H is the body of the nested loop. $\overline{I} = [I_1, \dots, I_n]^T$ is called the iteration vector.

The set $I \subseteq Z^n$ such that

$$I = \{(I_1, \dots, I_n) \mid S_1 \le i_1 \le E_1, \dots, S_n(I_1, \dots, I_{n-1}) \le i_n \le E_n(I_1, \dots, I_{n-1})\}$$ is the iteration space. To parallelize the loop, we need to know all the pairs of the iterations that are dependent and the relationship between them, such as the dependence vector. For a pair of vectors $\overline{I} = [i_1, \dots, i_n]^T$ and $\overline{J} = [j_1, \dots, j_n]^T$ such that $\overline{J}$ is dependent on $\overline{I}$, the vector $\overline{K} = \overline{J} - \overline{I} = [j_1 - i_1, \dots, j_n - i_n]^T$ is called the dependence vector. Methods of dependence analysis are considered in many papers, for example, in [1, 3, 10, 12].

Vectors $\overline{I} = [i_1,\dots,i_n]^T$ and $\overline{J} = [j_1,\dots,j_n]^T$ satisfy the condition $\overline{I} \prec \overline{J}$ iff there exists an integer k, $1 \le k \le n$ such that $i_1 = j_1,\dots,$ $i_{k-1} = j_{k-1}$ and $i_k < j_k$.

To find dependence vectors, a system of equations should be built for each pair of the same named variables $ID(A_1\overline{I} + B_1)$, $ID(A_2\overline{I} + B_2)$ that are located in the loop body on both hand sides of assignment statements – the right and the left – or on the left-hand sides only, where A_1, A_2 are matrices of dimensions $m \times n$, B_1, B_2 are m-dimensional vectors. This system can be written as follows

$$\begin{cases} A_1\overline{I} - A_2\overline{J} = \overline{B}_2 - \overline{B}_1 \\ \overline{K} = \overline{J} - \overline{I} \\ \overline{K} \succ \overline{0} \end{cases} \tag{1}$$

For a pair of dependent iterations, the source is the iteration that is lexicographically less.

In system (1), vector $\overline{I}$ describes all the iterations that form the sources of pairs of dependent iterations, while vector $\overline{J} = \overline{I} + \overline{K}$ describes the destinations of those, $\overline{K}$ is the dependence vector. To obtain correct results, all dependent iterations have to be executed in lexicographical order [1]. To determine vector $\overline{K}$, we have to solve system (1). From the second equation of system (1), we have

$$\overline{J} = \overline{I} + \overline{K} \tag{2}$$

Let us transform the first equation of (1), using (2), to the form

$$A_2\overline{K} + (A_2 - A_1)\overline{I} = \overline{B}_1 - \overline{B}_2 \tag{3}$$

and rewrite equation (3) as below

$$A\overline{X} = \overline{C} \tag{4}$$

were $A = [A_2 \quad (A_2 - A_1)]$ is a matrix of dimensions $m \times 2n$; $\overline{X} = [\overline{K}\,\overline{I}]^T$ is a $2n$–dimensional vector; $\overline{C} = \overline{B}_1 - \overline{B}_2$ is an m –dimensional vector. The solution to equation (3) is [4] $\overline{K} = V\overline{T} + \overline{V}_0 = \sum_{i=1}^{r}(\overline{V}_i t_i) + \overline{V}_0$,where $\overline{V}_0, \overline{V}_1,\dots,\overline{Vr}$ are n – dimensional vectors, coordinates of which are integers; t_i, $i = 1,2,\dots,r$ are free variables, values of which are arbitrary integers. Consider the following working loop

```
for (i = 1; i ≤ 4; i + +){
        for (j = 1; j ≤ 3; j + +){
            a[i][ j] = a[i + 1][ j] + a[i][ j + 1];
        }
}
```

Fig. 1. Working loop.

For this loop, there exist two dependence vectors, $\overline{K}_1 = \begin{bmatrix} 1 \\ 0 \end{bmatrix}$ and $\overline{K}_2 = \begin{bmatrix} 0 \\ 1 \end{bmatrix}$. Figure 2 presents dependences originated by these vectors.

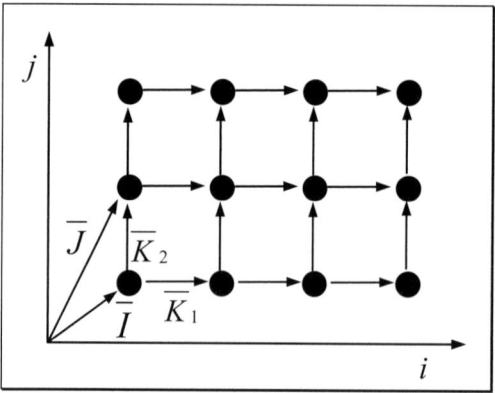

Fig. 2. Dependence vectors for the working loop.

The hyperplane method

In this section, we present the idea of a technique to be known as the hyperplane method, wave-front-method, or Lamport method [6, 7, 11].

Let $\overline{C}$ be the first row of matrix C, and $\overline{K} \succ \overline{0}$ be a dependence vector. If the inequality $\overline{C}\overline{K} > 0$ is satisfied for each dependence vector $\overline{K}$ originated by the loop, then for any given constant t, all the iterations $\overline{I}$ such that $\overline{C}\overline{I} = t$ can be executed in parallel. These operations belong to an affine hyperplane (wave-front) normal to $\overline{C}$. This is why $\overline{C}$ is called a strongly separating hyperplane. If for each dependence vector $\overline{K}$, the inequality $\overline{C}\overline{K} \geq 0$ is satisfied, $\overline{C}$ is a weakly separating hyperplane. To parellelize the loop, we should find one strongly separating hyperplane or a set of weakly separating hyperplanes satisfying all dependence vectors.

Let C be a matrix of dimension $m \times n$ whose the first n rows represent $n \leq m$ weakly separating hyperplanes for a perfectly nested loop of dimension m. When $n = m$, each hyperplane comprises the only iteration, that is, we have no parallelism. For each dependence vector $\overline{K}$, the following condition is satisfied $C\overline{K} \succ \overline{0}$. Two iterations $\overline{I}$ and $\overline{J}$ belong to the same hyperplane if the following constraint is satisfied $C\overline{I} = C\overline{J}$. For the loop presented in Figure 1, the following matrix C represents one strongly separating hyperplane $C = \begin{bmatrix} 1 & 1 \\ 0 & 0 \end{bmatrix}$, which permits us to parallelize this loop by the hyperplane method. Figure 3 shows iterations of the working loop belonging to each hyperplane built on the basis of matrix C attached above.

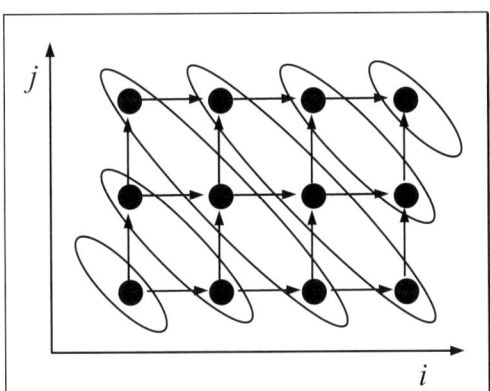

Fig. 3. Hyperplanes for the working loop.

To expose parallelism of the working loop, we should transform it to a loop whose the outermost nest enumerates hyperplanes sequentially while the innermost loop scans iterations of each hyperplane in parallel. Techniques of such a transformation are well-know [6] and are out of this paper scope. Figure 4 presents the iteration space of the transformed loop.

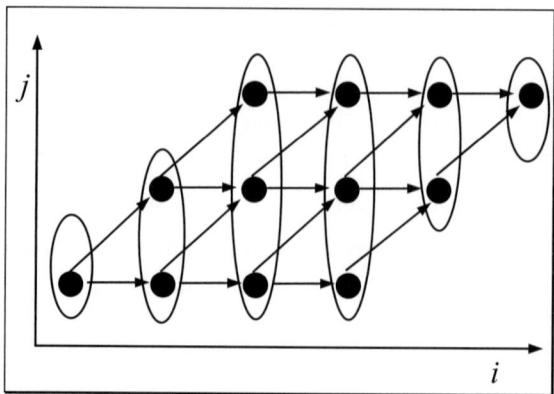

Fig. 4. Iteration space of the transformed loop.

The transformation is carried out by means of a transformation matrix T built on the basis of matrix C as described in [6]. Matrix T is of the form $T = \begin{bmatrix} 1 & 1 \\ 0 & 1 \end{bmatrix}$. Applying matrix T, we find iterations of the transformed loop $\overline{I}'$ as $\overline{I}' = T\overline{I}$, where $\overline{I}$ represents iterations of the original working loop. One can check that the transformation is valid since the condition $T\overline{K} \succ \overline{0}$, is satisfied for each dependence vector originated by the working loop

```
for (i = 2; i ≤ 8; i + +){
    for (j = max(i − 4,1);
        j ≤ min(i − 1,4); j + +){
            a[i − j][ j] = a[i − j + 1][ j] +
                           a[i − j][ j + 1];
        }
}
```

Fig. 5. Code of the transformed loop.

To find the bounds of the transformed loop, we form the following inequalities $1 \le T^{-1}\overline{I}' \le 4$ and resolve them by means of the Fourier-Motzkin algorithm [8]. The code of the transformed loop is presented in Figure 5.

Loop parallelization

In this section, we describe how our tool parallelizes loops written in the C language as well as limitations imposed on loops and structures of input and output files of the tool.

The loop parallelization process consists of the three following steps: (i) parsing a source program; (ii) loops parallelization; (iii) generating output files.

The goal of the first step is to reveal and check loops defined by the user to be parallelized. For each loop to be parallelized, lexical and syntactic analyses are carried out to verify whether loops can be parallelized, and if so, data is generated to be used in steps 2 and 3.

In the second step, dependence analysis is carried out for each loop to be parallelized. With this goal, the tool builds systems of equations as described in Section 2 and resolves them. Then hyperplanes are constructed for each loop to be parallelized, transformation matrices are derived, and, finaly, source loops are transformed to present the parallelism found with the hyperplane method.

In the last step, output files are generated. These files represent a parallel program to be compiled in the .NET environment. This program creates and synchronizes multiple threads to be run on the multiprocessor computer.

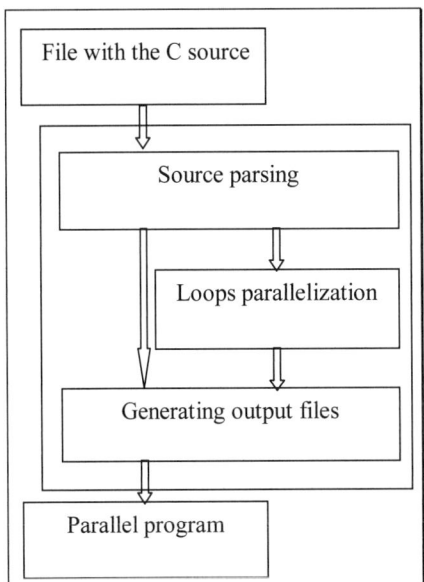

Fig. 6. Loops parallelization process of the C source.

Loops to be parallelized have to be declared by the user and must satisfy particular conditions as described below.

Each „for" loop to be parallelized has to be marked by the directives /*beforefor*/ and /*endfor*/, which for the convenient compiler are the comments and are ignored. In addition to these directives, applying the directive /*startfunc ... endfunc*/ is possible. It defines functions which cannot be called at the same time. These directives are recognized by our tool, which fulfils lexical and syntactic analyses of each loop within the directives /*beforefor*/ and /*endfor*/. If the loop body satisfies the conditions described below, the tool parallelizes this loop and generates output files. Figure 7 presents the skeleton of the code representing the loop to be parallelized by means of our tool. The loop to be parallelized must satisfy the following conditions.

- Be perfectly nested.
- Index variables are incremented with the stride equal to 1.
- Values of index variables cannot be modified within the loop body.

```
int main( ){
int i₁,i₁,···,iₙ;
...
/* beforefor * /
/* startfunc f1, f2,···, fn endfunc * /
for(i₁ = I¹ₘᵢₙ; i₁ ≤ I¹ₘₐₓ; i₁ ++){
    for(i₂ = I²ₘᵢₙ; i₂ ≤ I²ₘₐₓ; i₂ ++){
        ...
            for(iₙ = Iⁿₘᵢₙ; i₂ ≤ Iⁿₘₐₓ; iₙ ++){
                /* loop body * /;
            }
        ...
    }
}
/ * enfor * /
...
return 0;
}
```

Fig. 7. Skeleton of the loop to be parallelized.

- Names of different arrays cannot be the same within the loop body.
- The loop body cannot comprise the following statements: if, switch, continue, break, goto, return as well as the functions: exit() and longjump().
- Array expressions in the loop statements and the lower and upper loop bounds are affine functions of the iteration indices.
- To refer to elements of the array, only the operator [] can be used; the operator * is forbidden, for example, the form like $array\_name[\text{expr}_1]\cdots[\text{expr}_n]$ is permitted, but the expression like

$$*(...*(array\_name + \exp r_1) + .. + \exp r_n)$$ is forbidden.

- The loop body does not comprise any variable declaration.
- Different variables within the loop body does not have any common area in memory.
- The loop body includes only safe functions such that: (i) do not invoke static variables (local and global); (ii) do not cause any side effect; (ii) any parameter is no pointer.

Output files represent the code of parallelized loops in the C language and are to be compiled in the .NET environment. After compilation, we have executable code to be run on the multiprocessor system. The following section describes how multithreaded programs are generated in the .NET environment.

Using the .NET framework for building multithreaded programs

The .Net Framework provides a rich set of functionality to support multithreaded programming [9]. The System namespace contains fundamental classes and base classes that define commonly-used value and reference data types, events and event handlers, interfaces, attributes, and processing exceptions. The System.Threading namespace provides classes and interfaces that enable multithreaded programming. In addition to classes for synchronizing thread activities and access to data.

```
__gc class ThreadsControl
{
private:
    Manual Re setEvent * mainStartEvent;
    Manual Re setEvent * mainEndEvent;
    Manual Re setEvent * mainAfterCreateEvent;
    Manual Re setEvent * mainBeforeBarierEvent;
    Manual Re setEvent * mainAfterBarierEvent;
    int threadsCount;
    int threadsBeforeBarier;
    int threadsAfterBarier;
public:
    void CreateThreadsAndStart( int numThreads);
    bool virtual Continue(){ return false; };
    void virtual ChangeHyperplane(){};
    void virtual ExecHyperplane( int thredNum){};
private:
    void MyThread Pr oc();
    int AssignThreadId(void);
    void WaitOnBarier(void);
};
```

Fig. 8. Skeleton of the class TheadsControl.

Functionality in the System.Threading namespace allows you to write programs that perform more than one task at the same time. The Thread class represents a task, an isolated flow of execution in a program.

By default, when the program starts, it receives a single thread of execution. To create an additional thread, you create a newThread object and pass it a pointer to a method in your class via the ThreadStartDelegate.

To implement the hyperplane metod, the class ThreadsControl was written. The task of this class is to fork threads which are to execute in parallel iterations of each hyperplane as well as to synchronize them.

```
void CreateThreadsAndStart (int numThreads){

threadsCount = 0;

threadsBeforeBarier = 0;

threadsAfterBarier = 0;

mainStartEvent = new ManualResetEvent(false);

mainEndEvent = new ManualResetEvent(false);

mainAfterCreateEvent = new ManualResetEvent(false);

mainBeforeBarierEvent = new ManualResetEvent(false);

mainAfterBarierEvent = new ManualResetEvent(false);

for (int i = 0; i < numThreads; i++) {

    Thread * myThread = new Thread( new ThreadStart(this, MyThreadProc) );

    myThread - > Start();

    mainAfterCreateEvent - > WaitOne();

    mainAfterCreateEvent - > Reset();

}

mainStartEvent- > Set();

mainEndEvent- > WaitOne();

};
```

Fig. 9. Skeleton of the method CreateThreadsAndStart.

The skeleton of this class is presented in Figure 8. It comprises the following methods: CreateThreadsAndStart, Continue, ChangeHyperplane, ExecHyperplane, MythreadProc, AssignThreadId, and WaitOnBarrier.

The method CreateThreadsAndStart initializes attributes, creates the given number of threads, and waits on their termination. The skeleton of this method is given in Figure 9.

The method WaitOnBarier is to synchronize threads before to start executing each next hyperplane. The skeleton of this method is presented in Figure 10.

```
void WaitOnBarier(void){
    threadsBeforeBarier++;
    if(threadsBeforeBarier == threadsCount)
        mainBeforeBarierEvent->Set();
    mainBeforeBarierEvent->WaitOne();
    mainAfterBarierEvent->Re set();
    threadsBeforeBarier=0;
    threadsAfterBarier++;
    if(threadsAfterBarier == threadsCount)
        mainAfterBarierEvent->Set();
    mainAfterBarierEvent->WaitOne();
    mainBeforeBarierEvent->Re set();
    threadsAfterBarier=0;
};
```

Fig. 10. Skeleton of the method WaitOnBarier.

The method AssignThreadId is called at initializing each thread. It assigns a unique identifier to each thread. These identifiers are used to schedule iterations of hyperplanes. The skeleton of this method is described in Figure 11.

```
int GetThreadNumber(void){
    int thredNum,
    thredNum = threadsCount,
    threadsCount ++,
    return thredNum,
},
```

Fig. 11. Skeleton of the method AssignThreadId.

The method MyThreadProc executes the given number of hyperplanes defined by the user. It calls methods defined in the derived class which is responsible for executing the code of each hyperplane. The skeleton of this method is presented in Figure 12.

```
void MyThread Pr oc(){
    int thredNum;
    thredNum = GetThreadNumber();
    mainAfterCreateEvent->Set();
    mainStartEvent->WaitOne();
    while(Continue())
    {
        WaitOnBarier();
        if(thredNum==0 ) ChangeHyperplane();
        WaitOnBarier();
        ExecHyperplane(thredNum);
    }
    WaitOnBarier();
    mainEndEvent->Set();
};
```

Fig. 12. Skeleton of the method MyThreadProc.

The Methods defined in the derived class are the following.

The method Continue returns data informing whether continuing the threads execution is necessary.

The method ChangeHyperplane is responsible for the transition between hyperplanes. It is called only by the thread with the identifier equal to zero.

The method ExecHyperplane executes statements of the loop iterations.

```
for(i = 0; i <= 3; i ++){
    for( j = 0; j <= 3; j ++){
        Console::WriteLine(S"{0}",String::Format(
        S"Hiperplane: {0} Thread: {1}",
        __box(i), __box(j+1))
    }
}
```

Fig. 13. Loop to be parallelized with the hyperplane method.

Let us consider the loop presented in Figure 13. We assume that there are no loop-carried dependence in this loop. The code to execute this loop in parallel using multithreading is given in Figure 14.

```
__gc class Test2: public ThreadsControl {
public:
    int hyperplaneCount;
    int numIterations;
public:
    Test2() {
        hyperplaneCount = 0;
        numIterations = 3;
    };
    bool Continue() {
        return hyperplaneCount < numIterations;
    };
    void ChangeHyperplane() {
        hyperplaneCount ++;
    };
    void ExecHyperplane( int thredNum ) {
    Console::WriteLine(S"{0}",String::Format(
    S"Hiperplane: {0} Thread: {1}",
    __box(hyperplaneCount), __box(thredNum+1 )));
    };
};
void main() {
    Test2 *myTest = new Test2;
    myTest->CreateThreadsAndStart(3 );
}
```

Fig. 14. Code of the parallel loop.

The code presented in Figure 14 generates the following lettering:

Hyperplane: 1 Thread: 1
Hyperplane: 1 Thread: 2
Hyperplane: 1 Thread: 3
Hyperplane: 2 Thread: 2
Hyperplane: 2 Thread: 3
Hyperplane: 2 Thread: 1
Hyperplane: 3 Thread: 3
Hyperplane: 3 Thread: 2
Hyperplane: 3 Thread: 1

As we can see from the result, generated by the code in Figure 14, the order of executing hyperplanes is proper.

Conclusion

We have described the hyperplane method and its implementation in the .NET environment. Experiments with our tool shows that it can be applied to parallelize loops in many applications. But the following limitations restrict its use:

- The tool can parallelize loops written only in the C language.
- The tool can parallelize only perfectly nested loops.
- „ If " statements within the loop body prevent loop parallelization.
  We plan to carry out the following work on the tool to enhance its power:
- Extension of the lexical and syntactic analyses of the tool to permit parallelization of loops represented in the Visual Basic, C#, C++ languages.
- Extension of the dependence analyzer and applying affine transformations [6] to enable non-perfectly nested loops with if statements within the loop body to be parallelized.

References

[1] Allen, R, Kennedy, K.: Optimizing Compilers for Modern Architectures, Morgan Kaufmann, 2001

[2] D. Bacon, S. Graham, and O. Sharp. Compiler transformations for high-performance computing. Computing Surveys, 26(4):345-420, December 1994.

[3] U. Banerjee. Loop Transformations for Restructuring Compilers. Kluwer Academic, 1993.

[4] V. Beletskyy, M. Poliwoda. Parallelizing perfectly nested loops with non-uniform dependences. In Proceedings of the Advanced computer systems, pages 83-98, October 2002.

[5] H. Cameron , H. Tracey. Parallel and Distributed Programming Using C++. Prentice Hall Professional , 2003, 720 pp

[6] Darte, A., Robert, Y.., Vivien, F.: Scheduling and Automatic Parallelization. Birkhäuser Boston, 2000.

[7] L. Lamport. The Parallel Execution of DO Loops. Communications of the ACM, Vol. 17, No.2, Feb. 1974, pp. 83-93.

[8] Schrijver. Theory of Linear and Integer Programming. Wiley, Chichester, 1986.

[9] D. Watkins, M.Hammond, B. Abrams, Programming in the .NET Environment. Addison-Wesley, 2003.

[10] M. Wolfe. High Performance Compilers for Parallel Computing. Addison-Wesley Publishing Company,1995.

[11] M. E. Wolf and M. S. Lam. A data locality optimizing algorithm. In Proc. ACM SIGPLAN 91 Conference on Programming Language Design and Implementation, pages 30–44, June 1991.

[12] H. Zima and B. Chapman. Supercompilers for Parallel and Vector Computers. ACM Press, 1990.

On a Nonlinear Production-Inventory Problem

Stanislaw Bylka[1] and Ryszarda Rempala[2]

[1] Institute of Computer Sciences, Polish Academy of Sciences
ul. Ordona 21, 01-237 Warszawa, Poland
bylka@wars.ipipan.waw.pl
[2] Institute of Mathematics, Polish Academy of Sciences
ul. Sniadeckich 8, 00-956 Warszawa, Poland
ryszrem@impan.gov.pl

Abstract. The system under study is a multidimensional deterministic production-inventory system with a concave production cost and a linear holding cost. Demands should be satisfied without backlogging. An optimal production plan is determined by an algorithm closely related to some regeneration cycles.

Two multidimensional inventory problems can be solved by the method presented. The first is a production-distribution problem with one product and many distribution centers (warehouses). The second is a multiproduct inventory problem with the join setup cost.

Keywords: Multi-item, regeneration, lot-sizing, network

1   Introduction

In the paper two kinds of multidimensional deterministic inventory problems are discussed. First, the basic deterministic production-distribution inventory system is considered. A single producer (production center) produces a single item for many distribution centers (warehouses). The warehouses' demands appear at discrete time points and ought to be satisfied. The produced item is partitioned and shipped to the warehouses' stocks. All shipments (replenishments) are carried out immediately. In the model the production-replenishment plan for the i-th distribution center (warehouse) is treated as a decision variable. It is expressed by a nonnegative vector defined at the given instants $l_1, l_2, \ldots, l_m$ belonging to $[0, T]$, where T denotes a planning horizon. For simplicity we assume that $l_t = t$ for $t = 1, 2, \ldots, m$ and that $m = T$. The warehouse demands appear at the mentioned instants and are given by a nonnegative vector. The problem is to determine a general production-replenishment plan to meet the demands of all warehouses and to minimize the sum of production and holding costs. The production cost is described by a nondecreasing concave function $c : R^+ \to R^+$. In the model the jump $c(0^+) - c(0)$ denotes a set-up cost. It is assumed that the warehouse holding cost is linear in inventory levels. We can consider the presented problem as a member of the class of production-distribution planning problems in supply chains (see [7, 8]). The two main differences are the following: (1) the cost function is of aggregated quantity of individual replenishments and

(2) there is only common set–up cost of production and transportation (individual set-up costs are ignored).

The objective of the paper is to describe an algorithm for determination of an optimal general production-replenishment plan. The problem considered extends the results of the [4]. The algorithm relies heavily on the qualitative properties of optimal plans given in the mentioned paper. However instead of the standard dynamic programming method we present a more effective procedure which reduces the problem to a class of "smaller" subproblems.

The second kind of inventory problem is considered in Section 2. We show that a multi-product inventory problem with depreciations of the products can be solved by the presented procedure for the basic production-distribution system. The reason is that from the mathematical point of view the class of multi-product joint replenishment problems (see [2, 9, 10, 12]) can be transformed into the basic production distribution system considered in this paper.

The paper is organized as follows. In Section 2 we give a mathematical descriptions of the basic production-distribution problem and aforementioned multi-product inventory problems. In Section 3 we define some auxiliary problems and establish the properties of the solutions. The analysis of the properties leads to some necessary conditions of the optimal production-replenishment plan of the basic problem. By means of the conditions stated in Section 4 a network descriptions of the main production-distribution problem are given and the idea of an algorithm for the determination of the solution is presented. The algorithm is based on the regeneration points and on the forward optimal path procedure. In Section 5, a numerical example is presented and an other variant of description of the algorithm for a general case is considered. Some final remarks are offered in Section 6.

2   Production-inventory systems. Mathematical descriptions

The basic problem of the paper consists of determining the production plans ("replenishment" is omitted for simplicity) for n-warehouses over the horizon of T periods. The objective is to minimize the sum of production and inventory holding costs. The warehouses' demands are known and should be satisfied without backlogging.

Let $u_i(t)$, $t = 1, 2, \ldots, T$ denote a production plan for i-th warehouse and $d_i(t)$, $t = 1, 2, \ldots, T$ the demand of the i-th warehouse.

Moreover let $h_i > 0$, $i = 1, 2, \ldots, n$ with

$$h_i \geq h_j \text{ for } i < j \tag{1}$$

denote the unit holding costs of warehouses $1, 2, \ldots, n$ respectively and let $c : R^+ \to R^+$ be a given nondecreasing concave function which describes the production cost.

We consider the basic inventory problem (IP) of the form:

$$(IP): \qquad \min_{u_1, u_2, \ldots, u_n} \sum_{t=1}^{T} \left\{ c\left(\sum_{i=1}^{n} u_i(t) \right) + \sum_{i=1}^{n} h_i I_i(t) \right\} \qquad (2)$$

with the restrictions

$$I_i(0) = 0,$$

$$I_i(t) = \sum_{s=1}^{t} (u_i(s) - d_i(s)) \geq 0, \quad u_i(t) \geq 0, \qquad (3)$$

$$t = 1, 2, \ldots, T, \quad i = 1, 2, \ldots, n,$$

where I_i denotes the inventory process corresponding to the plane u_i.

Observe that the inequality $I_i \geq 0$ states that in the considered model the warehouse demand has to be satisfied without backlogging. The assumption the cost c is concave, means that the marginal production cost is nondecreasing and that a setup cost (if any) is described by the jump $\lim_{u \to 0+} c(u) - c(0)$. Note that in the model considered the warehouses' demands are given by any system of n nonnegative vectors and c is any non-decreasing concave function. We show that in such a case the solution of the n-dimensional problem (IP) can be given by a sequence of solutions of "smaller" subproblems. The main goal of this paper is to describe the corresponding algorithm.

As it was alredy mentioned the algorithm also allows to solve some n-product inventory problem $(nPIP)$ with a depreciation rate. The mathematical formulation is as follows:

$$(nPIP): \qquad \min_{z_1, z_2, \ldots, z_n} \sum_{t=1}^{T} \left\{ c\left(\sum_{i=1}^{n} a_i z_i(t) \right) + \sum_{i=1}^{n} H_i I_i(t) \right\}$$

under the conditions

$$I_i(0) = 0,$$

$$I_i(t) = \sum_{s=1}^{t} (z_i(s) - D_i(s) - \delta_i z_i(s)) \geq 0, \quad z_i(t) \geq 0,$$

$$t = 1, 2, \ldots, T, \quad i = 1, 2, \ldots, n,$$

where the following notation is used:

n	the number of products,
$z_i(s)$	the production plan for the i-th product at instant s,
$D_i(s)$	the demand for the i-th product at the instant s,
δ_i	the known rate of depreciation of the i-the product,
H_i	the unit holding cost of the i-the product,
$c(\sum_{i=1}^{n} a_i z_i(t))$	the production cost at instant t, $a_i > 0$,
δ_i	known depreciation rate of the i-th product, $\delta_i \geq 0$,
$I_i(t)$	the inventory level of the i-th product at instant t.

Note that by the transformation $u_i(t) = a_i z_i(t)$, $h_i = \frac{H_i(1-\delta_i)}{a_i}$, $d_i(t) = \frac{a_i D_i(t)}{(1-\delta_i)}$ we can reduce $(nPIP)$ to (IP).

In the literature (cf. [6, 5, 4, 2]) the similar n-product problem is considered with $\delta_i = 0$. Usually the n-product production (or ordering) cost consists of three components(cf. [3]): the joint constant setup cost, the individual constant unit production cost and the individual setup cost. The case (IP) considered here can be treated as the n-product problem without the individual setup costs but with the joint setup cost and the nonlinear joint production (or ordering) cost (cf. Section 5).

The scope of (IP) makes the problem important in inventory subjects. This is the reason we search for the new solution methods. The method considered here allows to find solution by a forward algorithm because we reduce the problem to determine optimal paths in some acyclic networks.

In the sequel it is convenient to keep the first interpretation of (IP) as a one product n-warehouses production distribution problem. The method of solution given here is similar to that presented in [7] for a solution of a one-item two-echelon dynamic lot sizing problem. The presented algorithm essentially exploits the so called regeneration points of an optimal plans. First, we discuss some necessary conditions for the solutions of (IP).

3   Auxiliary problems. Optimality properties

Before analyzing the necessary conditions let us introduce some notation. A period t is called a *replenishment period* of the i-th plan $u_i(t)$ if $u_i(t) > 0$. Additional, a period t is called a *regeneration point* of the i-th plan if $I_i(t) = 0$ (I_i is the corresponding i-th warehouse inventory process).

Let u_i^*, $i = 1, 2, \ldots, n$ be an optimal production plan (a solution of (IP)) and let I_i^*, $i = 1, 2, \ldots, n$ be the corresponding inventory processes. The following two propositions give the necessary conditions of the optimal solutions.

Proposition 1. *For every warehouse i the plan u_i^* is an optimal solution of the following 1-warehouse inventory problem $(IP)_i$*

$$(IP)_i : \quad \min_{u_i} \sum_{t=1}^{T} \left\{ c\left(u_i + \sum_{\substack{j=1 \\ j \neq i}}^{n} u_j^*(t)\right) + h_i I_i(t) + \sum_{\substack{j=1 \\ j \neq i}}^{n} h_j I_j^*(t) \right\} \quad (4)$$

with the restrictions

$$I_i(t) = \sum_{s=1}^{t} (u_i(s) - d_i(s)) \geq 0, \quad u_i(t) \geq 0, \quad t = 1, 2, \ldots, T. \quad (5)$$

Properties of the solutions of $(IP)_i$. Note that $c(u_i + \sum_{j=1, j \neq i}^{n} u_j^*(t))$ is nondecreasing and concave with respect to u_i. Thus by the known result for the single product problem (cf [2, 13]) the plan u_i^* and corresponding inventory process I_i^* has to satisfy the Wagner-Whitin condition:

$$\text{for every } i, \quad I_i^*(t)u_i^*(t+1) = 0 \text{ and } I_i^*(T) = 0. \tag{6}$$

Note that (6) describes the property of an optimal plan for every i-th warehouse $i \in \{1, 2, \ldots, n\}$. In particular, the property states that if $t+1$ is a replenishment period then t is a regeneration point.

The second kind of necessary conditions give a relation between k-th and l-th warehouse optimal plans.

Now put $u^* = u_1^* + u_2^* + \cdots + u_n^*$.

It is easy to see that for every pair of subscripts (k, l) the corresponding pair (u_k^*, u_l^*) solves a 2-dimensional linear allocation problem $(AP)_{k,l}$. More precisely we have the following proposition.

Proposition 2. *For every pair of warehouses (k, l) the optimal plans (u_k^*, u_l^*) solve the following allocation problem*

$$(AP)_{k,l}: \quad \min_{u_k, u_l} \sum_{t=1}^{T} \left\{ c(u^*(t)) + h_k I_k(t) + h_l I_l(t) + \sum_{\substack{i=1 \\ i \notin \{k,l\}}}^{n} h_i I_i^*(t) \right\}$$

with the restrictions

$$I_i(t) = \sum_{s=1}^{t} (u_i(s) - d_i(s)) \geq 0, \quad u_k(t) + u_l(t) = u_k^*(t) + u_l^*(t),$$

$$u_i(t) \geq 0 \quad \text{for } i = k, l, \text{ and } t = 1, 2, \ldots, T.$$

Properties of the solutions of $(AP)_{k,l}$. Let us consider two cases.

(i) If $h_k = h_l$ then any pair (u_k, u_l) which satisfy the constrains

$$u_k(t) + u_l(t) = u_k^*(t) + u_l^*(t),$$

$$I_i(t) = \sum_{s=1}^{t} (u_i(s) - d_i(s)) \geq 0, \quad i = k, l,$$

$$u_k(t) \geq 0, \quad u_l(t) \geq 0, \quad \text{for } t = 1, 2, \ldots, T$$

is a solution of $(AP)_{k,l}$. The solution is called allocation of the system $(u_k^*(t) + u_l^*(t), d_k, d_l)$.

(ii) If $h_k > h_l$ then by [4] the unique solution of $(AP)_{k,l}$ is so called optimal allocation plan of the system $(u_k^*(t) + u_l^*(t), d_k, d_l)$. So by Property 5' from the [4] (cf also [4, 11]) we know that the multidimensional Wagner-Whitin condition is satisfied

$$I_k^*(t) \cdot u_l^*(t+1) = 0 \quad \text{for } t = 0, 1, \ldots, T-1, \quad k < l. \tag{7}$$

Hence (7) and (6) state in particular that if $t + 1$ is a replenishment period of l-th plan then t is a regeneration point of the warehouse inventory processes $I_1^*, I_2^*, \ldots, I_l^*$.

Note that by the observation (i) there is no loss of generality in assuming that in the definition of (IP) the unit holding costs satisfy the strict inequality

$$h_1 > h_2 > \cdots > h_n > 0. \tag{8}$$

In fact, we have the following

Remark 1. If $h_i = h_j$ then we can reduce (IP) to $(n-1)$-warehouse problem without warehouse j but with $d_i := d_i + d_j$.

Thus in the analysis of (IP) we assume that (1) is replaced by the condition (8).

Finally we obtain the following conclusion.

Proposition 3. *The optimal plans (solutions) of the problem (IP) belong to the set of vector valued functions $(u_1(t), u_2(t), \ldots, u_n(t))$ which satisfy the conditions:*

1. $I_i(t) = \sum_{s=1}^{t} (u_i(s) - d_i(s)) \geq 0, \ u_i(t) \geq 0 \quad for \ t = 1, 2, \ldots, T,$
2. $I_i(0) = I_i(T) = 0,$
3. *If $I_i(t) > 0$ then $u_i(t+1) = 0,$ if $I_i(t) = 0$ then $u_i(t+1) = d_i(t+1) + d_i(t+2) + \cdots + d_i(t+\tau)$ for some $\tau \in \{1, 2, \ldots, T-t\},$*
4. *If $u_i(t+1) > 0$ then $I_1(t) = I_2(t) = \cdots = I_i(t) = 0.$*

Proof. 1 and 2 follow from the definition of the problem (IP) and (6), 3 is a consequence of (6), 4 is a consequence of (7).

A vector valued function $(u_1(t), u_2(t), \ldots, u_n(t))$ satisfying 1-4 of Proposition 3 is called the *standard production plan*.

Remark 2. There are some recursive relations between u_i and u_{i-1} in the standard plane. We try to explain that by considering some examples of standard plans.

Let
$$\begin{aligned} t &= 1\ 2\ 3\ 4\ 5\ 6 \\ d_1 &= 2\ 1\ 7\ 0\ 1\ 5 \\ d_2 &= 3\ 1\ 9\ 4\ 1\ 0 \\ d_3 &= 1\ 8\ 0\ 3\ 0\ 4 \end{aligned}.$$

Example 1:
$$\begin{aligned} t &= 1\ 2\ 3\ 4\ 5\ 6 \\ u_1 &= 3\ 0\ 7\ 0\ 6\ 0 \\ u_2 &= 4\ 0\ 9\ 5\ 0\ 0 \\ u_3 &= 9\ 0\ 0\ 7\ 0\ 0 \end{aligned}.$$

Example 2:
$$\begin{aligned} t &= \ \ 1\ 2\ 3\ 4\ 5\ 6 \\ u_1 &= \ \ \ 3\ 0\ 7\ 6\ 0\ 0 \\ u_2 &= 13\ 0\ 0\ 5\ 0\ 0 \\ u_3 &= 16\ 0\ 0\ 0\ 0\ 0 \end{aligned}.$$

Note that a standard plan is uniquely determined by these regeneration points which satisfy the conditions 2 and 3 of the Proposition 3.

Example 1: u_1 is determined by the regeneration points at $t = 0, 2, 3, 4, 6$, u_2 by $t = 0, 2, 3, 6$ and u_3 by $t = 0, 3, 6$. Example 2: u_1 is determined by the points at $t = 0, 2, 3, 6$, u_2 by $t = 0, 3, 6$ and u_3 by $t = 0, 6$. Figure 1 illustrates the relations between the regeneration points.

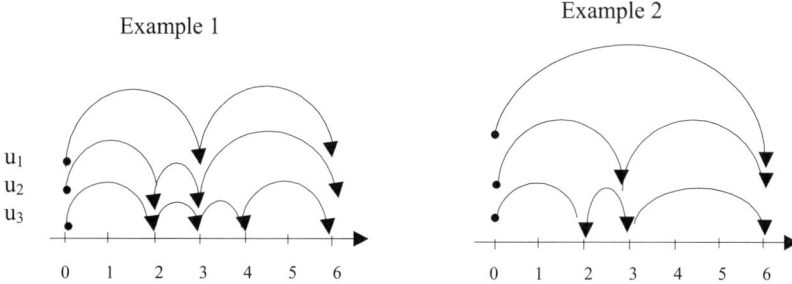

Fig. 1. The successive regeneration points determine the standard plans from Examples 1 and 2

4   A network description of the problem (IP)

Now we describe some acyclic networks and an idea of a selection of an optimal solution from the set of standard plans. In the method the optimal path procedure is applied many times.

Assumption: For simplicity assume $n = 3$.

A network is defined by: (i) a set of nodes, (ii) a set of arcs (a set of pair of nodes) and the cost function on the arc. We consider two kind of networks.

1. The network $G_{0,T}^3$ connected with a selection u_3^*.

(i) The nodes: time points: $0, 1, 2, \ldots, T$

(ii) The arcs: ordered pairs of nodes (i, j), $T \geq j > i \geq 0$, such that $d_3(i+1) + d_3(i+2) + \cdots + d_3(j)$ and if $i > 1$ then the sum is positive.

The pair of the arc nodes corresponds to two regeneration points of an inventory process $\widehat{I}_3$ with the plane $\widehat{u}_3(i+1) = d_3(i+1) + d_3(i+2) + \cdots + d_3(j)$, $\widehat{u}_3(i+2) = \widehat{u}_3(i+3) = \ldots = \widehat{u}_3(j) = 0$ ($\widehat{u}_3(i+1) > 0$ if $i > 1$).

(iii) As the cost q_{ij}^3 of the arc (i, j) we take the optimal cost of the following 2-warehouses problem

$$(IP)_{i,j}^3 : q_{ij}^3 = \min_{u_1, u_2} \sum_{t=i+1}^{j} \{c(u_1(t) + u_2(t) + \widehat{u}_3(t)) + h_1 I_1(t) + h_2 I_2(t) + h_3 \widehat{I}_3(t)\}$$

with the restrictions

$$I_1(i) = 0, \quad I_1(t) = \sum_{s=i+1}^{j} (u_1(s) - d_1(s)) \geq 0, \quad u_1(t) \geq 0, \quad t = i+1, \ldots, j$$

$$I_2(i) = 0, \quad I_2(t) = \sum_{s=i+1}^{j} (u_2(s) - d_2(s)) \geq 0, \quad u_2(t) \geq 0, \quad t = i+1, \ldots, j$$

If the arc cost is known then in the set of all paths from $t = 0$ to $t = T$ any path with the minimal cost determines the optimal plane for warehouse 3.

Note that the calculation of the cost q_{ij}^3 of the arc (i,j) requires solving 2-warehouse subproblem $(IP)_{i,j}^3$. This subproblem is restricted to the points $i, i+1, \ldots, j$ and to the warehouses 2 and 1. So the value q_{ij}^3 can be obtained by an optimal path procedure of the network below.

2. The network $G_{i,j}^2$.

(i) The nodes: time points: $i, i+1, i+2, \ldots, j$,
(ii) The arcs: the ordered pairs of nodes (k,l) with $j \geq l > k \geq i$ such that $d_2(k+1) + d_2(k+2) + \cdots + d_2(l)$ and if $k > i$ then the sum is positive.
    The pair of arc nodes corresponds to two regeneration points of an $\widehat{I}_2$ at $t = k, l$ with $\widehat{u}_2(k+1) = d_2(k+1) + d_2(k+2) + \cdots + d_2(l)$, $\widehat{u}_2(k+2) = \widehat{u}_2(k+3) = \cdots = \widehat{u}_3(l) = 0$, $\widehat{u}_2(k+1) > 0$ for $k > i$.
(iii) As the cost q_{kl}^2 of the arc (k,l) we take the optimal cost of the following one warehouse problem. (The methods of solutions are known in literature.)

$$(IP)_{kl}^2 : q_{kl}^2 = \min_{u_1} \sum_{t=k+1}^{l} \{c(\widehat{u}_3(t) + \widehat{u}_2(t) + u_1(t)) + h_1 I_1(t) + h_2 \widehat{I}_2(t)\}$$

with the restrictions

$$I_1(k) = 0, \quad I_1(t) = \sum_{s=k+1}^{l} (u_1(s) - d_1(s)) \geq 0, \quad u_1(t) \geq 0, \quad t = k+1, \ldots, l.$$

Having known the values q_{kl}^2 of the arcs of $G_{i,j}^2$ we are able to find the cost, say $\bar{q}_{ij}^3$, of the optimal path from i to j of the network $G_{i,j}^2$. Observe that

$$q_{ij}^3 = \bar{q}_{ij}^3 + \sum_{t=i+1}^{j} h_3 \widehat{I}_3(t).$$

Thus the network $G_{0,T}^3$ is completely defined and, as it was mentioned, any optimal path from $t = 0$ to $t = T$ determines the optimal plan for warehouse 3. Note that the initial nodes of the arcs of the optimal path give the regeneration points of I_3^* which uniquely determine the plan u_3^*. In this way we reduce the problem to 2-dimensional one with the cost function $\widehat{c}(u_1 + u_2) = c(u_1 + u_2 + u_3^*)$. Note that the 2-dimensional problem may be considered separately on each arc of the optimal path describing u_3^*.

5   A special example and the general case

Let $T = 10$ and consider the (IP) for $n = 3$ with cost function of the form:

$$c(u) = \begin{cases} 0 & \text{if } u = 0, \\ 5 + 2u & \text{if } 0 < u < 200, \\ 5 + 200 + u & \text{if } u \geq 200. \end{cases}$$

Note that the cost is concave with the set-up $c(0+) - c(0) = 5$.
Put $h_1 = h_2 = 0.3$, $h_3 = 0.1$ and

$t =$	1	2	3	4	5	6	7	8	9	10
$d_1 =$	60	70	1	10	150	20	50	0	20	30
$d_2 =$	40	130	0	10	50	80	150	1	30	20
$d_3 =$	100	100	10	20	100	100	100	20	10	20

The reduction of the problem to 2-warehouses case.

In this example $h_1 = h_2$, hence by the observation given in Remark 1 we first reduce the problem to the 2-warehouse case with the following data: $d_1 := d_1+d_2$, $d_2 := d_3$, $h_1 = 0.3$, $h_2 = 0.1$ and

$t =$	1	2	3	4	5	6	7	8	9	10
$d_1 =$	100	200	1	20	200	100	200	1	50	50
$d_2 =$	100	100	10	20	100	100	100	20	10	20

The optimal solution for the 2-warehouse case is given in the next table.

$t =$	1	2	3	4	5	6	7	8	9	10
$u_1^* =$	321	0	0	0	501	0	0	0	50	50
$u_2^* =$	230	0	0	0	350	0	0	0	0	0

Observe that $t = 1, 5$ are the *replenishment periods* of the plan $u_2^*(t)$ and $t = 1, 5, 9, 10$ are the *replenishment periods* of the plan $u_1^*(t)$. The points $t = 0, 4, 10$ are the regeneration points of I_2^* and $t = 0, 4, 8, 9, 10$ are the regeneration points of I_1^*.

By an allocation of u^* we obtain the following system $(\widehat{u}_1^*, \widehat{u}_2^*, \widehat{u}_3^*)$ which solves the initial problem (IP) with 3 warehouses (cf. Figure 2).

$t =$	1	2	3	4	5	6	7	8	9	10
$\widehat{u}_1^*(t) =$	141	0	0	0	220	0	0	0	20	30
$\widehat{u}_2^*(t) =$	180	0	0	0	281	0	0	0	30	20
$\widehat{u}_3^*(t) =$	230	0	0	0	350	0	0	0	0	0

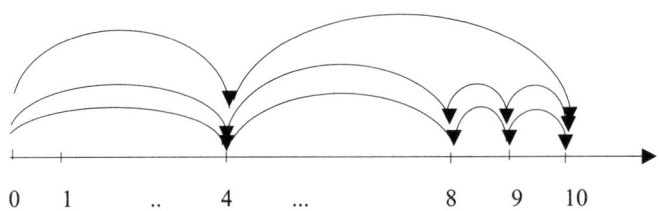

Fig. 2. The optimal plan for the special problem

For a general n-dimensional case it is possible to describe the procedure in somewhat different form. Consider the graph with sequences of natural numbers (regeneration points) as members of the set of nodes V and adequate cost function on arcs. For the case of n items, we define the network $\Gamma^n = (V, E, q)$:

$$V = \{(k_1, \ldots, k_n) \mid 0 < k_1 \leq k_2 \leq \cdots \leq k_n\} \cup \{(0, \ldots, 0)\}$$

and the set of arcs E as follows:

a pair of nodes $((k_1, \ldots, k_n), (j_1, \ldots, j_n)) \in E$ if and only if there exists r, $1 \leq r \leq n$ such that it satisfies:

1) $k_1 = \ldots = k_r < k_{r+1}$, where $k_{n+1} = \infty$,

2) $k_1 < j_1 \leq \cdots \leq j_r,$
3) $k_s = j_s,$ for each $s > r.$

Each path from the node $(0, \ldots, 0)$ to the node $(T, \ldots, T)$ defines a standard plan for the inventory problem (IP) and vice versa. For example, the optimal plan constructed in the above numerical example is represented as the path $((0,0,0), (4,4,4), (8,8,10), (9,9,10), (10,10,10))$ from $(0,0,0)$ to $(10,10,10)$ in Γ^3. All paths for the case of time horizon $T = 4$ in the network Γ^2 we can find in Figure 3.

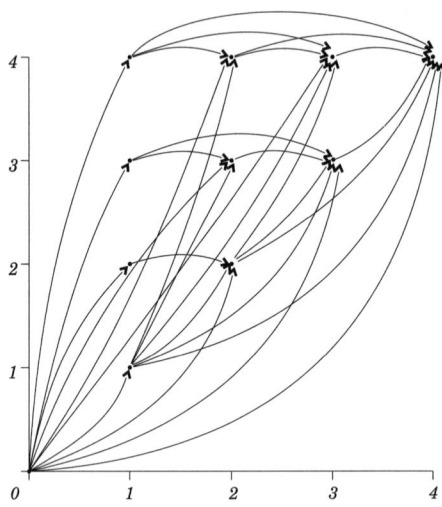

Fig. 3. The graph for the network Γ^2 for (IP) with $n = 2$ and $T = 4$

The costs will be equivalent if as the cost of an arc $e = \big((k_1, \ldots, k_n), (j_1, \ldots, j_n)\big)$ we take the cost

$$q(e) = c\left(\sum_{t=k_1}^{j_1} d_1(t) + \cdots + \sum_{t=k_n}^{j_n} d_n(t) \right) + h_1 \sum_{t=k_1}^{j_1} I_1(t) + \cdots + h_n \sum_{t=k_n}^{j_n} I_n(t).$$

The set of optimal plans for the inventory problem (IP) (as the set of the cheapest paths from the node $(0, \ldots, 0)$ to the node $(T, \ldots, T)$ in Γ^n) can be constructed by a standard procedure for the cheapest path in acyclic networks.

6 Final remark

In the paper we presented a method of determining an optimal plan for multi-dimensional inventory problem. In general (see [1]) such kinds of problems are NP-hard. The presented method is based on the regeneration point property and the optimal path procedure. Observe that the regeneration point property reduces the number of nodes in the corresponding graph. The algorithm is more effective in some special cases in which demands are equal to zero at many time points.

References

1. Arkin, E., Joneja, D., Roundy, R.: Computational Complexity of Uncapacitated Multi-Echelon Production Planning Problems. Operations Research Letters 8 (1989) 61–66
2. Bensoussan, A., Crouhy, M., Proth, J.H.: Mathematical Theory of Production Planning. North-Holland, Amsterdam (1983)
3. Boctor, F.F., Laporte, G., Renaud, J.: Models and Algorithms for the Dynamic-Demand Joint Replenishment Problem. Int. J. Production Research. **42** (2004) 2667–2678
4. Bylka, S., Rempala, R.: Multi-Product Inventory and Auxiliary Allocation Problem. Int. J. Production Economics. **71** (2001) 295–303
5. Bylka, S., Rempala, R.: Wybrane Zagadnienia Matematycznej Teorii Zapasów. Akademicka Oficyna Wydawnicza EXIT, Warszawa (2003)
6. Chan, G.H., Chiu, H.S.: A Simple Heuristic for Multi-Product Dynamic Lot Sizing Problems. Computers Operations Research. **24**, no 10, (1997) 969–979
7. Chan, L.M.A., Muriel, A., Shen Z.J., Simchi-Levi, D., Teo, C.P.: On the Effectiveness of Zero-Inventory-Ordering Policies for the Single warehouse Multi-Retailer Problem with Piecewise Linear Cost Structures. Management Science. **48**, no 11, (2002) 1446–1460
8. Erenguc, S.S., Simpson, N.C., Vakharia, A.J.: Integrated Production/Distribution planning in Supply Chains: An Invited Review. European J. of Operational Research. **115** (1999) 219–236
9. Frenk, J.G.B., Kleijn, M.J., Dekker, R.: An Efficient Algorithm for a Generalized Joint Replenishment Problem. European J. of Operational Research. **118** (1999) 413–428
10. Kirca, O.: A Primal-Dual Algorithm for the Dynamic Lotsizing with Joint Set-Up Costs. Naval Research Logistics. **42** (1995) 791–806
11. Rempala, R.: Joint Replenishment Multiproduct Inventory Problem with Continuous Production and discrete demands. Int. J. Production Economics. **81-82** (2003) 495–511
12. Sluis, E. van der: On Optimal and Heuristic Solutions for Multi Product Inventory System. AE-Report 0/2002, (2002)
13. Wagner, H.M., Whitin, T.M.: Dynamic Version of the Economic Lot Size Model. Management Science. **5** (1958) 89–86

INDEX

Printed in the United States of America